CW01667678

Manual of Digital Health

Informatics, Analytics, Therapeutics, Telehealth, and Regulations

Pushwaz Virk, MD

Manual of Digital Health. Copyright © 2024 by Pushwaz Virk. All rights reserved.

All rights reserved. No part of this work may be reproduced or transmitted in any form or by any means, electronic or mechanical, without the written permission of the copyright owner and the publisher except as permitted by U.S. copyright law. The content in this book is made available for educational purposes and readers' personal, noncommercial, educational, and scholarly use.

Every effort has been made to ensure that the content is accurate at the time of the writing. The views expressed in the book are solely of the author and do not imply any sponsorship, affiliation, endorsement, or association between any organization, corporation, committee, other group or individual, or other legal entity and the author or the publisher. All product, service, trade, and company names are trademarks and copyrights of their respective owners and are used only for informational purposes wherever possible. Trademarks have been identified in the relevant sections of the book. Please refer to the company websites for more details about the usage of the trademarks. The language of the regulations discussed in this book has been simplified. Readers are advised to refer to the original text of the regulation for accuracy. The regulations may not be current when this book is referenced.

The information in this book is presented on an "as-is" basis. The author or the publisher shall not have any responsibility liability due to any error, omission, or limitation, or with respect to any loss or damages due to the information in the book. The contents of this book should not be used as medical, legal, financial, or strategic advice. The author and publisher make no representations or warranties regarding the accuracy of the content of this book. Readers should seek counsel from experts experienced in their domain for business, professional, clinical, or contractual decisions.

No artificial intelligence (AI) generated content was used in this book. The use of the text in this book for generative AI or for training machine learning language models is prohibited.

U.S. edition printed in the United States of America.

First edition. 2024

Library of Congress Control Number: 2024916525

ISBN-13: 979-8-9886024-0-8 (Hardcover)

Update version: 2024.43

Published by Medeor University
548 Market St #80360,
San Francisco, CA 94104-5401
10 9 8 7 6 5 4 3 2 1

DEDICATION

This book is dedicated to my wife for supporting me during the writing journey, sharing feedback about the content, and providing constant encouragement. I would also like to dedicate this book to my children, who were extremely patient with me during my evening and weekend writing sessions.

ABOUT THE AUTHOR

Pushwaz Virk, MD, MBA, MPH, is an internal medicine physician, investor, and executive with experience in product management, clinical informatics, strategy consulting, business development, medical affairs, and clinical medicine. Pushwaz started his career as the founding member of the life sciences and healthcare practice of a multinational technology company, where he developed software for Fortune 50 pharma pharmaceutical and life science companies. He also set up international teams to validate clinical algorithms and manage back-office operations for global healthcare organizations. Since then, he has led the development and clinical validation of technology products and services, including chronic disease management, care coordination, and remote monitoring. He has also developed reimbursement models for innovative healthcare products and services. Pushwaz has a unique perspective on digital health as a developer, customer, and end-user due to the diversity of his roles as a Chief Medical Information Officer at a health system, Vice President of medical affairs at a software company, and the Medical Director of clinical product development and care innovation at a health insurance firm. He has evaluated, purchased, deployed, integrated, and scaled enterprise software at healthcare organizations. As a physician, Pushwaz has used six different electronic medical record and practice management software.

Pushwaz has a keen interest in healthcare innovation. He was the co-founder and board member of a healthcare and life sciences-focused angel investment group where he created a culture of mentoring first-time founders and conducting deep due diligence in partnership with industry experts. Pushwaz has supported over a hundred startups as an advisor or an angel investor. He has also served as the president and board member of Harvard Alumni Entrepreneurs, a 501©3 nonprofit promoting responsible entrepreneurship among Harvard alumni globally.

Pushwaz completed a Master of Public Health and a fellowship in healthcare administration at Harvard University, residency in internal medicine at Cleveland Clinic Akron General and has received a Master of Business Administration from the Faculty of Management Studies at University of Delhi. He is board-certified in internal medicine, lifestyle medicine, and clinical informatics and has certifications in software development and machine learning. Pushwaz's research has focused on global health innovation and health services research. Pushwaz is based in San Francisco Bay Area, California where he sees patients as a hospital medicine physician.

With his diverse background spanning clinical, administrative, and technical domains, Pushwaz offers an interdisciplinary perspective on digital health. This book reflects insights from his prolific career, offering a practical guide for those navigating the rapidly evolving digital health sector.

CONTENTS

ACKNOWLEDGMENTS

I would like to thank Dr. David Bates at Harvard Medical School, who encouraged me to pursue the path of clinical informatics and provided invaluable mentorship over last two decades. Dr. Michael Marino and Dr. Richard Carvolth at Providence Health and Dr. Michael Brown at Harvard University Health Services supported me in transforming healthcare delivery using technology.

I would also like to acknowledge my friends who, over the years, provided constant feedback, ideas, and encouragement. Dr. Anoop Rao at Stanford inspired me to write this book, Dr Vikram Sheel Kumar at Dimagi showed me the power of digital health to transform the world, and Dr Sandeep Sekhon at Clovis Community Medical Center who encouraged me to combine my careers in medicine and technology.

I am indebted to Prof. Venkat Raman from Faculty of Management Studies, Dr. Sumit Prasad from Columbia Africa, Dr. Anurag Duggal from Cleveland Clinic, Anupendra Sharma from Startup Leadership Program, Dr. Jasdeep Singh from DMC, Mr. Saurav Adhikari from HCL for supporting me at various junctures of my professional career.

I acknowledge that many more individuals have helped me in my academic and professional career and I remain grateful to everyone who has played a role in my journey.

CONTRIBUTION & FEEDBACK

The domain of digital health is rapidly evolving with new technologies, business models, regulations, and software applications. If you would like an invitation to join the digital health community of experts, researchers, entrepreneurs, and investors in digital health and clinical informatics where they share knowledge, resources, and job opportunities., please submit your information at *www.virk.md/contact.*

Domain experts from the industry and academia are invited to contribute to the next edition of the book. Please email us at *book@virk.md.*

ENTREPRENEURS & INVESTORS

The digital health ecosystem is growing across the world. Entrepreneurs looking for funding, advisors, domain experts, or employees for their early or late-stage startups can submit their information at *www.virk.md/resources.*

Angel and institutional investors who are interested in joining the investment group for global healthcare deals or partner on due diligence can get more information at *www.virk.md/resources.*

ERRATA

We have made a significant effort to keep the content of the book as accurate as possible at the time of writing. However, given the large scope of material covered in this book, there will likely be errors of omission and commission in the first edition, for which we apologize in advance. If you notice any errors or discrepancies, please contact us at *www.virk.md/contact* or email us at *book@virk.md.*

PREFACE

Digital health is predicted to bring the most profound change in the practice of medicine seen in the last 50 years. Digital health is transforming the practice of medicine and the healthcare industry. The last decade saw the adoption of technology by providers who moved from paper-based records to electronic systems. However, the exponential rate of innovation in health tech is accelerating with the adoption of health tech by consumers, advances in machine learning, and cloud computing infrastructure. The COVID-19 pandemic catalyzed the adoption of digital health and transformed the healthcare delivery landscape and society's mental model about how medicine can be practiced. Digital health technologies are enabling providers to incorporate more clinical diagnosis and treatment data.

Many introductory textbooks about clinical informatics focus on theoretical concepts, but no reliable material focuses on applied aspects. This book focuses on practical, real-world aspects of the digital health domain. The purpose of the book is manifold. It discusses advanced concepts about creating software for healthcare applications for professionals already working in healthcare or software development. It identifies opportunities for innovation in healthcare for entrepreneurs, researchers, and investors. It provides essential information for clinicians and technologists deploying digital health apps, telehealth products, and healthcare services at their organizations. The information in this book will hopefully motivate individuals to work in the digital health domain and contribute to improving the health and well-being of the population.

INTRODUCTION

Due to the broad scope of digital health and rapid developments in the field, writing a book that does justice to the subject is challenging. This book is one of the most comprehensive texts about applied digital health. While this book covers all the essential aspects of digital health, the discussion about developing digital health products and services will be available on the book's website, *www.virk.md*. Subscribe to the book mailing list at *www.virk.md/book* to be notified of updates.

Intended audience

This book intends to be a comprehensive reference about using technology in healthcare. It provides the background, challenges, solutions, and opportunities for developing digital health products and services. The book discusses concepts that anyone working with health technology needs to know and is targeted at a broad audience. It is aimed at clinical informaticists, healthcare professionals, including physicians and nurses, students studying healthcare or information technology courses, software developers, entrepreneurs, investors, and anyone else interested in developing digital products and services for healthcare. The book does not assume significant knowledge about healthcare or technology among the readers. However, individuals with some background in clinical informatics, software development, health care administration, or clinical medicine will find it the most useful. The book will significantly help entrepreneurs looking for opportunities for innovation in healthcare using technology and investors who are interested in learning more and investing in these ventures. The information in the book will also benefit Chief Medical Informatics Officers (CMIOs), Chief Information Officers (CIOs), Chief Nursing Informatics Officers (CNIOs), medical directors, hospital administrators, executives at software companies working in healthcare, insurance companies, and service providers to these organizations. The book also aims to provide adequate digital health background to medical, nursing, and computer science students interested in a digital health career.

Book layout

The book is divided into five units.

Unit 1 - Informatics

The first unit, Informatics, discusses the fundamentals of informatics and covers digital health applications for the enterprises. The chapter on digital health provides an overview of the digital health landscape and its future. It discusses the impact of the COVID-19 pandemic and the shift in digital health innovation funding.

The chapter on enterprise health informatics discusses the structure of hospital IT operations and factors that go into making a successful IT organization at a healthcare provider. Recommendations for successfully running a clinical informatics team at a hospital are included.

Healthcare interoperability is vital to digital health product and service development and implementation. This chapter provides a high-level overview of HL7® V2, V3, and FHIR standards. It also discusses common document exchange formats like CDA, CCD, and CCR.

Healthcare information needs to be codified for seamless and accurate data exchange. The chapter on healthcare terminology discusses the most common healthcare ontologies like SNOMED and LOINC. Apps and software use the interoperability architecture to connect to clinical data and use ontologies for interpretation.

Healthcare services are built on two foundational pillars – clinical care and payment for clinical care. Healthcare revenue cycle management is the end-to-end workflow for obtaining healthcare reimbursement. Health Information Management (HIM) departments at healthcare organizations manage the complete revenue cycle management suite in-house or outsource it to external vendors. The chapter provides detail about the revenue cycle management steps. It also discusses nomenclature used in RCM including DRG, CPT, HCPCS, and RBRV.

Health Information Exchanges (HIE) have played a key role in enabling interoperability between health systems and affiliated healthcare service providers. The chapter on health information exchanges provides an overview, including their structure, technology infrastructure, and data exchange formats.

FHIR is emerging to be the interoperability standard for the communication of healthcare information. The chapter on interoperability discusses the healthcare APIs, including SMART on FHIR, OAuth 2, OpenID Connect, and CDS Hooks.

The chapter on healthcare information standards discusses the data standards for medical data code sets, vocabulary standards, security standards, API standards, functional standards, transaction standards, transport standards and protocols, Universal Medical Device Nomenclature, and Global Medical Device Nomenclature.

The chapter on low-code and no-code applications introduce technologies that can empower healthcare enterprises to develop software applications in-house without hiring developers or contracting with software development vendors saving time and money. Organizations can configure pre-built templates for their specific needs without writing code.

The chapter on quality improvement discusses the major quality standards relevant to healthcare organizations and how digital health can be used to perform better on quality metrics. It discusses the quality metrics in the United States, Canada, UK, China, and India. These metrics provide a tremendous opportunity for digital health entrepreneurs, researchers, and innovators to develop products and services that can improve care delivery as measured by these metrics. The solutions developed for these geographies often apply to most other countries.

Virtual Reality (VR) and Augmented Reality (AR) are increasingly finding applications in healthcare. This chapter provides and overview of VR and AR technologies and how they have found use in healthcare.

Security and privacy are among the most critical considerations in developing and using technology in healthcare. The chapter on security and privacy practices highlights the best practices in security and privacy for healthcare organizations and for developers creating healthcare apps.

Unit 2 - Analytics

The second unit, Analytics, covers the basics of applied data analytics in healthcare organizations. It discusses the requirements for setting up an effective analytics team. It also provides multiple ideas for innovators to develop healthcare analytics products and services.

The first chapter introduces the fundamentals of health analytics and includes high-level technical and operational background for analytics projects in healthcare delivery organizations. The goal of this chapter is to cover concepts relevant to professionals working in healthcare delivery as well as innovators planning to develop analytics products and services. It covers analytical approaches, guidelines for developing analytics models, statistical concepts, and insights about analytics infrastructure and security.

Over the last decade, electronic health records adoption has significantly increased the clinical data available for research. The pharmaceutical industry is increasingly using this data in clinical trials. The chapter on real-world evidence discusses the applications of electronic medical records data in drug development and clinical research.

The chapter on machine learning and artificial intelligence provides an overview of machine learning techniques and the following two chapters discuss applications of machine learning in the domain of healthcare and clinical medicine including contemporary research.

Generative AI and Large Language Models (LLMs) have seen rapid adoption especially after the release of ChatGPT applications. An overview of Generative AI and LLMs along with their application in healthcare is discussed in the chapter on Generative AI.

Data governance is an essential function in any organization working with healthcare data. This chapter provides an overview of data governance as well as an overview of data security and safety.

Unit 3 – Digital Therapeutics

The third unit discusses the digital therapeutics currently on the market and those undergoing clinical trials. It also discusses digital diagnostics and digital biomarkers which are increasingly getting adopted in mainstream clinical medicine.

Consumer adoption of healthcare-focused mobile applications during the COVID-19 pandemic has attracted developer interest and the number of clinical apps available with or without prescription is increasing in quantity and quality. The chapter on mobile health apps discusses the quality and usability issues of these apps and provides examples of mobile applications that are doing well in the market.

Unit 4 - Telehealth

The unit on telehealth is broadly divided into telemedicine and remote patient monitoring. The introductory chapter discusses the impact on COVID-19 pandemic on telehealth. It discusses benefits of using telehealth applications as well as current challenges in the adoption of telehealth.

The chapter on remote patient monitoring provides a high level overview about remote patient monitoring. It goes into details about various remote patient monitoring applications, requirements for development of monitoring programs and important considerations about patient factors, sensors, analytics.

The other chapters discuss fifty-four types of telehealth in clinical and administrative scenarios under the categories of home health care, ambulatory care, acute care, mental health, rehabilitation, medical and surgical subspecialties.

The final chapter on telehealth reimbursement discusses Medicare and private payer coverage and codes used for remote monitoring claims as well as illustrative reimbursement rates.

Unit 5 - Regulations

The last unit explains, in simplified language, the healthcare regulations relevant to digital health. This unit will be beneficial for teams that are developing healthcare applications at software companies and healthcare organizations. It is important to note that the regulations are current when referenced, but they may be updated after the book has been published. Readers are strongly advised to check the source of the regulation for the most up-to-date information and to consult an attorney or regulatory expert if they plan to develop a digital health product or service.

Software as a Medical Device (SaMD) is essential in the FDA's regulation of software applications. The chapter on SaMD provides an overview of medical software regulation and software pre-certification programs. It also covers changes introduced in the 21st-century cures act and regulations enacted globally in digital health.

Clinical decision support is one of the most critical applications of information technology in healthcare delivery. The chapter on clinical decision support and regulation discusses what clinical decision support is, how it is used in healthcare applications, and the regulations governing its use.

The National Evaluation System for Health Technologies chapter provides an overview of the data quality framework and data quality maturity model, which is increasingly being adopted in the industry.

The Hitech Act of 2009 was an important milestone in promoting the adoption of Health IT in the United States. It was followed by Health IT Certification Program. Together, these two regulations formed the backbone of the software applications used in healthcare. The Health IT Certification program lists clinical processes, care coordination, clinical quality measures, privacy and security, patient engagement, public health, and electronic exchange.

Cures Act is the most recent substantial regulation directed at healthcare IT. The chapter discusses the impact of the Cures Act, updates to the 2015 Edition certification criteria, conditions of certification, and timelines for regulatory changes.

MACRA and MIPS are covered in the next chapter with details about eligible clinicians and reporting areas. These are gradually being replaced by alternative payment models.

HIPAA is one of the most significant regulations in healthcare and one of the most important laws impacting software used in healthcare settings. The chapter on HIPAA goes into detail about this necessary regulation covering all the requirements of the regulation.

Appendix

Career opportunities in digital health are increasing at a rapid rate. The chapter targeted at job seekers interested in careers in digital health provides an overview of the career opportunities available at healthcare systems, digital health companies, health insurance, research organizations, consulting firms, telehealth, pharmaceutical, and medical device companies.

UNIT 1: INFORMATICS

1 THE AGE OF DIGITAL HEALTH

Introduction

The use of technology in healthcare has previously been classified based on location (hospitals, home), users (providers, patients, consumers), purpose (diagnosis, treatment, wellness), and interface (mobile health, wearables). 'Digital health' is a broad term that refers to the use of software-based products and services in healthcare. Digital health includes enterprise healthcare applications, consumer digital apps as well as hardware including sensors, wearables, and novel computing interfaces. It also includes services and programs which improve the efficiency and efficacy of healthcare delivery programs including telehealth and remote patient monitoring. The goal of digital health is to augment the capabilities of healthcare professionals in managing medical conditions, as well as provide tools to individuals to reduce risks and promote their health.

The discipline of digital health includes 'clinical informatics', which is the research, development, and application of information systems in healthcare delivery as well as 'consumer health informatics' which is the use of healthcare technology by consumers for maintaining health or managing their medical conditions. 'Telehealth' is the provision of healthcare from a distance. 'Mobile health' (mHealth) is the application of mobile phones for healthcare purposes. The term 'Healthcare IT' has been used to represent all aspects of healthcare information technology, primarily referring to the commercial deployment of technology at healthcare enterprises. However, with increasing interoperability, the emergence of mobile medical apps, and advancements in telemedicine, the lines between these definitions have become blurry. Consumers have also started using healthcare-focused apps and connected devices, including fitness trackers and wellness apps which are also getting integrated into the electronic medical record systems, merging the consumer and enterprise side of healthcare. Further, the personalization afforded by the collection of multi-dimensional patient data allows the electronic medical record systems or software for computerized physician order entry and clinical decision support to use an individual's health profile for personalized recommendations.

'Clinical Informatics' is the study and practice of developing and deploying healthcare technologies used for healthcare delivery. It has also been defined as the application of information technology for clinical purposes or the use of information technology in healthcare by clinical providers. American Medical Informatics Association (AMIA) defines 'Clinical Informatics' as "the application of information technology to deliver healthcare services." It separates Clinical Informatics from Public Health Informatics. In its dictionary of Health Information and Technology Terms, Acronyms, and Organizations, the Healthcare Information and Management Systems Society (HIMSS) defines Clinical Informatics as a domain that "promotes the understanding, integration, and application of information technology in healthcare settings to ensure adequate and qualified support of clinician objectives and industry best practices." It further clarifies 'Clinical Informatics' as the "...application of informatics and information technology to deliver healthcare services. It includes a wide range of topics, from clinical decision support to clinical images, from clinical documentation to provider order entry systems, and from system design to system implementation, adoption, and optimization issues" (HIMSS, 2016).

Initially, clinical informatics used to be concerned with clinical systems which dealt directly with clinical data, like Electronic Medical Record (EMR) systems or Laboratory Information Management Systems (LIMS), etc. Over time, the professionals dealing with clinical informatics started overseeing other IT tools used in a healthcare organization, so the definition was expanded. Another term, 'Healthcare informatics', is "the integration of healthcare sciences, computer science, information science, and cognitive science to assist in the management of healthcare information" (Saba et al., 2015).

Expanding role of digital health

Digital health is augmenting traditional clinical interventions, including trained human capital, pharmaceuticals, and medical devices to improve health, prevent disease, and treat medical conditions. Innovations in digital health have accelerated with the increasing adoption of digital health tools by consumers and enterprise customers. The technologies which are classified under digital health have also expanded.

'Digital therapeutics' is the application of software for the treatment of medical conditions. Digital therapeutics products require approval by a regulatory body like Food and Drug Administration in the United States and are targeted at specific clinical conditions. Most digital health apps are considered low-risk by FDA. However, some software applications may be classified as Software as a Medical Device (SaMD), requiring formal FDA approval before public launch. Digital therapeutics products can be approved through De Novo Classification, Pre-Cert program, or 510(k) pathways in the United States or CE Mark in Europe. Most of these applications must demonstrate evidence through Randomized Controlled Trials (RCT), but many can access expedited access pathways or real-world data. Some of these may be available through prescriptions only and require oversight by a medical practitioner.

Digital health mobile applications are also becoming more sophisticated. By some estimates, more than 90,000 digital health were made available in mobile operating system app stores in 2020 (Deloitte. 2021), and this trend is accelerating. Health claims of most apps are unsubstantiated; however, a few peer-reviewed publications have demonstrated the effectiveness of digital health apps. Digital health apps are now used for disease prediction, including the risk of asthma and congestive heart failure exacerbations, diagnosis of medical conditions including atrial fibrillation and depression, promotion of health behaviors like healthy eating and exercise, monitoring health-related events, including falls and hypoxia, among many other uses.

Health insurance companies are catching up to the technology, and in the future, more digital health technologies and tools are expected to be covered by insurance reimbursement. The digital formularies of health insurance companies are incorporating digital therapeutics into their medical and payment policies.

Clinical research is adopting digital health at every stage of research and development through the adoption of real-world data and real-world evidence. Clinical trials tracking digital biomarker endpoints are growing and either have a human-in-the-loop or are automated by detecting abnormalities by machine learning algorithms. Remote patient monitoring is not only used in the practice of medicine but is also helping drug companies to collect data from clinical trial participants wearable sensors which allow for continuous tracking of human health state.

COVID-19 pandemic

The COVID-19 pandemic was a watershed moment in the digital health industry globally. Healthcare providers and patients rapidly adopted virtual visits and remote patient monitoring. Digital health evolved from an innovative idea to a necessity for millions. The regulatory changes, lobbied by trade organizations for years, were approved and implemented within weeks. According to estimates, the adoption of telehealth visits during the COVID-19 pandemic increased from less than 1% to over 50% within a few weeks (Amwell, 2020), catalyzed by the adoption of virtual visits by providers and patients, funding for public health data and reporting infrastructure, use of online media by patients and providers for information about the pandemic.

Clinical evidence for digital health

Health effectiveness studies increasingly are including digital health products and services to evaluate the application of digital health in various scenarios ranging from promoting a healthy lifestyle to clinical interventions.

A systematic review (Tang et al., 2020) concluded that wearable trackers improved physical activity in the short term, at least modestly. Another meta-analysis showed that mobile apps or trackers effectively promoted physical activity (Laranjo et al., 2021). A meta-analysis of mobile phone app interventions showed significant changes in body weight and body mass index (Islam et al., 2020). A systematic review and meta-analysis of randomized controlled trials showed that mHealth interventions improved total and LDL cholesterol values (Akbar et al., 2019). Another systemic review and meta-analysis of 20 studies showed that mobile health-based self-monitoring as part of a behavioral weight management approach resulted in a moderate decrease in weight and higher adherence to interventions. The effect of lifestyle mHealth interventions was pronounced compared to usual care, and smartphone-based interventions were the most effective mHealth interventions for weight management (Cavero-Redondo et al., 2020). For smoking cessation, a systematic review of randomized controlled trials showed that mhealth interventions improve smoking cessation compared to face-to-face interventions (Uthman et al., 2019).

Studies have also demonstrated applications of digital health in medical conditions. For example, in cardiology, a meta-analysis of smartphone-based cardiac rehabilitation programs showed that exercise capacity in patients with coronary artery disease improved (Murphy et al., 2020). A systematic review and meta-analysis of mhealth interventions included remote monitoring and clinical feedback for congestive heart failure, reduced mortality, and heart failure-related hospitalizations (Kitsiou S et al. 2021). A systematic review of app-based interventions in hypertensive patients showed reduced blood pressure and increased medication adherence (Xu H et al., 2020). Meta-analyses have also shown app-based interventions to be effective for chronic pain (Pfeifer et al., 2020) and medication adherence (Al-Arkee et al., 2021).

Digital health tools are also targeted at consumers who can use the apps to check their symptoms or create a shortlist of preliminary diagnoses. Studies have shown wide variation in the performance of these apps, and there is a significant opportunity for improvement.

Digital health funding

Venture capital, private equity, and public market funding saw a significant increase in digital health during and after the COVID-19 pandemic. Digital health venture funding was $14Bn in 2020, which was 72% higher than the previous high in 2018. This funding was spread over 440 deals which was also a record. The average deal size increased to $31.9 Mn. In 2021, the venture capital funding broke previous records and was close to $25Bn across over 600 deals, and deal size increased to close to $40Mn per deal (Rock Health. 2021). The impact of the increase in funding will be visible over the next few years.

2 ENTERPRISE HEALTH INFORMATICS

The procurement of software applications and services by healthcare systems is one of the largest categories of overall spending on healthcare technology. In 2018, healthcare organizations spent over $7 Bn on information technology (Beckers Health IT, 2018). The overall global healthcare IT market size was estimated to be US$ 180 billion in 2019, of which hospitals comprised the largest proportion of healthcare information technology buyers (Ugalmugle S et al., 2020).

Every hospital is unique in how it internally structures its information technology operations. A typical scenario is that the Information Services (IS) team manages the technology deployed at the hospitals. Some factors that influence the structure of IS department are whether the hospital is an independent free-standing facility or part of a more extensive network, the number of beds at the hospital or the health system overall, any affiliation with the university, or participation in informatics research. The departments operating under Information Services' purview and managing technology at a hospital or a health system are discussed below.

Hospital IT organization

Information technology

Information Technology, or 'IT' manages the computing infrastructure, including workstations, networking equipment, storage systems, bar code readers, printers, fax machines, etc. The spending on IT is one of the most significant capital expenditures in the information services departments. The enterprise infrastructure is updated to maintain compatibility with the ever-improving software. The healthcare applications are mission-critical in healthcare delivery and depend on > 99% uptime of the infrastructure. Most unplanned downtimes of hospital applications happen due to the failure of the infrastructure. These downtimes are not only disruptive to the work of the hospital but can also harm patient safety, hospital profitability, and reputation. It is vital to ensure that redundancies are built into the critical infrastructure.

Clinical informatics

The clinical informatics team oversees the software applications used by caregivers directly for delivering healthcare services. It primarily supports the Electronic Medical Record system, including implementation, training, optimization, governance, and maintenance.

The structure of the clinical informatics department within the overall IT division varies across the health systems. A chief medical informatics officer and, in many cases, the chief nursing informatics officer usually lead the clinical informatics team. They may report to chief medical officer, chief physician executive, or chief information officer. The clinical informatics team is closely aligned with the other teams within information technology.

Applications

The application team is responsible for procuring, deploying, and maintaining software applications. Generally, the management of EMR falls under the purview of clinical informatics, and the application team supports all the other applications used at the facility. These applications may include enterprise business management systems, including human resource management including talent acquisition, staff timekeeping, and payroll; financial management, including planning, accounting, budgeting, and forecasting; supply chain management, including procurement, contract, and payable management, inventory tracking; marketing and customer service; desktop applications including single sign-on, office suite productivity tools.

The applications team may also oversee specialized applications used by departments like dietary & nutrition, radiology including image management and PACS, analytics tools, labor and delivery applications including fetal monitoring, and applications for clinical specialties needs including endoscopy, orthopedics, etc.

Analytics

The presence of an independent analytics team is a relatively new concept in hospitals, which started to emerge in the second decade of the 21st century. The analytics department can report to the clinical organization, information services, clinical informatics, strategy, nursing, or the executive office. Analytics departments employ data scientists and analysts to develop dashboards, reports, and predictive models, integrate analytics services with other applications, manage data governance, and training. The applications used by or supported by the analytics team could include data warehouses, on-demand analytics platforms, front-end applications like visualization tools, integrated development environments, scripting tools etc. More details are available in the analytics section of the book.

Research

The informatics research departments are present in academic medical centers, universities, or independent research centers focused on health technology research. They may be part of clinical informatics or information services or exist independently. In all scenarios, there is a close collaboration with other departments. The research teams also create their own software applications that can be used in the affiliated hospitals or clinics. They are also more likely to spin out or collaborate with startup companies.

Biomedical engineering

The biomedical engineering department is responsible for installing and maintaining biomedical devices in the hospital. These include ventilators, dialysis machines, ICU monitors, infusion pumps, etc. Biomedical devices are increasingly managed with sophisticated software that can be controlled through device-based interfaces or separate PCs or mobile phones. The 'smart devices' are connected to the internet and include in-built clinical decision capability. They are also becoming more integrated with the rest of the technology infrastructure in the hospital. For example, ICU monitors may regularly export vital signs readings into the EMR systems. The lines between biomedical engineering managing medical devices, IT managing non-biomedical technology infrastructure, and clinical informatics dealing with clinical software applications are blurring.

Clinical informatics operations

The Clinical Informatics (CI) department is primarily responsible for acquiring and managing digital health tools in a hospital. A well-functioning clinical informatics team is essential to physician and nurse satisfaction and efficiency in clinical workflows and hospital operations.

Clinical alignment

Hospital departments have unique informatics needs because of their workflow, regulatory requirements, or dependence on a specific type of technology. Many hospital departments use specialized modules within the EMR, or they may have independent specialty-specific EMRs in addition to or instead of the organization-wide EMR system. It is vital that CI provides informatics support tailored to the needs of these departments.

CI team members can permanently be assigned to a few inpatient clinical departments and ambulatory sites. These team members can develop relationships with the providers and department admins. It also makes the job of communicating changes to the providers easier while at the same time helping to recruit clinical volunteers to serve in temporary or permanent informatics roles.

Some of the clinical departments which can be assigned dedicated clinical informaticists include:

- Ambulatory care (outpatient offices for primary care, urgent care, dental, outpatient specialties like dermatology or rheumatology etc., and outpatient practices of clinical departments like general surgery or ob-gyn etc.).
- Anesthesia
- Behavioral health and inpatient psychiatry
- Cardiology, echo, electrophysiology and catheterization lab
- Cardiothoracic Surgery
- Critical care and specialized ICUs including cardiac care, progressive metabolic care
- Emergency department
- Endoscopy
- General surgery and other surgical subspecialties like cardiothoracic surgery, neurosurgery
- Home health
- Hospital medicine, inpatient acute medical and surgical care
- Infectious disease and infection control

- Maternity services including labor & delivery, lactation, NICU, nursery, postpartum
- Nephrology and dialysis
- Neurology, EEG and sleep lab
- Nursing
- Obstetrics
- Oncology
- Orthopedics and trauma
- Pre and intra operative departments
- Palliative care & hospice
- Pediatrics
- Post-acute and long term care
- Post Anesthesia Care Unit (PACU)
- Rehabilitation and therapies including speech, physical, occupational and respiratory
- Trauma

Clinical informatics with or without the support of other IS departments, may also support applications used by the administrative departments such as:

- Admitting
- Bed control
- Billing and finance
- Biomedical
- Case management & social work
- Environmental services
- Health information management including coding and documentation integrity
- Materials management
- Patient scheduling
- Patient relations
- Patient financial services
- Pre-registration and registration
- Quality improvement
- Registration and patient scheduling
- Registries
- Security
- Transport

The ancillary departments are supported by a mix of teams from clinical informatics, IT, and biomedical engineering as these departments have a mix of deployed software applications and hardware devices:

- Blood Bank
- Chaplaincy
- Diabetes management
- Laboratory including clinical, microbiology, and pathology
- Nutrition & dietary
- Operating room

- Pharmacy
- Radiology and interventional radiology
- Radiation oncology
- Outpatient infusion

Clinical informatics team structure

The clinical informatics teams are structured based on the clinical informatics team's responsibilities and depend on the size of the team, healthcare system affiliation, presence of research programs, etc., as discussed previously. While the clinical informaticists may need to align with the clinical and operational departments, that segmentation may only sometimes be appropriate for the division of team roles. Typical clinical informatics roles include:

- Analytics and reporting
- Application training
- Clinical informatics operations
- Data exchange interface development and management
- Data warehouse and database administration
- EMR implementation and optimization
- EMR support

Information services success factors

An efficient and effective IS department works in the background to ensure that the users do not have to contact IS. An effective IS team reduces or eliminates any urgent needs to reach out to them by proactively anticipating and addressing the users' needs before issues arise. It is vital to ensure that no unanticipated breakdowns happen in technology that can impact operations, security, or safety. Healthcare organizations can create successful IS departments by adopting industry best practices. Some of these are discussed here.

Training & onboarding:

Establishing a robust and efficient onboarding process for the clinical staff is essential. According to a survey of 30,000 physicians, robust training provided before the first-time use of the EHR led to higher satisfaction with EHR (Jason, 2019). Other surveys have found that the onboarding training about EHR systems provided to the medical staff has generally been lacking due to inadequate training resources and inadequate allocation of training time (Brookstone, 2012). This is attributed to inadequate training resources and uncompensated training time leading to less than an inadequate allocation of training hours. The onboarding starts with access provisioning, including setting up user IDs, passwords, and authenticator apps. Third-party approvals may be required for the provisioning of electronic prescriptions and registration with RSA tokens or authenticator apps. The access control is tracked throughout the duration of employment of clinical and non-clinical staff using the applications. It is essential for safety and efficiency to ensure adequate and appropriate training has been provided prior to the first day of work. Training should be based on the user's role and scope of practice. It should be scheduled to minimize the impact on the provider's clinical workflow. Specialty-specific workflows should be incorporated into the training curriculum. EHR onboarding should be integrated with the overall onboarding process which includes human resources and employee health.

A sandbox environment may be necessary for adequate practice before the first day of work for providers unfamiliar with the EHR and other clinical applications at their new workplace. Physicians prefer live tutorials by their peers delivered either in person or via video calls. It is also helpful to provide the physicians and nurses with brief handouts to use as a reference until they become proficient. A refresher course, even of a smaller duration, two to four weeks after the start date, is helpful to reinforce the concepts. Sharing of best practices, efficiency tips, and shortcuts by experienced users with the new staff can be tremendously useful. A concise compendium of such clips can be made available to the staff at accessible locations bundled with self-directed learning modules. This is also especially helpful for traveling nurses who can save time and improve health care quality by incorporating efficient documentation and patient care practices in their workflows quickly based on such training.

Provider organizations should budget at least four to eight hours of training for providers new to the EMR or the site of care, subsequently supplemented by periodic refresher courses every few months. It is crucial that the residency programs also dedicate resources to training on clinical software applications, as the habits developed during the residency training are likely to continue post-residency. The initial training is also helpful in ingraining best documentation practices.

New EMR deployment projects should ensure that the rollout period includes formal training time followed by post-go-live support. Super users should be trained first, followed by the end users. Providers should pass a competency test before getting access to the EMR system. The EMR coaches can continue working with the providers for a few weeks post-onboarding and check in every few months with refresher material.

Efficient documentation practices can help reduce physicians' time spent on documentation time, increase billing accuracy, and improve their satisfaction with the EMR system. The Chief Medical Information Officer (CMIO) of the organization can aggregate tips and feedback from the most prolific and efficient users of the EMR system to share with the medical staff. This can include specialty-specific and targeted 'cheat sheets' which are distributed to the medical staff.

EMR personalization

Customization or personalization of EMRs using pre-built templates is a controversial topic. While it improves the efficiency and satisfaction of providers, it also makes it harder to achieve standardization across the organization. Different health systems have varying degrees of customization options ranging from individualized templates for every provider to one for the whole health system. A balance should be achieved by getting the departments' acceptance of the customized order sets, templates, favorites, etc. Frequent modifications should be avoided.

During the training during the onboarding process, commonly used shortcuts, standardized templates, and favorites should be provided to the new physicians. Organizations allowing more personalization options should revisit the templates after a few weeks when the providers better understand the EMR system and their needs.

Information security

Cyber-attacks on healthcare organizations are rising and will continue to increase as more health data is stored online and exchanged via the APIs. Robust processes need to be instituted for the collection, storage, and exchange of data. Periodic training should be mandatory for everyone who has access to health information systems. The staff should run comprehensive vulnerability analyses and do frequent drills to identify opportunities for failure and training. The security initiatives should be aligned with the organization's disaster mitigation and recovery efforts. Organizations can contract with cybersecurity consultants for a complete audit of their security processes and infrastructure. Please see the chapter on security for a detailed discussion about this topic.

Helpdesk

Information services' help desks are often overlooked in an organization. However, the technical helpdesk is one of the most important drivers of physician satisfaction. If the helpdesk cannot resolve a physician's complaint in the expected time, that can lead to dissatisfaction with the administration which can reduce physician engagement with the workplace. This experience is also relevant for other healthcare staff members.

Providers can contact the technology helpdesk for issues ranging from misconfigured or hung application sessions, forgotten or expired passwords, and EMR-specific issues, including errors during navigation, slow network access, or general usability. Other scenarios for helpdesk calls, in no particular order, include requests for access on their home computers and mobile phones, customization of the shortcuts, the configuration of favorite orders or dictation templates, malfunctioning hardware, including monitors, keyboards, etc.

One helpdesk phone number or ticketing system should be the providers' single point of contact for all technical issues. The staff should triage the issue and route it to the right team, like the EMR support team. The IT helpdesk, which oversees the hardware, and the dictation service, is usually managed by health information management or medical records departments. Organizations should create metrics like wait times, speed of ticket resolution, and qualitative and quantitative customer satisfaction surveys to evaluate the performance of helpdesks. Auditing help desk calls can help diagnose and mitigate recurring technical issues in time. Another tactic to improve the efficiency and effectiveness of the helpdesk is to assign help desk personnel to specific clinical units where they can build long-term relationships.

On-site support staff, in addition to phone support, increases provider satisfaction. It also improves the relationship between the providers and the clinical informatics department if the providers personally know the helpdesk staff.

Elbow support

Elbow support is the individualized, in-person support provided to hospital staff, physicians, and nurses, at their location of work. The informatics experts shadow the providers and share tips on improving efficiency through shortcuts and better documentation workflows. It can be provided for both inpatient and outpatient sites of care. The departments can also provide computers for physicians to use in the clinical informatics department, where they can sit adjacent to the informatics staff and physician informaticists and quickly get their queries addressed. Nurses or therapists who move into informatics roles after training on the EMR deployed at the hospital are particularly skilled in providing elbow support.

Downtimes

Information systems (IS) are the backbone of a healthcare system. Hospitals and ambulatory surgery centers are one of the very few organizations where the failure of computer systems can impact patient human safety. 'IS downtime' is defined as when computer systems are unavailable to the healthcare staff. These could be planned (scheduled) or unplanned (unscheduled) downtimes.

Scheduled downtime is needed for software or hardware upgrades. For a scheduled downtime, preparations are made in advance to ensure the continuity of operations. These are usually done overnight, and a downtime protocol is initiated, which may require migration to paper-based workflows. At the end of the downtime, the written documents are scanned into the patient record or manually entered into the system.

Unplanned system downtimes are one of the biggest challenges of hospital information services leadership. They can lead to delays in patient care, admission or discharges, surgeries, and diagnostic studies. The unplanned downtimes are critical, and a few reasons why they happen are:

- Power failures: This generally happens during prolonged power cuts and subsequent exhaustion of battery backups and generators, or in some cases, it is due to hospital equipment failure.
- Network failure: Failure of intranet or hospital network connectivity with the internet.
- Application failure: Sometimes, specific software applications cannot be accessed by the users. This may happen after an upgrade when an untested bug makes the system unstable or unusable. Sometimes it results from conflict between a newly installed application and an existing or hardware change. The software vendor usually works closely with the hospital to resolve the issue, which may require a rollback of the upgrade or installation of a patch or a workaround.
- Cybersecurity failure: Systems can be made unusable by ransomware or malware, which may encrypt the data and make the applications and databases inaccessible.

It is essential to conduct periodic drills testing various downtime scenarios and align them with the hospital disaster recovery and continuity plan. The IS leadership should hold workshops detailing the policies, procedures, protocols, and resources for downtime and training all hospital staff on downtime procedures.

Governance

Information system governance is essential in ensuring long-term strategic alignment of the technology strategy with the organizational goals. The governance team establishes priorities, assigns accountability, develops policies and standards, and allocates budgets. Responsibilities are assigned for operational targets, resource allocation, capacity planning, and project management. The governance framework is required for the dynamic allocation of resources based on the evolving needs of the organization, department, or a specific location. For larger health systems, the systemwide executive committees oversee program or clinical service line-oriented governance groups and geographically aligned committees.

The governance team may be subdivided into committees which develop policies for contracting, project funding, and tracking. They also create standardized processes for intake of requests, prioritization requests, allocation of resources, establishing timelines, and tracking success metrics. For example, any EMR enhancement decision should be based on provider feedback through advisory committees, physician champions, focus groups, or individual surveys. Focused, multidisciplinary workgroups can be created targeting specific areas like order sets, documentation, and clinical decision support.

3 INTEROPERABILITY

Multiple legislations were enacted in the 2000s and 2010s to address the lack of support for data sharing by providers, health systems, and health IT companies, especially electronic medical record companies. Lack of interoperability makes it difficult for a patient to seek care from a different provider if all their healthcare records are accessible to only one provider. The specific regulations introduced by the federal government to promote interoperability are discussed in the regulatory section of this book. Due to these legislations, EMR companies are creating app stores allowing other developers to create applications utilizing the data or workflows in their underlying EMR systems.

HL7®

HL7 International is an American National Standards Institute accredited, not-for-profit standards development organization. It provides a "comprehensive framework and related standards for the exchange, integration, sharing, and retrieval of electronic health information that supports clinical practice and the management, delivery, and evaluation of health services." (HL7. About HL7). HL7 is an international standard for exchanging clinical and health administration data between health providers. The "7" in HL7 refers to the 7th level of the International Standards Organization's Open System Interconnection Communication model (ISO-OSI). The seven layers are "Physical, Data Link, Network, Transport, Session, Presentation, and Application." HL7 has evolved through various versions, each of which uses a different messaging philosophy. The most current HL7 standard is HL7 Fast Health Interoperability Resources (FHIR) which is rapidly growing in adoption and is the culmination of a decade-long push to make HL7 standards easy to develop, adopt, and deploy.

HL7® and FHIR® are registered trademarks of Health Level Seven International, and their use in applications does not constitute endorsement by HL7. Please refer to the official documentation at www.hl7.org for current and detailed information about the HL7 standards.

HL7 standards include 1) Version 2 & 3 which provide specifications for clinical transactions, 2) Clinical Document Architecture (CDA) which provides specifications for clinical documents, 3) Continuity of Care Document (CCD) which provides specifications for most relevant administrative, demographic, and clinical information, 4) Structure Product Labeling (SPL) which is a standard to exchange product and facility information, 5) Clinical Context Object Workgroup

(CCOW) which is an specification for integration of applications and runtime environments, 6) Electronic Health Records (EHR) System functional model and profiles to create EHRs, 7) Fast Healthcare Interoperability Resources (FHIR), a standard for exchanging resources, 8) Arden Syntax which encodes medical knowledge and representation (HL7. Introduction to HL7 Standards).

HL7 implementation guides are available to define data standards and exchange mechanisms for FHIR-based digital Quality Measures. These include:

- US Core Implementation Guide, Quality Improvement Core (QI Core) Implementation Guide
- Data Exchange for Quality Measures (DEQM) Implementation Guide
- Quality Measure (QM) Implementation Guide
- Clinical Guidelines Implementation Guide.

HL7 also includes cross-paradigm or domain analysis models. These include (HL7. HL7 Standards – Section 1h: Cross-paradigm/Domain Analysis Models.)

- HL7 Business Architecture Model
- HL7 CDS Hooks
- CIMI Logical Model for Analysis: Analysis Normal Form
- HL7 Cross Paradigm Implementation Guide
    - UDI pattern
    - Behavioral health data exchange
    - Gender harmony – sex and gender representation
    - Medical device data sharing
    - Immunization
- HL7 Cross Paradigm Information Sharing for electronic long-term services and supports
- HL7 Cross Paradigm Specification
    - Health Services Reference Architecture
    - Clinical Quality Language
- HL7 Cross Paradigm Storyboard: Payer perspective, value based care
- HL7 Cross Paradigm Domain Analysis model
    - Vital records
    - Birth defects reporting
    - Common clinical registry framework
    - Emergency care
    - Intra-procedure anesthesia
    - Nutrition care
    - Patient centered care team
    - Specimen
    - Terminology harmonization in exercise medicine and exercise science
- HL7 Health Services Platform Marketplace

- HL7 Logical Model
    - o Standardized terminology knowledgebase
    - o Privacy and security logical data model
- HL7 Model-based Transformation Service

HL7® V2

HL7 V2 is currently the most common messaging standard supported by most EMRs. It has no documents, uses EDI/X12 messaging standard, and provides encoding rules, groupings, cardinality, and character sets. This version allows optional fields and additional messages to customize the needs of non-standard interfaces or those not covered by default specifications. V2 standard is backward compatible. V2 also allows hospital workflows to support administrative, logistical, financial, and clinical processes (HL7. HL7 Version 2 Product Suite).

Data is exchanged using the HL7 protocol through messages which could include patient information, billing information, or test results. The messages can exchange information including patient demographics, charges, accounting, insurance, clinical observations, registration, ADT (Admission, Discharge, Transfer), clinical services (Laboratory Tests, Surgical or Non-Surgical Procedures, Pharmacy, Consumables, or Supplies), test results, appointments, referrals.

V2 messages consist of segments separated by one-character delimiters. Segments have fields that have components and subcomponents. The delimiters can be carriage return, pipes (|), carets (^) to separate the components, ampersand (&) to separate subcomponents, hash sign (#) to separate truncation, and tilde (~) to separate repetition. Besides ADT, the other message types are ORM for Order Entry, ORU for Observation Results, MDM for Medical Documentation Management, DFT for Detailed Financial Transactions, BAR for Billing Account Records, SIU for Scheduling Information Unsolicited, RDS for Pharmacy / Treatment dispensing, RDE for Pharmacy/Treatment Encoded Order, and ACK for Acknowledgement Message.

Here is a sample HL7 message.

```
MSH|^~\&|EMR|EMRADT|SMS|SMSADT|201906100230| ADT^A01|9833899|D|2|
PID||975319^^MR|848482||Doe^John^^^^B|Doe^Jane^^^^|
NK1||DOE^JACK^^^^| (707)123-4567||EC|
```

HL7 messages have three components: Segments, Composites, and Sub-fields. A segment in an HL7 message has a specific category of information. For example, a segment could be patient identification or patient visit. Every segment is listed on a different line as it is separated by a carriage return. The name of every segment is listed in the first field of the segment and is three characters in length. In the above example, there are four segments, each starting with MSH, PID, NK1, and PV1 in that order. The first segment of every message has MSH, which identifies the message type. MSH is Message Header and contains information about the message, including the message type, sender, receiver, date, time, etc. The PID segment contains Patient Information. The NK segment carries information about the patient's Next of Kin. The PV segment includes information about patient visits, such as inpatient stays or outpatient visits.

Every segment of an HL7 message comprises composites or fields separated by a pipe character (|). A composite can contain other composites, known as sub- "composites or sub-fields" and separated by ^ character. A composite or sub-composite can be strings or numbers. In some cases, the sub-composite may also contain a composite, which is known as a sub-sub-composite. In the above example, it is listed as Patient Identification |Name|DOB|Address|. The Name can be split into |Surname|^|First name|. The Surname can further be divided into subcomponents|. In the above example, the HL7 message header example with six segments. John Doe is the patient name (PID-5). Doe is the family name. B indicates the type of name, and here it is Birth Name. The multiple ^ characters in the composites mean more than one sub-composite present. Every vendor and provider implementation can define their structure of composites and sub-composites.

The sub-fields are called sub-composites and are separated by (^) character. In the example above, the patient's name has sub-fields.

The delimiter characters are used to separate composites and sub-composites. These include pipe (|), which separates composites; (^), which separates sub-composites; ampersand (&), which separates sub-sub-composites; dash (-), which separates repeating fields; and escape (\), which is for escape commands. HL7 components can be repeatable, and some can have two values. e.g., Address1 ~ Address 2.

HL7® V3

HL7 V3 is an XML standard based on the HL7 Reference Information Model containing messages, documents, and services. It overcame some limitations of V2, like having too much flexibility and optionality, introducing inconsistency in information exchange, and difficulty creating conformance tests. It is not backward compatible with the V2 standard.

HL7 version 3 is based on Object Management Group's Unified Modeling Language based on the reference information model. It created data types and vocabulary specifications with a Reference Information Model. RIM is an information model representing HL7 clinical domains from which all information models and message specifications are derived. It consists of a set of classes subdivided into more specific health classes. It creates models for documents, data, and messages. It is the source for HL7 V3 standards and can be mapped to HL7 2.x message standard. V3 was based on semantic interoperability using standardized clinical contexts and shared between sending and receiving systems. V3 introduced concepts like trigger events, interaction designs, domain object models, and hierarchical message descriptors (HMDs) to the standard. V3 uses data types, vocabulary, and RIM for information modeling.

RIM is used with other coding systems like SNOMED-CT and LOINC to define CDA. RIM concepts include Entity, Actx, ActRelationship, Role, and Participation (HL7. HL7 Reference Information Model). The relationship between the concepts mirrors real-world scenarios. E.g., A person (entity) can play the role of a doctor in a downtown hospital, which is the scope of that role, and the same person may have the role of the patient at another hospital which will be a different scope for the (patient) role (Villegas et al., VICO).

- Entity: Entity refers to physical elements which could include person, organization, place, and material.
- Act: Act is the action which is of interest. It could include procedure, observation, account, supply, diet, document.
- ActRelationship: ActRelationship defines the relationships between the acts. It could include composition, preconditions, revisions

- Role: Role classifies the entities. For example, employee, patient, licensed entity.
- Participation: Participation defines association between specific roles and specific acts. For example, Entity (person) could be playing a role (physician) (Beeler, 2011).

HL7 V3 has been criticized for being overly complex and lacking clear documentation. It has been hard for the average developer to understand and incorporate it into the software. For example, the specifications for RIM had multiple layers requiring significant expertise for implementation. There have also licensing issues that constrained its initial adoption.

Clinical Document Architecture

Clinical Document Architecture (CDA) is a standard for exchanging clinical documents with structure, semantics, and encoding specifications. CDA is part of the V3 standard and is based on XML. CDA is commonly used in health information exchanges to share information. A CDA-based document could be a History and Physical, Discharge Summary, and Diagnostic reports for Radiology, Pathology, etc. The CDA documents are shared using HL7 Version 2 or Version 3 messages. It has a header, body, and section(s) with a narrative block and entry(s). Due to the nature of XML documents, these are human and machine-readable.

A clinical document is defined to have six characteristics: 1) Persistence, 2) Stewardship, 3) Potential for authentication, 4) Context, 5) Wholeness, and 6) Human readability (HL7. CDA. 2015). XML allows unstructured text and hyperlinks to other document types, including pdf, doc, and jpg. CDA is based on HL7 Reference Information Model. CDA document has human interpretable document content and RIM-based machine-readable structured content based on coding concepts like SNOMED. CDA allows the end users to design the complexity within the specification. For example, at the minimum, CDA could have XML-encoded metadata fields like provider name, document type, document identifier, and body having a MIME type with pdf, doc, or a jpg. This structure enables the filing, searching, and classification of the document. The text in a human-readable format is in the document body. It provides the ability to include data that is machine processable and can be used for decision support. The development work on CDA is ongoing. However, the HL7 FHIR standard is gaining more support.

Consolidated Clinical Document Architecture

Consolidated Clinical Document Architecture (C-CDA) is one of the most commonly used formats for exchanging health information in the United States. It was created after the harmonization of Health Information Technology Standards Panel HITSP Summary documents to streamline templates used in CDA. It is built on XML, CDA, and HL7 Reference Information Model (RIM) base standards and provides a collection of documents based on CDA format. The C-CDA standard has 11 document types (HL7. C-CDA):

- Care Plan
- Consultation Note
- Continuity of Care Document (CCD)
- Diagnostic Imaging Report
- Discharge Summary
- History and Physical
- Operative Note

- Procedure Note
- Progress Note
- Transfer Summary
- Unstructured Document

Continuity of Care Document

The CCD (Continuity of Care Document) is based on the architecture and XML templates from HL7s CDA (Clinical Document Architecture) and concepts and data models from CCR (Continuity of Care Record). The ASTM E31 committee, responsible for maintaining the Continuity of Care Record standard, helped develop CCD. It applies constraints on HL7 CDA standard and has US-specific requirements. Healthcare Information Technology Standards Panel has selected it as one of its core standards. The patient summary section of the document includes administrative, demographic, and clinical information about a patient providing a snapshot of the patient's information (ANSI. 2010). EHR vendors have implemented CCD in different ways, many of which are incompatible between different systems (D'Amore et al., 2011).

Clinical Care Record

Clinical Care Record (CCR) is another standard specification for health records which is developed jointly by ASTM International, the Massachusetts Medical Society (MMS), the Healthcare Information and Management Systems Society (HIMSS), the American Academy of Family Physicians (AAFP), the American Academy of Pediatrics (AAP), and other health informatics vendors (ASTM. 2012). CCR is a standard for summarizing patients' health summaries. It creates documents with relevant and timely information that caregivers can exchange (ASTM. 2013). CCR data set includes problems, medication list, allergies, health insurance information, care documentation, and care plan to provide a snapshot of patient's health information.

The mandated core elements in CCR are (Rhapsody. Understanding the Continuity of Care Record):

- Identifiers or Header
- Patient Identifying Information
- Financial and Insurance Information
- Health Status of the patient
- Care Documentation
- Care Plan Recommendation
- Advance directives
- Practitioners

CCR can be exported to other document types. CCR can provide basic information, and CCD provides more detailed information. CCR uses XML standard, which provides the flexibility to display CCR in the browser, HL7 message, PDF, HTML, and Word documents (Ferranti et al., 2006).

Arden syntax

Arden syntax is a markup language used to represent and share medical knowledge. The Arden syntax standard is overseen by Health Level Seven International. Arden syntax is organized in modules called Medical Logic Modules (MLMs), which are rules used to produce alerts, diagnoses, and interpretations in clinical decision support systems. Each MLM captures adequate logical information that can be used for a medical decision (Hripcsak, 1994). MLM syntax representation has four categories – maintenance, library, knowledge, and resources.

Arden syntax has diverse applications in healthcare. It is used to generate alerts for critical laboratory values or medication interactions, generate informational messages, generate messages triggered by events such as admission or discharges from the hospital, or manage messages. The advantages of Arden syntax are that it makes it possible to encode medical concepts (Song et al., 2009) in an easy-to-understand format. Some of the applications of Arden syntax have been in identifying nosocomial infections (Samwald et al., 2012), hypokalemia prediction, diagnosis support in rheumatology, etc.

Categories

- **Maintenance**: Maintenance module contains metadata about the module. It has nice slots
  - title: MLM title
  - mlmname: File which contains the mlm with extension .mlm
  - arden: Version of the Arden syntax
  - version: Version of MLM
  - institution: Institution which created the MLM
  - author: Creator of the MLM
  - specialist: Medical specialist who supervised the content of MLM
  - date: Date of creation or update of MLM
  - validation: Current status of the MLM with 4 states – production, research, testing, or expired
- **Library**: Library category contains information about the intended use of a specific MLM, it's workings, references to associated literature. It has the following slots
  - purpose: Clinical purpose of MLM
  - explanation: Description
  - keywords: Semicolon separated words used to search modules
  - citations: References to appropriate literature used in the module
  - links: URLs of other websites that are relevant to the module
- **Knowledge**: Knowledge category is the actual medical knowledge consisting of type, data, priority, evoke, logic and action slots.
- **Resources**: Resources category provides additional information like language.

These categories are used in this specific order in a single MLM. Categories contain slots arranged in a specific order which help to explain the logic (Samwald et al., 2012).

```
maintenance:
        title:                  ;;
        mlmname:        [required];;
        arden:          [required];;
        version:        [required];;
        institution:    [required];;
        author:                 ;;
```

```
        specialist:                  ;;
        date:               [required];;
        validation:         [required];;
library:
        purpose:                     ;;
        explanation:                 ;;
        keywords:                    ;;
        citations:                   ;;
        links:                       ;;
knowledge:
        type:            data_driven;;
        data:                        ;;
        priority:                    ;;
        evoke:                       ;;
        logic:                       ;;
        action:                      ;;
        urgency:                     ;;
resources:
        default:            [optional];;
        language:                    ;;
end:
```

Knowledge category slots include:

- Type slot indicates how MLM is used.
- Data slot defines the terms used in MLM slot.
- Priority describes the order in which MLM is invoked.
- Evoke slot indicates the process of activating the MLM.
- Logic slot describes the medical rule that is tested.
- Action slot creates the message sent to health care provider.

ArdenML (Arden Syntax Markup Language) is a schema for expressing Arden Syntax in XML format. Here is an example (Liu N, 2018):

```
maintenance:
      title: Checking the diastolic blood pressure;;
      mlmname: Hypotension;;
      arden: version 2.7;;
      version: 1.00;;
      institution: Latrobe University Bundoora;;
      author: Lakshmi Devineni;;
      specialist: ;;
      date: 2013-06-02;;
      validation: testing;;
library:
      purpose: check if the diastolic blood pressure of the patient is within
limits;;
      explanation: This MLM is an example for reading data and writing a
message;;
      keywords: hypotension; categorization;;
      citations: ;;
```

```
	links:http://en.wikipedia.org/wiki/Hypotension;;
knowledge:
	type: data_driven;;
	data:
	/* read the diastolic blood pressure */
	diastolic_blood_pressure := read last
	{diastolic blood pressure}; /* the value in braces is specific to your
runtime environment */
	/* If the height is lower than height_threshold, output a message */
	diastolic_pressure_threshold := 60;
	stdout_dest := destination
	{stdout};
	;;
	evoke: null_event;;
	logic:
	if (diastolic_blood_pressure is not number) then conclude false;
	endif;
	if (diastolic_blood_pressure >= diastolic_pressure_threshold) then
conclude true;
	else
	conclude false;
	endif;
	;;
	action:
	write "Your Diastolic Blood Pressure is too low (hypotension)"
	at stdout_dest;
	;;
resources:
	default: de
	;;
	language: en
	'msg' : "The normal range from 60 to 90";
	;;
	language: de
	'msg' : "Der Normalbereich von 60 bis 90";
	;;
	end:
```

Fast Healthcare Interoperability Resources

HL7's Fast Healthcare Interoperability Resources (FHIR®) specification is an interoperability standard for exchanging healthcare information. It defines a set of capabilities used across healthcare processes. HL7 International developed FHIR to simplify the HL7 data model, base it on contemporary web technologies, and improve usability (Grieve, 2011). FHIR® is a registered trademark of HL7 International.

The central theme of the FHIR standard is that the systems should be able to request only the information required at that time. "FHIR combines the best features of HL7's V2, HL7 V3, and CDA product lines while leveraging the latest web standards and applying a tight focus on implementability" (HL7. Introducing HL7 FHIR. 2018). FHIR defines the "data models, ontologies, and the method to exchange the information with FHIR server but does not use authorization or authentication" (Bloomfield Jr et al., 2017). FHIR can be used along with previous HL7 versions and other existing standards (HL7. Getting started with FHIR. 2019). In FHIR, documents are similar to CDA. They are packaged, sent, and received as a bundle which is a type of resource.

FHIR Resource

Clinical data in FHIR is represented as 'Resources' with well-defined fields and data types like Patient, Procedure, Condition, etc. Resources are structured data elements and are building blocks of healthcare data. Each resource has a human-readable part, a standard set of metadata, and a common definition and representation structure made of data types that are reusable patterns. FHIR resources can satisfy the majority of health interoperability needs. The resources link with each other to create a comprehensive look at the medical record. These resources can also be aggregated into documents to provide a detailed snapshot of a clinical record. The complete list of resources is available on the HL7 FHIR website.

Resources are organized into layers and categories based on common characteristics or patterns based on structures and behaviors. The top layer categories are the most common, and resources in these categories constitute the bulk of transactions. The layers and their resources are (HL7. Guide to Resources):

- Layer 1 **Foundation Resources**: Foundation resources are used for infrastructural tasks and are usually not referenced by other resources. These resources are related to:
    - Security
    - Conformance
    - Terminology
    - Documents
    - Other
- Level 2 **Base Resources**: These resources are most commonly used resource types. They are often referenced by other resources, but they themselves don't typically reference other resources. They include:
    - Individuals
    - Entities
    - Workflow
    - Management
- Layer 3 **Clinical Resources**: These resources are usually built on Layer 2 resources. If these resources are contextualized then they are referenced by resources in Layers 3, 4, and 5. These resources carry information about
    - Clinical
    - Diagnostic
    - Medications
    - Care Provision
    - Request and Response
- Layer 4 **Financial Resources**: These resources build on clinical and base resources and carry information about financial components of clinical delivery such as
    - Support
    - Billing
    - Payment
    - General
- Layer 5 **Specialized Resources**: These resources are less commonly used. They mostly serve as reference resources.
    - Public Health Research
    - Definitional Artifacts

    - Clinical Decision Support
    - Quality
- Layer 6 **Resource Contextualization**: This layer does not contain resources. It has two components
    - Profiles: Profiles are used to extend, constrain, or otherwise contextualize resources
    - Graphs: Graphs are compositions of resources, or webs of resource, that contain attributes of their own.

The resources have a fixed URL, which enables RESTful HTTP transactions. The operations are based on the CRUD methodology. Commonly used in web-based applications, CRUD operations stand for Create, Read (Retrieve), Update (Modify), and Delete, which can be enabled through SQL commands INSERT, SELECT, UPDATE, DELETE as well as HTTP queries PUT/POST, GET, PUT/POST/PATCH, and DELETE respectively.

The content of every FHIR resource is available on the HL7 website in multiple formats. These formats are some of the most used representations:

- UML (Unified Markup Language): UML helps to visualize the design of software systems by modeling the structure of FHIR resource.
- XML (Extensible Markup Language): XML provides rules used to encode documents into a machine-readable format while retaining human-readability.
- JSON (JavaScript Object Notation): JSON is a language independent data interchange format and a popular format to store and transmit data.
- Turtle (Terse RDF Triple Language): Turtle is a textual syntax for Resource Description Framework that is used to represent information on the Web. The information is represented in semantic triples which is made of subject, predicate, and object. Each item is expressed at Web Uniform Resource Identifier, commonly used as URL (Uniform Resource Locator) or web address.

As an illustration, the Patient resource in XML format is described below (HL7. Resource Patient – Content. 2019):

```
<Patient xmlns="http://hl7.org/fhir">
   <id value="[id]"/>
   <meta>
      <lastUpdated value="2021-01-02T22:15:24" />
      <versionId value="[id]"/>
      <source value="[uri]"/>
      <tag></tag>
      <security></security>
      <profile></profile>
   </meta>
   <language value="[code]"/>
   <implicitRules value="[uri]"/>
   <text></text>
   <contained></contained>
   <extension></extension>
   <modifierExtension></modifierExtension>
   <identifier></identifier>
   <active value="[boolean]"/>
```

```
    <name></name>
    <telecom></telecom>
    <gender value="[code]"/>
    <birthDate value="[date]"/>
    <deceased[x]></deceased[x]>
    <address></address>
    <maritalStatus></maritalStatus>
    <multipleBirth[x]></multipleBirth[x]>
    <photo></photo>
    <contact>
        <relationship></relationship>
        <name></name>
        <telecom></telecom>
        <address></address>
        <gender value="[code]"/>
        <organization></organization>
        <period></period>
    </contact>
    <communication>
        <language>language>
        <preferred value="[boolean]"/>
    </communication>
    <generalPractitioner></generalPractitioner>
    <managingOrganization></managingOrganization>
     <link>
         <other></other>
         <type value="[code]"/>
    </link>
</Patient>
```

- <id>: FHIR resource id to identify a specific resource within the repository. Different resource types will have an id and value. A resource can have multiple identifiers but only one id. Every resource type has an id, but not every resource type has an identifier. If an FHIR server stores many instances of resource data, then each of those instances on a server will have a unique resource id. The id value does not change once it is assigned. It can be created as a URI by combining the server base address, resource type, and the logical resource id (http://fhir.server.come/API/Provider/1001). The logical id of resource changes depending on its server.
- <meta>: Metadata about the resource.
- <versionId>: Resource may have multiple versions. The versionId helps to identify a specific version.
- <source>: Lists the source of origin of the resource.
- <tag>: Resource may have tags associated to reflect its relevance.
- <security>: Coding Security Labels which are applied to this resource.
- <profile>: The resource can conform to pre-existing profiles which are listed in this section.
- <language>: Language of the resource content.
- <implicitRules>: The set of rules which were used to create the content
- <text>: The human readable and interpretable summary of the resource.
- <contained>: Resource Contained, with the inline Resources.
- <extension>: It is the url / link to the resource definition. These can be multiple in a

resource. It provides additional content that is defined by various implementations.

- <identifier>: This identifier is different from resource id. It contains the standard data content of that instance of the resource. This identifier can be used across many resource types. So, in the above example of patient resource, the data under identifier is the instance of the resource on a specific date and time. The identifier assists in identifying the underlying concept across all related contexts. The identifier, or Business Identifier, is the preferred way to recognize the same content on different servers.
- <deceased>: It indicates if a patient is deceased and time of death, if known.
- <communication>: The preferred language used to communicate with the patient.
- <generalPractitioner>: Patient's primary care physician.
- <managingOrganization>: Organization which manages the patient's medical record.
- <link>: A link to another patient resource that is linked to this specific patient.

The same patient resource with some sample data in general readable text will appear like this.

id: example
identifier: Medical Record Number = 1021034
active: true
name: Jane A. Doe
telecom: ph: 123-999-1234(WORK), jane.doe@test.com
gender: Female
birthsex: Female
birthDate: May 25, 1993
address: 1 Pennsylvania Ave, New York, NY 10001
race: Asian
ethnicity: Indonesian

The same data in XML format is given below for illustration.

```
<Patient xmlns="http://hl7.org/fhir">
    <id value="example"/>
   <meta>
      <profile          value="http://hl7.org/fhir/us/core/StructureDefinition/us-core-patient"/>
   </meta>
   <text>
      <status value="generated"/>
      <div xmlns="http://www.w3.org/1999/xhtml">
         <p>
                  <b>Generated Narrative with Details</b>
         </p>
         <p>
                  <b>id</b>: example</p>
         <p>
                  <b>identifier</b>: Medical Record Number = 1020134</p>
         <p>
                  <b>active</b>: true</p>
         <p>
                  <b>name</b>: Jane A. Doe </p>
         <p>
                  <b>telecom</b>: ph: 123-999-1234(WORK), jane.doe@example.com</p>
```

```
        <p>
                <b>gender</b>: </p>
        <p>
                <b>birthsex</b>: Female</p>
        <p>
                <b>birthDate</b>: May 25, 1993</p>
        <p>
                <b>address</b>: 1 Pennsylvania Ave, New York, NY 10001
        </p>
        <p>
                <b>race</b>: Asian</p>
        <p>
                <b>ethnicity</b>: Indonesian</p>
    </div>
   </text>
   <extension url="http://hl7.org/fhir/us/core/StructureDefinition/us-core-race">
    <extension url="ombCategory">
        <valueCoding>
                <system value="urn:oid:2.16.840.1.113883.6.238"/>
                <code value="2028-9"/>
                <display value="Asian"/>
        </valueCoding>
    </extension>
    <extension url="detailed">
        <valueCoding>
                <system value="urn:oid:2.16.840.1.113883.6.238"/>
                        <code value="2038-8"/>
                        <display value="Indonesian"/>
        </valueCoding>
    </extension>
        <extension url="text">
          <valueString value="Mixed"/>
        </extension>
      </extension>
      <extension
        url="http://hl7.org/fhir/us/core/StructureDefinition/us-core-ethnicity">
        <extension url="ombCategory">
                <valueCoding>
                        <system value="urn:oid:2.16.840.1.113883.6.238"/>
                        <code value="2186-5"/>
                        <display value="Not Hispanic or Latino"/>
                </valueCoding>
        </extension>
        <extension url="text">
                <valueString value="Not Hispanic or Latino"/>
        </extension>
        <extension url="http://hl7.org/fhir/us/core/StructureDefinition/us-core-birthsex">
                <valueCode value="F"/>
        </extension>
<identifier>
        <use value="usual"/>
        <type>
                <coding>
                <system value="http://terminology.hl7.org/CodeSystem/v2-0203"/>
```

```
                        <code value="MR"/>
                        <display value="Medical Record Number"/>
                </coding>
                <text value="Medical Record Number"/>
            </type>
            <system value="http://thebesthospitalever.org"/>
            <value value="1021034"/>
        </identifier>
            <active value="true"/>
            <name>
                    <family value="Doe"/>
                    <given value="Jane"/>
                    <given value="A."/>
            </name>
            <telecom>
                    <system value="phone"/>
                    <value value="123-999-1234"/>
                    <use value="work"/>
            </telecom>
            <telecom>
                    <system value="email"/>
                    <value value="jane.doe@example.com"/>
            </telecom>
            <gender value="female"/>
            <birthDate value="1993-05-25"/>
            <address>
                    <line value="1 Pennsylvania Ave"/>
                    <city value="New York"/>
                    <state value="NY"/>
                    <postalCode value="10001"/>
                    <country value="US"/>
            </address>
</Patient>
```

FHIR Module

FHIR specifications are split into separate functional areas called 'Modules'. Modules are assigned to 5 broad categories called 'Levels', each catering to a distinct aspect of healthcare. The Resources are distributed within these Levels (HL7. Getting started with FHIR).

Level 1: FHIR specification is built on the framework in this module

- **Foundation**: It contains overall infrastructure and documentation of the specification. Importantly, all the other modules depend on the foundation module. It's framework elements are Resource, DomainResource, Basic, Binary, and Bundle. It contains Content Management resources which are Questionnaire, Questionnaire response, List, Composition, DocumentReference, and DocumentManifest. The Foundation module also includes Data Exchange Resourced which are OperationOutcome, Parameters, Subscription, MessageHeader, and MessageDefinition.

Level 2: These modules assist in the implementation of FHIR

- **Implementer Support**: Services to help implementers make use of the specification. It contains downloads, version management, use cases, and testing
- **Security & Privacy**: Documentation and services to create and maintain security, integrity and privacy
- **Conformance**: How to test conformance to the specification, and define implementation guides
- **Terminology**: Use and support of terminologies and related artifacts
- **Exchange**: Defined methods of exchange for resources

Level 3: This level has Administration module

- **Administration**: Basic resources for tracking patients, practitioners, organizations, devices, substances, etc.

Level 4: This level provides clinical content

- **Clinical**: Core clinical content such as problems, allergies, and the care process (care plans, referrals) + more
- **Medications**: Medication management and immunization tracking
- **Diagnostics:** Observations, Diagnostic reports and requests + related content
- **Workflow**: Managing the process of care, and technical artifacts to do with obligation management
- **Financial**: Billing and Claiming support

Level 5: This is an advanced module which provides functionality for analytics

- **Clinical Reasoning**: Clinical Decision Support and Quality Measures

Flat FHIR / Bulk Data Export

Flat FHIR is a standard to enable EHR population level data export to assist with population health efforts through data analysis (Gottlieb D et al. 2021). Population level data is known as 'Bulk Data'. The analysis of this data is important for population health management, improving quality of care, value-based care initiatives and research. Traditionally, the EHR data is an aggregation from multiple sources which is then manually cleaned, merged and exported in the desired format. Apps receive data via by FHIR by making an API request for each data point that is needed. This will not work for data sets capturing thousands of data points per patient and for thousands of patients. FHIR Bulk Data API specification was created to assist with this scenario.

In the ONC Health IT Final rule around interoperability in the 21st Century Cures Act, FHIR Bulk Data Access (Flat FHIR) API was adopted for group export criteria. SMART has made available bulk data reference server, client, tester and tools for APIs. These can be used for bulk export of notes from one health facility to other, integrating population health efforts with EHR systems, disease surveillance, accessing training data for machine learning, patient history import, querying using joins on JSON using Spark SQL or other data warehouses. SMART on FHIR is discussed more in detail in the chapter about Healthcare APIs. Bulk data is enabled by using FHIR Resources and a standard data model, FHIR Operation API to initiate data extracts. It uses SMART Backend Services Authentication and Authorization as the security model. App authorization can be done through token requests signed with private key, registered JSON Web Key Set public key or URL, direct app registration, or short-lived access tokens.

The flow of data in Bulk Data access scenarios is based on authenticated interaction between the client and the Bulk Data server

- Initially, Bulk Data client sends a kickoff request to Bulk Data server. The kick of request could be asynchronous request with status polling, FHIR operation requesting all data on the server, on all patients or a group of patients.
- The Bulk Data server responds with the content location.
- The Bulk Data client sends a GET request to the content location and gets a response if everything is in order and the server is getting the file ready. The second GET request to the content location provides the data file location. Final GET request from the Bulk Data client receives the FHIR resources file in response from the Bulk Data server.

The backend service admin sends the configuration public key and OAuth settings to Bulk Data server which responds with an OAuth client id. The Bulk Data client sends a signed token request to the Bulk Data server which provides an access token to the Bulk Data client.

FHIR Extensions

FHIR standards adhere to 80:20 rule, which means that the base specifications cover about four-fifths of all potential use cases. For everything else, developers can use the FHIR extensions which are child elements of the resource and represent additional information that is not part of the basic definition of the resource. Use of extensions requires adherence to strict requirements to ensure consistency. A general XML representation of extension structure is

```
<extension|modifierExtension xmlns="http://hl7.org/fhir" url="identifies the meaning of the extension (uri)">
        <value[x]><!-- 0..1 * Value of extension --></value[x]>
</extension|modifierExtension>
```

An example of this is given below where the name "Chief Red Cloud" is extended to have a name use code of "Indigenous" (HL7. Extensibility).

```
<name>
        <extension url="http://hl7.org/fhir/StructureDefinition/iso-21090-EN-use" >
        <valueCode value="I" />
        </extension>
        <text value="Chief Red Cloud"/>
</name>
```

Hypertext Transfer Protocol (HTTP)

FHIR is based on two widely used web concepts – HTTP and REST. HTTP is a protocol that enables the fetching of resources (Mozilla. An overview of HTTP). It is based on a client-server protocol where the client is usually the browser on web architecture and can exchange messages with a server. The client sends messages with a request, and the server sends the message with a response. HTTP can be used to transfer documents, images, and videos. On the web, a document is made of HTML with CSS, Web APIs, and Javascript embeddings. The HTTP protocol is based on the client-server model. The data storage and information processing are split between the client, the front-end interface for the user requesting resources or services, and the backend server, which provides resources or services. Servers provide processing, computational logic, and data storage (Reese, 2000). The main characteristics of HTTP are:

- **Simplicity:** Humans can easily understand HTTP messages.
- **Extensibility:** The protocol can be extended using headers which allow client and server exchange more information.
- **Statelessness:** Every request between the client and server is separate without any link between consecutive requests. To create contextual awareness, a browsing session becomes stateful through the use of HTTP cookies.
- **Connections:** HTTP relies on TCP standard which controls the connection at the transport layer.

Representational State Transfer (REST)

Representational State Transfer (REST) is a software architecture design with constraints that improve distributed systems' efficiency, reliability, and scalability (Barry DK. Service Architecture). REST is based on client-server architecture (Fredrich T. REST API Tutorial). Any web service API that adheres to the constraints of REST architecture is called RESTful API. A FHIR resource, which could be a document, is transferred along with its state and relationships through standardized operations through RESTful APIs. FHIR RESTful API does not deal with authentication, authorization, and audit collection.

REST API calls share some common characteristics:

- Base URI e.g., http://api.demo.com/list
- HTTP methods like GET, POST, PUT, PATCH, and DELETE
- Media type e.g., application/json. It consists of type and a subtype. Types include application, audio, example, font, image, message, model, multipart, text, and video. Subtypes are usually media formats. The format is type/subtype;parameter=value e.g. text/plain;charset=UTF-8 (Fielding RT. 2008).

REST framework imposes constraints in its usage. Some of these are:

- **Uniform interface:** The resource identifiers are used to identify individual resources using URIs. The resources returned are usually a modified form (e.g., XML, JSON) of the data stored on the server (e.g., RDBMS). Each message contains adequate information to process that message. The state is transmitted by the client system through content in the body, headers, query string parameters, and the requested URI with the resource name. The servers send state to the clients through content in the body, headers, or response codes.
- **Stateless:** The state required to process the request is contained with the request. This could be part of the URI which identifies the resource, body which contains the state of the resource, query-string parameters, body, or headers. State represents the data required for the current request. Resource is the data stored, typically in a database.
- **Cacheable:** The clients (browsers) can cache the responses received from the server and this process is made explicit so as to minimize client-server communication while at the same time prevent cache from getting out of date.
- **Client-server:** Separation of concern between client and server where server focuses on storing data and client focuses on usability and user interface. This allows for best design and resource allocation for both.

- **Layered system:** There may be intermediaries between client and the end server to improve scalability by using load-balancing and security by enforcing security policies.
- **Code on demand (optional):** Clients can sometime receive logic for processing from servers.

FHIR Interactions

Interactions are a set of operations performed on FHIR resources. The interactions and resources that are supported by the FHIR server are listed in the Capability Statement provided by the FHIR server. This statement can be used for compatibility testing, code generation, or conformance assessment. All the interactions are defined relative to service root URL so if address of any one FHIR resource on a system is known, address of other resources can be determined. In FHIR, the following interactions on the resources are defined as per documentation available on HL7 website (HL7. RESTful API):

Instance Level Interactions

GET

- ***read:*** *Current state*
- ***vread:*** *Specific version*
- ***history:*** *Change history*
-

PUT

- ***update:*** *Update or create by id*

PATCH

- ***patch:*** *Update by posting changes*

DELETE

- ***delete:*** *Delete a resource*

Type Level Interactions

GET

- ***search:*** *Search on specific criteria*
- ***history:*** *Change history*

POST

- ***create:*** *Create a resource with id assigned by server*
- ***search:*** *Search on specific criteria*

Whole System Interactions

GET

- ***capabilities:*** *Get system capability statement*
- ***history:*** *Change history*
- ***search:*** *Search on specific criteria*

POST

- ***batch/transaction:*** *Create, update or delete a set of resources*
- ***search:*** *Search on specific criteria*

The format of an interaction with a FHIR resource is *VERB [base]/[type]/[id] {?_format=[mime-type]}*

- **VERB**: REST based HTTP methods which identify the action performed on the resources. GET is for reading resources, POST is for creating a new resource at a location assigned by server, PUT is used to update a resource and DELETE removes a resource from a server.
- **base**: The location in the form of a url where all resources are stored. Format is *http{s}://server{/path}*
- **type**: The resource type identifier e.g. *https://server/path/Patient*
- **id**: Resource Logical ID
- **vid**: Resource Version id
- **mime-type**: FHIR mime-type is *application/fhir+xml, application/fhir+json* or *application/fhir+turtle*
- **compartment**: Logical grouping of resources sharing a common property. The compartment is used to perform a similar action on the group of resources instead of individually. Compartments include Patient, Encounter, RelatedPerson, Practitioner, Device etc.

Server errors

If an error is generated during any of the above mentioned procedures, the error response can help to deduce the reason for the error. Some server errors are and their descriptions from HL7 FHIR documentation:

- **400 Bad Request** – *"resource could not be parsed or failed basic FHIR validation rules (or multiple matches were found for conditional criteria)"*
- **401 Not Authorized** – *the authorization is required for the interaction that was attempted*
- **404 Not Found** – *resource type not supported or not a FHIR end-point*
- **405 Method Not allowed** – *the resource did not exist prior to the update, and the server does not allow client defined ids*
- **409/412** – *version conflict management*
- **422 Unprocessable Entity** – *the proposed resource violated applicable FHIR profiles or server business rules"*

FHIR Conformance

The FHIR specification rules provide optional features to allow for more flexibility in implementation. However, to ensure compatibility and interoperability, the FHIR applications are expected to choose the frameworks that they confirm to. These include:

- "RESTful FHIR": the RESTful API
- "FHIR messaging": Message based exchange
- "FHIR documents": Document based exchange

Conformance is implemented using StructureDefinition, CapabilityStatement and Implementation Guide. Three properties of data elements and data types allow implementation of conformance requirements (HL7. Conformance).

- Cardinality: Attribute count in one instance of the resource type. The cardinalities defined are 0..1, 0..*, 1..1, and 1..*
- Is-modifier: An element is considered to be a modifier if it cannot be safely ignored if there is a possibility that its containing element may not be considered as conforming to the definition of the element. It is used for status, active, refuted, or certainty elements.
- MustSupport: Support for the element.

United States Core Data for Interoperability

"The United States Core Data for Interoperability (USCDI) is a standardized set of health data classes and data elements for nationwide, interoperable health information exchange". (Marquard et al., 2021). Use of USCDI standard replaces the Common Clinical Data Set (CCDS). A USCDI "Data Class" is an "aggregation of various Data Elements by a common theme or use case. A USCDI "Data Element" is the most granular level at which a piece of data is exchanged. For example, Date of Birth is a Data Element rather than its component Day, Month, or Year, because Date of Birth is the unit of exchange." The USCDI v1 Summary of Data Classes and Data Elements list is included below for reference (ONC USCDI. 2020). Readers are encouraged to check the USCDI website for the most recent version of the standard.

- **Allergies and Intolerance**: Represents harmful or undesirable physiological response associated with exposure to a substance
    - Substance (Medication)
        - RxNorm
        - The Unified Code of Units for Measure
    - Reaction
        - SNOMED International, Systematized Nomenclature of Medicine Clinical Terms (SNOMED CT)
    - Substance (Drug Class)
        - SNOMED CT
- **Assessment and Plan of Treatment**: Represents a health professional's conclusions and working assumptions that will guide the treatment of the patient
    - SNOMED CT
    - Logical Observation Identifiers Names and Codes (LOINC)
- **Care Team Members**: The specific person(s) who participate or are expected to participate in the care team
- **Clinical Notes**:
    - Consultation Note: Contains the response to a request from a clinician for an opinion or advice from another clinician
    - Consult note (LOINC 11488-4)
    - Discharge Summary Note: Synopsis of a patient's admission and course in a hospital or post-acute care setting
        - Discharge Summary (LOINC 18842-5)
    - History & Physical: Documents the current and past conditions and observations of the patient
        - History and Physical Note (LOINC 34117-2)
    - Imaging Narrative: Contains a consulting specialist's interpretation of image data

        - Diagnostic Imaging Study (LOINC 18748-4)
    - Laboratory Report Narrative: Contains a consulting specialist's interpretation of the laboratory report
    - Pathology Report Narrative: Contains a consulting specialist's interpretation of the pathology report.
    - Procedure Note: Encompasses non-operative procedures including interventional cardiology, gastrointestinal endoscopy, osteopathic manipulation, and other specialty's procedures
        - Procedure Note (LOINC 28570-0)
    - Progress Note: Represents a patient's interval status during a hospitalization, outpatient visit, treatment with a LTPAC provider, or another healthcare encounter.
        - Progress Note (LOINC 11506-3)
- **Goals**: An expressed desired health state to be achieved by a subject of care (or family/group) over a period or at a specific time.
    - Patient Goals
        - LOINC
        - SNOMED CT
- **Health Concerns**: Health related matter that is of interest, importance, or worry to someone who may be the patient, patient's family or patient's health care provider.
    - LOINC
    - SNOMED CT
- **Immunizations**: Record of an administration of vaccination or a record of vaccination as reported by a patient, a clinician, or another party
    - CDC IIS: Current HL7 Standard Code Set, CVX -- Vaccines Administered
    - CDC National Drug Code (NDC) Directory – Vaccine NDC Linker Table
- **Laboratory**:
    - Tests: Examinations of specimens derived from humans to provide information for the diagnosis, prevention, treatment of disease, impairment of, or assessment of health.
        - LOINC
        - SNOMED CT
        - The Unified Code of Units for Measure
    - Values/Results: Outcome of the examination of a tested specimen
        - LOINC
        - SNOMED CT
        - The Unified Code of Units for Measure
- **Medications**:
    - Medications
        - RxNorm
        - The Unified Code of Units for Measure
    - Medication Allergies
- **Patient Demographics**:
    - First Name
    - Last Name
    - Previous Name
    - Middle Name (including middle initial)
    - Suffix
    - Birth Sex

        - Birth sex must be coded as per HL7 Version 3 (V3) Standard, Value Sets for AdministrativeGender and NullFlavor attributed as Male M, Female F, Unknown nullFlavor UNK
    - Date of Birth
    - Race
        - The Office of Management and Budget Standards for Maintaining, Collecting, and Presenting Federal Data on Race and Ethnicity, Statistical Policy Directive
        - CDC Race and Ethnicity Code Set
    - Ethnicity:
        - The Office of Management and Budget Standards for Maintaining, Collecting, and Presenting Federal Data on Race and Ethnicity, Statistical Policy Directive
        - CDC Race and Ethnicity Code Set
    - Preferred Language
        - Request for Comment (RFC) 5646, "Tags for Identifying Languages"
    - Current Address
    - Previous Address
    - Phone Number
        - ITU–T E.123 (02/2001) International Telecommunication Union E.123: Notation for national and international telephone numbers, e-mail addresses and web addresses
        - ITU–T E.164 International Telecommunication Union E.164: The international public telecommunication numbering plan
    - Phone Number type
    - Email Address
- **Problems**: Information about a condition, diagnosis, or another event, situation, issue, or clinical concept that is documented
    - SNOMED CT
- **Procedures**: An activity performed for or on a patient as part of the provision of care.
    - Health Care Financing Administration Common Procedure Coding System (HCPCS), as maintained and distributed by HHS.
    - Current Procedural Terminology (CPT), as maintained and distributed by the American Medical Association, for physician services and other health care services.
    - Systematized Nomenclature of Medicine Clinical Terms
    - International Classification of Diseases ICD-10-PCS 2020
    - Code on Dental Procedures and Nomenclature (CDT), maintained and distributed by the American Dental Association, for dental services
- **Provenance**: The metadata, or extra information about data, regarding who created the data and when it was created.
    - Author Time Stamp
    - Author Organization
- **Smoking Status**: Representing a patient's smoking behavior
    - SNOMED CT
- **Unique Device Identifier(s)**: A unique numeric or alphanumeric code for a Patient's Implantable Device(s) that consists of a device identifier and a production identifier.
    - UDI identifier as described by applicable FDA regulation.
- **Vital Signs**: Physiologic measurements of a patient that indicate the status of the body's life

sustaining functions.

- LOINC
- The Unified Code of Units for Measure
- Elements
  - Diastolic Blood Pressure
  - Systolic Blood Pressure
  - Body Height
  - Body Weight
  - Heart Rate
  - Respiratory Rate
  - Body Temperature
  - Pulse Oximetry
  - Inhaled Oxygen Concentration
  - BMI Percentile (2-20 years)
  - Weight-for-length Percentile (Birth - 36 months)
  - Head Occipital-frontal Circumference Percentile (Birth - 36 months)

USCDI+ initiative was launched to support identifying and creating domain specific datasets built on the core USCDI framework. For example, USCDI+ data specifications for quality measurement will harmonize multiple federal agency requirements.

Future direction

CMS is committed to improving the interoperability of healthcare data for quality measurement, quality improvement, clinical decision support, research, and public health. Standards-based data sharing can 'maximize interoperability, minimize burden, and facilitate the development and use of common tooling." The chapter on ONC 21st Century Cures Act discusses the requirements of certified health information technology including support for FHIR and USCDI. In the CY 2022 PFS final rule, CMS stated its goal of moving to the digital quality measurement for all CMS quality reporting and value-based purchasing programs starting with adoption of FHIR API technology and using FHIR standards for eCQM reporting. To achieve this, CMS well obtained electronic health record data through provider FHIR based APIs, redesigning the quality measures to be self-contained, establishing broad alignment of quality measure requirements (eCQI, 2022).

4 HEALTHCARE TERMINOLOGY

Healthcare IT systems use standardized healthcare nomenclature, which ensures that correct information is communicated to another entity and enables interoperability among different IT systems. This chapter will discuss the common terminologies, coding standards, and classifications used in healthcare.

Standards are of two types:

- **Syntax:** Standards that specify a uniform structure for sending messages and creating documents or APIs. e.g., FHIR, C-CDA.
- **Semantic:** Standards that provide a uniform vocabulary or code system. e.g., SNOMED CT, RxNorm, ICD.

Unified Medical Language System (UMLS)

Unified Medical Language System (UMLS) comprises of biomedical vocabularies and standards that enable interoperability among Health IT systems. It is made available as both data files and software. UMLS is maintained by a team under the aegis of the National Library of Medicine. UMLS is used by medical informatics developers. "It integrates and distributes terminology, classification and coding standards, and associated resources to promote creation of more effective and interoperable biomedical information systems and services, including EHRs" (Bodenreider, 2004).

UMLS has three knowledge sources that make the foundation of the standard:

Metathesaurus: This is the base of the UMLS and has over one million biomedical concepts and five million concept names from over 100 vocabularies and classification systems. The relationships can be in the form of hierarchies with "is a" for subclasses, "is part of" for subunits, and "is caused by" for associated relationships. This consists of vocabularies including LOINC, SNOMED-CT, ICD-10, CPT, RxNorm, and MeSH. Metathesaurus browser can search data through UMLS terminology services and access UMLS concept information, including Concept Unique Identifiers (CUIs), semantic types, and synonymous terms. Every concept is represented by a CUI (NLM. UMLS).

Semantic Network: These are broad categories (127 semantic types) and their relationship (54 semantic relations). The concepts in Metathesaurus are associated with one or more semantic types which are connected through semantic relationships. The Semantic Network Browser allows to "view the names, definitions, and hierarchical structure of the Semantic Network". The main semantic types are anatomical structures, biologic function, organisms, chemicals, physical objects, events, and concepts. Every semantic type has an identifier,

Specialist Lexicon and Lexical Tools: Syntactic lexicon is for "normalizing strings, generating lexical variants, and creating indexes" (NLM. UMLS).

Systematized Nomenclature of Medicine - Clinical Terms (SNOMED-CT)

Systematized Nomenclature of Medicine – Clinical Terms (SNOMED-CT) enables the standardized representation of clinical phrases generated by clinical providers and allows for automation and interpretation (National Library of Medicine. SNOMED-CT). SNOMED-CT allows for clinical interpretation of physician created content in EHRs and enables interoperability and reporting. It has over 300,000 concepts and over 1.3 million relationships.

SNOMED®, SNOMED CT® and IHTSDO® are registered trademarks of International Health Terminology Standards Development Organization. SNOMED-CT is maintained by International Health Terminology Standards Organization (IHTSDO). Details of the standard are available on SNOMED-CT website.

SNOMED is a clinically validated hierarchical taxonomy system classifying disease by its characteristics. It has been accepted as a national standard for a variety of use cases including public health reporting, meaningful use, health information exchanges, problem list generation in EHRs, genetic information resources, clinical research studies. The information can be captured with varying degrees of complexity while keeping consistency in terminology. SNOMED-CT is incorporated in Health IT systems and mapped to other coding systems like ICD-10 as it enables consistent and comprehensive clinical information representation.

Components

The content of SNOMED-CT is based on three types of components.

- **Concepts:** Concepts represent clinical ideas and are represented by a unique nine-digit concept identifier (SCTID). SNOMED CT concepts domains have clinical findings, including diseases, procedures, observable entities.
- **Descriptions:** Concepts have description that provides an unambiguous meaning and clarification of a concept in a human readable language. The description consists of a unique identifier and connects the concept to Fully Specified Name (FSN) which may have none to many synonyms. For example, *22298006* is a concept Id of myocardial infarction (FSN) having synonyms of "myocardial infarction, heart attack, infarction of heart, cardiac infarction, heart attack, myocardial infarct, MI – myocardial infarction" (SNOMED. SNOMED CT Starter Guide). Each concept also has one Preferred Term (PT) which is the most common way to express the meaning of the concept.
- **Relationships:** SNOMED CT relationships link concepts with some identifiable relationship. Every relationship has a unique relationship identifier. Every concept has at least one |is a|

relationship and can have multiple Attribute relationships. For example, Diabetes Mellitus type 2 (disorder) is a concept with relationship type | is a | of relationship Id 116680003 with concept Id 73211009 Diabetes Mellitus (disorder). At the same time Concept Id 425548001 abscess of heart (disorder) has an attribute relationship | associated morphology | with abscess 44132006 (morphological abnormality) and | finding site | relationship with 80891009 heart structure (body structure).

Concept Hierarchies

The SNOMED-CT Concepts are organized into hierarchies which are linked to the concepts using |is a| relationship. The hierarchies have broad as well as detailed concepts. The hierarchies include (SNOMED. SNOMED CT Starter Guide):

- **Body structure:** Normal and abnormal body structures. e.g. |Amputation stump|, |Sarcoma|, |B lymphocyte cell|, |Dendritic cell system structure|
- **Clinical finding / disorder:** Result of a clinical, observation, assessment or judgment including normal and abnormal states. Disorder is the sub-hierarchy of clinical finding. e.g. |fracture|, |normal bowel sounds|
- **Environment or geographical location:** Types of environments and locations e.g. |Medical floor|, |Derelict house|, |Canada|
- **Event:** Occurrences excluding procedures and interventions. e.g. |Abuse of partner|, |Earthquake|
- **Observable entity:** Question or assessment performed to obtain a result. There are four observable entities - Quality, Disposition, Function, Process. e.g. |diastolic blood pressure|, |color of sclera|
- **Organism:** Organisms of significance to human medicine. This concept is used in modeling cause of disease, document cause of notifiable disease, evidence-based infectious disease protocols. e.g. |Gram-negative bacterium|, |Salmonella enterica|
- **Pharmaceutical / biologic product:** Drug products. it has multiple smaller hierarchies. e.g. |Codeine sulfate|, |Bacitracin|
- **Physical force:** Physical forces that can cause injury when applied to the body. e.g. |radiation|, |altitude|, |motion|
- **Physical object:** Natural and man-made physical objects and devices. e.g. |Diagnostic imaging telemedicine system|, |Boomerang, device|
- **Procedure:** Indicates activities performed while providing health care. It includes clinical procedures, imaging, education, therapies, administrative procedures, medication administration. Regime/therapy is the sub-type of procedure which is a set of procedures for a single purpose on one patient over the period of time. e.g. |cholecystectomy|, |physical therapy|, |medical records transfer|, |anesthesia management|
- **Qualifier value:** Values for attributes that are not subtypes of other top-level concepts. e.g. |right|, |moderate|
- **Record artifact:** Entity created for providing other people with information about events or state of affair. e.g. |Clinical document|, |Cytology report|, |Duplicate report|
- **Situation with explicit context:** Concepts which contain clinical context within the concept definition. e.g. |past history of diabetes|, |tonsillectomy requested|
- **Social context:** Social conditions which are significant to health care. The subtypes are: ethnic group, lifestyle, occupation, person, racial group, religion/philosophy, social concept.

e.g. |Lower class economic status (social concept)|, |Eating habit (life style)|

- **Special concept:** Represents inactive and navigational concepts. e.g. |Intravenous administration of treatment|, |Duplicate concept|
- **Specimen:** Entities that are collected from the patient. Specimens can be further defined by attributes with procedure used to collect the specimen, source of the specimen, body structure from which specimen is obtained. e.g. |Mid-stream urine specimen|, |Soft tissue biopsy sample|
- **Staging and scales:** Assessment scales, symptom ratings, histological grading systems, and tumor staging systems. e.g. |Alcohol withdrawal scale|, |Tumor-node-metastasis (TNM) brain tumor staging|
- **Substance:** General substances, dietary substances, diagnostic substances, body substances, chemical ingredients of pharmaceutical or biological products. e.g. |Albumin|,|Tree pollen|, |Ice|

Concept Attributes

SNOMED-CT attributes or relationship types "are used to represent a characteristic of the meaning of a concept" (SNOMED. SNOMED CT Starter Guide). Domain of the attribute (or relationship types) is the set of concepts on which attribute is applied. Range of attribute is the allowed set of values for each attribute. The following are the attributes and their representations are provided in the SNOMED CT Starter Guide:

- **Clinical finding concepts:** Finding site, Associated morphology, Associated with, After, Due to, Causative agent, Severity, Clinical course, Episodicity, Interprets, Has interpretation, Pathological process, Has definitional manifestation, Occurrence, Finding method, Finding informer
- **Procedure concepts:** Procedure site, Procedure morphology, Method, Procedure device, Access, Direct substance, Priority, Has focus, Has intent, Recipient category, Revision status, Route of administration, Surgical approach, Using substance, Using energy
- **Evaluation procedure concepts:** Has specimen, Component, Time aspect, Property, Scale type, Measurement method
- **Specimen concepts:** Specimen procedure, Specimen source topography, Specimen source morphology, Specimen substance, Specimen source identify
- **Body structure concepts:** Laterality
- **Pharmaceutical/biologic product concepts:** Has active ingredient, Has dose form
- **Situation with explicit context concepts:** Associated finding, Finding context, Associated procedure, Procedure context, Temporal context, Subject relationship context
- **Event concepts:** Associated with, Occurrence

Concept Expressions

SNOMED-CT expressions are "a structured combination of one or more concept identifiers used to represent a clinical idea in a logical manner, which is automatically processable" (SNOMED. SNOMED CT Starter Guide). A SNOMED CT concept model provides alternatives for representing any information which is similar to recognized. For example, "|pneumococcal pneumonia| refined by |finding site||right upper lobe of lung| can be computed to have the same meaning as |right upper lobe pneumonia| refined by |causative agent||Streptococcus pneumoniae|." Clinical ideas not explicitly represented by SNOMED CT concepts can be created with compositional syntax. The basic process of creating SNOMED-CT composition can be broken down into following steps (SNOMED. SNOMED CT Starter Guide).

- For example, one SNOMED CT concept identifier is 80146002
- A term can be added to the concept identifier for reference. The term is separated from other parts of the expression by a pipe character. For example, the previous concept identifier can be represented as: 80146002|appendectomy|
- The concept identifier (along with the term) can be refined with additional attributes. These are separated from the concept identifier with a colon. For example: 80146002|appendectomy|:
- An expression refinement is part of the SNOMED expression which can provide additional details or refinements with one or more attribute-value pairs. Both the attribute and the value are represented by a concept identifier. An 'equals' sign separates the attribute from the value: 80146002|appendectomy|:260870009|priority|= 25876001|emergency|
- Commas are used to separate additional refinements with attribute-value pairs: 80146002|appendectomy|:260870009|priority|= 25876001|emergency|, 425391005|using access device|= 86174004|laparoscope|
- If the attributes need to be grouped together within a refinement, they can be grouped together with curly braces: 80146002|appendectomy|:{ 260686004|method|= 129304002|excision - action|, 405813007|procedure site - direct|= 181255000|entire appendix|}
- Attributes can be further refined through nesting by using round brackets: 161615003|history of surgery|:363589002|associated procedure|= (80146002|appendectomy|: 260870009|priority|= 25876001|emergency)

Logical Observation Identifiers Names and Codes (LOINC)

Logical Observation Identifiers Names and Codes (LOINC) is a code system and database about anything that is tested, measured, or observed about a patient. It is used for identifying laboratory tests, clinical observations and documents (LOINC. About LOINC). It is developed and maintained by Regenstrief Institute and is copyrighted by the Regenstrief Institute, Inc. It was initially released in 1995 and has grown to over 80,000 observations. Regenstrief Institute provides a free mapping program RELMA (Regenstrief LOINC Mapping Assistant) to assist with browsing of LOINC codes and mapping of test codes. As per LOINC website "LOINC is a rich catalog of measurements, including laboratory tests, clinical measures like vital signs and anthropometric measures, standardized survey instruments, and more. LOINC also contains codes for collections of these items, such as panels, forms, and documents....LOINC codes represent the 'question' for a test or measurement. Where needed, codes from other standards (e.g. SNOMED CT) represent the answer".

LOINC provides codes for single measures or observations or collections of measurements. The discrete measures and observations include patient measurement (e.g. weight, vital sign, fluid intake/output), lab test value (e.g. serum sodium mEq/L), survey question (e.g. What is your pain level from 1-10) or report element (physical findings of skin). The collections could include a panel of laboratory tests (e.g. Comprehensive Metabolic Panel), survey question (e.g. General life satisfaction survey), group of clinical measurements (e.g. heart rate panel), or a document or report (e.g. progress note). Currently, LOINC also includes patient care data sets, nursing interventions, nursing diagnosis, and outcomes classification.

LOINC Categories

Broadly, LOINC has two categories - Laboratory and Clinical. The Laboratory category includes is anything that we can test, measure, or observe about a lab specimen. It can include hematology, chemistry, microbiology, toxicology etc. The Clinical category includes physiological attributes that can be tested, measured, or observed about a patient without removing a specimen from them. e.g. vital signs, intake/output, EKG, echocardiogram, endoscopic procedures, provider notes include History & physical notes, Discharge summaries, Patient consents, Advance directives, Procedure notes, Flowsheets, Action plans, Prescriptions or Radiology reports.

LOINC also includes surveys and assessments. Some examples include Agency for Healthcare Research and Quality (AHRQ) surveys, Center for Medicare & Medicaid Services (CMS) surveys, Patient Activity Scale (PAS), Geriatric Depression Scale (GDS) survey, Morse Fall Scale survey, Nursing Management Minimum Data (NMMDS) survey etc.

LOINC Codes

LOINC provides a code and a formal name to every observation. Codes have 7-character field and are 3-7 characters in length with the last character (digit 0-9) separated by a hyphen. Every observation has a long formal name, short 30-character name and synonyms. LOINC Long Common Name is human readable text associated with every LOINC code. Short Name is used as column headers and for compatibility with older systems. Fully Specified Name (FSN) is used for mapping.

Every LOINC observation has six properties (LOINC. User Guide):

- **Component | Analyte:** The substance or entity that is being measured or observed (name of the measurement). e.g. Leukocytes: NCnc: Pt: CSF: Qn: Manual count. It has three subparts:
  - Principle name: The name of substance or entity. It can be further subclassified or identified with sub-analytes (e.g. Calcium.ionized, Births.preterm)
  - Challenge / Provocation: The information that can be used to interpret tolerance of tests. This could be time delay prior to observation, amount and route of administration with format (e.g. Breaths^1H post inhalation therapy)
  - Adjustment: These are the calculations that adjust the measured values. (e.g. Oxygen^^adjusted to patient's actual temperature, fentaNYL^^adjusted for lean body mass+urine creatinine)
- **Property:** Characteristic or attribute of the analyte. It can indicate different kinds of quantities (mass, substance etc.) and their subtypes including concentration, contents, ratios, fractions and rates. The properties could include MCnt (Mass content), MCnc (Mass concentration), RelSRat (Relative Substance Rate) e.g. Leukocytes: NCnc: Pt: CSF: Qn: Manual count. Here NCnc represents Number concentration
- **Time:** Time duration over which an observation was made (Point in time or measured over a time interval). Time could include 12H for 12 hour collection, 24H for 24 hour collection.e.g. Leukocytes: NCnc: Pt: CSF: Qn: Manual count. Here Pt referes to Point in time.
- **System:** The specimen or entity on which the observation is made. The system has two segments or parts. The initial segment contains name of the system and the next segment

contains name of a subpart of the sample that is not the patients. This could include Bld (whole blood), Ser/Plas (Serum or plasma). For tests run on a combination of types of systems, the codes are joined with "+". e.g. Leukocytes: NCnc: Pt: CSF: Qn: Manual count. CSF refers to Cerebrospinal fluid. if the sample was obtained from another source than the patient in context then super system notation is used. This includes Fetus, Donor e.g. WBC^BPU.

- **Scale:** This describes the nature of the observation value - Quantitative (Qn), Ordinal (Ord), Nominal (Nom), Narrative (Nar), Document (Doc). e.g. Leukocytes: NCnc: Pt: CSF: Qn: Manual count. Qn refers to Quantitative.
- **Method:** Method used to perform the test or how the observation was made. This property is optional. It includes MRI (Magnetic Resonance Imaging), IA (Immunoassay), Estimated, Automated. For example, Leukocytes: NCnc: Pt: CSF: Qn: Manual count. Here, manual count is the method.

Example of a LOINC observation (LOINC. Leucocytes):

- **Fully-Specified Name (FSN):** Leukocytes: NCnc: Pt: CSF: Qn: Manual count
- **Long Common Name (LCN):** Leukocytes [#/volume] in Cerebral spinal fluid by Manual count
- **Short Name:** WBC # CSF Manual

LOINC in HL7

In HL7, LOINC denotes Observation Identifier value (OBX-3 Observation identifier) HL7 code system name is 'LN'. e.g. (Vreeman DJ. 2012)

- OBX||CE||57131-5^Newborn conditions with pos markers^LN||7573000^PKU^SCT
    - CE : 'Coded element' to indicate coded answer
    - 57131-5 : Observation identifier
    - Newborn conditions with pos markers : Name of the observation
    - LN : Code for LOINC
    - 7573000 : Code for the answer
    - PKU : Phenylketonuria
    - SCT: Indicates that the code is from SNOMED-CT
- OBX||NM|26464-8^WBC # Bld^LN||3.24|10*3/uL
    - NM : 'Numeric' value to indicate the type of answer
    - 26464-8 : Laboratory identifier
    - WBC # Bld : Short name
    - 3.24 : Result
    - 10*3/uL : Units

RxNorm

RxNorm is the normalized nomenclature for clinical drugs (National Institutes of Health. RxNorm Overview). It assists in interoperability between clinical and pharmacy systems by providing unique identifiers to allow computer systems to communicate accurately. Drug names from eleven data sources are processed to create RxNorm which links these vocabularies to mediate messages between different systems. The normalized names are referenced as

SAB=RXNORM to clarify the source of drug name is RxNorm.

RxNorm is based on concept where drugs are grouped together into concepts. Each distinct ingredient, strength and dose form combination is assigned a unique RxNorm Concept Unique Identifier RXCUI. RxNorm does not include non-therapeutic radiopharmaceuticals, contrast media, food, dietary supplements, bulk powders, and medical devices. RxNorm is maintained by National Library of Medicine.

RxNorm concepts are created from the source data. Initially, similar versions of the source data are grouped into concepts. For example, Naproxen Tab 250 MG, Naproxen 250 mg tablet, Naproxen 250 MILLIGRAM In 1 ORAL TABLET. RxNorm normalized name is created for each concept. This name is made of ingredient, strength, and dose form. Branded versions of the drug appends brand names in square brackets at the end. Subsequently, RxNorm Concept Unique Identifier (RXCUI) and RxNorm Atom Unique Identifier are assigned. RxCUI is a code that identifies the concept. Every name obtained from source vocabulary is assigned an RXCUI. The drug name is the Atom. Additional characteristics like source, code assigned by the source, and term type are listed. Source data may include relationships that link drug names to ingredients, NDC codes, physical form information, images etc. Finally, RxNorm names and relationships are created. Along with clinical drug names, variations of the drug names are also created. For example, per NLM, "along with the RxNorm fully-specified name 'Naproxen 250 MG Oral Tablet', NLM creates: 'Naproxen', 'Naproxen 250 MG', 'Naproxen Oral Tablet' / 'Naproxen Oral Products' / 'Naproxen Pills'" These names are linked using relationships has_dose_form, ingredient_of, is_a, has_ingredient, has_tradename, part_of, dose_form_of, etc.

RxNorm Databases and Terminologies

RxNorm concepts are sourced from various databases and terminologies which are listed below along with their Source Abbreviation (SAB):

- Anatomical Therapeutic Chemical Classification System (ATC)
- CMS Formulary Reference File (MTHCMSFRF)
- Drug Bank (DRUGBANK)
- FDA Structured Product Labels (MTHSPL)
- FDB MedKnowledge (NDDF)
- Gold Standard Drug Database (GS)
- Medical Subject Headings (MSH)
- Micromedex Red Book (MMX)
- Multum MediSource Lexicon (MMSL)
- RxNorm Normalized Names and Codes (RXNORM)
- SNOMED Clinical Terms (SNOMEDCT_US)
- USP Compendial Nomenclature (USP)
- Vaccines Administered (CVX)
- Veterans Health Administration National Drug File (VANDF)

SAB-RXNORM uses term types (TTYs) to indicate drug names with varying specificity (National Institutes of Health. RxNorm Overview). For example:

TTY	Name	Description	Example
IN	Ingredient	A compound or moiety that gives the drug its distinctive clinical properties. Ingredients generally use the United States Adopted Name (USAN).	Fluoxetine
PIN	Precise Ingredient	A specified form of the ingredient that may or may not be clinically active. Most precise ingredients are salt or isomer forms.	Fluoxetine Hydrochloride
MIN	Multiple Ingredients	Two or more ingredients appearing together in a single drug preparation, created from SCDF. In rare cases when IN/PIN or PIN/PIN combinations of the same base ingredient exist, created from SCD.	Fluoxetine / Olanzapine
DF	Dose Form	Group Group of physical constitution types of the drug	Oral Solution
DFG	Dose Form Group	Group of physical constitution types of the drug	Oral Liquid
SCDC	Semantic Clinical Drug Component	Ingredient + Strength	Fluoxetine 4 MG/ML
SCDF	Semantic Clinical Drug Form	Ingredient + Dose Form	Fluoxetine Oral Solution
SCDG	Semantic Clinical Dose Form Group	Ingredient + Dose Form Group	Fluoxetine Oral Product
SCD	Semantic Clinical Drug	Clinical Drug Ingredient + Strength + Dose Form	Fluoxetine 4 MG/ML Oral Solution
BN	Brand Name	A proprietary name for a family of products containing a specific active ingredient.	Prozac
SBDC	Semantic Branded Drug Component	Ingredient + Strength + Brand Name	Fluoxetine 4 MG/ML [Prozac]
SBDF	Semantic Branded Drug Form	Ingredient + Dose Form + Brand Name	Fluoxetine Oral Solution [Prozac]
SBDG	Semantic Branded Dose Form Group	Brand Name + Dose Form Group	Prozac Pill
SBD	Semantic Branded Drug	Ingredient + Strength + Dose Form + Brand Name	Fluoxetine 4 MG/ML Oral Solution [Prozac]

PSN	Prescribable Name	Synonym of another TTY, given for clarity and for display purposes in electronic prescribing applications. Only one PSN per concept.	Leena 28 Day Pack
SY	Synonym	Synonym of another TTY, given for clarity.	Prozac 4 MG/ML Oral Solution
TMSY	Tall Man Lettering Synonym	Tall Man Lettering synonym of another TTY, given to distinguish between commonly confused drugs.	FLUoxetine 10 MG Oral Capsule [PROzac]
BPCK	Brand Name Pack	{# (Ingredient Strength Dose Form) / # (Ingredient Strength Dose Form)} Pack [Brand Name]	{12 (Ethinyl Estradiol 0.035 MG / Norethindrone 0.5 MG Oral Tablet) / 9 (Ethinyl Estradiol 0.035 MG / Norethindrone 1 MG Oral Tablet) / 7 (Inert Ingredients 1 MG Oral Tablet) } Pack [Leena 28 Day]
GPCK	Generic Pack	{# (Ingredient + Strength + Dose Form) / # (Ingredient + Strength + Dose Form)} Pack	{11 (varenicline 0.5 MG Oral Tablet) / 42 (varenicline 1 MG Oral Tablet) } Pack

RxNorm API provides access to RxNorm data using a SOAP/REST protocol. Use of RxNorm release files requires the UMLS Terminology Services account and use of non-SAB=RXNORM data requires licensing from the sources.

International Classification of Diseases (ICD)

International Classification of Diseases (ICD) is the global standard to systematically classify symptoms, diseases, and diagnoses. It is updated and maintained by the World Health Organization ((WHO. International Classification of Diseases). The current version is ICD-11 but ICD-10 is the currently deployed version in the United States. ICD-10-CM is the Clinical Modification of ICD developed and maintained by National Center for Health Statistics and is discussed below.

ICD contains description of all known diseases and injuries, each of which is assigned a unique code. The codes four alphanumeric characters from A00.0 to Z99.0 and are three to seven characters long. The first letter identifies a specific chapter. The three digits are the headings of the category codes and include up to seven characters. There are 68,000 codes and can indicate for laterality or anatomic location. For example:

- S72 - Fracture of femur

- S72.3 - Fracture of shaft of femur
- S72.32 - Transverse fracture of shaft of femur
- S72.321 - Displaced transverse fracture of shaft of right femur
- S72.321K - Subsequent encounter for closed fracture with nonunion

ICD-10 Chapters

ICD chapters classify the diagnosis based on anatomy or function. They group closely related concepts together and make it easier to find and apply the concepts. There are 21 chapters in total.

- CHAPTER I - Certain infectious and parasitic diseases (A00-B99)
- CHAPTER II - Neoplasms (C00-D49)
- CHAPTER III - Diseases of the blood and blood-forming organs and certain disorders involving the immune mechanism (D50-D89)
- CHAPTER IV - Endocrine, nutritional and metabolic diseases (E00-E90)
- CHAPTER V - Mental and behavioral disorders (F01-F99)
- CHAPTER VI - Diseases of the nervous system (G00-G99)
- CHAPTER VII - Diseases of the eye and adnexa (H00-H59)
- CHAPTER VIII - Diseases of the ear and mastoid process (H60-H95)
- CHAPTER IX - Diseases of the circulatory system (I00-I99)
- CHAPTER X - Diseases of the respiratory system (J00-J99)
- CHAPTER XI - Diseases of the digestive system (K00-K93)
- CHAPTER XII - Diseases of the skin and subcutaneous tissue (L00-L99)
- CHAPTER XIII - Diseases of the musculoskeletal system and connective tissue (M00-M99)
- CHAPTER XIV - Diseases of the genitourinary system (N00-N99)
- CHAPTER XV - Pregnancy, childbirth and the puerperium (O00-O99)
- CHAPTER XVI - Certain conditions originating in the perinatal period (P00-P96)
- CHAPTER XVII - Congenital malformations, deformations and chromosomal abnormalities (Q00-Q99)
- CHAPTER XVIII - Symptoms, signs and abnormal clinical and laboratory findings, not elsewhere classified (R00-R99)
- CHAPTER XIX - Injury, poisoning and certain other consequences of external causes (S00-T98)
- CHAPTER XX - External causes of morbidity (V01-Y99)
- CHAPTER XXI - Factors influencing health status and contact with health services (Z00-Z99)

Medical Dictionary for Regulatory Activities (MeDRA)

Medical Dictionary for Regulatory Activities (MedDRA®) is a clinically validated, standardized medical terminology to facilitate sharing of regulatory information internationally for medical products use by humans (ICH. 2022). It has been developed by International Council for Harmonization of Technical Requirements for Pharmaceuticals for Human Use (ICH). It is maintained by Northrop Grumman which acts like Maintenance and Support Services Organization contracted by ICH. MedDRA is used by pharmaceutical regulatory agencies during clinical research as well as post marketing activities including entry, retrieval, evaluation, and presentation of drug safety information. It is also used to classify adverse event data. MedDRA® trademark is registered by ICH.

MedDRA is organized by five structural hierarchical levels (ICH. MedDRA Hierarchy).

- **System Organ Class (SOC):** This is the highest level and consists of 27 levels classes which are categorized based on etiology (e.g. Infections and infestations), manifestation site (e.g. Gastrointestinal disorders), or purpose (e.g. Surgical and medical procedures). They are not mutually exclusive. A term can be represented by more than one SOC and also grouped under different classifications.
- **High Level Group Term (HGLT):** HGLTs are superordinate descriptors for one or more HLTs related by anatomy, pathology, physiology, etiology, or function. e.g. HLGT Vascular hypertensive disorders is linked to HLT Portal hypertension, Hypertension complication, Pulmonary hypertension etc. HGLTs are grouped into SOCs and must be linked to atleast one SOC and atleast one HLT. There are over 337 HLGTs.
- **High Level Term (HLT):** HLTs link PTs which are related to them by anatomy, physiology, pathology, etiology, or function. HLTs are used for data retrieval and presentation. HLTs are linked to HGLTs. e.g. Upper respiratory tract neoplasms, Pulmonary edema. There are over 1700 HLTs.
- **Preferred Term (PT):** Preferred Term described "symptom, sign, disease, diagnosis, therapeutic indication, investigation, surgical, or medical procedure, and medical, social, or family history characteristic". Every PT must have at least one LLT connected to it. Each LLT is linked to only PT. The clinical, pathologic or etiologic details are specified at this level. e.g. Meningitis viral, Meningitis bacterial, Meningitis cryptococcal, Meningitis aseptic. There are over 23,000 PT terms.
- **Lowest Level Terms (LLT):** They constitute the lowest level of the terminology. Each LLT is connected with only one Preferred Term (PT). They facilitate data entry and promote consistency by decreasing subjective choices. There are over 80,000 LLT terms. Their relationship with parent PT could be
    - Synonym: e.g. PT: Arthritis => LLT: Joint inflammation
    - Lexical variants: e.g. PT: Acquired Immunodeficiency syndrome => LLT: AIDS
    - Sub-concept: e.g. PT: Contusion => LLT: Bruising of face
    - Identical LLT: e.g. PT: Dementia Alzheimer's type => LLT Dementia Alzheimer's type

Here are two examples showing how it is used:

- Example 1
    - SOC: Gastrointestinal disorders
    - HLGT: Gastrointestinal signs and symptoms
    - HLT: Nausea and vomiting symptoms
    - PT: Nausea
    - LLT: Feeling queasy
- Example 2
    - SOC: Cardiac disorders
    - HLGT: Cardiac arrhythmias
    - HLT: Rate Rhythm disorders NEC
    - PT: Arrhythmia
    - LT: Cardiac Arrhythmia

Diagnostic and Statistical Manual of Mental Disorders (DSM)

Diagnostic and Statistical Manual of Mental Disorders (DSM) is a standardized taxonomy and coding system for psychiatric disorders. The copyright to DSM is owned by American Psychiatric Association and is managed by Division of Research of the Association. The DSM classification are used for treatment recommendations and payments.

DSM-5 is divided into 3 sections (American Psychiatric Association. 2013).

- Section I: Section I provides a background and overview of DSM.
- Section II: Lists the diagnostic criteria and codes. These include
  - Neurodevelopmental Disorders
  - Schizophrenia Spectrum and Other Psychotic Disorders
  - Bipolar and Related Disorders
  - Depressive Disorders
  - Anxiety Disorders
  - Obsessive-Compulsive and Related Disorders
  - Trauma- and Stressor-Related Disorders
  - Dissociative Disorders
  - Somatic Symptom and Related Disorders
  - Feeding and Eating Disorders
  - Elimination Disorders
  - Sleep-Wake Disorders
  - Sexual Dysfunctions
  - Gender Dysphoria
  - Disruptive, Impulse-Control, and Conduct Disorders
  - Substance-Related and Addictive Disorders
  - Neurocognitive Disorders
  - Personality Disorders
  - Paraphilic Disorders
  - Other Mental Disorders and Additional Codes
  - Medication-Induced Movement Disorders and Other Adverse Effects of Medication
  - Other Conditions That May Be a Focus of Clinical Attention
- Section III: Includes emerging measures and models, assessment measures and cultural formulation.

5 REVENUE CYCLE MANAGEMENT

Revenue Cycle Management (RCM) is the administrative process of evaluating the healthcare services delivered to the patients and converting them into codes, create claims to submit to the insurance companies and invoices for patients to receive outstanding payments. It requires an understanding of the clinical management, regulatory requirements around coding & billing, and a basic understanding of finance. There are tremendous opportunities to innovate in RCM, and digital health is being incorporated into many RCM functions.

The departments working on revenue cycle management vary from hospital to hospital but generally include health information management, patient access, billing, finance, and revenue integrity. Health information management could include coding, clinical document integrity, and medical records departments.

Revenue cycle management provides tremendous opportunities for innovation using digital health. Software applications are used to create documentation and capture clinical orders from providers, convert these into claims, process the claims, and manage payments. Current opportunities for digital health include faster and more accurate documentation, automation of workflows, communication between payers and providers, and accurate charge capture.

Health information management

The Health Information Management (HIM) or health information services department is responsible for the custody of patient health records. Any request for the release of medical records is received by HIM team and approved if accompanied by signed authorization and verified identity of the individual or an entity receiving the records per HIPAA and consent policies.

HIM also responds to legal subpoenas for patient health records which may be required in litigation, federal or state investigations, and law enforcement. They can also provide records for internal medical review, risk management, case management, utilization management, quality improvement, financial services, patient relations, or medical staff services. The other responsibilities of a health information management department include

- Storage, retention, and retrieval of medical records

- Coding and abstracting of records
- Identifying and rectifying deficiencies in clinical documentation
- Processing of medical records for reimbursement, analytics, or filing.

Documentation

Clinical documentation is the process of capturing a patient's health status and clinical information in an organized manner. The medical record has the patient's medical diagnoses, treatments, and test results. It captures the thought process of the providers and the justification for a treatment decision. The patient's medical record is a legal document and the basis for reimbursement. A medical service that is not documented will likely not be reimbursed.

Good documentation is essential for a variety of reasons. It accurately captures the physicians thinking at the time of evaluation and management of the patients for future reference, for communicating to other providers and caregivers who are also taking care of the patient at the same time, for accurate assignment of severity and risk of mortality scores to ensure that patient's condition is accurately conveyed to the regulatory and reimbursement organizations, to protect the physicians against a future malpractice claim, and use of the clinical data as real-world evidence.

The Clinical Documentation Integrity (CDI) department is usually within the health information management department. The focus of CDI is coding and quality control of the documentation. CDI specialists can guide the providers about good clinical documentation practices, especially those that improve coding quality for more accurate billing. They work closely with quality improvement and utilization management teams to create templates and training programs.

Healthcare revenue cycle

The revenue cycle management process depends on the site of care delivery. There are minor variations depending on whether the patient is in an acute care setting like a hospital, sees the physician in their office, or goes to a laboratory or a radiology center for a test. The general steps in each of these situations are generally the same.

Patient registration

The first step of revenue cycle management is patient registration. During this process, the patient's appointment is confirmed. The patient provides their demographic information, insurance, or any other evidence of financial responsibility for their treatment. The patient also agrees to disclosures around HIPAA provisions, sharing of medical data, and financial liability. The patient's eligibility and coverage with their health plan are verified based on the insurance card information. It includes the patient's general eligibility for benefits, copayment, or coinsurance at the time of service and if the visit is covered. Any requirements for preauthorization for the service are checked.

The HIPAA 270/271 transaction is used for getting information from the health plan through electronic eligibility verification. The response to eligibility inquiries is electronically communicated. It includes benefits information, insurance coverage dates, benefit units, coverage level, copay amount, deductible amount, out-of-pocket expenses, name of the primary care provider, etc.

Charge capture

The billing system creates an itemized list of all the charges incurred by the patient during their hospitalization or outpatient encounter. The charges are generated and sent to the charge router, which evaluates the charges sent to the billing department. The charges are checked and, if correct, are posted to the billing management system.

Coding

Coding is the process of converting the record of clinical activities into codes that can be processed and evaluated by the payers. Medical codes are assigned to diagnoses and procedures by the providers or coders. The assigned codes are verified and linked to justify the medical necessity of the care plan. Payers specify rules about billable codes; this information is used to prepare a claim.

The general inpatient coding workflow starts with triaging if a hospital account requires manual review or can be automatically coded. The uncoded account is sent to the coder for manual coding. The coder reviews the clinical documentation and uses an encoding system to encode diagnoses, procedures, and groupers. The biller then uses this information to generate charges which are evaluated by a charge router which are validated.

Claim processing

A claim could be a medical claim, pharmacy claim, dental claim, professional claim, inpatient facility claim, etc. The claim combines the information about the diagnoses, procedures, and charges into one document. It is a codified record of care provided to the patient. The professional fees are generally excluded from the hospital's charges and are billed separately by the providers to the insurance companies.

The billing information is formatted, checked for errors, and claims are generated. Clearinghouses help to standardize the claims generated from different software, formatted per state and payer requirements. These clearinghouses also aggregate the claim information and check claims that are sent to the payers for errors. The claims are submitted to the payer after the patient has been discharged. A healthcare provider may have to work with two dozen or more health plans, each having multiple plan types.

Claim adjudication

Adjudication is the process of reviewing healthcare claims and determining reimbursement based on the contract or the fee schedule, medical policies, and medical necessity guidelines. The claim could be paid fully, partially, or denied. Sometimes, the payers require more information from the provider to process the claim. The payer may reach back with questions, and outcomes could be payment, denial, underpayment, or overpayment.

Patient statement and collection

After the healthcare providers receive payment from the payer, they bill the patients for the remaining balance. If the bills are overdue, they are sent to collections.

Revenue cycle management data standards

Standardization of medical terminology is essential for facilitating electronic transactions and automation in revenue cycle management. The primary data standards are Diagnosis Related Groups (DRG), Current Procedural Terminology (CPT), Healthcare Common Procedure Coding Systems (HCPCS), and Resource Based Relative Value Scale (RBRVS).

Diagnosis Related Groups (DRG)

Diagnosis Related Groups (DRG) is a patient classification system used as a reimbursement tool linking the medical conditions treated in the hospital with the resources utilized for the treatment. Medicare payments are based on the DRG classification of an inpatient care episode and the estimated resources required by a typical patient. Sometimes, patients consume unusually high resources, and these are known as outlier cases which are looked at separately based on the outlier threshold and payment methodology applicable to an acute care facility. CMS is responsible for maintaining the DRG system. DRGs are assigned by the software 'Grouper,' which considers principal diagnosis (based on ICD), secondary diagnoses, procedures performed, patient age, gender, comorbidities, complications, and discharge status. DRGs can be further subclassified into non-CC (Complication and Comorbidity), CC, and major-CC.

DRGs are numbered from 000 - 999. They comprise 25 systems connected to major organs or etiologies grouped under major diagnostic categories. The codes could be medical or surgical. The DRG systems include (CMS. ICD-10-CM/PCS MS-DRG v37.0 Definitions Manual):

1. Diseases and Disorders of the Nervous System
2. Diseases and Disorders of the Eye
3. Diseases and Disorders of the Ear, Nose, Mouth and Throat
4. Diseases and Disorders of the Respiratory System
5. Diseases and Disorders of the Circulatory System
6. Diseases and Disorders of the Digestive System
7. Diseases and Disorders of the Hepatobiliary System and Pancreas
8. Diseases and Disorders of the Musculoskeletal System and Connective Tissue
9. Diseases and Disorders of the Skin, Subcutaneous Tissue and Breast
10. Endocrine, Nutritional and Metabolic Diseases and Disorders
11. Diseases and Disorders of the Kidney and Urinary Tract
12. Diseases and Disorders of the Male Reproductive System
13. Diseases and Disorders of the Female Reproductive System
14. Pregnancy, Childbirth and the Puerperium
15. Newborns and Other Neonates with Conditions Originating in the Perinatal Period
16. Diseases and Disorders of the Blood and Blood Forming Organs and Immunological Disorders
17. Myeloproliferative Diseases and Disorders, and Poorly Differentiated Neoplasm
18. Infectious and Parasitic Diseases (Systemic or Unspecified Sites)
19. Mental Diseases and Disorders
20. Alcohol/Drug Use and Alcohol/Drug Induced Organic Mental Disorders

21. Injuries, Poisonings and Toxic Effects of Drugs
22. Burns
23. Factors Influencing Health Status and Other Contacts with Health Services
24. Multiple Significant Trauma
25. Human Immunodeficiency Virus Infections

Payment calculation for a hospital is based on a base rate depending on its location, cost of living data, the severity of illnesses, and the complexity of medical care provided. Case Mix Index (CMI) is a relative value assigned to DRGs. CMI value allows comparison of an average cost per patient among various hospitals. The adjusted cost per patient or per day is calculated with reference to a value of 1. The risk of mortality and illness severity are other variables that try to assign complexity to a patient in the hospital.

Current Procedural Terminology (CPT)

Current Procedural Terminology (CPT®) is the national standard medical nomenclature for medical procedures, evaluations, surgeries, and diagnostic services. It is published and maintained by American Medical Association, which holds its copyright. Healthcare providers use the codes to inform the insurance payers about the services that need reimbursement. CPT was created in 1966 by American Medical Association. The Health Care Financing Administration (HCFA), which became the Centers for Medicare and Medicaid Services (CMS), merged Healthcare Common Procedure Coding System (HCPCS) with CPT. CPT® is a registered trademark of the American Medical Association.

Medical coders and billers use ICD codes to denote what diagnoses were identified on a patient and use CPT codes to inform what diagnostic tests and treatments were administered (AAPC. 2021). It has three categories of codes:

- **Category I: Most common and is used to identify inpatient and outpatient procedures. It has six sub-sections:**
  - Evaluation and Management: 99201 – 99499
  - Anesthesia: 00100 – 01999; 99100 – 99140
  - Surgery: 10021 – 69990
  - Radiology: 70010 – 79999
  - Pathology & Laboratory: 80047 – 89398
  - Medicine: 90281 – 99199; 99500 – 99607
- **Category II: Supplemental tracking codes for quality and performance management.**
  - Composite Measures: 0001F-0015F
  - Patient Management: 0500F-0575F
  - Patient History: 1000F-1220F
  - Physical Examination: 2000F-2050F
  - Diagnostic/Screening Processes or Results: 3006F-3573F
  - Therapeutic, Preventive or Other Interventions: 4000F-4306F
  - Follow-up or Other Outcomes: 5005F-5100F
  - Patient Safety: 6005F-6045F
  - Structural Measures: 7010F-7025F
- **Category III: Temporary codes for reporting and tracking new and emerging technologies, services, and procedures.**

A CPT code is composed of five alphanumeric characters. They are grouped numerically. The Category II codes are non-reimbursable and have four digits, followed by the letter F. Category III codes are four digits, followed by a letter I. For example:

- 99214 is one of the most frequent codes used for office visits. It is worth 1.5 RVUs. A provider can bill for this code if they spent 25 minutes face-to-face with the patient or if they satisfied two of the three documentation requirements - Detailed history, Detailed exam and Moderate complexity Medical Decision making.
- 12001 is used to bill for simple repair of superficial wounds that do not exceed 2.5 cm in length and is closed with single-layer closure.

Electronic Data Interchange (EDI)

Accredited Standards Committee X12 (ASC X12) is an electronic data interchange standards and XML schemas development and maintenance organization providing a standardized data exchange vocabulary. It provides the standards for HIPAA-mandated Electronic Data Interchange (EDI) transactions focusing on administrative and financial data. These include 270/271 for health care eligibility benefit inquiry and response, 276/277 for health care claim status request and response, 278 for a request for review and response examples, 820 for health insurance exchange-related payments, 832 for health care fee schedule, etc. (X12. 2021).

HIPAA Electronic Health Care Transactions and Code Sets (TCS) standards govern the electronic data exchanged between providers, health plans, and employers. These all follow the ANSI X12 format, which defines Electronic Data Interchange standards. The common standard transactions include

- **276/277**: Healthcare Claim Status Inquiry/Response
- **270/271**: Eligibility for a Health Plan Inquiry/Response
- **278**: Referral Certification and Authorization
- **837**: Healthcare Claims or Equivalent Encounter Information / Coordination of Benefits
- **835**: Healthcare Payment and Remittance Advice
- **820**: Health Plan Premium Payments
- **834**: Health Plan Enrollment and Disenrollment

Healthcare Common Procedure Coding System (HCPCS)

Healthcare Comon Procedure Coding System (HCPCS) is used to process claims for medical, surgical, and diagnostic services. It also includes durable medical equipment (DME), prosthetics, and ambulance rides. It is based on American Medical Association's Current Procedural Terminology (CPT) HCPCS Code range (HCPCS Codes Lookup, AAPC. 2021).

HCPCS Level II codes and descriptors are approved and maintained jointly by the alphanumeric editorial panel (consisting of CMS, America's Health Insurance Plans, and Blue Cross and Blue Shield Association). HCPCS has three levels of codes:

- Level I is AMA's CPT and is numeric.

- Level II codes are items, supplies and non-physician services which are not covered by CPT-4 codes (Level I). These codes are alphanumeric and are coded from A to V:
  - A0021-A0999: Ambulance and Other Transport Services and Supplies
  - A4206-A8004: Medical And Surgical Supplies
  - A9150-A9999: Administrative, Miscellaneous and Investigational
  - B4034-B9999: Enteral and Parenteral Therapy
  - C1713-C9899: Outpatient PPS
  - E0100-E8002: Durable Medical Equipment
  - G0008-G9987: Procedures / Professional Services
  - G1001-G1019: Clinical Decision Support Mechanism
  - G2021-G2058: Care Management Services
  - G2166-G2166: Physical and Cognitive Status
  - G2168-G2169: Therapy Maintenance Program in Home Health Setting
  - G2167-G2167: Performance Measures
  - G2061-G2063: Online Assessment by Qualified Nonphysician Healthcare Professional
  - G2064-G2065: Comprehensive Care Management Services
  - G2066-G2066: Cardiac Device Evaluation
  - G2067-G2075: Medication Assisted Treatment Program
  - G2076-G2081: Opioid Use Disorder - Evaluation and Treatment
  - G2082-G2083: Evaluation and Management Services
  - G2086-G2088: Opioid Use Disorder - Treatment (Office Based)
  - G2089-G2153: Functional Status
  - G2154-G2165: Immunization Status
  - H0001-H2037: Alcohol and Drug Abuse Treatment
  - J0120-J8999: Drugs Administered Other than Oral Method
  - J9000-J9999: Chemotherapy Drugs
  - K0001-K0900: Durable medical equipment (DME) Medicare administrative contractors (MACs)
  - K1001-K1005: Components, Accessories and Supplies
  - L0112-L4631: Orthotic Procedures and services
  - L5000-L9900: Prosthetic Procedures
  - M0075-M0301: Miscellaneous Medical Services
  - M1000-M1071: Screening Procedures
  - M1106-M1144: Episode of Care
  - P2028-P9615: Pathology and Laboratory Services
  - Q0035-Q9995: Temporary Codes
  - R0070-R0076: Diagnostic Radiology Services
  - S0012-S9999: Temporary National Codes (Non-Medicare)
  - T1000-T5999: National Codes Established for State Medicaid Agencies
  - U0001-U0004: Coronavirus Diagnostic Panel
  - V2020-V2799: Vision Services
  - V5008-V5364: Hearing Services
- Level III codes were local codes which have been developed by state Medicaid agencies, Medicare contractors, and private insurers. Their use has been discontinued (HCPCS Level II, CMS. 2018).

Resource Based Relative Value Scale (RBRVS)

Resource Based Relative Value Scale (RBRVS) is the physician payment system used by the Centers for Medicare & Medicaid Services (CMS) and other payers to make payments for physician services (RVS Update Committee, AMA). These are based on the relative value of the resources required to deliver physician services. Every medical service delivered is divided into three components, and payments are calculated by multiplying the combined costs of a service by a conversion factor determined by CMS and adjusted for geographical differences in costs.

- **Physician work:** Accounts for an average of 51% of the total relative value for each service and considers the time needed to perform the service, technical skill required, physical and mental effort required, judgment, and stress because of the potential risk to the patient.
- **Practice expense:** Accounts for an average of 45% of the total relative value for each service.
- **Professional liability insurance:** Accounts for an average of 4% of the total relative value for each service.

Each of the above is adjusted using Geographic Practice Cost Indexes (GPCI). GPCI is based on differences in the cost of living, prices of non-physician practice resources, and malpractice premium rates. To calculate total RVU, the formula used is: "Work RVU x Work GPCI + Practice Expense (PE) RVU x PE GPCI + Malpractice (PLI) RVU x PLI GPCI = Total RVU The corresponding Medicare payment will be: Total RVU x CY Conversion Factor (This was $36.0896 in CY 2020) = Medicare Payment" (AMA. Medicare Physician Payment Schedule).

6 HEALTH INFORMATION EXCHANGE

A Health Information Exchange (HIE) organization provides a network for storing and distributing healthcare data to capture, aggregate, and normalize data from electronic medical record systems. It includes both structured and unstructured data but is EMR and health system agnostic. It provides a longitudinal view of the patient across providers. Clinical information is securely exchanged over the Internet, promoting interoperability and care coordination. The health information exchange network can include acute care hospitals, ambulatory surgery centers, post-acute facilities, physician offices, laboratories, radiology centers, other HIEs, payers, and federal registries.

A health information exchange allows data input from multiple sources like HL7 V2, CDA, X12, and FHIR, to be aggregated in the HIE. The data can be normalized, translated, aggregated, deduplicated, and transformed after connecting with an HIE. After processing and manipulation, the data can be exported through V2, CDA, or FHIR connections. The patient index in HIE is critical to accurately match the patients across different health organizations and clinical settings.

Classification

HIEs can be classified based on their ownership or the triggers. The ownership can be of three types:

- Public-mediated: These are supported by the government funding.
- Private-mediated: These are supported by private non-profit or for-profit organizations.
- EHR vendor mediated: These are managed by EHR vendors.

HIEs can also be categorized into two categories based on the triggers for the exchange of data. These are based on push or pull:

- **Push-based exchange**: The sender of the information triggers the exchange of data. This information is used to create alerts, submit information to public health registries, and send results from labs or documents from provider encounters as soon as they are created. The push-based exchange can help close care gaps by providing updated information for care coordination. The push messages can be configured between two providers and can assist in setting up referrals. Direct messages between providers can be configured to carry protected health information.

- **Pull-based exchange**: This exchange type is also known as query-based exchange. The recipient of the information triggers the exchange of data.

Advantages

Significant investments have been made in HIE infrastructure over the last decade. It has improved the underlying infrastructure's performance, stability, and usability. The advantages of an HIE include:

- **Alerts**: HIEs can generate alerts based on pre-set criteria, including lab results (out of range / critical values), encounters (ED visits, hospital discharges), and procedures (endoscopy, MRI). The notifications can be sent based on the integrations with the alert engine (EMR messages, email). These alerts can be routed to the appropriate provider and are very useful in population health management, saving hours manually identifying the patients for outreach and communication.
- **Analytics**: HIE can provide comprehensive and up-to-date information about patients that helps in better clinical and administrative decision making.
- **Cost**: A single connection with an HIE avoids the cost and resource needs to build point-to-point connections between individual healthcare entities. Providers can avoid ordering duplicate tests by accessing historical information.
- **Data sharing**: HIEs enable provider-to-provider data sharing automatically on demand without manual interventions. The data sources could include hospitals, physician offices, skilled nursing facilities, and ambulatory surgery centers.
- **Disease management**: Providers can improve disease management by working with case managers, community health workers, and other providers.
- **Integration**: HIEs reduce the need for EMR systems to build connectivity with each other. A provider EMR can be connected to one HIE, connecting to other HIEs to enable data sharing.
- **Longitudinal Record**: Because an HIE can aggregate information across diverse sources and include historical and updated real-time data, it is possible to develop a longitudinal record.
- **Security**: Transmission of data directly into medical records is more secure than faxes and paper mail.

Legal agreements

Healthcare organizations are expected to sign participation or business associate agreements before connecting with HIE. These agreements are standardized for all participants and lay out policies, procedures, governance, and legal requirements. Participation in an HIE is also contingent on patient consent. Consent can be 'opt-out' where health information is available in HIE unless a patient explicitly decides to opt out of data sharing, or it can be 'opt-in' with a patient's information is available in HIE if the patient explicitly chooses to include their information.

Security

HIEs are repositories of all patient information accessed over the Internet, so their breach is a significant security risk. HIEs provide extensive security and privacy controls which include:

- User identification and authentication based on access privileges granted at the time of registration.
- Role-based access controls to ensure authorized access to data.
- Encryption of protected health information stored on exchange to provide end-to-end security.
- Maintenance of data integrity through multiple tiers of validation checks and hashing.
- Use of digital certificates to ensure secure transmission of messages and verification of senders.
- Extensive audit logs which include detailed information about which anyone accessing the exchange as well as their activity on the exchanged.
- Authorization of data sharing based on patient consent.

Data exchange

HIEs can share data in three ways:

Direct message: Direct push from the source of the document to the potential user of the document. The data sharing can be accomplished by using secure email or Cross-enterprise Document Media interchange profile (XDM).

Centralized storage and retrieval: In this scenario, the documents or hyperlinks to the documents are stored centrally. The provider for a healthcare entity needing information makes a manual request to get the document. Data sharing can be accomplished through Cross-enterprise Document Sharing profile (XDS).

Distributed storage and retrieval: The content is stored at and accessed by the entity which created the content. The individual requesting the document can query the healthcare entity to discover the document. The data sharing is accomplished through a Cross-Community Access profile (XCA).

HIE infrastructure is based on standardized data exchange formats. These allow electronic medical records to communicate with the HIE and connect one HIE with another. The systems can exchange messages via direct message or through direct integration. A direct message is used to send patient information via an email attachment encrypted with a Public Key and decrypted by the recipient using a Private Key. The format is usually XML-based CCD. The typical protocol used for file exchange is FTP and HTTP. A Secure File Transfer Protocol (sFTP) adds support for Transport Layer Security (TLS) and Secure Sockets Layer (SSL). Similarly, HyperText Transfer Protocol Secure (HTTP) combines Hypertext Transfer Protocol with SSL/TLS protocol for encryption and secure server identification. HL7 v2 is one of the most common data exchange formats of HIEs. It encodes multiple interfaces, including the ADT (Admission, Discharge, Transfer) and CCDA. The CCDA includes information about allergies and adverse reactions, encounters, goals of care, insurance information, immunizations, lab results, medications, plan of care, physician notes, problems, procedures, radiology reports, the reason for the visit, social history, and vital signs.

Applicability Statement 2 (AS2) is a B2B messaging protocol for transmitting Electronic Data Interchange documents. It uses hypertext transport protocol secure (http/s) to transport data securely. AS2 provides an envelope for data and can transport any document. Applicability Statement 3 (AS3) is based on a secure version of the FTP protocol and uses a client/server model instead of the peer-to-peer approach of AS2.

Documents and messages

It is essential to note the differences between the document and the message with respect to interoperability in healthcare. The documents are persistent, but messages are transient. Clinical documents include orders, physician notes like history and physical progress notes, diagnostic reports, and missing flowsheets. Documents represent the status of information regardless of when it was accessed. The content of the document does not change over time, and the context of a document is clear from the nature of the document itself. For example, the history and physical document is generated when a patient is admitted to an acute care setting. One document is considered a single legal unit of information.

Messages, on the other hand, reflect information when it is transmitted at a given point in time. In order to obtain the full context of the message, more information is needed than just the content, including the sender, recipient, and other associated metadata.

The data exchange standards in an HIE are primarily based on the specifications developed by Integrating the Healthcare Enterprise (IHE). IHE is a non-profit organization to improve health data sharing. IHE has created a technical framework that provides integration profiles for a specific clinical need. These integration profiles describe clinical information management use cases and specify how to use existing standards (HL7, FHIR, IETF, DICOM, OASIS, ISO, etc.) to address them (IHE Wiki. 2022). IHI domains address a specific area of healthcare, and IHE IT Infrastructure (ITI) domain is relevant to the healthcare data exchange. ITI has defined integration profiles that describe what content should be included in the documents about specific clinical use cases. For example, Patient Care Coordination (PCC) domain defines Medical Summary (XDS-MS) content profile for transferring patient care from one clinical site to another and the Emergency Department Referrals (EDR) content profile supports direct admission to an emergency department.

Document sharing profiles

The document sharing profiles "enable effective sharing of data among multiple, disparate systems in a way that minimizes the burden that data sharing imposes on those systems" (IHE. 2021). The metadata of the documents contains information about the patients. Patient identity management is essential to ensure that only the documents about the patient of interest are exchanged. Matching can be conducted before searching for patients, before sending patient information, or after receiving the patient information, depending on the method of sharing. IHI has developed integration profiles to locate information about a patient (IHE. 2021).

The Clinical Document Architecture (CDA) and Fast Health Interoperability Resources (FHIR) are two essential documents available from the medical record source systems. These are discussed in detail separately, but at a high level, the FHIR document type is newer and more standardized, but the CDA is more widely used. The documents can be shared in 3 ways:

- **Push**: Documents and metadata are transmitted directly to a previously identified recipient.

The relevant IHE profiles are Mobile Access to Health Documents (MHD), Cross-Enterprise Document Reliable Interchange (XDR), and Cross-Enterprise Document Medical Interchange (XDM).

- **Centralized Discovery and Retrieve**: Documents are retrieved from a custodian based on the location information stored with a centralized entity. The documents and their location are available to other systems that use the information to get the document. The relevant IHE profiles are Mobile Health Document Sharing (MHDS), MHD, and XDS.
- **Federated Discovery and Retrieve**: Documents of interest are located through queries sent to a network of connected entities. The source of documents can be found through manual queries or a directory. The relevant IHE profile is Cross-Community Access (XCA).

XDS: Cross-enterprise Document Sharing is used to find documents about a specific patient. XDS requires a governance structure and uses XDS Affinity Domain or Community as governance agents. The XDS Affinity Domain allows a group of organizations to exchange clinical information. XDS Affinity Domain Patient Identification Domain (XAD-PID) is the single Patient Identification used. This profile also enables registration or content and query and retrieve functions.

XDR: The Cross-enterprise Document Reliable interchange profile is commonly used for patient referrals. It is a point-to-point method to send documents and metadata using web-services-based transport.

XDM: The Cross-enterprise Document Media interchange profile is created for scenarios where data is transported through storage media instead of a network. The transport options include email, CD-ROM, and USB memory. Sending patient referrals is a common use case for this profile.

MHD: The Mobile access to Health Documents profile uses the FHIR REST push to send documents from point to point. The use case of MHD is when documents are required by a recipient. MHD can use a push API to transmit the documents.

XCA: Cross-Community Access Profile is used to share patient's health information between two communities, one of which is a patient's home community where they receive their care primarily and another where they may go for specialized services or during traveling. XCA is enabled through the use of gateways and uses a federated approach to querying each community for the documents.

XCDR: The Cross-Community Document Reliable interchange sends documents, including their metadata, from point to point.

The HIEs can use any of these infrastructures for data exchange. XDR, XDS, XCA, and MHD are legacy standards, and MHD is an API for publishing and consuming documents. XDS and XCA-based source systems can only be accessed with XDS and XCA infrastructure. The other advantage is that they allow asynchronous communication decoupling requests and responses. They also allow end-to-end security. MHDS and XDS enable the documents to be discovered from a central location; MHD is based on an API.

Patient identification profiles

A Patient Identifier is a unique identifier within an HIE domain that uniquely identifies an individual. One or more patient identifiers, along with demographic information and other authorized identifiers (driver's license number, social security number, etc.), comprise the Patient's Identity. Before sharing the information over an HIE, the parties agree on the patient identifier that will be used to acknowledge the patient. The patient identity management profiles enable document sharing using distributed management of patient identities.

PMIR: Patient Master Identity Registry is an FHIR-based system of patient identity resources that collaborate to keep patient master identity. The registry can be queried using Patient Demographics Query for Mobile (PDQm) or Patient Identity Cross-referencing for Mobile (PIXm).

PIX: Patient Identity Cross Reference is used to find the organization containing patient demographic information. This profile provides access to a registry of patient identities issued by assigning authority. These identities are cross-referenced using identifiers. The Patient Identifier is made of Patient Identity Domain or the assigning authority and Patient Identifier, which is assigned by the assigning authority. The identity domains could be primary care physicians, specialists, or hospitals. The matching algorithms enable the matching of information from each of those sources.

PDQ: Patient Demographic Query is used to identify a patient based on demographic parameters. The query can be executed with a limited set of demographic information to discover a patient. PDQm uses an FHIR standard.

XCPD: Cross-Community Patient Discovery is used to find the entities which contain data about a known patient. After identifying a patient, the XCA approach can be used to get the documents.

Privacy and Security

The Basic Patient Privacy Consents (BPPC) and Advanced Patient Privacy Cosents (APPC) Profiles can be used as a template for basic privacy consent controls. As per IHI, the examples of policies that can be made available for Patient Privacy Consents include (IHI. 2021):

- explicit opt-in,
- explicit opt-out,
- simplicity opt-in,
- explicit opt-out with an exception for emergencies,
- explicit opt-out for any sharing beyond local care,
- explicit authorization for research.

These profiles allow the communities to capture which specific type of consent has been provided by the patients. The Security and Privacy Profiles can work with any security and privacy policies developed by organizations. The profiles include audit trails and node authentication, consistent time, enterprise user authentication, cross-enterprise user assertion, essential patient privacy consents, personnel white pages, healthcare provider directory, document digital signature, and document encryption.

Transactions

IHE has defined a set of transactions which are defined in IHE IT Infrastructure Technical Framework. Each transaction has a specific role which is described in the specification (IHE ITI. 2022).

- ITI-01 Maintain Time
- ITI-02 Get User Authentication
- ITI-03 Get Service Ticket
- ITI-04 Kerberized Communication
- ITI-05 Join Context
- ITI-06 Change Context
- ITI-07 Leave Context
- ITI-08 Patient Identity Feed
- ITI-09 PIX Query
- ITI-10 Pix Update Notification
- ITI-11 Retrieve Specific Information for Display
- ITI-12 Retrieve Document for Display
- ITI-13 Follow Context
- ITI-14 Register Document Set
- ITI-15 Provide and Register Document Set
- ITI-16 Query Registry
- ITI-17 Retrieve Document
- ITI-18 Stored Query
- ITI-19 Authenticate Node
- ITI-20 Record Audit Event
- ITI-21 Patient Demographic Query
- ITI-22 Patient Demographic Visit Query
- ITI-23 Find Personnel White Pages
- ITI-24 Query Personnel White Pages
- ITI-25 Send Notification
- ITI-26 Receive Notifications
- ITI-27 Send Acknowledgement
- ITI-28 Receive Acknowledgement
- ITI-29 Cross Enterprise User Authentication (Cancelled in favor of ITI-40)
- ITI-30 Patient Identity Management
- ITI-31 Patient Encounter Management
- ITI-32 Distribute Document Set on Media
- ITI-33 Send Document Set (Unused)
- ITI-34 Retrieve Form
- ITI-35 Submit Form
- ITI-36 Archive Form
- ITI-37 Retrieve Clarifications
- ITI-38 Cross Gateway Query
- ITI-39 Cross Gateway Retrieve

- ITI-40 Provide X-User Assertion
- ITI-41 Provide and Register Document Set-b
- ITI-42 Register Document Set-b
- ITI-43 Retrieve Document Set
- ITI-44 Patient Identity Feed HL7 V3
- ITI-45 PIXV3 Query
- ITI-46 PIXV3 Update Notification
- ITI-47 Patient Demographics Query HL7 V3
- ITI-48 Retrieve Value Set
- ITI-49 Convey Printed Referral Request
- ITI-50 Request Referral
- ITI-51 Multi-Patient Query
- ITI-52 Document Metadata Subscribe
- ITI-53 Document Metadata Notify
- ITI-54 Document Metadata Publish
- ITI-55 Cross Gateway Patient Discovery
- ITI-56 Patient Location Query
- ITI-57 Update Document Set
- ITI-58 Provider Information Query
- ITI-59 Provider Information Feed
- ITI-60 Retrieve Multiple Value Sets
- ITI-61 Register On-Demand Document Entry
- ITI-62 Delete Document Set
- ITI-63 Cross Gateway Fetch
- ITI-64 Notify XAP-PID Link Change
- ITI-65 Provide Document Bundle
- ITI-66 Find Document Manifests
- ITI-67 Find Document References
- ITI-68 Retrieve Document
- ITI-69 Create Destroy Pull Point
- ITI-70 Pull Notification
- ITI-71 Get Authorization Token
- ITI-72 Incorporate Authorization Token
- ITI-73 Find Matching Services
- ITI-74 Query for Updated Services
- ITI-75 Care Services Free Busy Query
- ITI-76 Patient Location Tracking Feed
- ITI-77 Patient Location Tracking Query
- ITI-78 Mobile Patient Demographics Query
- ITI-79 Authorization Decisions Query
- ITI-80 Cross-Gateway Document Provide
- ITI-81 Retrieve ATNA Audit Event
- ITI-82 Retrieve Syslog Event

- ITI-83 Mobile Patient Identifier Cross-Reference Query
- ITI-84 Mobile Report Alert
- ITI-85 Query for Alert Status
- ITI-86 Remove Documents
- ITI-87 Submit File
- ITI-88 Search File
- ITI-89 Update Document Reference
- ITI-90 Find Matching Care Services
- ITI-91 Request Care Services Updates
- ITI-92 Restricted Update Document Set
- ITI-93 Mobile Patient Identity Feed
- ITI-94 Subscribe To Patient Updates
- ITI-95 Query Value Set
- ITI-96 Query Code system
- ITI-97 Expand Value Set
- ITI-98 Lookup Code
- ITI-99 Validate Code
- ITI-100 Query Concept Map
- ITI-101 Translate Code
- ITI-102 Introspection
- ITI-103 Get Authorization Server Metadata
- ITI-104 Mobile Patient Identity Cross-Reference Feed
- ITI-105 Simplified Publish
- ITI-106 Generate Metadata

As an illustration, a communication workflow with an HIE can have the following steps. These make use of profiles and transactions described above:

- Hospital A sends an HL7 ADT message to Hospital B HIE. This message includes the patient id (generally from the Master Patient Index) for PIXV3 Query. Another alternative is using the PDQV3 interface, which can include partial demographic information to get the list of patients.
- Hospital B sends the HIE PIXV3 Query/Response Interface (ITI-45) back to Hospital A.
- Hospital B sends HIE Cross-Enterprise Document Sharing XDS.b Document Query/Retrieve Interface (Stored Query ITI-18 and XDS.b Retrieve Document Set ITI-43) to Hospital A.
- Hospital A sends PIXV3 Query/Response Interface (ITI-45) to Hospital B HIE with authentication (SAML).
- Hospital A XDS.b Document Query/Retrieve Interface (Registry Stored Query ITI-18 and XDS.b Retrieve Document set ITI-43) to Hospital B HIE with authentication (SAML)

Major HIEs

HIEs can be regional connecting healthcare organizations in the state or a part of the state or national networks connecting healthcare organizations across state lines and regions. HIE can have a central hub, or it can be federated architecture providing standardized data exchange. Some of the common HIEs include:

Canada Health Infoway: Canada's digital health agency has created a national standard for exchanging medical information. It licenses, defines, and maintains standards to promote interoperability. It is developing pan-Canadian Patient Summary specifications, which define a summary of the record that can be shared to provide episodes of care.

Carequality: Carequality is an interoperability framework laying the foundation of national health data exchange. The members of this exchange are EHR vendors and some health information exchanges. It is provider-focused and provides peer-to-peer query-based exchange. The core elements of care quality are a requirement to adhere to the same set of rules, well-defined specifications, and a directory of participants.

CommonWell: CommonWell is another patient-centric network using centralized records which can be accessed through queries. Membership primarily consists of Electronic Health Record vendors.

Community HIE: The members include electronic health record vendors, pharmacies, laboratories, payers, and digital health companies. This exchange is patient-centric and provides alerts, reports, and analytic capabilities.

eHealth Exchange: This is the largest healthcare information network in the United States. The members of this exchange are primarily federal agencies, health systems, and other HIEs. It is provider-centric, and data is exchanged peer-to-peer using queries that allow participants to connect and share data over the Internet securely. A wide variety of data can be shared using common standards.

OpenHIE: The Open Health Information Exchange is supported by Regenstrief Institute and is a community of individuals and organizations working on health data sharing. The OpenHIE framework uses IHE profiles to describe digital health workflows.

The Sequoia Project: The Sequoia Project brings together government and private organizations to promote health interoperability and has spun out two organizations – eHealth Exchange and Carequality. It runs multiple projects, including - Interoperability Matters, which identifies, prioritizes, and collaborates on resolving challenges to national health information exchange; Patient Unified Lookup System for Emergencies (PULSE), which is a national disaster response platform; and RSNA Image share validation which is a conformity assessment program for exchange of medical images.

7 HEALTH APIS

SMART on FHIR

Substitutable Medical Apps and Reusable Technologies (SMART) App Launch Framework allows apps to connect with EHRs. The apps can be targeted toward clinicians, patients, and others and launched from inside or outside the EHR. The apps can be patient or provider apps and launch from a portal or be standalone (HL7 SMART App Launch. 2021).

The Office of the National Coordinator for Health Information Technology's Strategic Health IT Advanced Research Project funded the SMART project. (ONC. 2013). SMART aimed to develop an open platform for substitutable, interoperability-supporting, vendor-independent third-party apps. It also enables sandboxes for developers to test their apps in a controlled environment. The SMART team's goal was to use open web standards like REST API, which provided data access through a fixed uniform resource locator structure and using HTTP. Around the time that SMART was being developed, the HL7 organization was creating specifications for FHIR standards, so the SMART team closely collaborated with the development of FHIR. However, SMART created a way for health apps to connect to EHR systems using authorization, authentication, profiles, and UI integration (Mandel et al., 2016).

The 21st Century Cures Act requires a universal API for Health IT, which provides access to all elements of patient's records with no special effort. The Final rule from ONC published in 2020 specified SMART as the universal apps API to implement the 21st Century Cures Act.

SMART is based on FHIR (SMART Standards and Specifications. 2020). SMART uses the concept of FHIR profiles, adding to the base resource definitions while ensuring semantic consistency. The profiles can isolate the app developers from EHR-specific nuances. The apps and services which run in the background can use OAuth2 credentials to get authorization tokens for access to EHRs and automatically run queries and get data. SMART supports medication data encoded using RxNorm, observations encoded using LOINC, and problems encoded using SNOMED CT. The SMART reference implementation uses API, Authorization, and Apps servers. SMART supports Android, iOS, Windows, and web apps. The web-based apps can be embedded as an iframe to the web-based EHRs and as browser widgets or external browser windows for native client EHRs. EHRs can provide the context (which patient window was open) when a SMART app launches (Mandel et al., 2016).

SMART has also provided infrastructure to test and demo the apps. It has a Reference server implementation, Command line tool, and GUI client. Third parties have also made test servers available though these may not be live in the future. Some of these are:

- Microsoft https://github.com/microsoft/fhir-server
- HAPI https://hapifhir.io/
- IBM https://github.com/IBM/FHIR
- CMS Data at the point of care https://dpc.cms.gov/
- CMS ACO Beneficiary Claims Data https://sandbox.bcda.cms.gov/
- i2b2 http://fhir.i2b2.org/srv-dstu2-0.2/
- https://inferno.healthit.gov

SMART App Launch Framework

The SMART App Launch Framework provides an authorization platform for various apps, including those embedded within EHRs and mobile apps (HL7 SMART App Launch. 2021). The SMART profile is a method for apps to request authorization to access and retrieve FHIR resources securely. The profile does not deal with end-user authentication, session time-out, security auditing, accounting disclosures, and synchronization of patient context with EHRs. Apps use profiles to access FHIR resources using OAuth 2.0 framework. OAuth 2.0 authorization servers provide access based on institutional policies. Apps can be confidential and public depending on whether the app can protect secret keys, codes, or strings embedded in the app. The app's security is the responsibility of the developer. Some of the recommended security practices recommend that the apps:

- Ensure that authentication, authorizations, and tokens are transmitted over TLS-secured channels.
- Generate a random state parameter for each user session which is included with all authorization requests, validated for requests sent to redirect url and responses with access tokens.
- Ensure no input received as code is executed.
- Persist tokens in app-specific storage locations only.
- Avoid open redirection.
- Avoid storing unencrypted bearer tokens in cookies.

Registering SMART App with EHR

EHRs support for SMART has grown significantly since its launch. Apple's Healthkit App framework supports SMART. CMS's Blue Button supports SMART to provide API access to Medicare claim data.

Apps interfacing with EHR must be registered with that EHR's authorization service. EHR documentation specifies specific requirements for apps. SMART recommends OAuth 2.0 Dynamic Client Registration Protocol. The SMART apps are required to register zero or more fixed, fully-specified launch URLs and redirect_uri with EHR's authorization server.

The apps can be launched from within the EHR or independently. In order to request authorization, they connect to EHR's authorization server, which grants authorization and provides an authorization code to the app's redirect URL. In order to access an FHIR resource, the app uses the authorization code to get an access token sent to EHR's resource server. The details of these steps can be obtained from the HL7 site. In a production environment, in order to be able to complete health data sharing, legal agreements have to be completed between the providers and the app developers. These include but are not limited to Business Associate Agreements, Service Level Agreements, and Data Use Agreements.

SMART Markers

SMART Markers is a software framework to allow rapid deployment of apps that use patient-generated health data. It can be imported into apps to create an interoperable Patient-Generated Health Data (PGHD) system for patients and providers. Both can request data from EHR FHIR servers with the PGHD repository (Sayeed, 2020). SMART Markers have a Request and Report model with the functionality needed for providers to send PGHD requests to their patients, and patients can respond with data generated through their devices. The repository stores codified identifiers for data obtained from different sources.

The patient data can be generated from diverse sources including:

- **Questionnaires**: For example, PROMIS (Patient-Reported Outcomes Measurement Information System: a set of person-centered measures that evaluates and monitors physical, mental, and social health in adults and children), HRQoL (Health-related quality of life questionnaire for an individual's or a group's perceived physical and mental health over time)
- **API based data collection from devices**: e.g. Fitbit, step counters
- **Mobile health data aggregation platforms**: e.g. Apple HealthKit and ResearchKit, Google Fit

OAuth

OAuth is an authorization framework for HTTP services to provide defined, constrained access to users through third-party apps (Parecki. OAuth 2.0.). The user authentication is delegated to the user account hosting services, which authorize the third-party apps to access the user accounts. (Hardt D et al. 2012). OAuth provides an authorization layer. OAuth 2.0 is a public key-based authentication framework that uses the TLS / HTTPS / SSL infrastructure to encrypt client and server platforms.

OAuth Roles

The OAuth framework defines the following roles (Anicas, 2014)

- **Resource Owner**: User who authorizes that app to access their user account. The access granted is limited to the scope of authorization.
- **Resource & Authorization Server (API)**: Protected user accounts are hosted by the resource server. The identity of users is verified by the authorization server, which issues access tokens to the apps. These functions can be accessed through the APIs.
- **Client (App)**: The client or the app is authorized by the user to access the user account, and the resource and authorization server API validates the request.

OAuth Workflow

The OAuth workflow is a multi-step process starting with app registration and ending with a grant of access. These steps include

- **App registration with the server**: The developer provides the required registration information to the API service to register the app. The server then provides a client ID, which the service API will use to identify the application and create authorization URLs for the app to access. The client secret is the private string that will authenticate the app to the service API.
- **Request for authorization**: The app requests the authorization to access the resource from the user.
- **Grant of authorization**: The user authorizes the request, and the app is provided an authorization grant. An authorization grant is "a credential representing the resource owner's authorization and is expressed using one of four grant types or an extension grant type" (Hardt D. 2012). The grant could be:
    - Authorization code: Used with server-side applications where an authorization server authenticates the resource owner
    - Implicit: Used with mobile or web apps which are issued access tokens directly without an intermediate step of granting authorization code
    - Resource owner password credentials: Used with trusted apps where resource owner directly provides username and password to the client
    - Client credentials: Used with app API access and authorization scope is limited to controlled or previously authorized protected resources.
- **Request for token**: The application provides the authorization grant and authentication to the authorization server via the API to get access token.
- **Receipt of access token**: The authorization server issues an access token to the app. An *access token* is a string that represents an authorization issued to the client to access protected resources. The token defines a specific scope, lifetime, and other access attributes. The token specifies app permissions based on the context to ensure the right patient and correct encounter information is made available to the app. This authorization token can be attached to every REST API call.
- **Request for resource**: The app the requests the resource via the API from the resource server by presenting the access token.
- **Receipt of resource**: The resource server provides the resource to the app.

Launch context and scopes

OAuth scopes are used to communicate access requirements for three kinds of data: Clinical, Contextual, and Identity data. OAuth2 access scopes are targeted toward FHIR resource types that are needed. Read scopes allow read and search access, and write scopes allow FHIR to create, update, and delete access. Patient-specific scopes provide access to data about a single patient. User-level scopes allow access to specific data that a user can access. A wildcard scopes request all data for all available FHIR resources, even extending into the future.

The client requests launch context parameters which may or may not be granted. The launch context authorizes the apps to exchange data. Apps request launch context scopes to get context information from EHR like an open patient, currently open encounter, and active provider site in the EHR. The apps may be launched from within the EHR interface or outside the EHR if they are standalone apps.

An illustration of OAuth workflow is "An end-user (resource owner) can grant a printing service (client) access to her protected photos stored at a photo-sharing service (resource server), without sharing her username and password with the printing service. Instead, she authenticates directly with a server trusted by the photo-sharing service (authorization server), which issues the printing service delegation- specific credentials (access token)" (Hardt D. 2012). In a SMART situation, if an app is opened during an EHR session, the access token may contain the information about the patient (in context) and the permissions available to the app to access that specific patient's or encounter's health information.

OpenID Connect

OpenID Connect (OIDC) is a web standard for authentication (Sakimura N et al. 2014). When approved, SMART apps request an 'openid' access scope, which provides the app information like name, email address, and FHIR Profile URL in a signed OIDC identity token (Mandel JC. 2016). It is an identity layer deployed on top of the OAuth 2.0 protocol for user identity verification through authentication performed by the Authorization Server. OpenID supports web and mobile apps. The apps do not need to own or manage the password files. Google, Microsoft, Ping Identity, etc., have deployed OpenID Connect. Since it is based on OAuth 2.0 specifications, it uses REST/JSON message flows. OpenID allows for app interoperability, infrastructure security, ease of deployment for the developers, flexibility in implementation, and broader support. OpenID Connect uses the JSON Web Token (JWT) data structures.

CDS Hooks

CDS Hooks allow the introduction of decision support in EHRs by using clinical logic-based decision-making. The decision support workflows can be triggered within EHR sessions. The triggers could be specific medication or lab orders, lab results, or the opening of a patient record. These workflow-based triggers return CDS cards that display hyperlinks to launch SMART apps, provide additional information, or alternate workflow suggestions. The apps have access to the EHR data and can supplement the information EHRs provide users while matching the EHRs context.

8 HEALTH INFORMATION STANDARDS

Health interoperability has been made possible by the standardization of health information. This chapter lists the standards and protocols that have been adopted in the industry or have been recommended by relevant agencies of the United States government. The details have been simplified for easier understanding and the intention is to discuss them for general reference. Please check the latest guidelines from their source website before incorporating any of these in your products or services.

Medical data code sets

Medical data code sets have been discussed in detail in the chapter on Healthcare Terminology and Revenue Cycle Coding Systems. Here, we will provide a brief overview of code sets which constitute bulk of the health information standards that are required in healthcare.

International Classification of Diseases, 10th Revision, Clinical Modification (ICD-10-CM) is maintained and distributed by the Department of Health & Human Services (HHS), for the following:

- Diseases.
- Injuries.
- Impairments.
- Other health problems and their manifestations.
- Causes of injury, disease, impairment, or other health problems.

International Classification of Diseases, 10th Revision, Procedure Coding System (ICD-10-PCS) is maintained and distributed by HHS, for the following procedures or other actions taken for diseases, injuries, and impairments on hospital inpatients reported by hospitals:

- Prevention.
- Diagnosis.
- Treatment.
- Management.

Code on Dental Procedures and Nomenclature is maintained and distributed by the American

Dental Association for dental services.

The Current Procedural Terminology (CPT) is maintained and distributed by the American Medical Association for physician services and other health care services. These services include, but are not limited to, the following:

- Physician services.
- Physical and occupational therapy services.
- Radiologic procedures.
- Clinical laboratory tests.
- Other medical diagnostic procedures.
- Hearing and vision services.
- Transportation services including ambulance.

National Drug Codes (NDC) maintained and distributed by HHS, for reporting the following by retail pharmacies:

- Drugs.
- Biologics.

The Healthcare Common Procedure Coding System (HCPCS) maintained and distributed by HHS for all other substances, equipment, supplies, or other items used in health care services, with the exception of drugs and biologics. These items include, but are not limited to, the following:

- Medical supplies.
- Orthotic and prosthetic devices.
- Durable medical equipment.

HIT standards by standards organizations

The list of the standards, implementation specifications, and certification criteria adopted by Department of Health and Human Services for Health Information Technology Standards is included below. The version numbers of a specific standard have been omitted.

American National Standards Institute, Health Information Technology Standards Panel (HITSP)

- HITSP Summary Documents Using HL7 Continuity of Care Document (CCD)

ASTM

- ASTM E2147-18 Standard Specification for Audit and Disclosure Logs for Use in Health Information Systems

Centers for Disease Control and Prevention

- HL7 Standard Code Set CVX—Vaccines Administered
- Implementation Guide for Immunization Data Transactions using Health Level Seven (HL7) Standard Protocol Implementation Guide
- HL7 Implementation Guide for Immunization Messaging Release
- PHIN Messaging Guide for Syndromic Surveillance: Emergency Department and Urgent

Care Data, ADT Messages A01, A03, A04, and A08

- PHIN Messaging Guide for Syndromic Surveillance: Emergency Department, Urgent Care, Inpatient and Ambulatory Care Settings
- HL7 Implementation Guide for Immunization Messaging
- HL7 Standard Code Set CVX—Vaccines Administered
- National Drug Code Directory (NDC)—Vaccine NDC Linker
- CDC Race and Ethnicity Code Set

CMS

- CMS PQRI 2009 Registry XML Specifications
- 2009 Physician Quality Reporting Initiative Measure Specifications Manual for Claims and Registry
- Crosswalk: Medicare Provider/Supplier to Healthcare Provider Taxonomy
- CMS Implementation Guide for Quality Reporting Document Architecture Category I Hospital Quality Reporting Implementation Guide
- CMS Implementation Guide for Quality Reporting Document Architecture Category III Eligible Clinicians and Eligible Professionals Programs Implementation Guide

HL7

- Health Level Seven Messaging Standard, An Application Protocol for Electronic Data Exchange in Healthcare Environments
- HL7 Implementation Guide: Electronic Laboratory Reporting to Public Health
- HL7 Standard: Context-Aware Retrieval Application
- HL7 Implementation Guide for CDA®: IHE Health Story Consolidation
- HL7 Clinical Document Architecture
- HL7 Implementation Guide for CDA: Quality Reporting Document Architecture
- HL7 IG: Electronic Laboratory Reporting to Public Health
- HL7 Standard: Context Aware Retrieval Application
- HL7 Implementation Guide: Service-Oriented Architecture Implementations of the Context-aware Knowledge Retrieval
- HL7 Implementation Guide: Context-Aware Knowledge Retrieval
- HL7 Implementation Guide for CDA: Consolidated CDA Templates for Clinical Notes
- HL7 CDA Implementation Guide: Reporting to Public Health Cancer Registries from Ambulatory Healthcare Providers
- HL7 CDA Implementation Guide: Reporting to Public Health Cancer Registries from Ambulatory Healthcare Providers
- HL7 Version 3 Implementation Guide: Data Segmentation for Privacy
- HL7 Implementation Guide for CDA®—Level 3: Healthcare Associated Infection Reports
- HL7 Implementation Guide for CDA®: National Health Care Surveys (NHCS)
- HL7 Version 3 Standard, Value Sets for AdministrativeGender and NullFlavor
- HL7 CDA R2 Implementation Guide: C-CDA Templates for Clinical Notes
- HL7 FHIR Bulk Data Access
- HL7 FHIR SMART Application Launch Framework Implementation Guide
- HL7 FHIR Specification
- HL7 FHIR US Core Implementation Guide

Integrating the Healthcare Enterprise IGE

- IT Infrastructure Technical Framework

Internet Engineering Task Force (IETF)

- Network Time Protocol: Protocol and Algorithms Specification

International Telecommunication Union (ITU)

- ITU-T E.123, Series E: Overall Network Operation, Telephone Service, Service Operation and Human Factors, International operation—General provisions concerning users: Notation for national and international telephone numbers, e-mail addresses and web addresses
- ITU-T E.164, Series E: Overall Network Operation, Telephone Service, Service Operation and Human Factors, International operation—Numbering plan of the international telephone service

National Council for Prescription Drug Programs

- National Council for Prescription Drug Programs Prescriber/Pharmacist Interface SCRIPT Standard, Implementation Guide
- SCRIPT Standard, Implementation Guide

National Institute of Standards and Technology (NIST)

- FIPS PUB 140-2, Security Requirements for Cryptographic Modules
- FIPS PUB 180-4, Secure Hash Standard

Office of the National Coordinator for Health Information Technology (ONC)

- Applicability Statement for Secure Health Transport
- XDR and XDM for Direct Messaging Specification
- Transport and Security Specification
- ONC Implementation Guide for Direct Edge Protocols
- United States Core Data for Interoperability (USCDI)

OpenID Foundation

- OpenID Connect Core

Public Health Data Standards Consortium

- Public Health Data Standards Consortium Source of Payment Typology Code Set

Regenstrief Institute, Inc.

- Logical Observation Identifiers Names and Codes (LOINC®) Database
- The Unified Code of Units for Measure

The Direct Project

- Applicability Statement for Secure Health Transport
- Implementation Guide for Delivery Notification in Direct
-

U.S. National Library of Medicine

- International Health Terminology Standards Development Organization (IHTSDO) Systematized Nomenclature of Medicine Clinical Terms (SNOMED CT®) U.S. Edition
- RxNorm

World Wide Web Consortium (W3C)/MIT

- Web Content Accessibility Guidelines (WCAG) 2

Healthcare transaction standards

Healthcare collection is the exchange of information between two parties for the purpose of carrying out financial or administrative activities. The Department of Health and Human Services has standardized specifications for transactions using electronic exchange of healthcare data. These transactions include:

X12N 837: Submission of health care claim, coordination of benefits. It includes request to obtain payment, and the necessary accompanying information from a health care provider to a health plan or transmission of encounter information for the purpose of reporting healthcare, if there is no direct claim (CMS. Heath Care Claim or Equivalent Encounter Information).

X12N 835: Health care claim payment advice (or EFT, electronic funds transfer). The health care payment and remittance advice transaction is "the transmission of either a payment which includes information about the transfer of funds and payment processing from a health plan to a healthcare provider's financial institution or explanation of benefits or remittance advice from health plan to a healthcare provider." The electronic funds transfer, EFT, is the electronic message used by health plan to directly financial institution to transfer funds to providers account to pay for healthcare services. Electronic remittance advice (ERA) is an explanation from the health plan to provider to obtain payment. This includes reasons for any claim charge adjustments based on benefit coverage, co-pays, coinsurance, provided-payer contracts. These are explained through claims adjustment reason codes (CARCs) and remittance advice remark codes (RARCs) (CMS. Health Care Payment and Remittance Advice and Electronic Funds Transfer).

X12N 276/277: Health care claim status request or notification and response. A health care claim status transaction could be "an inquiry from a provider to a health plan to determine the status of a claim or response from the health plan about the status of a health care claim" (CMS. Health Care Claims Status).

X12N 270/271: Eligibility, coverage, or benefit inquiry/information. The eligibility / benefit inquiry transaction is used to obtain information about a eligibility and coverage for the plan for an enrollee. The plan required to respond to provider's eligibility questions in real time and share information about deductibles, co-pays, coinsurance, coverage information for specific services (CMS. Health Plan Eligibility Benefit Inquiry and Response).

X12N 834: Benefit enrollment and maintenance in a health plan. The enrollment / disenrollment transaction transmits subscriber's enrollment information from the sponsor of the benefits or insurance coverage plan to initiate or end insurance coverage (CMS. Health Plan Enrollment and Disenrollment).

X12N 278: Healthcare service review information including prior authorization and referrals. A referral certification and authorization transaction could be "a request from a health care provider to a health plan to obtain an authorization of healthcare, or a request from a health care provider to a health plan to obtain an authorization for referring an individual to another health care provider, or a response from a health plan to a healthcare provider about authorization and referral requests" (CMS. Referral Certification and Authorization).

X12N 820: Payment order/remittance advice/ explanation. "The health plan premium payment transaction is used to initiate a transfer payment the health plan premium payment transaction is used to initiate the transfer of payment for health insurance premiums and provide health plans with information about the transfer of funds, remittance details for individuals for whom premiums are being paid, and payment processing information" (CMS. Health Plan Premium Payments).

National Drug Codes (NDC)

National Drug Codes (NDC) are used for medicinal drugs in United States. NDC codes are developed and maintained by Food and Drug Administration and listed in Drug Registration and Listing System (DRLS) and published quarterly in NDC list. Pharmacies use the NDC code to fill the prescriptions through their pharmacy management system.

Every NDC code is a 10-digit number with 3 segments. NDC codes are in 4-4-2, 5-3-2 or 5-4-1 formats. They can be converted into 11-digit format by appending 0 in first, second or third segments. First segment is labeler code which identifies the manufacturer, repackager or distributor. Second segment is the product code that identifies the drug, its strength, medium, and formulation. The third segment is the packaging size. A drug can have multiple NDC codes. For example, 50580-496-98 indicates Johnson & Johnson Consumer Inc., McNeil Consumer Healthcare Division (50580) - Tylenol 325mg tablet (496) - 1 bottle, plastic in 1 carton with > 100 tablet in 1 plastic bottle. The NDC page for this provides detailed information about the drug including active and inactive ingredients, images of front and back of the tablet, physical description, drug uses (National Drug Codes List. Acetaminophen).

Universal Medical Device Nomenclature System (UMDNS)

The Universal Medical Device Nomenclature System™ (UMDNS) is "an international nomenclature and coding system that facilitates identifying, processing, filing, storing, retrieving, transferring, and communicating data about medical devices" (UMLS. UMD - Synopsis). UMDNS is owned and copyrighted by Emergency Care Research Institution (ECRI). It contains more than 12000 preferred terms and more than 29000 synonyms, entry terms, and related terms. UMDNS is used in applications for hospital inventory control, work order control, and medical device regulatory systems. It allows for error free data exchange between EHRs and devices, integration of devices into EHRs (UMLS. UMD – Statistics). It is updated monthly. UMDNS assigns a unique 5 digit numeric doe which corresponds to each preferred term. e.g. Code for bandages is 10274, blankets is 10415, 11218 is hemodialysis unit, 16488 is for portable blood glucose monitors,.

Global Medical Device Nomenclature (GMDN)

Global Medical Device Nomenclature (GMDN) is an international system of generic descriptors used to identify all medical device products including those products used for diagnosis, prevention, monitoring, treatment of disease or injury. GMDN was compiled based on ISO 15225 due to mandate by European commission and is maintained by GMDN agency (GMDN; ISO. ISO 15225:2010). GMDN is used for data exchange between manufacturers, regulators, and healthcare authorities, exchange of post-market vigilance information, inventory and supply chain management.

For example, surgical scalpel can be classified as

- Term name: Scalpel, single-use
- Code: 47569
- Definition: A sterile, hand-held, manual surgical instrument constructed as a one-piece handle and scalpel blade (not an exchangeable component) used by the operator to manually cut or dissect tissue. The blade is typically made of high-grade stainless-steel alloy or carbon steel and the handle is often made of plastic. This is a single-use device.

Unique Device Identification (UDI) system

Unique Device Identification System (UDI) is device identification system developed by FDA to identify medical devices from manufacturing to use by patients in United States (FDA, 2022c). UDIs can be issued by GS1 (www.gs1.org), Health Industry Business Communications Council (www.hibcc.org) and International Council for Commonality in Blood Banking Automation (www.iccbba.org).

In the past, medical devices including Digital Therapeutics products have used National Drug Codes (NDC) or Universal Product Codes (UPC) as identifiers and receive reimbursement as a pharmacy benefit. As per the UDI Rule, every medical device package and label distributed in the United States will need to have a UDI, unless exempted. This applies to all medical devices that are distributed through the pharmacies. The manufacturers submits the device information to the Global Unique Device Identification Database (GUDID) and the devices which have submitted to GUDID can be searched through a database called AccessGUDID available at https://accessgudid.nlm.nih.gov. UDI is added on the label both as text as well as machine readable form using automatic identification and data capture (AIDC) technology.

UDI Format

The Unique Device Identifier is alphanumeric code with the following components:

- **Device identifier (DI)**: Identifies the labeler or manufacturer and device model. It is mandatory and fixed in length. Device identifiers on UDIs issued by GS1 are numeric and 16 digits in length.
- **Product identifier (PI)**: This is of variable length and identifies:
    - Lot or batch number (GS1 format: alphanumeric, 22 digits)
    - Serial number (GS1 format: alphanumeric, 22 digits)
    - Expiration date (GS1 format: numeric, YYMMDD)
    - Manufacturing date (GS1 format: numeric, YYMMDD)
    - Identification code for a cell, tissue, or cellular and tissue-based product regulated as a device

UDI Benefits

UDI makes it easy to quickly identify a device and its key attributes to reduce medical errors due to misidentification or inappropriate use of the device. It also makes it easy to report adverse events, analyze adverse events, track medical devices at risk for adverse events, and implement recalls. Any communication about a medical device is likely to be clear, targeted, and minimize any confusion about which devices are recalled.

The AIDC technology enables rapid and accurate data acquisition, recording, and retrieval making it easy to integrate with health information system workflows. UDIs also enable better inventory management, easier access to relevant device manuals, identification of counterfeit devices, incorporation of the information in patients' personal health records.

Vocabulary standards

Healthcare vocabularies enable creation of standardized and structured terminology for health data. The common health data elements and their corresponding terminology standards are discussed below. The version number of a specific standard has been omitted.

- **Problems**
    - IHTSDO SNOMED CT
- **Procedures**
    - Code on Dental Procedures and Nomenclature
    - The combination of Health Care Financing Administration Common Procedure Coding System (HCPCS) and Current Procedural Terminology
    - International Classification of Diseases, 10th Revision, Procedure Coding System (ICD-10-PCS)
- **Laboratory tests**
    - Logical Observation Identifiers Names and Codes (LOINC)
- **Medications**
    - RxNorm, a standardized nomenclature for clinical drugs produced by the United States National Library of Medicine
- **Immunizations**
    - HL7 Standard Code Set CVX—Vaccines Administered
    - National Drug Code Directory (NDC)—Vaccine NDC Linker
- **Race and Ethnicity**
    - The Office of Management and Budget Standards for Maintaining, Collecting, and Presenting Federal Data on Race and Ethnicity
    - CDC Race and Ethnicity Code Set
- **Preferred language**
    - IETF BCP 47 Language Tag
- **Smoking status (*Removed in Cures Act 2020)**
    - SNOMED CT
- **Encounter diagnosis**
    - ICD-10-CM
- **Family health history (*Removed in Cures Act 2020)**
    - HL7 Version 3 Standard: Clinical Genomics; Pedigree

- **Numerical references**
  - The Unified Code of Units of Measure
- **Sex**
  - HL7 Standard Value Sets
- **Sexual orientation**
  - SNOMED CT and HL7 Standard Value Sets
- **Gender identity**
  - SNOMED CT and HL7 Standard Value Sets
- **Social, psychological, and behavioral data**
  - LOINC. Financial resource strain, Education, Stress, Depression, Physical activity, Alcohol use, Social connection and isolation, Exposure to violence
- **Patient matching**
  - Phone number standard. ITU-T E.123 & E.164
- **Provider type**
  - Medicare Provider/Supplier to Healthcare Provider Taxonomy
- **Patient insurance**
  - Public Health Data Standards Consortium Source of Payment Typology Code Set

Security standards

- **Encryption and decryption of electronic health information**
  - Any encryption algorithm identified by the National Institute of Standards and Technology (NIST)
- **Hashing of electronic health information**
  - A hashing algorithm with a security strength equal to or greater than SHA-2 as specified by NIST in FIPS Publication
- **Record treatment, payment, and health care operations disclosures**
  - The date, time, patient identification, user identification, and a description of the disclosure must be recorded for disclosures for treatment, payment, and health care operations
- **Synchronized clocks**
  - The date and time recorded utilize a system clock that has been synchronized following (RFC 1305) Network Time Protocol or (RFC 5905) Network Time Protocol
- **Audit log content**
  - ASTM E2147-18

Content exchange standards and implementation specifications

- **Patient summary record**
  - Health Level Seven Clinical Document Architecture (CDA), Continuity of Care Document (CCD)
  - ASTM E2369 Standard Specification for Continuity of Care Record
- **Electronic prescribing**
  - National Council for Prescription Drug Programs (NCPDP): SCRIPT Standard
- **Electronic submission to public health agencies for surveillance or reporting, immunization registries, lab results**

- HL7

- **Clinical quality measure data import, export and reporting**
  - HL7 Implementation Guide for CDA: Quality Reporting Document Architecture
- **Cancer information**
  - HL7 CDA Implementation Guide: Reporting to Public Health Cancer Registries from Ambulatory Healthcare Providers
- **Electronic incorporation and transmission of lab results**
  - HL7 Implementation Guide: S&I Framework Lab Results Interface
- **Clinical quality measure aggregate reporting**
  - HL7 Quality Reporting Document Architecture Category III, Implementation Guide for CDA Release 2
  - CMS Implementation Guide for Quality Reporting Document Architecture; Eligible Clinicians and Eligible Professionals Programs
- **Data segmentation for privacy**
  - HL7 Implementation Guide: Data Segmentation for Privacy (DS4P)
- **XDM package processing**
  - IHE IT Infrastructure Technical Framework
- **Public health—antimicrobial use and resistance information**
  - HL7 Implementation Guide for CDA: Healthcare Associated Infection Reports
- **Public health—health care survey information**
  - HL7 CDA Implementation Guide: National Health Care Surveys (NHCS)

Application Programming Interface (API) standards

- **HL7® Fast Healthcare Interoperability Resources (FHIR ®)**
  - HL7 FHIR US Core Implementation Guide
  - HL7 SMART Application Launch Framework Implementation Guide, including mandatory support for the "SMART Core Capabilities"
  - FHIR Bulk Data Access (Flat FHIR)
- **OpenID Connect Core**

Functional standards

- **Accessibility**
  - Web Content Accessibility Guidelines (WCAG)
- **Reference source**
  - HL7 Version 3 Standard: Context-Aware Retrieval Application.
  - HL7 Version 3 Standard: Context Aware Knowledge Retrieval Application.
  - HL7 Implementation Guide: Service-Oriented Architecture Implementations of the Context-aware Knowledge Retrieval Domain
  - HL7 Version 3 Standard: Context Aware Knowledge Retrieval Application, Knowledge Request.

Transport standards and protocols

- ONC Applicability Statement for Secure Health Transport

- ONC XDR and XDM for Direct Messaging Specification
- ONC Transport and Security Specification
- ONC Implementation Guide for Direct Edge Protocols
- ONC Implementation Guide for Delivery Notification in Direct

The health information standards generally stay the same over a number of years though they may have modifications over the years. It is possible that newer versions of the standards become available after the book is published. Readers are advised to check the source websites for the most recent standards.

9 VIRTUAL AND AUGMENTED REALITY IN HEALTHCARE

Virtual reality technology (VR) uses "interactive simulations created with computer hardware and software to present users with opportunities to engage in environments that appear and feel like real-world objects and events" (Weiss P et al., 2006). In virtual reality, complete immersion in the computer-generated environment is supplemented by artificial sounds and other stimuli (Sun P et al., 2023). The users can interact with the 3-dimensional computer-generated world by wearing headsets that track the motion of the head and provide a perspective of being in the computer-generated environment. The headsets can also track the body's position in the real-life 3-dimensional space, the position of hands, movements, or fingers, and in some cases, facial movement. Augmented reality (AR) or mixed reality (MR) refers to the merging of the display of a natural environment with a virtual, computer-generated environment (Milgram P et al., 1994). The digital images and the real world are displayed with computer-generated images aligned to real-world objects, enabling the perception of spatial presence (Sun P et al., 2023). Traditionally, VR and AR systems have used monitors as displays; however, with technological advancements, clinicians can experience virtual and augmented reality environments through head-mounted displays (HMDs). Virtual Reality (VR) and Augmented Reality (AR) have been used in healthcare for education, clinical evaluation, treatment, surgical support, and rehabilitation. With advancements in technology, virtual and augmented reality applications in healthcare are expanding. Together, they are called Virtual and Augmented Reality (VAR) technologies.

VR-AR concepts

Visual input

The visual information displayed in VAR can be obtained from a direct video feed of the patient through a digital camera, X-ray fluoroscopy, microscope, endoscope, or reconstruction from CT, MRI, or MRA images. Image-guided interventions can be enabled by displaying target organs (Okamoto K et al., 2015) and surroundings in the operating field along with the organs which are hidden from the direct field of view either because they are under superficial organs or outside the field of view (Ha H-G et al., 2016).

Markers

Surgeons have commonly used tissue markers, or fluoroscopic and CT-guided navigation, to assist them with accurate intraoperative localization. Both of these modalities provide a 2-dimensional view of the intervention plane. VR technologies can provide a 3-D view during preoperative training and planning, and AR technologies can provide real-time superimposed digital visuals. The surgeon can manipulate a 3-D anatomical model made from radiology images. The latest generation of HMDs eliminates the need to place markers on natural objects that must be tracked so that digital objects can interact with them. The fiduciary markers can be obtained through radiological images and registered manually or automatically. Optical registration tags and trackers to register pictures can also orient the radiological images. Registration accuracy is essential to avoid organ injuries and varies by the nature of the surgery and the organs on which it is performed. However, about 1 – 1.5 mm accuracy is the minimum expected for safe navigation (Citardi MJ et al., 2015). The tracking technologies use image recognition algorithms, depth perception sensors, and inertial measurement units (Genc Y et al., 2002).

Tracking

The image-guided systems based on 3-D models constructed from radiology images accurately map and superimpose the actual location of a patient's anatomy to the representation of the medical image. For registering a patient to the image-guided surgery system, anatomical landmarks are identified, and optical trackers or image recognition are used for tracking. Then, the radiology images are superimposed or registered in the surgeon's view to correlate with the actual anatomy for practice. The 3-D models enable the surgeons to look into the patient's body using digital representation (Wu JR et al., 2014), which can be tracked in real-time.

Applications in medicine

Behavioral and psychological Health

Anxiety and Depression

Studies have demonstrated a reduction in anxiety, fear, and negative thoughts after VAR treatments (Giglioli IAC et al., 2015). Multiple studies have demonstrated a reduction in participants' anxiety scores, fear, and avoidance behaviors after exposure (Juan MC et al., 2005). Interactive conversations with VR-based avatars where the avatars provide psychoeducation and encourage conversation about subjects' depression symptoms have been used to assess depression symptoms in patients with depression (Migoya-Borja M et al., 2020). In patients diagnosed with major depression, a randomized controlled trial demonstrated that virtual reality-based behavioral activation was found to reduce the severity of symptoms (Paul M et al., 2022). Another study demonstrated improved mood and reduction in hopelessness in VR environments (Habak S et al., 2020).

VR headsets can provide information about procedures, meditation, or pain management programs (Eijlers R et al., 2019) before stressful events like surgical procedures. They can also be provided to patients during or after surgery with pleasing and calming visuals to reduce pain and anxiety. Studies have found a reduction in the dose of sedatives and improved patient satisfaction in patients who use VR headsets (Haisley KR et al., 2020).

Mindfulness

Many mindfulness and relaxation applications are being developed for VAR technologies. Randomized Controlled Trials have demonstrated that participants with Generalized Anxiety Disorder produced higher alpha wave activity on EEG and lower galvanic skin response, indicating a lower stress state after exposure to a virtual reality environment (Wang TC et al., 2019).

Panic Disorders

VAR has also been combined with Cognitive Behavioral Therapy (CBT) for multiple disorders, including panic disorders (Shin B et al., 2021). This can be achieved through interaction with digital representations of individuals, commonly known as 'avatars' or 'virtual humans,' which are personalized to the specific needs of the patients. Avatars can be modeled after different professionals, personalities, ethnicities, and genders. They can provide emotional and cognitive support to patients experiencing emotional distress (Lisanne SP et al., 2022). The dialogue, speech, gestures, and facial expressions of these avatars can be modeled to achieve specific outcomes ranging from hallucinations (Leff J et al. 2014) to suicide ideation (Mozgai S et al. 2023).

Phobias

In the case of phobias, gradual exposure is provided to the source of the phobia. VAR has been applied to a wide variety of phobias, including aviophobia, acrophobia, arachnophobia, and animal phobia. For example, a study exposed subjects to virtual cockroaches and increased exposure to seeing, touching, and killing virtual cockroaches (Botella C et al., 2015). VAR-based exposure therapies for phobias work through extinction and habituation mechanisms (Wechsler TF et al., 2019). VR exposure therapy (VRET) is similar to in-vivo exposure therapy, but the phobic stimuli are presented to the subjects in a virtual environment. Other phobias that have been studied include claustrophobia (Malbos E et al., 2008), fear of driving (Costa RTD et al., 2018), fear of dental procedures (Gujjar KR et al., 2017), fear of procedures or exposure to blood or injections (Jian MYW et al., 2020).

Psychoses

VAR can also help in psychoses or body dysmorphic disorders since VAR can create self or environmental models that can mimic the abnormal reality models of the individuals (Metzinger TK., 2018).

Surgery

Image-guided surgical systems have been widely used in surgery since the early 2000s, and computer-aided technology has been shown to be accurate and consistent (Jud L et al., 2020). Surgery has been the most common use case of VAR in healthcare. The applications in surgery include preoperative planning, intraoperative guidance to surgical assistants, remote assistance to operating surgeons, patient education, and surgery resident training (Sun P et al., 2023). Currently, orthopedics, neurosurgery, and laparoscopic surgery are the most common specialties using VAR in surgical procedures; however, this could change as the technology evolves and more applications emerge (Zhao Z et al. 2021). It has been successfully demonstrated in hip arthroplasty (Fotouhi J et al., 2018), intramedullary nail placement (Ma L et al., 2018), pedicle screw placement (Gibby JT et al., 2019), vertebroplasty (Abe Y et al., 2013).

VAR technology can superimpose information on anatomy or medical instruments (Azuma R., 1997). This is useful for training surgeons using simulation or during actual procedures by guiding the path of instruments, placing implants, providing additional information within the field of view, and providing step-by-step assistance with the intervention steps. Virtual Reality can improve physicians' spatial awareness of patients' anatomical landmarks, reducing operating time and errors (Zhang J et al., 2023). The VAR systems can track instruments, identify and mark organs, and recreate the surgical steps using superimposed graphics. They can also reconstruct fine details of organs to assist in preoperative planning (Kockro RA et al., 2016).

Augmented Reality combines the information or visuals of the real environment with the virtual information or digital reconstruction. Surgeons can identify optimal location and orientation for placing implants, planes of resection, or insertion of screws or fixators. Augmented Reality enables surgeons to maintain their line of sight in the patient's surgical field instead of looking at the monitor (Gan A et al., 2019). Holographic overlays of surgical plans, implants, or organs are superimposed on the patient using shape or image recognition for registration. This helps to improve the identification of surgical landmarks in various surgery types, including laparoscopic endoscopy. Surgeons can create virtual trajectories to assess approaches to the tissue using superimposed images, which can be compared with actual trajectories (Gibby JT et al., 2019).

The advantages of VAR include reduced intraoperative radiation exposure, tracking of posture changes, and the ability to maintain the mapping of digital objects on the patient's anatomy throughout the procedure, avoiding the need for tissue markers for navigation. Other advantages are that the HMDs can be operated with voice commands, and physicians can collaborate in pre-surgical planning by discussing surgical approaches on anatomic models of patients constructed from radiological images. The AR is beneficial in minimally invasive surgery where the path of surgical instrumentation may not be directly visualized but could be guided by virtual 'rings' or 3-dimensional planes (Citardi MJ et al., 2015). Research is underway to ensure that VAR setup time does not prolong the duration of surgeries and that the VAR systems themselves and their attachments maintain the surgical field.

Rehabilitation

VAR technologies have been used in physical, occupational, speech, and cognitive rehabilitation. The rehabilitation techniques used in VAR include balance training, physical conditioning, sensorimotor exercises, task-oriented repetitive exercises, postural control, etc. (Vinolo Gil MJ et al., 2021). The technology has been used to improve balance, prevent falls, improve the function of limbs in stroke, and improve gait in Parkinson's, multiple sclerosis, and cerebral palsy patients.

While stroke has been the most common condition treated with VAR-based rehabilitation, the potential of these technologies is expanding as they become more advanced. Motor nerve disorders are emerging as the next common group of diagnoses. Notably, there has been a significant improvement in mobility in the geriatric population. The combination of virtual reality and conventional therapy has shown remarkable results in improving limb function and activities of daily living measures in stroke patients (Laver KE et al., 2017).

VR-based cognitive-motor rehabilitation has shown a better attention span and cognitive functioning than non-VR-based cognitive rehabilitation (Liao YY et al., 2020). Other randomized controlled trials have demonstrated improvements in memory, language, and visuo-constructional abilities in mild cognitive impairment (Manenti R et al., 2020) after patients received face-to-face cognitive virtual reality rehabilitation system treatment compared to conventional face-to-face treatment.

Besides improvement in clinical outcomes, VAR has been shown to increase (Vinolo GMJ et al., 2021) patient motivation and enjoyment in participation in therapies (Sveistrup H et al., 2004), provide home-based physical therapy (Lee H et al., 2018), and enable real-time monitoring and analysis (Borghese N et al., 2013).

Surgical simulation

Surgical training in virtual reality simulation to practice in environments and with instruments that they are familiar with reduces the learning curve and improves competency. VAR enables trainees to practice skills independently without constant supervision since there is a lower risk of injury to the trainee or the patient due to errors (Barteit S et al., 2021). Training about new medical devices can be provided through simulations in a VAR setting before the surgeons work on real devices on actual patients. The simulators can mimic skin, soft tissue, internal organs, bones, and vessels. They can also mimic the movement of different tissues and body fluids and the interaction of instruments with the tissues. Multiple variations can be created for the patient's environment, type of instruments, and patient clinical models. Instructors can also provide real-time feedback to the trainees. The educational modules can be gamified to increase interest, engagement, and retention.

VAR training can be provided on a wide range of procedures – from simple bedside procedures like placement of central lines, intubations, CPR, ultrasound guided biopsies, urine catheterization to complex surgeries like laparoscopies, joint replacements, neurosurgeries, and dental procedures. The downsides of using VAR technologies is limited ability to mimic all physiological and pathological variations, steep learning curve for trainees who have not used VAR technologies previously, significant investment required in creating VAR appropriate medical education content, need of research to evaluate long term retention between training on VAR environments vs live patient experience.

AR training can be combined with remote telepresence to create virtual interactive presence systems where a surgeon can remotely provide assistance to a trainee or less experienced surgeon virtually for intraoperative telecollaboration (Davis MC et al., 2016). Both the operating trainee surgeon and remote trainer surgeon see the same composite video with an overlay of digital information and images. The remote surgeon can guide the operating surgeon through audio as well as on-screen visuals.

Research studies have demonstrated positive outcomes from AR technologies. AR-based pre-surgery training for image-guided surgery has been shown to result in faster completion of navigation tasks, better accuracy, and more straightforward navigation of AR interfaces compared to standard of care (Glass HH et al., 2017). Immersive VR (Logishetty K et al., 2020) and AR (Nagayo Y et al., 2021) have been used for surgical training for open procedures. VR-based simulator training has been shown to reduce the time of laparoscopic surgery by half (Larsen CR et al., 2009). In another study, trainees using an overlay of images and laser guidance for placement of needles in joint injections demonstrated a better success rate and reduced potential for tissue damage compared to freehand insertions (Yeo CT et al., 2011).

Medical simulation

Physicians can receive training through VAR technologies for patient communication, medical counseling, patient assessment, and feedback. In these scenarios, patient encounters are simulated in VR or AR environments. VAR is also used in medical education, such as teaching gross and microscopic anatomy and physiological functions through 3D and 360-degree interactive models. Anatomic models created from radiological images and digital pathology slices enable a better understanding of organs, tissues, cells, and organelles.

Studies have demonstrated that VAR technologies may provide advantages compared to non-VAR training techniques. VAR can present complex medical content to students. It may reduce the need for equipment or lab equipment while reducing financial and resource constraints (Jensen L et al., 2017; Moro C et al., 2021).

Future of VAR

VAR technologies have progressed tremendously in the last few years. These advances will catalyze the development of VAR applications for healthcare, which will increase provider adoption and lead to more investment in VAR software and hardware R&D.

However, some challenges need to be resolved before the VAR technologies can have mass market adoption. Some of these issues have been addressed in the latest generation of headsets but many still remain in consumer grade hardware.

- The weight of VAR HMDs needs to be reduced to minimize neck and back fatigue due to wearing them for multiple hours
- The latency between tracking of head and hand movements and visual imagery displayed in the headset needs to be improved to reduce motion sickness
- The resolution of pass-through video and digital images needs to be improved to reduce headaches and improve immersion
- The navigation between virtual and augmented environments needs to be made seamless, without disruption
- The ergonomics and the range of motion of the controllers need to be improved to make them more useful
- The accuracy in matching the fiduciary markers and actual anatomic landmarks needs to be increased
- The field of view of HMDs needs to expand from the narrow field in currently available headsets
- The network latency needs to be improved, especially in telecollaboration applications to enable real time feedback during the procedures
- The privacy and safety of the software used in VAR technologies needs to pass the highest standards of healthcare safety and privacy standards.

10 QUALITY IMPROVEMENT

Digital health technologies and clinical informatics are playing a tremendous role in improving healthcare quality. An increasing number of healthcare services are now paid based on quality metrics, providing many opportunities for developing and deploying digital health tools. This chapter will discuss the generic framework around which quality metrics are created globally, with specific examples for United States, Canada, United Kingdom, India, and China. Details about particular quality indicators are available on this book's website. The discussion primarily focuses on healthcare delivery providers; however, some examples of quality indicators for healthcare insurance are discussed.

Healthcare quality measures are used to evaluate and guide healthcare delivery and health insurance industries. Understanding quality measures allows digital health companies to develop products and services that can help healthcare providers and insurance companies score better on these measures. Healthcare quality is studied by many organizations, many of which convert their assessment results into numerical measures. These scores or quality metrics can be used for reimbursement decisions, recognition, or released to the public for general information. Not all organizations are alike in the rigor of their methodology or recognition of their assessment. However, healthcare organizations must get good evaluations from significant quality rating organizations.

Healthcare organizations use metrics, measures, and indicators to track their organization's performance. Some of these are mandated by local, state, or federal recommendations; others are required for reimbursement by CMS and national healthcare accreditation bodies. The required st andards may change over time as the priorities of regulatory agencies or accreditation agencies evolve. Healthcare organizations can also choose to monitor their metrics and indicators. The healthcare organizations can be subject to regulatory oversight and financial penalties if they fail to achieve the metrics, so internally they use employment or contractual agreements with the healthcare providers, including physicians and nurses, as well as employees, to incentivize activities that help to achieve the metrics.

The essential requirement for any quality improvement project is data. The data is cleaned, combined, and analyzed to generate useful information. The information is shared, discussed, and interpreted in the organizational context, leading to the development of insights. These insights inform the strategy to generate and implement interventions. If everything feeding into this value chain is accurate, quality interventions can improve outcomes. It is vital for anyone working directly with data or acting on the intervention to understand the data itself. This information includes the source of data, who collected it, how it was collected, the assumptions in collecting it, and the limitations of the data. Frequently, data analysts must reach out to individuals who generated the data in the first place. These could be nurses documenting in the EMR, billers, and coders converting the healthcare activities into reimbursement, and laboratory technicians entering lab values.

Data-driven decision-making is getting adopted in healthcare after successfully improving quality in manufacturing and other service industries. Appropriate information communication via reports or dashboards is pertinent to ensure that right information is used for the right decisions. Ideally, these should be tied to the organizational priorities at that time. Ensuring that any metric or indicator is specific and actionable is essential. Frequent evaluation of the indicators guarantees that they continue to serve the original purpose for which they were identified. The analysts should ensure that the hypothesis behind the data collected for the indicators is unchanged, or if they do, it is suitably reflected in how the indicator is measured and tracked. For example, the calculation of several days a patient has had a Foley catheter placed in ED can be different depending on whether time t=0 is considered as the time of patient's presentation to ED, time of actual insertion, time of documentation, time when patient moved to the floor, end of shift time if the nurse documented Foley at the end of the shift. If the documentation practice changes at some point after the indicator has been introduced, it needs to be updated in the reports or dashboards. Presentation of analytics results is as important as ensuring that the data used to create those results is accurate and that the hypotheses are sound. The reports and dashboards should be concise, clear, and easy to understand and have 3-4 main takeaways at the maximum. Analysts should consider the level of understanding that the potential consumers of the dashboards will have. The analysts who have spent days looking at the data and running analyses on it need to make sure that those seeing the data for the first time are able to grasp the nuances.

Quality metrics

Digital health products, services, and interventions can be developed or implemented for healthcare quality improvement efforts, which can be based on clinical outcomes, medical protocols, operational workflows, financial metrics, patient safety, patient satisfaction, or compliance. The health care quality metrics are used in most countries around the world are quite similar. Some categories of quality metrics and examples of quality metrics under those categories are discussed below. Please note that the following are representative metrics. Please refer to the latest guidelines for updated information.

Medical protocols

- Inpatient care measures
    - Thrombolytic therapy for stroke patients
    - Sepsis management bundle
    - Elective deliveries
    - Alcohol use intervention provided or offered
    - Tobacco use treatment provided or offered
    - Influenza immunization discussion or administration

- Identification and treatment of moderate to severe protein calorie malnutrition
- Outpatient measures
  - Appropriate follow-up for outpatient procedures
  - Patient with low back pain having an MRI without trying other recommended treatments like physical therapy
  - Patients who got cardiac imaging stress tests before low risk outpatient surgery
  - Palliative care referrals for terminal cancer patients

Patient satisfaction

- Patient satisfaction tracking through surveys
  - Communication by the nurses
  - Communication by the doctors
  - Responsiveness of the staff
  - Pain assessment and discussion
  - Medication related communication
  - Hospital environment including cleanliness and quietness
  - Discharge assistance and information sharing
  - Assistance with care transition

Financial performance

- Hospital focused financial metrics
  - Bond rating metrics including days cash on hand, reserve funding, current ratio
  - Earning Before Interest Depreciation Taxes and Amortization
  - Loan ratios including Annual debt service coverage, Maximum annual debt service coverage, debt to capitalization
  - Claim denial rate
  - Appeals overturned rate
  - Reference lab costs
  - Negotiated rates for supplies and consumables
- Cost efficiency
  - Average spending per patient
  - Acute myocardial infarction payment per episode of care
  - Heart failure payment per episode of care
  - Pneumonia payment per episode of care
  - Direct cost per procedure (CABG, PCI, Arthroplasty, Laparoscopic cholecystectomy, Appendectomy, Colectomy etc.)

Compliance tracking

- Tracking external compliance
  - National accreditation requirements
  - Insurance reimbursement related metrics
  - State department of public health licensing requirements
- Tracking internal compliance
  - Healthcare personnel vaccination
  - Healthcare personnel hand hygiene

Operations

- HR metrics
  - Nursing turnover rate
  - Nursing vacancy rate
- Inpatient service volume
  - Admissions
  - Discharges
  - Patient days
  - Inpatient surgeries
  - Emergency visits
  - Number of emergency diversions
  - Average length of stay
  - Excess staffing
- Outpatient service volume
  - Outpatient surgeries
- Efficiency
  - Average annual bed turnover rate
  - Laboratory turnaround time
  - Time from transport request to patient pick up
  - Number of transport dispatches in an hour
  - Radiology turnaround time
  - MRI idle time
  - Patient discharged to bed cleaned
- Emergency department
  - Time from ED Arrival to ED departure for discharged patients
  - Patients who leave emergency department before being seen
  - Time from ED Arrival to admission to hospital bed
  - Time from ED Arrival to first physician contact
  - Head CT/MRI results for stroke patients within a specified time frame
- Operating room
  - Utilization
  - Turnaround times
- Laboratory services

Patient Safety

- Healthcare associated infections
  - Clostridium Difficile
  - Methicillin Resistant Staph Aureus bacteremia
- Surgical site infection
  - Colon surgery
  - Abdominal hysterectomy
- Healthcare associated device related infections
  - Central Line Associated Blood Stream Infections (CLABSI)
  - Catheter Associated Urinary Tract Infection (CAUTI)
- Surgical complications
  - Complication rate after Elective Primary Total Hip or Knee Arthroplasty

- 30-day acute care readmissions
  - Acute Myocardial infarction
  - Heart failure
  - Pneumonia
  - COPD
  - Total Hip Arthroplasty and total knee arthroplasty
  - Coronary Artery Bypass Graft surgery
  - Stroke
  - Hospital wide all-cause unplanned readmission
- 30-day mortality rate
  - Acute myocardial infarction mortality rate
  - Heart failure mortality rate
  - Pneumonia mortality rate
  - COPD mortality rate
  - Stroke mortality rate
  - CABG mortality rate
  - PCI mortality rate
  - Sepsis mortality rate

Population Health

- Disease segmentation in population
- Disease clustering in population
- Population risk stratification
- Trend analysis
- Chronic condition monitoring
  - Hypertension, Congestive Heart Failure, Asthma, Infection rates, Perinatal complications, Cancer
- Medical touchpoints monitoring
  - Office visits, Emergency room visits, SNF readmits, Telemedicine visits, Medication compliance

Health quality in United States

In the US, Centers for Medicare & Medicaid Services (CMS) develops the quality measures used for payments by the agency. These metrics are the most important quality indicators used by the healthcare delivery organizations. CMS quality measures are "used to measure healthcare processes, outcomes, patient perceptions, and organization structure and/or systems that are associated with the ability to provide high-quality health care and/or that relate to one or more quality goals for health care. These goals include: effective, safe, efficient, patient-centered, equitable, and timely care" (CMS. Quality Measures). These measures are used in CMS quality improvement, pay-for-reporting and public reporting programs

"Meaningful Measures" initiative was launched in 2017 to improve patient care through quality measurement and improvement efforts. The goal was to align the measures across programs and/or with other payers. The six goals were:

- Promote Effective Communication and Coordination of Care
    - Medication management
    - Admissions and readmissions to hospitals
    - Seamless transfer of health information
- Strengthen Person & Family Engagement as Partners in their Care
    - Care is personalized and is aligned with patient's goals
    - End of life care according to preferences
    - Patient experience and functional outcomes
- Make care safer by reducing harm caused in the delivery of care
    - Healthcare association infections
    - Preventable healthcare harm
- Promote Effective Prevention & Treatment of Chronic Disease
    - Preventive care
    - Management of chronic conditions
    - Prevention, treatment, and management of mental health
    - Prevention and treatment of opioid and substance use disorders
    - Risk adjusted mortality
- Work with communities to promote best practices of healthy living
    - Equity of care
    - Community engagement
- Make care affordable
    - Appropriate use of healthcare
    - Patient-focused episode of care
    - Risk adjusted total cost of care

CMS has created many programs to monitor quality metrics for healthcare delivery organizations:

- Hospital Compare
- Hospital Inpatient Quality Reporting
- Hospital Value-Based Purchasing
- Hospital Outpatient Quality Reporting
- Hospital Readmission Reduction Program
- Medicare and Medicaid Electronic Health Record Incentive Program for Hospitals and Critical Access Hospitals
- Medicare and Medicaid Electronic Health Record Incentive Program for Eligible Professionals
- Medicare and Medicaid Promoting Interoperability Program for Eligible Hospitals and Critical Access Hospitals
- Hospital Acquired Condition Reduction Program, Hospital Inpatient Quality Reporting
- Medicaid Promoting Interoperability Program for Eligible Professionals. The measures from the following programs are not included:
- Medicare Physician Quality Reporting System
- Physician Feedback/Quality Resource Use Report
- Physician Value-Based Payment
- Merit-Based Incentive Payment System (MIPS) Program

Hospitals

Hospital Compare from the Center for Medicare and Medicaid (CMS)

CMS has created a consumer-oriented website called Hospital Compare that helps consumers make informed decisions about the quality of care delivery at hospitals in the United States. Patients can select multiple hospitals and compare performance measures across various clinical indications. The mission of data to CMS is mandatory and impacts the financial bottom line through value-based payments.

Healthgrades

Healthgrades initially provided information on providers; however, it has expanded to providing hospital quality ratings based on clinical outcomes and most common procedures and conditions. It used over 45 million Medicare medical claims in the most recent three years from nearly 4500 hospitals nationwide. The hospital rating of the data is risk-adjusted for patient acuity. It provides awards for America's 250 best hospitals and specialty-specific awards.

Watson Health 100 Top Hospitals

Previously known as Truven Health Analytics 100 top hospitals, the IBM Watson Health 100 Top Hospitals® award measures hospital performance and leadership. The hospitals don't need to apply to this program. Public data sources are used to develop this ranking. Hospital performance measures include "inpatient and extended care quality, operational efficiency, financial health, and customer experience." The hospitals were classified into major teaching, teaching, large community, medium community, and small community hospitals. The 11 measures to select the 2020 winners were: "1. Risk-adjusted inpatient mortality index; 2 Risk-adjusted complications index; 3. Mean healthcare-associated infection index; 4. Influenza immunization rate; 5. Mean 30-day risk-adjusted mortality rate (includes acute myocardial infarction, heart failure, pneumonia, chronic obstructive pulmonary disease, and stroke); 6. 30-day risk-adjusted hospital-wide readmission rate; 7. Severity-adjusted average length of stay; 8. Mean emergency department throughput; 9. Case mix- and wage-adjusted inpatient expense per discharge; 10. Adjusted operating profit margin; and 11. Hospital Consumer Assessment of Healthcare; Providers and Systems score" (IBM. Watson Health).

National Surgical Quality Improvement Program

American College of Surgeons National Surgical Quality Improvement Program® Surgical Outcome Measures (ACS NSQIP) is a nationally validated, risk-adjusted, outcomes-based program to measure and improve the quality of surgical care. It uses data from the medical chart, which is risk-adjusted, case-mix adjusted, and based on 30-day patient outcomes. Report the outcomes through the CMS Hospital Compare website.

US News and World Report Best Hospitals

US News and World Report rankings are among the most well-known hospital rankings. Rankings are at the national level and state level. Children's hospitals get separate rankings. Hospitals are also ranked by specialty, including "cardiology and heart surgery, diabetes and endocrinology, gastroenterology and GI surgery, geriatrics, gynecology, nephrology, neurology and neurosurgery, oncology, ophthalmology, orthopedics, otolaryngology, psychiatry, pulmonology and lung surgery, rehabilitation, rheumatology, and urology."

Society of Thoracic Surgery National Database and Public Reporting Initiative

The participants in the Society of Thoracic Surgery national database and public reporting initiative can voluntarily report their surgical outcomes to the public. The scores are available for adult cardiac surgery, general thoracic surgery, and congenital heart surgery. More details are available at: https://www.sts.org/registries-research-center/sts-national-database.

American Hospital Association Survey

The American Hospital Association conducts an annual survey of the hospitals in the United States, which includes data on facilities and services, resources, utilization, staffing, revenue, expenses, managed care contracts, community health indicators, etc. the data provided by more than 6200 hospitals and more than 400 healthcare systems. As per AHA, this data can be used for population health, automated payment models, physician arrangements, telehealth, technology adoption and other critical IT indicators, hospital service lines and facilities, organizational structure, utilization including admissions, births, surgeries, ED visits, and staffing.

Becker's Healthcare 100 Great Hospitals in America

Becker's list is an internal analysis of ranking and awards from US News & World Report rankings, CareChex, Healthgrades, CMS star ratings, Leapfrog grades, and IBM Watson Health's top hospitals.

Medicare Five-Star Quality Rating System

CMS created a five-star quality rating system to help consumers, their families, and caregivers compare nursing homes more easily and get the information they need to choose a nursing home. "The Nursing Home Compare Web site features a quality rating system that gives each nursing home a rating of between 1 and 5 stars. Nursing homes with five stars are considered to have much above average quality, and nursing homes with 1 star are considered to have quality much below average." The rating source is Health inspections, staffing rating, and quality measures.

Agency for Healthcare Research and Quality Measures (AHRQ)

AHRQ is an agency of the Department of Health and Human Services. It develops quality indicators to measure quality and helps organizations identify quality concerns and areas for improvement and monitor changes over time. The Medicare and Medicaid Services quality indicators are used on the Hospital Compare website. Other federal programs also use these quality indicators to assess, incentivize, and report on quality improvement efforts. These include the National Quality Strategy (NQS), CMS Hospital Value-Based Purchasing Initiative, CMS Accountable Care Organizations, and CMS Meaningful Use Incentive Program.

AHRQ provides over one hundred quality indicators in four modules, which are Prevention Quality Indicators (PQIs), Inpatient Quality Indicators (IQI), Patient Safety Indicators (PSI), and Pediatric Quality Indicators (PDI). These indicators are used with illustrative hospital data unavailable for non-acute care settings, including family tree, emergency department, or outpatient settings. Some indicators can be used in ambulatory settings for adult and pediatric care.

Leapfrog

Leapfrog is a non-profit organization created by several large US companies and healthcare experts to improve healthcare quality and affordability. It measures and publicly reports hospital performance through the annual Leapfrog Hospital Survey of over twenty-five hundred hospitals.

It publishes a Leapfrog Hospital Safety Grade, which ranks hospitals nationally and for every state. The grade is calculated using some CMS national performance measures as well as its own survey. Critical access hospitals, federal hospitals, specialty hospitals, and some other hospital types are not included. The intended audience is payers, employers, consumers, and other healthcare-using entities. Leapfrog results are widely reported in news media, and even though there is no direct financial impact, the leapfrog ratings can be used by employers and payors in their contract negotiations. Leapfrog provides ratings on hospitals as well as surgery centers.

In 2019, a Leapfrog Ambulatory Surgery Center survey was launched. This survey evaluated process and outcome measures. The process or structural measures included (Source: Leapfrog):

- Computerized Physician Order Entry (CPOE)
- Bar Code Medication Administration
- ICU Physician staffing: It measures the use of intensivists in ICUs
- Patient Safety Practices
    - Culture of Safety Leadership Structures and Systems
    - Culture Measurement, Feedback, and Intervention
    - Nursing Workforce
- Hand Hygiene
- Hospital Consumer Assessment of Healthcare Providers and Systems (HCAHPS)

The outcome measures were focused on quality outcomes in acute care settings. These include:

- Healthcare Association Infections
    - Central line-association bloodstream infections (CLABSI) in ICUs and select wards
    - Catheter-associated urinary tract infections (CAUTI) in ICUs and select wards
    - Surgical site infections from colon surgery
    - Inpatient MRSA infections
    - Inpatient C.diff events
- Hospital-acquired conditions
    - Foreign objects retained after surgery
    - Air embolism
    - Falls & Trauma
- AHRQ Patient Safety Indicators
    - Pressure ulcer rate
    - Death rate among surgical inpatients with serious treatable conditions
    - Iatrogenic pneumothorax rate
    - Postoperative respiratory failure rate
    - Perioperative PE/DVT rate
    - Postoperative wound dehiscence rate
    - Unrecognized abdominopelvic accidental puncture/laceration rate

Health insurance

The health insurance companies are rated based on quality parameters, which have been developed at the federal level by CMS, other agencies like NCQA, and states.

Medicare Star rating

CMS has developed Star ratings for Medicare Advantage (Medicare Part C) and Medicare Part D prescription drug plans. A plan is assigned a rating between 1 and 5 stars, with 5 representing the highest quality (CMS. Part C and D Performance Data).

The Medicare Advantage Plans are evaluated in five categories:

- **Staying Healthy**: Measures preventive services like physical examinations, vaccinations, screening exams, etc., to keep members healthy.
    - Breast cancer screening
    - Colorectal cancer screening
    - Yearly flu vaccine
    - Monitoring physical activity
- **Chronic conditions management**: Measures care coordination and services for chronic conditions.
    - Members whose plan assessed their health needs and risks
    - Yearly review of all medications and supplements being taken
    - Yearly pain screening or pain management plan
    - Osteoporosis management
    - Eye exam to check for damage from diabetes
    - Kidney function testing for members with diabetes
    - Plan members with diabetes whose blood sugar is under control
    - Rheumatoid arthritis management
    - Reducing the risk of falling
    - Improving bladder control
    - The plan makes sure member medication records are up-to-date after hospital discharge
    - The plan makes sure members with heart disease get the most effective drugs to treat high cholesterol
- **Member experience**: Rates plans based on overall member satisfaction.
    - Ease of getting needed care and seeing specialists
    - Getting appointments and care quickly
    - Health plan provides information or help when members need it
    - Member's rating of health care quality
    - Member's rating of health plan
    - Coordination of members' health care services
- **Member complaints**: Member complaints, service issues, and change in plans influence the ratings
    - Complaints about the health plan (more stars are better because it means fewer complaints)
    - Members choosing to leave the plan (more stars are better because it means fewer members choose to leave the plan)
    - Improvement (if any) in the health plan's performance
- **Customer service**: Plans with responsive call centers, appeals, and grievance processes are rated higher.
    - Health plan makes timely decisions about appeals
    - Fairness of the health plan's appeal decisions, based on an independent reviewer
    - Availability of TTY services and foreign language interpretation when prospective members call the health plan

CMS also has a rating system for Prescription Drug Plans (PDP) and Medicare Advantage (MA) plans, which provide drug coverage. These ratings are divided into four categories:

- Member experience with the drug plan
  - Members' rating of drug plan
  - Ease of getting prescriptions filled when using the plan
- Member complaints and changes in the drug plan's performance
  - Complaints about the drug plan (more stars are better because it means fewer complaints)
  - Members choosing to leave the plan (more stars are better because it means fewer members choose to leave the plan)
  - Improvement (if any) in the drug plan's performance
- Drug Plan customer service
  - Availability of TTY services and foreign language interpretation when prospective members call the drug plan
- Drug safety and accuracy of drug pricing
  - Plan provides accurate drug pricing information for this website
  - Taking diabetes medication as directed
  - Taking blood pressure medication as directed
  - Taking cholesterol medication as directed
  - Members who had a pharmacist (or other health professional) help them understand and manage their medications
  - The plan makes sure members with diabetes take the most effective drugs to treat high cholesterol

Healthcare Effectiveness Data and Information Set (HEDIS)

National Committee for Quality Assurance (NCQA) developed the HEDIS®, a registered trademark of the National Committee for Quality Assurance (NCQA), which is a collection of performance measures for the managed care industry and is used by over 90 percent of the health plans enrolling about 191 million people (NCQA. 2021). HEDIS includes over 90 measures covering the effectiveness of care, access and availability of care, experience of care, utilization and risk-adjusted utilization, health plan descriptive information, and measures reported using electronic clinical data systems. The details about the measures are available from the NCQA website. For reference, the list of measures are:

Effectiveness of Care

- Prevention and Screening
  - Adult BMI Assessment
  - Weight Assessment and Counseling for Nutrition and Physical Activity for Children/Adolescents
  - Childhood Immunization Status
  - Immunizations for Adolescents
  - Lead Screening in Children
  - Breast Cancer Screening
  - Cervical Cancer Screening
  - Colorectal Cancer Screening
  - Chlamydia Screening in Women
  - Care for Older Adults

- Respiratory Conditions
    - Appropriate Testing for Children With Pharyngitis
    - Use of Spirometry Testing in the Assessment and Diagnosis of COPD
    - Pharmacotherapy Management of COPD Exacerbation
    - Asthma Medication Ratio (AMR)
- Cardiovascular Conditions
    - Controlling High Blood Pressure
    - Persistence of Beta-Blocker Treatment After a Heart Attack
    - Statin Therapy for Patients With Cardiovascular Disease and Diabetes
- Diabetes
    - Comprehensive Diabetes Care
- Musculoskeletal Conditions
    - Osteoporosis Testing and Management in Older Women
- Behavioral Health
    - Antidepressant Medication Management
    - Follow-Up Care for Children Prescribed ADHD Medication
    - Follow-Up After Hospitalization for Mental Illness
    - Follow-Up After Emergency Department Visit for Mental Illness
    - Follow-Up After Emergency Department Visit for Alcohol and Other Drug Abuse or Dependence
    - Diabetes and Cardiovascular Disease Screening and Monitoring for People With Schizophrenia or Bipolar Disorder
    - Adherence to Antipsychotic Medications for Individuals With Schizophrenia
    - Metabolic Monitoring for Children and Adolescents on Antipsychotics
- Medication Management and Care Coordination
    - Annual Monitoring for Patients on Persistent Medications
    - Medication Reconciliation Post-Discharge
    - Transitions of Care
    - Follow-Up After Emergency Department Visit for People With Multiple High-Risk Chronic Conditions
- Overuse/Appropriateness
    - Non-Recommended Cervical Cancer Screening in Adolescent Females
    - Non-Recommended PSA-Based Screening in Older Men
    - Appropriate Treatment for Children With Upper Respiratory Infection
    - Avoidance of Antibiotic Treatment in Adults With Acute Bronchitis
    - Use of Imaging Studies for Low Back Pain
    - Medication Management in Older Adults (DAE, DDE)
    - Use of Opioids at High Dosage
    - Use of Opioids from Multiple Providers
    - Risk of Continued Opioid Use
- Measures Collected Through the Medicare Health Outcomes Survey
    - Fall Risk Management
    - Management of Urinary Incontinence in Older Adults
    - Physical Activity in Older Adults
- Measures Collected Through the CAHPS® Health Plan Survey
    - Flu Vaccinations
    - Medical Assistance with Smoking and Tobacco Use Cessation
    - Pneumococcal Vaccination Status for Older Adults

Access / Availability of Care

- Adults' Access to Preventive/Ambulatory Health Services
- Children and Adolescents' Access to Primary Care Practitioners
- Annual Dental Visit
- Initiation and Engagement of Alcohol and Other Drug Abuse or Dependence Treatment
- Prenatal and Postpartum Care
- Use of First-Line Psychosocial Care for Children and Adolescents on Antipsychotics

Utilization

- Child and Adolescent Well-Care Visits
- Frequency of Selected Procedures
- Identification of Alcohol and Other Drug Services
- Mental Health Utilization
- Antibiotic Utilization
- HAI Standard Infection Ratio

Risk Adjusted Utilization

- Plan All-Cause Readmissions
- Acute Hospital Utilization
- Emergency Department Utilization
- Hospitalization for Potentially Preventable Complications

Measures Reported Using Electronic Clinical Data Systems

- Depression Screening and Follow-Up for Adolescents and Adults
- Utilization of the PHQ-9 to Monitor Depression Symptoms for Adolescents and Adults
- Depression Remission or Response for Adolescents and Adults
- Unhealthy Alcohol Use Screening and Follow-Up
- Adult Immunization Status
- Prenatal Immunization Status
- Prenatal Depression Screening and Follow-up
- Postpartum Depression Screening and Follow-up

Besides these, the individual states may have their own measures for the health plans like Medicaid Managed Care Accountability, Covered California Quality Transformation Initiative, New York State Managed Care Plan Performance Report, etc.

Health quality in Canada

About seventy five percent of healthcare in Canada is delivered through publicly funded system called Medicare which is administered by ten provincial and three territorial health systems (CIHI – National health expenditure trends). The overall healthcare system of the country is overseen by Health Canada which generates reports about health indicators in collaboration with the Canadian Institute for Health Information, Statistics Canada, and the Federal Health Partners Secretariat. The provinces are gradually moving towards quality linked reimbursement and alternative payment models for healthcare delivery.

Canadian Institute for Health Information (CIHI) is a not-for-profit organization that provides the data used to improve healthcare performance in Canada. It generates comparable and actionable information by working with government and health organizations. CIHI is also responsible for managing many Canadian health databases, including the National Physician Database, the National Health Expenditure Database, the National Prescription Drug Utilization Information System, the National Ambulatory Care Reporting System, the National Trauma Registry, and many others.

CIHI has developed many indicators to monitor healthcare delivery. These indicators provide a reference for healthcare organizations about areas they must focus on. These areas are a priority for healthcare organizations (CIHI. Indicator Library). The indicators are organized according to the Health System Performance Measurement Framework. The indicators below are categorized into quality-of-care themes. Measures or indicators listed below have been combined or omitted for brevity, to reduce redundancy, and to improve clarity. Please refer to the book website or CIHI website for the complete list.

- Appropriate and effective
    - 30-Day in-hospital mortality and readmission rate after cardiac procedures
    - Asthma emergency department visits
    - Average number of drug classes used by seniors
    - Caesarean section rate
    - Hospital readmission rate
    - Potentially inappropriate medications prescribed to seniors
    - Worsened physical functioning, worsened depressive mood, and experiencing pain in long-term care
- Person-centered
    - 30-Day readmission for mental illness, mood disorders
    - Hospitalization and repeat hospital stay for mental illness
    - Patient flow for hip replacement
    - Potentially inappropriate use of antipsychotics in long-term care
    - Restraint use in long-term care
- Health system resources
    - Age-adjusted public spending per person
    - Average gross clinical payment per physician
    - Cardiac revascularization and Coronary Artery Bypass Graft rate
    - Hip and knee replacement rate
    - Hysterectomy rate
    - Prescribed drug spending per capita
    - Physicians in rural areas
    - Transplants, by organ type
- Improve the health status of Canadians
    - Avoidable deaths from preventable and treatable causes
    - Hospitalizations entirely caused by alcohol, heart attacks, strokes
    - Incidence of end-stage kidney disease
    - Low birth weight rate (<2,500 grams, excluding 500 grams)
    - Perceived health

    - Self-harm hospitalizations
    - Small for gestational age rate
- Efficient allocation of resources
    - Corporate services expense ratio
    - Health care providers employed in direct care
    - Public drug program spending on generic drugs
- Efficiently delivered
    - Cost of a standard hospital stay
    - Inpatient rehabilitation length of stay efficiency
- Access to comprehensive, high-quality health services
    - Regular health care provider availability
    - Wait time for admission to inpatient rehabilitation
    - Wait time for physician initial assessment, disposition decision, and inpatient bed assignment in emergency department
    - Wait time for radiation therapy, cardiac and orthopedic surgeries
- Adjustment to population health needs
    - Epidural rate for vaginal deliveries
    - Assisted delivery rate among vaginal deliveries
- Safe
    - Falls in long-term care
    - Hospital harm
    - In-hospital sepsis
    - Obstetric trauma: vaginal delivery without instrument
    - Residents with new or worsening stage pressure ulcer
- Biological material, psychosocial, and behavioral factors of health
    - Heavy drinking
    - Obesity
    - Physical activity
    - Smoking
- Health system innovation and learning capacity
    - Percentage of seniors on public drug programs

Health quality in United Kingdom

The National Health Service of the United Kingdom maintains a quality and outcomes framework for primary care. The framework includes quality of care indicators, which cover multiple clinical domains. The edited list of indicators is included below for reference.

NHS Quality and Outcomes Framework

The NHS contractors are expected to maintain a register with records for all the patients with the conditions listed below (NHS Digital. 2021). This list is representative as some indicators have been simplified, shortened, or omitted. Every indicator has a time period that requires a percentage or proportion of patients to be reported. Each indicator specifies a period during which the intervention for the reported indicator is expected to have been performed. Please refer to the book website or NHS website for the complete and detailed list.

- Cardiovascular
    - Atrial fibrillation
    - Secondary prevention of coronary heart disease
    - Heart failure
    - Hypertension
    - Stroke and transient ischemic attack
- Respiratory
    - Asthma
    - Chronic Obstructive Pulmonary Disease
- High dependency on other long-term conditions
    - Cancer
    - Chronic kidney disease
    - Diabetes Mellitus
- Mental Health & Neurology
    - Dementia
    - Mental health
- Musculoskeletal
    - Osteoporosis: secondary prevention of fragility fractures
    - Rheumatoid arthritis
- Lifestyle
    - Smoking
- Public Health
    - Cervical screening

NICE Quality Standards

The National Institute for Health and Care Excellence (NICE) has established quality standards that can help with quality improvement, assurance, and monitoring. These are not mandatory but indicate priorities for quality improvement in health, public health, and social care (NICE Quality Standards). There are 197 quality standards currently which have been published. They help to identify areas for quality improvement, set benchmarks for clinical service lines, establish key performance indicators, and evaluate performance. The detail about each standard is outside the scope of this book but can be accessed at NICE Digital's website. The categories of standards are included below for reference.

- Abortion care
- Acute coronary syndromes in adults
- Acute heart failure
- Acute kidney injury
- Acute upper gastrointestinal bleeding in adults
- Air pollution: outdoor air quality and health
- Alcohol: preventing harmful use in the community
- Alcohol-use disorders: diagnosis and management
- Anaphylaxis
- Antenatal and postnatal mental health
- Antenatal care
- Antimicrobial stewardship

- Antisocial behavior and conduct disorders in children and young people
- Anxiety disorders
- Asthma
- Atopic eczema
- Atrial fibrillation
- Attention deficit hyperactivity disorder
- Autism
- Bedwetting in children and young people
- Bipolar disorder in adults
- Bipolar disorder, psychosis and schizophrenia in children and young people
- Bladder cancer
- Blood transfusion
- Brain tumors (primary) and brain metastases in adults
- Breast cancer
- Bronchiolitis in children
- Caesarean birth
- Cancer services for children and young people
- Cardiovascular risk assessment and lipid modification
- Care of dying adults in the last days of life
- Cerebral palsy in adults
- Cerebral palsy in children and young people
- Child abuse and neglect
- Children's attachment
- Chronic heart failure in adults
- Chronic kidney disease in adults
- Chronic obstructive pulmonary disease in adults
- Coeliac disease
- Coexisting severe mental illness and substance misuse
- Colorectal cancer
- Community engagement: improving health and wellbeing
- Community pharmacies: promoting health and wellbeing
- Constipation in children and young people
- Contraception
- Cystic fibrosis
- Decision making and mental capacity
- Delirium in adults
- Dementia
- Depression in adults
- Depression in children and young people
- Developmental follow-up of children and young people born preterm
- Diabetes in adults
- Diabetes in children and young people
- Diabetes in pregnancy

- Domestic violence and abuse
- Drug allergy
- Drug misuse prevention
- Drug use disorders in adults
- Dyspepsia and gastro-oesophageal reflux disease in adults
- Early years: promoting health and wellbeing
- Eating disorders
- Ectopic pregnancy and miscarriage
- Emergency and acute medical care
- End of life care for adults
- End of life care for infants, children and young people
- Endometriosis
- Epilepsy in adults
- Epilepsy in children and young people
- Fecal incontinence in adults
- Falls in older people
- Faltering growth
- Familial hypercholesterolemia
- Fertility problems
- Fever in children
- Flu vaccination: increasing uptake
- Food allergy
- Gallstone disease
- Gastro-esophageal reflux in children and young people
- Hematological cancers
- Head and neck cancer
- Head injury
- Headaches
- Healthcare-associated infections
- Healthy workplaces: improving employee mental and physical health and wellbeing
- Hearing loss in adults
- Heavy menstrual bleeding
- Hepatitis B
- Hip fracture in adults
- HIV testing: encouraging uptake
- Home care for older people
- Hypertension in adults
- Hypertension in pregnancy
- Idiopathic pulmonary fibrosis in adults
- Inducing labor
- Infection prevention and control
- Inflammatory bowel disease
- Intermediate care

- Intrapartum care
- Intrapartum care: existing medical conditions and obstetric complications
- Intravenous fluid therapy in adults in hospital
- Intravenous fluid therapy in children and young people in hospital
- Irritable bowel syndrome in adults
- Jaundice in newborn babies under 28 days
- Learning disability: behavior that challenges
- Learning disability: care and support of people growing older
- Learning disability: identifying and managing mental health problems
- Liver disease
- Looked-after children and young people
- Low back pain and sciatica
- Lower urinary tract symptoms in men
- Lung cancer in adults
- Lyme disease
- Medicines management for people receiving social care in the community
- Medicines management in care homes
- Medicines optimization
- Meningitis (bacterial) and meningococcal septicemia in children and young people
- Menopause
- Mental health of adults in contact with the criminal justice system
- Mental wellbeing and independence for older people
- Mental wellbeing of older people in care homes
- Metastatic spinal cord compression in adults
- Motor neuron disease
- Multimorbidity
- Multiple pregnancy: twin and triplet pregnancies
- Multiple sclerosis
- Neonatal infection
- Nutrition support in adults
- Nutrition: improving maternal and child nutrition
- Obesity in adults: prevention and lifestyle weight management programmes
- Obesity in children and young people: prevention and lifestyle weight management programmes
- Obesity: clinical assessment and management
- Oesophagogastric cancer
- Oral health in care homes
- Oral health promotion in the community
- Osteoarthritis
- Osteoporosis
- Ovarian cancer
- Pancreatic cancer
- Parkinson's disease

- Patient experience in adult NHS services
- People's experience using adult social care services
- Peripheral arterial disease
- Personality disorders: borderline and antisocial
- Physical activity: encouraging activity in the community
- Physical activity: for NHS staff, patients and care givers
- Physical health of people in prisons
- Pneumonia in adults
- Postnatal care
- Pressure ulcers
- Preterm labor and birth
- Preventing excess winter deaths and illness associated with cold homes
- Preventing unintentional injury in children
- Promoting health and preventing premature mortality in black, Asian and other minority ethnic groups
- Prostate cancer
- Psoriasis
- Psychosis and schizophrenia in adults
- Rehabilitation after critical illness in adults
- Renal and ureteric stones
- Renal replacement therapy services for adults
- Rheumatoid arthritis in over 16s
- Sarcoma
- Secondary prevention after a myocardial infarction
- Self-harm
- Sepsis
- Serious eye disorders
- Service user experience in adult mental health services
- Sexual health
- Sickle cell disease
- Skin cancer
- Smoking: harm reduction
- Smoking: reducing and preventing tobacco use
- Smoking: supporting people to stop
- Social care for older people with multiple long-term conditions
- Specialist neonatal respiratory care for babies born preterm
- Spondyloarthritis
- Stable angina
- Stroke in adults
- Suicide prevention
- Supporting adult care givers
- Surgical site infection
- Suspected cancer

- Suspected neurological conditions: recognition and referral
- Transient loss of consciousness ('blackouts') in over 16s
- Transition between inpatient hospital settings and community or care home settings for adults with social care needs
- Transition between inpatient mental health settings and community or care home settings
- Transition from children's to adults' services
- Trauma
- Tuberculosis
- Urinary incontinence in women
- Urinary tract infection in children and young people
- Urinary tract infections in adults
- Vaccine uptake
- Varicose veins in the legs
- Venous thromboembolism in adults
- Violent and aggressive behaviors in people with mental health problems
- Workplace health: long-term sickness absence and capability to work

NICE Quality Indicators

NICE has developed quality indicators to help identify opportunities for quality improvement, prioritize quality improvement efforts, track performance. Some of the indicators are used in Quality and Outcomes Framework or by Clinical Commissioning Groups (CCGs) to help the quality improvement schemes within the NHS. Some indicators which are similar to NHS quality and outcomes framework indicators have been omitted. Each indicator specifies a period during which the intervention for the reported indicator is expected to have been performed. Readers are advised to refer to the book website or NICE website for details about these indicators. The categories of indicators are:

- Accident and emergency services
- Alcohol use
- Angina and coronary heart disease
- Atrial fibrillation
- Bipolar, schizophrenia and other psychoses
- Cancer
- Care Givers
- Chronic Kidney Disease
- Chronic Obstructive Pulmonary Disease
- Contraception
- Depression and anxiety
- Diabetes
- Embolism and thrombosis
- Epilepsy
- GP services
- Gynecological conditions
- Healthcare-associated infection

- Heart failure
- Hip fracture
- Hospital services
- HIV and AIDS
- Hypothyroidism
- Immunizations
- Kidney conditions
- Learning disabilities
- Lipid disorders
- Liver disease
- Mental health conditions and services
- Mortality
- Multiple long-term conditions
- Myocardial infarction
- Obesity and weight management
- Order people
- Oral health and dental services
- Osteoporosis
- Outpatient and community care
- Patient safety
- Peripheral arterial disease
- Pregnancy and neonates
- Respiratory conditions
- Rheumatoid arthritis
- Smoking
- Stroke
- Surgical care

Health quality in India

India is rapidly evolving its healthcare quality measuring framework. The Ministry of Health and Family Welfare (MoHFW) is the national body responsible for administrating all health-related services in the country. It has the Department of Health and Family Welfare, which runs programs to prevent chronic diseases, tuberculosis, and other targeted programs. It also oversees the National Health Mission, which operates through the National Rural Health Mission and National Urban Health Mission. NRHM aims to create programs and services to address the health needs of underserved populations through strengthening health systems and communicable and non-communicable disease control programs.

MoHFW also oversees the National Health Authority, which implements national health insurance schemes and the Department of Health Research, which manages the premier Indian healthcare research organization - the Indian Council of Medical Research. MoHFW also manages the Health Technology Assessment sub-scheme, which is responsible for analyzing health technologies for their cost-effectiveness, clinical effectiveness, and equity (Department of Health Research, Health Technology Assessment in India). MoHFW also oversees the National Health

Systems Resource Center, which was set up to provide technical support and assist in policy and strategy development in providing and mobilizing technical assistance to the states and in capacity building for the Ministry of Health. The organization aims "to improve health outcomes by facilitating governance reform, health systems innovations and improved information sharing among all stakeholders at the national, state, district and sub-district levels through specific capacity development and convergence models" (NHSRC. About NHSRC). The public health administration function of the center is responsible for framing "national public health policies and programs by developing policies and strategies, cost-effective standards, designing a framework for their implementation, and providing certification and incentives."

The National Health Systems Resource Center (NHSRC) has identified key performance indicators and National Quality Assurance Standards for district hospitals, community, primary, and health and wellness centers. It has created a mechanism for scoring, assigning weights, and calculating net ratings (NHSRC. Quality Assurance Scores & Key Performance Indicators). These are used as a guide to gauge the performance of healthcare delivery organizations. These metrics allow digital health innovators to develop products and services targeted at one or more of these metrics.

The quality indicators have been developed for health and wellness centers, urban primary health centers, community health centers, and district hospitals. The indicators consider eligible population's absolute numbers, percentages, or proportions. The indicators below are representative and have been edited or omitted for readability and clarity. Please refer to the book website or NHSRC website for an accurate indicator list and description. The indicators for district hospitals, hospitals (emergency, outpatient, labor room, maternity room, laboratory, operating room, intensive care unit, inpatient department, radiology, pharmacy, general administration), and primary health centers are divided into productivity, efficiency, clinical care and safety, and service quality:

- Productivity
  - Ante Natal Care (ANC) rate
  - Bed occupancy rate
  - Cesarean-section rate
  - Emergency case rate
  - High-risk pregnancy/obstetric complication rate
  - ICU average length of stay
  - ICU readmission rate
  - Immunization rate per thousand
  - Outpatient clinic visits per day
  - Proportion of BPL (Below Poverty Line) patients
  - Rate of out-of-stock drugs
  - Trips per ambulance
- Efficiency
  - Ambulance response time
  - Cases referred to higher level of care
  - Cycle time for instrument processing
  - Down time rate of critical equipment
  - Initial assessment response time in emergency department
  - Missed ante-natal care
  - New-born skin-to-skin time

  - New-born resuscitation rate
  - Number of major surgeries per surgeon
  - Patients seen in outpatient clinic per physician
- Clinical care and safety
  - Adverse events rate
  - Antibiotic Use Rate
  - Average length of stay for normal delivery
  - Consultation time in outpatient clinic
  - Emergency, peri-operative, maternal, and neonatal mortality rate
  - High-risk pregnancy detection rate
  - ICU pressure ulcer incidence
  - ICU reintubation rate
  - Proportion of General anesthesia to spinal anesthesia
  - Re-exploration surgery rate
  - Sterilization failures and complications
  - Successful DOT (Directly Observed Therapy for TB) rate
  - Successful treatment of children with ORS (Oral Rehydration Solution) and Zinc
  - Surgical site infection rate
- Service Quality
  - Average consultation time at outpatient clinics
  - Average door to drug time
  - Left against Medical advice (LAMA) Rate
  - Patient satisfaction score
  - Registration to drug time
  - Surgical procedure cancellation rates
  - Waiting time at outpatient clinics

Health quality in China

The National Health Commission of China develops healthcare-related policies and oversees the Chinese Academy of Medical Sciences and Agencies for Disease Control and Prevention. Multiple rating and ranking systems have been developed in China to assess healthcare quality. Fudan University Hospital Ranking List (Xiong et al., 2017) ranks the top 100 hospitals in China. The list also includes the top 10 hospitals for 37 clinical specialties. The rankings are derived based on scores in infrastructure, service process, and service results categories. Chinese Academy of Medical Sciences ranks hospitals based on science and technology investment (Dai et al., 2016). China Hospital Development Institute has created a hospital performance measurement methodology (Dong et al., 2021). They evaluated the performance of hospitals based on Research and Development (Publications, Citations, clinical trials), Academic Reputation (Staff who are academicians of the Chinese Academy of Sciences or Chinese Academy of Engineering, Chief editors, National Association chairpersons, or have received significant awards), and Quality and safety (medical malpractice cases, National Health Commission's Diagnosis and Treatment Improvement of Rare Disease Program and national clinical specialty program). Hospital competitiveness ranking identifies hospitals based on medical service, academic impact, resource management, and hospital operations (Chong et al., 2016). The indicators used were for inpatient and outpatient facilities, beds, healthcare workers, length of stay, number and type of laboratories, and national awards.

The Chinese Medical Quality Indicator System (CHQIS) created by the Ministry of Health focuses on delivering medical services, safety, and continuous improvement. Regional efforts have created quality evaluation systems, including inpatient management, outpatient management, hospital-acquired infections, and patient satisfaction (Wu et al., 2017). The Medical Quality Control Committees created by the National Health and Family Planning Commission are responsible for developing standards and enforcing quality control in medical specialties, adverse effects, medical errors, and clinical pathways. They are supported by the National Medical Service Management and Guidance Center with technical support (World Bank Group. 2016).

The clinical specialties in China also create quality metrics for their specialty. For example, the Chinese Society of Critical Care Medicine (CSCCM) has developed guidelines for quality metrics in the ICU. These include (Rui et al., 2022). China has published over 1000 clinical practice guidelines (Yang et al., 2019; Chen et al., 2018; Wang et al., 2019). China also has developed medical databases, including the China Biomedical Literature Database, Wanfang Data Knowledge Service Platform, and China National Knowledge Infrastructure. Attempts have been made at the regional level to create more holistic clinical quality measures covering quality and efficiency. A pilot program evaluated hospitals based on disease-specific indicators, including compliance with treatment protocols, case mix index, and use of resources (Weiyan et al., 2014).

The hospitals in China are divided into three classes. Class I, II, and III hospitals. About 54 percent of hospitals and 84 percent of beds are public, and adding outpatient services accounts for 70 percent of hospital expenditures (National Health and Family Planning Commission. 2014. China Health Statistics Year Book).

- Class I hospitals are small hospitals in the community.
- Class II hospitals are larger secondary hospitals serving multiple communities, which may have 100-500 beds.
- Class III hospitals are tertiary-level hospitals that serve the whole city or district. They generally have over 500 beds (Wu et al., 2017).

China Health Reforms

In 2009, China started the process of healthcare reforms (CCCPC. 2009). Multiple changes were introduced during this period, including creating incentives for improving the quality of healthcare services. National Health Commission established Quality Indicators to improve the care of major clinical conditions as part of the National Specific Disease Monitoring System (Wang et al., 2021). As of 2015, China did not have a standardized clinical quality measurement system (Bradley et al., 2012). The performance-related data captured in the hospitals has focused on infrastructure rather than clinical outcomes. However, specialty medical organizations have created clinical performance evaluation systems. A quality assessment system was proposed based on condition-based outcome measures (Xu et al., 2015). It looked at four risk-standardized mortality rates (acute myocardial infarction, coronary artery bypass graft (CABG), pneumonia, stroke) and two risk-standardized post-procedural complication rates and failure-to-rescue rates of 20 post-procedural complications. By 2020, the National Health Commission had set up over 40 national and 1400 provincial quality control centers (NHCPRC. 2020). In 2023, the National Health Commission and the State Administration of Traditional Chinese Medicine launched a three-year comprehensive medical quality improvement initiative. This initiative encompassed other ongoing initiatives like the annual 10,000 Miles Medical Quality inspection tour, the ongoing initiative to improve the quality of medical services and make them patient-centered. The initiative's overall goal was to promote high-quality medical and general health services development, improve quality and safety, and develop high-quality training. The medical institutions were directed to create medical quality management working groups (NHC. 2023). The broad categories of work under this initiative were:

Strengthening basic healthcare processes

- Improve medical quality and safety management at the hospitals
- Improve access, training, and management of physicians, nurses, and medical technicians
- Strengthen monitoring of adverse events and utilization related to drugs, devices
- Standardization of medical technology at medical institutions
- Improve quality of emergency care, including pre-emergency triage, multi-specialty collaboration, and management of acute conditions
- Strengthen management and quality of day-to-day care in the hospitals
- Improving quality of outpatient care, including timely consultations, diagnosis and treatment services, and ancillary services like outpatient surgery and infusion centers
- Ensuring quality and safety of surgery, including preoperative assessment, anesthesia, surgical planning, surgical safety, and perioperative management
- Improve patient follow-up, including quality of frequency, form, and content of follow-up, assignment of resources for follow-up, prevention of readmissions after discharge
- Develop a 'patient-centered' and 'disease-oriented' approach for diagnosis and treatment of major diseases

Strengthening clinical processes

- Practice evidence-based medicine, follow clinical diagnosis and treatment guidelines, clinical pathways
- Strengthen patient assessment through standardized evaluation strategies, close monitoring of hospitalized patients, timely updates to diagnostic and treatment plans
- Improve the quality of inpatient rounding, advocating multidisciplinary rounds with medical teams, nurses, and pharmacists and joint rounds with traditional Chinese medicine teams.
- Promote rational drug use that is safe, effective, economical, and appropriate for medical conditions, including the use of resident clinical pharmacists and education of clinical staff
- Strengthen the quality and management of medical records, including education about good documentation practices standardization as applicable to outpatient records, ward rounds, surgical records, progress notes, discharge summaries, etc.
- Strengthen clinical consultations, including standardization of consultation requests, workflows, and tracking
- Strengthen patient safety, including reporting adverse events, analysis of safety concerns, and continuous quality improvement related to patient safety
- Provide high-quality nursing care

Strengthen quality management workflows.

- Improve quality control systems through the creation of quality control centers
- Sharing and disclosure of information related to quality and safety at medical institutions
- Include quality in performance appraisals of health personnel

- Create national, regional, and institution-specific quality-related goals
- Include quality and safety in the evaluation of hospitals, clinical specialties, disease-related programs
- Strengthen quality control of traditional Chinese medicine

In 2023, the General Office of the National Health Commission issued the National Medical Quality and Safety Improvement Goals (NHCPRC, 2023):

Goal 1: Improve the rate of reperfusion treatment for acute ST-segment elevation myocardial infarction
Goal 2: Improve the rate of reperfusion treatment of acute cerebral infarction
Goal 3: Improve the clinical TNM staging assessment rate before tumor treatment
Goal 4: Reduce perioperative mortality in hospitalized patients
Goal 5: Improve the reporting rate of medical quality and safety adverse events
Goal 6: Improve the standardized utilization rate of intravenous infusion among hospitalized patients
Goal 7: Improve the completion rate of preoperative multidisciplinary discussions for level 4 surgeries
Goal 8: Improve the completion rate of bundled treatment for septic shock
Goal 9: Improve the standardized prevention rate of venous thromboembolism
Goal 10: Reduce complications of vaginal delivery

The National Medical Quality Management and Control Information Network manages a National Clinical Improvement System, creating 367 indicators (in parenthesis) for 18 clinical categories. The details of the indicators are available on the book website.

- Emergency Department (10)
- Critical Care Medicine (15)
- Clinical Laboratory (15)
- Pathology (13)
- Infection Control (13)
- Data Quality Management and indicators on the home page of medical records (10)
- Obstetrics (10)
- Pulmonary Medicine (19)
- Neurology (74)
- Nephrology (32)
- Nursing (20)
- Pharmacy Management (15)
- Medical record management (27)
- Cardiology (11 conditions with a total of 105 indicators)
- Ultrasound diagnostics (13 indicators)
- Rehabilitation medicine (22 indicators)
- Nutrition (12)
- Anesthesia - 26

There are 17 categories for quality indicators for medical technology, with a total of 185 indicators. The number of indicators for each category are in parentheses:

- Lung transplant technology (12)
- Liver transplant (21)
- Kidney transplant (13)
- Heart transplant (12)
- Stem cell transplant (10)
- Homologous islet cell transplant (8)
- Allogenic structural tissue transplantation (5)
- Allogeneic corneal transplantation (12)
- Gender reassignment (11)
- Proton and heavy ion accelerator-based radiotherapy (7)
- Radioactive seed implantation treatment (9)
- Tumor ablation therapy (9)
- Ventricular assist technology (7)
- Artificial intelligence-assisted treatment (8)
- Extracorporeal Membrane Oxygenation (5)
- Autologous organ transplantation (18)
- Digestive endoscopy diagnosis and treatment (18)

There are two other categories with 23 indicators:

- Human Organ Procurement (13)
- Blood bank (10)

Diseases-specific indicators were also developed for over 45 medical conditions:

- Cardiovascular system
    - Acute myocardial infarction (15)
    - Congestive Heart failure (16)
    - CABG (18)
    - Atrial Fibrillation (14)
    - Aortic valve replacement (16)
    - Mitral valve replacement (16)
    - Atrial Septal Defect surgery (15)
    - Ventricular Defect surgery (15)
- Nervous system
    - Cerebral infarction (18)
    - TIA (15)
    - Intracerebral hemorrhage (17)
    - Meningioma (19)
    - Glioblastoma (20)
    - Pituitary Adenoma (18)
    - Subarachnoid Hemorrhage (20)
    - Convulsive Status Epilepticus (14)
    - Parkinson's Disease (16)

- Pulmonary system
    - Community-Acquired Pneumonia (32)
    - Acute Exacerbation of COPD (15)
    - Acute Asthma Exacerbation (31)
- Musculoskeletal system
    - Total Hip Replacement (15)
    - Total Knee Replacement (16)
    - Developmental Dysplasia of Hip Correction (13)
- Reproductive System
    - Cesarean section (17)
    - Ectopic pregnancy (15)
    - Uterine fibroids (14)
- Oncology
    - Lung Cancer (21)
    - Thyroid Cancer (17)
    - Breast Cancer (23)
    - Gastric cancer (23)
    - Cervical cancer (14)
    - Colon Cancer (23)
- Urinary system
    - Diabetic kidney disease (12)
    - End Stage Renal Disease – Hemodialysis (18)
    - End Stage Renal Disease – Peritoneal Dialysis (14)
- Oral surgery
    - Squamous cell carcinoma of the tongue (13)
    - Parathyroid gland tumors (14)
    - Oral Implantology (14)
- Ophthalmology
    - Primary Acute Angle-closure Glaucoma (13)
    - Complex retinal detachment (12)
- Other
    - Perioperative Infection Prevention (33)
    - Perioperative prevention of deep vein thromboembolism (42)
    - Hospital Based Inpatient Psychiatric Services (10)
    - Prevention of VTE in medium and high-risk patients (7)
    - Early treatment of septic shock (6)
    - Initial induction chemotherapy in acute lymphoblastic leukemia (16)
    - Initial chemotherapy for acute promyelocytic leukemia (16)
    - Thyroid nodules (13)
    - Intervention of HBV-infected mothers and infants during childbirth (13)

11 LOW CODE & NO CODE IN HEALTHCARE

Healthcare enterprises are developing customized software applications to support clinical, operational, and financial workflows. They are deploying an increasing number of automation tools adopted from other industries. Healthcare enterprises across providers, insurers, pharmacies, laboratories, etc., can either use off-the-shelf commercial products or outsource the development of applications to third-party software development companies. Most healthcare organizations do not have the resources to recruit a team of dedicated software developers who can develop new in-house applications. Also, the amount of work does not justify keeping a fully staffed internal team to develop and maintain these applications as this could be expensive and inefficient reducing the speed of deployment and enhancements.

Low-code and No-code platforms

The low-code and no-code platforms enable the development of production-quality application software without writing software code. These development platforms use graphical user interfaces and drag-and-drop features to create applications. They are based on visual programming, enabling applications to be created by manipulating program elements graphically instead of specifying them textually (Jost, 2014).

Using low-code and no-code (LCNC) platforms, healthcare enterprises can build anything from simple automation tools to mission-critical applications with complex workflows without any programming. The target users for LCNC tools are those in business, operational, and non-technical roles. However, these platforms are often used by non-technical professionals and professional software developers due to the speed of development and easier maintenance. These platforms primarily use application programming interfaces (APIs), templates, and open-access databases to integrate multiple workflows. There are minor differences between low-code and no-code platforms.

Low-code: The low-code platforms provide the ability to write code to augment the application created with the graphical user interface. The applications produced with low-code tools may be ready for production deployment at completion or require minor coding before production.

No-code: Like low-code development platforms, no-code development platforms use graphical user interfaces instead of programming scripts to create application software. However, no-code platforms aim to eliminate the need for hand-coded computer programming. The applications can be designed, created, tested, and deployed using visual tools. They can also be packaged into mobile apps for distribution as web apps or through mobile app stores.

Advantages

The LCNC platforms are rapidly developing in scope and features. Some advantages of using LCNC over traditional programming-based software development are:

- **Prototyping and deployment**: The LCNC platforms allow the rapid creation of applications. There is generally no need to hire developers, outsource software development, or train staff on programming. The existing staff can quickly move from idea to application with fast prototyping, testing, and launching in production.
- **Collaboration**: Due to the nature of application development, multiple teams can collaborate efficiently with faster decision-making.
- **Programming skills**: The users can create software applications without having any software coding knowledge. This enables functional experts who know business domains or workflows to create applications directly.
- **Industry best practices**: Most LCNC platforms are based on the reuse of templates. Organizations within the same industry can share these, enabling access to each others' best practices.
- **Cost**: The initial costs of setting up the development environment, training the users, deploying the applications, and ongoing maintenance are lower with the LCNC platforms.
- **Maintenance**: The applications developed on LCNC are relatively easier to maintain due to the visual nature of development, easier collaboration between multiple teams, and use of templates for commonly occurring workflows.

Disadvantages

Disadvantages of using LCNC platforms instead of traditional software programming using code are:

- **Complexity**: LCNC platforms are getting sophisticated. They always lag in the complexity of applications that can be created with traditional programming languages.
- **Speed**: For some applications, the speed of execution may be slower than coded applications. The caveat is that poorly written code can sometimes perform worse than a well-executed no-code or low-code app.
- **Cost:** Even though the net cost for the low-code and no-code apps may be less if the user base is small, the costs can rapidly increase as the number of users increases.

Types of tools

The types of LCNC platforms that are commercially available are increasing every year. At the time of the writing, these are some of the major categories of LCNC platforms:

- Application integration platforms

- Business process management and automation platforms
- Enterprise app development platforms
- Game creation platforms
- Marketing, customer service, sales automation platforms
- Mobile app development platforms
- Models and markup languages-based code generators
- Online database management
- Project management platforms
- Spreadsheet based platforms
- Website development platforms
- Workflow automation platforms

Healthcare applications

The applications of LCNC platforms in healthcare can be broadly divided into two categories. The first category is the industry sector agnostic applications. These applications are similar across different industries and include applications for human resources, finance, general project management, etc. The second category of applications is healthcare specific applications. These are custom created by or used in healthcare enterprises specifically for healthcare-specific workflows or clinical data. The applications which consume clinical data are required to be HIPAA compliant. They may also be expected to comply with other industry security certifications like SOC2, HITRUST, or ISO 27001. Healthcare-specific applications are also expected to be interoperable with other applications used in healthcare for the seamless exchange of data.

The LCNC apps can create hospital dashboards that combine clinical, financial, and operational data for the clinical unit managers. Health systems and outpatient provider clinics can use LCNC tools to create simple telemedicine and remote patient monitoring interfaces. Applications can be developed for use by patients – for example, providing them with intuitive access to their clinical data, including laboratory reports, clinical documents, etc. Providers can also use them for scheduling assistance, communication, patient information, clinical quality tracking, and compliance assistance.

Transition to full code

As the needs of healthcare enterprises grow and they discover they use cases or functions which cannot be satisfied with one or more LCNC platforms, they can decide to add software code to add the features or replace the LCNC platform with hand-coded computer software. The advantage are - minimal risk of failure as the end product is already available, quicker integration and migration, and lower costs as it is possible to get fixed bid contracts if the development is outsourced. We will continue to see more innovation and expansion in the scope of applications developed on LCNC platforms. The merger of artificial intelligence technologies with LCNC platforms will significantly increase the scope and capability of applications.

12 SECURITY & PRIVACY PRACTICES

Digital health companies, regardless of the type of product or service they offer, are expected to adhere to the highest standards of security and privacy practices. Enterprise applications may be subject to the requirements of the client organizations, and consumer applications may be subject to consumer protection laws. This chapter provides a high-level overview of the security and privacy practices for digital health but does not replace the need to have experienced security and privacy team members or consultants on the development teams.

Secure development practices

The safety and security of the software should start early in the software development life cycle (SDLC). Software developers should ensure that they follow secure design and coding practices through verification for both front-end and back-end applications. The development tools, especially those that are open-source, should be up to date and downloaded from reliable sources. The development environments, as well as the application software libraries, should be patched in time. Developers should ensure that the link between the front-end application and the back-end server or database is encrypted and transmitted over secure protocols.

The verification or testing of the applications should include security testing with code analysis, vulnerability scanning, fuzzy testing, source code scanning, and static and dynamic application security testing. Applications can use techniques like Runtime Application Self-Protection (RASP) tools to block malicious activity. The common vulnerabilities that have been exploited include SQL injection attacks, Cross Site Scripting (CSS) software attacks, broken access control security vulnerabilities, expression language injection, insecure configurations, and deserialization. However, new vulnerabilities are being discovered every day, including zero-day vulnerability, which is a security vulnerability discovered and used by hackers before the software manufacturer becomes aware of its existence and can take steps to mitigate it. The National Institute of Standards and Technology (NIST) (Black et al. 2021) has developed recommendations for software verification techniques. These include:

- "Threat modeling to look for design-level security issues
- Automated testing for consistency and to minimize human effort
- Static code scanning to look for top bugs
- Heuristic tools to look for possible hardcoded secrets

- Use of built-in checks and protections
- 'Black box' test cases
- Code-based structural test cases
- Historical test cases
- Fuzzing
- Web app scanners, if applicable
- Address included code (libraries, packages, services)."

Enterprise applications

Passing the security hurdle of a healthcare provider organization is essential for a digital health company targeting enterprise customers. The enterprise information services team requires a service agreement or a business associate agreement to be signed before commencing any work with the vendor team. It is also expected that the vendor will have similar agreements with its sub-contractors so that the security policies of the vendor (and the healthcare organization) are respected by everyone dealing with the healthcare organization's data. The sub-contractors will also be expected to have similar security provisions. Even if the company has been shortlisted, vetted, and a final contract has been signed, it cannot conduct business until the security team approves it. The security requirements will depend on the use case of the application. The assessment of security controls at the vendor site is rigorous if the vendor handles protected health information. The technical implementation of security practices is outside the scope of the book. However, readers are encouraged to review detailed guidelines on the Computer Security Incident Response Team website.

General expectations from the vendors who are handling health information include:

- Physical safeguards to reasonably protect confidentiality of client information
- Safeguards against unauthorized access of vendor's facilities and equipment
- Protection of data centers against unauthorized access or network breaches
- Presence and implementation of procedures and policies dealing with loss or theft of vendor equipment like mobile phones, laptops
- Asset management protocols and tracking of all authorized hardware and software used by vendor teams

The security practices targeted at professionals are focused on the vendor employees and contractor teams working with client data. The requirements may include:

- Background checks of employees and contractors working with client data
- Provision of safeguarding information in employment or subcontractor agreements
- Information security training for all employees and subcontractors
- Resources and practices for protection against and detection of identity theft
- Information security roles in line with industry best practices

The healthcare industry is one of the top targets of cyberattacks. Criminals are increasingly targeting vendors to get to the client organizations. The clients need to ensure that the vendors are held to the same high standards of security practices as their staff. The requirements from vendors could include:

- Provision of appropriate authorization and controlled access for all users with robust authentication, network login, and password management practices
- Periodic review of user access privileges and automatic updates in case of change in employment
- Recording and safekeeping of user activity logs and security events
- Manual and automatic review of audit logs and system activity

Mobile health apps

The health apps are expected to comply with data privacy laws applicable to all the jurisdictions where the app users reside. The two major mobile operating systems – Android and iOS, provide advanced security and privacy support, including authentication methods, secure folders, low-level libraries, app sandboxes, and storage encryption. The authentication methods inbuilt into the smartphone operating system include passcode, password, passphrase, fingerprint recognition, and face recognition.

The security settings of the apps should be configured to the highest security level by default. The user data should be stored in the in-built storage instead of SD cards or cloud storage unless it is HIPAA compliant with end-to-end encryption. The app developers should identify if the data collected from the app will be made available to third parties and, if so, whether there are data processing agreements with all partners. The personal data collected by the app should be encrypted during storage and transmission, using industry best practices, including dynamic encryption, secure containers, and standards like AES-256. The health applications should use, as applicable, session management (restricting access to a health application after a specific time of inactivity post-authentication), authentication (verifying the identity of the user), and authorization (enabling proper functionality for the user based on their access or permission level).

The apps should minimize the data collection from the users to just the essentials. They should limit the permissions required from the operating system to the minimum required for the stated functionality. The apps can generate identifiers that tie them to a specific computing device and, by proxy, to a specific user without using user's personal information. These identifiers are stored on the device itself, or they can be stored on a secure server. The data sent to the servers should be anonymized or pseudonymized. If needed, the data collected should be tied to the unique GUID or URI associated with the app installed on the phone instead of identifiable information. The sensitive data should be deleted from the servers once it is no longer needed for processing. In case of a breach, the app should be able to delete health information on mobile devices.

The design and development of health apps should be undertaken with appropriate security and data protection best practices. The security provisions of the mobile health app should be appropriate for the risk of health data that is processed on the app. The app's design should be as simple as possible, with appropriate documentation of trust boundaries. Any artifacts from the development version should be removed from the production version, including debug codes, ports, traces, etc. Secure coding practices relevant to the coding language used for app development should be used. The developers should use specific design patterns and components. Tools that evaluate the source code for security vulnerabilities, safe functions, secure toolchains, and error management are some techniques used to create secure software. The source code should be protected against unauthorized access, and other techniques like code obfuscation can prevent unauthorized source code modification. All the third-party software libraries integrated into the application should be from trusted sources. The developers should ensure that the app is installed if deployed through trusted channels (like app stores or the developer's own website) and signed with appropriate certificates.

The health app developers can get certifications related to security, including ISO/IEC 27001, ISO/IEC 27018, SOC2, HITRUST, etc. Furthermore, the app developers should test the app either by in-house experts or professional white hat firms which perform penetration testing to check for security vulnerabilities.

GDPR & CalOPPA

Health app users should be informed about how their data will be used and appropriate consent obtained. Modern mobile operating systems have standardized this process. The users should be given to erase their data. The General Data Protection Regulation (GDPR) (EU GDPR. Regulation 2016/679) and California Online Privacy Protection Act (CalOPPA) (Consumer Federation of California. 2015) regulations are the two most stringent privacy-related regulations currently active. CalOPPA applies to the operators of online services that collect personally identifiable information about individual California consumers. Online services include mobile apps. The personally identifiable information is defined as "a) a first and last name; (b) a home or other physical address, including street name and name of a city or town; (c) an e-mail address; (d) a telephone number; (e) a social security number; (f) any other identifier that permits the physical or online contacting of a specific individual; or (g) any information concerning a user that is collected online and maintained in personally identifiable form in combination with an identifier described above" (California Business & Professional Code §§ 22575-22579). The law requires that all mobile apps provide a notice of privacy practices which should include "a description of the types of PII collected and disclosed by the operator; a description of the process by which a consumer can access and request changes to his or her PII, if available; a description of the process by which the operator will notify consumers of material changes to the privacy policy; and an effective date."

GDPR applies to any app that processes personal data, defined as "any information that relates to an individual who can be directly or indirectly identified. Names and email addresses are obviously personal data." Location information, ethnicity, gender, biometric data, religious beliefs, web cookies, and political opinions can also be personal data. GDPR defines data protection principles, accountability, data security, and consent, and provides privacy rights of the individuals, which include the right to be informed, the right to access, the right to rectification, the right to erasure, the right to restrict processing, right to data portability, suitable to object, and rights related to automated decision making including profiling (EU GDPR. Regulation 2016/679). Besides personal data, GDPR applies to particular categories of personal, genetic, and biometric data. GDPR also includes the data minimization principle "Personal data shall be: adequate, relevant and limited to what is necessary in relation to the purposes for which they are processed." The apps should collect the minimum amount of personal data needed to fulfill the app's purpose. The app should provide a privacy notice which is "in a concise, transparent, intelligible, and easily accessible form; written in clear and plain language, particularly for any information addressed specifically to a child; delivered in a timely manner; and provided free of charge" (Proton Technologies. Writing a GDPR-compliant privacy notice).

GDPR requires specific information to be included in the privacy notice:

- "The identity and contact details of the organization, its representative, and its Data Protection Officer
- The purpose for the organization to process an individual's personal data and its legal basis
- The legitimate interests of the organization (or third party, where applicable)
- Any recipient or categories of recipients of an individual's data
- The details regarding any transfer of personal data to a third country and the safeguards taken
- The retention period or criteria used to determine the retention period of the data
- The existence of each data subject's rights
- The right to withdraw consent at any time (where relevant)
- The right to lodge a complaint with a supervisory authority
- Whether the provision of personal data is part of a statutory or contractual requirement or obligation and the possible consequences of failing to provide the personal data
- The existence of an automated decision-making system, including profiling, and information about how this system has been set up, the significance, and the consequences."

Risk management and business continuity

Risk management departments are common in healthcare organizations, but technology companies usually do not have a dedicated risk management unit. Digital health companies can work with risk management consultants who can also assist with regulatory compliance activities like:

- Compliance with data privacy, security, and confidentiality regulations
- Drafting policies for periodic review of compliance with applicable regulations
- Managing risk management program
- Conducting information security risk assessment
- Reporting and notification of security incidents, breach of confidential information, and unauthorized access

A business continuity plan is a good practice for any organization; however, for digital health vendors working on sensitive patient data, ensuring data protection in cases of unforeseen disasters is vital. At the minimum, digital health companies should have a business continuity plan with information security provisions and a disaster recovery strategy.

One of the advantages of SaaS-based products and services is the opportunity to use APIs to exchange data. It also allows for quick updates of applications in cases of newly discovered security vulnerabilities. Further efficiencies can be gained by using a single sign-on application for multiple applications improving user variance. Cloud-hosted applications with a global data center for backup also improve redundancy and reliability.

Ransomware

Ransomware is a malicious computer program restricting access to an organization's applications and data for extortion. Ransomware has emerged to be a critical threat to health systems. As per a US government report, there are 4,000 daily ransomware attacks (US Department of Justice.

United States Government Interagency Guidance Document). Ransomware encrypts the data, which the hacker can only unencrypt, generally after the ransom is paid in cryptocurrency. The security practices required to prevent ransomware attacks are similar to the recommended security practices for the safety and security of data or the prevention of computer viruses.

HIPAA regulations also require that organizations implement procedures to conduct risk analysis, identify vulnerabilities, and prevent and detect malicious software. Security Management Process is a HIPAA security rule standard that has requirements for covered entities and business associates. This concept is discussed in more detail in the chapter on HIPAA.

Prevention is the best strategy against ransomware attacks. Prevention includes educating employees against clicking links on suspicious emails. The IT administrators can enable spam filters to catch emails with phishing links and executable files from reaching the end users. Firewalls can block suspicious IP addresses. Test phishing emails can be sent to the users to train the end users. Email spoofing can be prevented by using authentication technologies like DomainKeys Identified Mail (DKIM), Domain Message Authentication Reporting and Conformance (DMARC), and Sender Policy Framework (SPF). The operating systems, application software, computer firmware, and network-connected devices like routers, security cameras, and printers should be patched and updated. The applications can be run in virtual machines or containers and restricted through Software Restriction Policies. Restricting access to the systems by employees based on the least privilege principle is a successful strategy. The users should be assigned minimal permissions to system applications and data files required to complete their work. Digital health firms should also work with security consulting firms to conduct penetration testing and vulnerability assessments.

Besides safeguarding the data from ransomware attacks, healthcare organizations can do frequent data backups with periodic test restorations. These backups should be physically separated from the networks. HIPAA security rule also provides recommendations for disaster recovery planning, emergency operations planning, and business continuity planning.

UNIT 2: ANALYTICS

13 FUNDAMENTALS OF HEALTH ANALYTICS

Introduction to analytics

Analytics is the science of using data to assist with decision-making. Data analysis allows individuals and organizations to find solutions for current problems and develop insights for future scenarios (Kalé et al., 2015). A more applied definition of analytics is "the use of tools and techniques on data in order to develop an understanding of the current performance and to develop future plans by identifying patterns and relationships in the data." Using analytics, organizations can make decisions based on the correct information provided to the right people at the right time, made available in the proper format, and with the assistance of the right tools for that individual and the problem at hand (Strome TL, 2013). Business Intelligence is a framework that uses system architecture, databases and data warehouse sales, analytical tools, and applications to assist with decision support (Sharda R et al., 2014). Healthcare analytics is typically used for clinical data and processes, while business intelligence is used for traditional business functions like supply chain, finance, and operations.

Healthcare organizations are becoming more sophisticated and complex, and the data they process daily continues to increase. Analytics departments have been created within healthcare organizations to support clinical quality programs mandated by regulations and improve the efficiency of care delivery and clinical outcomes. The source of the data in healthcare organization can be electronic health records, medical device imports, medical coding and billing software, human resource applications, financial applications, or obtained directly from patients. Technology companies are creating user-friendly tools to assist with the data analytics, but there are still tremendous opportunities for innovation in this area.

Objective of analytics

The objective of analytics is to assist organizational leaders in making decisions that are rational, data-driven, transparent, verifiable, and robust (Saxena R et al., 2013).

- **Rational**: Teams within complex healthcare organizations represent diverse skill sets, training, and cultural backgrounds. Rational decision-making processes incorporate continuous learning and feedback and empower everyone on the team.

- **Data Driven**: Clinicians are trained to make evidence-based decisions. These clinical leaders expect a healthcare organization's administrative and operational decisions to be based on data. In a data-driven approach, decisions are based on facts and verifiable evidence.
- **Transparent**: If the data chain from sourcing to hypothesis generation to modeling to visualization is accessible to all, decision-making can become transparent. Analysts can help break information and data silos by combining data from multiple sources. For example, the lab ordering frequency for a particular diagnosis can be combined with the cost or reimbursement data and clinical outcomes data to provide evidence of clinical waste.
- **Verifiable**: The accuracy of source data, data integration, decision-making criteria, and selection of the correct outcome can be verified by anyone at any point in time.
- **Robust**: Using analytics helps eliminate biases from the decision-making process. Some biases could be due to missing data, incorrect hypotheses due to lack of knowledge, myopic view of problem-solving, etc. Continuous improvement allows for standardization and improving the robustness of the process.

Analytics is the fundamental tool for quality improvement in healthcare organizations. Just like clinical protocols in healthcare are based on evidence, healthcare organization decisions are becoming data-driven and evidence-based. As healthcare delivery shifts towards value-based care and reimbursement linked to quality metrics, the analytics teams occupy center stage in any healthcare organization's decision-making.

Analytics layers

The analytics layers provide an excellent framework for thinking about the structure that needs to be put in place to create an effective analytics organization. These layers are aligned with each other to create an effective analytics program supporting the organizational goals. Healthcare analytics can be divided into five layers (Strome TL, 2013).

- **Business context**: The business context is the primary layer that provides the objectives and goals for the organization. The context drives the decision-making and allocation of resources in the organization. The business context usually is a function of the mission of the organization, the size of the organization, whether the organization is standalone or part of a larger system, and unique demographic, social, regulatory, reimbursement, and competitive challenges in the local geographic region.
- **Data**: To achieve the business objectives, appropriate and required data needs to be accessed. The data streams from multiple sources need to be integrated to run analytics. These could be multiple Electronic Health Records (inpatient, outpatient, home health), billing and financial systems, human resource systems, etc.
- **Analytics**: Analytics layer consists of all the resources and infrastructure needed to develop actionable insights to achieve organizational goals. The analytics infrastructure is required for a functioning analytics layer, including software tools, trained data scientists or data analysts, stakeholder buy-in, and involvement of front-line managers and operators, and project managers.
- **Quality and performance**: It is essential to establish a baseline for any metric that needs to be improved. The famous management thinker Peter Drucker has said, "You cannot manage what you cannot measure." The workflows and healthcare processes from which the data is sourced are documented to clarify the assumptions behind data collection, and comparisons are made about the data collected from different departments. Workflow process variability

often has consequences for how the data is interpreted. The quality or performance indicators are identified, and target goals for the indicators are set. It is crucial to have a consensus among the stakeholders around the goals. Quality improvement models are implemented throughout the organization. These include Plan-Do-Study-Act (PDSA), which has been created by Institute for Healthcare Improvement combining Total Quality Management (TQM) and Rapid-Cycle Improvement (RCI) (IHI. 2021), Six Sigma (ASQ. 2021), which is used to reduce variation and defects, and Lean (IHI. 2005) which is an approach to improve efficiency and reduce waste in work processes.

- **Presentation**: This layer is the end user-facing view of analytics. It may be in the form of dashboards, spreadsheets, or reports. Analysts need to customize their output such that it is understood by the executives, managers, physicians, or other end-users of the analysis. In recent years, many exciting presentation layer tools have emerged, making it easier to visualize data and insights.

Analytics steps

The end-to-end data analytics process includes problem definition, data collection, cleaning or preparation, analysis, and interpretation.

Problem definition

Before embarking on any analytics-related activity, it is important to develop a clear understanding of the problem that is to be solved. This could be a business problem or a hypothesis that needs to be proven or disproven. A well-defined objective keeps the rest of the analytics process efficient and focused.

Data collection

Data can be collected from three different sources:

First party data (1P): This is the data that is directly collected by the organization. The collection and content of data are within the organization's control. This data includes data from EMR systems, patient surveys, etc.

Second party data (2P): The organization obtains Second-party data from another trusted source. The examples include data from contracted billing companies, website analytics, etc.

Third party data (3P): This is the data collected by a third-party organization with no relationship with the team or organization working on the analytics project. The data could be structured or unstructured. It may be proprietary or in the public domain. Examples of this data include government surveys, prescription data, etc.

Data cleaning

After the raw data is collected, it is converted into a format that can be used for analysis. It is cleaned by fixing data that needs to be consistent, complete, correct, deduplicated, and free of outliers. Unless collected in a very controlled environment, data cleaning is one of the most time-consuming data analysis steps. Data from multiple sources may also be combined during this process.

Data analysis

A wide variety of techniques used for data analysis have been discussed separately, including exploratory, descriptive, diagnostic, predictive, and prescriptive analyses.

Data interpretation

The analytics and business teams collaborate during the interpretation step. Insights from this phase create a feedback loop back into the previous steps. Data is interpreted using visualization, reports, dashboards, or statistical metrics.

Analytics types

The experts have divided the practice of analytics into four types (Morr CE et al., 2019) – Descriptive, Diagnostic, Predictive, and Prescriptive. Sometimes, exploratory analytics is conducted first to get more information about the data before the analysis process.

Exploratory analytics

Exploratory data analysis is developing an intuition about the data set. It is used for a high-level overview of the data to check for trends, outliers, and overall sense of the data set. Analysts use visual tools such as graphs and summary statistics, including mean, median, and quartiles. For example, it can help to answer questions like 'What is the profile of a typical patient,' 'How much variation is present for different parameters,' and 'Are there any obvious segments or classes that patients could be classified into,' 'Is there a way to aggregate different observations,' etc. Exploratory data analysis can also be used to analyze data over time. For example, the data sets could change blood pressure values over time. If the patient has had episodes of dizziness during the time of the data samples, they could be plotted and reviewed. Exploratory data analytics helps us construct metrics that are of interest and create new variables by aggregating data points within an observation. It also provides a general idea of what statistical learning method we may want to employ to get the desired result.

Descriptive analytics

Descriptive analytics is used to capture the metrics and indicators within an organization. Here, past and current data is used to produce a snapshot of the state of the organization. It frequently uses visualizations to provide a comprehensive map of the available data. Descriptive statistics are used to provide information about the data. These include measures of central tendencies and variation. The standard measures of central tendencies include mean, median, and mode. The measures of variation include variance and standard deviation. Descriptive analysis is presented through reports, dashboards, charts, and tables. The goal is to find patterns to identify problem areas in the organization. Healthcare organizations use description analytics for issues like tracking emergency department wait times, identifying patients with hospital lengths of stay exceeding the expected number of days, and immunization compliance.

Diagnostic analytics

Diagnostics analytics is used to identify problems and their cause. Analysts can use business intelligence tools to isolate the problem areas and confounding variables. Various techniques are used for the analysis, including cause and effect analysis (Fassett WE, 2011; Ursprung R et al., 2010), root cause analysis (Uberoi RS et al., 2004), and cluster analysis (Liao M et al., 2016; Everitt BS et al., 2011).

Predictive analytics

Predictive analytics is used to forecast the probability of occurrence of any event in the future using statistics and algorithms. This assessment helps organizations to create forecasts, develop business strategies, and allocate resources based on data science. The techniques used for predictive analytics include predictive modeling (Hijazi HH et al., 2018; Safaee MM et al., 2018), machine learning (Baessler B et al., 2018; Karisani P et al., 2018; Schadler MR et al., 2018), and neural networks (Wu Y et al., 1993; Zhang ML et al., 2017).

Prescriptive analytics

Prescriptive analytics is used to select the best course of action by analyzing what has happened in the past and why it happened that way. It uses advanced analytical techniques and experiential information to guide decision-making. Prescriptive analytics provides a course of action to attain a goal by simulation. Prescriptive analytics provides a rationale for suggesting a specific course of action. Some prescriptive analytics approaches include switching neural networks, logic learning machines, rule-based systems, and decision trees. Prescriptive analytics has been extensively used in the healthcare domain (Alexander GK et al., 2017; Lee M et al., 2018) developing what-if-scenarios, graph analyses, simulation, stochastic optimization (El-Rifai O et al., 2015; Jeremic A et al., 2015; Legrain A et al., 2015), and non-linear programming (Christodoulou MA et al., 2008; Saffer SI et al., 1976; Simmons GH et al., 1975). It is also used in clinical scenarios that recommend a specific treatment plan. For example, a study to estimate the efficacy of recommendations for optimal brace correction for patients diagnosed with Adolescent Idiopathic Scoliosis found that using the model-generated recommendations during brace fitting likely improved outcomes (Chalmers E et al., 2015).

Statistical inference

Statistical inference is the process of extracting data from healthcare activities and then using the insights derived from the data to influence these healthcare processes and activities. The smallest unit of analysis in statistics is an observation. It is the individual measure or characteristic of an entity of interest. A data set is composed of N observations where N is the total number of observations in the data set. A sample is a small subset of the data set of observations and is used to develop insights about the whole population of observations. A sample allows the analysts to assume the underlying data. Samples make computing more manageable and allow practical applications of statistical methods on data, at the cost of increasing bias and reduction in accuracy. It is important to be cognizant of the biases present in the sampling process. A model is a simplified representation of a complex entity. A model could be of physical phenomena, biological processes, chemical reactions, mathematical theories, etc. The data model is a structural representation of the data. Statistical models use statistical theories and methods to develop inferences about a quantified problem.

Analytics infrastructure

Healthcare organizations have made varying degrees of investments in the tools and technologies supporting analytics efforts depending on the size of the organization and the organization's priority for analytics. However, the following infrastructure elements are generally present:

- Data analytics tools
- Data discovery and visualization tools
- Data warehouse and data mart
- Enterprise search platform
- RDBMS with OLAP
- Reporting tools
- Web based dashboards

The source of data that feeds analytics can be inpatient or outpatient Electronic Medical Record (EMR) systems; Enterprise Resource Planning (ERP) systems; Revenue Cycle Management (RCM) systems which include billing, coding, and claims information; financial data from accounting applications; supply chain data; research data if the organization supports a research department; patient information from customer service and marketing; human resource systems including payroll management, benefits, etc. The data can be pulled from standalone SQL databases, applications, or third-party sources. The data is then aggregated into a data warehouse, a distributed file system, or an RDBMS. A data access layer connects data services, including business logic, and a security layer with logging and monitoring. The data is presented via dashboards, reports, and queries and served through API, desktop, or mobile interfaces.

Analytics security

Patient data security and HIPAA compliance is an essential issue in healthcare. There is an exception in HIPAA that allows access to PHI for operations. While healthcare organizations have implemented safeguards and created infrastructure to protect PHI in EMRs, the same rigor must be implemented on analytics infrastructure. For example, a general-purpose analytics or visualization tool is used by analysts to import data from the EMR database into the analytics tool or data warehouse. These tools may not have access logs, and it may not be easy to fine-tune which particular data element can be displayed to which user. For this reason, it may be safer to use the analytics tools inbuilt into the EMRs, which allow access based on user specific permissions.

The analytics governance team may need to develop security tiers for various reports and classify anyone having access to the BI tools created for end users. The other option is role-based access, with every consumer of analyst reports assigned a role. In this case, the analysts can control the access by restricting the access to specific roles. For example, physician leaders, super users, and quality team leaders can have higher privileges than operational managers, who can have higher privileges than all other hospital employees with generic access privileges for the self-service reports. Training may be required for each user category to ensure they understand the underlying data, business context, and appropriate use.

Self service

Self-service reporting platforms can reduce the operational work of the analytics teams. Using a self-service approach, the end users can directly work with data and generate analytics reports for their needs without requiring knowledge of statistics or analytics. Simple and recurring requests like finding several procedures or visits and pulling quality metrics for providers are ideal for consideration of self-service. Before deployment of self-service tools, adequate research needs to be conducted to ensure that the specific configuration of the platform serves a broad swathe of future users' needs.

Self-service can be one of the most powerful interventions in a healthcare organization. If done right, it can empower end-users at every level to be more effective. However, if not executed well, it can reduce satisfaction and an increase workload for the analytics team with a deluge of requests for updates and troubleshooting.

Predictive Model Markup Language (PMML)

Predictive model markup language (PMML) is an interchange format for predictive models based on XML. It is used to exchange predictive models created by machine learning algorithms. The models can be transferred through an XML configuration file. It is currently developed and hosted by Data Mining Group (DMG. PMML 4.4.1). The elements of PMML are:

- **Header**: Contains information about the PMML document
- **Data Dictionary**: Definitions for the fields in the model
- **Data Transformations**: Used for mapping of the model data. These could include normalization, discretization, value mapping, functions, and aggregation
- **Model**: Data mining model definition. It contains specific model attributes
- **Mining schema**: Fields used in the model with information about each field like name, usage type, outlier treatment, missing value replacement policy etc.
- **Targets**: Used for post-processing of the predicted value or in classification tasks
- **Output**: Used to name the output fields expected from the model

Portable Format for Analytics (PFA)

Portable Format for Analytics (PFA) is an open statistical and machine learning model standard. PFA is based on the concept of a scoring engine which is an executable with an input, mathematical function, and an output. It uses JSON and enables the exchange and execution of complex predictive models. Data Mining Group (DMG. 2022) currently develops and hosts PFA. The algorithms can be deployed by developers on their own applications and analytics tools using PFA. PFA specification defines the structure of JSON documents which contains control structures and user-defined functions. Library functions can be combined in various permutations to create complex structures. A simple PFA example is:

```
{"input": "double",
 "output": "double",
 "action": [
   {"+": ["input", 100]}
```

]}

14 REAL WORLD EVIDENCE

Introduction

Real World Evidence (RWE) is the inference about the risks and benefits of medical products based on data collected in a routine clinical practice setting obtained by analysis of Real World Data (RWD). Real-world data is data about a patient collected during routine healthcare delivery. RWD is the health data not collected for clinical research but is repurposed for clinical research activities. It is obtained from electronic medical records (EMR), medical claims data, pharmacy sales data, product and disease registries, or personal wearable devices. EMR systems contain individual patient health records maintained by healthcare providers providing clinical care. They contain patients' medical history, diagnoses, treatment plans, immunizations, allergies, radiology images, pharmacy records, and laboratory data.

RWE is increasingly gaining acceptance from regulatory agencies and pharmaceutical companies for drug development. RWE is used to develop insights and generate evidence for developing pharmaceutical and medical device products by extracting data elements from electronic health records' structured and unstructured sections. These specific data models and developed using data analytics and statistical methods. The real-world data researchers work closely with clinicians and scientists to establish clinical requirements and develop analysis plans. RWE can also be used for health services research, clinical patient care, outcomes research, quality improvement activities, surveillance for safety, and conducting effectiveness studies (Sherman RE et al., 2016).

The pharmaceutical industry uses RWE after the market launch of the product to further demonstrate the product's effectiveness or expand the original label. It takes advantage of the fact that the patients' information in the real-world data sets more closely reflects the population receiving the drug. Other applications of real-world evidence include clinical trial design, clinical trial recruitment, developing marketing insights, and value-based care delivery model design.

While Randomized Controlled Trials (RCT) work well in standardizing the treatment protocols and reducing variability in patients and the research process, they also create artificial treatment environments very different from how the drug or device is essentially used in practice. The narrow scope of the RCT environment could limit the generalizability of the results. RCTs are also time-consuming and expensive. The cost of these trials limits the number and type of therapies that can be developed, as pharmaceutical companies select only those with the highest return on investments.

RWE allows the clinical environment to be considered when evaluating treatment efficacy. These include the clinical settings for treatment, payer & provider characteristics, and patient preferences. RWE is based on a heterogeneous sample, which is assumed to be sufficiently large to provide valuable and meaningful insights. However, frequency data may need to be included in RWD, necessitating statistical manipulation to fill the gaps or reject incomplete data. A blanket exclusion of the missing data may lead to bias in the selected data sets. For example, if the patient stopped picking up their prescription from the pharmacy and that has been used as an indicator for the patient getting treatment, then it becomes hard to identify the causality behind this retrospectively – did they change to a different pharmacy, did they suffer side effects, did they move to an alternate medication because of the cost, did they see a TV ad about potential harm which led them to discontinue the therapy etc.

Applications

RWD is used in randomized clinical trials to capture clinical data. It can also be used for collecting post-market safety data. RWD and RCT can be complementary as the study group is homogenous in RCT and is heterogenous in RWD. In RCT, the trial is conducted by a few designated investigators, but in RWE, there are many clinical practitioners whose data collection is used for evaluation. The comparison arm in RCT is a placebo or a preselected alternative; however, in RWE, many alternatives can be used as control arms. RWE-based trials can be performed much more quickly as they do not need any time spent on patient recruitment or enrollment. RWE is also used in trials that cannot be done using RCT, such as those exploring safety in high-risk groups. RWE can detect uncommon side effects, which may or may not be possible with RCT depending on the size of the population under study. Machine learning and artificial intelligence techniques can be used on RWD to widen the scope and validity of data.

RWE can be incorporated in submissions to FDA, including an existing Investigational New Drug (IND), or as an adjunct to an NDA (New Drug Application) or BLA (Biologics License Application). Clinical trials can use RWE for post-marketing review to evaluate safety or effectiveness. Clinical research protocols can be created for single-arm trials, incorporating RWE as an external control.

RWE uses observational studies that generate real-world evidence to support the expansion or change in efficacy label. This could include "adding or modifying an indication, change in dose, dose regimen, or route of administration; use in a new population, adding comparative efficacy information, adding safety information; and other labeling changes" (FDA. Framework for FDA's Real-World Evidence Program). RWE is also used in observational studies to develop hypotheses for prospective trials (Gradman AH et al., 2014). It is used for quality improvement in healthcare delivery, safety surveillance (Cantlupe J., 2016; FDA MedWatch), and generalize findings from conventional clinical trials (Tavris DR et al., 2005).

Source of data

Electronic Health Record (EHR) systems are the primary source of RWD. RWE research data is increasingly being sourced from more frequent measurements of patient-specific clinical elements and which requires massive data processing capabilities. The ultimate goal is targeted therapeutics using precision medicine.

EHR systems that have been certified for the requirements of the ONC health IT certification program are preferred for collecting R. EHR systems are not under the control of FDA-regulated entities, including clinical research sponsors and clinical investigators. FDA has provided guidance when EHRs are used as sources of data and clinical investigations, providing them the ability to verify the quality and integrity of the data. FDA requires that the sponsors follow privacy and security controls, including policies and processes for the use of EHR systems at the investigation sites, limiting access to an electronic system to authorized users, establishing the identity of authors generating the data, ability to track interview audit trails, ability to retain the records for FDA inspection when requested.

Data elements can be transferred from electronic health records to case report forms, which can then be submitted to the FDA. It can be accomplished using interoperable data exchange or manual abstraction. This process is straightforward if the EHR systems are interoperable with the electronic data capture system used in clinical research. The structured data elements are collected from EHR based on the data collection plan defined in the protocol. The unstructured data is reviewed to ensure acceptable reliability and quality to FDA. It is essential to have a quality management plan which includes standard operating procedures, change control procedures, and protocols to review the integrity and security of the data.

Benefits

The most common use case currently uses real-world evidence for post-marketing surveillance or research, used to develop predictive models. Observational studies based on real-world evidence can provide useful insights without needing to conduct large-scale double-blind, randomized control studies. These findings can improve standards of clinical care by quickly incorporating into the clinical protocols, providing support for relevant value-based payment models, informing formulary decisions, expanding the drug labels developed from randomized clinical trials.

RWE provides many other benefits for the clinical research process. RWE can improve the power of randomized controlled trials for endpoint analysis. It is increasingly being used in regulatory, reimbursement, and clinical decision-making. Patient recruitment is done through cohort identification using structured data and natural language processing on unstructured data. Advanced statistical techniques, including machine learning, are used to create trial arms. The protocols in RWE include a focus on the security of data and data analytics methodology. Similarly, IRB approval is focused on security and privacy practices compared to a randomized controlled trial that is focused on clinical practices.

The cost of conducting traditional clinical research is increasing every year. At the same time, patient data is also exponentially increasing. RWE provides a more targeted and, in many cases, more comprehensive information than that can be solely obtained from clinical trials.

Limitations

The data collected during clinical encounters is not structured for research purposes. It limits the analysis that can be performed on this data set that can sustain the rigor of regulatory review. Data analytics coupled with an improved understanding of real-world evidence augmented by advanced machine learning techniques, including natural language processing and data modeling, are starting to generate accurate insights from medical records data.

One of the biggest challenges for RWE is data quality, or lack thereof. The accuracy of EHR data from different providers is generally quite variable, so data analysts and clinical informaticians are needed to clean and tag the data. Study protocols establishing minimum accuracy requirements must be implemented to ensure valid data is used for RWE. Extracting meaningful insights from primarily unstructured text-based documentation and laboratory values with no predominant standard across systems is still very challenging. Also, the rigor in data collection for routine healthcare practices differs from the one deployed during clinical trials.

Data cleaning is one of the most time-consuming and resource-intensive activities of RWE. RWE also requires data analysis expertise which is not commonly available. RWE requires specific precautions before the analysis to avoid issues of privacy or confidentiality. There are concerns about the introduction of bias when using real-world data. It requires significant expertise, time, and resources to collect, organize, and analyze the data obtained from medical records.

Process

The patient data in the electronic medical record systems at academic health centers and community health systems is essential for developing real-world data sets. Over the years, the consolidation of electronic medical record systems has made it easier for pharmaceutical companies to access data from multiple health systems as they are on relatively few electronic medical record systems.

Integration of disparate data sets is vital for using real-world data. Health systems that invest in creating data warehouses have an advantage in attracting partnerships with pharmaceutical companies. The data sources include phenotypic data from electronic health records, sensor data from medical devices, outcomes data from medical claims, treatment data from pharmacy systems, etc.

Once the data sets are identified, the research team reviews the patient's medical records to evaluate if they meet the inclusion criteria for the specific studies as outlined in the protocols. They work with the medical record abstractors and extract patient records' structure, concepts, and content. They develop, implement, and update the research and standard operating procedures and protocols.

Regulations

The first regulatory approval based solely on real-world evidence was granted to extend the labels for the oncology therapy Palbociclib in 2019. Proof of this drug's efficacy in male breast cancer treatment was provided to FDA through analysis of electronic health records and medical database data. Since then, the FDA has created workgroups to guide real-world evidence-based clinical research. Over the next couple of years, more drug and device approvals will be based on RWE.

15 MACHINE LEARNING & ARTIFICIAL INTELLIGENCE

Introduction

The word 'learning' in machine learning denotes that the machine can learn new knowledge and improve its performance by observing examples from the world. These examples are provided as input and output pairs, which help the machine build a model that can then be used to predict outputs for future inputs. The model is iteratively refined with appropriate 'feedback' until it can predict with the desired accuracy. In this case, the machine refers to computer programs that can perform statistical computations.

Machine learning (ML) is used to make predictions, classify or assign data to clusters. For example, we can predict a patient's chance of being readmitted to the hospital. In this case, the readmission probability is the 'output variable.' It is also called a 'dependent variable.' The output or dependent variable may be dependent on multiple factors like existing patient diagnoses, demographics like age, gender, social, economic status, income, or support factors like the presence of a primary care physician, full-time caregiver, etc. These factors are called 'input variables' or 'features' or 'predictors.'

In most statistics texts, the input variables are represented by X and the dependent variable with Y. The relationship between X and Y is expressed as a function f and expressed as an equation $Y = f(X) + e$. e is a random error term with a mean value of zero (Gareth J et al., 2013). Statistical tools are used to estimate f. The error term is considered 'reducible' if it can be reduced to improve the accuracy of the output variable or 'irreducible' if it cannot be reduced. 'Loss function' measures how well the statistical model can map the inputs to the outputs. It is a measure of actual value versus the estimated value. 'Variance' is the expected squared deviation from the mean.

The goal of machine learning methods is to find f while minimizing e. This is achieved by finding predictor variables that most influence the output variable, finding the extent of their influence, and shortlisting the equation that accurately explains the relationship between the predictive variables and the output variables. This equation is called a 'model'. Besides accuracy, other considerations for the selection of a model are the time taken for processing the model, called runtime, the time taken to train a model, and the time taken to apply the model every time to a new data set. With the availability of auto ML tools, machine learning as a service, and plug-and-play software for running the data set through multiple machine learning algorithms at the same time, data analysts can work on machine learning with reasonable proficiency and, in many cases, with a basic understanding of the machine learning process and the algorithms. The models are developed on training data and validated on test data. 'Training data' is the set of observations used to create a machine learning model. 'Test data' tests the model's accuracy generated from the training data.

The methods can be classified into two types:

- **Parametric**: Parametric methods estimate a set of parameters. In this approach, initially, we select the type of shape of the function f being linear, log, or other. Once the model is selected, the parameters are estimated for each variable. This can be expressed as $f(X) = b_0 + b_1X_1 + b_2X_2 + b_3X_3 + ... b_pX_p$ if there are p dimensions or input variables. The disadvantage of this approach is that for simplistic models, the obtained f may not be very accurate.
- **Non-parametric**: Non-parametric methods do not pre-select any particular form of f. So they try to produce an f which matches the observations as much as possible. The disadvantage of this approach is that it can provide overfitting and require many observations.

Generally, all the data available for analysis is not used in the model for various reasons. Common reasons for this are that the predictor variables may be correlated, they may not be relevant to the problem at hand, and the variables may be redundant or erroneous. The 'feature selection' process is used to identify the data used in the model. The subset of data is used in the model as a predictor or dependent variable. For example, in an EHR dataset, the record of an individual patient may be an observation. However, the associated diagnoses, list of medications, and vital signs are the dependent variables or predictors.

The prediction may involve finding a discrete or continuous output value. Common techniques for this approach are linear and logistic regression. However, sometimes a categorical or qualitative output value may be required. This may be desired in classification problem for example, predicting if a patient is in a high-risk or a low-risk category. Another application could be clustering problems where we may want to group data elements with specific characteristics—for example, grouping patients with similar gene expression profiles. The predictor variables can be quantitative or qualitative. The quantitative variables are numerical and denote an individual's height, weight, blood pressure, etc. The values of qualitative variables are categories to which the variables belong. These could include the disease diagnosis, gender, and risk status (high, medium-low).

The workflow of a machine learning project at a healthcare organization is similar to any data analytics project. The project goes through the following stages in general - problem definition, data collection, data cleaning, selection of analytic approach, model development, model validation, model implementation, and interpretation of results.

In healthcare, the machine learning model must be interpretable to clarify the rationale behind the outcome. FDA requires the interpretability of the model as one of the factors for classifying software as a medical device.

Machine learning is broadly split into two types – Supervised learning and Unsupervised learning. In recent years, deep learning or reinforcement learning, considered a part of unsupervised machine learning, has been considered separate from machine learning. Deep learning uses neural networks to generate output.

This book summarizes topics in machine learning and artificial intelligence, especially as they relate to applications in healthcare. Please refer to specialized books on machine learning for information about statistical theory, creating machine learning models, and deploying machine learning in research or production.

Supervised learning

Supervised learning uses input data and output results to represent how inputs are mapped to the outputs. It can be used for Classification as well as Regression. Classification is the process of assigning data into previously identified categories. For example, data may classify patients into high and low risk for a disease or health outcome. The machine learning techniques used for classification include:

- Discriminant Analysis
- Naïve Bayes
- Nearest Neighbor
- Neural Networks
- Support Vector Machines

Regression is the process of identifying the relationship between the input variables and the output variable. For example, data may be used to calculate a risk score for a patient based on the effect of different input variables. The machine learning techniques used for regression include:

- Decision Trees
- Ensemble
- Gaussian Process Regression
- Linear Regression
- Logistic Regression
- Neural Networks
- Support Vector Regression

Unsupervised learning

Unsupervised learning uses only input data to group data elements into clusters of similar data or to create associations between data elements. The algorithm learns the patterns in the input data without any explicit feedback. For example, imaging data may be used to cluster images with a diagnosis of a tumor, or clinical information may be used to cluster patients into similar phenotypes. The machine learning techniques used for unsupervised learning include:

- Association Rule Mining
- Hierarchical
- K-Means
- Mixture Model

- Neural Networks
- Principal Component Analysis

Besides the above, some techniques are applicable in supervised and unsupervised scenarios. Examples include various types of Markov models.

Reinforcement learning

The 'learning' in reinforcement learning happens by providing positive or negative feedback ('reinforcement') to the algorithm, which it uses to update itself to maximize the positive feedback. In this technique, the feature extraction and classification steps are merged and iterate on themselves through a feedback loop before producing an output. This technique is based on neural networks, which can broadly be classified into Deep Neural Networks (DNN), Recurrent Neural Networks (RNN), and Convolutional Neural Networks (CNN).

The differences between these three categories have become blurry over time. There may be a combination of techniques that use elements from each method. The details of these techniques are discussed below.

Supervised learning

Supervised learning creates models and outputs based on one or more input values. Supervised learning is used for prediction and inference. Prediction is the mechanism to predict the outcomes of a phenomenon in the future. Inference is the process of inferring how the output is created as a function of input data so that we can learn about the data generation process. In this technique, both the input variables and the correct output are provided to the machine learning algorithms. The algorithm creates a model by learning from the training data set with inputs and outputs and applying the same model to the input variables for which the output is unknown. The algorithms using supervised learning either use classification or regression techniques.

- **Classification**: The machine learning models classify the output into a category out of two or more options. These categories could be pre-determined, or they could be auto-generated by the model. This technique is used for problems like spam email recognition, natural language processing to predict words based on spoken sound, classifying patients into low-risk or high-risk, and diagnosing cancer from radiology or pathology images. Many observations or data points are categorical - race, symptoms, insurance status, and side effects of drugs. In these situations, classifiers are used to predict the probability of each category of a qualitative variable. The classification techniques are used for discriminant analysis, knowledge extraction, and outlier detection, including fraud detection, medical diagnosis, customer retention, and pattern recognition, with applications in speech recognition, image recognition, and biometrics detection (Alpaydin E., 2014; Jha V., 2017). Classification is used in healthcare to select categorical predictors. For example, it could be a risk category (High, medium, low) or a diagnosis based on lab values and symptoms. The response or output is a qualitative response variable. A response with two options can be obtained by linear regression using dummy variables with 0 and 1 coding. Training observations are used to build the classifier, and test observations are used to test the classifier. The classification techniques include:
    - Classification trees

- Discriminant Analysis
- Ensemble methods
- Fuzzy classification
- Generalized Additive Models
- K-Nearest Neighbors
- Logistic Regression
- Naive Bayes
- Neural networks (Deep Learning)
- Random Forest
- Support Vector Machines

- **Regression**: Unlike the classification technique, where the model's output is a category, linear regression techniques' output is a numerical value. This technique is used in healthcare to predict cases like the expected length of stay of a hospitalized patient, the number of no-show appointments for a physician's office, the expected number of staff members needed at some point in the future, or to estimate costs of one or a cohort of patients in the future, or predict life expectancy for specific diagnoses. The regression techniques include:

  - Bayesian networks
  - Decision trees
  - Ensemble methods
  - Gaussian regression
  - Linear Regression
  - Logistic Regression
  - Neural networks (Deep Learning)
  - Support vector regression

Unsupervised learning

Unsupervised learning helps to understand the structure and relationships in the data. In unsupervised learning, the model does not use any supervising output. It is used where we do not have output values for a set of input values to train the algorithms. Instead, the algorithms try to generate hypotheses through pattern matching and then use this insight to predict future output from future inputs. The common techniques used in unsupervised learning are clustering and dimension reduction.

- **Clustering**: In this technique, the data is separated into clusters. If the data set comprises patients, we can cluster the patients into groups based on the input variables. This technique is commonly used for image recognition, market research, and risk assessment. The techniques can help identify high or low utilizers for different healthcare services (Lefèvre T et al., 2014). Other applications include developing recommendation systems, image compression, document clustering, and DNA analysis (Alpaydin E., 2014). The algorithms used for clustering include:

  - Hidden Markov models
  - Hierarchical clustering
  - K-means clustering
  - Mixture model

- Neural networks

- **Dimension reduction:** This technique reduces the number of input variables or factors to improve the efficiency of large data sets without significantly compromising the algorithm's accuracy. This is especially important in clinical scenarios with many input factors like demographics, previous diagnoses, and lab values, so generating a predictive model for readmission and propensity for a complication can quickly become cumbersome. Dimension reduction is used to reduce the number of variables, usually doing a 'gut check' on these variables and then using them in subsequent models. A similar approach is used in image recognition, especially in the context of self-driving cars, which need to interpret large amount of data quickly. The algorithms used for dimension reduction include:
  - Linear discriminant analysis
  - Multidimensional statistics
  - Principle Component Analysis

Machine learning techniques

Linear regression

Linear regression is one of the most common algorithms used to make predictions when the predictor variable or feature and an outcome variable or response have a linear relationship. The mathematical concept is that there is a straight line called the regression line that minimizes the distance between all the observations in a geometric space. The goal of that line is to 'minimize the residual sum of squares,' which is the sum of squares of the vertical distance from the regression line to each data point. The variability in the model is captured with the addition of an error term for noise. The error term captures the variance 'sigma square' of the model. We use 'mean squared error' as an estimator for the variance. The model is evaluated using p-values, R-squared, and cross-validation.

Simple linear regression

Linear regression is a machine learning technique that uses the concept of least-squares to predict a quantitative output. It is a supervised learning method. This model assumes a linear relationship between the predictor variable X and the output value Y. The equation used to model the linear relationship between the predictor and response variables is:

$$Y = \text{coefficient}_0 + \text{coefficient}_1 * \text{variable } X + e.$$

This equation may be familiar because it represents the equation of a straight line where b0 represents the intercept and coefficient is the slope. coefficient0 + coefficient1 * X represents the linear function, and the error term is the aggregate current predicted outcome variable compared to the actual or expected outcome. The line generated by the model is based on least squares.

The accuracy of the model is evaluated by using goodness-of-fit measures. Residual Standard Error (RSE) is the absolute measure of the distance of the data points from the regression line. It measures how well the regression model fits the observations. It is the standard deviation estimate of the error term 'e'. The residue standard error is small if the predicted variable is close to the outcome. So, RSE provides an estimate of the effect of the model on the data. R-squared statistic (RSS) is the proportion of variability in the outcome variable that can be explained using the predictor variable. It evaluates how well the model fits the data. Its value is between zero and one, where zero means that the model did not explain the variability in the variable. RSS is the square of the value of the correlation between the outcome and the predictor in simple linear regression.

If the predictor variable is qualitative and has two possible values, e.g., insurance status - insured or uninsured, then the qualitative predictor is replaced by a proxy or dummy variable, which takes a value of either 0 and 1 or -1 and 1, indicating the two options. If the qualitative predictor variable has more than two options, we create dummy variables, each representing the presence or absence of the qualitative value. e.g., if the type of insurance option has the possible values of Private, Medicare, Medicaid, or Uninsured, then Insurance1 could be 1 if Private and 0 if not Private, Insurance2 could be 1 if Medicare and 0 if not Medicare, etc. These variables are plugged into the linear model.

Linear regression has many advantages as a machine learning technique. It is easy to compute, there are generally small numbers of coefficients that are easy to interpret, and it is easier to perform tests of significance on the model.

Multiple linear regression

Linear regression is used to predict the response using one predictor variable. In real-life scenarios, there is usually more than one predictor. For example, a patient's hospital readmission risk could depend on age, disease diagnoses, educational status, social, economic status, support system, etc. Multiple regression also helps to rule out confounders. Multivariate regression predicts the value of an outcome variable based on multiple independent variables. It is also used in cases of continuous outcome variables—for example, blood pressure or cost of treatment (Sylvia ML et al., 2018). Multiple linear regression uses a linear equation to predict a dependent variable as the outcome from one or more independent input variables. The outcome function could be expressed as

Output Y = coefficient_1 x variableX_1 + coefficient_2 x variableX_2 + coefficient_3 x variableX_3 + constant.

For example, risk of complication = a * (age of the patient) + b * (previous hospitalization) + c * (Carlson Comorbidity Score) + d. The training data is used to identify the coefficients a, b, c, and d. Then those coefficients are used in this equation for the prediction. Non-numeric variables like previous hospitalization are coded as a binary number (e.g., no=0, yes=1). This is a simplistic example of multiple linear regression in practice (Fahl J., 2017; Sylvia ML et al., 2018; Christo EM, 2019).

Least-squares approach can be used to derive the regression coefficients. The regression coefficients are calculated based on minimizing the residual sum of squares. 'F-statistic' evaluates the relationship between the predictor variable and the output. Its value is 1 if there is no relationship between the predictor variables and the output. If the F statistic is large, it means that at least one of the predictor variables has a relationship to the response. We generally check for the p-value of the F-statistic to evaluate whether its value is statistically significant.

In a multiple linear regression situation, a response is related to more than one predictor, but not all the predictors are included in the regression equation. So, to select the best predictors through a process known as 'variable selection,' we calculate the F-statistic for the predictors and look at the associated p-value. Variable selection is done by generating models with all permutations of predictor variables and selecting the model which performs the best. However, this process can be very onerous as a data set with 20 predictors will generate 1,048,576 models. So, we use techniques like forward selection, backward selection, and mixed selection to make selecting features more efficient.

- **Forward selection**: In this technique, a model is created with no predictor variables, and gradually, one predictor or feature is added at a time. Iterations of simple linear regressions equal to the number of predictor variables are conducted. Then predictor variable, which improves the model the most, usually by finding the lowest RSS to the model is added and the process is started again till the data scientist is satisfied with the number of predictor variables added to the model or when the addition of a feature starts to make the model worse.
- **Backward selection**: This is the reverse of the forward selection. This process starts with the model, which includes all features or variables. Then the least statistically significant predictors or predictors whose removal improves the selection criteria are iteratively removed. This continues until a defined condition is met, usually when the model selection criteria worsen.
- **Mixed selection**: This approach combines forward and backward selection. The process starts like forward selection, but if the p-value of any of the predictor variables in the model increases beyond a threshold, it is removed. The process continues till the p-values of all variables inside the model have been minimized.

The multiple linear regression model fit can be done using the R-square statistic. R-square is the square of the correlation between the linear model and the response. It increases with the addition of more variables to the model. A value close to 1 means that the model explains a higher amount of variance in the output variable. In addition to R-square, Residual Standard Error can also be used. Models created as we add more variables may increase Residual Standard Error (RSE) if the Residual Sum of Squares (RSS) falls less than the increase in p-value.

'Prediction intervals' can also be calculated for the response obtained from the multiple regression model. Prediction intervals estimate the difference between predicted and true values by incorporating reducible and irreducible errors.

In scenarios where any change in one variable also affects the second variable, i.e., there is an interaction between variables, an interaction variable that is the product of the interacting variables is introduced; the interaction variable gets its own coefficient, 'Interaction Effect.' The case for an interaction is strong if the interaction variable p-value is significant. In such a scenario, including the interacting variables separately is recommended, even if their p-value is not-significant.

Limitations

- Even though linear regression is straightforward to understand and easy to deploy, it has shortcomings. There may not be a linear relationship between the predictors and the model output or response. One way to verify this is to create a residual plot of residual values against the predicted outcomes. 'Residual value' is the vertical distance between a single data point and the regression line. Log, square root, and squared transformations are alternatives to the linear approach.

- Model output may be flawed if the error terms have a correlation among them.
- If the variance of the error term increases with the value of the predicted outcome, then a transformation may need to be applied to the response variable by taking a log or square root of the output value.
- Variance Inflation Factor (VIF) can be computed to check for a correlation between the predictors. If VIF shows correlation, then either one of the variables is eliminated, or both are combined into one variable.

Going beyond linear regression, many non-linear approaches are available. These include generalized additive models, smoothing splines, step functions, polynomial regression, and regression splines. These are advanced topics and readers are advised to refer to specialized textbooks for further information.

Logistic regression

Logistic regression is used when the outcome is a binary - yes or no, healthy or sick, success or failure. It can be used in classification, where the output is the probability that the response belongs to one group or category. A simple logistic regression has one binary outcome and one independent variable. In multiple logistic regression, there is a single binary outcome and multiple independent variables. Multiple logistic regression is used when the outcome is of a categorical type. For example, risk of readmission (high/low), blood type, gender, or city. Here the output is a chance that the output variable represents one of the categorical options. The process of creating an equation is similar to multiple linear regression (Fahl J., 2017; Sylvia ML et al., 2018; Morr CE et al., 2019).

Logistic regression uses a logistic function whose output is between 0 and 1 for all values of the predictor variables. 1 represents that outcome of interest is present, and 0 represents the absence of the outcome of interest. The logistic function or the model can be represented as follows:

$$\text{p (Predictor variable X)} = \frac{(e^{\wedge(\text{coefficient0} + \text{coefficient1} * \text{Predictor variable X1})})}{(1 + e^{\wedge\text{coefficient0} + \text{coefficient1} * \text{Predictor variable X2}})}$$

Like linear regression, the predictor variables in the logistic function have coefficients. The difference is that the coefficients obtained from the model indicate a change in the expected log odds for every unit of change in the predictor variable if other predictor variables are kept constant. The odds ratio can be obtained by getting an antilog of the regression coefficient.

The first step in logistic regression model development is to estimate the coefficients. It uses the 'maximum likelihood method' to generate the model in which the coefficients maximize the likelihood function. The accuracy of the estimated value for the coefficients is obtained by checking the z-statistic, which is considered statistically significant if the p-value is small. For variables with binary values or True/False, Male/Female type options, dummy variables with 0/1 coding can be used. The response variable can have more than two classes, but logistic regression is not commonly used in those scenarios. The other drawback of logistic regression is that in scenarios where the categories or classes are quite separate, logistic regression is unreliable. If regression is used for classification, we look at the model's predicted probability and classify it as 1 if the probability is over 0.5 and 0 if it is less than 0.5.

Multivariable logistic regression has been used to develop the LACE index, which is used to predict early death or unplanned readmission after discharge from the hospital. The input variables for this score are the length of stay at the hospital in days (L), acute admission (A), comorbidity (C - Charlson comorbidity index score), and number of visits to the emergency departments in the previous six months (E). The Odds Ratio associated with each of these variables is 1.47, 1.84, 1.21, and 1.56, respectively. The increase in LACE score by 1 increased the risk of unplanned readmission by 18% and early death by 29% (van Walraven C et al. 2010).

Discriminant analysis

Linear Discriminant Analysis (LDA)

Linear Discriminant Analysis (LDA) is preferred if there are more than two response classes and there is a separation between the classes. The assumption is that the underlying data within each class belongs to a multivariate Gaussian distribution. LDA classifier can be used for multiple predictors, which are assumed to represent a multivariate normal distribution (Gareth J et al. 2013). This scenario uses a linear discriminant function based on the Bayes classifier. The bayes classifier uses Bayes theorem to estimate the conditional distribution of response for any predictor variable. The classifier assigns the observation to the category with the highest posterior probability of having that observation.

Classification is achieved by changing the threshold of the posterior probability of an outcome. The optimum classifier threshold value changes on a case-to-case basis, and it is selected based on the error rates, true positive and false positive rates of different threshold values. Alternatively, LDA attempts to find a Bayes classifier with the least error rate by having the lowest number of total misclassifications. Please refer to a textbook on Bayes Theorem to get more details.

In order to make the prediction, LDA calculates the mean and variance parameters for the class. The performance of a classifier is obtained by looking at Area Under the Curve (AUC) of the Receiver Operating Characteristics (ROC) curve. Good classifiers will have a ROC curve close to the top left corner and a larger AUC. The ROC curve plots the true positive rate against the false positive rate. The model performance can be objectively assessed by evaluating the area under the ROC curve as the AUC of different classifiers can be compared. It performs better in linear relationships between predictor and response or outcome.

Quadratic Discriminant Analysis (QDA)

The difference between Quadratic Discriminant Analysis (QDA) and LDA is the treatment of the covariance matrix. The classes in LDA share a common matrix, while in QDA, every class has its unique matrix. QDA is preferred in large training sets. LDA has a lower variance and is better in cases of few training observations, so it is important to minimize the variance. QDA performs better in more situations because most real-world problems are not linear.

K-Nearest Neighbors (KNN)

K-Nearest Neighbor (K-NN) classifier is used to get the conditional distribution of an outcome variable given a predictive variable and then use the probability to assign the observation in the data set to the category of interest. K-NN classification technique can help answer whether a patient is at high, medium, or low risk for a disease or medical condition. Using linear regression for such problems is difficult as the output is continuous, but we still need a categorical output variable. The KNN model combines most similar items in the observation set based on their attributes or features. To achieve this, we define the similarity of some parameters based on domain knowledge and then check the similarity between all the label items provided in the data set. The most similar items are called neighbors and help determine the classification of the unlabeled items. The number of neighbors is denoted by the pre-determined number K. This number is changed during various runs of the model, and the best output based on similarity measure or distance metric is selected. The 'similarity measure' is generally defined by Euclidean distance in the geometric space. The other options are Cosine similarity, Hamming distance, etc. The original labeled data in the data set is divided into training and test data. An evaluation metric, for example, the misclassification rate, was selected to assess the model's performance. The algorithm is run a few times in the value of K, which provides the best evaluation measure selected. Using these values, we run the model on test data.

KNN uses the Bayes rule for classification. The KNN regression method is related to the KNN classifier. The model identifies a specified number of training observations around a given prediction data point in this approach. Then a model function is estimated using the average of these training observations. If K is small, then the model fit is flexible, having low bias but high variance. For example, if K is 1, every data point is used to generate a prediction. As the K value increases, there is less variability because an average of larger (K) observations is used for prediction. On the contrary, this increases bias as some data points may be ignored. KNN performance decreases as the number of predictors increases because the sample size per prediction becomes smaller. The observations nearest to the observation of interest are selected to predict if a K training observation belongs to a specific class. The observation is allocated to the class to which the probability of belonging is the highest. KNN performs better than LDA and logistic regression in non-linear situations. Since there are no coefficients in KNN, there is no way of knowing if some predictor variables are more important than others.

Support Vector Machines (SVM)

Support Vector Machines (SVM) are generally used when the data needs to be classified into two classes. However, with extensions, it can be applied to problems requiring more than two classes. SVM is based on the concept of hyperplane, which is a geometrical concept separating the observations into distinct regions, thereby classifying them. A maximum margin hyperplane is created by calculating the largest minimum distance of the training observations from the margins of the hyperplane. The test observations are then classified depending on the side of the hyperplane on which they end up. If the hyperplane cannot cleanly separate all the observations such that some observations end up in the wrong region, a Support Vector Classifier (SVC) is used. SVC is used when it is impossible to separate the training data into two classes or regions cleanly, and some observations are misclassified. It is influenced by the observations that are on the margin or in the wrong region, and these small quantities of observations in the training data are the ones that influence the model. Support vector classifier can be applied to problems with non-linear boundaries between the classes. In these scenarios, quadratic, cubic, or higher-order polynomial functions can be used (Gareth J et al., 2013). SVMs can also be used for classification requiring more than two classes using one-versus-one and one-versus-all techniques.

Unsupervised learning

Decision trees

Decision trees are used for regression as well as classification. These methods segment the observations into regions of predictor space. In these approaches, multiple trees are created, which are finally combined. The regions are called terminal nodes or leaves. Decision trees are built using attributes that maximize the information gained from the model. Simplistically, linear regression is better if there is a linear correlation between input and output variables. However, decision trees are better if these two have a non-linear or complex relationship. Linear regression generally has lower variance in typical scenarios compared to decision trees. Decision trees are broadly classified into two types of trees:

- **Regression Trees**: The standardized training data splits the observations into distinct non-overlapping regions called terminal nodes or leaves. Regions are created by finding the areas with the minimum RSS. A response is predicted using the training observation mean values for the regions or terminal nodes with test observations. This approach is called recursive binary splitting or top-down, in which the process starts with one region (stem) and then splits into two smaller regions (branches) at every step. Smaller trees have lower variance, so to avoid making the trees complex, tree pruning is used. After the tree is made using the above approach, a sub-tree sequence is selected using cost complexity pruning. Cross-validation is used to select the appropriate tuning parameter.
- **Classification Trees**: Classification trees are used if the output response is qualitative. Recursive binary splitting is used to create the classification tree. Every new data element is attached to the most common class in its region. So, both class prediction and class proportions of the assigned training observations are considered. Gini index, entropy, or classification error rate can be used as a selection criterion for classification trees. The Gini index measures the variance across the total number of classes. The classification error rate is the proportion of training data elements in a specific region that are not in the most common class in that region. Entropy is the uncertainty in the variable's possible outcomes.

Deep learning

Deep learning (DL) is a machine learning approach that can improve the algorithm's performance without requiring ongoing human input for model improvement. Deep Learning is made of a multi-layer representation of learning architecture. The first layer is activated through a data input or a sensor, which activates the next layer; each subsequent layer processes the representation non-linearly, advancing the schema (LeCun Y et al., 2015; Schmidhuber J et al., 2015). This is a different approach compared to the general machine learning task-specific algorithms. DL is used in visual recognition, speech recognition, and language classification. DL is also called black box decision-making because the input data undergoes a complex transformation, and the result is produced. How exactly the algorithm came up with an answer is currently unknown and is one of the most significant downsides of DL.

Conventional machine learning techniques require domain expertise and engineering for feature extraction to develop an appropriate representation of the data, which can be used to generate a classifier. Deep learning is based on computational learning techniques that allow algorithms to ingest raw data automatically to identify the representations required for classification (LeCun Y et al., 2015). Deep learning can create complex functions by stacking up multiple non-linear transformations, which convert the representation of the raw input into a more sophisticated, abstract representation at every step. The system learns by prioritizing the specific aspects of the input that are important for the outcome and suppressing variations that play a minimal role.

A typical DL algorithm is a mathematical function with many parameters, making visualization or developing a conceptual map exceedingly tricky. Clinicians and researchers are used to using evidence that peers have scientifically validated before introducing any changes to diagnosis or treatment flows. There may be mistrust on the part of physicians to trust the algorithm's output if they cannot understand how the output was obtained. Also, the performance of an algorithm could change for experiments done with the same initial conditions because of randomization in the internal conditions.

DL has the advantage of uncovering previously unknown patterns, highlighting features that may not have been considered necessary in clinical guidelines, or identifying patterns that may not be detectable by the human eye in radiological or pathological images. DL algorithms program themselves by learning from an allowed set of examples that indicate the required outcome without explicitly creating any decision logic or rules (LeCun Y et al., 2015). The structure of the deep learning algorithm is in the shape of multiple non-linear layers or stacks of modules that transform the input to output by gradually improving the performance of the algorithm by "increasing the selectivity and the invariance of the representation" (LeCun Y et al., 2015). These interconnected modules are then able to create complex functions.

In deep learning, the initial activity is collecting a large data set, usually labeled with the category to which it belongs. This is an example of supervised learning. For example, for the algorithm to identify skin cancers, the initial task will be to collect hundreds or thousands of labeled skin cancer images and labeled normal images and feed them to the algorithm. The algorithm analyzes the image and generates a mathematical vector or score for each classification category. An objective function measures the difference between this output and the actual or desired output during every iteration. This difference could be the distance between the vectors or an error term. The algorithm then automatically modifies its parameters repeatedly until it can minimize this difference or error. It makes minor weight adjustments and checks the error for all the parameters or weights generated in the function. For example, a common method is stochastic gradient descent in which multiple small input sets are provided to the algorithm many times, each process leading to adjustment in weights. The process is continued till the average error of the whole data set or the average of the objective function has been minimized.

The deep learning network consists of many connected layers which perform feature extraction or classification. The layers are arranged in sequence, and one layer can feed its output into the next in both forward and backward directions. These layers combine to create increasingly complex representations of the input data. In the case of image detection, the earlier layers of the network may identify the edges of the image. Subsequent layers can identify other concepts from images like parts of the face or body or characters like numbers and alphabets. These layers, called neural networks, are mathematical constructs with stacking elements called nodes. Each node performs a simple mathematical function and non-linear transformation. Stacks of nodes combine to form a layer.

Unlike traditional machine learning, deep learning algorithms learn features automatically through the neural network by optimizing the algorithm using techniques like backpropagation.

'Back propagation' is a technique based on the chain rule of derivatives in which the derivatives or gradients start from the module's output and are propagated through the modules to the input module. In a non-linear function called Rectified Linear Unit (ReLU), unsupervised pre-training is not required for training a deep supervised network (Glorot X et al., 2011).

Convolutional Neural Network (CNN)

A Convolutional Neural Network (CNN) is a feed-forward network using multiple layers. CNNs have been used in image recognition and text classification tasks. They have been used in many studies on image recognition, like dermatology, histology, and other medical specialties. They are based on the concept of convolutional layers, which detect small areas of feature combinations from the previous layer and following layers that merge similar features. An image is a representation of pixels. CNN nodes allow the recognition of a single feature within the image. The deep learning algorithm may learn features in the first layer to detect edges in the image. The second layer may detect patterns and look for arrangements of edges or colors. The next layer may combine these patterns into subparts of familiar objects. The next layer may combine the subparts into full-fledged objects and learn the context of these objects within the whole image. Combining image motifs, parts, or objects creates the mathematical concept of an image within the network (Krizhevsky A et al., 2012; Farabet C et al., 2013; Tompson J et al., 2014). In Natural Language Processing (NLP), CNNs are used for classification like sentiment classification or topic categorization and have been replaced by Recurrent Neural Networks for most tasks. Examples of CNN models include LeNet, AlexNet, ResNet, VGG, Inception, and Xception.

Recurrent Neural Network (RNN)

A Recurrent Neural Network (RNN) is a deep learning technique with applications in speech and language tasks like translation apps, chatbots, and voice recognition apps. The speech recognition accuracy is improving as more speech data is getting collected worldwide (Mikolov T et al., 2011; Hinton G et al. 2012; Sainath T et al. 2013). Along with natural language understanding, it is now possible to create intelligent agents who can interact with humans purely by voice (Collobert R et al., 2011; Bordes A et al., 2014; Jean S et al., 2015; Sutskever I et al., 2014). RNN is also increasingly used in life sciences, including drug development and genetic analysis (Ma J et al., 2015; Leung MK et al., 2014; Xiong HY et al., 2015).

RNNs have improved the quality of text classification compared to conventional machine learning models. Long Short Term Memory network (LSTM) (Sepp H et al. 1997) or Gated Recurrent Unit (GRU) (Junyoung C et al. 2014) are a type of RNNs that can remember large quantities of text for context compared to a CNN (TextCNN) which can only remember a few words at a time. RNNs can perform better on language modeling and machine translation because keeping a larger number of words in memory and creating context among the sentences creates semantic dependency (Dzmitry B et al., 2014; Sutskever I et al., 2014). Due to this advantage in sequence modeling, RNNs can more accurately predict which word will come next in a sentence. RNNs were further improved by using the 'Attention mechanism' (Bahdanau D et al. 2014), which assigned weights to important words in a paragraph or sentence, improving the accuracy of the output.

The sequence-to-sequence models used in RNNs are based on the concept of transforming a sequence of input values into a sequence of output values. They have two main components –

'encoders' which process the input, and 'decoders', which convert the processed input into the output. Word embedding algorithms convert the input sequence (sentence, image, etc.) into mathematical vectors. The vector captures the meaning of the words with words similar in meaning clustered together. They also add another input vector called the hidden state, which is updated with every step in the encoder. After the encoder has finished processing, the input vector and final hidden state from the encoder are passed to the decoder as a context vector. The RNNs have a significant limitation that due to the sequential processing of the text, the processing time increases as the length of the input increases.

Newer architectures like Transformers are discussed in a separate chapter of the book.

Model performance

- **Mean Squared Error**: Determination of the performance of a machine learning model is a critical step in machine learning model development. One of the common techniques to determine the difference between predicted response and true response in statistical models using regression is Mean Squared Error (MSE) which is small if there is a slight difference between observed and predicted output. The MSE can be obtained for the training as well as the test data. For classification methods, the training or test error rate is the ratio of incorrectly classified training or test observations.
- **Variance**: The variance of a statistical method is the amount of change in the output of the predictive function if a new training data set is used. Small changes in the predictive function and output value are expected by using different training data. However, if there is a significant change in the predictive function (and subsequently the output value) due to a minor change in the training set, the statistical method is considered to have high variance.
- **Bias**: Bias is the amount of error in the predictive function due to using a simpler statistical method. Ideally, the method should have low variance and bias; however, they go in the opposite direction in real life. The key is to find a balance where one decreases a lot more than the increase in the other. A simple model has a high bias, and if we add more data, it will not improve the performance of the model. A complicated model has high variance, which can cause overfitting.

Feature selection

A domain expert can look at the variables and make a shortlist of any that seem remotely interesting or relevant. However, this introduces subjective bias and may prevent the discovery of unique insights. Ranking based on specified criteria and using that to select a smaller subset of features can be useful. However, this may end up providing correlated features. Feature selection is the technique of selecting the most promising predictors or input variables or attributes in a machine learning algorithm. Feature selection can be achieved through multiple techniques.

- **Filter method**: Filter methods select a subset of features based on their relationship with output and use statistical tools like correlation coefficient, Fisher's score, Chi-square test, etc.
- **Wrapper method**: Wrapper feature selection may have better accuracy than filter methods and use stepwise regression, in which features are selected by adding or removing features in a regression model. The approaches are Forward selection, Backward selection, and Mixed selection, which are discussed separately.

Model selection

Selecting one machine learning model for production use out of many options is a challenging problem in machine learning. Model Selection is the process of finding a model with the required level of applicability for a specific problem and the data available to solve that problem. Model selection is different from model assessment, which is simply the process of evaluating the performance of a model. Model selection is based on many factors, including model performance, model scalability, model generalizability, model deployment effort, model generation and deployment complexity, and model maintainability.

The evaluation of the model is based on the intended application of the model. For example, some data scientists prefer a model which minimizes false-negative as in the case of cancer diagnosis prediction. Evaluation is important to consider the model's sensitivity, specificity, accuracy, and precision.

- **Sensitivity**: Sensitivity is also known as recall and is the true positive rate or probability of correctly diagnosing someone with a disease when they do have it.
- **Specificity**: Specificity is the probability of correctly diagnosing a patient to be disease-free when they do not have the disease. It is also referred to as a true negative rate.
- **Precision**: Precision is the ratio of true positive results over all positive ones. It is the probability that a patient diagnosed with the disease had the disease.
- **Recall**: Recall is the ratio of the number of true positive results divided by the total number of individuals who truly had the disease, including those who have false-negative results. It is a probability that the algorithm identifies any person with a disease.
- **Accuracy**: Accuracy checks how often the correct outcome is predicted. It is the probability that the model predicts the correct answer and is the ratio of true positives and true negatives over the total number tested.
- **F-score**: F-score is the harmonic mean of precision and recall. These metrics are combined to get the misclassification rate.

Two broad categories of approaches are used for model selection – Probabilistic techniques and Resampling methods.

Probabilistic model scoring techniques

Probabilistic techniques score a model on various criteria based on training and test errors as well as the complexity of the model. Errors can be improved with predictors having the smallest RSS and the largest R-squared. The best overall models have the lowest test error, estimated by adjusting the training error or using cross-validation. Usually, this penalizes the complexity of overfitted models. A simpler model has fewer parameters and better generalizability. Probabilistic model selection approaches include:

- **Akaike Information Criterion (AIC)**: Calculated using the number of parameters in the model and maximized value of the log-likelihood. It also adjusts RSS and is proportional to Cp, so only one is used. Lower AIC is preferable.
- **Bayesian Information Criterion (BIC)**: BIC is another approach to modify RSS and has low values in good models. It is calculated using several parameters in the model, a number of

observations, and maximized value of the log-likelihood. It has a greater penalty than the above options for models with a larger number of variables. Lower BIC is preferred.

- **Adjusted R-squared**: A larger Adjusted R-squared value indicates a small test error. It is better than R-squared as its value is lower if the model contains unnecessary or less-than-optimal variables. R-squared is simply a measure of the variance that can be accounted for by the model.
- **Mallow's Cp**: It adjusts RSS by adding a penalty that increases proportionately to the number of predictors. A better model is the one with the lowest Cp.
- **Others**: These include Structured Risk Minimization and Minimum Description Length.

Resampling methods

Resampling is picking up multiple samples from the training data and fine-tuning the model on every sample. Usually, this is done by splitting the training dataset into many training and testing subset samples and fitting the data on the training subset while evaluating it on the test subset.

- **Cross-validation**: Cross-validation (CV) is an effective, and simple-to-deploy technique where the smallest cross-validation error estimate is calculated for the generated models. The test error in CV for classification is estimated from the number of misclassified observations. Cross-validation attempts to fix the shortcomings of a validation set strategy in which the available data is randomly divided into a training set and a validation set of equal size. The training data set is used to fit the model. The data from the validation set tests the resulting model by getting the test error. The drawback of the technique is that it may have a variable test error rate depending on the data distribution in the training and validation sets. If the training set has more observations than a test set, it may create a less-than-optimal model. CV is used to evaluate the performance of a model by estimating its test error. Two common techniques are Leave-One-Out Cross Validation and k-Fold Cross Validation
  - **Leave-One-Out Cross-Validation (LOOCV)**: LOOCV can be used with most learning methods like Logistic Regression or LDA. In this approach, the validation set consists of just one observation from the data set, and the rest are put into the training set. This is like k-fold cross-validation if k=1. This process is repeated by selecting a different observation into the validation set on every iteration. The test error estimates the average of MSEs over all the iterations. Statistical techniques can significantly reduce the computation required for the LOOCV method. LOOCV has a lower bias than the validation set approach or k-fold CV as it does not overestimate the test error rate, but compared to the k-fold CV, LOOCV has a higher variance.
  - **k-Fold Cross-validation**: In this approach, the observations are randomly split into 'k' equal-size groups or sets, where k is usually 5 or 10. One set is labeled as a validation set, while the others are labeled as training sets. The MSE is estimated on the observations which are in the validation set. The process is iterated over all the k groups. The k-fold CV estimate is the average of MSEs of all the k groups.
- **Bootstrap**: Bootstrap is a technique to computationally create new sample sets from the original data and estimate the variability of these samples. Data sets are generated through multiple sampling techniques. Bootstrap is applicable to many learning techniques and helps with the accuracy of a parameter estimate of a model.

Model fitting

Model fitting is a process to measure how well any machine learning algorithm performs on a data set that is similar to the data used to train the algorithm. The goal of model fitting is to reduce variance. Other techniques for model fitting include shrinkage and subset selection. A mathematical function is created to explain the observations or collected data. An algorithm that under fits does not match the training data as closely as necessary, while the algorithm that overfits matches the data used for training quite well and may not generalize to real-world data or a new set of data. Various techniques are used for model fitting. Dimension reduction is used to reduce the number of input variables using techniques like Principal Component Analysis, Singular Value Decomposition, Linear Discriminant Analysis, etc. The least squares approach for model fitting is based on finding predictor coefficients that minimize the RSS.

Subset selection

Subset selection selects a smaller number of variables and has three main types – best subset selection, stepwise selection, and dimension reduction. These are discussed in detail below:

- **Best subset selection**: In this approach, various subsets of the predictor variables are used to generate models, and then the best model is selected from this shortlisted group. The least squares regression is checked for all combinations of predictor variables, and the model with the smallest RSS and largest R-squared value from each subset is identified. Subsequently, the best model from these is selected using adjusted R-squared, Cross Validated prediction error, or other probabilistic model scoring techniques. The downside of the approach is that as the number of predictors increases, the number of models increases exponentially.
- **Stepwise selection**: There are three common types of stepwise selection methods
    - **Forward stepwise selection**: This approach is more efficient than the best subset selection as it starts with a model with no predictors. It adds one predictor at every step if it improves the model by having the lowest Residual Sum of Squares or the largest R-squared. Once all the models have been created, one of them is selected using model scoring techniques.
    - **Backward stepwise selection**: This approach starts with the least squares model having all the predictors included. At every step, one predictor contributing the least to the model is removed. The model with the lowest Residual Sum of Squares or the largest R-squared is shortlisted. In the final step, the top-performing model is selected using error detection or model scoring techniques (Gareth J et al., 2013).
    - **Mixed approach**: The mixed approach adds variables like forward selection but also removes any variable at every step that does not contribute to the model fit.

Shrinkage methods

Shrinkage methods fit the model by shrinking the estimated coefficients to small values as close as zero. Model is fit using many techniques, commonly least squares to a model (linear, logistic, etc.) with fewer predictors. The two techniques used for shrinkage are Ridge Regression and Lasso.

Dimension reduction

In this approach, the predictor variables are transformed and then the models based on transformed variables are fit using least squares approach.

- **Principal Components Analysis (PCA)**: The principal components are generated from standardized predictors, which capture the most variation in the data. Statistically, principal components are vectors or directions of variability in the data set. So, for example, the first principal component indicates the vector in which the observations have the most variability. These principal components are then incorporated as predictors in the algorithm, typically by linear regression, and are subsequently fit using the least squares approach. The regression variation increases along with an increase in the number of principal components; however, the bias decreases. If a few predictors account for most of the variation, then PCA produces good results. PCA is discussed in more detail in the unsupervised learning section.

- **Partial Least Squares**: Partial Least Squares (PLS) generates a smaller set of new variables or features from the original predictors using a supervised approach instead of an unsupervised one, as in PCA. These new features are then used to fit the linear model, where by using a supervised approach, the new features consider both predictors and responses.

Improving predictions

Many machine-learning techniques are used to improve the accuracy of predictions. These can be applied to both regression as well as classification methods. Some of the common ones are:

Bagging

Bagging is a variance-reduction technique based on bootstrapping. It does this by generating multiple samples from training data. In the case of regression, the model is trained by fitting a decision tree on each bootstrapped sample. Finally, the predictions which are generated are averaged. This technique can reduce both bias and variance. However, it is harder to interpret. In the case of classification, the most frequently predicted class in every tree is taken for every observation, and then the overall most frequently predicted class is selected. Test error is calculated by finding the MSE or classification error of the set of observations that are not used to find the fit of the tree.

Boosting

Boosting is similar to bagging but does not use the bootstrapping technique. Every tree is created by including the information from the previous trees. Boosting fits a decision tree to the model residuals instead of the outcome. The tree which is obtained is then incorporated into the function. The parameters used to tune the function include the number of trees, the number of tree splits, and the shrinkage parameter.

Random forest

This technique is like bagging in that bootstrapping generates samples from the training set. However, when creating a split in the trees, a random subset of predictor variables is used for the split. This approach reduces the effect of any strong predictor in the predictor set, which may influence all the downstream trees if it is part of the initial branch, and this process is called de-correlation. This approach is also helpful if the predictor variables are reasonably correlated in a set. Their drawback is that they are challenging to interpret.

Causality

The models built for prediction are not created to understand the causality behind the features. It is well known that correlation does not imply causation. A correlation between two variables is insufficient to prove causation, and additional validation is necessary. If we want to understand whether particular behavior leads to a specific outcome, then we need to be able to find the cause and effect. Such analysis helps assess the effect of treatment on health outcomes or understanding the effect of drugs in controlling infection. It can also help answer questions about medication non-compliance, the efficacy of public health interventions, and promoting healthy behaviors. 'Causal inference' can help with making these assessments. Specialized techniques are used to assess for causality.

- **Randomized Controlled Trials (RCT)**: The best way to check for causality is through randomized experiments such as Randomized Controlled Trials. In these experiments, subjects are randomly assigned to a treatment group that gets the intervention and a control group that does not. The outcome is measured between both groups. During the design of the experiment and setting up of groups, an attempt is made to make the groups as identical as possible and remove confounders to make the statistical analysis valid. In the case of clinical trials, 'clinical equipoise' is the uncertainty among the clinical investigators about which intervention group is better. If it is discovered that one group is better than the other, then it is the ethical responsibility to offer that treatment to everyone. Conversely, providing an intervention that is harmful to the subjects is unethical. The drawbacks of RCTs are that they are expensive, complicated to manage, and sometimes infeasible.
- **A/B Testing**: This is widely used in software and web development to divide the users into two groups, present two different product options to each, and measure the impact. Software product managers use this approach to test which version of the website, product, or prototype the people prefer.
- **Observational Studies**: These are undertaken to understand cause and effect in situations where it is not possible to do controlled experiments. These are the most common type of studies as they are relatively easier to perform. In observational studies, we only have access to the data from the intervention arm. The assignment of intervention in observation studies is not random. For example, if 1000 subjects were in an intervention - like taking a drug or being exposed to a chemical. Say 10 percent of them developed an outcome - they got cured of the disease or developed a side effect. Since we did not have a control arm, we wanted to see what would have been the rate of outcome if they were not on a drug or exposed to a chemical. We use a technique called 'Propensity Score Matching' (PSM) in which a synthetic control group mimics a randomized experiment. 'Propensity score' is the probability of a subject being assigned to a particular intervention group given the observed covariates. The synthetic control group comprises subjects considered similar to the intervention group. With PSM, we can mitigate the effects of treatment assignment bias and do pseudo-randomization by generating a sample of subjects that received the intervention, which is similar on all covariates to a sample of subjects that did not receive the intervention. PSM is used when we want to study a causal connection due to the conditions of the outcome where there are not many subjects in the non-intervention group comparable to the intervention group, and selecting the control groups is difficult due to the complexity of matching the characteristics. For example, to study the effects of smoking, we may do an observational study on subjects already smoking and find subjects in the control group who match the subjects in the smoking group. This type of study is required as we cannot create an experiment in which we select a subject population and randomly assign them to a smoking and non-smoking group (we cannot ask subjects to start smoking). For analysis, we use logistic regression to develop a model to find the probability of every subject's chance of getting the intervention. The

outcome or dependent variable is whether a subject participated or not in the observation study. We select the possible confounders and get an estimate of the propensity score. Then we verify that the propensity score and covariates are balanced across the intervention and the control groups. Every subject in the intervention group is matched to one or more subjects in the control group on propensity scores using techniques like k-nearest neighbors, caliper matching, or stratification matching. The covariates are compared across the intervention and the comparison groups in the matched sample. Finally, multivariate analysis is performed to arrive at the result.

Guidelines for developing models

This chapter covered major concepts of machine learning at a relatively high level. Readers are recommended to consult a specialized textbook on machine learning to get more information and practice applying the algorithms to actual or sample data.

To build effective models, one needs to understand the data well, analyze the model output, perform a feasibility check, and retry as many model iterations as possible. A good analysis is independent of choosing the best computing hardware statistical package or the most complex model. It is based on a clear problem statement, clean data, readable code, the suitable model for the problem, and the data set.

In most scenarios, a simple model is better than a complex model. Simple models are easier to create and interpret. Most of the time, simple models provide acceptable accuracy, and using additional complex models may only increase the accuracy by a few percentage points. It may not be worth the extra effort and difficulty in interpretation. It is worthwhile to try multiple algorithms before selecting one. For many situations, ensemble models work well.

It is also essential to develop an understanding of probability. Many good books and online courses cover the statistical concepts required for basic healthcare analytics. Probability is the statistical representation of natural and physical processes. For example, the height distribution in the population helps us answer the question – if we randomly pick a person from a population, what is the chance of finding someone over 6 feet in height? The associated concepts are the 'mean' and the 'median' of the population, which gives us the centeredness of the population, 'standard deviation,' which gives us the spread or distribution of the population. There are many named probability distributions, but the common ones are normal distribution, t distribution, and exponential distribution. More details can be studied in a book on statistics.

The data scientists should study the data before feeding it into the algorithm. It is helpful to have someone with knowledge of the domain on the team to validate the addition and removal of features. It is also vital to identify biases, gaps, and correlations. The model creation and validation should be an ongoing process. The output should be monitored periodically to improve the model over time.

16 ARTIFICIAL INTELLIGENCE FOR HEALTHCARE ADMINISTRATION

Introduction

Our understanding of intelligence is evolving. Human intelligence is unique due to the speed of complex computations, short-term memory, and the ability to form accurate and retrievable long-term memories (Jensen AR. 1998). "Artificial intelligence is the science and engineering of making intelligent machines, especially intelligent computer programs. Intelligence is the computational part of the ability to achieve goals in the world" (McCarthy J., 2007). In the case of artificial intelligence, some unique traits which have been proposed are:

- **Logical condition intelligence**: The software assesses all options and takes an action based on the most appropriate to achieve the end goal.
- **Search**: The software examines large number of possibilities.
- **Pattern recognition**: Software program tries to match the new observations with a pattern.
- **Inference**: The software can infer some facts after a selection of facts is presented to it. This includes ordinary logical reasoning.
- **Representation**: Software represents the facts about the world.
- **Common sense knowledge and reasoning**: currently, the software available are limited in their ability to achieve this.
- **Learning from experience**: Software based neural nets are able to learn from previous experience. The goal of artificial general intelligence is to expand on this capability.
- **Planning**: Software programs develop a strategy to achieve a goal based on given set of general facts, details about specific situation and description of the goal.

As per analysis by Accenture, the market opportunity for AI in healthcare will be $150Bn by 2026 with the market value of individual categories (Accenture. Artificial Intelligence)

- Administrative Workflow Assistance: $18Bn
- Automated Image Diagnosis: $3Bn
- Clinical Trial Participant Identifier: $13Bn
- Connected Machines: $14Bn
- Cybersecurity: $2Bn

- Dosage Error Reduction: $16Bn
- Fraud Detection: $17Bn
- Preliminary Diagnosis: $5Bn
- Robotic Assisted Surgery: $40Bn
- Virtual Nursing Assistants: $20Bn

The process of generating machine learning algorithms has been discussed in the previous chapter, but at a high level, machine learning-based model development can be divided into three parts: 1) Preparation, 2) Training, and 3) Evaluation. In the preparation phase, the task is defined in which the inputs and outputs are identified (Rajkomar A et al., 2019). The input variables are called features, and the output values are called labels. Then, a raw data set containing both the variables assumed to influence the output and the output values themselves is collected. This data is cleaned and validated to ensure it contains all the variables needed to create the model. This step is usually performed by domain experts with some background knowledge. However, in many cases, scientists without domain expertise can also run this step by using all the available variables. The observations or data are split into two sets – one for training used to create a model and the second for testing used to test the model. The features are then run through the machine learning algorithm with a matched output value, and the algorithm fine-tunes its parameters till it comes up with an equation that maximizes the probability of predicting the correct output given inputs similar to the ones in the training set. In the third step, model evaluation, the data from the test set is run through the model to create predictions that are compared with the actual results. The second and third steps are run repeatedly till the evaluation step produces results to the data scientist's satisfaction.

In this chapter, we will discuss applications of machine learning in healthcare. Currently, most applications in healthcare are for quality improvement, operational efficiency, clinical support, etc. Specific applications in clinical decision-making for medical and surgical specialties are discussed in the next chapter.

It is important to remember that new predictive models are being developed daily for healthcare applications, and their accuracy is improving. The newer algorithms are building on the learnings from previous research, collecting better data, and using more sophisticated algorithms to push the accuracy bar higher. The discussion in this and the following chapter provides illustrative cases for the type of problems machine learning is solving and the types of algorithms used to address those problems.

The general considerations for machine learning model selection also apply to healthcare data. In general, simpler models are preferred over more complicated ones as simpler models can explain significant amount of variation in most use cases. Simpler models are also easier to understand, explain, modify, and deploy with less computational and human resource needs. If the number of predictor variables is smaller, a simple regression model can be used to predict, for example, nurse staffing needs, the need for rapid response activation in the hospital, etc. Simpler models are also relatively easy to integrate into clinical guidelines as well as point-of-care calculators. Many such predictor models are widely used in clinical settings, for example, the Acute Physiologic and Chronic Health Evaluation (APACHE) score to estimate mortality, Atherosclerotic Cardiovascular Disease (ASCVD) risk calculator to estimate the risk of atherosclerotic cardiovascular disease over the next 10 years, HAS-BLED score for bleeding risk in patients with Atrial Fibrillation, etc.

If the data has a lot of noise and it is difficult to get clean, structured data, a complicated model can filter through the noise and provide more accurate predictions. For situations requiring multiple predictor models with complex interrelationships in scenarios like image recognition on pathology slides, CT scans, or invasions, more complicated models, including deep learning models, may be required. Complicated models have the disadvantage of being unable to be explained easily to clinicians. These 'black box algorithms' may work in image recognition but are a challenge in clinical predictions. Clinicians want to be able to explain why they chose a particular diagnostic or therapeutic option. In cases of adverse events, it may not be possible to reverse engineer why a particular prediction based on deep learning was followed, creating challenges in medical-legal cases.

Increasingly, organizations are developing proprietary predictive models for clinical scenarios, the details of which are not shared with clinicians or the general public. The developers of these models may not publish the underlying data, features, and coefficients in the model, making it very hard to reproduce and validate by third parties. There is a risk that, over time, medical decision-making may become expensive if it is based on subscription-based predictive models leading to further increases in the cost of healthcare.

Health data collection and preparation

The use of electronic health records has benefits and challenges as the data source for analytics (Goldstein BA et al., 2017). The data is available in multiple formats, including structured and unstructured data, multiple predictor variables, objective data like lab values and vital signs, and subjective interpretations, including pain levels and symptoms.

A significant proportion of the time spent on an analytics project is spent on data cleaning, merging, and customizing. According to a survey, 60% of the effort of data scientists is spent on cleaning and organizing data. About 20% of the time is spent collecting data sets (Press G., 2016). Techniques have been developed to quickly deploy machine learning models on raw EHR data to be used at multiple institutions without much local data preprocessing. This involves automatically extracting the entire EHR, including unstructured data with free text and structured data, into a standardized format and deploying predictive models about clinical outcomes, clinical quality of care, resource utilization, and patient characteristics.

Predictive models with high false positive and false-negative predictions quickly lose acceptance within the provider community. False positive outcomes may create unnecessary alerts and alarms, and false-negative outcomes may cause patient harm (Drew BJ et al., 2014; Chopra V et al., 2014; Kaukonen KM et al., 2015).

The Electronic Health Records (EHR) data is recorded inconsistently with different formats. In many cases, biases like ascertainment bias (Newton KM et al., 2013) can reduce variation between EHRs deployed at multiple sites. According to an analysis in 2017, most predictive analytics models created using EHR data have typically used data sets from one health system, are created using simple algorithms, and have used less than 30 variables (Goldstein BA et al., 2017). Attempts are ongoing to make semantic conversion easier to integrate

EHRs from heterogeneous sources. (Sum H et al., 2015). EHRs provide an opportunity for patient stratification, patient phenotype-genotype assessment, and discovering disease correlations

(Jensen PB et al., 2012). Researchers are applying unsupervised deep learning methods to EHR data to automatically identify patterns and dependencies and create a general-purpose patient representation for clinical predictive modeling classifiers and other predictors (Miotto R et al. 2016). In a study by Miotto et al, a deep neural network with a stack of denoising autoencoders created patient representations from the EHR using inference. To minimize variance, the values of the features in the data set were normalized between zero and one. The layers of autoencoders and sigmoid activation functions were used with 500 hidden units per layer. Five hundred features represented each patient in the data set. Additional techniques with similar complexity were used for comparison - Gaussian mixture model (using 200 mixtures and full covariance matrix), k-means clustering (using 500 clusters), principal component analysis (using 100 principal components), and 100 principal components in independent component analysis. A random forest classifier was trained for each disease using a data set of 200,000 patients to predict the probability of a patient developing a disease. This approach achieved an average AUC – ROC of 0.773 and outperformed other approaches. It also achieved an AUC-ROC of 0.907 for diabetes mellitus with complications and was used on multiple other diseases. Such an approach can create personalized treatment recommendations and clinical trial recruitment.

In another study, researchers deployed a deep learning approach on the entire raw EHR dataset to create a structured FHIR-compatible dataset. This was subsequently used on multiple predictive scenarios within the hospital. In this analysis, electronic health record data of over 200,000 patients were used to predict inpatient mortality 24 hours after admission with an AUC of 0.95, readmissions within 30 days with an AUC at discharge of 0.77, and long length of stay 24 hours after admission with an AUC of 0.86, inferring discharge diagnoses at admission, 24 hours after hospitalization and time of discharge with weighted AUC 0.87 (Rajkomar A, 2018).

Compliance

Machine learning models have been developed to assess compliance with clinical recommendations, healthcare regulations, and guidelines. In one project, analytics was used to predict medication adherence in elderly patients with chronic diseases. This approach compared logistic regression with a support vector machine. In this scenario, support vector machines had much higher accuracy and 97.3% compared to 71.1% or logistic regression (Lee SK et al., 2013).

Hand hygiene has been one of the common compliance requirements from the medical staff. Hand hygiene is essential for reducing hospital-acquired infections. To assess compliance with hand hygiene, researchers have used computer vision and image recognition to monitor healthcare staff behavior. Multiple image recognition architectures like AlexNet, VGG-16, and ResNet-152 have been used for image recognition research and in commercial products. In one project, researchers used images that provided a de-identified 3D data set. Training data was generated by hand annotating images and videos of hand-hygiene and non-hand-hygiene events. 150,400 images were used to generate the classifier with an 80% - 20% training-test split. The system detected persons and recognized tracking activity of using a hand sanitizer. The algorithm's accuracy was 75% compared to proximity algorithms which had 18%, and covert observation by 3 people at 72%. For the classification of hand hygiene activity, ResNet-152 achieved an accuracy of 95.5%, precision of 95.3%, sensitivity of 96.7%, and specificity of 94.5% when using depth, foreground, and pose inputs and using a spatial transformer network (Haque A et al., 2017).

Diagnosis and therapy selection

Machine learning models for automated diagnosis based on symptoms, vital signs, and other data like laboratory tests or radiology information have been commercially launched. A few illustrative examples of different approaches that have been taken are discussed below.

Machine learning has been applied to diabetes for disease diagnosis using binary classification and prediction models, including decision trees (Varma KVSRP et al., 2014), ensemble methods (Zhu J et al., 2015; Patil BM et al., 2010), feed-forward neural networks (Park J et al., 2001; Wang C et al., 2013), and support vector machines (Barakat N et al. 2010). It has also been used for treatment efficacy prediction with binary classification using decision trees (Huang Y et al., 2007), k-nearest neighbors, Naive Bayes, SVM (Kang S et al., 2015), as well as multi-class classification using ensemble methods (Kang S et al. 2017). Recurrent neural networks are increasingly used to guide clinical decision support for therapy selection. In patients with type 2 diabetes mellitus, sequential modeling using sequential dependencies was undertaken at the patient level to find the efficacy of prescriptions and help with clinical decision support. Recurrent neural networks based on a sequence of previous prescription records were used to develop prediction models. The baseline model was implemented with Feed-forward neural network (FNN) and a new model with RNN (Kang S et al. 2018). In the RNN, a hidden layer with sigmoid activation functions and LSTM having 100 hidden units was used, followed by a dropout layer with a dropout rate of 0.5. The output unit used a linear function for regression and a sigmoid function for classification. The loss function during backpropagation was mean squared error for regression and binary cross-entropy for classification analysis. The networks were implemented on Tensorflow. RNN outperformed in regression with an RMSE value of 0.652 compared to 0.624 and in classification with AUC 86.67 compared to 84.94. In a research project, Long Short-Term Memory (LSTM) hidden units-based recurrent neural network was trained to classify 128 diagnoses using 13 clinical measurements. The model achieved an AUC of 0.9966, F1 of 0.8571, precision of 1.0000, and recall of 0.7500 on diabetes mellitus for ketoacidosis. The model was also used on 300 other diagnoses; however, the results could have been more impressive (Lipton ZC et al., 2015).

The healthy baseline state varies amongst individuals, and the trajectory and speed of change in a disease stage are unique for everyone. A deep convolutional machine learning technique was used on lab data to detect early temporal disease signatures. The research group created a prediction model based on a multi-resolution convolution network and an imputation model based on the differentiable formulation of non-parametric density estimation. The model created AUC for each disease on convolution vs. multi-layered perceptron vs. logistic regression using 18 lab tests for 3 years. The highest AUC was 0.933 for Supervised Other normal pregnancy (ICD V22.1), 0.899 for irregular menstruation (ICD 626.4), 0.888 for Anemia in chronic disease (ICD 285.21), and 0.876 for chronic kidney disease not otherwise specified (ICD 585.9) (Razavian N et al., 2015). In similar research by the same team, Long Short Term Memory RNN was trained for multi-task prediction of disease onset on lab test data obtained from claims for 133 conditions (Razavian N et al., 2016).

One of the benefits of automated machine learning algorithms is the possibility of embedding these algorithms directly into the electronic medical record system to link medical concepts. These can provide inputs to physicians as well as patients through symptom checkers. In a project, an automated process was developed to link the disease with symptoms based on the knowledge extracted from electronic medical records using logistic regression, a naïve Bayes classifier, and a Bayesian network using noisy OR gates. Knowledge graphs were constructed, compared, and validated against opinions from physicians and knowledge graphs from Google. The noisy OR model produced a precision of 0.85 for a recall of 0.6 (Rotmensch M et al., 2017). Using similar approaches, clinical decision tools can be made more robust.

Disease progression

Tracking the progression of chronic diseases, especially those that evolve over a long period, have complex pathophysiology, and present with heterogeneous signs and symptoms, is a challenging problem. The predictive modeling of disease progression with computational methods is used in preventive medicine, drug development, and clinical guidelines. Disease progression research has been done for diseases ranging from Alzheimer's (Ito K et al., 2010) to coronary atherosclerosis (Exarchos K et al., 2013). Disease progression models encounter the limitations of heterogeneous covariate progression trajectories, incomplete medical records, heterogeneous intervals for discrete observations, and difficulties in longitudinal data collection (Kwon BC et al., 2021). In order to address some of these challenges, an unsupervised disease progression model was demonstrated using a three-layer model consisting of Markov jump process, Markov chains, and noisy-OR network. This model was applied to chronic obstructive pulmonary disease and was used to discover medically meaningful comorbidities in COPD patients (Wang X et al., 2014).

An end-to-end deep dynamic memory neural network, DeepCare, was developed, which extracted data from medical records, stored existing and previous illness history, and made predictions about future outcomes (Pham T et al. 2017). The algorithm was created on Long Short Term Memory (LSTM), a recurrent neural network that stores past experiences. The input to the model were a sequence of diagnosis, interventions, admission types, time lapse. The outputs were the diagnoses at discharge, interventions during the current admission, and readmission risk. The model was not based on manual feature engineering. The diagnoses were aggregated through a time-decayed multiscale pooling strategy. Finally, the neural network analyzed the pooled diagnoses to generate future prognoses. The model was used on a cohort of diabetes patients representing over 7000 individuals, over 53000 admissions, 243 diagnoses, 773 procedures, and 353 medication codes. The mental health cohort contained over 6000 patients and over 52000 admissions with 247 diagnoses, 752 procedures, and 319 medication codes. For intervention recommendation, the model showed 78.7 percent precision for the diabetes cohort and 71% for the mental health cohort. The model had an F-score of 79% for predicting future risk for unplanned readmission.

Cardiovascular disease is the leading cause of morbidity and mortality. Several simplistic risk assessment tools are available to the clinicians. A machine learning approach was used to understand relationships between predictor variables to improve the detection of at-risk individuals. 10-year anonymized data from clinical practice research datalink was used for this analysis. Eight established variables were supplemented with additional 22 variables, considered as potential risk factors. 75 - 25 split between training and validation cohort was used. Logistic regression, gradient boosting, random forests, and neural networks, were used for analysis. All of these individuals were free from cardiovascular disease at baseline. Over the 10-year follow-up. Over 370,000 patients were included in the analysis. There were 24,970 incidents of cardiovascular disease. New risk factors not listed earlier in this prediction tool were identified, including COPD, severe mental illness, oral corticosteroid prescriptions, and triglyceride levels. The AHA/ACC baseline model had a sensitivity of 62.7%, and the poster's predictive value of 70.1% random forests algorithm had a sensitivity of 65.3% with a positive value of 17.8%. Logistic regression had a sensitivity of 67.1% and a positive predictive value of 18.3%. Gradient boosting machines and neural networks had a sensitivity of 67.5% and a positive predictive value of 18.4% (Weng SF et al., 2017).

In another project, recurrent neural networks were used to predict an initial diagnosis of heart failure in time-stamped data from EHR. Over the 12-month observation window, AUC of 0.777 was achieved, which was better than 0.747 for logistic regression, 0.765 for multilayer perceptron, 0.743 for SVM, and 0.73 for K-nearest neighbors. RNN AUC over the 18-month window was 0.883. Similar models have been developed using LSTM (Maragatham G et al., 2019). The superiority of RNN for predicting the future diagnosis of heart failure has been replicated in other studies (Chen R et al., 2019).

Telemedicine approaches are combined with predictive analytics tools for earlier diagnosis, more targeted interventions, and effective monitoring. A supervised machine learning model was used to predict the probability of developing PTSD after trauma based on the symptoms displayed between 10 and 20 days post-trauma. Multiple machine learning binary classifiers, including logistics regression, naïve Bayes, support vector machines, random forests, and ensemble methods, including hard voting and weighted average probabilities, were used. Subsequently, feature reduction was used. Scoring was performed based on the holdout method and k-fold cross-validation. SVM outperformed other single classifiers, and performance was noted to be improved with feature reduction. The ensemble method had better performance compared to the single classifier methods (Wshah S et al., 2019).

In another project, longitudinal laboratory test data was used to predict Diabetes onset using LSTM, RNN, and CNN for 133 conditions based on 18 lab tests. An ensemble of neural networks performed the best compared to logistic regression, CNN, and LSTM. The ensemble model's AUC for End stage renal disease was 0.920, Anemia of chronic disease 0.879, and Diabetes Mellitus Type I without complications 0.829 (Razavian N et al., 2016).

EMR data was used in deep learning to identify patients who will most benefit from palliative care interventions. The algorithm predicted the mortality of a patient in the next 12 months. Supervised learning techniques were used on data obtained from the clinical data warehouse of a tertiary care hospital spanning years from 1995 to 2014. Over 177,000 records were used for training, 22,139 for validation, and 22,134 for testing. A deep neural network was used with an input layer of 13,654 dimensions and 18 hidden layers, each with 512 dimensions and a scalar output layer. The Scaled Exponential Linear Unit (SeLU) activation function was used at each layer, along with the Logistic Loss function at the output layer. Adam optimizer was used with a batch size of 128 examples. The algorithm was implemented using the PyTorch framework and scikit-learn library (Avati A et al., 2018). Area Under Precision-Recall Curve was used for model selection. AP score was 0.69, and recall was 0.34 at 0.9 precision. AUROC obtained was 0.93.

Documentation

Context-aware voice recognition algorithms can transcribe a physician's dictation and convert it into structured data or execute commands such as placing orders or lab tests. Similarly, medical chatbots are being used for the triage of patients and reduce the load on the nurse triage lines while at the same time gathering more detailed information than what is possible through the short call with the nurse. In a study, a semi-supervised learning method using a recurrent neural network was used to improve clinical documentation (Kannan et al., 2018). The method was tested on clinical documentation tasks that required locating and classifying symptoms in a doctor-patient conversation. This model was based on a single-layer bidirectional LSTM with 512 hidden notes.

Natural language processing (NLP) is increasingly being used to parse free text in doctors' notes. Increasingly, these products are being made available in commercial programs. In a project, NLP was used to identify cancer patients receiving palliative gastrostomy and assess documentation of end-of-life process measures in EHR. Regular expressions were used to identify the procedure and process measures by using ClinicalRegex software which looks for keywords or phrases in clinical notes. The NLP keyword library was used to find the instances of documentation at specific periods. The library included the following words for limited resuscitation status: "dnr, dnrdni, dni, do not resuscitate, do-not-resuscitate, do not intubate, do-not-intubate, chest compressions, no defibrillation, no endotracheal intubation, no mechanical intubation, shocks, cmo, comfort measures; full code status: full code confirmed, full code d/w, full code discussed, full code verified, would like to be full code, wishes to be full code, would like to remain full code, wishes to remain full code, wish to be full code, remaining full code, full code; goals of care discussions: Goals of care, goc, goals for care, goals of treatment, goals for treatment, treatment goals, family meeting, family discussion, family discussions, debility/ goals of care, goc/coping, patient goals." The natural language processing algorithm found patients with 95.8% sensitivity and 97.4% specificity, with over 85.7% sensitivity and 96.7% specificity for end-of-life measures (Lindvall C et al., 2019).

Another research project demonstrated the advantages of using unstructured free text, vital signs, and demographic data to predict the presence of sepsis. This study divided over 200,000 patient visits into training, validation, and test data sets. The free text was represented by a bag of words model and a topic model. The free text was initially preprocessed using bigram and negation detection. Then the prediction model was built using a linear support vector machine. L2-regularized logistic regression, naïve Bayes, and random forest models were developed for comparison purposes. Four models were trained - most models included vital signs and demographic variables, the second model had chief complaints along with vital signs, the turn model had a chief complaint in nursing assessment along with vitals, and the fourth model had a set of clinical conditions or 'topics' inferred from the patient's dataset was included along with vitals. The project demonstrated that with the addition of free text, the AUC increased from 0.67 to 0.86 to identify sepsis in emergency departments. There was no significant difference between the bag of words and topic-based models (Horng S et al., 2017).

Length of stay

Reducing inpatient length of stay is one of the most common quality improvement programs at a hospital. Increased length of stay incurs more cost for the hospital, requires more staffing, and exposes patients to hospital-acquired infections. Using diverse approaches, machine learning approaches have been used to develop models to predict the length of stay. A systematic review studied 74 studies predicting the length of stay in patients admitted to the hospitals. These studies were conducted from 1972 to 2019. 64.9% of the studies used regression, 20.3% used other machine learning approaches, and 17.6% used deep learning with machine learning and deep learning approaches more common from 2010 onwards. The regression models used were linear regression, logistic regression, lasso regression, ridge regression, and binomial regression. One study used linear discriminant analysis. The mixed model and survival model were used by three studies each. Machine learning approaches included decision trees, support vector machines, fuzzy art maps, random forests, bagged regression trees, restricted cubic splines, piece-wise exponential models, ensemble learning, Bayesian networks, and Markov models (Lequertier V et al., 2021). The studies used different measures to assess performance. R2 was used in about half the studies with a median value of 0.31; the rest of the studies, which considered the length of stay as a continuous variable, were equally divided between measuring mean square error (median 0.37) and mean absolute error (median 4.68). The studies which considered the length of stay as categorical had median accuracy of 0.8, AUC median of 0.8, and sensitivity median of 0.82.

Researchers have also used machine learning for length-of-stay predictions for specific subsets of patients or clinical diagnoses. Researchers developed prediction models to predict the length of stay of cardiac patients. They used decision trees, neural networks, support vector machines, and ensemble algorithms. The support vector machine had the best accuracy of 96.4% and the best specificity at 97.3%. The ensemble algorithm had the best performance, with a sensitivity of 98.2%. The support vector machine also extracted the most important factors influencing the length of stay with an accuracy of 99.1%. These included drugs, previous diagnoses of coronary artery disease, most recent ejection fraction, sex of the patient, family history, smoking history, comorbidities, and type of insurance (Hachesu PR et al., 2013).

Triana et al. used random forests and artificial neural networks to predict the length of stay of coronary artery bypass graft patients (Triana et al., 2021). In a scoping review of predictive models to predict the length of stay for pediatric patients, the machine learning approaches were diverse for preprocessing, variable selection, and cross-validation. The performance metrics used included R2, which ranged from 0.04 to 0.9415, Root Mean Square Error (RMSE) with values from 0.296 to 18.8 days, and Mean Absolute Error (MAE) with values ranging from 2.5 to 14.6 days (Medeiros et al., 2021).

Nutrition

Machine learning approaches are being used in image recognition of food products for matching nutritional needs based on individual phenotypes, energy expenditure, or early detection of nutritional allergies and specific food products. Multiple research groups have tried to identify food from pictures, present its properties, and provide nutritional advice (Subhi MA et al., 2019). Food image datasets consisting of up to 100,000 images are available. Various food segmentation approaches have been used in research and commercial applications. These include spatial relationship, semantic texton forest, bounding box using CNN with GrabCut segmentation, and DeepLab model. Food-specific feature description approaches include Local Binary Patterns, Gabor filter, color information, and Scale Invariant Feature Transform. Classification approaches have included Support Vector Machines and K-Nearest neighbors. Deep learning classification algorithms that have been used include Food-101, GoogleNet, Inception V3, DeepFood, Ensemble Net, Arch-D, VGG, and DCNN. Volume estimation approaches have included 3D reconstruction, stereo analysis, depth estimation, and predefined food container volume analysis.

Outcomes

Predicting the deterioration of clinical conditions of hospitalized patients can help in reducing inpatient mortality. Early signals of patient deterioration can lead to timely life-saving interventions, reduce rapid response and code blue alerts, and keep patients out of the ICU. There are multiple early warning system algorithms that have been developed. In one example, a discrete-time logistic regression model was developed on a data set of over 370,000 patients. A risk score was developed, which included physiological data, health service indicators, care directives, neurological status, severity of illness, and comorbidity indices (Kipnis P et al. 2016). This algorithm had an AUC of 0.82 compared to 0.79 for electronic Cardiac Arrest Risk Triage (eCART) and 0.76 for National Early Warning Score (NEWS).

Risk assessment scores have been developed for a wide variety of clinical complications. For example, more than 40 risk assessment scales have been developed for predicting pressure ulcers (Nixon J et al. 2001). Schoonhoven et al. identified independent predictors for the development of pressure ulcers in hospitalized patients using logistic regression analysis and bootstrapping techniques with an AUC of 0.7 and predictors including age, weight at admission, abnormal appearance of the skin, friction and sheer, and planned surgery in the coming weeks (Schoonhoven L et al. 2006). Another research team used logistic regression with a random under-sampling model with predictors of gender, age, surgical duration, and on-admission total Nursing Needs Score with an AUC of 0.84 (Nakamura Y et al. 2015).

Models have been developed targeting morbidity and mortality risk associated with a specific medical condition. Heart failure is one of the most common reasons for inpatient hospitalization. Seven machine learning algorithms were compared, out of which Laboratory-Based Acute Physiology Score (LAPS2) and Premier model with administrative data outperformed the clinical models with a 95% CI of 0.79-0.83 (Lagu et al., 2016). Most algorithms used variations of generalized estimating equation (GEE) logistic regression models, and one used the classification and regression tree (CART) method to develop a decision tree. A Gated Recurrent Unit (GRU) based model developed by Che et al could make mortality predictions in real time on MIMIC-III time series data with an AUC of 0.70 (Che Z et al., 2016).

In another study, a recurrent neural network-based model was created with data extracted from 12,000 patients admitted to pediatric ICU to predict mortality risk based on real-time EMR data integrated into the dynamic model. It dynamically ingested over 300 variables. The results were compared with PIM2 and PRISM3 models available in the EMR and logistic regression and multi-level perceptron-based models. The RNN-based model achieved an AUC of 93.4%, which was better than all other models. The multi-level perceptron was developed on static data and had an AUC of 88% (Aczon M et al. 2017). This research also demonstrated the importance of temporal data.

Patient characterization

Developing models on raw clinical data is hampered by resource requirement of labeling. Halpern et al develop a methodology to estimate a patient's clinical state based on unlabeled data in electronic medical record. Instead of using labeled data which is labor-intensive to obtain, the researchers created machine learning models on large quantities of unlabeled data. They used domain experts to identify anchor variables which are assumed to stay stable between institutions. These are then used to assist in the unsupervised learning technique. In this process the data from clinical databases his first mapped to standard ontologies like SNOMED-CT, LOINC, ICD-10 etc. Clinical state variables were created based on patient history, present illness, clinical trajectory etc. in this technique, the noisy data labels are identified using domain knowledge and using machine learning model. Classifiers were used to develop the model. This was compared to a supervised method trained using logistic regression. The unsupervised learning algorithm was able to generate accuracy as good as a supervised prediction algorithm (Halpern Y et al. 2014).

'Electronic phenotyping' is defined as the process of identifying a medical condition by searching an electronic document using a defined set of data elements and logical expressions (NIH. HCSRC. Informed Consent). This process is used to create cohorts of patients with similar characteristics. Researchers use this approach to replace the rule-based manual phenotyping by experts with automated feature extraction from knowledge sources using natural language processing. They proposed a software framework for phenotyping using supervised or semi-supervised learning of phenotype models (Banda JM et al. 2017). There are multiple other examples around phenotyping including using standard topic modeling (Ghassemi M et al. 2014), tensor factorization (Ho JC et al. 2014), latent topic analysis (Arnold CW et al. 2010), and inductive logic programming (Peissig PL et al. 2014).

Patient monitoring

Patient monitoring is increasingly used for signal detection to provide real-time intervention using streaming or temporal healthcare data. An early detection system using the EMR data was developed and piloted at two hospitals to provide real-time indicators that triggered rapid response team evaluation or intervention (Escobar GJ et al., 2016). This approach was superior to a widely used scoring system called Modified Early Warning Score (MEWS) (Escobar GJ et al., 2012). The team developed another model to predict risk-adjusted hospital mortality (Escobar GJ et al., 2013). The model used Laboratory-based Acute Physiology Score, version 2, and Comorbidity Point Score, version 2. The model was developed based on over 200 million individual data points from 650,000 hospitalizations. The elements included in the model were age, sex, hospital unit, admission location, days already spent in the hospital, care directive orders, admission status, vital signs, neurologic status, laboratory test results including anion gap, bicarbonate, glucose, hematocrit, lactate, blood urea nitrogen, creatinine, sodium, troponin, white blood cell count, ICD diagnosis codes attached to patient records in preceding 12 months. The output from the model was directly included in the EMR for bedside decision-making.

Temporal models are used in an increasing number of clinical predictions. A generalized predictive model was developed using longitudinal data from EHRs and RNN techniques to predict diagnoses and medication orders. It achieved a recall of 79.58% for diagnoses and 85.53% for treatment (Choi et al., 2016). Similarly, clinical intervention prediction models were developed in the ICU setting based on LSTM and CNN techniques for real-time performance and to enable clinical interventions. The model targeted 5 clinical interventions (ventilation, vasopressor use, non-invasive ventilation, colloid bolus, and crystalloid bolus) and 4 actions (onset, weaning, stay off, and stay on) (Suresh et al., 2017).

Automated monitoring of patients is a challenge due to the need for certified sitters, which are in short supply and, in many cases, are not affordable by nursing homes, assisted living facilities, or families at home. Image recognition can be used to monitor patients. In a study of the surgical ICU, 62 hours of image data were recorded and classified into 109 segments from eight patients using sensors. The software analyzed the sensor data and assigned mobility scores. The weighted kappa statistic between the algorithm and physicians was 0.86. A convolutional neural network detected if an image was a patient. The algorithm learned the patient's position and identified the patient as lying down, sitting, or standing. Motion analysis was used to assign a mobility score using Support Vector Machine (Ma AJ et al., 2017).

Patient safety

Machine learning algorithms are increasingly being developed to improve patient safety. Besides predicting adverse outcomes or triggering early warning systems, they also evaluate socioeconomic and disease susceptibility risks. A few representative examples of models for patient safety are discussed in this section.

Off-label use of drugs can sometimes create patient safety risks. Natural language processing methods have been used to find the 'used-to-treat' relationship between drugs and indications obtained from the medical chart (Chapman WW et al., 2011). An SVM classifier was developed to recognize 'used-to-treat' relationships for the population by finding the frequency of instances where a drug and an indication are listed together in the patient chart and comparing that to expected co-mentions just on the basis of chance. In this approach, inputs were obtained from drug databases about drug usage, drug targets, and mechanism of action. Classifier was used to predict a 'used-to-treat' relationship between the condition and the indication. The SVM classifier was trained using positive and negative examples. This trained model was used to identify used-to-treat relationships in over two million drug-disease pairs. By removing the known indications, about six thousand novel usages were identified, which were presumed to be off-label (Jung K et al. 2014). A similar approach has been used to detect drug-drug interactions (Iyer SV et al., 2013).

In another case, a model was developed on a statewide claims database to assess a patient's risk of getting a future diagnosis of domestic abuse. Naïve Bayesian classifiers were used to classify patients into low-risk and high-risk classes. The data was split into a training set and a test set. An overall risk score was developed with different models for men and women. The AUC of the model was 0.88 for the narrower case definition and 0.82 for the broader definition. Tools developed on such models can be used for screening in the emergency department or physician's office (Reis BY et al., 2009).

Postop complications

Postoperative complications are a significant reason for unplanned hospitalizations. A data set of over 50,000 patients undergoing major surgery was used to evaluate the performance of logistic regression, support vector machines, naïve Bayes, and generalized additive models for predicting postoperative sepsis in acute kidney injury. 285 demographic, socioeconomic, clinical, laboratory, pharmacy, and administrative variables were used for the initial input. These were a mix of continuous, binary, and nominal variables. These were combined into groups and subgroups. Over 3000 ICD-9-CM codes were converted into 187 groups. Least Absolute Shrinkage and Selection Operator (LASSO) and Principal Component Analysis (PCA) techniques were used for feature detection. A 70/30 cross-validation was used to assess model performance. The AUC of the models varied between 0.797 and 0.858 for acute kidney injury and 0.757 and 0.909 for sepsis. Overall, the support vector machines and generalized additive models generated the best models (Thottakkara P et al. 2016).

Readmissions

Prediction of hospital admissions and readmissions has been one of the most common commercial applications of machine learning (Kansagara D et al. 2011; Futoma J et al. 2015). The inpatient readmission rate has been included in multiple value-based payment models. Unanticipated readmissions due to complications also cause patient inconvenience and, in many cases, increased costs. Machine learning approaches to predict hospital readmissions have looked at administrative claims data (He D et al., 2014). They have used logistic regression, logistic regression with heuristic variable selection, random forests, penalized logistic regression, random forest, support vector machines, and deep learning. The models obtained an AUC of 0.828 for the dataset with 3 million admissions and over 8000 admissions. Deep learning models had better AUC and positive predictive value than penalized logistic regression for the common conditions CMS penalizes for readmissions, including Pneumonia, COPD, CHF, AMI, and THA/TKA. AMI and THA/TKA were the hardest to predict.

Zhou and colleagues conducted a systematic review of the literature on predictive models for 28-day or 30-day unplanned hospital readmissions. The models' area under the curve for validation studies ranges from 0.53 to 0.83 (Zhou et al., 2016). Similarly, Low et al. created a regression model and compared its performance with the well-known LACE index to predict 30-day readmission (Low LL et al. 2015).

Utilization

Staffing costs make up a significant category of healthcare costs. Hospitals also have chronic nursing shortages, so healthcare organizations are trying to predict the future demand for healthcare services to be able to match the staffing and resource availability with the demand. In one study, over 50,000 patients were analyzed at UCSF and patient data fields collected from the EMR included "demographic data (age, sex, race-ethnicity, primary payer, primary care clinic location, primary care clinician), primary care office visits billed for more than 5 minutes, missed appointments, emergency department visits, emergent hospitalizations, elective hospitalizations, infusion and transfusion center visits, medical and surgical subspecialty visits, diagnostic and interventional radiology visits, telephone encounters with any member of their assigned primary care team, urgent care visits, and electronic messages with their primary care team through the EHR secure messaging system" (Rajkomar A et al. 2016). Clustering of patients using k-means clustering was a better indicator of predicting the number of primary care visits than the conventional case-mix index or predictive models based on regression of one-year visit data. The utilization phenotype clusters were merged into weighted primary care work clusters, which were applied to the patient data. A visit vector was created for every patient that was entered into the training set by adding the number of encounters, which included "adjusted number of primary care visits, telephone encounters with the primary care office, missed appointments to the primary care office, urgent care visits, emergency room visits, emergent hospitalizations, routine hospitalizations, medical and surgical specialty visits, infusion center visits, transfusion center visits, diagnostic and interventional radiology visits, and electronic messaging." This method was able to predict better the number of primary care visits in the following year compared to conventional approaches.

Summary

The discussion about the application of machine learning in various healthcare use cases above was representative of the diversity of ongoing work in this space. Readers are encouraged to refer to the original publications in the references. It is impossible to present a comprehensive view on this topic due to the hundreds of thousands of publications in this domain exponentially increasing yearly. Reinforcement learning is being increasingly used on clinical data, for example, in the management of sepsis, schizophrenia (Shortreed SM et al., 2011), mechanical ventilation (Prasad N, 2017), etc. The machine learning approaches are also being used to target one or more indicators of quality for hospital performance which are discussed in the chapter about quality. The AI for Clinical Medicine chapter will specifically focus on machine learning applications for diagnosis, treatment, and prevention in medical and surgical specialties.

There are still many challenges to the adoption of artificial intelligence in healthcare. Research has shown that AI can hardwire the inherently present biases in the healthcare system or society. Medicine is still grappling with the disparity in healthcare access and delivery. Building AI models on existing structures will institutionalize these issues. Natural language processing is still error-prone. The bar for accuracy is much higher in medicine where, for example, "to" can be interpreted as the t0 stage of cancer. It is also possible that situations arise where an inappropriate cause is ascribed to an effect. For example, an algorithm may trigger an alert based on clinician action rather than deterioration in the patient condition itself.

17 ARTIFICIAL INTELLIGENCE FOR CLINICAL MEDICINE

Introduction

In medicine, machine learning enables data processing at a scale that is impossible for a single physician or a team of physicians to process in a reasonable time frame or with reasonable accuracy. Historically, rule-based systems have been created to assist with diagnostic decision-making as well as the planning of treatment. However, medicine is too complex and dynamic for static rules to predict accurate outcomes in all unforeseen situations. Machine learning approaches where the software-generated algorithm learns from examples instead of hardcoded decision rules have been demonstrated to work quite well, especially in sensors where the inputs and their meanings do not change over time. The characteristics or 'features' of an image or correlated with the diagnoses or 'labels.' With enough examples, the algorithm can create a sufficiently accurate model of image representation which can be used to interpret previously unseen images. This kind of work has been successfully deployed in dermatology, radiology, and increasingly in, pathology. The next innovation will be to create similar models for videos collected from medical procedures.

The principles of biostatistics and epidemiology are foundational elements in the practice of medicine. As more computational power becomes available to medical researchers and clinicians, advanced machine-learning techniques are increasingly applied to various clinical problems. Machine learning algorithms have been applied to radiology image recognition, predicting clinical events, predicting treatment responses, finding at-risk populations, etc. In this chapter, we will discuss machine learning projects in clinical specialties. Many are based on image recognition, primarily used in radiology, dermatology, and pathology, but they are finding more applications outside of these specialties. Models are applied on MRI images followed by histology, CT, Ultrasound, and X-rays. Increasingly, retinal images and dermoscopy are also being explored. Multiple anatomic systems have been studied using deep learning techniques. Common anatomic systems for radiology image analysis are the brain, lung, abdomen, breast, heart, bones, and retina (Litjens G et al. 2017). The tasks for these analyses include organ or substructure segmentation, object detection, and classification. The common algorithms used are Convolutional Neural Nets, Recurrent Neural Networks, Restricted Boltzmann Machines, and auto-encoders.

Generally, applying deep learning methods to medical images requires preprocessing, like segmentation or extraction of visual features, before applying machine learning techniques. Deep learning performance correlates to the quantity of training data available to train the algorithm. For example, in a project on detecting skin cancers, the training data set used for the skin malignancy classification and diabetic retinopathy algorithms had more than a hundred thousand images. Smaller data sets lead to overfitting. Machine learning specialists use data augmentation to generate new training images from the original set. As artificial intelligence applications increase and techniques mature, more imaging data sets are available. More recently, large language models have been developed using transformer architecture. These have found rapid use in language applications like chatbots, intelligent search agents, etc. The following sections provide more detail about machine learning applications in each specialty. The examples discussed in this chapter provide a sample of the wide variety of applications of artificial intelligence in clinical medicine. Thousands of research and commercial projects are currently active in this area globally, pushing the boundaries of machine learning capabilities.

Cardiology

As smartwatches become more ubiquitous, they will play an increasing role in monitoring the wearer's health status. They are already being used for the detection of previously undiagnosed atrial fibrillation as well as the detection of atrial fibrillation episodes in patients with paroxysmal atrial fibrillation. Such innovations can help provide diagnostic information using widely available equipment and, in many cases, without blood tests. In a study using smartwatch signals, a heuristic pre-training approach validated against a standard electrocardiograph was used to train a deep neural network on a cohort of patients undergoing cardioversion. Individuals with a self-reported history of persistent atrial fibrillation provided their smartwatch data to validate the algorithm. Over 130 million heart rate measurements were used to train a deep neural network. The c-statistic of the algorithm was 0.97, with a sensitivity of 98% and specificity of 90.2% (Tison GH et al., 2018). Another study used a smartphone-based electrocardiogram to detect hyperkalemia based on ECG leads I and II (Galloway CD et al. 2018). A deep neural network was developed using a data set of over 700,000 patients, over 2 million ECGs, and 4 million serum potassium values.

A cardiac arrest is a serious, life-threatening event in the hospital. A machine learning model was developed to preemptively identify patients likely to go into cardiac arrest using data from electronic medical records consisting of demographic information, hospitalization history, and vital and laboratory measurements. Overall 0.5% were found to go into code blue. The vital sign information from the last 24 hours was used to estimate trends and temporal properties of the recorded variables. The observations were divided into timed windows. Subsequently, classification was performed using logistic regression with lasso penalty and support vector machine with the radial kernel. The model achieved an 80% recall and a 20% false positive rate four hours before the event. The algorithm could predict code blue better than the current standard of care, a modified early warning score (MEWS) in terms of mean recall, false positive rate, and AUC (Somanchi S et al. 2015). A similar effort developed a cardiac arrest risk triage (CART) score to predict cardiac arrest using a stepwise multivariate logistic regression with backward elimination. The model achieved AUC of 0.84 versus 0.76 of MEWS (Churpek MM et al. 2012).

Coronary Artery Disease (CAD) is the leading cause of mortality in the world. Multiple scores have been created to predict the risk for coronary heart disease, like the Framingham risk score from NIH, Prospective Cardiovascular Munster (PROCAM), Atherosclerosis and Cardiovascular Disease (ASCVD) risk estimator from the American College of Cardiology, Systematic COronary

Risk Evaluation (SCORE) from European Society of Cardiology, Reynolds risk score, etc. The Coronary Heart disease prediction models have used algorithms including artificial neural networks, fuzzy inference models, decision trees, Bayesian theory, and genetic algorithms (Kim J et al. 2015; Palaniappan S et al. 2008; Anooj PK. 2012; Khatibi V et al. 2010; Krishnaiah V et al. 2015). Similar approaches have been used to diagnose coronary heart disease (Mohammadpour RA et al., 2015; Das R et al., 2009; Vanisree K et al., 2011). CT Angiogram images have been used to classify coronary artery plaque (Rajendra Acharya U et al. 2019).

Machine learning approaches have been applied to sensor data, vital sign measurements, and cardiac imaging. Electrocardiogram data has also been used for the classification of myocardial infarction, coronary disease, and congestive heart failure (Lih OS et al., 2020) as well as blood pressure measurement from one-channel electrocardiogram signal (Miao F et al. 2020).

Dermatology

There is a worldwide shortage of dermatologists, and the prevalence of skin conditions is increasing. Deep learning algorithms are currently used for many common and serious dermatological conditions. Dermoscopy images are surface images of skin which are captured through specialized instruments and used to train machine learning algorithms. Large sample of images is required to mitigate the variability in image capture factors such as lighting, angle, etc. (Masood A et al. 2013; Rosado B et al. 2003; Burroni M et al. 2004). Other projects involving the classification of images have approached similar problems for dermatological (Kittler H et al. 2002; Codella N et al. 2015) and histopathological applications (Binder M et al. 1998; Schinderwolf T et al. 1993).

In one of the earliest applications of deep learning in dermatology, convolutional neural networks were used to classify skin lesions using a convolutional neural network trained from images directly using a data set of about 130,000 images of over 2000 diseases. The algorithm was compared against reading by board-certified dermatologists on clinical images which had undergone biopsies. Binary classification models were tested to identify keratinocyte carcinomas versus benign seborrheic keratosis and malignant melanoma versus benign nevi. The CNN performed on par with experts for both tasks (Esteva et al., 2017).

Gastroenterology

A common approach for applying machine learning in gastroenterology is the application of image recognition algorithms on images captured from endoscopic procedure videos. A systematic review analyzed polyp detection, localization, and segmentation method using deep learning. For detection, the approaches used were classification (using CNN, C3dNet, CDDN, VGG19, ResNet50, GAN techniques), bounding-box (using VGG16, VGG19, R-CNN techniques), semantic segmentation (using Y-Net, FCN-AlexNet, FCN-GooLeNet techniques), and hybrid approaches (using AlexNet, CNN techniques). For localization, bounding-box, classification, and patch-based semantic segmentation approaches were used. For segmentation, patch-based and semantic segmentation were used (Encoder-decoder, FCN-8s, SegNet, U-Net++, AlexNet). In most cases, publicly available datasets were used. Data augmentation was performed in a few studies. Various metrics were used, including accuracy, precision, recall, AUC, F1 score, F2 score, Matthew correlation coefficient, and Dice coefficient (Sánchez-Peralta LF et al., 2020). This foundational work paves the way for real-time lesion detection during the procedures.

In a prospective randomized controlled trial for automatic polyp detection during colonoscopy, the colorectal adenoma detection rate increased from 20% to 30% using machine learning (Wang P et al. 2019). A deep learning-based polyp detection algorithm during colonoscopy was created with SegNet architecture-based convolutional neural network, which had an area under the curve of 0.984. The Computer-Aided Detection (CAD) group used a real-time automatic polyp detection system, and the control group had a routine colonoscopy. The system processed each frame and identified the detected polyp location during the withdrawal phase of the colonoscopy procedure (Wang P et al., 2018). Similar studies have been done by other research groups (Mori Y et al. 2018), and over time the impact of machine learning on live video studies will increase (Alagappan M et al. 2018; Mori Y et al. 2017).

Genetic medicine

Researchers use machine learning to match genotypic and phenotypic data to disease models. In a study of patients with chronic-phase myeloproliferative neoplasms and myelofibrosis, prognostic models were created by integrating 63 clinical and genomic variables to generate tailored predictions of clinical outcomes (Grinfeld J et al. 2018). The research team sequenced 69 genes, single nucleotide polymorphisms, germline loci associated with myeloproliferative neoplasms from 1887 patients and whole-exome sequencing in 148 patients. Bayesian modeling was used to 'identify genomic subgroups with maximum within-group similarity and maximum between-group discrimination.' Markov chain Monte Carlo method was used for cluster analysis. The analysis found that mortality in the chronic phase was primarily dependent on age, with genomic features having small predictive power. However, genomic features were important in progressing from chronic phase myelofibrosis into acute leukemia transformation. The model also created specific risk predictions around long-term survival, mortality and chronic phase disease, and milofibrotic and leukemic transformation. This analysis held up after internal and external cross-validation.

Neurology

A significant number of neurological diagnoses are made with brain imaging, electroencephalography (EEG), and electromyography (EMG). Machine learning applications for brain imaging, including CT and MRI scans, have been discussed in the section on radiology. Machine learning techniques have been used to analyze EEG recordings to assess the complexity of epileptic seizures using convolutional neural networks and recurrence quantification analysis (Gao X et al., 2020). SVM classifier has been used for the automated detection of schizophrenia from EEG signals (Jahmunah V et al., 2019). Deep learning has been used to develop human-computer interfaces using electrooculogram input (Teng G et al., 2020).

Obstetrics

Machine learning algorithms are being used for a variety of obstetrical applications. These include predictions for neonatal outcomes, preterm deliveries, delivery routes, fetal weight or growth abnormalities, aneuploidy, postpartum complications, gestational age, and preeclampsia prediction (Dhombres F et al. 2022). Systematic reviews have found the use of machine learning to predict perinatal complications (Bertini A et al., 2022). Another systematic review evaluated the application of machine learning algorithms in predicting preterm birth (Akazawa et al., 2022). Machine learning is also being used to augment the tools available to obstetricians in fetal evaluation. One study used an ensemble approach with Random Forest, XGBoost, and LightGBM to predict fetal weight at various gestational changes without ultrasound examination (Lu Y et al., 2020).

Oncology

Prostate cancer is one of the most common malignancies. Without codification, the staging of cancer from the structured elements of electronic health records is a manual process. A machine learning project used the Observational Health Data Sciences and Informatics (OHDSI) feature vector framework to classify patients based on the cancer stage. Four machine learning models were trained – logistic regression with LASSO penalty, random forest, gradient-boosted trees, and extreme gradient boosting. Compared to ICD code search, which used ICD codes indicating metastases, the machine learning models had better precision up to 0.9. However, the machine-learning models had a low recall (Seneviratne MG et al., 2018). Similar other efforts have used Natural Language Processing on pathology reports (Warner JL et al., 2016; Strauss JA et al., 2013; Nguyen AN et al., 2010).

Ophthalmology

Medical conditions diagnosed based on visual inspection of the retina were some of the first applications of artificial intelligence techniques in ophthalmology. Deep learning is being used on fundus photographs and optical coherence tomography to detect diabetic retinopathy, glaucoma, macular edema, and macular degeneration for screening and monitoring. Other deep learning applications in ophthalmology have included red lesion detection in fundus images, in which features learned by CNN are augmented by incorporating hand-crafted features. In one study ensemble approach was used to identify actual lesions using a random forest classifier (Orlando JI et al., 2018).

A deep learning algorithm was used to detect diabetic retinopathy and diabetic macular edema in images of the retina (Gulshan V et al. 2016). Convolutional neural network Inception-v3 was trained using 128,000 retinal images, classified into diabetic retinopathy and diabetic macular edema. Diabetic retinopathy severity was greater in non-, mild, moderate, severe, and proliferative. The data set consisted of 9900 images. De-identified macular-centered retinal fundus images were used from two data sets. The data was preprocessed by scale-normalizing the input images. The performance of the algorithm showed a sensitivity of 91% and specificity of 98.2% and moderate or worse diabetic retinopathy only, a sensitivity of 84% and specificity of 98.8% in severe or worse diabetic retinopathy only and a sensitivity of 90.8% and specificity of 98.7% on diabetic macular edema only in the EyePACS-1 data set. The algorithm also had a sensitivity of 93.9% and a specificity of 90.9% for detecting fully gradable images.

Orthopedics

The specialty of orthopedics is very reliant on radiographic images. Many machine learning efforts are targeted toward diagnosing and treating skeletal conditions. Compression fractures are prevalent in the elderly age group and are sometimes difficult to diagnose on plain X-rays. A study was conducted to diagnose vertebral compression fractures on CT scan images. For this, the images of the spinal column were segmented, and sagittal patches were extracted (Bar A, 2017). The data set was collected from over 3700 individuals, reviewed by a radiologist, and assessed for vertebral compression fractures. Spine segmentation and preprocessing were performed to extract positive and negative samples. The binary classification was performed on these patches using a convolutional neural network to predict vertebral fracture. Patches were rescaled to 32 x 32 pixels. The convolutional neural network architecture created multiple layers, including 3x3 convolutions, ReLU, 3x3 max pooling, drop out, fully connected, and softmax. Single-layer LSTM-based RNN with 128 cells was used for classification leading to 89.1 % accuracy, 83.9% sensitivity, and 93.8% specificity.

Similarly, deep learning algorithms have been used to identify injuries on MRI images with accuracy ranging from 72.5-100% (Siouras A et al. 2022). D'Antoni and colleagues systematically reviewed deep learning approaches on spinal images from different modalities (MRI, CT scan, X-ray, ultrasound, X-rays). They evaluated the results obtained with deep learning and digital image processing and found that the best-performing models for segmentation of spinal structures achieved Sørensen–Dice scores over 90% (D'Antoni F et al. 2021). Other systematic reviews have looked at detecting implants (Ren M et al. 2021). Machine learning approaches have also been used in optimizing patient selection preoperatively, predicting and managing postoperative outcomes (Lopez CD et al. 2022).

Pathology

Like radiology, image recognition algorithms are the most common applications of machine learning in histopathology. With the increasing adoption of digital pathology, deploying these algorithms on pathology images has become easier. The current commercial applications of machine learning is to improve pathology workflows by identifying normal or challenging slides so they can be triaged appropriately. Nagpal et al used a deep learning algorithm for grading prostate cancer from biopsy specimens. The algorithm outperformed general pathologists on the metric of agreement with subspecialists (71.7% vs 58%). The deep learning system and general pathologists, were found to have similar outcomes in distinguishing nontumor from tumor biopsies (Nagpal K et al. 2020).

Pathology data sets have been used in research competitions for image recognition algorithms. In a research competition (Camelyon16), multiple algorithms were used to identify individual metastases in whole slide images and classify whole slide images into positive or negative for containing sentinel lymph node metastases. These included architectures GoogLeNet ResNet CNN with pre-trained network, VGG-16, VGG-Net, SegNet, 4-layer CNN, AlexNet, U-Net, CRFasRNN, Random Forests, SVM & Adaboost, Rule-based, 7-layer CNN and Agg-Net. The algorithms improved their output with techniques like network ensemble, stain standardization, fine-tuned pre-trained networks, invariances to augment training data, addressing the class imbalance between normal versus abnormal tissue, and using the output on the discriminative classifier to add weights to the scores. Some deep learning algorithms performed better than the pathologist working within time constraints. The AUC for the algorithms range from 0.5562 to 0.994, with the top-performing algorithm achieving a lesion level, true positive fraction comparable with that of the pathologist working without time constraints. The best algorithm performed better than the pathologist in whole slide image classification (Ehteshami et al., 2017).

Another group of researchers obtained whole slide images from two datasets and developed an algorithm called Lymph Node Assistant (LYNA) which obtained an AUC of 99% on the whole slide area and a sensitivity of 91% at the level of tissue patches. The images from the database were divided into a grid of 128 x 128 pixels, as current machine-learning models cannot work on images larger than 1000 x 1000 pixels. Non-tissue regions were eliminated using the average grayscale value threshold. The training dataset of 270 slides was split 80:20 into training and tuning sets. A slimmed-down version of Convolutional Neural Network Inception V3 was used on the Tensorflow platform without pre-training. The weights of CNN were adjusted with stochastic gradient descent by reducing softmax cross-entropy loss. Data augmentation strategies used were random rotation and mirroring of images and random changes in brightness, saturation, hue, and contrast of the image. Finally, the ensemble method was applied to improve the prediction. They could also detect micro-metastases on two slides labeled normal by the conventional independent laboratory (Liu et al., 2019). LYNA was unaffected by poor fixation, overstaining, chatter, and coverslip bubbles. It falsely identified giant cells, germinal centers, and histiocytes as tumors. Overall this algorithm performed better than the best algorithm in the Camelyon16 challenge.

Psychiatry

Depression is diagnosed based on self-reported symptoms via surveys and interviews. Machine learning techniques are being used to augment the current techniques to diagnose depression. In a study, data captured from variable wristbands and sensors in the smartphone was used to predict the Hamilton Depression rating scale. The input data included sleep behaviors, motion, location changes, phone communication, electrodermal activity, and phone usage patterns. Questionnaires about mood, stress, anxiety, sleep, alcohol/drug/caffeine usage, and overall health were collected. Positive and negative affect schedule was used to measure affect. The initial feature set contains 700 features on which PCA and SVD methods were used for dimension reduction. The regression methods used were lasso, ridge, and elasticNet with L1 and L2 regularization. RMSE obtained was 4.5 on the imputed Hamilton Depression rating scale, demonstrating the feasibility of continually measuring depressive symptoms using passive data captured from sensors (A. Ghandeharioun et al. 2017). Other research efforts using machine learning to predict depression include using voice to predict symptoms of depression and PTSD (Place S et al. 2017).

Pulmonology

Deep learning is used for image recognition in lung diseases ranging from tuberculosis, pneumonia to cancers and interstitial lung diseases. High-resolution CT and MRI scans have made it possible

There are challenges in interpreting a high-resolution CT scan due to dependency on skills of the interpreting physician. In a case-cohort study, a database of 1157 high-resolution CT scan with diffuse fibrotic lung disease was used for classification based on idiopathic primary fibrosis diagnostic guidelines. The algorithm performance was checked using accuracy, prognostic accuracies, and the rated K coefficient of interobserver agreement on the two test sets was compared with the majority vote of 91 specialist thoracic radiologists. These were reclassified according to Fleischner Society diagnostic criteria for idiopathic pulmonary fibrosis. The algorithm was retrained, and performance was compared with four specialist thoracic radiologists using the weighted K coefficient of interobserver agreement. It was found that the accuracy of the algorithm on the first test set was 76.4%. The accuracy of the algorithm on the second test set was 73.3%, and the median accuracy of thoracic radiologists was 70.7%. The algorithm outperformed 66% of thoracic radiologists. Interobserver agreement between the algorithm and radiologists' majority opinion was good and outperformed 62% of thoracic radiologists. In this study, a tensor flow-based machine learning library was used with Inception-ResNet-v2 CNN. Categorical cross entropy was used as a loss function which was minimized using the Adam optimization algorithm. The hyperparameters were the learning rate, the exponential moving average of the gradient, and the exponential moving average of the square gradient. The image size was 350 x 350 pixels. More than 200 algorithms were trained in the study (Walsh SLF et al., 2018). Such an analysis could be useful for hospitals with limited thoracic imaging expertise and for a clinical research study. There have been many other studies that have predicted prognosis rather than diagnostic information. In these studies, feature engineering is used, where expert radiologists annotate the imaging data. Overall, there have been multiple approaches used for image analysis of radiology images with idiopathic pulmonary fibrosis (Maldonado F et al., 2014; Salisbury ML et al., 2017; Humphries SM et al., 2017; Kim HJ et al., 2015; Jacob J et al. 2017).

Natural Language Processing has been used for automated chart review to mine the Electronic Health Records to assess asthma status in children (Kaur H et al. 2018). A training data set of 87 patients was used with the validation and test data set of 427 patients. The input variables were a collection of symptoms, diagnoses, patient history, and lab test values. An open-source NLP algorithm MedTagger was used to annotate and label the datasets. A manual chart review was used to compare the output of validation data and measure sensitivity, specificity, positive predictive value, and negative predictive value. The algorithm was able to predict asthmatic status with a sensitivity value of 86%, specificity of 98%, a positive predictive value of 88%, and a negative predictive value of 98%.

Machine learning algorithms are also used on pulmonary imaging. Chest X-rays are one of the most common diagnostic tools available to clinicians and the most common imaging exam globally. Deep learning approaches have been used to diagnose and classify many chest X-ray findings. Some have achieved impressive results. Researchers used Faster Region-based Convolutional Neural Networks to detect images of interest on CT axial slices for detecting pulmonary nodules. Subsequently, they used three-dimensional CNN to reduce false positives. The FROC score was 0.89 (Ding J et al. 2017). Multiple other approaches are used for pulmonary nodule detection, one of the most common incidental findings on chest X-rays (Setio AAA et al., 2016; Pesce E et al., 2019).

Some recent research has been done to diagnose tuberculosis, a severe disease in developing countries (Lakhani P et al., 2017; Maduskar P et al., 2013). Bar et al. trained CNNs on non-medical datasets used on chest X-rays to identify different pathologies in chest rays and achieved an AUC of 0.87 to 0.94 expanding the possibilities of conventional algorithms for medical applications (Bar Y et al. 2015). Cicero et al used CNNs to achieve sensitivity and specificity of 91% with an AUC of 0.964 for classifying a study as normal and AUC of 0.962 for pleural effusion, 0.868 for pulmonary edema, 0.850 for consolidation, and 0.875 for pneumothorax (Cicero et al., 2017). Another team developed a 121-layer CNN-based network to detect the presence of 14 pulmonary pathologies and used cardiothoracic specialist radiologists as reference standards. The algorithm was trained and validated on NIH's ChestX-ray8 dataset, which contains over 100,000 posteroanterior and anteroposterior chest X-rays of over 30,000 patients. The images were resized to 512 pixels by 512 pixels and normalized based on images in the ImageNet training set. The parameters were trained using Adam, a stochastic gradient descent variant. The algorithm achieved radiologist-level performance on 11 pathologies. The algorithm performed better than the radiologist in detecting atelectasis, and there was no statistically significant difference between the algorithm and radiologist for consolidation, edema, effusion, fibrosis, infiltration, mass, nodule, pleural thickening, pneumonia, and pneumothorax (Rajpurkar P et al., 2018).

Radiology

In medicine, machine learning has been most successfully applied to radiology so far. Large data sets are being collected and annotated for training machine learning models. The machine learning applications in radiology have been extensively discussed under sections about other specialties.

Typically, a large dataset based machine learning model is constructed typically like the one where a mammography-based deep learning model was developed from a data set of over 88,000 mammograms from 39,000 patients. The model was provided full field mammograms and information about breast cancer diagnosis within 5 years of the mammogram. The patients were assigned to training, validation, and test sets. Every mammogram was associated with risk factors. Multiple models were developed – a risk-factor-only model used logistic regression, an image-only deep learning model used a convolutional neural network on a 1664x2048 pixel view of the image, and a hybrid deep learning model combined information in the above models. The model was more accurate than the Tyrer-Cusick (TC) model, the current clinical standard, by identifying 31% of patients with future breast cancer in top risk decile compared to 18% by the TC model. The hybrid model performed the best and obtained an AUC of 0.71 (Yala A et al., 2019).

18 GENERATIVE ARTIFICIAL INTELLIGENCE & LARGE LANGUAGE MODELS

Generative Artificial Intelligence (Gen AI) is the ability of AI systems to create new, original content. Non-gen AI-based deep learning models are focused on a single task, which could include regression, classification, or segmentation, as discussed in the chapter on machine learning. For example, deep learning models have been used to predict mortality from EMR data (Avati A. et al., 2018) and disease progression based on imaging data (Yim J et al., 2020). The generative AI models can create output, which is text, images, video, sound, computer code, etc., based on the Large Language Models (LLM) concept.

Transformers

Transformers, the foundation of Large Language Models, were introduced in 2017 as a powerful and efficient alternative for natural language processing tasks like machine translation or language modeling. With their encoders and decoders coupled with attention mechanisms, Transformers offer a more streamlined approach to learning and processing dependencies between distant positions. This efficiency is achieved by avoiding recurrence or convolution, which reassures data scientists about their ability to handle complex language tasks with ease.

In recurrent models, the computation required to learn dependency between two positions increases linearly or logarithmically. The 'Attention' mechanism allows data scientists to overcome this limitation and removes restrictions on modeling a dependency between any two positions on input or output sequences. So, in a long text with 100 words, it is easier for a transformer-based model to establish dependency between the first and last word than a recurrent model. Therefore, by using attention, the complexity, computations, and processing time can be reduced.

In the 'Attention' approach, the Encoders pass all hidden states that the encoder has produced to the decoder, increasing the amount of information passed from the encoder to the decoder through the context vector. The decoder ranks the hidden states so that the most relevant hidden state is used for the output. Transformers use Encoder and Decoder stacks of neural layers, which are essentially multiple layers of neural networks, to process the input and generate the output. These layers are designed to capture different aspects of the input and output, allowing the model to learn complex patterns and dependencies. Both Encoders and Decoders have self-attention and feed-forward layers. Transformer models include keys, values, and queries, the discussion of which is beyond the scope of this book. Transformers include feed-forward networks and linear transformations with ReLU activation and SoftMax functions (Alammar J., 2018).

The applications of Transformers have been broadened with fine-tuning algorithms, which enable Transformers to adapt to new tasks without having any prior exposure to those tasks using transfer learning on pre-trained models. Examples of Transformers include BERT (Bidirectional Encoder Representations from Transformers), LaMDA (Language Model for Dialogue Applications), LLaMA (Large Language Model Meta AI), PaLM (Pathways Language Model), GPT (Generative Pre-trained Transformer), ViT (Vision Transformer), BART, Chinchilla, Diffusion models, PaLM (Pathways Language Model), GLM (General Language Model), Transformer XL (Amatriain X., 2023).

ChatGPT-3 and ChatGPT-4

ChatGPT-3 and ChatGPT-4 aree among the most well-known commercially available deep-learning models based on Transformers. ChatGPT-3 has an estimated 175 billion parameters and was trained on a corpus of 570GB of data, including content from the Internet like Wikipedia, books, etc. ChatGPT-4 was a multimodal algorithm estimated to have one trillion parameters (Albergotti R., 2023).

Natural Language Processing (NLP)

In data science, natural language processing (NLP) activities include information retrieval, named entity recognition, classification, topic modeling, translation, speech tagging, reading comprehension, text entailment, question answers, semantic labeling, syntax analysis, word sense disambiguation, etc. Natural language processing (NLP) algorithms have evolved. Till recently, NLP algorithms were based on word vectors and created for specific tasks using single-layer representations. Deep learning techniques like RNNs use multiple layers of representations for specific tasks. More recently, transformer-based large language models (LLMs) have used general pretraining and subsequent fine training for specific tasks instead of task-specific architectures (Brown TB et al., 2020). LLMs are created using principles of deep learning and transfer learning.

Traditional deep learning techniques depend on labeled data to train. However, LLMs can build a linguistic model on unlabeled data. Large Language Models are created using semi-supervised or supervised learning. In contrast to traditional deep learning methods, LLMs also attempt to understand the concepts present in the collection of words. LLM deduces these concepts from the training data or knowledge base.

Most NLP algorithms try to predict the next word in a sequence. In the case of LLMs, the initial word or sequence of words is a prompt, and the algorithm tries to predict the following sequence. LLMs generate words with the highest probability of appearing next in a sentence. The first word is generated in response to a prompt provided by the user. The model then iterates over the whole text to generate yet another word with the highest probability of occurring next, and this loop continues. The probability is determined based on the context created from the input parameters, training data, and information provided in the prompt. For example, it means different things in medical versus non-medical contexts.

LLMs can generate rationale and reasoning when solving a problem (Wang B et al., 2022). Pretraining of language models allows them to develop broad pattern recognition skills. Large

Language Models are considered foundation models because they are trained on many data types but can be configured or finetuned to various applications (Bommasani R et al., 2021). With adequate computing resources, using word-level, phrase-level, and sentence-level semantics or embeddings has enabled better performance of LLMs. Unfortunately, like deep learning, we do not have a good explanation for the outputs of LLMs.

Training data

While different organizations have developed different types of LLMs, the most critical factor for the performance of an LLM remains the quality and size of the training data. Medical data has many formats. It contains free text physician notes, structured data, which could include clinical data like diagnoses or lab results, etc., or genomic data, images like radiology or pathology. The data that is used for training may exist in different record systems and formats. Research is ongoing on the best approach to train the Generative AI models on various data types (train separately and combine through APIs, train on a combined data set, etc.). The hope is that one grand algorithm could create a unified picture of an individual's health, risks, and appropriateness of specific treatments.

The healthcare-specific data could be used for pretraining or finetuning. Common datasets for pretraining include:

- Electronic health record information, including progress notes and procedure notes (Johnson AE et al., 2016). Many of these are free text dictations categorized into sections
- Transcriptions of conversations between physicians and patients around clinical matters (Chiu CC et al., 2017)
- Transcriptions of conversations between healthcare staff and patients around administrative matters
- Case studies published in medical journals
- Multiple choice style questions patterned on US Medical Licensing Examination like MedQA (Jin D et al., 2021)
- Answers to consumer health questions by NLM (Abacha AB et al., 2017), Google (HealthSearchQA), and MedicationQA (Abacha Ben A et al., 2019)
- Disease information databases (MedicineNet – Diseases & Conditions, MalaCards)
- Procedures and Tests (MedicineNet – Procedures & Tests)
- Medications (MedicineNet - Medications)
- Summaries of doctor-patient conversations (Ben Abacha A et al., 2023) (Ionescu B et al., 2023)
- Generating vignettes about clinical conditions for training

Generative AI Concepts

Context length

Context length (also called context window) is the size of the information the LLM processes in one go. It includes the input tokens submitted via the prompt and the output tokens generated as a reply. The larger the context length, the more considerable the amount of contextual data that a model can consider in its response. For example, this enables a model to remember a larger chat conversation with a user or a larger document from which LLM can process or answer questions. Conversation that a model can remember. The context length is expressed in terms of the number of tokens and ranges from four thousand to over two hundred thousand. The context length increases over time with increasing computational resources and mathematical optimizations.

Finetuning

Finetuning is the process of customizing a pre-trained model by adjusting the parameters of a previously trained LLM to make it perform better on a specific task or adapt it for a specific domain of knowledge. It uses the concept of transfer learning, where the model builds on the knowledge gained during pretraining for a specific task based on the content of data used for finetuning. Finetuning generally uses labeled data and increases the performance or effectiveness of the model on a specific task compared to a model trained on general data.

Inference

Inference is using the pre-trained LLMs on new data or prompts. Because LLMs have billions of parameters, inference requires many computing resources. Inference is used interchangeably with prediction but is a preferred term in the context of LLMs. In machine learning, inference is the study of the impact of predictors on the output function, while prediction is finding the value of the output function.

Instruction tuning and in-context learning

These are similar approaches in which specific instructions and examples are provided within the prompt itself to tailor the model's output in a specific format. It does not update the weights of the pre-trained model. It provides examples or demonstrations in the prompt to the model containing examples of inputs and example outputs.

Parameters

Parameters represent the capacity of transformer models. Some recent ones have been in the trillions. One of the earliest open-source models, LlaMA, had over 65 billion parameters. GPT-3, which was related to ChatGPT, had 175 billion parameters, which were created from about 500 billion tokens, with one token roughly representing 4 characters. It was estimated that over 700GB of memory was required to train a model of this size.

Precision

Precision is the accuracy of number representation. In machine learning, floating point numbers are used for mathematical calculations. Floating point numbers represent real numbers and include a sign (positive or negative), exponent (magnitude), and mantissa (significant digits of the number). Floating Point 32 (FP32) means 32 bits are used to represent a number, FP(16) uses 16 bits, int8 only uses 8 bits (one byte), and int4 uses 4 bits. FP32 is single precision and uses 32 bits with 1 bit for the sign, 8 bits for exponent, and 23 bits for mantissa for a total of 7 decimals of precision. Double precision (FP64) uses 64 bits, with 1 bit for signs, 11 bits for exponents, and 52 bits for mantissa, a total of 15 decimals of precision. The use of double precision improves the accuracy of models while also increasing computation and memory requirements.

Pretraining

Pretraining is the initial step in creating large language models, which process large amounts of data to develop a general understanding of the language and communication based on the content and the concepts. During this process, the LLM understands language representation, grammar, sentence structures, reasoning, etc. This helps in natural language processing tasks like named entity recognition, answering specific questions, and establishing relationships between sentences. Pretraining is achieved using the transformer architecture, unsupervised learning, and masked language modeling techniques. In masked language modeling, a model tries to guess certain missing words in a sentence. Some pre-trained LLMs include the GPT series from OpenAI, Gemini from Google, Claude from Anthropic, BERT from Google, LLAMA from Meta, and Mistral from Mistral AI. For these foundation models, pretraining has been done using data from scraped web pages, Reddit discussions, Wikipedia, and online books and journals. The Generative Pre-Trained Transformers use the finetuning approach to pre-training all parameters using unidirectional language models. For example, GPT-3 used about 570GB of filtered text data from 45TB raw text data for pretraining.

Prompts

The prompt is an instruction or input provided to an LLM that generates an output as a response to the instruction or input. Prompts can be in the form of questions to get specific answers, a dialog or observation to have an ongoing conversation about a topic, a text to summarize or critique it, a software code for finding errors, etc. Prompts can use zero-shot or few-shot techniques. In zero-shot prompting, the model produces an answer with an initial prompt, which does not include any example or demonstration of how the answer should be arrived at or how it should look. In the few-shot technique, examples of the potential response are provided in the prompt to refine the output. Chain of thought prompting is a technique where the prompt instructs the model to include the reasoning steps that the model used in creating the output. This approach of reasoning prior to presenting a response breaks down the complex tasks into simpler concepts and improves the model output.

Quantization

The size of the large language model is a function of several parameters and the precision of the weights in the trained model. Quantization is modifying the precision of weights of large language models to reduce their size. This allows the models to be run on less powerful computers with a minor hit to performance and accuracy. Newer quantization techniques are being developed over time. Some common ones currently are Post-Training Dynamic and Static Quantization and Quantization Aare Training. For example, using quantization from FP16 to INT4, a model size can be reduced by 70%.

Reinforcement Learning from Human Feedback (RLHF)

Reinforcement learning is the process of learning the best outcome by repeatedly making decisions and getting rewards or penalties for right and wrong answers, respectively. An example of reinforcement learning is when a machine learning model learns to play Chess or Go by playing millions of times with itself using different approaches and learning which works best from the outcomes. Reinforcement Learning from Human Feedback (RLHF) is a technique to improve the performance of LLMs by providing human feedback (Christiano P et al. 2017). RLHF is generally used in scenarios where there is no one indisputable correct answer. The goal is to ensure that the LLM output aligns with society's preferences, laws, and expectations to make interacting with them more 'human-like." RLHF is a model-tuning technique that relies on humans to score the default LLM outputs, which are then incorporated into future model outputs. For example, multiple outputs from a specific prompt are presented to a human labeler who selects the best option. This is then provided back to the LLM, which incorporates the feedback into the model through reinforcement learning. This technique is different from the supervised learning approach, where the correct answer is provided along in the training data set. RLHF techniques have improved the accuracy and relevance of complex outputs from Transformer models.

Retrieval Augmented Generation (RAG)

Retrieval Augmented Generation (RAG) is the ability to augment LLMs by connecting them with data that was not previously used to create or train the model. RAG is used to add domain-specific knowledge to the model or to update the knowledge initially used to train the model. RAG avoids the need to retrain the model from scratch whenever a new data source must be included in an LLM. RAG's other benefits include improved output accuracy and reduced hallucinations.

Tokens

A token is the smallest unit of data in a large language model. Tokens are common sequences of characters present in words. In most scenarios, one token is equivalent to one word, but in some cases, a word could be split into multiple tokens or words, and a punctuation mark could be in one token. LLMs use tokenizers to convert texts into tokens.
through APIs, train on a combined data set, etc.). The hope is that one grand algorithm could create a unified picture of an individual's health, risks, and appropriateness of specific treatments.

Generative AI Applications

The applications of Generative AI in healthcare and clinical medicine are evolving rapidly. Just like other machine learning techniques, Gen AI applications can be used for administrative or clinical purposes. They can be for information retrieval, content creation, or task agents. Below are typical and representative applications of LLMs in healthcare that have been demonstrated. Some are research projects, while others are commercial products or services.

Administration

One of the earliest applications of LLMs in healthcare has been for administrative use cases. This is attractive because of the large amounts of healthcare data, complexity of workflows, and less impact of hallucinations on administrative applications compared to clinical applications. LLMs are being used both by healthcare providers and healthcare payers. Examples include

- **Claims adjudication:** A large amount of information necessary for appropriate claim adjudication can quickly be processed in near real-time.
- **Eligibility and benefits**: Health plans have a large combination of benefits for every line of business. LLMs can help identify and match eligibility and benefits information for procedures, drugs, and clinical services. This could be for the members, providers, or payers.
- **Fraud detection**: The use cases for fraud detection in healthcare include intentional incorrect billing, identification of suspicious patterns in documentation and claims, medically inappropriate services, and non-delivery of billed services.
- **Medical coding**: On the provider side, billing codes are identified from clinical documentation in the electronic medical records and the list of services provided to the patients. On the payer side, ensuring the codes are accurate and correctly bundled.
- **Prior authorization:** Prior authorization requests and decisions on prior authorization

requests can be made using LLMs. They can also be used to conduct an initial review or evaluate previous authorization decisions.

- **Utilization management**: The utilization management teams of providers and payers can perform medical necessity reviews and management of appeals and grievances.
- **Value-based payments**: The administrative overhead of managing the delivery and monitoring of value-based programs is high. LLMs can assist with such use cases.

Clinical documentation

Physician-patient communication is the foundation of medical practice. It is used to collect data for diagnostic and therapeutic decisions, provide patient education, and address patient queries and concerns; LLM-based systems are being developed to improve the interactions between physicians and patients. These models can understand medical terms and clinical context and engage in appropriate conversation to achieve a prognostic, diagnostic, or therapeutic goal. Most medical AI models start with a foundation model, finetuned with transcripts of medical encounters, case studies, and question-answers. They can be integrated with electronic health records or can be standalone software applications. LLMs can get initial patient information, convert free text into structured conversations, and create summaries for patients and referred providers. They assist with real-time documentation to convert physician-patient interaction into clinical visit notes and diagnostic and treatment recommendations in assessment and plan.

Clinical management

The applications of LLMs in clinical management have been slower due to issues around hallucinations and privacy. Many of these are research projects that are not currently available in the commercial domain. Some interesting applications include

- **Clinical decision support**: Evidence-based clinical decision support, best intervention for patients, health coaching, and diagnoses based on symptoms or clinical data.
- **Clinical risk assessment**: LLMs can identify and predict high-risk members in advance and recommend enrollment in appropriate preventive services.
- **Disease management**: Natural language processing, along with LLMs, can identify relevant medical information from the text of medical charts, physician dictation, or patient conversations. For example, they can identify diagnoses, symptoms and their characteristics, disease progression timelines or chronology of significant events, differentiate past and current issues, identify drug names with dosages and frequency, and understand medical procedures, abbreviations, and laboratory values.
- **Personalized medicine**: As more health data becomes available for individuals, LLMs can combine medical diagnoses, genetic risk, insurance coverage, and lifestyle data to create personalized recommendations.
- **Quality improvement**: Detection and tracking of gaps in recommended care, including screenings, healthcare services, consultations, and medication compliance.
- **Triage recommendations**: AI-assisted symptom checkers were one of the earliest applications of machine learning in medicine. A systematic review found that the highest diagnosis accuracy of the top 3 diagnostic possibilities was 70.5% compared to 82.1% for general practitioners (Gilbert S et al., 2020). The symptom checkers have been better at triaging, with triage accuracy reported to be as high as 97.8% (Wallace W et al., 2022). With large language models, the accuracy of symptom checkers will increase because they can consume regular conversations instead of yes or no or single-word answers. Text or voice-

based chatbots can collect patient information, conduct assessments, and make preliminary recommendations.

Customer service

LLMs have demonstrated significantly improved reasoning and communication compared to previous machine-learning approaches. The customer service tasks in other industries are seeing the most impact from LLMs in a commercial environment. LLMs can replace human customer service reps or make them more efficient. They can assist with routine tasks like booking appointments, managing referrals, and getting eligibility and billing information. Voice- or text-based chatbots can answer queries from physicians' offices or patients. They are used in patient communication and can provide patients with automated, personalized, coordinated information.

Research

The traditional approach to searching medical terms or related concepts in the medical corpus was keyword matching. Over time, it improved to consider synonyms to identify concepts in medical terminologies. However, LLMs allow a natural language-based search that can infer relationships between diagnoses, symptoms, and treatments from unstructured data without direct mapping between terminologies. Physicians can query medical records in natural language, and models can process complex queries through multi-step analysis.

The applications of Generative AI in healthcare and clinical medicine are evolving rapidly. Just like other machine learning techniques, Gen AI applications can be used for administrative or clinical purposes. They can be for information retrieval, content creation, or task agents. Below are typical and representative applications of LLMs in healthcare that have been demonstrated. Some are research projects, while others are commercial products or services.

Medical LLMs

Large language foundation models are trained on a wide variety of data sources and can be used in a variety of applications. These foundational models are trained on general English text to understand the basics of communication. Then, they are trained on domain-specific documents from electronic medical records or research studies to generate domain-specific answers. At a technical level, the model weights from the pretraining process are used for transfer learning on the new data set. The models are constantly upgrading as more training data, computing, and finetuning are available. Healthcare data sets previously used for machine learning include MIMIC, EHRSHOT, CRADLE, etc. While the discussion below focuses on clinical LLMs, many are being created for biology, genetics, proteomics, drug discovery, etc. These include Geneformer for transcriptomes (Theodoris CV et al., 2023), scGPT for single-cell biology (Cui H et al., 2024), and AlphaMissense for genetic missense variants (Cheng J et al., 2023).

The list of models below is representative and current as of this writing. Readers are advised to refer to the documentation of each model for details about it.

Articulate Medical Intelligence Explorer (AMIE)

Articulate Medical Intelligence Explorer (AMIE) (Tu T et al., 2024) was trained on publicly available datasets of medical licensing exam Q&As, transcripts of conversations between physicians and patients, summaries of EMR data, and simulated conversations created from medical databases. AMIE was developed using a self-play-based simulated diagnostic dialogue environment, automated feedback, and a chain-of-reasoning strategy where the model analyzed patient information and selected the best response based on previous questions and answers. The model had a detailed evaluation framework and was evaluated on a) Differential diagnosis accuracy and quality which included differential diagnoses comprehensiveness, appropriateness of differential diagnoses, management plan, escalation recommendations, investigation recommendations, treatment recommendations, follow-up recommendations, and confabulations; b) Patient-Centered Communication Best Practice which included relationship fostering, gathering information, providing information, decision making, enabling disease and treatment related behavior and responding to emotions; c) Practical Assessment of Clinical Examination Skills which included ability to elicit presenting complaint, systems review, past medical history, family history, medication history; ability to explain clinical information accurately, clearly, comprehensively, professionally and in a structure way; manage patient concerns by showing understanding and addressing concerns in an empathetic manner; d) differential diagnosis accuracy and quality; d) diagnosis and management with sound clinical judgment and focus on patient welfare. It was demonstrated to perform better than primary care physicians on most evaluations. AMIE was also used as a differential diagnosis aid to the clinicians and was demonstrated to improve the differential diagnosis accuracy of clinicians compared to those using internet search (McDuff D et al., 2023)

BioBERT

BioBERT (Lee et al., 2020) was created by training a BERT model on a biomedical research corpus consisting of PubMed abstracts and full texts. BERT (Bidirectional Encoder Representations from Transformers) was created by pretraining a deep bidirectional transformer by randomly masking some tokens from input and trying to predict "the original vocabulary id of the masked word based only on its context" and using a "next sentence prediction task to pre-train text-pair representations" (Devlin J et al., 2019) BERT is pretrained on unlabeled data. The finetuning of initialized pre-trained parameters is done with labeled data from downstream applications. For the original BERT model, pretraining was done on 800M words of BooksCorpus and 2500M words from Wikipedia. BioBERT performed better on the F1 score than contemporary models on biomedical named entity recognition and biomedical relation extraction and a higher MRR score on biomedical question answering.

BiomedCLIP

BiomedCLIP is a multimodal foundation model adapted to biomedical vision-language processing (Zhang S et al., 2023) using Contrastive Language-Image Pretraining (CLIP). It is trained on the PMC-15M data set, which contains 15 million biomedical image-text pairs from 4.4 million articles. Similar models that have used CLIP for image-text pretraining are PubMedCLIP (Eslami S et al., 2021) and MedCLIP.

BiomedGPT

BiomedGPT (Zhang K et al., 2023) is a multimodal biomedical LLM that was pretrained on curated biomedical datasets. It is based on BART implementation using a transformer with a multi-head attention mechanism. BiomedGPT can be used for disease classification, medical language understanding, text summarization, image captioning, and visual question answering (VQA).

BioWordVec

Before transformer-based models like BERT, word representation models like Word2Vec, ELMo, and GloVe (Wwang Y et al., 2018) were used for biomedical NLP. Word vector representations have been used for other biomedical applications like medical synonym extraction (Jagannatha A et al., 2015), named entity recognition (Tang B et al., 2014), chemical-disease relationship (Jiang Z et al., 2015), drug-drug interaction (Liu S et al., 2016), protein-protein interaction (Jiang Z et al., 2016), gene-gene interaction (Alachram H et al., 2021). Word2vec (word2vec., 2013) uses continuous bag-of-words and continuous skip-gram algorithms to produce word vectors as outputs. Word vectors have been created for biomedical data (Biomedical natural language processing. http://bio.nlplab.org/), including PubMed and PubMed Central, which contain 5.5 billion tokens from 14 million abstracts and 700,000 full-text articles (Pyysalo et al., 2013). A variant called BioWordVec has used a subword embedding model on biomedical literature and domain knowledge contained in the Medical Subject Headings (MeSH) database (Zhang Y et al., 2019). Another approach, ELMo, is based on the Bidirectional-LSTM language model that has been finetuned on clinical content. Some examples included extracting clinical concepts (Zhu H et al., 2018) and de-identifying patient notes (Khin K et al., 2018). LSTM has also been combined with other approaches like conditional random fields for biomedical data analysis (Habibi et al., 2017).

ChatDoctor

Open-source LLMs like LLaMA have allowed the creation of clinical models for the research community. Yunxiang and colleagues (Yunxian L et al., 2023) finetuned an instruction-following LLaMA version from the Stanford Alpaca project (Stanford Alpaca) by using anonymized 100,000 patient-doctor dialogues resulting in significant improvement in the model's capability to provide appropriate responses to the patients.

ClinicalBERT and ClinicalBioBERT

ClinicalBERT was trained on a BERT base model, and Clinical BioBERT was trained on a BioBERT-fine-tuned model (Alsentzer E et al., 2019). They use a corpus of clinical notes from the MIMIC-III database, which includes 1.2B words from over 3 million patient records obtained from EHRs.

Clinical Camel

Clinical Camel was created by finetuning a LLaMA model using the QLoRA technique on public and synthetic chat conversations (Toma A et al., 2023). The team converted clinical review articles and MedQA questions into conversations to train the model.

DoctorGLM

DoctorGLM is a medical language model optimized for the Chinese language. It was trained on the Chinese translation of the ChatDoctor (Yunxiang Li et al., 2023) dataset. It is based on the ChatGLM model, which was fine-tuned using low-rank adaptation for medical purposes. ChatGLM is a Chinese and English large language model pre-trained on 1 trillion tokens based on the General Language Model (GLM) framework (Zeng A. et al., 2022). It also included supervised finetuning, feedback bootstrap, and RLHF (Hou Z et al., 2024). DoctorGLM has a prompt designer module that converts the input prompt into keywords and adds additional information about those keywords depending on whether the keywords are symptoms, diagnoses, or treatments. This additional information is presented to DoctorGLM along with the original prompt.

HuaTuo (华驼)

HuaTuo is a Chinese biomedical LLM trained on Chinese medical knowledge graph (CMeKG) (Wang H et al., 2023). The model uses instruction data for supervised finetuning.

LLaVA-Med

LLaVA-Med is an open-source significant language and vision model trained on biomedical data. The model was created using the curriculum learning method and focused on open-ended biomedical question-answer tasks (Li C et al., 2024). It was trained on the PMC-15 dataset, which comprises 15 million biomedical image-text pairs at PubMed Central. The goal of this project was to create a biomedical chatbot.

Med-PaLM

Med-PaLM, developed by Google, is a proprietary model trained on healthcare data (Singhal K et al., 2023). It was one of the first Large Language Models (LLM), scoring over 60% on questions patterned on the United States Medical Licensing Examination that medical students take to graduate medical school. Google made a derivative of Med-PaLM called MedLM available to the general public and enterprises. MedLM is a collection of multiple models each of which is tuned for a specific task. For example, one model could classify radiology images, another could help to answer questions about patient medical history, and another could identify and provide a chronological list of patient conditions, medications, etc.

MedAlpaca

MedAlpaca has been created by finetuning the Stanford Alpaca version of LLaMA (Large Language Model Meta AI) with medical data (Han T et al., 2023). The data sources included Wikidoc, Anki flashcards, biology-related questions from StackExchange, and question-answer pairs from ChatDoctor. MedAlpaca is targeted at medical Q&A and medical dialogues.

Meditron

Meditron (Chen Z et al., 2023) is based on LLaMA and was developed through continuous pretraining and finetuning on clinical practice guidelines, paper abstracts, and RedPajama datasets.

PMC-LLaMA

PMC-LLaMA (Wu C et al., 2023) is based on the open-source LLaMA foundation model and was found to perform better than the base LLaMa model on medical benchmarks like MedQA and MedMCQA. It was created using medical domain-specific knowledge injection, instruction tuning, biomedical academic papers, and textbooks.

RadOnc-GPT

The availability of open-source models has enabled researchers to create domain-specific LLMs. RadOnc-GPT (Liu Z et al., 2023) was finetuned on radiation oncology patient records. The model is designed to be used as a chatbot by patients to get information post-radiotherapy. The team used instruction tuning to create treatment regimens, identify the best radiation treatments, and provide ICD-10 codes.

Benchmarks

Healthcare-oriented LLMs have been created using diverse base foundation models, data sets, and finetuning techniques. Standardized benchmarks and evaluation data sets are used to compare the performance of these models. The performance of the healthcare LLMs is tested in zero-shot or multiple-short accuracy. Benchmarking allows developers to compare the effectiveness of different approaches. Select benchmarks that have been used are discussed below. Some of these are for generic LLMs, while others focus on medical ones.

AgentBench

AgentBench (Liu et al., 2023) has evaluated LLM agents' capabilities in eight domains. These include operating systems, databases, knowledge graphs, digital card games, lateral thinking puzzles, householding, web shopping, and web browsing. It tests LLM agents' reasoning and decision-making capabilities.

BenchMD

BenchMD (Wantlin K et al., 2023) is a data set created by a consortium of universities and used to assess AI models across multiple modalities, including medical images and sensor data. It contains 19 datasets and 7 medical modalities, including sensor data, images, and volumetric scans from electrocardiograms, electroencephalograms, chest X-rays, retina fundus images, dermoscopic images, CT scans, and mammograms.

ClinicalBERTScore

Benchmarks have been proposed for clinical speech recognition. BERTScore (Zhang T et al., 2019) is based on semantic similarity between two sentences. ClinicalBERTScore (Shor J et al., 2023) modifies this by using weighted scores on medical terms in the text obtained from Google's Knowledge Graph (Singhal A, 2012) and tuning it to match the clinician transcript dataset. Other metrics for medical speech recognition include Word Error Rate (WER), BLEU (Bilingual Evaluation Understudy), and METEOR (Metric for Evaluation of Machine Translation Output).

HaluEval

Even though HaluEval is not specific to healthcare, it has been included here because LLMs are known to have the issue of hallucinations. Hallucination Evaluation (HaluEval) benchmark data set can test LLMs' ability to recognize hallucinations across dialogue, summarization, and general domains (Li J et al., 2023).

MMLU

Measuring Massive Multitask Language Understanding (MMLU) is a dataset for general reasoning, but subsets have been created related to medicine and biology. The datasets are based on multiple-choice questions. The subsets include over 1000 questions covering clinical knowledge, college biology, college medicine, medical genetics, professional medicine, and anatomy.

MedMCQA

The MedMCQA dataset is based on multiple-choice questions from Indian medical entrance examinations. It has over 180,000 questions in the training set and over 6,000 in the test set. The answers are explained.

MedNLI

MedNLI (Romanov A et al., 2018) dataset contains annotations by physicians performing natural language inference on the MIMIC III dataset. It has over 14,000 unique sentence pairs and has training, development, and testing subsets.

MedQA

The MedQA dataset is based on multiple-choice questions patterned on the United States Medical Licensing Examination (USMLE). The current version has over eleven thousand questions in the development set and over one thousand in the test set. In 2023, The commercial GPT-4 Medprompt model achieved an accuracy of 90.2% on this benchmark.

MultiMedBench

MultiMedBench is a multimodal benchmark created by Google to evaluate biomedical AI. The benchmark has 12 de-identified datasets (Tao T et al., 2024), including clinical documents, genomic data, radiology, pathology, and dermatology images. It evaluates performance in answering medical questions, summarizing findings in radiology reports, answering visual questions on radiology and pathology images, generating reports from chest X-rays, and classifying chest X-rays, photos of skin lesions, mammograms, and genomic images. The data sets included MedQA representing multiple choice US medical licensing exam style multiple choice questions, MedMCQA representing multiple choice Indian medical entrance exam questions, PubMedQA representing multiple choice biomedical literature questions, MIMIC-III (Medical Information Mart for Intensive Care III) with de-identified information about forty thousand patients admitted to critical care units, and MIMIC-CXR including chest x-rays and associated reports.

Med-VQA

The Medical Visual Question Answering benchmark is based on the PathVQA dataset, which includes over 30,000 question-answer pairs representing 5000 pathology images (He X et al., 2020). The datasets were created from publicly available pathology textbooks.

PubMedQA

PubMedQA is a dataset with over 1,000 question-answer pairs, with PubMed abstracts split between training and testing. Answers include yes, no, maybe, and long answers.

ROUGE

Recall-Oriented Understudy for Gisting Evaluation evaluates the text-generating capability of LLMs compared to reference texts. It assesses text generation, summarization, translation, and document retrieval.

Risks and limitations of Generative AI

Despite LLMs' advantages, several risks and challenges limit their broader adoption. Efforts are underway to mitigate some of these risks and limitations.

Training data

The data used in the foundation models has not been made public in most proprietary as well as currently available open source models. There is a risk that underlying data used to train the model may contain incorrect or outdated medical information. This may lead to erroneous outputs from LLMs, potentially having serious adverse effects.

Context length

Context window or context length is the amount of content that an LLM can keep in its memory or consider in its response when answering queries. A large context window or length means the model can answer questions about large documents or long conversations without forgetting initial details. A typical outpatient record is less than 2100 words (Huang AE et al., 2018). Assuming a patient generates 10 notes equivalent content per year for 30 years, the total medical record size will be about 25 megabytes or 800k tokens without including any media. Models with larger context windows have typically been less accurate than smaller ones.

Hallucinations

The ability of LLMs, which makes them especially attractive for creative tasks, also creates a problem called hallucination. Hallucination is a phenomenon where the GenAI algorithm makes up facts or conveys inaccurate information as valid. They can generate false, inaccurate, or nonsensical information but present it as if it were true, including incorrect citations in many cases. This can be dangerous in critical domains like healthcare, where incorrect information can lead to harmful outcomes. For example, LLMs have created made-up articles and references and displayed them as valid scientific studies or provided advice that could be life-threatening. Hallucinations remain among the most significant risks to deploying generative AI in healthcare.

Computational resources

LLMs require significantly more computational resources for training and inference, putting them out of the reach of many users. They also use more energy every time they are used, increasing the energy demands on the grid and running costs.

Data safety, security, and privacy

Due to the sensitive nature of healthcare data, prompts entered into an LLM need to be safely secured in compliance with HIPAA guidelines. It is also important to ensure no PII is used in the training data, as that can unexpectedly be displayed in an LLM response.

Generative Artificial Intelligence (Gen AI) is the latest technique in a long list of machine learning approaches. Due to the success of Gen AI in consumer applications, there will be more investments in foundational research and newer techniques are expected to emerge over the next few years.

19 DATA GOVERNANCE, SAFETY & SECURITY

Data stewardship, governance, and ownership in healthcare are essential because of data quality, security, and privacy issues. As per one definition, "Data Governance is a collection of practices and processes which help to ensure the formal management of data assets within an organization" (Knight M, 2021). Data Governance Institute (DGI) defines data governance as "a system of decision rights and accountabilities for information-related processes, executed according to agreed-upon models which describe who can take what actions with what information, and when, under what circumstances, using what methods" (The Data Governance Institute, 2021). A well-functioning analytics organization requires a well-defined data governance policy and a data governance committee. The role of the data governance committee is to create data governance policies, monitor data quality, resolve conflicts, and enforce good data management practices and compliance.

Every analytics organization must establish a data governance policy to guide data management. The healthcare analytics teams work with individuals' health information, which requires specific protections as outlined in the Health Information Portability and Accountability Act (HIPAA) chapter.

Data quality and governance

The foundation of quality and performance improvement teams is accurate data. The organization must have trust in any information created by the analytics teams. Data quality is the most crucial factor for the success of an analytics organization. The computer science concept of 'Garbage-In Garbage-Out' holds true for the data analytics domain. If the underlying data is not accurate, consistent, or reliable and does not represent the hypotheses made for analytics, then any dashboard, report, or algorithm developed from this data will not be acceptable. This can impact business decisions and reimbursements, eventually leading to regulatory penalties. As a practice, anytime a new report is created, or a new data source is accessed, the analysts must evaluate the quality of the data.

Good data management practices are vital in ensuring good data quality. The primary data source in a healthcare organization is from electronic medical record systems in the form of physician notes and data from pharmacy, laboratories, radiology, and billing. The other data is similar to any other organization, like financial records, human resource records, supply chain, etc.

Canadian Institute for Health Information (CIHI) has developed an Information Quality Framework (CIHI, 2017). CIHI defines 'information quality' as the "quality of the statistics, indicators, analytical reports, electronic reporting tools and other information products generated by the organization" and 'data quality' as the "quality of the underlying data that is collected and used to produce these outputs." Information quality is the broader concept that "considers how the information is accessed, presented and can be interpreted; how information from different sources fits together to paint a coherent picture; and how the processes involved in transforming data into information are effectively managed." If the information quality is successfully managed, there is increased knowledge, trust, use, and quality of the analytics department.

CIHI uses five dimensions of quality:

- **Relevance**: The degree to which information meets the current and potential needs of clients, users, stakeholders, or the audience.
- **Accuracy and reliability**: The degree to which the information correctly and consistently describes the phenomena it was designed to measure.
- **Comparability and coherence**: The degree to which information is comparable over time and across jurisdictions, produced using common standards and methods, and can be combined with other sources.
- **Timeliness and punctuality**: Timeliness refers to how quickly information is made available after the end of the reference period; punctuality refers to whether the information is delivered on the dates announced.
- **Accessibility and clarity**: The degree to which information, including supplementary explanatory information and metadata, is easily obtainable and presented in a way that can be understood.

CIHI has developed four quality management activities to produce relevant, high-quality information products:

- **Prevent**: The ideal goal should be to prevent the quality issues from occurring in the first place. Activities to ensure prevention include
    - Consistent data capture by using technical, data and clinical standards
    - Ensuring that the vendor specifications for the products comply with the standards
    - Adequate and appropriate training to ensure accurate and standardized data capture
    - System audits to validate the captured data
- **Monitor and control**: Activities to monitor and control the submitted data
    - After validation of the captured data, error reports and corrections are generated and feedback is shared with the data suppliers
    - Data stewards are provided access to reports which list quality issues. Data stewards are data stakeholders who make data related decisions. Data stewards ensure high-quality and highly reliable data. There could be one or multiple data stewards within a healthcare organization representing their department or functional area
    - Use of machine and learning and statistical techniques to flag augment manual detection capabilities
- **Evaluate and document**: After the project is completed, the information management process is evaluated and documented
    - Documentation and metadata about the production, interpretation and use of the data

- Evaluating the quality of the data using the DSAT
  - Evaluating indicators using the indicator life cycle
  - Stakeholder interviews to get feedback about the output
  - Validation studies targeting specific aspects of quality
  - Publication and sharing of data and information quality metrics, indicators and reports
- **Improve**: The continuous improvement cycle is an iterative process
  - Collaboration with stakeholders including data providers to ensure correct data is collected and submitted
  - System changes by incorporating knowledge gained from the feedback into the standards, processes, resource materials, and training

Governance team

The data governance team is responsible for the oversight of the use of healthcare data within the organization. It manages the data governance program, including developing policies and standards for the data processes, roles, and relationships. The strategy, goals, and success metrics created by the governance team lays the foundation for the scope of governance. The governance team also creates data controls to minimize the risk of data breaches and increase data security.

The data governance team should have broad representation from clinical and business leaders. The data governance committee members are interested in how data is created, collected, stored, analyzed, or used. The team generally includes representatives from departments like information technology, informatics, legal, security, risk management, compliance, and quality. Key influencers should be identified and play a leadership role within the governance team. The senior leaders from clinical informatics, information services, strategy, and research should be included. The governance team can have multiple sub-committees like the data quality council and data quality workgroup. A subgroup of the governance team should be available for any urgent prioritization requests. The responsibility and accountability of governance team members is clearly defined. Data governance teams can be within IT, Informatics, Analytics, Compliance, or Quality teams. Ideally, they should report to an entity with enforcement jurisdiction within the healthcare system. The committees should develop an annual roadmap with priorities, goals, and success metrics. Frequent re-evaluation is required to respond to the organization's evolving needs. The data governance efforts must have buy-in from the senior leadership. Enough resources need to be allocated to data governance to be effective.

A dedicated governance team is required if the organization is sufficiently large and has analytical teams doing many custom projects sourcing data from multiple data sources or if specific regulatory compliance or contractual issues need focused oversight over data governance. Not every healthcare organization needs a data governance committee. A separate data governance committee may be optional in smaller organizations like physician practices and smaller hospitals. Since the health analytics team is primarily responsible for working with healthcare data, the analytics teams can take on data governance responsibilities.

The data governance team develops the data management policy of the organization. At the minimum, it defines the data's ownership, access, integration, sharing, and use. The team may also develop dashboards, reports, and self-service tool recommendations. The governance team is responsible for data management, including creating and overseeing data dictionaries, data definition, and mapping codes as needed. Data integrity is critical to an organization, and the governance team ensures the quality and accuracy of the data. The governance team can also create and monitor policies to prioritize analytics projects. Recommendations for prioritization of analytics projects have been discussed separately.

Data dictionaries

The use of healthcare data for analytics is challenging. Multiple data sources generally result in more than one definition for the data fields. For example, readmission rate, length of stay, and ER wait time. There are also differences in the interpretation of business nomenclature used within the organization. The policies may have unclear terminology, which makes it difficult to be used as a reference for analytics products. The data dictionary or data glossary helps to define terminology across the business units. It is used to define the business concepts for the organization and is vendor independent. The data dictionary provides information about the data elements within the database or data warehouse. It can include attributes, data properties, etc. It can include information like data type, size, allowed values, constraints, the purpose of the data field, etc. Using a business glossary helps to easily connect different data sources and user interfaces and improve communication across departments or organization units.

Data safety & security

Data safety and security are vital for healthcare data. Three main concepts are important to understand:

Confidentiality

The law recognizes confidentiality as "privileged communication between two parties in a professional relationship, such as with a patient and a physician, a nurse or other clinical professional" (Naseem M et al., 2022). Healthcare organizations are expected to prevent unauthorized access to non-public information that two or more parties have agreed to restrict. Confidentiality is "the question of how personal data collected for approved purposes shall be held and used by the organization that originally collected it, what other secondary or further uses may be made of it, and when consent by the individual will be required. To further the patient's willing disclosure of confidential information to doctors that the law of privileged communications was developed" (Westin AF, 1976).

Security

Security is "a number of measures that organizations implement to protect information and systems. It includes efforts not only to maintain the confidentiality of information, but also to ensure the integrity and availability of that information and the information systems used to access it" (National et al., 1997). "Security of data involves an organization's ability to keep its promises of confidentiality." (Westin AF, 1976). HIPAA provides the framework and standards for protecting health information.

Privacy:

In his 1967 book Privacy and Freedom, Alan Westin defined informational privacy as "the claim of individuals, groups or institutions to determine for themselves when, how and to what extent information about them is communicated to others" (Westin AF. 1967). "Privacy," according to Lawrence Gostin, "is the right of individuals to limit access by others to some aspect of their persons" (Gostin LO, 1995). The U.S. National Information Infrastructure Task Force 1995 formulated it as, "Information privacy is an individual's claim to control the terms under which personal information—information identifiable to an individual—is acquired, disclosed, and used" (Information Infrastructure Task Force. 1995). Alan Westin clarified: "Privacy is the question of what personal information should be collected or stored at all for a given function. It involves issues concerning the legitimacy and legality of organizational demands for disclosures from individuals and groups and setting of balances between the individual's control over the disclosure of personal information and the needs of society for the data on which to base decisions about individual situations and formulate public policies" (Westin AF., 1976).

Per Westin, "privacy policies help to answer the question of what personal information should be collected or stored for a given function. It involves issues concerning the legitimacy and legality of organizational demands for disclosures from individuals and groups and setting of balances between the individual's control over the disclosure of personal information and the needs of society for the data on which to base decisions about individual situations and formulate public policies" (Westin AF. 1976).

Privacy is the "fair and authorized 'processing' of personally identifiable information that can be used to identify or contact an individual or be reasonably linked to a specific individual, device or computer" (Dennedy MF et al., 2014). Personally identifiable information refers to any data that can be used to identify an individual. General Data Protection Regulation (GDPR) defines 'personal data' as "any information relating to an identified or identifiable natural person ('data subject'); an identifiable natural person is one who can be identified, directly or indirectly, in particular by reference to an identifier such as a name, an identification number, location data, an online identifier or to one or more factors specific to the physical, physiological, genetic, mental, economic, cultural or social identity of that natural person." GDPR defines 'processing' as any operation or set of operations which is performed on personal data or sets of personal data, whether or not by automated means, such as collection, recording, organization, structuring, storage, adaptation or alteration, retrieval, consultation, use, disclosure by transmission, dissemination or otherwise making available, alignment or combination, restriction, erasure or destruction" (EU GDPR, 2016).

Federal Trade Commission of United States has been involved in online privacy issues and has developed principles of privacy protection. Fair Information Practice Principles are (FTC, 1998).

- **Notice / Awareness**: Individuals are given notice about organization's information practices before any personal information is collected.
- **Choice/ Consent**: Individuals are given option about how any personal information collected from them may be used or disclosed to third parties.
- **Access/Participation**: Individuals are able to access information about themselves with the organization and correct any mistakes.
- **Integrity/Security**: Organizations collecting data need to ensure data integrity and security through administrative, technical and physical safeguards.
- **Enforcement/Redress**: A mechanism for enforcement and redress is put in place.

The readers are encouraged to refer to the chapter on HIPAA for more details about data privacy, confidentiality, and security.

UNIT 3: THERAPEUTICS

20 DIGITAL THERAPEUTICS

Introduction

Digital Therapeutics (DTx) refers to software applications that prevent, treat, or manage medical conditions. These software applications can be accessed through mobile phones, desktop or laptop computers, virtual reality devices, etc. Digital therapeutics software can be packaged with health care services like personalized counseling or offered with conventional drug or device-based treatments and provider-led therapies.

One key difference between Digital Health products and Digital Therapeutics (DTx) is that DTx has clinical evidence and real-world outcomes to support their use. DTx products are based on evidence-based interventions for clinically recognized disease states with a validated software-based approach. DTx are evaluated by regulatory agencies and are offered to patients as outlined in their regulatory filings. All DTx offered in the United States are expected to have regulatory oversight through FDA. They may or may not require a prescription by a provider before being made available to the end users. The strength of clinical evidence varies by product. The gold standard for clinical evidence is a randomized controlled trial in which the DTx is compared against a current standard of care or a placebo. Due to challenges with reimbursement and evolving regulatory framework, large-scale clinical trials are still limited for DTx. Systematic reviews have found digital health to be effective for the self-management of respiratory diseases (Morrison D et al., 2014), cardiovascular diseases (Widmer RJ et al., 2015), diabetes (Greenwood DA et al., 2017), and behavioral health. They are also used for supportive care in oncology (Aapro M et al. 2020) and neurology (Abbadessa G et al. 2022).

DTx are available in multiple forms based on how they're used. These include:

- **Standalone**: Standalone DTx are used alone and are not dependent on or used with any other therapeutic intervention.
- **Adjunctive**: DTx products added to an existing standard of care treatment to improve compliance, effectiveness, or reduce adverse effects of the standard of care treatment.
- **Combination**: DTx products combined with another drug, device, or diagnostic. These combination products are tested together in clinical trials to ascertain their efficacy as a combination.

DTx can be used for three types of interventions in medicine:

- **Prevention**: DTx is used to prevent the occurrence of pathology, disease, adverse outcome, or complication. This is generally accomplished through improved compliance, improvement in lifestyle factors, reduction in risk exposure, etc.
- **Treatment**: DTx for behavioral disorders using CBT techniques has emerged as one of the most common applications. The treatment can be provided just by the standalone app or as a combination or an adjunct product.
- **Ongoing management**: DTx apps can be crucial in managing chronic diseases or pathologies. These can track symptoms, increase medication adherence, and provide care coordination or education.

Based on the analysis of clinical trials from www.clinicaltrials.gov, currently the largest proportion of digital therapeutics are in the clinical domain of psychiatry, followed by cardiovascular, endocrine, neurology, and respiratory (Burrone V et al. 2020).

Considerations

The DTx products should comply with industry-accepted best practices for digital health around design, software development, software life cycle management, quality, interoperability, communication standards, good manufacturing practices for software as a medical device, computer systems validation, privacy and security safeguards, risk management, and usability. The DTx product usability considerations should include the digital literacy of the patients, localization in the patient's language, accommodations for disabled individuals, and users' health literacy. The DTx design should be based on industry-standard user experience and user interface design principles with clear instructions, detailed documentation, or tutorials.

Regulation

Most countries regulate DTx under medical device or Software as a Medical Device (SaMD) regulations. In the US, FDA currently regulates digital therapeutics under a precertification program. In Europe, European Union Regulation 2017/745 regulates medical devices, and European Medicines Agency and European Commission have started doing preliminary work in this area.

Evidence

DTx products are expected to demonstrate evidence for clinical outcomes collected through clinical trials. Evidence published in peer-reviewed, high-impact journals and incorporated in clinical guidelines created by medical societies or disease-focused working groups carries more weight. This evidence forms the basis for regulatory approval after evaluation of efficacy and safety as well as reimbursement or coverage decisions by payers. For reimbursement, inclusion of DTx in an evidence-based clinical guideline serves as the gold standard. Sometimes instead of the specific product, the general approach used by the DTx can be substituted in the clinical guideline. While this is a positive indicator by itself, the inclusion of the specific DTx is a more direct clinical endorsement. The significance of the level of evidence of a new DTx can vary based on whether an existing standard of care exists for the same condition. If so, the DTx can either be adjunct to the standard of care or replace the standard of care.

Evaluation

DTx evaluation is conducted by regulatory agencies for regulatory approval, health insurance (federal, state, or private) for coverage, medical associations, and healthcare providers for incorporation in clinical guidelines. Risk-benefit and cost analysis are key components of all these analyses. The cost analysis could include cost-benefit, cost-utility, or cost-minimization analyses.

Clinical application

The type of clinical use will be important for the risk-cost-benefit assessment. A DTx could be used to prevent a disorder, manage an existing disorder, or treat a disorder. The DTx can be used just by itself as a therapeutic, as an adjunct to an existing treatment, drug, or device as support, or additive. DTx can be used for a disorder for which no treatment exists, for a disorder for which treatment is less than satisfactory due to efficacy or side effect profile, or for a disorder for which a satisfactory treatment exists. However, the introduction of DTx further improves efficacy, reduces cost or side effects, or improves patient or provider experience.

Patient access

Prescription DTx can only be made available with a prescription from qualified providers. Wellness-related DTx can be accessed by patients directly without requiring any approvals from third parties. Between these two extremes is the DTx, which needs approval from employers or needs a recommendation from a payer or provider to be made available to individuals.

Clinical evidence

The gold standard for the highest quality of clinical evidence remains a randomized controlled trial. Some DTx products have come on the market with other variations, including non-randomized controlled trials, open-label trials, prospective single-arm trials, crossover studies, and head-to-head trials). Any endorsement through practice guidelines or clinical society position statements strengthens the case for the DTx approval and adoption. Real World Evidence provided by the DTx developer can help bolster the clinical evidence. Monitoring programs can be created through ongoing literature review or tracking of efficacy among the patients using DTx through patient-reported outcomes or symptoms, standardized questionnaires, or data sets from real-world data.

Regulatory approvals

DTx products receive market authorization after regulatory review by FDA. Some products may not need regulatory review or market approval, and for these cases, analysis of the intended use should be undertaken to ensure that the absence of regulatory review is appropriate.

Technology

It is important to ensure that the technical requirements of DTx do not preclude it from being usable by a large number of eligible patients. The hardware, network, and operating system requirements and the technical expertise required to operate the DTx by end users are important factors in the evaluation. The DTx may be standalone or may need to integrate with other software, medical devices, or data sources like EMRs, or sensors. The DTx may need a regular smartphone or a computer, or another hardware repurposed or custom developed for the DTx. These could include sensors, medical devices, virtual reality headsets, wearables, etc. Some applications may require constant internet connectivity.

The technology evaluation will also review the type of technical support available to the users, providers, or sponsors (health plans or employers). The evaluation may include the impact of the need for technology infrastructure like a mobile phone, a laptop, or a desktop computer may also influence the decision as not all patients may have access to them. The product should provide disaster recovery plans in cases of errors or malfunctions. Provisions for data access, backup, and maintenance should be to industry standards. The DTx should provide estimates of expected downtime over a time period.

Privacy and security

The DTx providers are expected to have robust information security risk management and governance framework, preferably with certifications from industry-standard certifying bodies. The privacy framework should align with industry best practices, including HIPAA and GDPR and the other guidelines and recommendations for patient data protection. The software and firmware should be updated with security patches and cybersecurity techniques to protect against malicious actors. Similarly, industry-standard security practices and certifications like HITRUST, SOC 2, or ISO/IEC 27001, etc. The product also needs appropriate authentication and authorization mechanisms to ensure users access the right information. The privacy practices of DTx manufacturers should address patient data collection, processing, usage, sharing, protection, storage, and retention.

Clinical review by providers

Hospitals and health systems conduct clinical reviews of a drug, device, or a digital therapeutic before making it available through hospital pharmacies. The Pharmacy & Therapeutics (P&T) Committee is created by healthcare providers, most commonly acute care hospitals, to evaluate and select therapies that are made available at the institution. P&T committees review the published evidence and use the clinical judgment of the committee members, including clinical pharmacists and physicians, to develop policies around therapy access. The committees increasingly use reimbursement, quality, and access in determining formulary decisions. DTx are increasingly making their way into agendas of P&T Committees and undergoing similar approval processes as has been followed for drugs and biologics.

Success criteria

The single biggest marker of the success of a digital therapeutic is improvement in clinical outcomes. To be able to achieve a good clinical outcome, a DTx should demonstrate the following characteristics:

- **Availability**: The digital therapeutic needs to be made available to the consumers in a format that works for them and is suitable for the type of outcome that is being targeted.

- **Affordability**: The DTx needs to be affordable for end users who may need to pay deductible or copay, or coinsurance; they need to be affordable for the employers who may bear the cost of DTx if they are covering it for their employees; they need to be affordable for the health plans themselves so that they can cover it without needing to significantly increase premiums.
- **Convenience**: The sign-up process and ongoing access for the DTx should be simple and convenient. For example, if an employer offers a DTx to their employees as a benefit, then in order to be able to access a therapeutic, the user may need to undertake three levels of authentications – first, for the health plan; second, for the employer; and third, for the actual product itself. Technologies at the backend using single sign-on are trying to make this process seamless, but it highlights the need to make workflows convenient.
- **Usability**: The DTx should use best practices for developing user experience/user interface (UX/UI). Motivated users may stop using the product if the user experience is not on par with what they are used to with other products and services.
- **Consistency**: The users prefer a consistent experience, especially if the digital therapeutic is supplemented with services including counseling or telehealth visits delivered by therapists or other healthcare workers.

Challenges

Unlike medical devices and drugs, DTx have not universally demonstrated consistent outcomes at Level I evidence through randomized control trials, which are adequately powered with statistically significant outcome differences compared to control groups. This research should be conducted with clinical trials following Good Clinical Practices with results reported using Consolidated Standards of Reporting Trials.

Examples of digital therapeutics

DTx have been commercially available as standalone software products or as part of digital health programs. In most commercial digital health programs, services are provided to the patient for the management of clinical conditions by human experts through digital interfaces, including mobile applications or apps. Examples include services for managing diabetes or obesity by nutritional counselors, dietitians, or health coaches. National organizations like CDC have developed frameworks for some clinical areas like Diabetes Prevention Program. In these programs, the software application is used as the interface to connect with human experts without any inherent preventive, therapeutic, or management intervention by the software itself.

It is also important to consider that DTx companies go to market for a specific clinical indication or disease condition but slowly expand the application of the underlying technology to multiple indications. So, while they may have one product with FDA approval and reimbursement on the market, they may have clinical trials in pipeline for other conditions.

Disclaimer: The discussion about commercial DTx is for illustrative and educational purposes. All products and services discussed in this section are registered trademarks owned by their respective registrants, owners, or licensees. The author does not endorse or vouch for the clinical validity of any products or services listed here. The indications of the products were accurate at the time of the writing but may change over time.

Abdominal pain

Regulora

metaMe Health is developing prescription DTx for chronic conditions. Regulora is an FDA-cleared app using gut-directed hypnotherapy to treat Irritable Bowel Syndrome (IBS) pain. The treatment is undertaken for 2 months with lessons up to 30 minutes. It is used as an adjunct to another standard of care treatment. The company is also developing DTx for heartburn, ulcerative colitis, and functional dyspepsia.

Anxiety

Daylight

Daylight is a CBT-based app that has demonstrated improvement in anxiety in a randomized controlled trial on patients over 18 with moderate-to-severe generalized anxiety disorder (GAD) symptoms. The CBT app is used for 10 minutes daily for about 10 weeks. The app is an adjunct to medical care but can be used by itself (Carl JR et al., 2020). The skey tudy enrolled 256 participants who were followed up for 6 weeks with an additional 26th-week follow-up. It used MINI and SCID for diagnosis and GAD-7 for severity. Per the indications, Daylight can be used under the supervision of a healthcare professional and in adjunct to their usual medical care for GAD. The app delivers a quiz to patients and then follows up with personalized techniques. The product is available in the US without prescription under the FDA's enforcement discretion rule but not as an FDA-cleared medical device. It is available under the Class I CE mark in the UK through self-referral or from GPs.

Asthma and COPD

Propeller

Propeller is a sensor attached to an inhaler and a smartphone app that tracks medication usage and provides individualized recommendations to patients with persistent asthma and stage II-IV COPD. The platform provides information about symptom triggers, air quality forecasts, in-app medication refills, medication adherence reminders, and progress reports. The providers can monitor medication usage and review symptoms. In the US, it is available as FDA class II medical device in Canada and the EU as a class I medical device. Clinical studies have demonstrated a 35% reduction in COPD-related ED visits (Alshabani K et al. 2020) and asthma-related ED visits by 53% (Merchant R et al. 2018).

Sonde Health

A vocal and respiratory biomarker has been developed by Sonde Health which tracks and predicts respiratory symptoms, including the risk of exacerbation of Asthma or COPD. Same voice biomarker technology is also used for mental health conditions.

Others

Some other DTx include AsthmaTuner, ProAir and AirDuo Digihalers, BreatheSmart spirometer and inhaler tracker sensors, NuvoAir spirometer, cough counters and inhaler sensors.

Attention Deficit / Hyperactivity Disorder (ADHD)

EndeavorRx
EndeavorRx is a prescription-based video game that FDA has approved as a class II medical device. It is targeted to improve focus and multitasking ability in children 8-12 years old with primarily inattentive or combined type ADHD with demonstrated attention issues. The patients spend about 25 minutes daily in one sitting over 4 weeks. The 3-month prescription is sent to a specialty pharmacy where the patient completes registration and payment to get an activation code. The app is available for $99. EndeavorRx has been shown to be effective in research studies. An open-label effectiveness study shows improvement in ADHD Impairment Rating Scale after 4 weeks of using EndeavorRx (Kollins SH et al., 2021). This technology is also being studied through randomized controlled studies to evaluate for improved sustained attention measured by the Test of Variables of Attention in adults with depressive disorder and cognitive impairment (Keefe RSE et al., 2022).

Others
Another products available for attention impairment is TALi.

Chronic pain

HelloBetter Chronic Pain
HelloBetter Chronic Pain is a pain reduction program based on Cognitive Behavior Therapy (CBT) and Acceptance and Commitment Therapy (ACT) delivered online or through an app as a course. It targets adults with chronic pain for at least 3 months and carries a diagnosis of persistent somatoform pain disorder, chronic pain disorder with somatic and psychological factors, fibromyalgia, dorsalgia, and chronic intractable pain. The program lasts for 12 weeks, split into 7 units of about an hour each. A randomized controlled trial showed reduced pain interference, measured with Multidimensional Pain Inventory (MPI) (Lin J et al. 2017). It is available in Germany and Switzerland as a Class I CE mark eligible for a prescription for reimbursement.

Depression

deprexis
Praxis is an automated CBT-based adjunctive treatment for patients over 18 experiencing a depressive episode and having recurrent depression or depressive disorders as a primary or secondary diagnosis. It is an app or web-based program with modules and messaging features and is recommended to be used for at least half an hour per session, 1-2 times per week, for 12 weeks. The program costs $399 and provides behavioral modification tips, biweekly patient health questionnaire analysis, guided meditations, and mindfulness exercises. A meta-analysis has demonstrated a clinically relevant reduction of depressive symptoms over 8-12 weeks (Twomey C et al. 2020). Patients with bipolar disorder, psychotic disorder, or suicidal risk are not advised to use it. Users can select if they want to share information with their providers. It is available in the US under FDA enforcement discretion and CE-marked in a few EU countries.

Woebot Health
AI-powered, prescription-only Chatbot by Woebot received FDA breakthrough device designation as a digital therapeutic for treating postpartum depression. It is based on CBT and Interpersonal psychotherapy (IPT) and helps to reduce depression symptoms (Darcy A et al., 2022). The product is also being investigated for Adolescent depression (Nicol G et al., 2022).

Others

Other DTx available for depression include SparkRx, HelloBetter Diabetes and Depression. Ensemble is a 10-week program with 2 CBT-based activities 15-30 minutes daily.

Diabetes

BlueStar

BlueStar and BlueStar Rx mobile and web applications have been FDA approved as Class II medical devices to provide digital coaching for patients with Type 1 and Type 2 Diabetes. The system reads blood glucose readings and recommends insulin dose adjustments, personalized messages to reduce Hemoglobin A1c. The products are indicated for use by healthcare providers and their patients aged 18 years and older, not pregnant, and not using continuous glucose monitors. The BlueStar insulin management features available with prescription are listed below as sourced from the company:

- *"For bolus insulin users with type 1 or type 2 diabetes, BlueStar includes an insulin dose calculator to allow patients to use their prescribed regimen to calculate a dose of bolus insulin for a given amount of carbohydrates and/or glucose value.*
- *For basal insulin users with type 2 diabetes, BlueStar includes an Insulin Adjustment Program (IAP) which calculates appropriate long-acting basal insulin doses for titrating insulin levels based on configuration by a healthcare provider. The healthcare provider must activate the IAP and configure it with patient-specific parameters.*
- *For bolus insulin users with type 2 diabetes, the BlueStar IAP calculates appropriate dose adjustments of bolus insulin based on configuration of a healthcare provider. Qualified type 2 diabetes patients are those who are not achieving glycemic targets despite optimization of their basal insulin dose or their current bolus insulin regimen.*
- *For premixed insulin users with type 2 diabetes, the BlueStar IAP calculates appropriate dose adjustments of premixed insulin based on the configuration of a healthcare provider. Qualified type 2 diabetes patients are those who are not achieving glycemic targets and who do not take other types of insulin."*

A 3-month randomized control study of thirty patients with type 2 diabetes demonstrated reduction in 2.03% reduction of hemoglobin A1c (Quinn CC et al. 2008).

d-Nav

d-Nav is also a prescription FDA-approved app for Type 2 diabetics, which provides insulin dosage recommendations based on patients' blood glucose levels. Clinical studies have demonstrated a reduction in Hemoglobin A1c after 3 months and no increase in the risk of hypoglycemia (Schneider JE et al., 2018; Bergenstal RM et al., 2019). The personalized insulin dose recommendations are coupled with virtual care management support.

Insulia

Insulia is a prescription-only DTx that is used to aid in the management of type 2 diabetes. It is indicated for use with insulin detemir, insulin degludec, and insulin glargine. It is based on the algorithm that works with insulin to recommend dose titration. Insulia is available as FDA Class II medical device, EU as a Class IIb CE mark, and in Canada as a Class II MDL.

Better Therapeutics

BT-001 is a software-based nutritional cognitive behavioral therapy to treat patients with type 2 diabetes. The goal of the application is to reduce Hemoglobin A1c after using the application for 90 days. A clinical trial demonstrated a mean A1c reduction of 1.3% in half the number of patients in the intervention arm at 180 days, with an overall mean reduction of 0.4% compared to the standard of care. The higher-dose subgroup showed greater A1c improvement compared to the low or moderate-dose use group. The product is expected to be approved by FDA through de novo classification.

Others

Other examples of DTx for diabetes include Dario smart meter and app and iSageRx from Amalgam, which has a CE mark.

Disease self-management

Sidekick Health has a platform that is being used for atopic dermatitis (SK351) to help patients self-manage the symptoms of mild to severe Atopic Dermatitis. The app provides medication reminders, educational resources, behavior modification techniques, physical activity, management of side effects, and symptom tracking. A similar approach is used for Psoriatic Arthritis (SK-341), Rheumatoid Arthritis (SK-331), Ulcerative Colitis (SK-311), Crohn's Disease (SK-321), Breast Cancer (SK-421 in trial NCT05459454), High-risk pregnancies (SK-811).

Insomnia

Sleepio

Sleepio is a mobile and web-based DTx that helps manage insomnia in adults by providing six sessions for about 20 minutes per week and a daily sleep diary. It is available in the US under FDA's enforcement discretion and in the UK under the Class I CE mark. Clinical studies have shown a 54% reduction in time to fall asleep and 62% less time awake at night (Espie CA et al). Sleepio is available as an adjunct to usual medical care under a medical provider.

Nightware

Nightware is a prescription DTx to reduce sleep disturbance related to nightmare disorder or nightmares due to PTSD in adults. It is classified as a Class II medical device and has been authorized by FDA under breakthrough device designation. The app works in combination with smartphones and smartwatches. It has clinical research (NCT03934658, NCT03828656) to support its clinical evidence.

Others

Another product for insomnia is Somryst which is a 9-week CBT based program with 6 lessons for adults 22 years or older with insomnia.

Irritable Bowel Syndrome (IBS)

Mahana

Mahana is an FDA-cleared class II medical device using CBT-based treatment for Irritable Bowel Syndrome (IBS). It is an app-based provides personalized counseling with lesson plans for 3 months. The app is available with a prescription and can be covered by insurance. A clinical study demonstrated that the IBS symptom severity score was 61.6% less in the intervention arm compared to treatment as usual after 12 months of follow-up (Everitt AH et al., 2019).

Maternity care

Invu
Nuvo's Invu non-stress test remote monitoring device, approved by FDA under 510(k) for fetuses, provides personalized education, risk assessment, and remote management of pregnant patients. Invu system includes wireless maternal and fetal heart rate monitors, comparable to the current standard of care (Mhajna M et al. 2020).

Twill Health
DTx solutions for pregnancy provide self-guidance and symptom management, including stress and anxiety. Twill Health uses CBT for positive psychology and mindfulness, education, personalized care journey, and live coaching.

Medication adherence

Medication adherence has been one of the earliest applications for digital health applications. Some DTx available for medication adherence includes Health Beacon for injectables, Abilify MyCite from Proteus Therapeutics, and Lid Sync for daily medication intake tracking and reminders.

Migraine

Nerivio
Nerivio is a prescription-based remote electrical neuromodulation stimulation device and associated smartphone app for treating migraine with or without aura in patients over 12. The device is applied to the upper arm when the patient feels the onset of migraine. The small nerves in the arm are stimulated, which causes the release of pain-inhibiting neurotransmitters relieving migraine attacks. Treatment is continued for about 45 minutes. In a randomized, double-blind, sham-controlled clinical study, 66.7% of patients achieved pain relief within 2 hours (Yarnitsky D et al. 2019). It is available under De Novo FDA authorization in the US and class IIa CE mark credentialed by Dekra in the EU.

Musculoskeletal

Sword Health
Sword Health provides a digital therapist program for musculoskeletal conditions, including an app, a motion sensor, home-based education, and remote physical therapy monitoring. The wearable motion sensors are class II medical devices approved by FDA. The physical therapists communicate with patients three times a week. A clinical study has demonstrated digital rehabilitation with better outcomes than conventional in-person rehabilitation (Correia FD et al., 2018).

Panic disorder / PTSD

Freespira

Freespira is an adjunctive treatment for PTSD and/or panic disorder symptoms. The app targets patients over the age of 13 years with PTSD, panic disorder, or episodes of panic attacks associated with other medical and behavioral health conditions. It provides a tablet, sensor, and an app to patients who complete two 17-minute sessions daily for 28 days. The sensor attached to the nasal cannula measures real-time carbon dioxide and respiratory rate, and the app provides feedback about breathing at different rates. Freespira also provides clinically supervised remote coaching as needed. FDA has cleared it as a class II medical device and requires authorization by a licensed healthcare professional but does not require a prescription. Clinical studies have demonstrated that 68% of patients were free of panic attacks 12 months post-treatment (Meuret AE et al., 2008). 89% of patients reported decreased PTSD symptoms 6 months post-treatment (Ostacher MJ et al., 2021).

Others
HelloBetter Panic is another DTx available for panic disorders.

Pelvic disorder

Vaginismus Plus
Vaginismus Plus is a CBT-based 12-week online course approved in Germany and Switzerland as a Class I CE mark for genito-pelvic pain/penetration disorder. A randomized controlled trial that tested eight modules and a booster session delivered through an eHealth platform found that 31% of participants could engage in penetrative sex and experienced reduced pain and anxiety (Zarski AC et al., 2021).

Others
Another DTx for pelvic health is Bloom for pelvic floor muscle exercises.

Stroke

Constant Therapy
Constant Therapy has developed a DTx to assess speech, language, and/or cognitive deficits for patients with stroke, for which it has received FDA breakthrough designation. It is also conducting clinical research for applications in Traumatic Brain Injury, Mild Cognitive Impairment, Alzheimer's disease, Multiple Sclerosis, Parkinson's disease, Major Depressive Disorder, and Epilepsy.

Substance Use Disorder (SUD)

reSET
reSET is a class II FDA-approved prescription CBT for substance use disorder. reSET is based on Community Reinforcement Approach (CRA) neurobehavioral therapy adjunct to contingency management and fluency training. The intervention is provided through modules, each of which can be completed in 10-20 minutes. The modules are available for twelve weeks per prescription for adult patients with substance use disorder who are under treatment for addiction to stimulants, marijuana, cocaine, alcohol with other substances, opioids, and others. A clinical study has demonstrated improvement in retention rates of all patients and a doubling of abstinence rates in patients whose primary addiction was not opioids (Campbell AN et al., 2014).

DynamiCare
DynamiCare has received a breakthrough device designation for DCH-001, which is DTx for treating tobacco use disorder during pregnancy. A study demonstrated 2.8 times the likelihood of smoking cessation in women. The product includes a smartphone app, a breath CO sensor, periodic cotinine tests in saliva, and a debit card that uses the CBT technique of contingency management. The product is also being evaluated for stimulant use disorder (NCT04162132) and alcohol use disorder (NCT03701204). It is undergoing a clinical study in Japan to use their app for alcohol use disorder.

Connections
Connections is based on Addiction-Comprehensive Health Enhancement Support System (A-CHESS) smartphone application developed to help patients with abstinence, provide strategies to navigate cravings and withdrawal symptoms, and avoid triggers for relapse. It uses the concepts from self-determination theory and provides decision-making tools, educational content, and connection with a support system. The eRecovery module provides peer support and care management tools; the intervention module connects individuals with mental health and SDOH services; and the ePrevention tool for community screening and evidence-based interventions. The app has demonstrated improvement in patients staying in treatment (Johnston DC et al., 2019) and increased outpatient addiction treatment (Glass JE et al., 2017).

Other
reset-O received a breakthrough designation approval from FDA for opioid use disorder as an 84-day prescription digital therapeutic. CureApp SC Nicotine Addiction Treatment App and Carbon MonoxideCheckerr is available in Japan as PMDA-cleared class II medical device. Vorvida is a web-based CBT for alcohol use for 180 days, used 1-2 times a week for at least 30 minutes.

Symptom monitoring and management

Digital technologies are effective for capturing patient symptoms and patient-reported outcomes for managing medical conditions. They have been demonstrated to improve symptom support, reduce hospitalizations, improvement of quality of life measures (Aapro M et al. 2020).

Kaiku
Kaiku is an online or app-based platform for patients with cancer to report symptoms, receive self-care instructions, communication, and education. Healthcare professionals can use the platform for non-urgent communication, routine oncology care, and research studies. Kaiku captures and processes data on multiple cancers and is compatible with multiple cancer pathways. A randomized controlled trial of 766 metastatic cancer patients undergoing chemotherapy showed 5.2 months longer medial overall survival, improved quality of life, and reduced hospitalization with digital symptom monitoring (Basch E et al. 2017). In the US, Kaiku is made available under FDA's enforcement discretion, a Class IIa medical device in the EU.

Voluntis
Voluntis has developed a symptom monitoring and management platform for various indications. Oleena is a prescription DTx to report symptoms analyzed by the application for severity and provides recommendations. Oleena has CE marked as a Class IIa medical device in Europe and FDA authorized in the US. The company's other investigational product, eCO, that allows patients with cancer to self-report symptoms like hypertension and diarrhea.

Urinary incontinence

Leva

Leva Pelvic Health System is an FDA class II medical device available with a prescription used for strengthening, rehabilitation, and training of pelvic floor muscles, mixed and mild to moderate urgency urinary incontinence, including overactive bladder in women. It is available as a combination of an app paired with an intravaginal motion sensor. The motion sensor records signals during pelvic floor muscle exercise and transmits them to the app on a smartphone. The app provides guidance for 3-5 minute long exercise sessions twice a day for 8-12 weeks. The randomized controlled trial has demonstrated a reduction in incontinence episodes and an improvement in symptoms (Weinstein MM et al., 2022). The prescription for the device is available after a video or audio consultation.

21 DIGITAL DIAGNOSTICS & DIGITAL BIOMARKERS

Improvements in computing technology and sensors have created opportunities for digital tools to be used in clinical medicine. Progress in digital diagnostics and digital biomarker technologies is expanding their applications in clinical practice, consumer wellness, and clinical research. This chapter provides an overview and potential clinical applications of digital diagnostics and biomarkers.

Digital diagnostics

Digital diagnostics are technology products that collect and measure any data from the patient. Digital diagnostics may be used with automated interventions or provide information or data to healthcare professionals who then rely on their judgment for potential interventions. Digital diagnostics collect digital biomarkers through software applications, specialized standalone sensors, or through integration with drug delivery devices. A digital diagnostic can have a combination of hardware, software, and/or digital application. For our discussion, we will exclude digital imaging devices which use digital cameras to take images of anatomical organs or create images based on the interpretation of electromagnetic waves. These digital devices include:

Radiology: Digital acquisition of images using techniques such as Magnetic Resonance Imaging (MRI), Computer Tomography (CT), Fluoroscopy, or X-Rays can be used to create 2D or 3D imaging data sets of tissues, organs, or organisms.

Pathology: Digital pathology uses slide scanners, creating a whole slide digital image of formalin-fixed paraffin-embedded tissue or frozen section. Similarly, fluorescence confocal microscopy using digital imaging can be used for collecting digital images (Cimadamore A et al., 2021).

Molecular: Most molecular diagnostics are based on 'lab-on-chip' or microfluidics technology, which can detect chemicals, proteins, or amino acids. These diagnostics can generate, process, and store data (Digital Diagnostics for Africa Network. 2022). Molecular digital diagnostics have the ability to multiplex, which is the capability to process multiple analytes, pathogens, immunoassays, and biomarkers in one sample at one time.

According to a survey of specialists in laboratory medicine conducted by the International Federation of Clinical Chemistry and Laboratory Medicine (IFCC) Committee on Mobile Health and Bioengineering in Laboratory Medicine, digital diagnostics were divided into 10 market segments (Desiere F et al., 2021):

- **Laboratory management software**: Lab automation and workflow management tools
- **Laboratory performance analytics**: Data analytics for medical, operational, financial information
- **Laboratory information systems**: Lab data management solutions
- **Digital after-sales service**: Tools targeting end-customers
- **Clinical workflow automation**: Workflow tools for clinical collaboration
- **Clinical decision support**: Recommendation engines or alerts
- **Electronic health records**: Patient care coordination, data, and flow management tools
- **Digital disease prevention**: Patient self-monitoring tools or applications
- **Digital disease self-management**: Patient self-testing, diagnosis, or management tools or applications
- **Population health management**: Tools to track linked to quality of care

Biomarkers

As per FDA, a *biomarker* is defined as "a defined characteristic that is measured as an indicator of normal biological processes, pathogenic processes or response to an exposure or intervention" (FDA-NIH Biomarker Working Group. 2016). World Health Organization defines *biomarkers* as "any substance, structure or process that can be measured in the body or its products and influence or predict the incidence of outcome or disease" (WHO. 2001). Biomarkers can refer to anatomic functions (e.g., tidal volume), body chemistry (e.g., blood glucose, d-dimer, etc.), or physiological characteristic (e.g., heart rate, blood oxygen saturation, etc.) measured to track a specific biological outcome like a medical condition or a disease state. Biomarkers can be molecular, physiological, radiographic, histological, biochemical, or digital. Biomarkers have been divided into diagnostic, monitoring, response, predictive, prognostic, safety, and risk (FDA-NIH Biomarker Working Group. 2016).

Diagnostic biomarker: A diagnostic biomarker is "used to detect or confirm the presence of a disease or condition of interest or to identify individuals with a subtype of the disease" (FDA-NIH Biomarker Working Group. 2016). For example, continuously elevated blood pressure readings in adults may be used to diagnose a patient with essential hypertension. An ideal biomarker will have 100% specificity, which means that the individuals who do not have the disease would be diagnosed (no false positives), and 100% sensitivity which means that every individual with a disease who is tested will get diagnosed (no false negative). However, in practice, this is not easy to achieve. The biomarkers should be reliable, precise, and repeatable (Califf RM. 2018).

Monitoring biomarker: Per FDA's definition, "a biomarker measured repeatedly for assessing the status of a disease or medical condition or for evidence of exposure (or effect of) a medical product or an environmental agent." For example, INR values monitor response to anticoagulation therapy with Warfarin. Respiratory rate may be used as a monitoring biomarker for nebulizer therapy. These biomarkers are used to assess treatment response, monitor disease progression or physiological parameters, and the emergence of new abnormalities. They are also used to develop new treatments and conduct drug safety studies.

Response biomarker: A response biomarker is a "biomarker used to show that a biological response, potentially beneficial or harmful, has occurred in an individual exposed to a medical product or an environmental agent." These biomarkers can be used in clinical research as pharmacodynamic or surrogate endpoint biomarkers.

Predictive biomarker: A predictive biomarker is "used to identify individuals who are more likely than similar individuals without the biomarker to experience a favorable or unfavorable effect from exposure to a medical product or an environmental agent." For example, BRCA1/2 gene mutation may be predictive for certain breast cancers, or skin changes may be predictive biomarkers for skin tumors. In clinical practice, predictive biomarkers may be used for treatment selection or treatment titration, and in clinical research, predictive biomarkers are used to select patient cohorts or for patient segmentation.

Prognostic biomarker: Prognostic biomarker is a "biomarker used to identify the likelihood of a clinical event, disease recurrence or progression in patients who have the disease or medical condition of interest." For example, a fall in blood pressure or pulse oximetry may indicate a worsening prognosis in patients with heart arrhythmia.

Safety biomarker: A safety biomarker is "measured before or after an exposure to a medical product or an environmental agent to indicate the likelihood, presence, or extent of toxicity as an adverse effect." These biomarkers are used as early indicators for adverse events to therapies, toxins, or products in development.

Susceptibility or risk biomarker: A risk biomarker "indicates the potential for developing a disease or medical condition in an individual who does not currently have a clinically apparent disease or the medical condition." This biomarker is generally tested in patients to prevent the development of a disease or condition in the future. For example, measuring LDL for future coronary artery disease risk.

Biomarkers may or may not correlate with a patient's subjective well-being or clinical state. In clinical research, it is essential to evaluate if the biomarker can replace clinical or surrogate endpoints through validation. FDA can designate biomarkers that are useful indicators as qualified biomarkers. Clinical endpoints "directly measure what matters most to people – whether they feel or function better or live longer" (FDA. 2017i). FDA considers improvement in clinical endpoints as a criteria to recommend therapies. Surrogate endpoints are proxies for clinical outcomes and are validated to correlate with clinical benefit. Per FDA, 45% of new drugs were based on surrogate endpoints between 2010 and 2012. For example, a validated surrogate endpoint measured by a digital diagnostic device could be systolic blood pressure correlated to clinical outcome. Surrogate endpoints allow clinical research studies to be conducted with smaller groups of participants over a shorter duration than clinical endpoints.

Digital biomarkers

Digital biomarkers refer to any quantifiable data generated by physiological processes, captured through behavioral measurements or patient questionnaires, and collected using digital devices to diagnose, monitor, or treat clinical conditions. A digital biomarker has been defined as "a characteristic or set of characteristics, collected from digital health technologies, that is measured as an indicator of normal biological processes, pathogenic processes, or responses to an exposure or intervention, including therapeutic interventions" (Vasudevan et al., 2022). Digital biomarkers capture the biomedical state of an individual. They track health status or medical conditions, monitor treatment efficacy, and detect remission or flares of chronic conditions. Digital biomarkers can be collected through "portable, wearable, implantable or digestible sensors" (Babrak LM et al., 2019). Like traditional biomarkers, digital biomarkers need regulatory approval. They need to be validated, and their feasibility for the condition of interest assessed based on established guidelines.

Studies have demonstrated the role of biomarkers in improving general health in reducing mortality (Elkaryoni et al., 2019). The future course of a disease or medical condition can be predicted by applying machine learning algorithms to digital biomarker data (Shin EK et al., 2018). Digital biomarkers are also finding applications in clinical medicine and research (Hartl D et al. 2021). In clinical research, they can be surrogate endpoints (Arnerić SP et al., 2017) used in setup of decentralized trials (Khozin S et al., 2019), reduces duration of research studies, and provide early feedback during the trials (Bakker JP et al., 2019).

Digital biomarkers can collect established biomarkers like heart rate or create new biomarkers, which would be impossible without digital technologies like tapping smartphone tests for Parkinson's disease severity (Zhan A et al. 2018). Digital biomarker information is collected through sensors. These can be self-contained or embedded in other devices like mobile phones. Broad categories of technologies used to collect digital biomarkers include (Saner H et al. 2020):

- **Imaging sensors**: Cameras can record in the visible spectrum or non-visible spectrum including infrared, radio waves or radars. They are being used for cardiovascular measurements using plethysmography for vascular pulses, body temperature using infrared, gait evaluation etc.
- **Pressure sensors**: Piezoelectric sensors convert mechanical pressure into electrical charges. These sensors can be used to detect weight, breathing cycles, blood pressure etc.
- **Electrical sensors**: These sensors measure subtle changes in electrical activity in the body. These include electrocardiogram for heart rhythm, electroencephalogram for brain waves etc.
- **Sound sensors**: These sensors record audio and are used for speech analysis, breath sounds etc.

Digital biomarkers based on sensors can be categorized based on the placement of sensors (Saner H et al. 2020):

- **Wearable sensors**: Worn on the body of individual from whom the biomarker data is being collected. Such sensors have been used in conditions like atrial fibrillation.
- **Object sensors**: Attached to the object used by the individuals whose data is being collected. For example, pillboxes which are used to evaluate medication adherence.
- **Ambient sensors**: Placed in the environment around the individuals to collect data about the individual. Examples of ambient sensors include passive infrared sensors, piezo-electric force sensor arrays, radars to evaluate movement.

Considerations

Digital biomarkers have many advantages over non-digital biomarkers. Digital biomarkers are generally non-invasive, easier, and less expensive to collect. They make it easier to collect longitudinal data without increasing the frequency of patient visits (Guthrie NL et al., 2019). Continuous physiological data can be collected more cost-effectively. Continuous data collection helps to titrate therapy in real time or more frequently than periodic data collection. Digital biomarkers can generate large amounts of data, which has the advantage that it can be leveraged for training machine learning algorithms. Continuous data collection matched with machine learning algorithms for trend analysis can detect anomalies earlier compared to human review. In clinical research, this allows for improvement in statistical power, sensitivity, and specificity (Dodge HH et al., 2015). The real-time collection and sharing of digital biomarker data using internet-connected digital diagnostic devices at an individual or population level can be analyzed in real-time. It is also easier to share this data in real-time with multiple recipients across the globe at minimal additional cost. Digital diagnostics can integrate with electronic medical records and disease registries for bidirectional data exchange. Integrating external data elements like gender, age, and past medical history can improve the accuracy of the output and personalize it for an individual for precision health. Decision support can be built right into the diagnostic itself. Digital biomarkers are also finding use in clinical research. They enable easier collection of real-world evidence, which can help with new product development, label extensions, and adverse event monitoring of products already on the market. Since digital biomarkers are quantified, multiple biomarkers can be combined for a composite view of an individual (Coravos A et al., 2019).

The disadvantages of digital biomarkers are primarily related to the cost of sensors and management of data compared to analog diagnostics. While digital biomarkers have expanded the potential applications of biomarkers, they may require patients to play a more active role in sensor management and data collection, which may exclude some patients. Due to the nature of digital data, digital biomarkers require large amounts of storage, which need appropriate safeguards per HIPAA. One of the advantages of digital biomarkers is the potential to apply machine learning algorithms to the data. However, this makes the analysis complex and challenging to explain to providers and patients.

Artificial intelligence in digital diagnostics

Using predictive analytics using machine learning has improved the scope of potential applications and the accuracy of digital biomarkers. For example, a systematic review found that the most common machine learning algorithms used in wearables tracking mental health include support vector machines, k-nearest neighbor, random forests, artificial neural networks, logistic regression, decision trees, bayesian network, linear discriminant analysis, and principal component analysis (Long N et al. 2022). In another study on mild cognitive impairment, the machine learning algorithms used on biomarker data included an adaptive neuro-fuzzy inference system, decision trees, convolutional neural network, generalized linear model, K-nearest neighbor, logistic regression, LSTM, naive Bayes, non-negative least squares, reinforcement learning, ROC, support vector machines. Validation methods included 5-fold and 10-fold cross-validation, leave-one-out cross-validation, and leave-two-subject-out cross-validation (The SK et al., 2021).

Artificial intelligence algorithms can combine multiple digital biomarkers representing different modalities into a single predictive output. Predictive models can be developed for better accuracy than a single biomarker by using supervised deep learning with dimensionality reduction on multiple models. For example, in a study, a convolutional neural network for unsupervised representation learning of multivariate sensor data from an accelerometer for activity, photoplethysmography for heart rate, respiratory rate, heart rate variability, blood perfusion, temperature, galvanic skin response, the barometer was used with random forest trained on the subject reported physical fatigue labels to quantify measures of fatigue (Luo H et al. 2020). Machine learning algorithms can also fine-tune the digital diagnostic output to the differences in underlying baseline physiology due to age, gender, etc.

Evaluation of digital biomarkers

The V3 framework recommended by Goldsack et al. has recommended verification, analytical validation, and clinical validation as a framework to evaluate digital measurement tools (Goldsack JC et al., 2020). The framework applies to tools that "identify, measure, or predict the clinical, biological, physical, functional state, or experience."

Verification

Verification is the process of evaluating the hardware and sensors using electronics to check that the signal from the sensor is converted into appropriate sensor output. This could include sensors on smartphones, wearables, or remote monitoring devices. The verification goal is to ensure that the hardware is sensitive enough to capture the biomarker of interest and that there is minimal signal noise, no environmental interference, etc. The manufacturers of the sensors perform verification. In the United States, FDA (FDA. 2021k) has provided guidelines about verifying sensors used in healthcare settings. A similar function is performed by CE (Conformité Européenne) mark in the European Union (European Commission.) The activities in the verification phase could include assessing the sensor's precision, accuracy, and consistency. The error rate is compared against widely accepted industry standards.

Analytical Validation

Analytical validation evaluates the algorithm that converts the sensor output into a measurement of interest. Analytical validation aims to check that the physiological measurements are detected as intended. The hardware or sensor manufacturer performs validation if the sensor is offered along with an interpreted output value, or it could be performed by organizations that source the sensors and develop their algorithm for the output value used in the product or service. These algorithms are targeted toward the biomarkers of interest and include efficacy and safety data for regulators. The United States and European Medicine Agency's FDA provides guidelines for validating algorithms. The activities in analytical validation may consist of comparing the accuracy of the output of sensor-algorithm combination against industry-standard equipment and comparing against industry or regulatory best practices, standards, or guidelines.

Clinical Validation

Clinical validation is the process of evaluating the clinical relevance of the digital biomarker. The goal is to ensure that the biomarker has clinical utility and that the measurements produced from the sensor contribute to the diagnosis, management, or prevention of a specific clinical condition. The clinical validation is conducted either during the development of new products or new applications of existing products. The activities in clinical validation may consist of evaluating whether the digital marker detects, predicts, diagnoses, or monitors a clinical condition.

Applications of digital diagnostics

Digital biomarkers using digital sensors have been used for a myriad of physiological measurements across multiple organ systems (Motahari-Nezhad H et al., 2022). These include:

- Cardiovascular system
  - Blood pressure
  - Heart rate
  - Heart rhythm and rate variability
  - Physical activity
  - Weight
- Respiratory
  - Lung volumes including tidal volume
  - Pulse oximetry
  - Respiratory effort including FEV_1
  - Respiratory rate
  - Respiratory rhythm
  - Respiratory sounds including cough and wheeze
- Metabolic syndrome
  - Blood glucose
  - Foot steps
  - Hormone levels
- Musculoskeletal
  - Body and mobility measurements
  - Movement and gait
  - Muscle stimulation
  - Posture
  - Swallowing
  - Wrist or finger based actigraphy
- Neurology
  - Brain activity
  - Cognitive functions
  - Neuropsychiatric changes
  - Pain
  - Speech
- Ophthalmology
  - Intraocular pressure
  - Visual acuity

Digital biomarkers have been used in multiple of medical conditions. Some of the widely researched areas are discussed below.

Disclaimer: The evidence listed is illustrative and not a comprehensive review of all potential digital biomarkers in research or on the market for a specific medical condition. The discussion is for illustrative and educational purposes. All products and services discussed in this section are registered trademarks owned by their respective registrants, owners, or licensees. The author does not endorse or vouch for the clinical validity of any products or services listed here. The characteristics of the products were accurate at the time of the writing but may change over time.

Asthma

Evaluation of breath sounds using a stethoscope has been one of the earliest biomarkers used in medicine. Digital stethoscopes have created new opportunities for remote and automated lung function assessment. Digital biomarkers studied in asthma have included respiratory rate, oxygen saturation, and cough sounds (Rassouli F et al., 2020). Cough sounds are also being studied for pneumonia (Boesch M et al., 2023).

Atrial fibrillation

Photoplethysmography has been used on wearables to detect atrial fibrillation (Greiten L et al., 2017)). Mobile phone apps have been developed to differentiate the arrhythmia signals obtained by smartphones (McManus DD et al., 2016). Elevated heart rate detected through the same sensors used for atrial fibrillation can be used to detect other medical conditions like vasculitis (Gkikopoulos N et al., 2022), supraventricular tachycardias (Sequeira N et al. 2020), and heart block (Overbeek DL et al., 2019).

Cognitive impairment

Cognitive impairment is a spectrum from mild cognitive impairment to severe dementia. Digital biomarkers tested in conditions with cognitive impairment include memory tests, handwriting or drawing tasks, games, and digital version of test batteries (Ding Z et al., 2022). There have been efforts to detect mild cognitive impairment in the community setting using passive infrared sensors and door contact magnetic sensors (Akl A et al. 2017), triaxial accelerometers (Rahimi H et al., 2018), circadian activity, speech, gait analysis, handwriting, and movement (The SK et al., 2022).

Fatigue

Smartphone-based eye tracking to measure gaze fatigue has been postulated to predict mental fatigue (Tseng WV et al., 2021). Mental fatigue has been linked to medical conditions impacting general well-being (Penner I-K et al., 2017; Pawlikowska T et al., 1994) or physiological conditions such as sleep deprivation (Dawson D et al., 2015).

Heart failure

Heart failure is an excellent example of a clinical condition where the exacerbations can be easily captured through biomarkers and early interventions to prevent hospitalizations. Rapid increase in weight measured using an internet-connected weighing scale has traditionally been a common biomarker to predict the onset of heart failure exacerbation. Kramer et al. evaluated sensors collecting information about physical activity, tissue impedance, heart rate, respiratory rate, patient-reported outcomes, and lab tests as biomarkers in heart failure patients (Kramer F et al., 2020). Measuring intrathoracic impedance using wearable bioimpedance monitors have shown to predict heart failure exacerbations (Abraham WT et al., 2011).

Huntington's disease

Machine learning algorithms applied to inertial sensors attached to shoes have been used to create digital biomarkers of patients' gait, correlated with the Unified Huntington's Disease Rating Scale, Total Motor Score (TMS), and Total Functional Capacity (TFC). Digital gait analysis has examined stride length, gait velocity, stride, and stance time (Gaßner H et al., 2020).

Mental health

Digital biomarkers have been used for anxiety, stress, and depression (Hickey BA et al., 2021). Wearable devices have been shown to capture emotional states (Laureanti R et al., 2020). A study demonstrated that using sleep, physical activity, stress metrics, neurocognitive assessments, EEG, and ecological momentary assessments delivered via smartphone could predict depression (Shah RV et al., 2021). Most approaches studying applications of digital biomarkers in mental health have used a multimodal approach to measuring stress through wearables. Stress-specific digital biomarkers have included cardiac activity, respiratory activity, respiratory activity, and using wearable electrochemical immunosensors to detect biofluids for cortisol (Kang M et al., 2022). In studies, heart rate variability has been shown a better predictor of stress than heart rate (Hernando D et al., 2018). Electrodermal sensors combined with other biomarkers have been found to increase stress detection accuracy (Seoane F et al. 2014). Electrodermal sensors have been used to detect social anxiety in individuals (Shaukat-Jali R., et al., 2021). Other psychiatric disorders where biomarkers have been used include bipolar disorders (Valenza GL et al., 2015), PTSD (Tsanas A et al., 2020), and Schizophrenia (Ben-Zeev D et al., 2016)

The use of biomarkers in mental health disorders also has special challenges. They require consideration for safeguarding privacy while tracking mental health disorders using sensors and biomarkers. It is also challenging to establish standardized outcome measures due to subjectivity in assessing mental health conditions among individuals, as the sensors capture the physiological response due to underlying mental health conditions, which may be influenced by individual and environmental factors (Sheikh M et al., 2021).

Metabolic syndrome

Digital biomarkers used in metabolic syndrome have included sensors measuring blood glucose, weight, waist circumference, and physical activity (Lee J-H et al., 2022). Physical activity, one of the most common digital biomarkers, has been shown to impact glucose control (Ozaslan B et al., 2020). Smartphone-connected continuous blood glucose monitors have been used for diabetes monitoring for many years. A research team used smartphone-based photoplethysmography coupled with deep neural networks as a non-invasive biomarker to diagnose diabetes (Avram R et al., 2020). Self-monitoring using blood pressure monitoring wearables has been shown to lower hypertension (Yen HY et al., 2022).

Neurological disorders

Multiple sclerosis impacts the brain, spinal cord, and nerves, with symptoms affecting vision, muscle movement, and sensations. Testing fine motor functions on smartphone screens provides detection of subtle changes in motor functions. Cameras and accelerometers can be used for gait analysis, including step count, walking speed, coordination, and balance. Cognitive assessments performed by digital tools can check for cognitive changes in MS, including executive functions, memory, verbal fluency, and information processing speed (Rao SM et al., 1991). Eye trackers have been used for eye-related biomarkers like saccadic initiation time (Nygaard GO et al., 2015) and pursuit of ocular movement frequency (De Santi L et al., 2010). Digital biomarkers like measurement of the peripapillary retinal fiber layer can be used to monitor the progression of Multiple Sclerosis (Dillenseger A et al., 2021). Assessment of contrast vision assessed by mobile devices can be another useful digital biomarker. Vocal biomarkers obtained from speech analysis have been used to evaluate acoustic speech and language (Noffs G et al., 2020). Smartphone-based apps have been developed to assess motor functions in MS. For example, the Digital Self-Assessment Multiple Sclerosis mobile app (MSCopilot) to assess MS progression using the Multiple Sclerosis Functional Composite score has obtained a CE mark in Europe. It collects over 350 digital biomarkers on physiological and behavioral characteristics. Other apps for MS include Floodlight (Roche, Switzerland), Konectom (Biogen, USA), and MS Sherpa (Orikami, The Netherlands) (Dillenseger A et al., 2021).

NMOSDCopilot is an app used for self-assessment of Neuromyelitis Optica Spectrum Disorder (NMOSD). The measurements conducted by the app include tests to assess gait, vision, cognition, and dexterity, as well as questionnaires for pain, fatigue, quality of life, depression, bladder, and bowel dysfunction. This app was evaluated in a clinical study that compared the results of at-home e-tests with in-clinic standard tests (NCT05566769).

Neuromuscular disorders

Digital biomarkers are effective in early diagnosis, monitoring treatment, and adverse effects in neuromuscular disorders (Youn BY et al., 2021). Chen et al. studied upper limb movement using hand velocity, arm lifting angle, and elbow angle for Spinal Muscular Dystrophy (Chen X et al., 2017). Le Moing et al. used magneto-inertial sensors to check the angular velocity of the wrist, the ratio of the vertical component of acceleration to overall acceleration, and computer power in patients with Duchenne Muscular Dystrophy (Le Moing et al., 2016). Studies have demonstrated the value of using physical activity using home sensors, heart rate variability, and speech in ALS patients (Garcia-Gancedo L et al., 2019). ME&MGopen mobile app is used to monitor symptoms of myasthenia gravis by the patients using questionnaires assessing breathing, speaking difficulty, drooping eyelids, and arm or leg weakness. The clinical studies assessing it were NCT05564936 and NCT05566964. Smartphone sensors have been used to track fluctuations in symptom severity and medication response in Parkinson's disease (Sieberts SK et al., 2021). Video recordings of patients' gait have also been used as a biomarker to analyze motion patterns and assist in the diagnosis (Rangel E et al., 2022).

Post-surgical monitoring

Post-surgery tracking of recovery or early detection of adverse events is important for improving surgical outcomes. For example, wearable sensors were used in patients who had undergone sternotomy to measure chest expansion as a digital biomarkers (Wang C et al., 2020). Similarly, gait analysis is being used for post-surgical physical therapy.

Vision impairment

The OdySight Care app is used to develop clinically validated visual acuity score to provide medical advice and guidance about the ophthalmic health. The app is used to track ocular toxicities in chemotherapy or targeted immunotherapy.

22 CLINICAL RESEARCH IN DIGITAL HEALTH

Clinical research is ongoing in multiple domains of digital health and digital therapeutics. The clinical trials may take years before FDA clears the product, and is made available to the patients directly, or gets reimbursement codes and is incorporated into payer benefits if reimbursed through the health plans.

The discussion of the clinical trials is for illustrative and educational purposes only. The studies may be planned for the future, actively recruiting, completed, terminated, or in an unknown state. They are listed in two categories – standalone digital health or digital therapeutics products and combination products, where the digital health product is combined with a drug or medical device.

Standalone products

Acute Coronary Disease (ACD)

CardiCare mobile app is in clinical trials for the post-acute coronary syndrome. It includes a physical activity recommendation engine, personalized physical activity recommendations, symptom tracking, monitoring of physical activity, and education to improve VO2 max. The app is used in conjunction with an Actigraph.

Autism

eGOLIAH (Gaming Open Library for Intervention in Autism at Home) study (NCT05271955) provides children aged 3 to 6 years with usual care and video games. Video games can be combined with speech therapy and/or psychological care.

Cancer related anxiety and depression

Multiple clinical studies have been conducted to assess the efficacy of the treatment of BNT-003 from Blue Note Therapeutics to treat symptoms of anxiety and depression related to cancer (NCT05032404). A double-blind, randomized efficacy trial of Dreamland, a psychological mobile app, versus Cerena, a medical information app, in improving patient's experience after diagnosis of Acute Myeloid Leukemia was conducted. Dreamland (BNT200) provides supportive psychotherapy, psychoeducation, psychosocial skill-building, and self-care. Cerena provides general wellness education, nutrition, exercise, and cancer prevention information.

(NCT05501171). BNT001 is a cognitive behavioral stress management app for cancer patients to treat anxiety and depressive symptoms related to cancer diagnosis (NCT04705025). Randomized, registrational study (NCT04862195) and randomized controlled trial (NCT05227898) have been conducted to compare the effectiveness of the CBT app Attune and educational app Cerena in managing cancer symptoms.

Melanoma

Melanoma Surveillance Photography (MSP) uses total body photography and digital dermoscopy (NCT04385732) for reducing false positives biopsies in high and very high-risk individuals due to high naevus counts.

Multiple Sclerosis (MS)

A study (NCT04445116) is evaluating the use of a video game 5 days a week for 8 weeks, about 25-30 minutes daily, using a mobile device to evaluate the impact of cognitive deficits in adolescents and young adults with pediatric-onset Multiple Sclerosis.

Musculoskeletal conditions

Sword Health is studying (NCT05417685) the impact of remote monitoring of rehabilitation exercises performed by patients at home. Trained professionals monitor the patient groups, including acute, post-acute, and post-surgical musculoskeletal conditions. Instruments used for measuring primary outcomes include Self-reported Pain (NPRS); Short version of the Disabilities of the Arm, Shoulder and Hand questionnaire (QuickDASH); Oswestry Disability Index (ODI); Neck Disability Index (NDI); Short form of Foot and Ankle Ability Measure (QuickFAAM); Short form Hip Osteoarthritis Outcomes Score (HOOS-PS); Short form Knee Osteoarthritis Outcomes score (KOOS-PS); Fear Avoidance Beliefs Questionnaire - Physical Activity (FABQ - PA); Neck, lower spine, shoulder, elbow, ankle, hip and knee range of motion (ROM). The instruments used for secondary measures include Self-reported Pain (VAS); Self-reported fatigue (VAS); Self-reported Surgical intent; Self-reported consumption of painkillers; General Anxiety Disorder-7 (GAD-7); Patient Health Questionnaire-9 (PHQ-9); Work Productivity and Activity Impairment Questionnaire (WPAI).

Heart failure

BiovitalsHF is conducting a clinical study (NCT04191330) to assess the effectiveness of a digital platform to titrate Guideline-Directed Medical Therapy for heart failure with reduced ejection fraction with the primary outcome of improvement in optimal therapy score. SideKick Health is conducting a clinical study of SK-141 for behavior change, lifestyle change, and remote symptom monitoring digital app in heart failure patients to improve the frequency of symptoms, quality of life, medication adherence, and self-care with the primary outcome as a change in Kansas City Cardiomyopathy Questionnaire (KCCQ-12) scores. The app uses gamification, altruistic rewards, and content and is used with the standard of care therapy. (NCT05193344)

An unblinded 4-arm parallel group RCT (NCT04394754) evaluated three digital health technologies to improve heart failure patients' management and quality of life. The technologies were a smart scale (BodyPort), a personalized diet and weight management coaching app (Noom), and an automated conversational platform for patient motivation and education (Conversa). The primary outcome is improved quality of life after 90 days, measured by KCCQ.

Hypertension

CureApp HT for the management of essential hypertension using an app and home BP monitoring (HBPM) demonstrated a reduction in blood pressure compared with patients under physician management and HBPM in a randomized controlled trial - HERB-Digital Hypertension (Kario K et al. 2022). The app analyzes home BP measurements and guides behavioral lifestyle changes. The app has been approved and reimbursed for the management of hypertension in Japan.

Non-Alcoholic Fatty Liver Disease (NAFLD)

CureApp is developing a DTx for patients with NASH undergoing clinical trials in Japan. The app will use behavior modification, education about diet, and exercise therapy. Sidekick Health's (SK-241) clinical trial is evaluating its digital behavioral change program for patients with metabolic derangements and non-alcoholic fatty liver disease (NAFLD) through lifestyle changes, including improving diet, increasing physical activity, stress reduction (NCT05426382).

Stuttering

A software application that uses euphonic music tracks with broad-spectrum binaural beats using the concept of auditory neuro modulation to induce selective EEG spectral power changes is being investigated in a single-group assignment interventional study (NCT05339906). The participants are exposed to the stimuli for 5 minutes, and biosignals consisting of EEG and ECG are recorded before, during, and after exposure. The study will measure speech disfluencies before, right after, and 10 minutes after auditory stimulation.

Substance abuse

A clinical trial is evaluating (NCT05031416) remote smoking cessation DTx targeted at individuals with serious mental illness, which integrates nicotine replacement therapy with a smoking cessation app and social support provided through social media. Another trial (NCT04948307) on a combination of a DTx OXD01 (MODIA) with sublingual buprenorphine/naloxone for the treatment of opioid use disorder is based on digital therapy for 1-2 times per week for 15-30 minutes each for a total duration of 6 months.

Suicide prevention

A double-blind, parallel assignment randomized clinical trial (NCT04775160) evaluated two smartphone applications based on Ecological Momentary Intervention to prevent suicidal thoughts and behavior. The apps MEmind and eB2 were used in the intervention group, along with treatment as usual with psychiatric follow-up. The app provides a safety plan with coping strategies, an enhanced contact intervention with customized messaging, and a mental toolbox with relaxation techniques.

Combination products

Combination products combine therapeutic and/or diagnostic modalities to provide a joint intervention. These could be drug-device, drug/device-diagnostic, drug/device-biomarker, drug/device-digital therapeutic, or similar combinations.

Anxiety

ALISA study (NCT05510804) is evaluating the efficacy of app-based CBT using virtual reality headsets and scheduled therapist sessions for anxiety disorders, including agoraphobia with or without panic disorder, social anxiety disorder, or panic disorder.

Asthma

A Phase 4 study (NCT04997304) was conducted to develop predictive models for AirDuo and ProAir Digihalers combination products with sensors and apps attached to the inhaler devices to predict asthma exacerbations and medication response.

Cardiac amyloidosis

Some combination trials include a service component as an adjunct to usual care. For example, NCT05098665 will add telemonitoring using digital scales to track body weight changes and intervene early in acute and subacute decompensated heart failure cases in patients with cardiac amyloidosis.

Insomnia

Menopause After Cancer Study (Citalopram +/- Gabapentin + Sleepio + support person): This study (NCT04766229) is currently recruiting women "with vasomotor symptoms of menopause and a prior cancer diagnosis, for whom conventional menopausal hormone therapy (MHT) is contraindicated." The intervention adds a digital therapeutic using CBT to standard drug treatment for insomnia to evaluate for improvement in quality of life.

Medication adherence

A smartphone app TransMedAx and QR code technology on extended-release Tacrolimus are being evaluated to improve adherence and reduce intra-patient variability in kidney transplant recipients (NCT04711291).

Schizophrenia

Ability MyCite combination (Drug + Sensor + Transmitter + Mobile App) combines the drug Abilify (Aripripazole) used to treat schizophrenia with an ingestible sensor that tracks when the pill was taken by sending a message wireless to a wearable patch. The patch sends information to a mobile app on the phone to track the ingestion of the drug, which can be shared with providers and caregivers. Similar combinations can be used with any other drug where ingestion tracking is important for clinical outcomes (NCT03881449).

Similarly, a Phase 2 interventional study on 112 participants to assess if a digital therapeutic (PEAR-004) could reduce the symptoms of schizophrenia using psychosocial intervention CBT along with the standard of care with antipsychotic medication (NCT03751280).

23 MOBILE HEALTH APPS

The use of mobile phones in healthcare was initially described as 'mHealth' by the Global Health Observatory of the World Health Organization (WHO). As per WHO, "mHealth is a term used for medical and public health practice supported by mobile devices, such as mobile phones, patient monitoring devices, Personal Digital Assistants (PDAs), and other wireless devices. mHealth applications include the use of mobile devices in collecting community and clinical health data, delivery of healthcare information to practitioners, researchers, and patients, real-time monitoring of patient vital signs, and direct provision of care" (WHO Global Observatory for eHealth. 2011). With the advent of smartphones, almost all health applications are being enabled through mobile apps. The mobile phone apps are distributed through the app stores. However, some companies may directly offer app downloads through their company websites or their partners, health insurance companies, or employer portals. Consumers are using health apps to monitor and manage their health and well-being. They find health apps by directly searching for them on the app stores, reading blogs or wellness sites, with prescriptions from their providers or referrals from their health insurance providers or employers. Physicians like to see peer-reviewed evidence of benefit or inclusion in professional guidelines to make prescription recommendations, and most mobile health apps do not cross this bar. Unless an app has been recommended as a standard of care, the providers are also concerned about data privacy/security, liability issues, health equity concerns for patients without smartphones or proficiency with technology, and costs associated with the app.

There were over 300,000 health apps (Aitken, M. 2017) per an analysis conducted in 2017. Millions of health-related apps are downloaded every year from the app stores. The health apps can be broadly categorized into apps that provide:

- Wellness information targeted at general consumers
- Medical information targeted at health care providers
- Healthcare related coaching
- Medical record information and recommendations based on these records
- Interface to medical devices or electronic medical record systems
- Data collection interface for the patients
- Telehealth capabilities

According to a study (IMS. 2013), about two-thirds of the apps are targeted at consumers, and one-third are targeted at healthcare professionals. The consumer apps are wellness apps that target fitness, stress, diet, nutrition, and lifestyle. Most of the consumer apps were targeted at women's health, followed by children's health, and then senior health. About a quarter of the apps were for disease management, with the largest categories being mental health, diabetes, blood, circulatory, musculoskeletal, and nervous system.

Many apps collect personal information from users without oversight. While some apps have demonstrated benefits to the users, there are concerns about misinformation and unvalidated claims by most others. Organizations are developing standards and guidelines to assist with evaluating health-related apps. There is no formal evaluation process for the apps claiming any health or medical benefit unless they voluntarily seek approval under medical device regulations.

Clinical apps

The discussion about Software as a Medical Device (SaMD) in this book includes more information about which apps qualify to be considered medical devices per regulations in the United States. These devices address a health issue and can cover preventive, diagnostic, and therapeutic indications. It can also be used for disease management, patient rehabilitation, or supporting an organ or bodily function. Generally, any app that qualifies as a medical device must follow rigorous processes during and post-development. The app developers are expected to include documentation of evidence that the app is a medical device as per the regulatory definition of a medical device in the jurisdiction where the medical app will be operated. A high-quality app is developed based on evidence from peer-reviewed scientific studies and discussions with qualified health professionals and potential users. It is also important to evaluate and address ethical concerns or inadvertent biases and outcomes from using the app.

Prescription apps are the holy grail of health. These are applications that are only available to users if they are prescribed by a healthcare provider. Such apps can claim higher reimbursement from the payers and be included in the treatment protocols, thereby significantly increasing their use and market share and collecting data that can further strengthen their value proposition. Some common therapeutic areas in which mobile apps have been used clinically are weight loss, physical activity, diabetes, and mental health.

There are over 700 clinical studies currently underway which are using mobile apps in some capacity for a multitude of clinical conditions. A sample of outcomes of studies which are in Phase 1-4 include:

- Caregiver training
- Case management of homeless individuals
- Cognitive behavioral therapy for management of depressive symptoms,
- Digital therapeutic for diabetes improvement
- Improve adherence to medical therapy
- Improve diabetes care
- Improve eating disorders
- Improve heart failure outcomes
- Improvement of mood
- Improving patient distress in serious medical conditions
- Intervention to increase physical activity

- Interventions to reduce drug and alcohol use
- Measure cognitive impairment due to psychoactive substances
- Mobile app to improve health of cancer survivors
- Patient education app for chronic diseases
- Reduce gestational diabetes
- Reduction in alcohol consumption using app and device.
- Smoking cessation intervention

Apps focused on mental health have become increasingly popular over the last few years. A systematic review looked at RCTs of app-based interventions to reduce anxiety. These apps used breathing retraining, Cognitive Behavioral Therapy, and the meta-analysis found a reduction in total anxiety scores due to the intervention. (Firth, J. et al. 2017). A systematic review studied RCTs and feasibility studies for behavior change (Payne HE et al., 2015) using self-monitoring, cue to action and feedback, or social support. Eight out of ten studies reported increased physical activity, nine reported decreases in BMI and weight loss, and the mental health apps showed decreased depression levels and better stress ratings.

Metabolic disease is a major public health issue in the developed world and increasingly in developing countries. A meta-analysis of RCTs showed a mean reduction in glycated hemoglobin by 0.4 (Bonoto BC et al., 2017). A systematic review and meta-analysis found a reduction of 1.04 kg of body weight by using a mobile phone app-based intervention (Flores Mateo G et al. 2015). The strategies used by apps included calorie counting, physical activity monitoring, and automated reminders. The apps had an attrition rate of over 30%, and the usage of apps was minimal after a month of using them. Another systematic review examined randomized control trials, controlled trials, and pre-post studies (Schoeppe, S. 2016). The results of included studies were mixed. An app promoting increased vegetable consumption was able to demonstrate increased consumption of vegetables. An app promoting increased activity among seniors demonstrated increased gait velocity and cadence during walking. However, a study based on gamified exercises failed to improve physical activity or cardiorespiratory fitness significantly.

Quality

Hundreds of thousands of apps are available on app stores making assessment of quality of their content difficult. Apps are likely more reputable if FDA has approved them, are published by a reputable software company or publishing house, and are sourced from reputed published sources which are peer-reviewed. Conventional mobile apps are rated based on the score on the app score provided by the users who review the apps. The other source is the articles from industry publications where experts select a handful of apps. Assessing the quality of health apps becomes challenging because, besides the conventional metrics used to assess an app, the apps also need to be evaluated based on the accuracy of their content.

The app stores contain large number of apps with questionable health benefits. It is imperative that the apps clearly state their health benefits supported by evidence. The apps should also address any concerns about health risks or harms due to using the app. These should be clearly stated to the users of the app. If the app needs to be restricted to a specific subset of users, mechanisms should be implemented to enable such restrictions.

If an app relies on health information as its core functionality, it is vital to ensure the developers are current on the latest developments. Medicine is rapidly advancing, and the discoveries related to health and wellness may either change the initial hypothesis on which the app was based or nullify it. The apps that use clinical algorithms must demonstrate their functioning to the regulatory authorities. These apps could include medical calculators, recommendation engines, treatment details, and artificial intelligence-based predictive analytics. The apps should have checks and balances against erroneous data entry and appropriate use of predictive models in the proper context.

IMS Institute for healthcare informatics has developed a scoring system based on an independent and objective assessment of healthcare app functionality (Aitken M et al. 2013). The IMS app functionality score is calculated based on information provided by the app for the following categories (Mortara A et al., 2020).

- Information to the patient in multiple formats
- Instructions pertinent to the user
- Ability to collect, share, and evaluate health data
- Reminders or alerts based on data collected or for targeted behavior change
- Graphical display of user entered data
- Guidance or recommendations based on user-entered data including potential diagnosis, treatment plan, or triage
- Communication between healthcare professionals and patients

Another quality rating criterion is the Mobile App Rating Scale (MARS), which measures quality with indicators under aesthetics, function, engagement, information quality, and subjective quality. Every indicator is rated on a five-point scale, with score of one denoting inadequate to five denoting excellent. Indicators under 'engagement' include checking if the app is entertaining, engaging, providing customization, interactive, and appropriate. Indicators under 'functionality' check for the app's performance, user interface, ease of use, and navigation, including workflow for most common tasks. The indicators under 'aesthetics' evaluate the app's layout, quality, and appropriateness of graphics and fonts. Indicators under the 'information' category evaluate the accuracy of the app's description in the quality of content. There are points for subjective preference for the app and for the impact of the app on the "user's knowledge, attitudes, intentions to change and the likelihood of behavior change" (Stoyanov SR et al., 2015).

Data sources

Smartphone apps allow collection health data, including physiological, social, emotional, and behavioral, in real time (Bush NE et al., 2019). Self-reported data for self-assessments can be collected to improve patient engagement, symptom tracking, and providing feedback. Data can be entered into a questionnaire or a series of questions with branching logic (Ben-Zeev D et al. 2015). Performance data can be collected based on the patient's interaction with the app. The app can personalize the intervention based on the data in real-time. Predictive analytics models can be deployed on the collected data. This approach has been used in neuro and behavioral health applications to collect data about cognitive processing speed (Brouillette RM et al., 2013) or assessing short-term memory (Timmers, C et al., 2014).

Phone-based sensor data using inbuilt GPS, accelerometer, audio, and video recording capabilities enhance the data pool, which can be used by mobile applications to provide clinical interventions. The sensor-based data has been demonstrated in clinical publications to predict mood (Saeb S et al., 2015), to check activities of daily living (Stucki RA et al., 2014), or to monitor behavioral health to predict the risk of depression (Ben-Zeev, D et al. 2015).

Smartwatches or wearable sensors worn on the body can supplement mobile phone data through standalone sensors or those integrated with smartphones. Such approaches have been demonstrated to be used for biofeedback (Dillon A et al., 2016), sleep tracking (Domingues A., 2015), and bipolar disorders (Puiatti, A. 2011).

Usability

The usability of healthcare apps ensures that they are used as intended. The apps should follow mobile accessibility guidelines like those proposed by Web Content Accessibility Guidelines (WCAG). The thirteen guidelines are based on 4 principles – perceivable, operable, understandable, and robust and provide the goals and success criteria. As of this writing, most recent version of the guidelines is 2.1, which covers mobile applications, including orientation, timeouts, and motion activation (W3C. 2008).

"Perceivable

- Provide text alternatives for any non-text content so that it can be changed into other forms people need, such as large print, braille, speech, symbols or simpler language.
- Provide alternatives for time-based media.
- Create content that can be presented in different ways (for example simpler layout) without losing information or structure.
- Make it easier for users to see and hear content including separating foreground from background.

Operable

- Make all functionality available from a keyboard.
- Provide users enough time to read and use content.
- Do not design content in a way that is known to cause seizures or physical reactions.
- Provide ways to help users navigate, find content, and determine where they are.
- Make it easier for users to operate functionality through various inputs beyond keyboard.

Understandable

- Make text content readable and understandable.
- Make web pages appear and operate in predictable ways.
- Help users avoid and correct mistakes.

Robust

- Maximize compatibility with current and future user agents, including assistive technologies."

The apps should be designed based on the context in which the apps are expected to be used. Information should be collected about potential users through ethnographic research or interviews to understand the user experience. The app developers should ensure that future users with disabilities, language barriers, skill constraints, and resource-poor settings can use the apps.

Developers should get input from potential users in the design and development of the application. There should be easy-to-reach links for the help section with instructions about using the app. This can be supplemented with user forums where users can ask questions and email or chat-based support to respond to user queries. After the app has been launched, the developers can continue to get feedback from the users to improve the app's functionality.

UNIT 4: TELEHEALTH

24 INTRODUCTION TO TELEHEALTH

Telehealth is the use of digital tools to deliver a healthcare service from a distance. Telemedicine refers to the delivery of medical care by healthcare providers to their patients from a distance using telecommunication technologies. According to World Health Organization, telemedicine is "…the delivery of health care services, where distance is a critical factor, by all health care professionals using information and communication technologies for the exchange of valid information for diagnosis, treatment and prevention of disease and injuries, research and evaluation, and for the continuing education of health care providers, all in the interests of advancing the health of individuals and their communities" (WHO. 1998). Department of Health and Human Services defines telehealth as "use of electronic information and telecommunications technologies to support and promote long-distance clinical health care, patient and professional health-related education, public health and health administration. Technologies include video-conferencing, the internet, store-and-forward imaging, streaming media, and terrestrial and wireless communications" (HealthIT.gov, 2020).

A simplified and abridged version of the definition of telemedicine, as defined in Title 21, United States Code, Controlled Substance Act, states that the term 'practice of telemedicine' means the "practice of medicine in accordance with applicable Federal and State laws by a practitioner (other than a pharmacist) who is at a location remote from the patient and is communicating with the patient, or health care professional who is treating the patient, using a telecommunications system, which practice:

- is being conducted while the patient is being treated by, and physically located in, a hospital or clinic by a practitioner acting in accordance with applicable State law; and registered in the state in which the patient is located
- is being conducted while the patient is being treated by, and in the physical presence of, a practitioner
- is being conducted during a public health emergency declared by the Secretary and involves patients located in such areas, and such controlled substances, as the Secretary, with the concurrence of the Attorney General, designates" (United States Code Controlled Substances Act).

Telemedicine allows the distribution of specialized expertise more effectively through remote consultations with patients located far from the specialist physicians. As telemedicine becomes a more prevalent modality of patient care, efficiency studies have been done to evaluate best practices and create metrics like consultation times for acceptable standards of quality and efficiency (Ellis et al., 2006).

Types

Telehealth technologies are continuously evolving as more healthcare and clinical processes move to remotely managed or delivered workflows. These modalities can be performed in isolation or in combination with other healthcare workflows like chronic condition management, counseling, patient education, care coordination, medication management, etc. Here are some major categories of telehealth:

Synchronous Televisit: A live encounter between a healthcare provider and an individual conducted over a telecommunication platform, including a phone or video call. In some cases, email or chat-based encounters are also considered under tele-visits.

Asynchronous (Store and Forward) interaction: Asynchronous televisit interactions are not real-time and include communication between a provider and a patient over email or chat. It can also include transmitting questionnaire information, image, symptoms, and health data to a provider to review the information later to create a diagnosis or treatment plan.

Telemonitoring: Collection, transmission, evaluation, and tracking of patient health data remotely. The data could include vital signs, symptoms, and lab values and can be collected using wearable sensors, implantable devices, mobile phones, or other wireless devices. Telemonitoring may be real-time or asynchronous. Telemonitoring is covered in more detail under the section on Remote Patient Monitoring.

Telesupervision: Oversight or supervision of a healthcare provider by another who is usually better trained, more experienced, or is in a supervisory role.

Teleconsultation: Discussion between one healthcare provider with another via telephone, chat, or video call. The consulting provider may be a specialist in a particular disease area or who may be more familiar with the patient's medical background.

Teleinterpretation: Interpretation and/or diagnosis performed remotely based on transmitted patient laboratory results, imaging procedures, etc. Teleinterpretation can be performed by healthcare providers or third-party organizations which set up remote centers to collect and analyze data generated at healthcare organizations. The clients of these services are healthcare organizations, not individual patients.

As of this writing, CMS has identified three types of virtual visits that can be provided to Medicare beneficiaries (CMS. 2020a):

- **Medicare Telehealth visits**: A visit with a provider that uses telecommunication systems between a provider and a patient. The common telehealth services include 99201-99215: Office or other outpatient visits; G0425-G0427: Telehealth consultations, emergency department or initial inpatient; G0406-G0408: Follow-up inpatient telehealth consultations furnished to beneficiaries in hospitals or SNFs. These could be for new or established patients. Medicare allowed these visits to be used for new patients during COVID public health emergency.

- **Virtual check-in**: A brief (5-10 minutes) check-in with the patient's practitioner via telephone or other telecommunication device to decide whether an office visit or other service is needed. A remote evaluation of recorded video and/or images submitted by an established patient. These are for established patients. The codes used for these are G2012, G2010.
- **E-visits**: A communication between an established patient and their provider through an online patient portal. The codes used are 99421-99423, G2061-G3063.

Telehealth can also be categorized based on the location of the providers.

Inpatient telemedicine

Telehealth technologies are increasingly finding more use within hospitals. Traditional video-based teleconferencing was previously most used in outpatient settings, with inpatient scenarios limited to teleconsultation with specialists at hospitals where specialty services were unavailable. During the Covid-19 pandemic, due to logistical constraints, isolation requirements, and hospital investments in technology infrastructure, along with the growth in traditional inpatient telemedicine, newer applications of telehealth emerged and became mainstream. Telerounding by physicians from emergency medicine, acute care, critical care, and post-acute care significantly rose in deployment worldwide. Rounding on admitted patients using video-conferencing by providers, nurses, case managers, etc., reduces infectious exposure to the care teams and the overall rounding time. The downside of this shift is the investment required in infrastructure for both video conferencing equipment in the rooms and the increased requirement of network bandwidth. There are also occasional challenges in communication due to difficulty in hearing in noisy hospital environments over video conferencing, or with patients having hearing deficits. Portable video conferencing equipment, which is wheeled from one patient room to another, required adequate cleaning to prevent the spread of infection. It is also challenging to set up the telemedicine link with the provider and the interpreter for patients requiring language translation. Once the patients are discharged from the hospitals, telehealth is used for follow-up of patients who are discharged from the hospital (Moreno et al., 2020).

Disaster telemedicine

Another application of telemedicine is for providing care during disasters at remote places (Augusterfer et al., 2013), including recovery and management (Ajami et al., 2014b), and assist in future disaster preparedness (Alverson et al., 2010). Mobile technologies are becoming specially important (Case et al., 2012). Providers have also deploying telemedicine to prepare for mass casualty events (Farmer et al., 2019) and wars (Merrell et al., 2008).

Public health telemedicine

Surveillance of an area by community health workers via mobile phones is used for early detection of endemic epidemics in rural areas. This has particular relevance in global health, where the public health infrastructure may not have enough resources to manage wider outbreaks of illnesses (Meyers et al., 2016).

Market size and opportunity

There are over 8.5 billion physical and virtual doctor visits in OECD countries annually, costing up to $520 billion. Patients over the age of 65 account for over 30% of all doctor's office visits in the US (Ashman et al., 2019) despite being only 17% of the US population. Global visits are estimated to cost US$700 billion annually (Deloitte. 2021).

The telehealth market is predicted to grow at a yearly rate of 38% over the next five years (Becker's Hospital Review. 2020). Other surveys have shown that 46% of US consumers used telehealth in 2020 compared to 11 percent in 2019 (McKinsey COVID-19 Consumer Survey, April 27, 2020). There was a decrease in telehealth visits after COVID-19 subsided, but the new baseline was still significantly higher than before the pandemic.

The type of services offered through telemedicine has grown exponentially. These include services that traditionally used telemedicine but have now expanded their service offerings, as well as those that did not have any telehealth presence before the pandemic. Many technological innovations are also improving telemedicine care. These include technologies like smart glasses (Romare et al., 2020) for consultations or procedures (Pérez Alonso et al., 2017). These cloud-connected ultrasounds can create 3-D models which can be interpreted remotely (Arbeille et al., 2014). Smartphones have made it inexpensive and convenient to share images with patients and healthcare providers, which specialist physicians can remotely evaluate (Boissin et al., 2017). Voice assistants integrated with electronic medical records and remote healthcare delivery infrastructure are being used to augment the health service capacity (Sezgin et al., 2020).

Recent surveys show that about 50% of Americans prefer providers offering phone- or web-conference consultations (Business Wire. 2020). Virtual consultations have also reduced the waiting times for seeing specialists (Brooke LeVasseur. 2020).

COVID-19 pandemic

COVID-19 pandemic was one of the biggest drivers for the adoption of telehealth. During the pandemic, adoption of telemedicine increased by almost 300% between 2018 and 2020, according to national surveys (Merritt Hawkins. 2020). Telemedicine visits increased from less than 1% to over 65% at some sites. The studies did not show a reduction in the quality of care metrics (Berlin et al., 2021). The usage of telemedicine increased across specialties, practice types, and regions. 43.5% of all US Medicare primary care visits were conducted via telehealth consisting of video calls, phone calls, emails, and non-video-based methods compared to 0.1% before the pandemic (DHS. 2021). Similarly, the Department of Veteran Affairs Video Connect system increased to 120,000 visits per week from 10,000 per week a year before (Department of Veterans Affairs. 2020). During the COVID-19 pandemic, patients over the age of 65 had to rapidly learn to use video conferencing tools not just for healthcare but also to keep in touch with family members and friends. By the end of 2020, over 75% of the 65-plus population was connected to the Internet (Pew Research Center. 2021).

While there was an increase in virtual visits by specialized telehealth providers, a larger proportion of virtual visits were conducted by providers in traditional practices, as almost all of their in-person visits converted to virtual. So providers who never had conducted telehealth visits previously were forced to become comfortable with telehealth. There were multiple catalysts for the surge:

1) Widespread smartphone adoption and consumer experience with video calls
2) Ease of deployment, scheduling, and enterprise integration of video conferencing tools
3) Cloud connected, mobile friendly, and inexpensive electronic medical record systems
4) Restrictions on entry into healthcare facilities due to COVID-19's contagiousness as well as disproportionate effect on individuals with chronic and immune-compromised conditions
5) Patients' concern about visiting healthcare facilities due to the risk of exposure
6) Strict lockdowns nationwide making it difficult to travel to healthcare facilities
7) Significant and swift regulatory changes promoting the use of telehealth
8) Mature telehealth companies which were able to ramp up quickly.

Regulatory changes

The regulatory changes had the most profound impact in driving telehealth adoption. During the COVID-19 public health emergency, the requirements of provider & patient telehealth-based relationships were relaxed. CMS expanded the telehealth benefit under the 1135 waiver authority and Coronavirus Preparedness and Response Supplemental Appropriations Act. "Under this new waiver, Medicare can pay for an office, hospital, and other visits furnished via telehealth across the country, including in patient's places of residence starting March 6, 2020. A range of providers, such as doctors, nurse practitioners, clinical psychologists, and licensed clinical social workers, can offer telehealth to their patients." Also, HHS Office for Civil Rights (OCR) waived penalties for HIPAA violations against healthcare providers that served patients in good faith through everyday communications technologies, such as FaceTime or Skype, during the COVID-19 nationwide public health emergency. The 1135 waiver also allowed the Secretary to authorize telephones with audio and video capabilities for furnishing Medicare telehealth services. Under billing, the distant site providers could use the Place of Service (POS) 02 code for Telehealth. Medicare paid the facility rate on all services billed with POS 02.

Reimbursement changes

Medicare introduced parity in reimbursement for telehealth services with in-office visits for all diagnoses (AMA. 2020). Access to telehealth was expanded by reimbursing telemedicine delivered to patients in all settings across the country, including urban and rural areas. Consent for telehealth services is required only once annually. Medicare also allowed telephone-based telehealth visits, audio-only for evaluation, and management visits for new and established patients. The types of visits that could be provided with telehealth were expanded, including emergency department visits and medical screening exams. CMS removed the frequency limitation on the number of Medicare telehealth services. Remote patient monitoring services to new and established patients for acute and chronic conditions and patients with only one disease were covered. Medicare expanded telehealth access to other nonphysician providers. Drug Enforcement Administration permitted physicians to prescribe controlled substances, including buprenorphine, for patients under treatment for opioid use disorder based on telehealth visits if they follow the state laws and have appropriate waivers. The patients were also allowed to self-report their vitals from home for the Medicare Annual Wellness Visits (AWV) conducted via telemedicine (Moore. 2020). Physicians could provide telehealth services from their homes without updating their addresses on Medicare enrollment files. Physicians licensed in one state could provide telemedicine services to Medicare beneficiaries in different states, provided they followed state licensure guidelines.

Before 2020, Medicare Advantage plans were able to offer more telehealth benefits than original Medicare. Before COVID-19, Medicare reimbursed real-time audiovisual visits between a patient and healthcare provider in which the patient's location was a qualified rural or underserved area, including a rural census track, health professional shortage area, and a region outside the metropolitan statistical area. The provider could provide services from a hospital, physician's clinic, skilled nursing facility, or federally qualified health center. The provider categories included physician, advanced practice provider (PA, NP), psychologist, licensed clinical social worker, and registered dietitian. However, due to COVID-19, Medicare expanded the scope of telemedicine visits.

Healthcare delivery changes

Prior to the Covid-19 pandemic, the bulk of outpatient telemedicine in the United States was driven by large telemedicine companies. All the health systems combined had a minuscule share of the total telehealth market. The telehealth services that were offered were largely limited to inpatient consultations. However, during the pandemic, almost all medical centers, as well as medical groups, adopted telemedicine for outpatient consultations.

There was a rapid increase in the number of direct-to-consumer startups, which provided convenient and, in many cases, more affordable options to patients to get care for simple ailments. All the top five technology companies by market capitalization are aggressively entering the healthcare market with each entering the market using its strengths and expanding into offering more products and services.

Another trend that accelerated during COVID was the emergence of specialized telemedicine companies and medical practices. These were venture or private equity financed and focused on a specific subset of the patient population like post-menopausal women, pediatrics, and African-Americans on specific disease states like diabetes, behavioral health, obesity, musculoskeletal health, and hypothyroidism. While previously, most telemedicine activities were dominated by primary care providers treating simple conditions, additional types of providers started offering their services via telemedicine, including dietitians, physical therapists, and behavioral therapists. Surgical specialties like orthopedics, plastic surgery, and neurosurgery, joined medical specialists like cardiologists, endocrinologists, etc., to offer care virtually.

Virtual pharmacies were one of the biggest beneficiaries of stay-at-home restrictions as they provided an interface to virtual care providers and mail those medicines to patients' homes. There were also technologically advanced compared to traditional pharmacy chains and provide easy-to-use mobile apps to track and manage medications.

Benefits

- **Cost savings**: Telemedicine has shown an overall reduction in the cost of healthcare for healthcare systems, providers, and patients. A study in 2014 showed that global telemedicine visits can save as much as $5Bn (Lee et al., 2014). Though this number was likely to increase with the rapid adoption of telemedicine during the Covid pandemic. Cost savings accrue from patients not missing work to see their physicians, physicians' ability to provide consultations without the expense of office, and reduced need for support staff.

- **Improved access to care**: Telemedicine reduces the no-show rate, which was calculated to be over 20%, with an average cost per patient of approximately $200 (Kheirkhah et al., 2016). This has come down in recent years. It enables access to health care for patients living in remote locations, those who don't have assistance to get out of the home. Telemedicine allows patients living in rural or remote areas to get access to specialists.

- **Improved health outcomes**: Studies have demonstrated that telemedicine visits are more effective in adherence to health programs than in-person visits (Halpren-Ruder et al., 2019). Canadian Agency for Drugs and Technologies in Health evaluated the use of telemedicine for urgent conditions and found a reduction in resource use and increased quality of care in urgent care (Canadian Agency for Drugs and Technologies in Health. 2015a) and long-term facilities (Canadian Agency for Drugs and Technologies in Health. 2015b). Studies targeting individual conditions have demonstrated telemedicine visits as effective as in-person visits for asthma (Portnoy et al., 2016), diabetes mellitus (Shea et al., 2009), and chronic disease management of congestive heart failure, stroke, and chronic obstructive pulmonary disease (Bashshur et al., 2014).

- **Improved patient satisfaction**: Multiple studies have shown patient satisfaction with telemedicine due to factors like reduced cost and need to travel (Powell et al., 2017) or convenience and perceived high quality of care (Polinski et al., 2016).

- **Patient safety**: While the telemedicine modalities may increase errors due to communication, with adequate safeguards, they may also be able to reduce or prevent errors. Due to the absence of barriers of geography, there may be closer, continuous, and more frequent communication between the patient, caregivers, and healthcare professionals. Telehealth and remote monitoring technologies can aggregate multiple data points and patient information for better diagnosis and treatment decisions. Specific telemedicine interventions like tele-ICU or teleconsultation provide the advantage of a second opinion with a specialist.

Challenges

Despite the increased adoption of telehealth during the COVID pandemic, there are still significant challenges in the broader deployment of telehealth (Yellowlees et al., 2020). The challenges are related to patients, providers, health institutions, and technology infrastructure (Elliot et al., 2017).

- **Incomplete information**: Due to the inability to perform an in-person physical exam, the providers may miss essential signs or physical exam findings. Patients uncomfortable with video conferencing may be unable to share complete information on a video call, leading to erroneous diagnoses or treatment plans. Physicians may have difficulty estimating patients' health status during telehealth visits (Bos et al., 2021).

- **Technological challenges**: Patients may not have computers or smartphones to conduct video visits. Those who have the hardware may not be technically savvy enough to configure the software and successfully join the video call at a scheduled time. The internet connectivity may also be inadequate to support video calls. There are concerns that telehealth visits may worsen health equity by making healthcare access harder for a subset of patients with technological challenges. These challenges can also exist for providers who are not technologically savvy. They may not have access to a dedicated and appropriately equipped office to conduct a remote visit. The physicians also need hands-free headphones to make phone calls, an electronic medical record system with electronic prescription and lab test ordering capability.

- **Logistical challenges**: Providers may be unable to reach the patients via video or phone. Patients may also have more distractions at home, especially if they are caregivers of young children or ill family members.

- **Communication barriers**: Patients with conditions like cognitive impairment, neurological conditions, and hearing issues may be unable to communicate over the phone or video. There may also be a language barrier and technical difficulty in incorporating a translator into the encounter. Patients may not be able to understand the physician. They may be less forthcoming in admitting their inability to comprehend over the phone or via video calls to avoid stalling the visit. Patients may also hesitate to ask questions for similar reasons and have difficulty describing their condition in a tele-visit. Phone visits may not provide adequate body language signals to indicate to the physician whether the patient understood the physician's recommendations. Along with a lack of information, misunderstanding the message may also be challenging.

- **Depersonalization**: The telehealth visits may appear monotonous and depersonalized, especially if the providers are not trained in good communication strategies. Patients may get the impression of reduced empathy and quality of the physician-patient relationship.

- **Security and privacy risks**: Privacy of telehealth encounters may be compromised if anyone else besides the patient or the physician is in the vicinity and can overhear the conversation. Hackers may get access to live or recorded video visits (Fernandez et al., 2020).

- **Fragmentation of care**: The care of patients is spread over different direct-to-consumer telemedicine providers or within the same provider or multiple practitioners billing to reduce informational continuity, relational continuity, and management continuity (Haggerty et al., 2003). Concerns have been raised around limited information obtained over telemedicine encounters, especially regarding examination, shorter duration of typical appointments, and lack of access to patient comprehensive medical records by providers. The medical boards have cautioned against routine direct-to-consumer telemedicine because that can lead to fragmentation and quality of care (Conners et al., 2017).

- **State licensing**: Regulations mandate that the provider is licensed in every state where their patient is located. Some states have joined to create a licensure compact for physicians and other providers. The onerous paperwork requirements dissuade physicians from obtaining licenses for more states and deprive patients outside their state of access to their expertise. Hopefully, more states will join the inter-state compact and move towards one national licensing system.

- **Credentialing and privileging**: Credentialing is the process of verifying and assessing previous experience and qualifications of the providers. Privileging authorizes the healthcare practitioner to provide clinical services within a defined scope of practice. Joint Commission "allows an originating site (where the patient is located) to use the credentialing and privileging information from a distant site when making final privileging decisions for telemedicine practitioners" (Final Revisions to Telemedicine Standards. Joint Commission Perspectives®, January 2012, Volume 32, Issue 1). During the pandemic, the joint commission clarified that "Licensed Independent Practitioners (LIPs) currently credentialed and privileged by an organization, who would now provide the same services via a telehealth link to patients, do not require additional credentialing or privileging. The medical staff determines which services would be appropriate to be delivered via a telehealth link. There is no requirement that 'telehealth' be delineated as a separate privilege." With the change in regulations and telemedicine reimbursement by CMS, the credentialing and privileging practices standards are evolving.

- **Reimbursement:** Medicaid and private insurance reimbursement varies by state. This creates challenges for healthcare providers operating in more than one state to track reimbursement policies of all insurers in every state they do business.

- **Physician-patient relationship**: With the increasing prevalence of on-demand mobile phone-based video calls between the patients and providers offered by telehealth companies, patients are not able to establish a physician-patient relationship with one provider. Continuity of care is broken as patients see a different provider at every visit. This could be especially problematic for patients with chronic conditions.

25 REMOTE PATIENT MONITORING

Remote patient monitoring (RPM) captures, records, and transmits a patient's physiologic data to healthcare professionals or machine learning algorithms for review, diagnosis, or clinical intervention. Remote patient monitoring is rapidly advancing, with healthcare organizations and private companies providing services for monitoring patients with congestive heart failure, asthma, chronic obstructive pulmonary disease (COPD), hypertension, pregnancy, metabolic syndrome, and many others.

Remote patient monitoring can be achieved using smartphone or mobile apps, implantable or wearable sensors, and software systems, including electronic health records. Remote patient monitoring has become more effective with novel, smaller, connected, accurate, integrated sensors with increasingly better battery life. Sensors are now available that continuously measure blood glucose, electrolytes, hormones, muscle activity, neural activity, etc. They are also getting integrated into clothes, watches, shoes, beds, toilet seats, and mirrors (Sarasohn-Kahn et al., 2021). Biometric measurements that have been tracked in RPM programs include respiratory rate and rhythm, spirometry, oximetry, heart rate, heart rate variability, single-lead electrocardiogram, blood glucose, weight, blood pressure, temperature, activity, falls, body posture, body acceleration, body position, limb and torso orientation, gait, physical location, voice, speech, galvanic skin response, sleep patterns. Many others are in advanced stages of research and development.

Advantages

As more use cases are discovered for remote patient monitoring and monitoring and interpreting technology gets more sophisticated, the advantages of RPM will continue to grow. Here are some of the major ones:

- **Replacement of home health visits**: Remote home monitoring in combination with telehealth can provide the ability to replace home visits by healthcare personnel, improving the response times and productivity of healthcare staff.
- **Individualized and dynamic allocation of resources**: Most home health programs assign the same amount of time and frequency of visits to all patients. However, with remote monitoring, patients can receive care depending on their health needs as assessed remotely. Stable patients may not need to be seen for months, while patients with rapid deterioration or fluctuating disease course may have more frequent care touch points. Alternatively, triggers

can be identified to initiate more intensive monitoring, in-person visits, or additional diagnostic or therapeutic interventions.

- **Real time remote analytics**: Machine learning algorithms can play an important role in remote monitoring programs. For example, separating signal from noise, early identification of disease decompensation, predicting disease trajectory, and selecting the best intervention are some of the things possible using artificial intelligence and machine learning.
- **Command centers**: Centralized command centers can remotely monitor and manage multiple patients, programs, and clients. These command centers can serve more patients and be staffed with specialized providers who can supervise field staff.
- **Acute and post-acute facility monitoring:** Patients can be monitored while they are admitted at the hospital or at a post-acute care location. This allows for closer observation, intervention, and planning for discharge. Additionally, baseline data can be collected at the facility, which can help inform decisions about discharge.
- **Patient engagement**: Patients are more engaged with their care if they feel that someone is keeping a close eye on them and will respond quickly if something goes wrong.

Applications

The benefits of RPM have been demonstrated in several medical specialties, as discussed below. The applications of RPM are expanding every year with advancements in technology and clinical research. The list below captures some illustrative applications:

Cardiology

Mobile cardiac monitoring devices can be used for up to a month for ambulatory telemetry. When connected to a central monitoring station, these devices can alert appropriate individuals in case of any events or emergencies. Mobile telemetry has been shown to be superior to memory loop recorders in confirming the diagnosis of clinically significant arrhythmias (Rothman et al., 2007). Pacemakers and cardioverter-defibrillators can store and transmit data about any cardiovascular event, which can be remotely monitored for early identification of arrhythmias and device malfunctions. These devices have the advantage over in-person monitoring over longer duration of monitoring, allowing the patient to be in their routine instead of the controlled setting of a hospital or physician's office. The combination monitors have been facilitated by the introduction of mobile phones. Heart rhythm monitors are combined with sensors that measure acceleration, oxygen saturation, doppler flow, electrical skin impedance, heart rate variability, physiological sounds, blood pressure, temperature, and blood glucose.

RPM combined with personalized feedback for risk factor modification has been demonstrated in patients with coronary heart disease to reduce lower-density lipoprotein, smoking, systolic blood pressure, and body mass index (Chow et al., 2015). RPM has also demonstrated reduced mortality from complications in chronic heart failure patients (Nakamura et al., 2014).

Metabolic syndrome

Continuous glucose monitoring in patients with diabetes is becoming more pervasive with multiple direct-to-consumer products and services launched in the last few years. In children with type I diabetes, CGM devices can alert families and health professionals of hyperglycemic and hypoglycemic events with 24-hour monitoring. In scenarios where real-time monitoring is unavailable, glycemic information can be sent regularly to monitoring centers (Tauschmann et al., 2016). Integrated intervention in diabetes patients using a mobile app for semi-personalized guidance messages associated with blood sugar logs and health coach intervention has demonstrated a decline in hemoglobin A1c (Quinn et al., 2011).

Neurology

Remote patient monitoring has been successfully applied in geriatric populations. Smartphone apps can evaluate movement disorders in Parkinson's patients and assist with independent living (Kostikis et al., 2011). Mobile applications coupled with RPM enable tracking and monitoring of patients with dementia to prevent them from getting lost (Sposaro et al., 2010). Home-based monitoring is also used in cases of mild cognitive impairments and mild Alzheimer's disease for assessment and intervention (Piau A, 2019). Similarly, medical devices integrated with RPM programs can be used for rehabilitation and preventing falls and stroke patients (Edgar et al., 2010).

Pulmonology

A meta-analysis demonstrated a reduction in ER visits, hospitalizations, and patients with chronic obstructive pulmonary disease (McLean et al. 2012). Besides COPD, patients with asthma and be monitored to evaluate their adherence to inhalers (Chan et al., 2015). Wearable devices collect vital signs, including respiratory rate, heart rate, temperature, coughing, and wheezing, and step data has been used to predict asthma control and healthcare utilization (Rhee et al., 2015). RPM is being combined with data from weather services and predictive models to predict asthmatic attacks and guide preemptive intervention. Another application is diagnosis and evaluation of treatment responses in obstructive sleep apnea (Bsoul et al., 2011).

Critical care

RPM has been used for real-time monitoring and interventions at distant ICUs (Field et al., 2002), improving critical care. Automated algorithms to identify early symptoms of deterioration are being integrated into the monitoring systems as false positive alarms have been considered a major disadvantage (Poncette AS, 2020).

Psychiatry

RPM has also been used in psychiatry for monitoring patients with bipolar disorders using smart phone connected wearable sensors (Puiatti et al. 2011).

Nephrology

Patients who receive artificial kidney transplants can be remotely monitored to assess proper functioning of the artificial kidney (Rosner et al. 2011).

Post Marketing Surveillance

Medical devices need FDA approval before making them available to physicians and patients. After the necessary regulatory approvals have been obtained and the medical device is launched in the market, the medical device manufacturers must continuously monitor their safety and efficacy. The clinical trials are conducted on a limited set of patients. However, the actual use of the device may be on thousands or millions of patients and for a longer duration, which may expose safety concerns that could not be identified during the clinical studies. FDA requires post-market surveillance to ensure that the medical devices perform as they were intended and that any unanticipated adverse effects are detected early. Physicians, patients, or manufacturers can report the adverse effects. FDA can receive the reports directly or extract them through patients' medical records after obtaining authorizations and permissions from the patient and the providers.

Program development

The goals and incentives for a remote patient monitoring program depend on whether the monitoring entity is an insurance company, health system, private medical clinic or federally qualified health center, or home health agency. The reason for remote patient monitoring could be driven by clinical, administrative, or financial outcomes.

Setting up an RPM program requires strategic analysis and evaluation of business and technical challenges unique to RPM to ensure the long-term viability and sustainability of the program. While the technology is immensely beneficial, patient safety and medico-legal concerns need to be mitigated. The clinical or therapeutic areas targeted for RPM should be carefully selected based on the healthcare entity's competency, target patient population, market need, technical expertise, provider interest, and alignment with overall organizational strategy.

The healthcare organizations which plan to offer RPM need clear policies about what types of data monitoring devices are eligible to participate in their programs. With the ubiquity of smart watches collecting EKG information, mobile phone-connected thermometers, and weighing scales, it may be tempting for all consumer devices to hook into the organization's RPM program. While this has the benefit of lowering the rollout costs, it adds significant downsides. Many of these consumer devices or applications collecting physiologic information are not FDA-approved and may have questionable reliability. Even if the smart devices are standardized to one vendor, healthcare organizations will depend on vendor-specified data feed, which may limit the flexibility around data processing. Other issues are around device maintainability, ownership of the data, who bears the cost of repairs, who decides when to replace the device etc.

The RPM programs are categorized based on two criteria. First is the duration of patient participation in the program. The RPM program can be time-bound, or it can be ongoing. Time-bound programs have a finite end either based on achieving a milestone (HgA1c <6.5) or pre-specified time duration (for example, 1 year). Second is the frequency of patient monitoring. The frequency can be continuous or intermittent. Continuous programs collect data continuously (e.g., 24x7, daily), while intermittent programs either have pre-defined triggers or schedule when the data is collected.

Patient factors

Patient Eligibility

The eligibility criteria for patients should be carefully developed to ensure maximum benefit from the assigned resources. The selection criteria may include clinical risk, past medical history, connectivity, and understanding of the limitations.

Patient education

Patient participation is critical to the success of the RPM program. Patient education should be initiated before the rollout and supplemented with ongoing check-ins as part of the ongoing RPM workflow. Patients should learn to use the devices and maintain them, periodically evaluate that their devices are functioning correctly and transmitting data, and perform basic troubleshooting in case of issues.

Device usage

Once a patient is enrolled in the RPM program, monitoring devices are distributed to the patients. The sponsor of the project can purchase remote monitoring devices. The sponsors can store the inventory or contract with manufacturers or distributors to directly ship the devices to the patients as they are enrolled. The devices need to be tested and calibrated to ensure that they perform accurately. The project sponsors can recruit staff for installation and end-user training. Alternatively, it can be outsourced to third-party providers specialized in managing medical devices for remote patient monitoring. The outsourced service providers vary in the complexity of their services. They can range from logistics providers who just do the installation, end-user training, and troubleshooting to full-fledged remote monitoring companies who do all of these but also receive the data, process the data, validate the accuracy of alerts, respond to alerts, and provide actionable insights to the project sponsor. RPM companies also need to track, collect, and clean RPM devices after use.

Sensors

With advances in miniaturization, micro-electromechanical systems (MEMS), battery technology, and processing power, healthcare applications for connected devices continue to grow. The sensors provide physiological information in real-time or based on pre-determined criteria to the providers. Many sensors can be integrated into wearables which can be constantly worn or the body or are attached to mobile devices to transmit the data. The range of connected sensors now available include

- Basic Vital signs
    - Heart rate and heart rate variability
    - Blood pressure
    - Pulse oximetry
    - Weight
    - Respiratory rate
- Sleep
    - Sleep duration and stages
    - Sleep apnea
- Cardiac function
    - EKG
- Metabolic function
    - Blood glucose with intermittent or continuous glucose monitoring
    - Blood alcohol with wearables or using breathalyzers

    - Hormone levels using wearables
- Muscular function
    - EMG
    - Movement analytics for rehabilitation, therapy, falls, diagnosis or monitoring of symptoms of movement disorders using smart clothes or limb sensors using accelerometer, gyroscope and inertial measurement unit
    - Swallow analytics using EMG or airflow sensors
    - Posture sensor
- Brain function
    - EEG for seizure activity
    - Apps to assess dimensions of cognitive function
    - Neuropsychiatric changes through wearables or app based instruments, voice or face analysis
    - Speech impairment with phone-based speech analytics
- Pulmonary function
    - Digital stethoscopes or apps analyzing breath sounds
    - Point of care ultrasounds with image recognition
    - Continuous respiratory rate using smart clothes, chest movement sensors or capnography
- Eye function
    - Visual acuity assessment with smartphone apps
    - Intraocular pressure

Remote data analysis

EHR integration of remote patient monitoring programs leads to efficient workflows, higher staff satisfaction with all patient data, and a single source of truth. However, it may be a challenge if the EHR does not support the integration and storage of RPM data. Importing low-value data into EHR without filters may lead to complaints of information overload by providers as the signal-to-noise ratio can be very low.

Healthcare organizations can partner with vendors providing data screening and data analytics on monitoring services to identify relevant events recorded by the sensors and contact the providers through escalation protocols. Either the vendor or the healthcare organization can set up a help-desk team for troubleshooting. Healthcare organizations can define protocols and ensure that care episodes are appropriately triaged to providers capable and available to address the emergent interventions. It is important to identify concerning trends in the physiologic data as soon as possible using manual or automated reviews.

Traditionally, providers have resisted collecting remote patient data without supporting infrastructure which can respond appropriately to any adverse signal which requires immediate action as soon as it is available to healthcare providers. If a patient has an urgent medical condition and they are under the impression that it has been communicated to the provider, they may not seek alternative sites of care. So, triaging of remotely collected data based on potential severity of interventions is critical. As an example, provider offices often have voicemail messages dissuading patients from leaving any messages about any urgent or critical conditions as provider office staff may not access the messages in time.

26 TELEMEDICINE REGULATION

The practice of telemedicine is governed by federal and state laws. In 2020, during the COVID-19 pandemic, multiple new regulations around telehealth were introduced in 2020. Most of these were planned to be temporary but have been extended as of writing this edition. Telehealth regulations are rapidly evolving at the federal and state levels. Readers are advised to check the most recent guidelines from CMS, state legislatures, state healthcare departments, state medical boards, and insurance companies for up-to-date information. The jurisdiction of the state law applies to the location of the patient, not the provider, so it is important to review the state law in which the provider is planning to practice (CCHP. Professional requirements).

The rules around using an online or internet-based questionnaire to replace an actual physician-patient encounter are evolving. Currently, these are considered insufficient to establish a patient-provider relationship and e-prescribe drugs. A telehealth-based physical exam is allowed in some states, and some states have limited restrictions for prescribing controlled substances and medication-assisted therapy using telehealth.

Licensure requirements

In United State, telehealth rules and regulations are different in every state. Telehealth practices must comply with state guidelines, reimbursement policies, and clinician licensure requirements of the state where the patient receives care. Malpractice must cover clinical practice in every state the provider sees the patients in. During the COVID-19 public health emergency, 49 out of 50 states relaxed requirements for across-state telehealth. This may change once the public health emergency is lifted. The licensure and reimbursement are the challenges in scaling the telehealth business. Interstate licensure compact is an easy way to get clinical privileges in multiple states in one application.

As of this writing, the state medical boards of forty-nine states, the District of Columbia, Puerto Rico, and the Virgin Islands require that the physicians providing telemedicine are licensed in the state where the patient is located. Twelve state boards issue a special purpose license or a telemedicine license to practice medicine across state lines. This allows an out-of-state provider to counsel via telemedicine in a state where they are not physically present. Six state boards require physicians to register to practice across state lines. 28 states, the District of Columbia, and Guam have adopted the Federation of State medical boards (FSMB) interstate medical licensure compact for physicians. 34 states have nurses licensure compact, 28 have physical therapy compact, 15 have a psychology inter-jurisdictional compact, five have an audiology and speech-language pathology interstate compact, and 20 have an emergency medical services personnel licensure interstate compact. As of this edition, 41 states had introduced waivers in their regular licensing process. The state-by-state regulations are available on the Federation of State Medical Boards website (FSMB. 2021).

State telemedicine laws

The Medicaid program is administered at the state level with differences in every state's approach, coverage, and schedule. This state-by-state variation is also reflected in telehealth-related policies. The states have continued to advance their telehealth reimbursement policies, which were significantly expanded by telehealth changes during the COVID-19 pandemic. Even though many of these changes were labeled as temporary but efforts are underway to make some or all of those permanent (Medicaid.gov., 2021). The Medicaid reimbursement policies have been more permissive than Medicare (CCHP. Current State Laws & Reimbursement Policies). All states and Washington DC reimburse some form of live video through Medicaid fee-for-service. The Medicaid programs in 18 states reimburse store-and-forward, 21 states provide reimbursement for RPM. Medicaid programs in Alaska, Arizona, Maine, Minnesota, Missouri, New York, Oregon, Texas, and Virginia reimburse live video, store-and-forward, and RPM. These could change in the future as regulatory environment evolves.

Payer coverage

The general trend over the last decade has been the expansion of telehealth reimbursement despite state-to-state disparities in reimbursable modality, services, and patient location. The Medicaid reimbursement for live video is higher than store-and-forward and remote patient monitoring. During the Covid 19 epidemic use of telephones has been considered for reimbursement, though it is unclear how many states will make this provision permanent. States have also expanded the lists of providers eligible for telehealth reimbursement. For example, reimbursement for physical, occupational, and speech therapy has expanded during the pandemic.

68% of Americans have private health insurance as their primary source of health coverage (U. S. Census Bureau. 2020). During the COVID-19 pandemic, private national insurance carriers expanded telehealth coverage temporarily during the pandemic. Almost all of them waived cost-sharing for COVID-19-related telehealth services. The private-payer telehealth coverage has no federal regulatory framework but depends on state regulations. 43 states and the District of Columbia govern private-payer telehealth reimbursement policies. Similar to Medicaid coverage of telehealth, private-payer laws have significant disparities in the extent and form of coverage. Almost every health insurer offered some telehealth coverage in 2019 (AHIP. 2019), and the private payers used third-party vendor platforms for providing telehealth services (CCHP. 2021).

27 TECHNOLOGY ENABLED HOME HEALTHCARE

Medical practitioners have been delivering care at home for centuries around the world. As clinical care became more complex and hospitals or infirmaries became more resourced, there was a shift to providing medical care at these dedicated facilities. However, with the aging population, the emergence of digital health, and advancements in telemedicine, more care is being shifted outside the traditional hospitals. The COVID-19 pandemic has accelerated the adoption of telehealth technologies and increased research exploring non-traditional clinical delivery sites. Home healthcare generally includes services delivered at home by visiting nurses who may visit as much as twice daily to once a week. The common historical use cases of these services have included infusion of IV medications, wound care, rehabilitation, skilled therapies, (add more) but are now rapidly expanding. These services are being complemented by advances in remote patient monitoring from home. The newly emerging models include the full spectrum of clinical care the patient would have received at the hospital delivered in the home setting, including physician consultation, nursing care, and diagnostic and therapeutic services.

Home-based primary care is well established with clinical provider visits at home augmented by technology. Home-based urgent care has gradually seen wider adoption over the last few years. Hospital level services delivered at home is a relatively recent concept poised to accelerate with regulatory changes announced in 2020. The hospital-at-home model enables patients to stay at their homes and receive acute-level care, which previously would have been delivered in the hospital setting. 'Hospital at home®' is registered trademark of Johns Hopkins University.

Introduction to Hospital-level Care At Home

This chapter will focus on a Hospital-level Care At Home (HCAH) concept, a new type of telehealth intervention. HCAH delivers clinical care, including diagnosis and treatment, at a patient's home instead of an acute care hospital. While healthcare services have been delivered at home for hundreds of years, HCAH services allow for managing clinical conditions that previously were only treated in a hospital setting. The common conditions have been community-acquired pneumonia, urinary tract infection, congestive heart failure, diabetes, chronic obstructive pulmonary disease, asthma, cellulitis, and venous thromboembolism. Studies have demonstrated that HCAH leads to higher patient and family satisfaction compared to usual hospital care, increases the efficiency of care, improves patient safety, reduces practice variation, and improves patients safety (Frick KD et al., 2009; Leff B et al. 2006; Leff B et al. 2005). Besides the clinical services, HCAH programs provide administrative support, including care coordination, patient education, and appointment scheduling.

History

The provision of hospital-level services in a non-hospital setting has been explored globally for the last few decades. A 1993 study evaluated the efficacy and safety of intravenous antibiotic therapy for treating streptococcal endocarditis in outpatient clinics in Switzerland, France, and Belgium (Francioli P et al. 1992). Subsequent studies in the United States evaluated the safety and efficacy of antibiotic therapy for streptococcal endocarditis in the home setting (Colford JM Jr et al., 1993). In 2004, a study conducted in Italy demonstrated lower admissions rates for patients who received home treatment from a geriatric home hospitalization service compared to a general medical ward after an acute uncomplicated first ischemic stroke (Ricauda NA et al., 2004). Research in other countries like Australia demonstrated the safety and efficacy of hospital-level care at home (Montalto M., 1998). In 1999, a Johns Hopkins study of 17 patients who were provided hospital care at home otherwise would have required acute hospitalization for cellulitis, chronic obstructive airway disease, chronic heart failure, or community-acquired pneumonia was demonstrated to be safe, feasible, satisfactory, and cost-effective (Leff B et al. 1999). The other early trials explored the feasibility of early discharge of patients from the hospitals to reduce the length of stay (Richards SH et al., 1998).

Health conditions evaluated in the studies about HCAH have included medical diagnoses like hip replacement, antibiotic therapy, COPD, pressure ulcer management, and stroke. Post-surgical care of patients includes hip and knee replacement and hysterectomy (Leff B., 2001).

CMS Approach

The HCAH concept got a boost when the Acute Hospital Care at Home program was launched by the Centers for Medicare and Medicaid Services (CMS) in 2020 to enable hospitals to provide patients with another option to receive acute care. The rules and waivers were initially introduced to increase the care sites during the COVID-19 pandemic which allowed the hospitals to transfer patients to ambulatory facilities, including ambulatory surgery centers, inpatient rehabilitation hospitals, hotels, and dormitories, to deliver care. These services were allowed to be billed at the same rate as the inpatient services delivered at acute care hospitals. The guidelines also allowed lab technicians to go to patients' homes to collect specimens for COVID-19 testing (CMS. Additional Background: Sweeping Regulatory Changes to Help US Healthcare System Address COVID-19 Patient Surge). A few months later, CMS announced the Acute Hospital Care At Home program, allowing hospitals to provide hospital care for eligible patients at their homes. CMS identified up to 60 conditions, including asthma, congestive heart failure, pneumonia, and chronic obstructive pulmonary disease, that could be treated in patients' homes with appropriate treatment protocols and in a safe manner. (CMS. CMS Announces Comprehensive Strategy to Enhance Hospital Capacity Amid COVID-19 Surge). These efforts were in addition to expanding the scope of the telehealth services, with coverage increasing to 135 services, including emergency department visits, initial inpatient and nursing facility visits, and discharge day management services. Subsequently, CMS allowed hospitals that had treated at least 25 patients to apply for a waiver from the requirement of nursing services on-premises 24 hours a day, 7 days a week, and immediate availability of a registered nurse for the care of any patient. Initially, six healthcare systems were approved for providing acute hospital care at home, expanding to 53 systems covering 116 hospitals by 2021 (CMS. Acute Hospital Care at Home Program). Acute hospital care programs were required to be integrated within a hospital to ensure rapid escalation of care.

CMS laid out specific requirements for the hospitals that wanted to participate in the program:

- Patients can be admitted from the emergency departments and inpatient hospital beds.
- In-person evaluation is required prior to starting services at the patient's home. The inpatient hospitalist or admitting provider could perform the in-person exam documenting the history and physical and entering the admission orders before the transfer to home.
- Patients satisfying both inpatient admission criteria, as well as observation status patients, could be enrolled in the program.
- Establish criteria to ensure that only patients who require acute-level care are treated in the program.
- Screening protocols assessing medical and non-medical factors prior to the home base care
- Daily evaluation by a physician or advanced practice provider in-person or remotely
- Daily evaluation by a registered nurse in-person or remotely
- Two in-person visits daily by either registered nurses or mobile integrated health paramedics based on the nursing plan and hospital policies
- 30-minute response time to attend to a decompensating patient
- Immediate and on-demand audio connection to an RN or MD facilitated by an Acute Hospital Care at Home team member
- Tracking safety metrics with periodic reporting to CMS, including patient volume, unanticipated mortality during an acute episode of care, escalation rate
- A local safety committee that reviews patient safety data
- Provision of all services that are required during inpatient hospitalization be provided directly or through contractors.

Types of Hospital-level Care At Home (HCAH) programs

The HCAH model is broadly categorized into 1) acute care and 2) post-acute care. Acute care is the provision of care provided at acute care hospitals. The post-acute care includes medical services delivered at long-term acute care hospitals (LTACH). The HCAH stay for acute inpatient care is generally 3-5 days. The observation unit at home is for a 1-day acute observation level of care at home, which may or may not transition to home.

The HCAH services are set up under two common models:

Hospitalization avoidance

These programs can avoid hospitalization entirely and provide medical care at the patient's home. Patients who require admission to an acute care hospital for a targeted illness are enrolled directly into HCAH either from the emergency department or ambulatory site.

Early discharge

In these programs, patients get a part of their medical care at the hospital, which is then transferred to the home setting. The transfer may happen after a diagnostic test or a therapeutic intervention that cannot be performed at home. Home-based recovery provides recuperative and rehabilitative services at home using telehealth and remote patient monitoring tools.

Benefits

The benefits of the hospital care at home (HCAH) include reduced risk of complications like hospital-acquired infections. It can also reduce the total cost of treatment though the payment models for hospitals at home are still in their early stages of rollout.

Comfort: Studies have documented reduced stress in their caregivers in HCAH (Leff B et al., 2008) and higher satisfaction levels for patients and family members than in acute hospital inpatient care (Leff B et al., 2006). Patients prefer staying at their own homes, which is especially helpful to patients in the geriatric age group who may have difficulty adjusting to the unfamiliar hospital environment. The patients can maintain a relatively higher level of physical activity at home compared to the hospital due to familiarity with their home setting. Patients may also prefer to be with their pets and maintain social contact with friends and family members who may find it easier to visit the patient at home compared to the hospital.

Safety: If implemented appropriately, the HCAH models are safe while preventing complications acquired at hospitals. Studies have shown reduced complication rates in HCAH models (Leff B et al., 2005). Hospitalizations have been shown to cause adverse events like falls, delirium, functional decline, and hospital-acquired infections in the elderly (Creditor MC, 1993). Another international study demonstrated that delirium episodes in geriatric patients were earlier, of longer duration, and more severe in patients admitted to geriatric hospital wards compared to geriatric home hospitalization service (Isaia G et al., 2009).

Cost Effective: Studies have demonstrated cost savings of about a third (Leff B et al., 2005). A small, randomized control study of 91 patients demonstrated the mean cost of care for acute care episodes to be 38% lower and the 30-day rehospitalization rate for patients in home hospitals compared to acute care facilities (Levine DM et al., 2020). These savings can go up with advanced care algorithms and the use of technology. A study found a hospital home model was 38% less expensive than similar in-hospital care (MacIntyre CR et al., 2002).

Efficacy: The studies have evaluated common diagnoses like congestive heart failure and COPD (Frick KD et al., 2009). Hospital care at home has shown higher efficacy compared to acute care hospitalization in multiple studies. A meta-analysis of randomized control trials showed reduced mortality with an odds ratio of 0.81, aggregating admissions for medical, surgical, rehabilitative, or psychiatric reasons (Caplan GA et al., 2012). Studies have also demonstrated better improvements in Activities of Daily Living (ADL) for patients in HCAH care for community-acquired pneumonia, chronic heart failure exacerbation, or chronic obstructive pulmonary disease (Leff B et al. 2009). HCAH can also reduce the need for post-acute care, like placement at skilled nursing facilities.

Empathy: Physicians can see the patients in their home setting and provide recommendations that may not be available if they do not have an insight into the patient's living situation.

HCAH workflow

In a typical HCAH workflow, the patient gets all the usual hospital-based services at home, including oxygen, intravenous fluids, medications, radiology studies, and sample collection for laboratory studies. They also get respiratory, physical, and occupational therapy and get consultations from wound care. Broadly, the workflows encompass the following activities:

Enrollment

Enrolling the appropriate patients is critical for the success of the HCAH program. The HCAH should develop well-defined inclusion and exclusion criteria. The patients must be carefully selected to ensure that they have acute needs, require a hospital level of care, and have a diagnosis that can be appropriately managed at the patient's home. The eligibility considerations include patient acceptance, insurance coverage, and safety issues at home. It is important to note that patients need to consent to receive treatment at home.

Evaluation

After the eligible patients are enrolled in a HCAH program, they are evaluated by the HCAH physician in the ED, ambulatory site, or at home. In some programs, preliminary treatment to stabilize the condition and initial labs may be done in the ER before transitioning to home. Patients are transported by the hospital or contracted third party.

Integration

The telehealth technology in HCAH should ideally be integrated into the hospital's technology infrastructure. The healthcare providers at home should be able to enter data captured at home directly into the enterprise EMR of the hospital through their laptop or tablet devices. Telemedicine applications can directly run off the hospital infrastructure. If multiple vendors are used to support the technology for the HCAH program, they should seamlessly integrate with each other and the parent hospital's information systems.

Management

After the patients are short-listed, evaluated, and admitted to the program, HCAH nurses are dispatched to the patient and provide patient care at home. The number of hours of nursing care varies depending on the program and the acuity of the clinical condition. Patients are also educated about collecting vital signs and watching for concerning symptoms. Routine evaluation by physicians can be conducted through virtual rounds, which may be multidisciplinary and can include the nurse, pharmacist, case manager, or HCAH coordinator. The vital signs are transmitted to the provider via telemetry. They are manually entered into the EMR or automatically recorded via an interface. The treatment team provides daily input and creates a provision for 24-hour care coverage and protocols to respond to urgent visits. Patients can be transported to the hospital and back home for advanced testing for diagnostic studies or procedures not available at home during the HCAH program. It is also important to ensure that the staff has experience and comfort in treating patients in HCAH.

Equipment

DME equipment is sent to patients' homes, including hospital beds, walkers, spirometers, pulse oximeters, and compression devices. Patients who require oxygen get oxygen cylinders or concentrators. It is important to note that patients may require education about using these services.

Telehealth

Telehealth is an important component of the HCAH model. The providers are connected via phone, video for synchronous and asynchronous consultations. Continuous monitoring of physiological telemetry data from biosensors enables the remote provider teams to respond in near real-time. Analytics which can be supplemented with machine learning for signal detection, provides intelligent alerts and recommendations. The information capture and processing infrastructure is modified to support patients in geographically separate areas connected via different networks with varying bandwidths.

Skilled therapies and supportive services

The HCAH model provides the ability to deliver physical and occupational therapy at home. The services can be provided by hospital staff or by third-party contractors. Patients can also be evaluated by social services. Nutrition and dietary experts can provide appropriate meals for the patient when needed. Patients can get food from the hospital kitchen or contract outside services like Meals on Wheels.

Pharmacy support

IV medications are delivered and administered at home. This process is usually performed by the home health division or outsourced to a home infusion service partner. They are responsible for installing the necessary infrastructure, supplies, and monitoring. The oral medications and inhalations can be delivered from the hospital's inpatient pharmacy. The hospital's pharmacists are responsible for the ultimate home medication administration program oversight. All administration is documented in the EMR, similar to the inpatient bedside documentation.

Laboratory

The specimens collected from the home are processed in the hospital laboratory using the same protocols as inpatient samples. The results are made available in the EMR system. Protocols are developed around specimen collection, handling during transportation, and turn-around times. Clinical conditions with a high probability of requiring laboratory studies which may be difficult to collect at home and process accurately, like lactic acid or arterial blood gas, may need to be excluded from the HCAH program.

Radiology services

A mobile X-Ray or CT scan collecting system is required to collect radiological images. These could be read by radiologists on staff or third-party contracted companies. Other studies like venous ultrasounds and echocardiograms may be performed at home if transportation and testing infrastructure are available.

Security

The security practices should be outlined in the HCAH policies. The portable computing devices should be secured. The hospital staff should have their network connectivity through mobile phones or hotspot connections. The 24x7 home monitoring devices may use patients' Wi-Fi secured through a VPN connection.

Quality metrics

The most significant quality metrics are clinical outcomes and patient satisfaction. However, many other process outcomes have been studied (Leff B et al., 2005). These have included time for the initial physician evaluation, nurse visit, initial medication administration, physician and nursing visits per day, total nursing hours, length of stay, and use of healthcare services 30 to 60 days after HCAH. Other proposed metrics include serious falls, medication errors, and pressure ulcers. For evaluating the program, the post-HCAH measures could include readmission to the hospital or return to emergency, length of days of HCAH treatment, and patient satisfaction.

Post discharge

Some HCAH programs follow the patients for up to 30 days post-hospitalization at home to support the transition of care to the primary care physician. The follow-up could include regularly scheduled follow-up calls, home visits, care coordination with a multidisciplinary team, medication reconciliation, and referral assistance (Morano B et al., 2020).

Post acute care

Post-acute care could be offered to patients after they are discharged from the HCAH. They could also include services provided at home but traditionally offered at dedicated facilities. These services include those provided at long-term acute care hospitals, skilled nursing facilities, and rehabilitation hospitals and could be transitioned to home in certain settings.

Conclusion

Hospital care at home will get increasingly popular in the future. COVID-19 accelerated the adoption of the concept, which had been tested over the last 20 years. Coupled with technological advances, wider installation of fast home internet connectivity, and innovative payment models, more clinical conditions will be safely managed at home.

28 TELEHEALTH FOR ACUTE CARE

Telehealth has been used in outpatient settings for many decades. In the inpatient setting, ICUs and radiology departments were among the earliest and most prolific users of telehealth. However, in recent years telehealth use has increased across multiple inpatient departments.

TeleCritical care

ICUs face shortages of intensivists who are also increasingly reporting burnout due to high workloads (Lilly et al., 2019). The shortage is not limited to the United States and has been reported in many countries worldwide. In the United States, only about 1/3 of the patients in the ICU are treated by a critical care board-certified physician (Angus et al., 2000). Most intensivists working in the ICUs work part-time (Pronovist et al., 2007). Evidence from studies shows that ICUs staffed by intensivists have lower lengths of stay and mortality rates (Pronovost et al., 2002).

To address the shortage, hospitals have set up teleICUs which are remote monitoring centers serving other hospitals within the same healthcare system or other unaffiliated hospitals. TeleICUs (also called eICUs) had been one of the most common and successful applications of telemedicine prior to the pandemic. Patients can be monitored 24 x 7 or only at nighttime when an in-house intensivist is unavailable. Besides being available on call, these teleICUs can monitor patients and detect early deterioration through alerts and reminders (Scurlock et al., 2015). TeleICUs also allow intensivists to manage multiple ICUs by the audiovisual interface, document on the site-specific EMR, and enter orders via a computerized physician order entry system for the local nursing, laboratory, or pharmacy.

TeleICUs can be set up as networks where a single hub provides telecom services to multiple locations or as a point-to-point arrangement where smaller or understaffed hospitals are staffed by specialists from a larger healthcare facility in the same health system. TeleICUs can be configured into continuous, episodic, remote monitoring, and response care-based systems depending on the need of the site (Herasevich et al., 2019).

In a continuous care model, remote monitoring of any ICU is 24 x 7. The hub can be staffed by ICU physicians, ICU-trained Nurse Practitioners, and RNs. The episodic care model provides remote care for intermittent needs, for example, during daily rounds, shift changes, or unforeseen absenteeism. A responsive care model is a reactive, episodic care arrangement where remote consultation is requested by a facility on a case-by-case basis. This may be initiated by a hospitalist from the hospital where there is no intensivist coverage at all or at certain hours during the night when an intensivist is not physically present at the location.

Besides routine monitoring, emergency or critical care-trained physicians use telemedicine to remotely manage critical events like cardiac arrests (Barbash et al., 2020). Meta-analysis of teleICU has demonstrated reduced ICU mortality, hospital mortality, and ICU length of stay after teleICU implementation (Chen et al., 2018). TeleICUs have also demonstrated increased patient safety due to adherence to a standard of care for deep vein thrombosis prophylaxis, stress ulcer prophylaxis, cardiovascular protection, and ventilator-associated pneumonia (Purnell et al., 2021). Burn units often use telemedicine as they may have varying censuses (Ajami et al., 2014a).

TeleICUs have expanded their services beyond initial evaluation and episodic monitoring of critical patients. The remote critical care teams manage post-operative ICU patients (Collins et al., 2017) and conduct family conferences and palliative care consultations with the families of critically ill patients (Menon et al., 2015). Due to the remote nature of care teams in these teleICUs, families are provided with online decision tools to participate in their family members' care remotely (Cox et al., 2015). In some situations, limited telecritical care services can be provided for remote monitoring of ventilators, patient monitors, pumps, etc. The remote teams assist the hospitalists or other providers without intensivists (Ambrosino et al., 2016). Tele ICU centers have also started to provide telenursing services to ICU-trained nurses who work closely with onsite bedside nurses to provide intensive care support (Goran et al., 2011).

It is vital that the hospitals planning to set up an eICU program conduct a detailed cost-benefit analysis (Kruklitis et al., 2014) before launching the program. Studies have demonstrated that often these programs are clinical, financial, and operational successes (Gorman et al., 2013). As the number of patients with multiple chronic diseases grows and value-based payment incentives expand, telemedicine services will continue to expand.

TeleEmergency medicine

Emergency rooms are one the busiest departments in a hospital. TeleEmergency care is one of the emerging areas for telehealth application in an acute care setting (McKinney et al., 2015). Telemedicine can be used for remote diagnosis (Castellano et al., 2015) and treatment consultation.

74% of stroke cases die outside of the hospital (Norris et al., 1998), and studies have demonstrated improvement in the level of care if stroke evaluation is completed through teleconsultation with emergency medical services (Rogers et al., 2017). Multiple studies have found reduced treatment time if the diagnosis is developed while the patient is in prehospital transport. Telehealth technology integrated into the ambulance significantly impacts the critical care process. These ambulances can be connected over cellular signals, wireless broadband Internet, or radio communication. Teleemergency management has multiple clinical and operational benefits. For incoming patients, teleemergency allows the ED to be connected with the EMS services. Telemedicine in ED can triage the patients at home, preventing unnecessary emergency room visits by integrating with the EMS personnel (Champagne-Langabeer et al., 2019). The emergency departments can support the EMS personnel by providing remote supervision of intubation with video laryngoscopy (Sibert et al., 2008) or for managing specific emergent conditions like stroke (Lumley et al., 2020). The two most common delivery methods for EMS telemedicine are video-conferencing and store and forward (Winburn et al., 2018). In a survey of paramedics, the majority agreed or were neutral about telemedicine's role in improving hospital diagnosis, destination decisions, and patient satisfaction. The concerns about using telemedicine by EMS personnel include background noise, connection issues, and interference with routine care. Telemedicine was believed to be most beneficial for unclear acute stroke diagnoses, trauma center criteria, and STEMI criteria (Simon et al., 2020).

Teleemergency applications include exchanging real-time audiovisual data and image transfers for physician-to-physician communication with an ED physician providing consultation to non-physicians at distant locations or to multiple smaller EDs at distant locations (Mueller et al., 2014). A typical application is communication between an ER and a specialist, including neurology, trauma, and ophthalmology (Ward et al., 2015). The communication can also be between an ED physician and another staff member, including ED nurse, Nurse Practitioner, or Clinical Staff for teleconsultation, telepresence, or teleradiology.

The other advantage of telehealth in emergency medicine is reduced ED door-to-provider time using ED-based telehealth (Mohr et al., 2018). During the surges in ED, TeleICUs can work with EDs to improve throughput (Lilly et al., 2019). Having remote clinical teams on standby in emergency or critical care units has a beneficial impact on outcomes (Scurlock et al., 2016), improving the quality of care.

Poisoning is one of the most common household accidents. Teletoxicology is used for evaluating and managing these patients (Chai et al. 2014), primarily by emergency medicine physicians. The Sexual Assault Nurse Examiners (SANE) affiliated with the emergency departments have used teleSANE for the evaluation of sexual assault victims (Walsh et al., 2019).

TeleHospital medicine

While critical access hospitals benefit from telehospitalist coverage (Kuperman et al., 2018), any hospital or skilled nursing facility can augment their staff using telehospitalist services. Hospitalists can round on their patients using telerounding, which is not only limited to hospital medicine but can be used for inpatient rounding in any medical or surgical specialty. Telerounding can be done using fixed cameras and monitors in the patients' rooms or telepresence robots with wheels that can be navigated to patients' rooms. Telerounding has been shown to improve the quality of care and reduce medical errors (Ellison et al., 2007).

TeleNursing

Telenursing activities include conducting initial telephonic assessment interviews, educating patients, triaging patients' needs, including home assistance, care coordination, assessing patients' clinical condition, and reviewing vital sign data collected from home. Telenursing can coordinate with primary care physicians, private nurses, pharmacists, and home care facilities (Ferrua et al., 2021). The triage systems using telenursing have been shown to benefit from improving access and reducing costs. Studies have shown no clinically significant difference in quality and satisfaction between remote triage and traditional nurse triage and physician triage using telepresence (Gidora et al., 2019). Telenursing can also be used for surveillance and tracking in the ICU, augmenting the in-person staff (Rincon et al., 2017)

Telenursing is also used to provide direct care interventions to patients, including providing information about chronic diseases, providing emotional support and words of encouragement, addressing clinical issues based on patient data like blood glucose or blood pressure, medication adjustments, and providing general lifestyle or health information. (Wakefield et al., 2013). The indirect care interventions provided by telenursing include reporting patient information to the primary care provider, providing social contacts, addressing system issues, including medication refills, clinic appointment reminders, and troubleshooting blood glucose meters. Telenursing can also assist with non-patient care interventions, for example, fixing telemonitoring devices, responding to false alarms, streamlining nursing schedules, etc.

29 TELEHEALTH FOR AMBULATORY CARE

Ambulatory care applications for telehealth have expanded beyond primary care and now include telegenetics, teledermatology, and others. One advantage for most scenarios is the opportunity to use asynchronous methods to deliver care. This chapter discusses some exciting applications of telehealth in ambulatory care settings.

TeleAllergy & TeleImmunology

The telehealth applications for teleallergy care are viable both for diagnosis and monitoring. Teleallergy medicine has constantly been used for asthma in pediatric patients, but its scope is expanding to other allergic and immunological disorders, including allergic rhinitis, food allergies, and urticaria. Prick tests for diagnosis can be monitored remotely by allergologists as long as adequate resources are available on-site for any possible anaphylactic reactions (Staicu et al., 2018). Telemonitoring combined with allergology allows the practitioners to monitor the patients at their homes using smartphone diaries or images captured with smartphones. Patients and providers have expressed high satisfaction with telehealth visits for telephone consultation, follow-up visits, interpretation of laboratory results, and preauthorization reviews (González-Pérez et al. 2021).

TeleConsultation

An electronic referral (e-referral) is a request by a treating healthcare provider (referring provider), most commonly a primary care provider, to another healthcare provider (referred provider), most commonly a specialist, to evaluate and/or treat a patient. After the electronic referral is placed, the patient can see the referred provider through telemedicine or an in-person visit. The most common consultation requests are from primary care physicians to specialists, but the consultations can also be inter-specialty or intra-specialty. Primary care physicians can request clinical input from the specialists without sending the patients to the specialist's office for an in-person visit or a separately scheduled telehealth visit. Algorithms can be created for the automatic triggering of referrals of patients to specialists. For example, patients with a hemoglobin A1c above a certain threshold can automatically be referred to an endocrinologist. Patients with a diagnosed malignancy can automatically be referred to a hematology-oncology service. Similar automated patient referrals can be put in place for patients with diagnoses ranging from HIV to infectious disease, uncontrolled hypertension to nephrology, and skin lesions to dermatology.

The referral management systems are specialized applications for the referral management process. They improve efficiency by providing the providers with relevant clinical history and managing the end-to-end referral workflow. They sometimes require that the refereeing providers use a separate portal if these systems are not automatically integrated into the EMR ordering process.

An electronic consultation (e-consult) is an exchange of clinical information, most commonly inputs about diagnostic workups or treatment plans, between two healthcare providers about the care of the mutual patient or between a patient and a consulting provider. Electronic consultation can be done through email, phone, or video calls without the patient needing to see the preferred provider directly. Specialty-specific consultation requests and responses can be created using templates to improve efficiency. Depending on the need, the consultations can be written, provided over the phone, or converted into a bidirectional video call with or without the patient's participation. The consulting specialists can identify the symptoms or diagnoses for which the consultation can be requested. The healthcare systems are increasingly adopting e-referrals and e-consults due to the increasing complexity of medical treatments, increased demand for specialty care, reduced availability of specialist physicians, higher quality of care, improved efficiency, and reduced cost of care.

For specialties like hematology, endocrinology, and dermatology, over 50% of in-person visits can be avoided using e-consults (Keey et al., 2013). E-consults reduce inappropriate clinic visits and unnecessary follow-up visits (Kim-Hwang et al., 2010). E-consults also reduce the wait times to get access to specialists. They help to retain the patients within the same health system network. Care coordination and inter-specialty communication are enhanced by using a specialized consultation management system. The tracking of consultations also assists with tracking billing and payments for consultations, especially if insurance companies do not reimburse them. There is still some outstanding skepticism about medico-legal liability for providing e-consultation, but the case law will become clearer as the prevalence of e-consultation increases.

TeleDentistry

Traditionally, dentistry has not been considered conducive to telehealth due to the need for in-person examinations and hands-on procedures. However, specific business use cases emerged during the pandemic, which expanded on the rise in direct-to-consumer orthodontics businesses.

Teledentistry is based on conventional telemedicine technology platforms, including video or phone calls for teleconsultation or specialist triage, telediagnosis using dental images, and telemonitoring using serial communication with patients to assess treatment progress (Ghai et al., 2020). Teledentistry can be used for remote screening, diagnosis, consultation, treatment planning, and monitoring. Published systematic reviews of tele-dentistry have shown comparable diagnostic performance to the standard alternatives (Estai et al., 2016). A wide variety of dental conditions are conducive to teledentistry. Some of these include evaluation and treatment; monitoring of malocclusions like open bite, overbite, crossbite, and tooth irregularities; oral lesions like dental caries, leukoplakia, candida, ulceration, ulcers, granulomas; dental trauma; gum pathologies like gingivitis (Daniel et al., 2013). Research studies have shown no statistical difference between screening for dental caries through teledentistry versus in-person visits (Kopycka-Kedzierawski et al., 2007). The examinations performed through teledentistry have found the need for orthodontic referral with the same effectiveness as clinical examinations (Mandall et al., 2005). Studies have also demonstrated that phone-based teledentistry is more cost-effective when incorporating the cost of time away from work and overnight accommodations for distant patients (Scuffham et al.,

2002).

Teledentistry services have focused on risk evaluation, early dental lesion detection, timely treatment of oral diseases, oral health education, and reducing barriers to access. The teledentistry models include store-and-forward teledentistry as well as real-time interaction. A typical staffing model could be a dental hygienist and a dental assistant physically evaluating a patient with a remote dentist or a dental specialist (Nichols et al., 2019). For routine evaluations, patients can send their photographs taken on smartphone cameras via secure messaging services (Giudice. 2020).

The services provided by non-dentist dentistry practitioners depend on state-specific regulations and reimbursement models. For example, the ability of dental hygienists to place cavity liners and bases, install and remove temporary restorations, install and remove temporary crowns, and place and finish amalgam and composite restorations is dependent on the scope of practice allowed by the state (ADHA. 2016).

Teledentistry reimbursement is still a work in progress, with wide variation between states' insurer policies. Two teledentistry Current Dental Terminology (CDT) codes were created in 2018 for reporting dental services and procedures: D9995 (synchronous "real - time." encounters) and D9996 (asynchronous "store-and-forward" encounters). Besides reimbursement issues, there are also regulations around licensing. Dentists who participate in tele-dentistry across state lines must obtain licensure in every state their patient is physically located.

According to the surveys conducted during the pandemic, the majority of the patients expressed a strong preference to use teledentistry. The diversity in teledentistry applications and business models has expanded during the pandemic. It has successfully provided community-based dental care in elementary schools and low-income childcare programs. They typically are based on store-and-forward technology, where the community dental team gathers background information about the patient, obtains intraoral pictures of all services of each tooth and surrounding soft tissue, performs a head and neck exam, and takes radiographs. The tele-dentist reviews the information and makes a treatment plan, including whether the patient needs a referral to a dentist (Nichols et al., 2019).

TeleDermatology

The specialty of dermatology has been one of the most impacted by the consumer adoption of telehealth, improvements in image capture and transmission infrastructure, and innovation in business models. Studies have demonstrated teledermatology consults to be accurate and valuable (Keller et al., 2020). Most teledermatology consultations are based on the store-and-forward method and depend on accurate image capture of dermatological lesions. With better smartphone cameras, specialized equipment is no longer required for most lesions. However, appropriate diagnosis and treatment require accurate lighting, coloring, and measurements. Experts have developed guidelines for taking high-quality medical photographs (Muraco et al., 2020) and demonstrated that patients can acquire clinically useful images of their lesions. Studies on teledermoscopy have shown that 97% of patients can acquire baseline and follow-up images of their skin lesions which are considered valuable by the dermatologist. Though dependent on operator characteristics, it is possible to create teledermatology solutions dependent on the patient's acquisition of images using a mobile dermascope attached to a mobile phone for store-and-forward telemedicine (Wu et al., 2015).

Teledermatology for simpler dermatologic issues like acne is one of the most common indications for consumer-initiated teledermatology. A review of teledermatology consultations over three years, where store-and-forward teledermatology was used, showed that patients were able to avoid about two-thirds of potential dermatology visits, the median wait time was reduced by almost half, and the no-show rate was reduced by one-third. Biopsy rate was more than double (Dobry et al., 2021). Research has shown that most patients are satisfied with their encounters with the providers after video-call visits (Ruggiero et al., 2020). Besides routine clinical consultation about wounds, teledermatology is also used for serious conditions like dermatologic emergencies (Villa et al., 2020) or even diagnosing and treating cutaneous skin cancers like melanomas (Nahm et al., 2021). This approach is instrumental in the short-term monitoring atypical melanocytic lesions (Altamura et al., 2008). A review of studies has demonstrated sensitivity ranging from 73% to 97% and specificity ranging from 73% to 83% for teledermatology diagnosis accuracy compared to face-to-face diagnosis and/or histopathological results. Most of the studies demonstrated high concordance between teledermatologists and face-to-face dermatologists. Patients who were provided with educational teledermatology demonstrated improvement in the severity of their skin conditions, higher adherence to therapy, higher quality of life scores, and reduced anxiety compared to the usual care (Oliveira et al., 2017).

Systemic reviews have shown good diagnosis and treatment between a teledermatology diagnosis and face-to-face and/or histopathological diagnosis coupled with face-to-face assessment. The reliability of teledermatology has been shown to depend on factors like imaging skills and equipment, availability of comprehensive and relevant history, and skills of the tele-dermatologist and the referring physician (Levin et al., 2009).

Dermatology is primarily an office-based specialty, but there are many situations when hospitalized patients need dermatological evaluation, and dermatologists are unavailable for inpatient rounding and consultation. It is important to appropriately triage the patients who need a dermatology consultation in these situations. At the same time, they are admitted to the hospital versus the patients who can safely follow up with a dermatologist post-discharge. Algorithms have been created to help with this decision-making and triage the patients into three categories - telemedicine consultation only, intermediate-risk dermatology consultation, and high-risk dermatology consultation. These algorithms are better if they include information from electronic medical records and use them to capture, store, and share high-quality photos of the lesions taken by trained nurses and ancillary staff (Kyle et al., 2020).

TeleGenetics and TeleGenomics

An increase in the prevalence of DNA genotyping or sequencing is leading to increased identification of mutations that can predict disease risk. This sets up a positive feedback loop where the utility of these genetic tests increases, leading to more individuals getting their genome sequencing done. Traditionally, geneticists and genetic counselors consulted individuals and couples with hereditary risk at tertiary academic medical centers. However, increasingly, direct-to-consumer telegenetics and telegenomics service providers are connecting genetics counselors and genomic researchers with patients directly via telehealth platforms. The services provided include cancer genetic services, reproductive genetics, genetic counseling about the risks of disease, cardiac genetics counseling, diagnosis of genetic diseases, and management of genetic diseases. This has the primary benefit of increasing access to genetic counseling services for the patients and providers. Genetic counselors have set up practices leveraging telemedicine technologies to provide remote counseling to individuals and families about their hereditary risk for developing malignancies (Mahon. 2020), reducing the barrier to the adoption of telehealth technologies.

The Covid-19 pandemic had a mixed impact on telegenetics. In data published by one group, the no-show rate for telephone genetic counseling improved during the pandemic while maintaining service capacity. At the same time, there was reduced compliance with sample return and higher rates of sample failure (Shannon et al., 2020).

Telegenetics also provides access to clinical genetics services to pediatric populations in underserved regions (Kubendran et al. 2017.) The geneticists work closely with the pediatricians, where the pediatrician conducts a disorder-specific physical exam, provides an overall health assessment, and provides overall health recommendations. The genetic counselors analyze the family and medical history, coordinate genetic testing, and provide genetic counseling. (Lopez et al. 2014). Geneticists help with dysmorphology exams, review disorder-specific physical exams, and provide disorder-specific recommendations.

While the telegenetics field is rapidly progressing, outstanding issues still need to be addressed. Privacy and security of genetic information are a big concern (Du et al. 2018). It is also unclear if industry standards will emerge regarding the use of patients' genetic information collected through direct-to-consumer genetic tests for research purposes.

TelePediatrics

Telemedicine applications in pediatrics can be categorized based on the clinical setting. For acute inpatient care, the primary, specialty, and consulting physicians use telehealth to see patients using live or intermittent bedside encounters in emergency departments or inpatient wards. Telemedicine is used to monitor neonates and children in community hospitals by neonatologists and intensivists using monitors and videoconferencing. Besides clinical management, telemedicine improves shared decision-making by connecting families and community members to patients and caregivers.

Telemedicine plays an important role in the perinatal and newborn care. Physicians can provide antenatal consultations in high-risk pregnancies. High-risk mothers can be monitored remotely during the hospitalization and the labor and delivery process. Neonatal resuscitation can be supported and stabilized in newborns with complications like pre-term birth, perinatal asphyxia, etc. Post-delivery, bedside subspecialty consultations can evaluate distress and triage any needs for transfer to another center (Marcin et al., 2016). Telemedicine can also augment the management of high-risk infants (Gray et al., 2000) directly or by supporting their parents (Tan et al., 2012). Digital technologies like noncontact photo plethysmography can be combined with telemedicine to assist in remote evaluation of infants' heart rate in the NICU without contact and reducing the risk of infection.

Timely, high-quality, and evidence-based tele counseling about breastfeeding can be critical to the health of infants. Telehealth interventions for breastfeeding have been demonstrated using group videoconference social network sites, SMS-based programs, video conference and phone combined programs, and internet-based interactive breastfeeding monitoring systems (Marcucci et al., 2018). Studies have demonstrated the performance of telehealth interventions compared to the usual standard of care (Ferraz Dos Santos et al. 2020).

The incidence of retinopathy of prematurity is increasing due to the increasing survival of very low birth weight infants. The screening requires a thorough examination by a pediatric ophthalmologist. Unlike diabetic retinopathy, the window of time available to intervene is much shorter to prevent bad clinical outcomes. The technical expertise needed to image the fundus of premature infants for reasonably accurate reading is much higher (Graham et al., 2014). Studies evaluating the use of telemedicine for retinopathy of prematurity have shown that high-quality images can be obtained after appropriate training of health personnel capturing the images, and telemedicine can help in obtaining a faster turnaround time. The reading can be augmented by computer analysis of the images that may not be available at all centers (Makkar et al., 2020).

Telemedicine also assists with routine subspecialty care in pediatrics. There is a shortage of trained pediatric emergency physicians. Telemedicine helps to fill the gap wherever there is a shortage of trained practitioners. For example, it can enable consultations with trained pediatric emergency medicine physicians in smaller hospitals or remote locations (Gattu et al., 2016; Dharmar et al., 2013).

Pediatric hospitalist programs have also adopted telemedicine to provide consultations between specialists and hospitalists (Labarbera et al., 2013). Inpatient teleconsultation can be provided to pediatric patients who are in isolation. Patients can be evaluated for activity, alertness, tone, and signs of respiratory distress. Bedside nurses assist with digital stethoscope auscultation. Lactation support and counseling are provided via videoconferencing to the mothers. Other inpatient services and occupational and social work can reach the isolated patients and their families through videoconferencing (Umoren et al., 2020). The application of telemedicine in trauma, emergency care, and surgical management has undergone significant advancements in the last few years. Systematic reviews have found reduced travel times, improved continuity of care, and provision of specialist care in medically underserved and rural areas (Lewis et al., 2012).

Pediatric telecardiology has been shown to reduce the length of stay of low birthweight infants, cost savings, improved diagnostic accuracy, and unnecessary referrals. Pediatric cardiologists can perform confirmatory testing of critical congenital heart disease using telemedicine after a positive screening exam or concerning symptoms.

Fetal teleechocardiography can be performed by pediatric cardiologists, maternal-fetal medicine specialists, or obstetricians to screen for congenital heart disease and fetal arrhythmias. It can be used for screening fetal heart diseases to increase prenatal diagnosis of congenital heart disease (Sharma et al., 2003). Such interventions can improve post-delivery surgical and heart transplantation outcomes by early referral of pregnant mothers to appropriate clinical centers. Generally, store-and-forward technologies used for fetal ultrasound or echocardiogram images via a secure network can be sent to a tertiary care fetal heart center for consultation and management advice. Remote fetal tele-echocardiography service can transmit live images for real-time maternal-fetal medicine consultations. Fetal teleechocardiography can also guide and monitor pharmacotherapy and fetal arrhythmias.

School-based telehealth models help increase student healthcare access, reduce ER visits, and improve children's health status with acute and chronic illnesses. The programs that have been implemented include diabetes, speech and language impairment or learning disability, fluency disorders, asthma, hearing screening, and attention-deficit / hyperactivity disorders (Sanchez et al., 2019). Pediatric telepsychology interventions are equivalent to face-to-face treatment in areas like "therapeutic alliance, weekly progress, child/family engagement, establishing rapport" (Wade et al., 2019). There may be some advantages in pediatric populations, like convenient scheduling of appointments, a better understanding of the family's home environment, and reduced caregiver stigma in issues related to behavioral care at home.

For ambulatory care, direct-to-patient videoconferencing encounters and remote patient monitoring can provide access to consultants. Studies have demonstrated that adding video data can improve the triage efficacy of pediatric phone triage systems (Freeman et al., 2017) and increase patient satisfaction. Subspecialists provide synchronous consultations to primary care offices or asynchronous evaluation of patient data for second opinions or subspecialty consultations. School-based clinics and rural health centers are connected to remote multispecialty clinical teams for acute and chronic disease management of diabetes and obesity. Common primary diagnosis subgroups for direct-to-consumer pediatric telemedicine have included sinus infections, sore throat infections, ear infections, eye infections, skin disorders, respiratory infections, gastroenteritis, fever, respiratory disorders, viral illnesses, psych or behavioral disorders (Alessandrini et al., 2010).

Digital interventions promoting adolescent health management have improved medication adherence, asthma control, quality of life, and reduced healthcare utilization. Examples include automated telephone calls triggered by overdue refills, text messages based on personalized schedules, sensors, and monitors providing a range of reminders, interactive websites providing assessment and feedback tools, electronic daily diaries, symptom scores, peak flow variability assessment modules, educational websites, mobile apps coupled with connected nebulizers and peak flow meters (Ramsey et al., 2020).

In the nurseries, videoconferencing tools improve communication and interactions between healthcare staff of neonatal ICUs, infants, and their parents. Teleneonatology has been successfully used during newborn resuscitation (Beck et al., 2008; Fang et al., 2016). Besides close monitoring of pre-term babies, routine management of ventilators of neonates and children can be assisted by respiratory therapists through telemedicine (Bell et al., 2016).

TelePrimary Care

Teleprimary care is the largest application of direct-to-patient telemedicine by the number of visits annually. Its adoption has increased with the emergence of direct-to-consumer companies which have leveraged mobile phones to connect the providers directly with the patients. American Telemedicine Association has developed guidelines for the implementation of telemedicine in primary and urgent care and other related areas (Gough et al., 2015). Various telehealth interventions have been implemented with additional use cases introduced during the COVID-19 pandemic.

It is important that the office staff at the primary care offices appropriately triages the patients into in-person versus video-based primary care visits. Usually, telemedicine visits are selected due to patient-dependent factors. For example, it may not be feasible for the patient to travel due to ambulatory issues and lack of availability of transport options; patients may have a family-related issue like family need to be with a child or a parent or grandparent or inability to leave work. As discussed earlier, telemedicine visits bring their unique logistical challenges. Patients need to have hardware, software, and connectivity at their preferred location to participate in telemedicine. Patients may be required to conduct some part of the physical exam, like checking their vital signs or performing maneuvers independently or with assistance from an attendant or a parent

(Sturesson et al., 2018). Studies have demonstrated that local, practice-based telephone triage services result in fewer patient referrals to ED or primary care doctors compared to regional or national telephone triage services (Rushton et al., 2019).

Telehealth allows physicians to remotely monitor the patient's chronic conditions and provide more frequent interventions versus waiting for the patient to arrive in the office. Chronic care management is a critical component of primary care and includes activities outside the typical primary care office. The services which make up chronic care management include discussion and review of medical records, communication of test results, providing education and support, sharing patient's health information, including their electronic health plan with the patient's other health care providers, management of care transitions, coordination of home or community-based services. These services can be provided by professionals other than physicians, including nurse practitioners, physician assistants, certified nurse midwives, and clinical nurse specialists, and at any site, including federally qualified health centers, rural health clinics, and critical access hospitals. It is easier to identify new symptoms and intervene early in case of the emergence of new symptoms. Usually, patients wait for their symptoms to worsen before making an appointment to travel to their physician's office. As of this writing, the reimbursement under the CCM program requires management, provision, accounting, and documentation of the 20 minutes or more spent by staff providing non-face-to-face care. The traditional chronic care management services are billed under 99490, 99491, 99487, 99489, G0511, and 99439. Per CMS, patients eligible for chronic care management are "Medicare fee-for-service and dual eligible beneficiaries with two or more chronic conditions expected to last at least twelve months or until the death of the patient, when those conditions place the patient at significant risk of death, acute exacerbation / decompensation, or functional decline" (CMS. Connected Care Toolkit).

Multiple studies have demonstrated the effective use of telehealth in the management of chronic diseases (Parker et al., 2018). Patients with depression can get cognitive behavioral therapy through telehealth. Phone or video-based counseling interventions can be provided for losing weight and increasing physical activity in patients with diabetes. Home-bound medically frail older patients with COPD, CHF, CKD, or vulnerable groups like at-risk veterans with comorbid depression can get daily monitoring, protocol-driven in-home messaging, and telehealth-based depression care management. Tele-behavioral interventions include techniques for problem-solving, behavioral activation, self-management, response to treatment, and intervention in cases of premature discontinuation of medications. American Heart Association has acknowledged multiple digital health interventions that target reduction in weight, blood pressure, cholesterol, and smoking (Burke et al., 2015).

Telehealth is also being deployed in the domain of preventive medicine. An analysis of 25 randomized control trials which looked at multifactorial dietary interventions in patients with chronic disease showed that telehealth-delivered dietary interventions which targeted whole foods or healthier dietary patterns improved the quality of the diet with an increase in fruit and vegetable intake. They also demonstrated reduced blood pressure, weight, BMI, and total cholesterol levels (Kelly et al., 2016). A similar analysis looking at telehealth interventions for the secondary prevention of coronary artery disease demonstrated lower rehospitalization or cardiac events (Jin et al., 2019).

Home blood pressure readings generate automated or human-generated customized messages via email, SMS, and mobile apps. Some programs integrate these interventions with telephone consultations with physicians or nurses and run parallel to the standard of care drug therapy and other lifestyle changes.

A systematic review of mobile phone-based messaging to improve medication adherence in secondary prevention of cardiovascular disease showed beneficial effects on medication adherence in coronary artery disease patients (Adler et al., 2017). Cochrane review of telemedicine studies has found lower glycated hemoglobin in patients with diabetes, improved quality of life in heart failure patients, and decreased LDL and blood pressure (Flodgren et al., 2015).

For patients who cannot access telehealth from their homes, teleconsultations can be set up with specialists like psychiatrists directly from the primary care offices reducing barriers to receiving specialist care (Fulford et al., 2016). These services can be augmented by integrating ancillary providers like community health workers who can cost-effectively drive coaching and goal setting via web applications and telephone calls. Similarly, family planning clinicians can provide contraceptive counseling services to patients without needing in-person visits, increasing provider and patient satisfaction (Stifani et al., 2021).

Primary care providers are using digital tools to communicate with patients. This targeted digital client communication has been defined as the "transmission of targeted health content to a specified population, or to individuals within a predefined health or demographic group" (Ames et al., 2019). Examples of such communication include targeted health education or a combination of alerts, notifications, and reminders to a patient for cases like appointment reminders and lab alerts. Telehealth allows multimodal delivery of individually tailored plans which can be delivered via SMS, email, mobile app notifications, interactive voice response, voice calls, instant messengers, multimedia messages or MMS, or video calls. The communication can be individualized, dependent on a patient's unique situation, or standardized with predetermined content sent to a subgroup of the population.

Increasingly, telehealth interventions collect physical activity data from smart watches and pedometers. Phone or video calls are combined with disease-specific sensors and instruments, tracked remotely by nurses or technicians. The data collection can be automated or manually entered into the disease management programs driven by care protocols and algorithms. The interventions can be delivered through smartphone apps, combining automated health management with personalized health coaching. Programs promoting physical activity have combined mobile phone or email reminders with real-time feedback about physical activity levels. Body-worn sensors with personalized weight management coaching based on self-monitoring of daily food intake, lifestyle activity, and emotional state have been implemented. The self-monitoring programs that have remotely delivered real-time feedback using dietitians or exercise physiologists have shown benefits. Some interventions use group therapy with online forums. Social cognitive theory-based approaches have been incorporated into telehealth apps.

Technology interventions have been deployed in primary care settings for interventions for substance use disorders (Tofighi et al., 2018). These include smartphone apps, text messages, and web-based interventions. Studies on smoking cessation have used SMS, email, interactive voice response hotlines, mobile apps, and video messages to communicate with the participants. Other studies have demonstrated the effectiveness of using messages for behavioral change, supportive communication for quit-date targeted goals, and delivering personalized advice. These treatments can be administered at patients' homes and reduce barriers to access (Uscher-Pines et al., 2020). Studies have also demonstrated that automated telephone communication systems which deliver voice messages and collect health information from patients through a voice recognition software or touch-tone keypad can change patients' health behaviors, improve clinical outcomes, improve quality of care by improving immunization rates, screenings, compliance with medications or lab tests, and reduce no-shows for medical visits (Posadzki et al., 2016).

Teleprimary care has also shown increased access to healthcare in rural populations, especially for older adults and children, people with disabilities, substance use disorders and/or mental health conditions, inmates, tribes, island populations, and people in disaster zones. The benefits of teleprimary care are varied depending on the primary care site. Federally qualified health centers are resource-constrained healthcare delivery programs that have adopted telemedicine to improve access. The utilization of telehealth technologies by FQHCs and patient adoption increased during the pandemic and will likely persist in the future (Sodhi. 2020). There have been concerns that telehealth-based interventions may exclude patients with limited phone access or who were on a limited quota of text messages or data. However, these concerns have been minimized with the broader adoption of mobile technologies and government-subsidized mobile phone plans. The patients have also expressed concern about privacy and confidentiality when receiving such communication. Some strategies to mitigate these issues include using neutral or nonspecific language in the content of the message and changing the timing and frequency based on individual recipients' preferences.

TeleRadiotherapy

The specialized clinical practice of radiation oncology saw significant adoption of telehealth during the COVID-19 pandemic. Even though radiation therapy is performed in person, telehealth is used for remote contouring, remote treatment planning, and overall teleradiotherapy consultations (Fernández et al., 2020). Telehealth allows for easier multidisciplinary discussion with multiparty video or phone calls.

Teleradiation oncology workflows mimic the traditional in-person process (Maroongroge et al., 2020). The initial consultation is a video call that may have a physical exam component facilitated by a local healthcare provider or patient's attendant. The preliminary work-up, including laboratory or imaging tests, is usually complete by the time a patient presents to the radiation oncologist. The patients must be physically present at the radiation therapy facility to get the radiation treatment, but many ancillary activities can be performed virtually. The treatment simulation using standardized patient indexing, treatment planning, and quality assurance can be coordinated with centralized dosimetrists via phone, video, or email. After treatment sessions, video or phone-based follow-ups can be conducted with the patients.

Notably, some radiation oncologists have raised concerns about worsening health equity for those with low technical comfort with technology or those who lack access to the internet regarding their access to radiotherapy specialists who are available via telemedicine (Franco et al., 2020).

TeleSleep medicine

Multiple approaches have been used to monitor sleep, including sensors on the finger, wrist, head, pillow, mattress, and table stand, with varying degrees of success. Software applications combine data from these sensors with other data elements to provide personalized coaching to individuals. Home-based sleep studies have been gaining popularity due to their ease of use and lower cost. Wearable devices can be combined with smartphones to diagnose sleep-related breathing disorders remotely at home. Sleep specialists can diagnose and monitor sleep apnea and response to CPAP therapy using tele-sleep medicine.

Advanced home sleep apnea monitoring can be implemented by using multiple sensors worn on the body to create a Body Area Network. Multiple sensors are also used for real-time monitoring of alertness in individuals who require a high level of vigilance in their occupation. These instruments capture EEG, EOG, and ECG signals which can be interpreted remotely in real-time or at a later date or linked with automated algorithms for real-time alerts (Kim et al., 2009). Other emerging telehealth applications in sleep medicine include diagnosing and monitoring restless legs syndrome, insomnia, and narcolepsy (Singh et al., 2015).

Telemonitoring monitors adherence to continuous positive airway pressure (CPAP) therapy in patients with sleep apnea. Internet-connected CPAP machines can provide real-time data about usage time, apnea incidents, airway pressures, and air leakages (Singh et al. 2015). The CPAP machines transmit this data to medical service providers, who can triage based on clinical scenarios. Patients with low usage of CPAP can be contacted to assess for limitations and take mitigating steps to improve their compliance (Woehrle et al., 2018). Telesleep medicine is also used in pediatric patients to diagnose obstructive sleep apnea and follow up to monitor CPAP adherence (Paruthi, 2020). Internet-based cognitive behavior therapy for insomnia (CBTI) has increased sleep-related parameters in children (de Bruin et al., 2018).

TeleSports medicine

Telesports medicine can provide access to clinical care for professional and amateur athletes. Sports injury cases that need in-person examination can be triaged via telehealth to save time. Telehealth approaches can be easily and efficiently used for making diagnoses, follow-ups, and routine health monitoring. Multidisciplinary consultations can be arranged with other supporting specialties. For example, sports teams may need access to orthopedics, neurosurgery, cardiology, radiology, pharmacy, nursing, dentistry, nutrition, performance coaching, etc. These can be easily arranged through telehealth instead of having the athlete visit every specialist in their office (Dijkstra et al., 2020).

About 2 million children sustain concussions every year in the United States. Tele-concussion can provide an evaluation of the patients suspected of concussion. Patient symptoms are collected through this process, and screening and testing tools, including Post-Concussive Symptom Checklist (PCSS), Vestibular Ocular Motor Screener (VOMS), and computerized neurocognitive testing, are administered digitally. Whenever required, the provider can remotely guide the patient through movements they replicate independently (Caze et al., 2020).

TeleUrgent care

Phone-based triage has been successfully implemented by the poison control centers for many years. (Law et al., 2014). In the last few years, many companies have been set up to provide virtual visits to manage common acute illnesses. Studies have found wide variations in the quality of clinical care among these providers. This is an opportunity for standardization as virtual urgent care visits become more mainstream (Schoenfeld et al., 2016). A recent study examined a virtual urgent care service that was staffed by emergency medicine physicians. The service used a custom electronic health record to provide 24-hour coverage. As per the analysis, 76.4% of the patients who sought care from this service had an existing primary care provider. Only 3% of the visits could not be completed due to no-shows or technology issues. The common comorbidities among the patients included obesity, asthma, coronary artery disease, COPD, diabetes mellitus, hyperlipidemia, hypertension, and malignancy. The median age of the patients using the service was 40 years compared to the median age of 43 years for patients discharged from a corresponding ED. Out of all the patients seen virtually, 6.1% were referred to the ED for further evaluation (Smith et al., 2021).

TeleWound care

Wound management includes assessment and measurement of the wounds. Precise area measurement requires accurate identification of wound margins using contact or digital tracing. Wound volume requires measurement of wound depth. For example, the clock method technique is a "linear measurement using the face of an imaginary clock to measure the greatest risk, longest length and greatest depth of the wound with 12 o'clock being the head position" (Swezey. 2021). Mobile phones are increasingly used for evaluating wound characteristics and making decisions about management (Van Dillen et al., 2013). Many smartphone apps are available for measurements of wounds (Shamloul et al., 2019). Commercially available mobile phone apps can be used to identify foot ulcers early, assess burn wounds, or track wound healing. Studies have demonstrated shorter healing times and reduced costs using telehealth for chronic wounds (Le Goff-Pronost et al., 2018).

The international working group on diabetic foot recommends that telehealth be used for ulcer assessments, providing self-care or advice to patients and their caregivers, check for foot offloading and dressings (International Working Group on the Diabetic Foot. 2021). Guidelines have been developed to determine which conditions can be safely evaluated with home telemedicine. These include improving foot ulcers, inactive Charcot foot, uncomplicated venous leg ulcers, recently healed foot ulcers, healed amputation, and for diabetic foot risk assessments (Lee et al., 2020).

A study comparing in-person wound evaluation with teleconsultation showed high concordance between in-person and electronic consultations. A physician examined the patients face-to-face, photographed the wounds, and sent the images to a remote wound specialist for teledermatological assessment. The concordance for wound features was 84% for slough, 98% for necrosis, and 76% for granulation tissue formation (Salmhofer et al., 2005). Another study found no difference between the management of forefoot ulceration through telemedicine and in-person diabetes foot in average ulcer healing time, the percent of ulcers healed in 12 weeks, and the adjusted healing time ratio (Wilbright et al., 2004). High-risk patients without any active diabetic foot ulcer can be monitored at home by remote patient monitoring to assess for impending tissue loss, presence or absence of infection, and compliance with footwear or therapy. Additional hardware like smart socks, smart insoles, smart mad, smart offloading, and smart thermography imaging remote monitoring can augment visual inspection (Najafi. 2020).

Stoma care services can also be provided through telehealth. These include consultations for mechanical bowel preparation, transanal irrigation, training for patients with fecal incontinence and constipation, stoma care, including first visit and follow-up, and stoma care complications (Dinuzzi et al., 2021).

Telewound care has limitations and cannot be applicable to all wound-care scenarios. Video and photos may not provide enough information for accurate evaluation. Static images have shown low validity and reliability as a standalone remote assessment method for remote diabetic foot ulcer assessments (van Netten et al., 2017). The virtual encounters may not provide information about wound smell, the texture of the skin, the extent and nature of the swelling, or manipulation of the wound to assess for subcutaneous paths. Most wound evaluations also need some intervention – cleaning, dressing change, etc., which requires in-person visit. Appropriate care must be taken to triage patients to telewound visits to minimize multiple visits for the same issue.

As healthcare delivery is shifted to ambulatory settings from hospitals, telehealth technologies are playing an increasing role in supporting this migration. Procedures which were previously performed in hospitals can now be performed in ambulatory care coupled with remote monitoring in some cases.

30 TELEHEALTH FOR HOME & POST ACUTE CARE

Telehealth can bridge the geographic divide between a clinician's office and a patient's home. Telehealth is augmenting home-based clinical services and increasing the scope of activities for post-acute care. This chapter discusses the applications of telehealth in home-based or post-acute care scenarios.

TeleCaregiver support

Telehealth-based caregiver support programs have demonstrated significant advantages compared to non-telehealth-based interventions (Bergström et al., 2018). These programs have been delivered through telephone, video, web portals, and text messaging. The interventions have targeted caregivers of patients with Alzheimer's disease, stroke survivors, cancer patients, patients with chronic medical conditions, elderly and frail patients, and caregivers of patients in hospice.

A systematic review of telephone-based counseling for informal caregivers of patients with dementia has demonstrated benefits in reducing depressive symptoms in caregivers. Such counseling included information about dementia, education about coping skills and self-care, psychosocial support, and opportunities to develop social support for caregivers (Lins et al., 2014). Similarly, phone-based support interventions, delivered by health professionals and targeted toward informal caregivers, can reduce anxiety and preparedness to care for patients (Corry et al., 2019). The interventions for caregivers include individual telephone counseling sessions, telephone-based support groups, video sessions, self-care activities, relaxation and breathing techniques training, and identification of pleasing daily activities to offset emotional distress. Caregivers also receive education about problem-solving skills, navigating behavioral issues, managing complex caregiving challenges, organizing care routines, and specific topics like empathy, normalizing, validation, venting, role play, bibliotherapy, cognitive reframing, coping strategies, behavioral activation, thought-stopping, and distraction techniques.

TeleGeriatrics

With the aging population, governments and healthcare systems face a shortage of resources to make healthcare services available to all elderly. Telehealth is one of the effective solutions that can efficiently provide acute and chronic care services to elderly patients (Shah et al., 2013). Telehealth technologies can also be integrated with other ancillary services created to combat loneliness in the geriatric population (Zubatsky et al., 2020).

Telehealth in geriatrics clinics has demonstrated productivity and clinical benefit. These are cost-effective, save transport costs, reduce visit cancelation rate, help with medication rationalization, and reduce hospitalization (Murphy et al., 2020). At home, the elderly are increasingly using computers or smartphones to access the internet, communicate with their family and friends, track their health and fitness, manage their finances, etc. These platforms can be leveraged for a diverse set of telemedicine activities. Mobile technologies have been developed to support the elderly with dementia in activities of daily living, location tracking, health monitoring, and social interaction (Koo et al., 2019). Telehealth is used to provide telemental health programs (Gould et al., 2020) to elderly individuals at high risk or those who have already been diagnosed with psychiatric disorders. Teledermatology services can be provided to geriatric patients as the incidence of skin malignancies increases with age (Simpson et al., 2020). Community paramedic personnel can use telemedicine to care for older adults with multiple chronic conditions for evaluation and treatment at home (Abrashkin et al., 2016).

There are mixed results about cognitive evaluation using telehealth to measure performance scores using tools like MMSE compared to in-person visits. This may be because of their dependence on patient and provider comfort with technology or lack of adequate supporting infrastructure (Sekhon et al., 2021). However, the management and tracking of dementia is a critical application for the deployment of telehealth in the elderly and can be integrated into a suite of services provided by an integrated team of internists, neurologists, behavioral health specialists, social workers, case managers, and home health nurses. The functional and clinical evaluations could include activities of daily living, medication review and compliance with primary care workup, new behavioral disturbances and change in any neuropsychiatric symptoms, state of social determinants of health, emerging mobility issues, and concerns related to caregiver support and burnout.

Projects that successfully implemented telehealth solutions for geriatric patients with dementia have conducted detailed neurobehavioral exams via video. It is possible to evaluate a patient's motor, sensory, and cognitive functions and psychiatric state. In some cases, assistance from the patient's caregiver or primary care physician may be required. The assessments obtained via video or phone encounters have included "orientation, concentration, memory, language, mood, affect, insight and judgment, thought content/ process, cranial nerve function, coordination and balance" (Weiss et al., 2021). Targeted instruments can be used to assist with such examinations, such as Blessed Orientation Memory Concentration Test, Picture-Based Memory Impairment Screen, etc.

TelePalliative medicine

About 60% to 70% of patients on hospice receive care at home (NHPCO., 2016). This care is delivered by hospice providers, including physicians, nurses, social workers, spiritual care counselors, volunteers, and informal caregivers, including spouses, children, relatives, and friends. Per the Medicare data, hospice nurses see patients about two times every week on average (Phongtankuel et al., 2018). Over 30% of the patients do not have any contact with a hospice provider during the last week of hospice care (Gozalo et al., 2017).

Studies have shown that video call-based therapy for informal hospice caregivers is not inferior to a face-to-face encounter (Demiris et al., 2012). The well-being of the patient and their caregivers can be tracked in real-time remotely, and additional needs can be identified quickly.

Before the pandemic, palliative care was considered a high-touch specialty ill-suited for telehealth, but during the pandemic, the benefits of telehealth became more apparent. These included avoiding hospitalized immunocompromised patients (Stockdill et al., 2021), augmenting palliative care teams, and increasing flexibility in scheduling multi-party conferences.

Telehealth can also improve administrative workflows in hospice medicine. Hospice recertification visits are required by hospice physicians or nurse practitioners before the 180th-day recertification and subsequently for 60-day recertification to assess a patient's eligibility for continued hospice care. During the pandemic, these visits were conducted through telehealth and showed no statistically significant difference in hospice care reauthorization between recommendations of in-person providers compared to providers conducting telehealth visits (Moore et al., 2020).

Pediatric palliative care, which frequently is integrated with pediatric oncology, offers outpatient services through telehealth clinics (Winegard et al., 2017). Telehealth enables parents from remote areas to connect with specialized expertise, which is unavailable in most regions in the United States. It also enables an increased number of family members to attend the appointments making it easy to coordinate visits with multiple caregivers and providers. Due to the sensitive nature of the conversations, discretion must be employed during the triage of the patients to telehealth vs in-person visits (Brock et al., 2019).

Telephone-based telepalliative consultations have been conducted on patients with cancer and heart failure with in-person consultation followed by phone sessions with advanced practice nurse coaches and care navigators. Another project set up video consultations with newly diagnosed patients with cancers and those newly admitted to hospitals with serious chronic illnesses in small rural hospitals (Watts et al., 2021). Nurse-led tele-palliative programs with focused interventions can be effectively deployed at a larger scale. For example, these programs have been used to identify a surrogate decision maker, conduct and document Advanced Care Planning conversations, and address caregiver burden in cases of high Caregiver Strain Index (Tan et al., 2021). Smartphone-based palliative care telehealth visits have demonstrated high satisfaction for patients and their families. These visits are based on the concepts of shared decision-making (SDM) and value, acknowledge, listen, understand, and elicit (VALUE) approach to discuss issues like discharge planning and withdrawal of life-sustaining treatment (Wu et al., 2020).

TeleSNF care

By 2030, 20% of Americans will be over 65 (United States Census Bureau. 2020). Currently, over 1.3 million patients live in over 15,000 nursing homes (National Center for Health Statistics. 2020). Skilled Nursing Facilities are resource constrained with rising expenses and declining reimbursements and are turning to telehealth to bolster the quality and efficiency of their operations. The Affordable Care Act did not provide additional funding to skilled nursing facilities to upgrade their technology. So, post-acute care facilities have been relatively less technologically savvy compared to acute care hospitals.

However, telehealth has found numerous applications in post-acute and long-term care settings. In the past, healthcare providers have also been reluctant to adopt technology and new models of care in the nursing home setting (Gagnon et al., 2012). During the COVID-19 pandemic, nursing homes were severely hit and multiple telehealth strategies were used nationwide to minimize the transmission risk and augment clinical staffing at post-acute care facilities. Real-time decision support was provided for the emergent management of COVID-19 patients. Clinical providers used telemedicine for routine evaluation of patients to improve access and reduce COVID-19 exposure. The facilities were able to connect with Infectious Disease specialists who could direct treatment at the sites. Telemedicine services integrated with emergency medical services allowed rapid triage to emergency rooms or alternative care destinations.

Before the COVID-19 pandemic, Medicare telehealth services were only reimbursed if they met specific requirements, including originating site and geographic location requirements. Originating site requirement stated that the patient needed to be located at an approved originating site when telemedicine service was delivered. Skilled Nursing Facilities (SNF) were one of the allowed originating sites. The other originating sites were Physicians' or practitioner offices, Hospitals, Critical Access Hospitals (CAH), Rural Health Clinics, Federally Qualified Health Centers, Hospital-based or CAH-based Renal Dialysis Centers, and Community Mental Health Centers (CMHC). The originating site also needed to be in a Health Professional Shortage Area (HPSA) or a rural area unless there was an exception. Most SNFs were not in rural areas, so their residents could not obtain services due to a lack of reimbursement from Medicare. During the pandemic, originating site location requirement was waived. This also helped home health agencies that provided services to patients in their homes. Medicare also expanded the services that could be reimbursed to over 80 new types, including audio-only codes. For SNFs, these included initial nursing facility visits with CPT codes 99304, 99305, and 99306 and discharge day management with CPT codes 99315 and 99316. Before the pandemic, these services were prohibited from being performed through telehealth. CMS also waived the requirement that telehealth visits for subsequent care in SNFs could be reimbursed once every 30 days and allowed the use of CPT codes 99307-10. Physical therapy, occupational therapy, and speech-language pathology services could also be provided via telehealth for the patients admitted to the SNFs. Medicare Advantage, Part C program, allows beneficiaries to choose their care and treatment to be delivered through private health plans. CMS has been open to allowing telehealth platforms at SNFs for these beneficiaries. This may be a catalyst of telehealth growth post-pandemic.

Medicare has paid for virtual check-ins and e-consults from 2019 onwards. Virtual check-ins are short patient-initiated communications with a healthcare provider. Per the requirements, the patients must have an established relationship with a physician or other practitioners, check-ins unrelated to a medical visit within the previous 7 days, and do not lead to a medical visit in the next 24 hours. The providers can respond to patients' questions by phone, audio-video calls, secure text messages, email, or through the patient portal. HCPCS codes G2010 or 2012 can be used. E-visits are non-face-to-face patient-initiated communications, usually through an online patient portal with providers who already have a physician-patient relationship with the patients. Per the requirements, the patient must initiate the query, and communication can occur over 7 days. Billing codes that can be used are 99421-23, G2061-63.

Telemedicine can be used in nursing homes for tele palliative care, teledermatology, telepsychiatry, and other medical and surgical subspecialties (Driessen et al., 2016). The other telehealth applications include ongoing monitoring of patients and urgent medical care delivery to improve clinical outcomes and reduce costs (Razak et al., 2020). Hospice facilities can use telehealth instead of face-to-face encounters for hospice certifications.

The number of potentially avoidable hospitalizations in nursing home patients for short-stay skilled nursing home residents is 690 per 1000 patient-years, and for long-stay nursing home residents, 285 per 1000 patient-years (Segal et al., 2014). SNFs often lack access to qualified healthcare providers who can assist with managing complicated conditions at SNFs. Most facilities also lack advanced decision management tools such as Interventions to Reduce Acute Care Transfers (INTERACT)-compatible order sets (Ouslander et al., 2014). SNFs can avoid avoidable emergency department visits for emergency consultations using telehealth, reducing patient transfer costs. It also improves the quality of care by providing access to specialist physicians, improves value-based program payments by reducing readmissions, and reduces patient inconvenience.

Telehealth can also help with coverage of nighttime calls at SNFs. Conventionally, there is reduced staffing during the night shifts. Studies have shown a reduction in hospitalization rates in facilities that are more engaged in after-hours telemedicine coverage, leading to average savings of over $150,000 for each nursing home (Grabowski et al., 2014).

SNFs can also access primary care physicians through telehealth more easily, which has been conventionally difficult when trying to transport residents to PCP offices for every visit. The primary care providers affiliated with long-term care facilities can do eConsults with specialists. According to one study, the most frequently consulted specialties included, in decreasing order of frequency, dermatology, geriatric medicine, infectious diseases, gastroenterology, neurology, rheumatology, cardiology, ENT, surgery, pharmacy, endocrinology, obstetrics and gynecology, orthopedics, pain medicine, urology, wound care, hematology, and nephrology (Helmer-Smith et al., 2020). Residents of SNFs who require multidisciplinary consultations can use telemedicine for group consultations. For example, oncology clinics can conduct coordinated consultations with the participation of a surgeon, medical oncologist, and radiation oncologist (Grenda et al., 2020).

31 TELEHEALTH FOR MEDICAL SPECIALTIES

Medical subspecialties like cardiology and neurology been early adopters of telehealth tools and techniques. In recent years, most other medical subspecialties have started using telehealth. This chapter captures some salient examples of telehealth implementations in multiple medical subspecialties. Research and technology development is progressing rapidly in this area, so many previously unseen applications will likely emerge over the next few years.

TeleCardiology

Cardiovascular disease is one of the leading causes of morbidity and mortality. In the United States, one person dies every 36 seconds from cardiovascular disease (CDC, 2018). Telehealth can be used to screen, treat, and monitor cardiovascular diseases. Cardiovascular telehealth can be used for hospitalized patients, visiting their primary care physicians or having cardiac symptoms at home. Paramedics responding to 911 calls can be supported for managing patients with heart attacks in the field for diagnostics (Brunetti et al., 2015) or with treatment (Brokmann et al., 2016). Early intervention can improve the outcomes of the patients and reduce subsequent complications. The management of STEMI is time-critical, so telehealth is effectively used to shorten the time to treatment (Rasmussen et al., 2014). EMS providers routinely consult with Emergency Departments from the field for triage and initial consultation. This is being augmented by integrating cardiovascular and other critical care specialists.

Telecardiology can also be used to manage chronic conditions. Congestive heart failure is a common chronic cardiovascular condition responsible for more hospitalizations than pneumonia or heart attacks in adults over 65 (McDermott et al., 2017). In several studies, managing congestive heart failure through telemedicine has demonstrated value (Ahmed et al., 2020). Remote monitoring coupled with targeted virtual visits can potentially be used for congestive heart failure management (Mohebali et al., 2021). Remote monitoring technologies for congestive heart failure have targeted vital signs, including weight, heart rate, and blood pressure; lung congestion through thoracic impedance and dielectric sensing; hemodynamics through pulmonary artery pressure measurement and left atrial pressure measurement. Telemonitoring and structured telephone support have been shown to reduce all-cause mortality and heart failure-related hospitalizations in congestive heart failure patients (Inglis et al., 2009).

Frequently, cardiac patients need rehabilitation after a heart attack or severe congestive heart failure. Tele-cardiopulmonary rehabilitation connects patients with physical therapists, respiratory therapists, cardiologists, and pulmonologists from their homes. Patients are provided other equipment exercise apparatus, incentive spirometer, pulse oximeter, cough assistive device, and blood pressure monitor to collect data (Bryant et al., 2020). They can upload their vital signs and get instructions and feedback about exercising and using the rehab equipment. Studies have demonstrated improvements in exercise capacity with tele-cardiac rehabilitation, especially when used with mobile apps, heart rate monitors, etc.

Surveillance of patients for abnormal heart rhythms can also be achieved using telemedicine (Chen et al., 2017). Remote patient monitoring of cardiac patients using implantable electronic devices, implantable loop recorders, and wireless implantable pulmonary artery pressure sensors has been a safe alternative to in-person-only visits (Miller et al., 2020). An international consensus statement has recommended that all patients with implantable cardioverter–defibrillator (ICD) should be offered the option of remote monitoring (Slotwiner et al., 2015). The alerts collected could be related to lead dysfunction, ventricular arrhythmia, atrial arrhythmia, and heart failure. Wearables like smartwatches are becoming more sophisticated in their monitoring capabilities and are going beyond heart rate measurement by adding the detection of various arrhythmias.

Most telehealth programs provide sensor kits to patients, which are integrated into the telemedicine service. For example, for pediatric patients with cardiac complications like single ventricle heart disease, and ventricular assist devices, many families do not possess the necessary medical equipment to obtain reliable vital signs at home. They are provided with pre-packaged kits with pulse oximeters and pediatric blood pressure cuffs, allowing the kids to be monitored at home (Chowdhury et al., 2020).

Telecardiology also includes remote diagnostic services. ECGs are remotely interpreted (Hsieh et al., 2012) with electronic ECG capturing ability at most hospitals. Tele echocardiography allows the echocardiogram reports to be accessed and read by the cardiologists off-site. However, it requires proper equipment, trained personnel, and adequate transmission bandwidth. Tele-auscultation is a cost-effective alternative to tele-echocardiography in many situations for remote murmur evaluation using digital stethoscopes. This approach can be deployed in synchronous and asynchronous settings with overall accuracy similar to face-to-face evaluations (Rajakumar et al., 1999). Computer-aided auscultation using machine learning techniques can be used to provide decision support to non-cardiologist providers.

As telemedicine adoption becomes widespread, there is criticism that it may accentuate health disparities, especially for folks with inadequate technical skills or appropriate internet connectivity. This is a serious concern in telehealth programs for critical conditions like cardiovascular disease. Studies have shown reduced telemedicine use in females and those with a median household income of less than $50,000 (Eberly, 2020). Resolving these issues will require a concerted effort from telehealth providers, health systems, and the government.

TeleEndocrinology

Telehealth has been used to manage diabetes since the early 1990s (Billiard et al., 1991). With the advent of connected continuous glucose monitors and mobile apps, self-management of diabetes has undergone a significant change. Commercial products and services have been launched which provide mobile app-based services combining monitoring with diabetes health coaching or insulin adjustment consultation. Mobile apps have the advantage of being able to interface with a wide array of insulin pumps, smart pens, continuous glucose monitors, and glucose meters. Patients can easily upload data and in some cases, no intervention is required on the part of the patient. The apps can calculate trends, identify patterns, and develop individualized recommendations for a specific patient (Battelino et al., 2019).

Continuous Glucose Monitors (CGM) have been integrated with virtual visits and remote monitoring platforms to prevent serious complications like diabetic ketoacidosis in people with type 1 diabetes (Peters et al., 2020). Similarly, patients with gestational diabetes mellitus are managed through telemedicine and smartphone apps integrating machine learning for personalized feedback (Capel et al., 2020). CGM metrics that can be collected include the number of days CGM is worn, percentage of time CGM is active, mean glucose, estimated A1c, glycemic variability, time in various blood glucose ranges, low and high blood glucose indices, hypoglycemia, and hyperglycemia episodes. Smartphone apps targeted towards people with diabetes, which capture blood glucose data and other self-reported factors, can improve glycemic control in patients with type 1 and type 2 diabetes (Cafazzo, 2019; Wu et al., 2017).

Multiple studies have demonstrated improvement in the management of diabetes with telemedicine with reductions in HbA1c (Huang et al., 2015). Video-based endocrinology visits heavily depend on patient data, including laboratory results, glucose measurements, and insulin pump records. As more and more glucose monitors get integrated with smartphones, remote management of diabetes will become increasingly commonplace (Ahn et al., 2020). The expanding use of remote Diabetes Self-Management Education and Support (DSMES) and Medical Nutrition Therapy (MNT) services have shown increased adoption during and post-COVID-19 pandemic (Kerr et al., 2020).

Endocrinologists also use telemedicine to manage severe conditions besides diabetes, like pheochromocytoma and thyroiditis (Run Y., 2020). Patients with hypothyroidism typically get their serum thyroid hormone levels measured every 4-6 weeks until stable and every three months. If the condition does not stabilize after a year or year and a half, surgical removal or radioiodine ablation of the gland is considered (Bartalena et al., 2018).

TeleInfectious Disease

The COVID-19 pandemic increased the use of telemedicine in infectious diseases specialty. Hospitals, clinics, and patients needed to connect with infectious disease experts to get current information about treatment guidelines and COVID-19 patient treatment strategies. Broadly, opportunities in infectious diseases include inpatient consultations, live video consultations, store-and-forward consults for images, physician-to-physician telephone consultations, antimicrobial stewardship, monitoring and supervision of outpatient parenteral antimicrobial therapy, pre-exposure HIV prophylaxis, and chronic management of conditions like HIV, HCV, TB (Abdel-Massih et al., 2019).

Telemedicine also allows infectious disease physicians to collaborate with other specialties for the multidisciplinary care of patients. For example, opioid use disorder patients on methadone undergoing hepatitis C treatment can have an integrated opioid substitution therapy program with participation from a hepatologist and infectious disease specialists (Talal et al., 2019). The treatment of chronic hepatitis C has demonstrated higher rates of initiation of therapy in patients who were using telemedicine compared to in-person treatments.

With the rapid advancement in antimicrobial therapies and wider use of therapeutics platforms like interferons, mRNA, and emerging infectious disease outbreaks like Ebola, Zika, SARS, Covid-19, etc., tele-infectious disease services will continue to be a vital requirement for every health system.

TeleGastroenterology & TeleHepatology

Common acute gastrointestinal complaints like constipation or abdominal pain can be evaluated and treated through a virtual visit. Common chronic digestive diseases that can be managed through telemedicine include chronic abdominal pain, celiac disease, chronic constipation, cyclic vomiting syndrome, dysphagia, eosinophilic esophagitis and gastroenteritis, food protein–induced enterocolitis, gastrostomy tube care, inflammatory bowel disease (IBD), and irritable bowel syndrome (IBS). When a gastroenterology-related physical examination is needed, a visual physical exam, either done by the patient or with assistance from a bedside provider, is possible via telehealth.

Telemedicine interventions have improved the overall quality of life, vitality, emotions, and social functioning in patients with digestive diseases. Similarly, studies have shown that physiological biomarkers of disease activity and symptom severity scores improved in telemedicine intervention groups (Helsel et al., 2018). Teleconsultation services allow patients and primary care providers to connect with gastroenterology experts, including hepatologists (Tahan et al., 2016) and gastroenterologists (Regueiro et al., 2014). Specialized care management is made available through video interactions to improve the quality of care for gastrointestinal disorders like Inflammatory Bowel Disease (IBD) (Li et al., 2016). Patients with chronic diseases with flares can use symptom diaries and home telemanagement. A home telemanagement system allows patients to follow their self-care plans, helps providers monitor patients' self-management process based on clinical guidelines, and provides ongoing patient education (Finkelstein et al., 2003). This system has been applied to chronic diseases such as asthma, heart failure, diabetes mellitus, and IBD. It can be used as an adjunct to other methods of detecting and tracking disease flares, medication compliance, and adverse events (Cross et al., 2006).

Telemedicine is used for many other digestive disorders. Dysphagia is a common gastrointestinal complaint. Screening and assessment of swallowing as well as training and monitoring have been conducted through telemedicine in dysphagia patients (Ku et al., 2020). Telemonitoring has also been used to assess gastrointestinal motility disorders (Spiegel et al., 2015) as well as in inflammatory bowel diseases (IBD), including ulcerative colitis (Cross et al., 2012) and Crohn's disease (Kosinski et al., 2016). Telemonitoring of patients with IBD was found to be as effective in improving the quality of life as an outpatient visit while being more cost-effective (Heida et al., 2018). In another example, a home automated tele-management system was successfully deployed for patients with ulcerative colitis, which used text messaging via mobile phones to exchange patient data (Castro et al., 2006). This type of system is linked to a networked computer and electronic rate scale, which transmits patient data to a central server and generates alerts and reminders for patients resulting in a customized action plan (Cross et al., 2012). A study on celiac disease patients showed that most were satisfied with the remote consultations (Siniscalchi et al., 2020).

A systematic review of telemedicine for chronic liver disease has found applications in hepatitis C treatment, periprocedural management in liver disease, evaluation and management of hepatocellular carcinoma, and remote monitoring of patients after liver transplants (Serper et al., 2017). Patients with significant or worsening GI or liver issues are best evaluated in person.

However, telehepatology has the advantage that it can more reliably identify patients with psychosocial or other barriers to transplantation. Telemedicine can improve the evaluation efficiency for stable patients with chronic liver disease or benign liver lesions. For patients with liver disease who decompensate, telehepatology can enable rapid evaluation and intervention (Fix et al., 2020).

Virtual tumor boards can help with efficient and expedited multidisciplinary management of patients with chronic gastrointestinal conditions like hepatocellular carcinomas. Teleconsultations have also been shown to prevent relapse and reduce hospitalizations in cirrhosis patients. Liver transplant departments routinely use telemedicine to improve communication between transplant teams and patients post-transplant (Piao et al., 2019).

For patients undergoing endoscopies and colonoscopies, phone consultations in endoscopy-related clinics have improved failure-to-attend rates and patient satisfaction. The need for in-person follow-up consultations and physical examinations is also reduced (Zorron et al., 2020). In cases of elective colonoscopies, tele-education through telephone calls about bowel preparation has resulted in successful bowel prep and higher rates of polyp detection (Liu et al., 2014).

Successful telemedicine consultations have been conducted for pediatric patients with chronic digestive diseases like chronic abdominal pain, celiac disease, chronic constipation, cyclic vomiting syndrome, dysphagia, eosinophilic esophagitis, gastrostomy tube care, IBD, and irritable bowel syndrome (Berg et al., 2020). The shortage of pediatric gastroenterologists can be ameliorated by the use of telemedicine to improve the care accessibility and quality of care (Stone et al., 2018).

TeleNephrology

Telemedicine has shown effectiveness in the management of many chronic diseases. Even though metabolic syndrome, including hypertension, diabetes mellitus, and obesity, are considered the largest opportunities for chronic disease management, chronic kidney disease management is another area where telemedicine can have a significant positive impact. Telenephrology is beneficial for long-term screening of at-risk patients or early referral of patients to specialists (Gómez-Martino et al., 2008). The common conditions managed in a telenephrology program are hypertension, chronic kidney disease, diabetic nephropathy, renal polycystic disease, nephrolithiasis, congenital malformation obstructive nephropathy, chronic glomerulonephritis, and urinary tract infection. Telenephrology intervention has improved kidney disease quality of life and medical outcomes surveys (AlAzab et al., 2016).

Randomized clinical trials have shown that telemedicine services have caused improvement in hospitalizations and ED visits, patient satisfaction, the patient-reported quality of life measures, improvement in Depression, Anxiety, and Stress Scale (DASS) in patients with chronic kidney disease, those on hemodialysis or home peritoneal dialysis therapy (Raina et al., 2021). Another randomized controlled trial in patients with chronic kidney disease showed that management by an interprofessional team consisting of nephrologists, nurse practitioners, nurses, clinical pharmacists, psychologists, social workers, and dietitians using mobile tablets to communicate with the patient was not inferior to the usual care on all-cause mortality, hospitalization, emergency department visits or nursing home admissions (Ishani et al., 2016).

Telenephrology programs focusing on arresting the progression of chronic kidney disease, supporting patients on hemodialysis or peritoneal dialysis, and tracking post-kidney transplant patients are gaining traction. Real-time video and audio have been used for group sessions to improve patients' compliance with therapy and train nurses working with dialysis patients. For patients on hemodialysis, by using teleconferencing to implement home-based preventative care, nephrology groups have reduced hospitalization and hospital stay incidence, reduced overall cost of care, and improved quality of life (Berman et al., 2011).

The number of active home hemodialysis systems is increasing every year. This technology enables patients to perform hemodialysis at home by themselves and allows for frequent nocturnal hemodialysis, which has significant clinical and lifestyle benefits (Pauly et al., 2009; Heidenheim et al., 2003). The home hemodialysis devices are integrated with a digital platform connected with clinics and care teams. Peritoneal dialysis patients can perform home dialysis with assistance from remote monitoring. This became especially attractive during the pandemic because that could reduce the risk of infection during in-person hemodialysis treatment and dialysis centers (Alfano et al., 2020). Patients on peritoneal dialysis over followed at home using telemedicine showed reduced rates of hospitalizations (Gallar et al., 2007). Physicians can remotely evaluate volume status and dialysis access through photographs or video. Social workers can also use telemedicine for check-ins to discuss emotional distress, caregiver burnout, and medical resource acquisition and management. Trained nurses can troubleshoot catheters with remote nephrologists (Lew et al., 2021).

TeleNeurology

Neurology is one of the most common and effective use cases of telemedicine in the inpatient setting. Telestroke has been widely adopted in hospitals with good outcomes (Switzer et al., 2009). Patients with acute stroke are evaluated by neurologists, saving critical time for evaluation and advising on the management (Whetten et al., 2018). Such telemedicine implementations are cost-effective nationally (Ehlers et al., 2008). American Heart Association has endorsed remote evaluation of patients with stroke in underserved areas (Schwamm et al., 2009). Besides stroke evaluation, telemedicine platforms are used to evaluate patients with depressed consciousness, encephalopathy (Adcock et al., 2017), seizures, and other neurological conditions. Studies have validated the use of remote NIHSS (NIH stroke scale) evaluation (Wang et al., 2003). Multiple studies have also demonstrated remote thrombolysis to be safe (Pervez et al., 2010). Patients requiring endovascular therapy can be quickly and appropriately identified using telestroke infrastructure and transferred to the tertiary care centers as part of a "drip, ship, and retrieve strategy."

There are multiple options available for setting up a telestroke service. One option is advisory teleconsultation by a remote neurologist over the phone or video with treatment responsibility and liability of the patient (Bowry et al., 2015). Another option is that the remote specialist closely monitors and manages the patient's care, including telethrombolysis if needed. The final model is a close integration of a remote neurology department with a hospital where a remote team participates in patient care. The patient may continue at the referring site or be transported to the neurologist's local hospital. With the rising adoption of telemedicine in neurology, specialized roles are also emerging, like teleneurohospitalist for admitted patients (Freeman et al., 2012).

Out of all medical subspecialties, neurology likely has the highest dependence a physical examination. A near-complete neurological exam can be performed through telemedicine by the remote telemedicine provider or with an in-person healthcare provider (Meyer et al., 2008). Neurologic examination components which are assessable through telemedicine depend on the skill of the clinician and the presence of a trained chaperone with the patient. The components of examination that can be conducted remotely are mental status evaluation, including orientation, memory, cognition, and language; motor function evaluation, including facial palsy, shoulder shrug, tongue movement, aphasia, dysarthria, gross strength, tremor, coordination; sensory examination including hearing, vision. The examination is more effective if performed with the assistance of a care partner or family member with the patient rather than by the patient themself (Daggubati et al., 2020).

Telehealth has also been successfully used to assess, treat, and monitor neurodevelopmental disorders, including autism spectrum disorders (ASD), attention deficit hyperactivity disorders (ADHD), communication disorders, and tic disorders. Telehealth services have generally been found to be equivalent to face-to-face services. Telehealth visits with multiple sclerosis patients were shown to provide similar information to in-person visits, with consistent assessments of optic, bowel and bladder, and cerebral functions, while cerebellar and brain stem functions were the least consistent (Corea et al., 2021). Parent training interventions for ASD have been shown to improve caregiver knowledge, competence, and child participation and reduce problem behaviors (Valentine et al., 2021). Due to the chronic and slowly progressive nature of neuromuscular disorders, they are good candidates for evaluation and management via telemedicine. Besides televisits, digital tools like personalized questionnaires can be used for surveillance and patient triage to assess symptoms (Bonavita et al., 2020) remotely. However, the standard evaluation scales and examination methods may not work when administered remotely. Experts have suggested using ALSFR-R for motor neuron diseases, MG-ADL for neuromuscular junction diseases, Myo-FRS (M-FRS) for myopathies and Nerve-FRS (N-FRS) for neuropathies (Garibaldi et al., 2021). The conventional neuro-assessment scales are being modified or adopted for telemedicine with variations. The Unified Parkinson's Disease Rating Scale can be performed remotely without rigidity and postural instability testing (Abdolahi et al., 2013). The Montreal Cognitive Assessment (MoCA) is feasible in patients with movement disorders (Abdolahi et al., 2016). Real-time evaluation of motor functions has been demonstrated to be feasible using the remote Unified Huntington'sHuntington's Disease Rating Scale (Bull et al., 2014).

TeleObesity medicine

Obesity is a major risk factor for coronary artery disease, diabetes mellitus type 2, stroke, and certain cancers. Many studies have demonstrated the cost-effectiveness and efficacy of telemedicine for weight reduction using behavioral weight loss treatments. These studies have used video conferencing and phone calls in urban and rural settings and adult and pediatric patient populations (Brown et al., 2020).

Chronic disease management requires uninterrupted follow-ups for the long-term success of the therapeutic intervention. Obesity clinics have transitioned to hybrid programs with initial in-person evaluation and telemedicine-based encounters. Obesity clinics are usually staffed by an obesity medicine-certified clinician, nurse coordinator, registered dietitian, trainer, and a pediatric developmental psychologist in pediatric cases. As an example, one pediatric obesity medicine program transitioned to telemedicine which required 26 hours of intervention over 12 months. These were split into eight weekly to eight bi-weekly to six monthly visits followed by individualized maintenance appointment schedules. Patients have positive telemedicine experiences as they can share details about their home environment, including their kitchen, food, and exercise areas. The counselors can involve more family members in the intervention (O'Hara et al., 2020).

Video or phone-based technology coupled with mobile phone apps based tracking can provide patients with discreet, personalized monitoring, counseling, and medical treatment (Rivera et al., 2016). These apps provide self-monitoring, goal setting, physical activity support, healthy eating support, weight assessment, personalized feedback, motivational strategies, and social support. The patients can get support for weight control, exercise tips, dietary recommendations, and addictive behaviors. Telehealth also makes it easier to connect with peers for support. The Obesity Medicine Association has developed an algorithm for assessing, diagnosing, educating, prognosis, and treating obesity.

Centers for Medicare and Medicaid Services (CMS) reimburses primary care providers who provide intensive behavioral therapy (IBT) visits for weight loss in a primary care setting over one year. In order to continue to remain eligible for the program, the beneficiaries are expected to lose 3 kg weight during the first 6 months. It includes coverage for physicians, associate providers, and clinical nurse specialists (NCD. 2021). Dietitians have been using telehealth to provide nutritional advice for the general population and patient groups with metabolic syndrome (Benson et al., 2019) or those on total parenteral nutrition. Many commercial direct-to-consumer companies have launched apps for mobile phones where the dietitians provide weekly, monthly nutritional plans customized for individuals, monitor progress, and provide resources and feedback. Most of these target weight loss but can be incorporated into other clinical use cases.

TeleOncology

Traditionally, oncology has lagged behind most other medical specialties in adopting telemedicine. However, incorporating telehealth, remote monitoring, digitally enabled care, and therapeutics development may significantly impact the oncology practice (Kaye et al., 2020). Using telemedicine, oncologists can schedule clinical visits for initial evaluation, follow-up visits, and clinical trial intake visits. Supportive care to oncology patients can also be delivered through telemedicine. A multidisciplinary team of social workers, psychologists, therapists, and dietitians can work with the patient to provide a gamut of services. The subdomain of integrative oncology has seen good responses through online practitioner–patient interactions (Ben-Arye et al., 2021). Before the initiation of treatment and during the treatment course, patient education about chemotherapy and radiation therapy can be provided to patients remotely. Oncology offices can also monitor patients for patient-reported symptoms and outcomes and support self-care (Liu et al., 2020). Virtual visits can also be used for ancillary services like palliative care, genetic counseling, and fertility counseling. Telemedicine approaches are also useful in supporting patients with cancer around issues like body care, supporting healthy lifestyles, social and psychological aids, and general life questions (Jansen et al., 2015). A systematic review of telephone interventions to support self-management of cancer-related symptoms validated the use of telephone-based interventions for managing depression, anxiety, emotional distress, and fatigue. These can be augmented with video calls, face-to-face encounters, or digital materials (Ream et al., 2020).

Oncologic care is multidisciplinary, involving medical oncologists, radiation oncologists, ablative and reconstructive surgeons, radiologists, pathologists, supportive and palliative care professionals, speech-language pathologists, nutritionists, and physical and occupational therapists. Multidisciplinary conferences are key pillars of oncology care. They allow for a detailed evaluation of every case, from diagnosis, staging, treatment planning, clinical trial enrollment, care coordination, complications, response monitoring, and adverse events. Multidisciplinary conferences have been shown to reduce delays in diagnosis and treatment, increase the frequency of evaluation by provider teams, improve referral coordination, and reduce the burden of travel on patients and providers. Virtual multidisciplinary conferences are preferred over in-person sessions by the majority of participants in studies (Dharmarajan et al., 2020).

The telemedicine infrastructure and protocols developed during the pandemic will continue to enhance cancer care and provide earlier access to care for patients with cancers, especially common cancers like breast cancer requiring multidisciplinary care (Cadili et al., 2020). Based on the learnings during the pandemic, home screening of cancer is likely to be more widely adopted in the future. This approach will add more cancer diagnoses over time; however, in the short term, colorectal and cervical cancer will see an immediate impact (Gorin et al., 2021). It will also spur other innovations like differentiated triaging systems for specific types of cancers to triage patients into urgent appointments based on historical patterns and clinical needs for optimal patient management (Paleri et al., 2020).

The digital health ecosystem in oncology is integrating telehealth with remote patient monitoring, mobile apps, and passive data collection. The data is collected from patients through sensors in devices like mobile phones, activity trackers, and smart weighing scales. For example, performance status and early warning indicators of toxicity can be assessed in patients undergoing chemo-radiotherapy (Garg et al., 2018). Chest-mounted devices are being used to monitor patients with lung cancer receiving radiation therapy (ClinicalTrials.gov identifier: NCT03340714). Internet-connected nonbillable devices like smart weighing scales have been used with face-to-face sessions in breast cancer survivors to monitor weight (Valle et al., 2017). Digital platforms focusing on capturing Patient Reported Outcomes (PROs) have shown an association with performance status and treatment adherence. These have been integrated into Patient-Reported Outcomes-Common Terminology Criteria for Adverse Events item bank and serve as a companion to Common Terminology Criteria for Adverse Events (Basch et al., 2014).

Teleoncology is also being bundled with teleradiology and telepathology to provide bundled services. Multidisciplinary management using multiple modalities of treatment lead to improvement in function, quality of life, and survival. Mobile microscopy is combined with telemedicine for screening which can be applied to multiple types of cancers. These use tablet or phone-based mobile microscopes, which combine cameras, illumination, and motors to scan slides and capture high-resolution images of stained brush biopsy samples. The images are then remotely interpreted using telepathology (Skandarajah et al., 2017). The surgical oncology specialties are also integrating telemedicine into their workflows. For example, neurosurgical oncology clinics are using telemedicine to evaluate patients virtually. The benefits of this approach are quicker triage and prioritization, minimum exposure for immunocompromised patients, and the ability to do quick inpatient consultations for admitted patients (Daggubati et al., 2020).

Besides the advantages discussed above, the tele-triage process can help detect patients with infections and reduce the chances of the spread of infection at oncology clinics and wards because of the immunocompromised status of patients in oncology clinics and inpatient wards (Indini et al., 2020).

TelePulmonology

Remote monitoring of patients with respiratory diseases is achieved by using many sensors, including respiratory signal monitors, activity trackers, environmental sensors, pulse oximeters, and other physiological parameters like temperature, heart rate, etc. The respiratory monitors include spirometers and forced oscillation technique devices. Respiratory movement can be sensed by respiratory inductance plethysmography and breathing monitors based on resistance or capacitance for respirations. Newer research focuses on non-contact monitors and sensors embedded in the clothes. Besides these, sensors for detecting carbon dioxide and blood oxygen levels are helpful in patients with chronic respiratory diseases and acute decompensation of respiratory function (Angelucci et al., 2020). Telehealth-based spirometry assessments have been used in patients with cystic fibrosis. The spirometers are connected to a computer or mobile device. The patients share their screens with the respiratory therapist, who can see the flow-volume tracings and provide real-time feedback to the patient or their family. The patients can use remotely supervised spirometry to collect baseline values, routine home-based or outpatient monitoring, or during symptomatic episodes (Logie et al., 2020). Similar interventions have been tried for COPD, asthma, and idiopathic pulmonary fibrosis patients.

COPD is one of the leading causes of hospital readmissions, with readmission rates of up to 20% (Shah et al., 2015). The digital management of COPD encompasses self-management, in-hospital care, post-discharge care, and at-home care. Telemonitoring interventions have been shown to reduce hospitalizations (Cruz et al., 2014). Post-discharge care programs have also been shown to reduce hospital readmissions (Alshabanat et al., 2017). In one such project, patients were enrolled within 24 hours of hospital discharge into a telehealth program and were provided with a computer with a webcam, microphone, pulse oximeters, and spirometers. The post-discharge telemedicine system was led by a nurse who remotely assessed the patients and provided interventions to prevent exacerbation showing significant reductions in 30-day readmissions (Sorknaes et al., 2011). In another study, a telehealth program demonstrated a 75% reduction in 30-day hospital readmissions in COPD patients based in rural communities (Hillock. 2020).

A systematic review of telehealth interventions for asthma has provided evidence of improvement in the quality of life of asthma patients. The telehealth interventions are based on videoconferencing, remote monitoring, and store and forward techniques through smartphone apps. Some common use cases have included interactive web-based portals which provide education, recording of symptoms, monitoring of lung function, personalized asthma action plan, feedback, and protocols for self-management and adherence to medical treatment regimens. The effectiveness of telehealth interventions is evaluated using asthma-specific measures like the Asthma Control Test (ACT), Asthma Control Questionnaire – 5, and Asthma Quality of Life Questionnaire, as well as other outcome measures including asthma medication use, asthma-related hospital or ED visits, school absence due to asthma, preventative medications prescriptions, chronic disease self-efficacy scale, number of severe exacerbations, number of days of systemic corticosteroid treatment, PHQ-9 questionnaire, lung function tests including FEV1, PEF, FVC, FEF 25-75%, and therapeutic and diagnostic treatment adherence. Interactive telehealth interventions improved QOL outcomes. Tailored telehealth management incorporating education for asthma patients has shown to be more effective than one-way approaches (Snoswell et al., 2021). A Cochrane review did not demonstrate any important differences between face-to-face and remote asthma checkups when considering exacerbations, asthma control, or quality of life (Kew et al., 2016).

Virtual pulmonary rehabilitation through live video conferencing has reduced the frequency of hospitalizations in patients with COPD. Besides COPD, pulmonary rehabilitation is also recommended for patients with bronchiectasis and interstitial lung disease. In a systematic review, virtual pulmonary rehabilitation demonstrated statistically significant improvements in disease-specific quality of life questionnaires and functional exercise through incremental shuttle walk test (ISWT). It also improved generic questionnaires, depression, anxiety, and breathlessness scores (Knox et al., 2019). Home-based pulmonary rehabilitation programs using telehealth have shown improved patient adherence, lower dyspnea intensity, improved quality of life, and 12 min walk distance (Ding et al., 2019). Physicians can administer exercise tests to people with chronic lung diseases at home or in the office as part of their annual baseline monitoring. The tests which have been used at home include six-minute walk test (6MWT), Sit-to-Stand (STS) tests including 1 minute (1minSTS), 5 times (5STS), and 10 times (10STS), 6-minute stepper test, 3-minute step test (3MST) and Timed Up and Go (TUG) (Holland et al., 2020).

Digital stethoscopes can be used to transmit real time or recorded respiratory sounds. However, this technique is limited due to operator training and the higher expense of digitally connected stethoscopes. Portable, mobile phone-connected ultrasounds are also getting incorporated into the telemedicine practice. Trials have been successfully performed with lung ultrasound with a handheld ultrasound device in which real-time remote support by an expert operator is provided through two-way audio and video to guide the patient to obtain correct views. The same ultrasound can also be used for cardiac and intraabdominal imaging. This technology can significantly improve remote diagnostic accuracy (Pivetta et al., 2020).

TeleRadiology

About 70% of US hospitals use teleradiology for preliminary readings during off-hour emergencies (Krupinski. 2014). Teleradiology has been one of the most successful commercial applications of telemedicine. This has been enabled partly due to the nature of radiology, making it easy logistically and technically to be offered via telemedicine. It does not generally matter that the radiologist reading the images is located in the reading room of the hospital or at a remote site unless they are performing or supervising a procedure. The American College of Radiology and the European Society of Radiology have recommended that the teleradiology services be supplemental to the on-site radiology practice. The radiologists at remote sites should follow the same professional, quality, and safety standards of the radiology practice or the local hospital where they are contracted. Teleradiology can provide nighttime readings (nighthawk services), overflow interpretation during heavy workloads, and nonemergency backlog interpretations to clear work lists. The radiologists must be licensed in the state where the images are captured.

Handheld and portable ultrasounds have recently been launched, providing clinically useful diagnostic information at the point of care. These are directly connected to remote experts who can help with the (Nelson et al., 2011). Remote interpretation is also valuable for trauma cases when radiology expertise is unavailable on-site (Al-Kadi et al., 2009). Tele-ultrasonography is becoming popular as it can be performed at the bedside, does not require ionizing radiation, and the scanners are small enough to connect to mobile phones (Constantinescu et al., 2018; Crawford et al., 2012).

TeleRheumatology

A comprehensive physical exam is an essential component of a rheumatological assessment. One of the significant limitations of telerheumatology is dependent on a remote physical exam. The physical exam is especially important for the diagnosis of new conditions. A remote exam may be more acceptable during the subsequent visits to maintain therapy. For this reason, video consultations are preferred by rheumatologists over phone or text-based communication. The information provided by videoconference, like body habitus, body language, facial expression, and nonverbal cues, provides additional information to the provider. The patients can also visually self-assess joint or skin pathologies. It may be better that the patients use a physical exam facilitator who has some background training in physical exams to be present with the patient during the telerheumatology consultation (Gkrouzman et al., 2020).

Video-based telemedicine has been combined with clinometric questionnaires, which are administered by nurses during the virtual visit to assess the disease activity, the impact of the disease on the health status, and other associated symptoms. Some of the standard questionnaires used are The Assessment of SpondyloArthritis International Society Health Index (ASAS HI) and Bath Ankylosing Spondylitis Disease Activity Index (BASDAI) for spondyloarthritis, Rheumatoid Arthritis Impact of Disease (RAID) and Patient Reported Clinical Arthritis Activity (PRO-CLARA) for rheumatoid arthritis, The Psoriatic Arthritis Impact of Disease (PsAID) for Psoriatic arthritis, Beck'sBeck's Depression Inventory (BDI) for depressive symptoms, Fibromyalgia Rapid Screening Tool (FiRST) for Fibromylagia, State-Trait Anxiety Inventory (STAI) for Anxiety disorder, Visual Analog Scale (VAS) pain scale for assessment of pain. Telerheumatology consultations are also sought by primary care practitioners, orthopedicians, and dermatologists. Generally, common questions for a rheumatologist are related to selecting an appropriate drug, indications or goals for treating a particular condition, assistance with diagnosis, and management. As per one study, the reasons for consultation in descending order of frequency were osteoporosis, joint pain, inflammatory polyarthritis, osteoarthritis, rheumatoid arthritis, abnormal serological markers, crystal arthropathy, polymyalgia rheumatic, inflammatory monoarthritis, fibromyalgia (Rostom et al., 2018).

In pediatric patients, a Video-pGALS (pediatric Gait, Arms, Legs, and Spine) assessment has been proposed to conduct a physical exam over a video consultation. V-pGALS is a structured approach that includes maneuvers from pediatric regional musculoskeletal system examinations. The V-pGALS amends and supplements maneuvers to the pGALS exam, which has components from the pREMS (Pediatric Regional Examination of the musculoskeletal system) (Shenoi et al., 2020). The V-pGALS has questions for joint, muscle, or back pain, morning stiffness, difficulty dressing or undressing, walking, or going up or downstairs. It has maneuvers to assess gait, arms, legs, and spine (Pediatric Musculoskeletal Matters International). Studies have also demonstrated tele-rheumatology's effectiveness in diagnosing and managing autoimmune/inflammatory rheumatic diseases (McDougall et al., 2017). In a randomized controlled trial, no differences in disease activity were found between in-person or video-based telemedicine visits in patients with controlled rheumatoid arthritis (Taylor-Gjevre et al., 2018). Rheumatology is a complex disease with baseline variations among disease presentations. This also introduces diagnostic variation between rheumatologists in research studies complicating the findings. Few studies have compared the effectiveness of tele-rheumatology with standard-of-care in-person treatments. Per one study, the satisfaction rate with telehealth visits was over 90% in patients and physicians (Leggett et al., 2001).

32 TELEHEALTH FOR SURGICAL SPECIALTIES

Surgical specialties have not adopted telehealth with the same intensity as medical subspecialties. However, during the COVID-19 pandemic, they were forced to switch to telehealth visits, and subsequently, there was significant adoption in telehealth among surgical subspecialties. Specific use cases have emerged within every specialty that fits telehealth well. This chapter highlights some salient telehealth applications in surgical subspecialties. These are continuing to evolve at a rapid pace.

Several studies have evaluated the effectiveness of telehealth in surgical patients. In a group of patients who had undergone thoracotomy, remote monitoring of symptoms by using automated telephone calls coupled with severity-based email alerts to the care team showed a reduction in reports of serious symptoms (Cleeland et al., 2011). In another project, vascular surgeons implemented remote monitoring using a blood pressure cuff, thermometer, weighing scale, image capture, and pulse oximeter after a revascularization procedure for the lower limb. The data was subsequently reviewed by care managers. The remote-monitoring patient group had increased satisfaction and no difference in 30-day readmissions or surgical site infection compared to the group without remote monitoring (Mousa et al., 2019). A randomized controlled trial at a pediatric surgical outpatient clinic evaluated the patients who had video visits versus in-person follow-ups. The data showed that the video visit group did not miss any clinical findings. The telehealth group also had lower travel time, days off from school or work (Goedeke et al., 2019).

Remote telemonitoring can be combined with smart sensors and machine learning algorithms for early identification of complications. For example, using accelerometer data as a proxy of physical activity, researchers have demonstrated a good correlation with post-operative activity in patients who eventually had complications like readmission, sepsis, ED visit, operation, wound complication, and death (Panda et al., 2019). Patients can also submit photos of surgical incisions in lieu of in-person visits for post-operative monitoring. In a randomized controlled trial of patients who had undergone breast reconstruction surgery, there was no difference in 30-day complication rate, patient satisfaction or the total number of 30-day in-person visits to primary care physicians, operating surgeons, or emergency department, or for patients who had used a smartphone app for submitting photographs of incision and reporting pain symptoms instead of making an in-person visit to the physician (Armstrong et al., 2017).

Multiple studies have demonstrated that telehealth can replace in-person post-operative care (Williams et al., 2018). In most low-risk situations, routine follow-ups with the surgeon can be replaced entirely by a video visit. In high-risk surgeries, telehealth interventions may allow for more frequent data gathering and monitoring of patients post-op. Post-operative use of telehealth also reduces the length of stay and re-hospitalization. For example, patients with surgical drains placed at the hospital can be discharged home with telehealth monitoring and physician-guided home drain removal. These drains need routine monitoring to check for complications at the insertion site, monitoring for blockages, and evacuation of air. Patients are typically kept in the hospital till the drains can be removed, or they are discharged home and returned to the office for monitoring and drain removal. Prior to discharge, patients are provided with instructions and instructional infographics. In one project, patients could safely remove the drain with real-time, remote physician guidance and caregiver support, and no complications were noted (Go et al., 2020). In another study, patients underwent accelerated discharge after their minimally invasive colectomy using Telehealth for Enhanced Recovery After Surgery protocol leading to lower overall length of stay without increasing severe adverse events. Their home recovery was monitored using tablets, computers, post-operative tele-visits, and instant messaging (Bednarski et al., 2019). Another surgical team had a stoma nurse follow patients discharged after stoma creation by video teleconsultation. There were no differences in quality of life measured by 30-day readmissions or the EQ-5D index (Augestad et al., 2020).

Transplant recipients who require chronic follow-up visits can also be enrolled in telehealth programs. In a study, kidney transplant recipients showed improvement in blood pressure control and medication adherence post-transplant in a randomized controlled trial. They were provided a smartphone app integrated with a blood pressure monitor and pillbox (McGillicuddy et al., 2013). In another study, liver transplant patients had a lower 90-day readmission rate compared to the standard of care when they were provided with a tablet that enabled instant messages and periodic video visits and which was connected to a device that could measure and transmit vital signs (Lee et al., 2019). The transplant patients' televisions can be scheduled in advance or urgently in case of acute development of concerning symptoms. The urgent visits enable appropriate triage to the surgeon's office, urgent care, or emergency department (Chang et al., 2020).

Post-surgical follow-ups via telehealth can be rolled out for many surgical conditions. Studies have found no difference in the secondary outcomes, patient satisfaction, or additional physician office or emergency department referrals between the patients receiving follow-up visits by video or in-person office who have undergone laparoscopic appendectomy, inguinal hernia repair, and laparoscopic cholecystectomy (Cremades et al., 2020). Synchronous real-time audiovisual visits during consultations and follow-up visits have been demonstrated successfully for cosmetic surgery, rhinoplasty, maxillofacial trauma, reconstruction, and flap monitoring (Shokri et al., 2020). Virtual visits have been used in outpatient settings to conduct monthly post-surgery group sessions. The switch to telemedicine resulted in an increased volume of follow-up visits for advanced practitioners and a reduction in the no-show rate for follow-up visits (Brown et al., 2020).

Surgeons are also using telehealth for teleintraoperative consultations and telementoring. The surgeons can contact their colleagues or specialists during the surgery for consultations about intraoperative findings. These consultations can include verbal guidance over the phone, telestration, where a consultant can follow along with the procedure on a monitor and mark certain areas of the anatomy on the screen to assist the operating surgeon, and telementoring, where an experienced surgeon can guide the operating surgeon during complicated procedures.

A systematic review that studied the treatment of neurosurgical patients via telehealth found that the treatment was successful in 99.6% of the patients. Most of the failures were attributed to technology failures. The types of telemedicine services studied in the systematic review included transfer triage of adult and pediatric patients, post-operative outpatient follow-up, remote programming of neuromodulation devices, stroke trial enrollment, and thrombolytic administration for stroke. Telemedicine encounters were also similar or superior to in-person visits in 15 of 16 studies (Eichberg et al., 2020).

Lastly, telehealth technologies are also being used for telesurgery, which is the process of conducting a surgical procedure on a patient by a surgeon from a distance. Surgical robots have made telesurgery accessible. Studies have demonstrated that telesurgery is feasible with the same efficiency achieved regardless of the distance. Telesurgery has been performed for robotic percutaneous renal access, laparoscopic Nissen's fundoplication, laparoscopic hemicolectomies, sigmoid resections, and inguinal hernia repairs (Anvari et al., 2005). Network latency is the most significant limiting factor for telesurgery. Research has shown that a less than 300ms latency is generally acceptable, with ideal latency being less than 200ms (Xu et al., 2014).

There are some constraints in using telehealth which are applicable across specialties. Like all telehealth modalities, it is not easy to conduct a complete physical exam, and, in some cases, vital sign information may not be available at the time of prescription order. Providers may also be unable to provide all available therapeutic options during the limited encounter through the mobile app.

TeleCardiac surgery

Telemedicine has been used to manage cardiac surgery patients for triaging, preoperative, and post-operative care. The applications of telemedicine in cardiac surgery include teleconsultations for diagnosis or treatment recommendations, remote prehospital triage for cardiac surgery, remote monitoring of health status and management of cardiac parameters in cardiac surgery candidates, remote management of post-operative patients, including wound management, and remote analysis of cardiac procedures like coronary angiograms, echocardiograms, cardiac MRI, ECGs (Ajibade et al., 2020).

TeleGynecology & TeleObstetrics

Telehealth has increased access to prenatal care, contraception, abortion, etc. It reduces the barriers to healthcare access for women from lower socioeconomic status who may have difficulty getting to in-person appointments due to transportation or childcare issues. Virtual prenatal care visits and consultations can replace many in-person visits. Maternal-fetal medicine consultations have been successfully transitioned to telemedicine. They have also included remote monitoring of ultrasound recordings, including fetal echocardiograms, management of chronic medical diseases, and genetic counseling (Shields et al., 2020). Patients use blood pressure cuffs, scales, and fetal dopplers at home for obstetric telemonitoring. The monitoring can include fetal heart rate, uterine activity, and blood glucose in patients with gestational diabetes mellitus. It has been shown to reduce healthcare costs, low neonatal birth weight, unscheduled in-person visits, and decreased risk of neonatal intensive care unit admissions (Lanssens et al., 2017). Telehealth can also augment provider support during delivery (Zork et al., 2020).

Transitioning to obstetrical telehealth requires some adjustments in the prenatal care protocols. For example, one practice created a virtual prenatal care protocol combining eight in-person visits with six virtual nursing units and an asynchronous online website for questions and patient education (de Moois et al., 2018; Fryer et al., 2020). Peahl et al. created a patient-centered care pathway where in-person prenatal visits were replaced with five in-person and five virtual visits (Peahl et al., 2020). The virtual visits were during intake and then weeks 16, 24, 32, and 38 and focused on getting the entire history, prenatal labs, vital signs, fetal heart rate, and pregnancy symptoms. The in-person visits were during weeks 8, 19, 28, 36, and 39 and, depending on the week included a physical examination of the mother and the fetus, vital signs, ultrasound, vaccinations, cancer screenings, pregnancy symptoms, diabetic screen, and lab tests.

Telephone-based support to women during pregnancy and six weeks post-partum has been implemented in multiple projects. Most projects include outreach from healthcare professionals, but peer-to-peer telephone support has also been implemented. These interventions have been shown to reduce anxiety and depression during pregnancy and post-partum. They have shown improvement in quality-of-care parameters, such as an increase in the duration of breastfeeding. Preliminary evidence indicates that these proactive phone-based interventions may help prevent smoking relapse and low birth weight (Lavender et al., 2013). A targeted text message or voice-based interventions have shown increased utilization of healthcare services like vaccinations or HIV care (Palmer et al., 2020).

Consumer-directed telehealth companies provide prescription medications directly to patients after a video, phone, or chat-based encounter primarily conducted through a mobile app. In many cases, the prescriptions are dispensed after a self-administered questionnaire. Studies have demonstrated the effectiveness of this approach, where a self-administered checklist acts as a filter to screen for contraindications to prescriptions (Zuniga et al., 2020). For prescribing hormonal contraception, the approach of using self-screening questionnaires has been found to be effective (Shotorbani et al., 2006); however, it is unclear if the self-screening questionnaires are as accurate as a provider's interview. In patients with HIV, telehealth programs have improved compliance rates with antiretroviral therapies and clinic attendance. Some platforms allow for at-home diagnostic testing of sexually transmitted diseases by kits sent via mail.

In patients suspected of having a urinary tract infection, empiric antibiotic therapy ordered in a telehealth visit was effective with lower costs; however, some studies have shown that it may result in a higher incidence of prescriptions, which may lead to worsening antibiotic resistance in the community. With stricter guidelines created by telehealth companies, newer studies show no difference in antibiotic prescribing. (Murray et al., 2020). It is recommended to evaluate patient-specific factors in any telemedicine visit. In the case of urinary tract infections, these could include parameters like age, immune suppression assessment, diabetes mellitus, catheter use, number of urinary tract infection the previous year, and recent exposure to antibiotics. These can be used to triage to an in-person visit appropriately. Anyone suspected of having a severe infection can be referred to an in-person evaluation (Grimes et al., 2020).

Ambulatory telegynecology has traditionally focused on risk stratification and triaging based on patient complaints or past medical history. Common conditions include urinary tract infections, sexually transmitted diseases, breast symptoms, cancer screening, and follow-up. Other telegynecology applications include screening and assessment of intimate partner violence, screening for depression and anxiety, counseling patients on birth control and prevention of unintended pregnancies, preconception counseling, and counseling related to abortion procedures (Cohen et al., 2020). Telemedicine consultation can also be provided for menopausal issues like the management of climacteric symptoms, screening for concerning symptoms, and titration of medications.

Telehealth has also been successfully implemented in the rehabilitation of female pelvic floor dysfunction by improving symptoms, such as a reduction in the number of incontinence episodes, improvement in pelvic floor muscle strength, and improvement in the quality of life (da Mata et al., 2021). Patients with urinary incontinence can be managed by nonsurgical approaches, including telemedicine-based behavioral therapy and smartphone applications for teaching and tracking kegel exercises. Behavioral modification counseling, as well as teaching intermittent self-catheterization techniques, can be done over videoconferencing. Patients with pelvic organ prolapse can use virtual pelvic floor exercises, internet-based pelvic floor training, and smartphone apps coupled with biofeedback devices which are used to train muscles (Grimes et al., 2020). In the geriatric age group, telemedicine also helps older adults avoid travel for in-person visits reducing morbidity in patients with arthritis or a history of falls (Gloria et al., 2020).

There are many areas in the United States where access to abortion is limited, with no provider within 100 miles. Direct-to-patient telemedicine has been used for providing abortion services, including medications that are sent via mail (Upadhyay et al., 2019). This approach connects a videoconference call with the clinician, and pretreatment laboratory tests and ultrasounds are ordered if needed. The medication packet containing mifepristone and misoprostol is sent along with instructions via mail. This model of tele-abortion is safe, effective, efficient, and satisfactory to the patient's several providers (Raymond et al., 2019). A systematic review studied mobile phone-based intervention to improve the use of contraception, promote specific methods of contraception or improve adherence to contraception via text messages, voice messages, or mobile apps. The evidence supports that interactive voice messages and counselor support can improve post-abortion contraception, and a combination of unidirectional and interactive messages can improve overall adherence to oral contraceptives. (Smith et al. 2015).

TelePlastic surgery

Plastic surgery has seen tremendous growth with the advent of smartphones and in-built video chat applications, wider adoption of photo apps, and increased video calls (Padley et al., 2021). The use of telemedicine in plastic surgery has also continued to grow. Remote plastic surgery consultations are conducted for evaluation (Hoppe et al., 2014) and post-op monitoring. The aesthetic procedures are generally reimbursed out-of-pocket, so patients do active research about providers and, in many cases, travel to a different state or country to get the procedure done. Teleconsultations provide an opportunity for both the surgeons and the patients to have a preliminary discussion without the need for the patient to travel. On the inpatient side, the management of burn patients has relied on telemedicine due to a shortage of burn specialists and burn units. Acute plastic surgery trauma and burns-related consultations can be quickly conducted via telemedicine (Jones et al., 2004). American Telemedicine Association has developed guidelines for managing burn patients (Theurer et al., 2017), which can also be undertaken with the help of a smartphone app (Wallis et al., 2016). Studies have shown that 70% of plastic surgeons had favorable opinions about telemedicine. Post-operative complications can be assessed remotely. Patients can send images to physicians after the surgery (Fryer et al., 2020).

TeleOphthalmology

Teleophthalmology has been used in global health but is increasingly popular in developed countries. The shortage of ophthalmologists has accelerated the adoption of telehealth for remote consultations with ophthalmologists in multiple clinical settings, including inpatient and emergency departments (Tauber et al., 2020). About one-third of approximately two million people visiting EDs for ophthalmic complaints are in nonmetropolitan settings, where about half of the EDs do not have in-house ophthalmologists (Channa et al., 2016). With the increasing popularity of teleophthalmology, multiple ophthalmological indications can be evaluated or monitored through telemedicine. These include blepharitis, chalazion, dry eye syndrome, conjunctival laceration, corneal abrasion, stable post-penetrating keratoplasty patients, allergic or viral or bacterial conjunctivitis, stable glaucoma, active glaucoma, red eye, cranial nerve palsy, optic neuropathy, nystagmus, anisocoria, pre-septal cellulitis, orbital cellulitis, eyelid lesion, ptosis, thyroid eye disease, flashes and floaters, macular degeneration, diabetic retinopathy, and iritis. These conditions can be evaluated remotely using virtual examination maneuvers (Bowe et al., 2020). Corneal abrasions, foreign bodies, and urgent infections like macular conjunctivitis can be remotely diagnosed by sharing images from anterior segment cameras (Bhopal et al., 1993).

Remote diagnosis is used for screening conditions like diabetic retinopathy and prematurity retinopathy and monitoring chronic diseases like glaucoma (Rathi et al., 2017). Teleglaucoma programs are used for screening, diagnosis, and treatment monitoring over the longer term. Retinopathy is a common complication of diabetes that requires examination of the fundus of the eye. Health providers, after training, can take photos of the fundus oculi with non-mydriatic fundus cameras (Solomon et al., 2017). Multiple countries are now using telemedicine to screen and diagnose diabetic retinopathy (Galiero et al., 2020). High-resolution images of the fundus rated by retina experts remotely can increase the impact of the screening programs (Cameron et al., 2009). In children, retinopathy of prematurity is one of the leading causes of irreversible visual impairment. The data captured from retinal images is used to screen prematurity and low birth weight babies. Similar techniques are applied to pediatric ophthalmic conditions like retinoblastoma, shaken baby syndrome, etc. Teleophthalmology allows patients in remote rural areas to be connected to tertiary care centers for specialized access resulting in early diagnosis and appropriate treatment. Virtual visits are conducted with visual acuity testing applications that provide accurate calibrations, conventional optotypes, and standard notations (Kapoor et al., 2020).

Opthalmology sub-specialties are also using telemedicine to enhance patient care. Oculoplastic consultants can evaluate patients over video consultations for a variety of conditions. These include thyroid eye disease, eyelid lesions including basal cell carcinoma, melanoma, seborrheic keratosis, retention cyst, and chalazion, orbital pathologies like orbital inflammation, orbital sarcoidosis, orbital lymphoma, dacryoadenitis, carotid-cavernous fistula, and orbital amyloidosis, lid pathologies like blepharitis, lid swelling, lid asymmetry, ptosis, trichiasis and entropion, orbital foreign body, orbital trauma, epibulbar lipodermoid, scleritis, dry eyes, chronic progressive external opthalmoplegia, facial nerve palsy and socket related problems (Kang et al., 2020). OCT scanners are noninvasive medical devices used to capture real-time imaging of the layers of the retina. The images captured by nurses and optometrists are sent to ophthalmologists for evaluation and initial treatment of age-related macular degeneration. These images are also useful for diagnosing glaucoma and have been successfully deployed globally in virtual glaucoma clinics.

There is a need for more neuro-ophthalmologists, with only one neuro-ophthalmologist per 1.63 million people in the United States and a median wait time for an appointment of approximately 6 weeks. Telehealth can supplement in-person neuro-ophthalmologic care using digital optical fundus photography and mobile vision testing. Mobile applications are available for visual acuity, color vision, visual fields, torsion, esotropia, and heterophorias. Nonmydriatic ocular fundus photography can be used in urgent care with remote teleophthalmologist consultations (Ko et al., 2020).

Studies have proven a good cost-to-efficacy ratio of teleophthalmology and have found the usefulness of teleophthalmology consultations, especially in triage in emergency departments (Wedekind et al., 2016). Other studies have found that post-operative consultations after eye surgeries like vitrectomy for retinal detachment repair conducted via telemedicine after the surgery have demonstrated high patient and provider satisfaction (Shahid et al., 2021).

TeleOrthopedics

Teleorthopedics had been used to evaluate trauma at remote sites by the US Army for many decades, but the wider adoption was accelerated during the COVID-19 pandemic. US Army has used various telemedicine modalities, including asynchronous communication like email from the deployed healthcare providers to subspecialty consultants for fractures, sprains, neuropathies, and tendon injuries. These programs have reduced the number of unnecessary evacuations from the battlefield for in-person evaluation. Similar programs are feasible in resource-constrained settings in civilian environments (Blank et al., 2011).

Opportunities exist for post-surgical follow-up or rehabilitation after orthopedic interventions. Patients undergoing total knee and hip arthroplasty have shown promising results for follow-ups and rehabilitation through telehealth (Pastora-Bernal et al. 2017). In another program, shoulder surgeons demonstrated the benefits of post-surgical follow-up via telehealth following arthroscopic rotator cuff repair (Kane et al., 2020).

Telemedicine has challenges, especially in specialties heavily reliant on physical exams like orthopedics. Even if, based on initial triage, a visit is deemed appropriate for the virtual consultation, during the visit, the physician may realize that a hands-on physical exam is required, and another visit may have to be scheduled. The scenarios could include the assessment of fractures, cast wedging, pin removal, or adjusting hardware (Carter et al., 2020). If patients' cooperation is required in the physical examination, in some cases, patients may not be able to perform maneuvers due to joint pathologies, requiring an assistant or a caregiver.

Multiple studies have evaluated the accuracy of patient assessment and virtual physical examination. Some studies have shown good reliability between in-person assessment vs. teleassessment of back pain, which included back muscle endurance assessment, lumbar spine mobility, and lumbar motor controls (Palacín-Marín et al., 2013). Other studies have found variability in differences between in-person orthopedic exams vs. telemedicine physical exams on post-operative total knee arthroplasty patients when comparing swelling, knee range of motion, and scar appearance (Cabana et al., 2010). Another study showed good reliability in making correct ankle pathology diagnoses in patients with ankle pain based on in-person vs. virtual physical examination of ankle range of motion, single-leg squat, and gait (Russell et al., 2010). There is a variation between examiners for subjective evaluations, exacerbated during the telehealth-based exam making direct comparisons or longitudinal assessment quite tricky. Standardization and validation of remote examination is an ongoing research question. Best practices are emerging around physical examinations conducted virtually. Practitioners have published recommendations for specific examinations like knee, hip, shoulder, elbow (Tanaka et al., 2020), and spine (Iyer et al., 2020).

Randomized control trials have shown that patient satisfaction and patient-reported outcome measures were on par between ortho televisits and in-person visits. In one study, questionnaires enquired about changes in patient's mobility, self-care, usual activities, pain or discomfort, and anxiety or depression, and the outcome measures were evaluated using the EQ-5D index and EQ-VAS (Buvik et al., 2019a). In another study, orthopedic specialists had high satisfaction with video-assisted consultations (Buvik et al., 2016). Another randomized controlled trial showed that video-assisted orthopedic consultations in remote clinics cost less than standard outpatient consultations if there is enough volume to support the creation of a remote teleconsultation platform (Buvik et al., 2019b).

In remote patient monitoring, there is this question of how much remote monitoring is adequate for good clinical outcomes while balancing the risk of added reporting and alert burden for caregivers and patients. In a randomized controlled trial of patients who underwent total knee replacement, patients who used a smartphone app with daily instructions using push notifications had lower pain scores, higher quality of life, better activities of daily living, and higher satisfaction compared to patients who received instructions twice a week (Timmers et al., 2019). It is a balancing act to ascertain the extent of adequate and appropriate remote monitoring for good clinical outcomes. Generally, after any major surgery, patients will prefer more communication instead of less. Remote monitoring and interventions can be dialed down for stable chronic conditions.

Pediatric orthopedics visits may be difficult because of the need to provide instructions to the parents of the patients for assistance in the physical exam. Similarly, physical exams may be challenging to perform and evaluate remotely in children having neuromuscular or special needs. Some of this can be ameliorated by providing detailed and visual instructions to the parents before the virtual visit. Condition-specific recommendations may have to be developed and sent to the patients or their families to facilitate the virtual exam. For example, experts have developed condition-specific recommendations to improve the quality of pediatric orthopedic telehealth visits (Carter et al., 2020). For rotational abnormalities, parents are asked to film the child walking over a clear walking space with a hard surface. Parents' cooperation may be required to assist in the examination for scoliosis evaluation. For joint pains or injuries, an active range of motion demonstration can generally be performed by children and adolescents. In the case of children, family members can assist with passive range of motion or bony tenderness. Foot evaluation may require elevated foot placement for adequate visualization through the desktop, laptop, or mobile phone camera. The telehealth visits may be challenging in cases of cerebral palsy, developmental dysplasia of the hip in newborns, or conditions requiring neuromuscular exams. In these situations, telehealth visits can focus on discussions, counseling, education, or monitoring during follow-up visits.

TeleOtolaryngology

Almost 62% of all ENT-specific outpatient presentations have been considered appropriate for telemedicine. However, this number is expanding as more specialized equipment is connected to the Internet and is being made available to providers (McCool et al., 2018). Telelaryngology has been aided by the development of small-caliber flexible endoscopes which can be connected to smartphones (Lozada et al., 2018). Remote examination of the upper airway can be conducted through a coupling device connected to a mobile phone and a nasopharyngolaryngoscope. A remote otolaryngologist can remotely review the recording or live stream to evaluate the nasopharynx, oropharynx, tongue base, larynx, and airway patency (Miller et al., 2020). Video recordings of nasal passages via endonasal endoscopy have been used for the examination and evaluation of chronic rhinosinusitis (Yip et al., 2017), nasal obstruction (Klapan et al., 2008), and nasal sinus surgery (Athanasiadis et al., 2008).

The smartphone-based otoscopic attachments make it possible for the patients to obtain images of the tympanic membrane at home and forward them to the providers (Jayawardena et al., 2020). Smartphone-connected otoendoscope can capture the image of the patient's eardrums which are combined with other clinical information and sent to ENT consultants for review. This enables primary care physicians to get ENT specialist advice for complicated cases. Primary care physicians get quicker consultations for their patients without the need for signing the patients for in-person appointments requiring long wait times to see the specialists. This technology allows for real-time evaluation and the recording of images and transmission in batches to the contracted specialist for the practice (Cottrell et al., 2020). Video otoscopy is also used in pediatric populations for remote evaluation and therapeutic intervention in hearing-impaired children (McCarthy et al., 2010). Studies have found that correlation between video otology and in-person examination in the range of 49 and 100 percent (Beule et al., 2019).

Teleaudiology can also assist with screening for ototoxic side effects of chemotherapy (Dille et al., 2015). Using a special device, the patient can do remote hearing monitoring during chemotherapy treatment, and the results are communicated to the audiologist. Remotely supervised teleaudiometry evaluation in combination with a computer-assisted audiometer can be used to expand the geographic reach of audiometric examinations, especially in resource-poor settings with high reliability both for speech audiometry (Yao et al., 2015) as well as tone audiometry (Skarzynski et al., 2016). Remote fitting of hearing aids is another use case in audiology though it is subject to licensing and reimbursement constraints (Penteado et al., 2012). Telemedicine has been successfully used to fit individuals with cochlear implants (Ramos et al., 2009). It can also be used for initial fitting, set up, and follow-up of digital programmable and signal processing devices (Wesendahl. 2003).

Post-operative use cases include examination of surgical incisions and follow-up post-head and neck surgeries. In outcome studies, a high correlation has been found in 80% of encounters between teleconsultation and face-to-face contact with the patients, and 50% of the in-person ENT visits were deemed viable by telemedicine (Yulzari et al., 2018).

TeleTrauma

Rural areas are resource constrained when it comes to healthcare resources. This is especially acute for emergency issues like trauma. Telemedicine is effective in the management of rural trauma patients (Lapointe et al., 2020). Telemedicine in trauma has been used for teleradiology evaluation, trauma assessment, diagnosis accuracy, triage, trauma monitoring, trauma treatment advice, trauma follow-up, and patient engagement. Technologies include store-and-forward live interactive video, remote monitoring, and mobile health applications (Said et al., 2020). Smartphones enable high-quality image and video capture to evaluate trauma patients (Zangbar et al., 2014).

TeleUrology & TeleReproductive medicine

Urologists are adopting virtual tools to evaluate and communicate with patients. Besides clinical evaluation for diagnosis and management, virtual visits are also helpful for lifestyle counseling, reproductive techniques, genetic counseling, psychologic services, follow-up discussions of results, treatment plans, or sales cycles.

Teleurology workflow at a fertility practice can begin with an initial telehealth visit to obtain a detailed history of both partners. This can include thorough medical, sexual, and social history as well as a review of previous medical records. A limited physical exam can be conducted on male and female patients (Berg et al., 2020). A subsequent lab visit may sometimes be required for semen analysis, hormone profile, genetic testing, or other bloodwork. An office visit may be required for physical, pelvic, or scrotal ultrasound, hysterosalpingogram, or other procedural intervention.

Teleurology can be provided to adult, pediatric, veterans, and incarcerated patients. Studies have shown effectiveness, safety, and high patient satisfaction with teleurology video visits (Castaneda et al., 2020). Teleconsultations for patients with prostate cancer can be for follow-up of postprostatectomy patients and prostate cancer survivorship care. Patients with catheters can get telenursing consultation for chronic home-based intermittent catheterization. Pediatric patients can get consultations for neurogenic bladder or telemonitoring of prenatally diagnosed urologic anomalies. Patients can also store and forward video clips of voiding to help evaluate urinary symptoms or photos of voided urine to assess for hematuria.

Similarly, patients who undergo the creation of a urostomy can be followed at home through telemedicine using real-time phone or video calls and photographs of the stoma. These patients can be referred to other surgical specialists and called into the office based on a remote evaluation (Sims et al., 2020). Studies have documented improved sexual functions due to internet-based psychosexual therapy in patients with erectile dysfunction or premature ejaculation. Telemedicine interventions have been used to monitor symptoms and individualize follow-up in patients with benign prostatic hyperplasia or overactive bladder (Novara et al., 2020).

Studies have shown clinical equivalency, safety, and acceptable patient satisfaction (Connor et al., 2020). As per one study, over 54% of urology patients were eligible for a telemedicine visit. The common reasons for telemedicine consultations noted were for andrological conditions, bladder pain syndrome, testicular cancer, incontinence or bladder dysfunction, reconstructive urology, penile cancer, prostate cancer, urothelial cancer, urolithiasis, and urinary tract infection (Boehm et al., 2020). Patients who had a video visit instead of an in-person visit after radical prostatectomy showed similar visit efficiency, patient satisfaction, and reduced patient cost (Viers et al., 2015). Another study showed a 90% concordance between the diagnoses made during telemedicine and in-person visits. However, there was no discordance in the diagnosis of malignancy. The most common diagnoses for telemedicine visits in this study were noted to be benign prostatic hyperplasia or lower urinary tract symptoms, benign testicular lesions, hematuria, urinary infections, urethral strictures, elevated PSA, kidney stones, urological malignancy, sexual dysfunction. This study also found that about half of the patients who underwent telemedicine were subsequently called in for an in-person visit (Sherwood et al., 2018). The need for an in-person visit following the initial telemedicine encounter depends on multiple variables – lack of proper triage, new findings discovered during the telehealth visit, and lab or imaging results following the initial visit requiring an in-person visit. A study showed that for certain conditions, up to 92% of initial telehealth visits did not require a subsequent in-person visit (Castaneda et al., 2020).

33 TELEHEALTH FOR MENTAL HEALTH

Telehealth is very practical for mental and behavioral health consultations. This chapter discusses four common telehealth applications – behavioral health, addiction medicine, psychiatry, and psychology.

TeleBehavioral health

Videoconferencing is one of the most common telehealth platforms for behavioral health interventions. Studies have demonstrated promising outcomes for motivational interventions (Celio et al., 2017), cognitive processing therapy (Moring et al., 2020), cognitive behavioral therapy (Waller et al., 2020), prolonged exposure therapy (Wells et al., 2020), and behavior analysis (Zoder-Martell et al., 2020). Cognitive behavioral therapy has wide-ranging applications. Studies have demonstrated the effectiveness of telemedicine in reducing alcohol consumption, improving depression, increasing patient satisfaction, improving accessibility, improving quality of life, and reducing the cost of care (Kruse et al., 2020). One of the most important use cases is to reduce suicidal ideation, where internet-based platforms have been shown to be effective (Büscher et al., 2020).

Twenty percent of all children have behavioral illnesses, and most go untreated. Telebehavioral health can effectively be used for pediatric interventions (Gale et al., 2015), including eating disorders (Datta et al., 2020). Telehealth has been used to initiate and continue assessment or treatment for feeding disorders like avoidant/restrictive food intake disorders in children with outcomes equivalent to in-clinic services (Peterson et al., 2021).

Digital technologies can also be used for peer support interventions in patients with serious mental illness (Fortuna et al., 2020). Similarly, mobile apps are available for managing obesity or anxiety though more effective and integrated apps targeting these comorbidities are still not widely available (Gómez-de-Regil et al., 2020).

There are over one thousand psychosocial wellness and stress management apps on Android and iOS platforms targeting mindfulness meditation, positive psychology, and goal setting (Lau et al., 2020). The direct-to-consumer digital psychotherapy services have raised questions about accountability, liability, informed consent, safety, and data protection. With the broader adoption of telebehavioral health, more research will be needed to address these issues (Martinez-Martin et al., 2018).

TeleAddiction medicine

Telemedicine is increasingly important in managing the opioid epidemic (Yang et al., 2018). Telehealth for treating substance abuse disorders is promising because of the treatment characteristics of tele-addiction interventions. Addiction is chronic, and its treatment requires long-term contact between patients and clinicians. The treatment does not rely on physical examination in most scenarios. There is a stigma around visiting an addiction treatment center and a scarcity of trained clinicians. Tele-addiction interventions have used multiple platforms for providing interventions. These include telephone-based care for treatment support, web-based screening encounters or ongoing interventions, computer software-driven treatment protocols, videoconferencing sessions with mental health providers, smartphone apps targeted at specific disorders, and virtual worlds with avatars. Mental health support apps have become increasingly sophisticated and use machine learning to tailor interventions to individual patients. Chatbots created with cognitive behavioral therapy foundations can dynamically change treatment protocol based on the patient's progress. They are also available 24/7. Many apps also have an automated interface connected to a human expert who can intervene via chat, call, or email. Telehealth can provide recovery support, relapse prevention, continuing care, and family education (Molfenter et al., 2015). Telemedicine-assisted medication-assisted treatment provides direct-to-patient or specialty consultation services remotely addressing the opioid epidemic in rural areas (Yang et al., 2018).

The use of telehealth to manage opioid agonist therapy has demonstrated a higher likelihood of uninterrupted treatment retention (Ho et al., 2018). Traditionally, federal regulations have restricted the behavioral health services that can be delivered via telemedicine, but many were relaxed during the pandemic. Federal guidelines have prohibited providers from prescribing buprenorphine without a federal 'waiver.' There is also a limitation on number of concurrent patients that can be treated at a given time. This is enshrined in the Ryan Haight Act, which specifies that a prescriber can only prescribe a controlled substance after s/he has conducted an in-person examination. Traditionally, this has created barriers to access for those patients who cannot physically travel to the prescriber's offices. This requirement of the Ryan Haight Act was waived during the COVID-19 emergency when Drug Enforcement Administration (DEA) allowed the initiation of buprenorphine, creating an opportunity for tele-buprenorphine (Harris et al., 2020). Other changes during the pandemic were the authorization of telephone consultations and the waiver that DEA-registered providers obtain a separate DEA registration in each state where they practice. The guidelines developed by the DEA are available from the Department of Health and Human Services (DHHS. 2021).

A survey was administered to the senior executives of substance use disorder treatment centers in which they were asked to identify the technologies that were of interest to them. The technologies in the descending order of interest were: computerized screening/assessments, appointment reminders via text messages, web portals for patients, mobile apps for posttreatment recovery, video-based therapy, telephone-based recovery support, recovery support chats, telephone-based therapy, texting motivational messages, mobile apps for treatment, virtual worlds (Molfenter. 2018). Telemedicine technologies that have demonstrated success in their application in substance use disorders include telephone-based treatment support (McKay et al., 2005), web-based treatment support (Marsch et al., 2016), text messaging (Mason et al., 2015), videoconferencing (Young. 2012), mobile apps (Gustafson. 2016), and virtual worlds (Molfenter. 2015).

TelePsychiatry

Telepsychiatry is one of the most common applications of telemedicine. Telemedicine has increased the available opportunities for delivering on-demand telepsychiatry services (Arevian et al., 2018). According to the American Psychiatric Association (APA), telepsychiatry may be preferable in patients with severe anxiety disorders, geriatric patients with physical limitations, and immune-compromised patients (Hilty. 2020). Virtual psychiatry can be employed in scenarios where it is difficult for the patient to make in-person visits helping patients who are unable to ambulate, those who are caregivers and cannot leave home, patients who cannot take leave from work for in-person appointments, patients in remote areas, or women who need perinatal mental health treatment (Dossett et al., 2019).

The telemedicine-based interventions for remote psychiatric care delivery have been expanded through digital health tools. Programs integrating reminders, support messages, social support engagement, and psychoeducation have been deployed to improve medication adherence in adult mental health and substance use disorders (Steinkamp et al., 2019). Digital health interventions can be accessed through smartphones or computers. The common digital interventions for mental health include – standalone mental health apps, self-guided or professional-led web-based interventions, and online support groups. Web-based behavioral interventions combining interactive therapy, peer-to-peer social networking, clinical moderation, and on-demand web chat with clinicians are more effective than routine care combined with routine care (Alvarez-Jimenez et al., 2020). Telepsychiatry consultation provided in real-time (synchronous telemedicine) is comparable to in-person consultation or asynchronous telepsychiatry, where a video recording of a standardized interview is sent to the psychiatrists for review (Yellowlees et al., 2017). Similar interventions have also been used for severe psychiatric conditions like schizophrenia relapse prevention (Brunette et al., 2016).

Telemedicine-based interventions have improved problematic symptoms in veterans with posttraumatic stress disorder in a randomized, noninferiority trial comparing telemedicine with in-person visits (Morland et al., 2010). Telebehavioral health interventions can provide services to the victims of domestic and intimate partner violence (Emezue et al., 2020), including therapy and support (Gray et al., 2015). Studies have shown that by using telemedicine, practitioners can reduce the trauma during the medical and psychological evaluation of abuse victims (Arnold et al., 2013). Telehealth incorporating video has been deployed for patients at high risk of suicide (McGinn et al., 2019). Clinical guidelines and safety protocols are being developed based on rigorous clinical research for assessing and managing suicidal patients using telehealth (Luxton et al., 2014). Schools offer telepsychiatry services focused on children and adolescents to expand mental health access to students (Stephan et al., 2016). The advantage of telemental health in this age group is that it can be provided to children and adolescents in the privacy of their homes (Myers et al., 2017)

In-hospital telepsychiatry is a significant opportunity, and many healthcare systems have started offering telepsychiatric services to other health systems (Varrell et al., 2015) for admitted patients. There is also a significant demand for telepsychiatry services in emergency rooms (Yellowlees et al., 2008), especially in scenarios where the remote practitioner can evaluate psychiatric emergencies using video conferencing (Trondsen et al., 2014). Timely evaluation in such cases is helpful for the appropriate placement of patients on 5150 holds. Interestingly, studies have not found any benefit of telepsychiatry in reducing psychiatric readmissions. This presents an opportunity for innovation and rethinking the telepsychiatry approach to patients with severe psychiatric disorders (Koblauch et al., 2018).

TelePsychology

Psychologists are adopting telehealth using videoconferencing, email, and text messaging in their clinical practice (Barnett et al., 2013). Smartphone apps targeting psychological health have increased in popularity and sophistication (Bush et al., 2019). During the COVID-19 pandemic, there was an increase in the adoption of telemedicine among psychologists, and telemedicine tools are expected to continue post-pandemic (Marra et al., 2020). Telepsychology can also be used with a specific subset of clients, like those in the criminal justice system and affected by substance abuse addiction (Batastini et al., 2016).

Telemedicine provides multiple advantages in psychiatry and psychology (Uscher-Pines et al., 2020). Using telemedicine, practitioners can see patients' home environments, which can be valuable in assessing patients' home situations and better ability to tailor interventions that accommodate patient-specific factors. Patients are also more relaxed in their home setting compared to the office environment of psychology or psychiatry practices. For patients with logistical challenges in reaching provider offices, telemedicine allows for better access to care.

The tests commonly used in neuropsychology were initially developed for in-person testing. However, novel assessments can be created using technology instead of just digitizing existing tests. These can be used for administration, scoring, and generating new data points like the measurement of responses over time; number, length, and positional pauses; amplitude and frequency of tremulousness at rest or during movement. These tests can be administered over a tablet with an electronic pencil and can be remotely monitored. Tests like picture naming tests, visual-spatial construction tasks, verbal fluency tasks, reaction time assessments, episodic memory evaluation, free recall, nonverbal learning, and memory assessment can be coupled with computer adaptive testing and modern psychometric theories like item response theory to evaluate item-level performance in real-time (Miller et al., 2017).

Significant progress has been made in developing telephone-based cognitive assessment. The assessment tools include screening measures, batteries, and tests (Gosselt et al., 2020; Carlew et al., 2020). Some of the commonly used ones are

- Addenbrooke's Cognitive Examination – revised (ACE-R)
- Adult Lifestyles and Function Interview (ALFI)
- Age-Related Eye Disease Study (AREDS) Telephone Battery
- Brief Screen for Cognitive Impairment (BSCI)
- California Verbal Learning Test (CVLT)
- Cognitive Assessment of Later Life Status (CALLS)
- Computer-Assisted Administration (CATI) of the TICS-M
- Frontal Assessment Battery (FAB)
- Heidelberg Cohort Study of the Elderly (HeiDE) assessments
- Late-Onset Alzheimer's Disease (LOAD) Study Battery
- Memory and Aging Telephone Screen (MATS)
- Memory Impairment Screen by Telephone (MIS-T)
- Modified Minnesota Cognitive Acuity Screen (MCAS-m)

- Philadelphia Brief Assessment of the Cognition (PBAC)
- REGARDS (Reasons for Geographic and Racial Differences in Stroke) Study Battery
- Short Orientation-Memory-Concentration (SOMC)
- Short Portable Mental Status Questionnaire (SPMSQ)
- Structured Telephone Interview for Dementia Assessment (STIDA)
- Successful Aging after Elective Surgery (SAGES) battery
- Swedish Adoption/Twin Study of Aging (SATSA)
- Telephone Cognitive Assessment Battery (TCAB)
- Telephone Information-Memory-Concentration Test (TIMC)
- Telephone Interview for Cognitive Status (TICS)
- Telephone Modified Mini Mental State Examination (Tele MMSE)
- Telephone Montreal Assessment of Cognitive Status (T-MoCA)
- Telephone Screening Protocol (TELE)
- Telephone-Assessed Mental State (TAMS)
- UCSF Cognitive Screening Battery (UCSF – SB)

Telehealth is increasingly used to assess autism spectrum disorders (Dahiya et al., 2020). Based on the literature, if guided appropriately, parents can collect evidence of the target behaviors of their children, which can be later submitted for evaluation. Store-and-forward technology can be used for remote analysis of videos and applying Autism Diagnostic Observation Schedule – Generic (ADOS-G) protocol, resulting in classification accuracy of 96.8, 94.1% sensitivity, and 100% specificity (Fusaro et al., 2014).

At-risk children can be administered surveillance protocols through standardized tests and interviews to assess cognitive, adaptive, social, and communicative functioning. Parents can assist with eliciting and recording specific behaviors for autism spectrum disorder symptom assessment in different scenarios. Such approaches have resulted in a high agreement between the telehealth and in-person assessments, getting 88.2% agreement, 84.9% sensitivity, and 94.4% specificity (Smith et al., 2017). Remote surveillance protocols have been developed using a combination of online interviews and video registration of parent-child play to screen for autism spectrum disorders (Conti et al., 2020). The providers use a variety of instruments for assessment. Some of these questionnaires include the Child Behavior Checklist; MacArthur–Bates; Communicative Development Inventories; Early Motor Questionnaire; First Year Inventory; Infant–Toddler Social and Emotional Assessment; Language Use Inventory; Modified Checklist for Autism in Toddlers; Parenting Stress Index, Third edition; Italian Questionnaires of Temperament; Repetitive Behavior Scale-Revised; Sensory Profile (Conti et al., 2020) The remote surveillance protocol received positive feedback from practitioners as well as parents in a research study.

There have been other notable outcomes using telemedicine interventions. Family-based treatment delivered via telemedicine was shown to be as effective as treatment for anorexia nervosa (Anderson et al., 2017). In another study, no differences were found between videoconferencing psychotherapy (VCP) and face-to-face therapy, with significant improvements noted in panic disorder, agoraphobia, fear of sensations, and depressed mood (Bouchard et al., 2020).

There are also some downsides to using telemedicine by these practitioners. The home environment may provide less privacy and more distractions to the patients. The providers cannot use all the senses during the encounter to support the diagnosis and treatment. The collection of vital signs may be unreliable, and there are constraints with the physical examination. It may be challenging to control conversation flow using video or phone calls. Also, there may be technology issues with the videoconferencing tools, internet connectivity, or general patients' comfort with the technology. Additional challenges for evaluating patients with bipolar disorders may be present. Changes in speech volume or tone, voice prosody, and emotion may be harder to ascertain over the phone or video call due to low resolution, lag, etc. (Burgess et al., 2020).

34 TELEHEALTH FOR REHABILITATIVE THERAPIES

Physical medicine and rehabilitation providers are using telehealth for a variety of disorders. This includes both initial assessments as well as monitoring. Telerehabilitation is the "use of information and communication technologies as a medium for the provision of rehabilitation services to sites or patients that are at a distance from the provider" (Rogante et al., 2010). Telehealth for rehabilitation is used in patients with neuromuscular disorders or post-trauma. Patients can undertake rehabilitation-related services like physical, speech, and occupational therapies remotely through telerehabilitation. For activities of daily living-related functions, telerehabilitation has shown outcomes comparable to face-to-face therapy and usual care (Laver et al., 2013). This chapter discusses the applications of telehealth for physiatry, occupational therapy, physical therapy, and speech therapy.

TeleOccupational therapy

Occupational therapy provides preventative, habilitative, or rehabilitative interventions to patients. Telehealth in occupation therapy is used to "develop skills; incorporate assistive technology or adaptive techniques; modify work, home, or school environments; and create health-promoting habits and routines" (Telehealth. 2013). The therapists can also monitor patients' ADLs, adherence to intervention programs, cognitive changes, and fall risk. Examples of specific telehealth interventions include evaluation for wheelchair or adaptive equipment prescription, home modification, and ergonomic assessment. The Occupational therapy specific assessments like the Kohlman Evaluation of Living Skills and the Canadian Occupational Performance Measures, the Functional Reach Test, and European Stroke Scale, the Unified Parkinson's Disease Rating Scale, Jamar Dynamometer, Nine-Hole Peg Test, Preston Pinch Gauge have been validated, and considered reliable when administered through telehealth modalities.

Randomized control studies have demonstrated the effectiveness of telehealth for children with disabilities (Camden et al., 2019). Occupational therapists working with children with disabilities use different telehealth strategies for specific interventions. Some potential telehealth interventions have included parent-focused activity instructions based on specific toys and upper-limb sensory-motor tasks in children with unilateral cerebral palsy. These children can also use gamified exercises using wearables or interactive platforms with interactive toys tailored to the child's therapy goals. Online platforms employ coaches to support parents and child therapy goals in children with motor difficulties (Camden et al., 2021). Early interventions can also be provided to infants and toddlers with disabilities and developmental delays using telehealth to improve their quality of life. (Cason et al. 2011).

There is an advantage to using telehealth in school-based scenarios. The therapists can observe from a distance and work with the teacher to plan and implement interventions. Evidence shows that telehealth-based occupational therapy can be provided to schools for evaluation and intervention (Gallagher. 2004). Students who have sustained traumatic brain injury can be reintegrated into the schools after completion of acute rehabilitation using a telehealth platform (Verburg et al., 2003).

Telehealth-based interventions can also be provided to home-bound elderly. Remote monitoring and self-management strategies have been demonstrated to reduce hospitalizations and nursing home length of stay (Bendixen et al., 2009). Occupational therapists can use home monitoring devices to monitor patients' occupational performance and recommend environmental modifications and interventions (Mann et al., 2005).

Occupational therapists can also provide tele-ergonomics services to corporate clients at their workplaces remotely and provide individualized workstation modification recommendations, which reduce workplace discomfort, fatigue, and injury and improve productivity (Baker et al., 2013).

TelePhysiatry

Telemedicine-based physical rehabilitation can be image-based, sensor-based, virtual environments, or virtual reality telerehabilitation (Russell et al., 2007). In a systematic review, telemedicine interventions for neurological, cardiac, spinal cord injuries, and speech-language impairments have shown outcomes that are at least similar to or better than alternative interventions. Telerehabilitation has been found to have high compliance, high patient satisfaction, longer consultation times, and potential cost savings (Kairy et al., 2009).

Telerehabilitation has proven to be beneficial in multiple complex clinical conditions (Steel et al., 2011), including multiple sclerosis (Finkelstein et al., 2008), cognitive rehabilitation (Mantovani et al., 2020), stroke (Khan et al., 2015), and chronic pain management (Emerick et al., 2020). Telerehabilitation for patients with multiple sclerosis has been proposed through multiple channels, including physical activity, educational, behavioral, and symptom management programs. Systematic reviews have demonstrated positive outcomes in stroke survivors with at-home therapies leading to a reduced risk of deterioration, improved activities of daily living, reduced costs, and duration of rehabilitation (Khan et al., 2015). In these studies, patients were regularly monitored, and a range of services were provided at patients' homes. The outcome measures studied in various programs improve baseline function, reduce impairment and symptoms, and increase participation. Telemedicine plays an important role in chronic pain management in primary care settings (Fulford et al., 2016) or when patients cannot make in-person visits to pain specialists (Emerick et al., 2020).

There is evidence that telerehabilitation improves functional activities, including physical activity, balance, and postural control, compared with baseline, and there is some benefit in improving walking and physical activity. There are short-term benefits, like improving impairments such as fatigue, and long-term benefits, like improving pain and insomnia.

There are several instruments and tests that are used to monitor and track rehabilitation outcomes. Their focus includes symptoms, motor function, sensory function, and functional capacity. Some of the scales include (Khan F et al. 2015) Action Research Arm Test (ARAT), Berg Balance Scale (BBS), Computerized Dynamic Posturography (CDP), Composite Equilibrium Score (CES), Dynamic gait Index (DGI), Exercise Self-Efficacy Scale (EXCE), Fatigue impact scale (FIS), Fatigue severity scale (FSS), Godin Leisure-Time Exercise Questionnaire (GLTEQ), International Physical Activity Questionnaire (IPAQ), Late-Life Function and Disability Instrument (LL-FDI), McGill Pain Questionnaire (MPQ), Modified Fatigue impact scale (MFIS), Motor Control Test (MCT), MS related symptom check list, Multidimensional Outcomes Expectations for Exercise Scale (MOEES), Multiple Sclerosis Walking Scale – 12 (MSWS-12), Nine-Hole Peg Test (NHPT), Physical Activity Readiness Questionnaire (PARQ), Pittsburgh Sleep Quality Index (PSQI), Sensory organization Test (SOT), Six Meter Walk Test (6MWT), Tineti Scale (TS), Timed Up and Go (TUG), Two Meter Walk Test (2MWT), Twenty-five Foot Walk Test (25-FWT), Visual Preference Ratio (VPR).

The quality of life-based outcomes measures include the Centre for Epidemiologic Studies Depression Scale (CES-D), Energy Conservation Questionnaire (ECQ), Exercise Goal Setting Scale (EGS), Expanded Disability Status Scale (EDSS), Hamburg Quality of Life Questionnaire in Multiple Sclerosis (HAQUAMAS), Hospital Anxiety and Depression Scale (HADS), Leeds Multiple Sclerosis Quality of Life Scale (LMSQOL), Multiple Sclerosis Impact Scale (MSIS-29), Quality of Well- Being Scale (QWB), 36 items Short Form Health Survey Questionnaire (SF 36), Symbol Digit Modalities Test (SDMT). Other outcome measures found in the literature are muscle strength, Patient Determined Disease Steps (PDDS), Self-Efficacy for Energy Conservation (SEEC), Satisfaction with the intervention, and Visual Analogue Scales (VAS).

A physical exam is an essential component of physical medicine and rehabilitation. Recommendations have been developed to conduct and document a physical exam via telemedicine. The physical exam primarily focuses on neurological and musculoskeletal systems, but comprehensive examination documentation is required for appropriate billing. Some of the components of the physical exam may be performed without assistance. However, some require assistance from a caregiver or attendant who can help perform exam maneuvers on the patient (Verduzco-Gutierrez et al., 2020).

Pediatric telerehabilitation medicine visits are conducted in patients' homes (Rabatin et al., 2020). They may require durable medical equipment, toys, and other household items to aid in the exam with assistance from the patient's caregivers. It is helpful to have an adequate flat floor to evaluate gross motor skills, including sitting, creeping, walking, running, jumping, or skipping. The patient may need to be examined for range of motion, strength, and postural reactions. Fine motor skills can be assessed using toys that can be pushed, pulled, opened, pieced together, or otherwise physically manipulated. Reflexes may be tested depending on the caregiver's comfort. Patients may need to demonstrate clothing manipulation with zippers, buttons, books for turning pages, paper, and writing instruments. The musculoskeletal exam will assess mental status, speech and language, cranial nerves, balance, coordination, gait, reflexes, gross motor, fine motor, strength, sensation, and muscle tone. Caregivers can inspect joints, including the spine, check for joint range of motion, and palpate musculoskeletal structures to assess for pain. Special maneuvers may be required for the musculoskeletal exam of infants.

Chiropractors also use real-time video conferencing for consultations. Chiropractors can collect medical history, conduct health behavior risk assessment for home ergonomics and assess physical activity. Typically, the physical examination requires modifications of assessments conducted over the video. Patients can palpate their body regions by following instructions. Verbal guidance is provided to the patients so they can perform provocative and orthopedic tests. For treatment, the patients have explained the exercises needed and are asked to perform them immediately to demonstrate their understanding. Towels, elastic bands, and canned food can be used for resistance exercises. Studies have demonstrated high validity with in-person assessment for postural examination, active range of motion virtual assessment, and directional movement preference for assessing and treating low back pain and chronic musculoskeletal conditions (Green et al., 2020).

The common use cases for telerehabilitation currently in the market are chronic pain management, coordination and referral to physical therapy, discussing imaging results, non-opioid medication management, and post-procedure care. Other emerging use cases include the evaluation of new patients referred by other providers, cancer pain management, perioperative pain management, post-procedural care, detoxification from chronic opioid therapy, and medical cannabis certification.

As per the current recommendations, the inappropriate use of telemedicine includes evaluation of established patients who are at risk for opioid misuse, abuse, or overdose; new or established patients who require in-person evaluation due to acute or evolving symptoms; patients with unclear diagnosis and those with high medical complexity, psychosocial complexity, or suspected medication misuse (Emerick et al., 2020). For any new or worsening problems, the providers prefer an in-person visit. Generally, the issues more amenable to telemedicine include medication prescription, titration or medication, and education or counseling of patients (Chang et al., 2021).

The major advantage of telerehabilitation is that the therapy can be delivered at a location and time convenient for the patient, feedback can be provided in real-time as well as asynchronously after reviewing the data, and patients can participate regardless of whether they are at home, skilled nursing facility or residential care facility (Salawu et al., 2020).

TelePhysical therapy

Virtual physical exams are gaining mainstream acceptance as telephysiotherapy adoption increases. Clinicians are also developing recommendations about conducting virtual examinations of the musculoskeletal system (Tanaka et al., 2020). Researchers are trying to develop best practices for patient-assisted physical examination without caregivers at the bedside. In a typical scenario, a physical examination consists of inspection or observation, palpation, range of motion testing, neurological examination, muscle strength testing, and special tests depending on the joint involved. The common joints evaluated include the shoulder, spine, neck, hip, knee, elbow, and ankle (Laskowski et al., 2020).

Telephysiotherapy projects can use live video or apps to send written and video tutorials to patients. The asynchronous data from the patients consisting of images and videos is used to monitor exercise measurements and performance. Physiotherapists use live video to evaluate patients at home remotely. Instead of specialized tools available at the physiotherapy clinics, patients use regular household furniture as treatment tools. In the case of children, parents assist with teaching exercise techniques under physiotherapists' guidance (Negrini et al., 2020). Studies have proven compliance, symptom relief, and an overall positive experience using telehealth for exercise (Morrison et al., 2020).

TeleSpeech therapy

Speech therapy is suitable for telemedicine as it uses audio and visual clues for diagnosis, management, and monitoring. Studies have demonstrated the efficacy of speech therapy delivered via telehealth. The interventions can target speech, voice, swallowing, reading or writing, and cognition (Molini-Avejonas et al., 2015). Virtual therapies for patients with aphasia, dysarthria, and apraxia of speech can be monitored in real-time (Keck et al., 2014). Over video, therapists can provide directions to the patients and evaluate their responses. The therapist may hold print materials in front of the camera or email the print materials to the client in advance and work on the materials together in real time, creating a treatment plan collaboratively. The other advantage is that the therapists, family members, or teachers can record and review the video sessions. Multiple web-based and mobile app-based software programs based on speech therapy principles are available to the patients. Some studies have shown better outcomes among children who received speech therapy via telehealth than in-person therapy based on National Outcomes Measurement System Functional Communication Measures data (Towey et al., 2012). Telehealth is also used by speech pathologists for assessments and interventions for cognitive and communication impairments stemming from complex medical issues like brain injury, phonological alexia, Parkinson's disease, dementia, and dysphagia (Weidner et al., 2020). Other telehealth-based speech pathology interventions have focused on children with cleft lip or palate. Pre- and post-operative speech evaluations have been conducted with speech therapy using video-based telehealth.

Telespeech therapy allows for therapeutic interventions in disorders like stuttering for pediatric and adult populations (Sicotte et al., 2003). The speaking disorders are remotely evaluated using microphones to capture voice, preferably as part of a video conferencing system (Jessiman. 2003). Speech therapy assessments and follow-up in stuttering cases can be done using both asynchronous and synchronous modalities. Studies have demonstrated positive outcomes with reduced stuttering frequency and severity and reduced situation avoidance (Bayati et al., 2021). Learning rehabilitation patterns using asynchronous communication is sometimes easier for patients with stuttering as it provides enough time to practice speech techniques and error correction (Carey et al., 2010). Telehealth has demonstrated better adherence to treatment protocols as patients feel more comfortable in their home setting (Carey et al., 2014).

Systematic reviews have found telehealth effective and viable for aphasia (Hall et al., 2013). There is a high degree of agreement between remote and in-person diagnoses for dysphagia or aphasia. Telehealth-based interventions for aphasia include progressive cueing hierarchies to target word retrieval, script training, constraint-induced language therapy, Promoting Aphasic Communication Effectiveness (PACE) therapy, Verb Network Strengthening Treatment (VNeST), and Semantic Mediation. There were comparable outcomes in patients with Parkinson's Disease using traditional Lee Silverman Voice Treatment (LSVT LOUD®) speech treatment. For adults with traumatic brain injury, Facial Affect Recognition Intervention (FARI), cognitive rehabilitation, compensatory techniques for attention and memory, self-monitoring and self-regulation, and problem-solving were feasible.

Swallowing assessments have also been conducted over telehealth, and patients have been provided cues for postural or compensatory strategies. For patients with voice disorders, intensive voice intervention has been provided. Telemedicine allows swallowing therapy through remote assessment of the swallowing function and penetration–aspiration rates (Malandraki et al., 2011).

It can also be used for second opinions and asynchronous care of home-based swallowing therapy. Similarly, for patients on chemo-radiotherapy, intensive prophylactic swallow therapy can be performed via telemedicine (Wall et al., 2017). It provides an alternative to clinician-directed face-to-face therapy and has been shown to have higher adherence than independent patient-directed therapy. The recommendations obtained via telemedicine are highly correlated with in-person evaluations in most cases.

Telespeech therapy can help mitigate waiting lists for accessing specialists and provide a flexible work environment for therapists. It enables cost and time savings, increases access to patients with motor impairments, and provides the ability to create a flexible treatment schedule. There are still challenges similar to other telehealth-based clinical interventions, including the inability to perform in-person physical exams, the risk of inaccurate assessment, and difficulty in communication over audio or video in certain situations (Bayati et al., 2021). However, with increasing use and familiarity with telehealth, and technological innovations are reducing the impact of these limitations.

35 TELEHEALTH FOR CLINICAL SERVICES

Clinical services include administrative, ancillary, and clinical support services in acute or outpatient settings. Telehealth is increasingly being deployed in these departments to improve productivity and efficiency.

TeleCase management

Telehealth is increasingly getting deployed in clinical support departments like case management. Such use cases include setting up hospital telehealth coordinators (Edirippulige et al., 2016). Case managers can remotely speak with patients post-discharge from the hospital to support their transition. Community health workers can also work with high-risk patients to ensure they are connected with appropriate support services. Nursing facility-based case managers can provide support with remote evaluation of patients by remote physicians for appropriate triaging.

TeleMicrobiology

Telemicrobiology is the remote interpretation of microbiological samples. It allows for remote evaluation of microbiological slides and digital plates of microbiological cultures for faster diagnosis (Rhoads et al., 2015). The remote interpretation can be preliminary or confirmatory. Besides diagnostic support, telemicrobiology has been used for remote supervision, quality assessment, and microbiology laboratories (McLaughlin et al., 1998).

Telemicrobiology offers multiple advantages to healthcare providers. These include rapid access to specialists, reduced risk of physical damage to the specimens, lower risk of loss of specimens, and reduced costs (in most cases). The images captured with telemicroscopy and sent for telemicrobiological evaluation must contain enough information for reliable interpretation. Besides requiring multiple images of the area of interest, this can include capturing information like patient history, suspected diagnosis, type of specimen, data collection, stain used, lens magnification used, and patient identifiers (Rhoads et al. 2016a).

Telemicrobiology can be implemented using static capture telemicroscopy, whole slide imaging, video telemicroscopy, or a combination. Video microscopy may involve a live human at the slide preparation site, a robot operating video at the source site, or a recorded video of the slide. (Rhoads et al. 2016a). Static image telemicrobiology is used for evaluating simple stains like gram stains in microbiologic preparations. This technique can be quite accurate. For example, no statistically significant differences were found in a study comparing the diagnostic accuracy of digital video images of these slides with conventional in-person light microscopy. The technique of slide prep also plays a significant role in the accuracy of the final diagnostic interpretation. For example, studies have shown the quality of interpretations between high-magnification digital slides using oil immersion and glass slides (Rhoads et al., 2016b).

Due to the rapid progress in digital imaging, advanced whole-slide imaging scanners are continuously being developed to assist with telemicroscopy to ensure high-resolution images and appropriate depth of field. They are spawning more specialized applications of telemicroscopy. Specialized applications of telemicrobiology are being developed, including telebacteriology, televirology, and telepathology. With the advancement in camera technology in mobile phones, attachments have been developed for mobile phones, which convert them into microscopes. This allows for the creation of a portable device that can be easily put together for quick image capture and transmission. Computer-aided diagnosis techniques enable the digitally captured images for telepathology, or tele-microbiology, to be augmented using computer algorithms, especially machine learning techniques.

The disadvantages include errors in capturing the relevant area of the slides, inability to visualize multiple Z-planes of the slide, and inability to change or quality of the slide by the interpreting specialist. Poor-quality images usually result from poor focus, inappropriate magnification, poor image exposure, poor cropping, or too few images for reliable diagnosis. The other downside is that, in some cases, the end-to-end process for telemicrobiology may increase the time required to prepare images suitable for remote review.

TelePathology and TeleCytology

The digitization of histopathology slides, advancements in digital pathology, and the development of robotic-assisted microscopy has dramatically expanded telepathology applications. With the digitization of slides, physical proximity to the slides is not required for interpretation. Alternatively, for tissue telediagnosis, pathology labs can upload digitally scanned images of glass slides which can be remotely evaluated by pathologists.

Telepathology includes digital microscopy, telemicroscopy, video microscopy, and whole-slide imaging (Pantanowitz et al., 2014). Telepathology allows for remote interpretation of pathology material, including "H&E-stained paraffin tissue sections, frozen sections, cytology or hematology slides, microbiology specimens, clinical fluids, electron micrographs, electrophoresis gels, and cytogenetics images." Telepathology applications include "primary diagnosis, intraoperative consultation, rapid cytology, secondary consultation, specialized studies, archival review, quality management, tumor board conference." The specialty guidelines recommend that the devices used to facilitate telepathology be approved by the FDA. Telepathology can work for both anatomic and clinical pathology and has been used for the initial interpretation of specimens, providing second opinions and education.

Static image telepathology refers to the storing and forwarding process of pathology images. It is an asynchronous technique for image capture for later viewing (Weinstein. 1996). Robotic telepathology is the ability to remotely control an image-capturing device, which is then used to view glass slides (Dunn et al., 2009). Video microscopy is the technique of streaming microscopic images from a video camera (Buxbaum et al., 2012). Whole Slide Imaging scans the entire glass slide to be viewed subsequently, similar to conventional microscopy (Ghaznavi et al., 2013). This usually results in a large image file requiring larger storage systems. For example, a WSI with x20 magnification can be over 20 gigabytes which is then compressed for transmission (Krupinski et al., 2012). Telepathology can exist independently or combined with other sub-specialties like teledermatopathology for specific use cases.

Rapid On-Site Evaluation (ROSE) of cytology has also helped the planning process during minimally invasive procedures. Synchronous real-time telecytology using robotic microscopes uses remote cytotechnologists and cytopathologists to evaluate the specimens prepared, including smears and stained by interventional radiologists. The remote specialist uses robotic microscopy to view the specimen via the network (Sirintrapun et al., 2017). The cytotechnologists perform adequacy assessments and do not provide the final cytologist diagnosis. The specialists evaluate whether the cellular and tissue material is adequate for flow cytometry, molecular studies, and immunohistochemistry. This process reduces the need for repeat procedures and effectively triages material for ancillary studies. The remote dynamic robotic function has been used for frozen section diagnosis and non-cytology teleconsultation (Thrall et al., 2014; Vitkovski et al., 2015).

TelePharmacy

A systematic review done in 2018 demonstrated that clinical pharmacy services can be provided effectively via telemedicine (Strnad et al., 2018) to improve patient outcomes. Before the COVID pandemic, telepharmacy was authorized in 23 states in some capacity. Other states had pilot programs or waivers, leaving about one-third of the states that did not have pilot programs or waivers (Tzanetakos et al., 2018).

Pharmacists on telemedicine service can monitor patient symptoms and provide counseling services or address patient concerns (Yap et al., 2013). It allows for flexible pharmacy staffing while providing pharmacist services in remote areas. Pharmacists can counsel patients at the point of care or on discharge from the hospital. Patient counseling activities of a telepharmacist could include discussions with the patient to improve therapy. These discussions between a pharmacist and a patient could be conducted over video, phone, and chat and include discussing description of the drug, dose, route of administration, duration of therapy, the intended effect of the drug and expected response, precautions, possible side effects, or adverse effects, contraindications and interactions, storage and disposal of unused medication, refill information, missed doses. Such interventions can improve medication adherence and provide avenues to reduce patient costs. They can also educate patients about their medications or providers who need specific pharmacist input.

Telepharmacy allows pharmacists to be available at multiple pharmacy locations. In the inpatient setting, telepharmacists work as an extension of the in-house pharmacy by providing 24 x 7 coverage or fill-in coverage during peak hours. They can provide remote order entry for an inpatient pharmacy or hospital. They can also review medication orders before the hospital staff administers medications to the admitted patients. Inpatient pharmacies can also use tele pharmacists in the IV-admixture rooms to review the IV admixture remotely. Telepharmacists providing services to retail community pharmacies or outpatient pharmacies can supervise the pharmacy technician, review prescriptions, and provide remote patient counseling.

Telepharmacists can perform various non-dispensing functions like patient education, review of patient profiles and medication histories, remote prescription verification, medication therapy management, and drug utilization review. For prospective drug utilization review, the telepharmacist obtains the patient's medical records and reviews known allergies, therapy contraindications, appropriate duration and route of administration, directions for use, adverse drug reactions, drug-disease contraindications, drug-food interactions, drug-drug interactions, therapeutic duplication, evidence of abuse or misuse, and drug appropriate utilization. Medication adherence monitoring services and intervention programs promote medication compliance, self-monitoring and reporting, and improved drug options.

Telepharmacists also participate in research and quality improvement projects. The ambulatory care services that can be performed include prior authorizations, evaluation of medication therapy monitoring, and responding to medication-related questions from providers, patients, or other pharmacists. (Elson et al., 2020).

Telepharmacists can also be engaged in "patient assessment and evaluation, assessing health plan and medication eligibility and coverage, administering drugs, vaccines, or biologics, performing peer review and peer consultations, reviewing, selecting, and developing formularies or practice guidelines, providing patient referrals, performing medication therapy management, ordering lab tests" (Telepharmacy Task Force Report. 2017). The National Association of Boards of Pharmacy amended its Model Act based on the task force's recommendations. These changes further clarified provisions around telepharmacy. Per the Act, telepharmacy "means the practice of pharmacy by registered pharmacies and pharmacists located within US jurisdictions through the use of telepharmacy technologies between a licensee and patients or their agents at distances that are located within US jurisdictions. The Practice of Telepharmacy is deemed to occur within the jurisdiction in which the patient is located and the jurisdiction(s) in which the pharmacist and, if applicable, pharmacy are located; therefore, such practice will be subject to the Pharmacy practice regulations of all jurisdictions' Boards of Pharmacy". Telepharmacy technologies refers to "secure electronic communications, information exchange or other methods that shall meet applicable state and federal requirements." (National Association of Boards of Pharmacy Model State Pharmacy Act). The Act also specifies a valid patient-practitioner relationship which becomes complicated in telemedicine scenarios.

In order to run a telepharmacy, the pharmacy needs to obtain a resident or a non-resident permit issued by the Board and comply with appropriate federal and state controlled substance laws and rules. The remote dispensing sites are required to have a pharmacist in charge who is responsible for all operations. The sites must have either a pharmacist or certified pharmacy technician on-site. There is also the requirement for a video and audio communication system between the supervising pharmacy and the remote dispensing site personnel and patients or caregivers.

As per the requirement of state medical boards, pharmacies providing pharmacist services to individuals should be licensed within the state where the individual is located. Pharmacists outside the state of the individual providing pharmacist care services through telemedicine or outside of a licensed pharmacy must register with the state where the individual is located to engage in the non-resident practice. 'Pharmacist care services' are defined as "the provision by a pharmacist of patient care activities within this State or into this State, as defined by the rules of the board, with or without the dispensing of drugs or devices, intended to achieve outcomes related to the cure or prevention of a disease, elimination or reduction of a patient's symptoms, or arresting or slowing of a disease process."

TelePresence

Telepresence robots consist of video conferencing equipment mounted on a motorized trolley which can be remotely or autonomously navigated (Marttos et al., 2013). These are becoming increasingly common hospital sites as they are a less expensive option compared to a fixed videoconferencing equipment mounted in front of every patient bed.

TeleQuality improvement

Hospitals can use telemedicine technologies to impact many quality-of-care metrics, like reducing readmissions (Ray et al., 2016). Telemedicine can reduce healthcare disparity and provide care in resource-constrained settings (van Veen et al., 2019).

TeleSimulation

Telemedicine programs used simulation even before COVID, but this trend accelerated during the pandemic due to social distancing requirements. The simulation-based teaching of procedures can complement in-person learning. Mannequins have been demonstrated to be an effective teaching tool when coupled with telehealth technologies (Hayden et al., 2018).

UNIT 5: REGULATIONS

36 DIGITAL HEALTH REGULATION

Introduction

The regulation of digital health products and services falls primarily under the purview of the FDA. FDA has developed recommendations for the type of software applications regulated in the federal Food, Drug, and Cosmetic Act (FD&C Act). The regulatory oversight by FDA is targeted towards software functions considered medical devices because of the risk to patients' safety if they do not function as intended. Most digital health software and mobile apps are not eligible for regulatory oversight by the FDA, so it is important to understand the exclusion criteria. Per the guidelines, software intended for maintaining or encouraging a healthy lifestyle unrelated to the diagnosis, cure, mitigation, prevention, or treatment of a disease or condition is not considered a device. The general wellness software functions that are not considered devices include

- General wellness software functions related to a specific disease or condition, such as those promoting relaxation, mindfulness, reducing stress, fatigue, feelings of isolation
- General wellness software function related to sleep such as promoting good sleep, improving sleep experience
- General wellness software function related to mental health or psychiatric conditions due to increased public awareness related to the pandemic
- Software functions that provide reminders add the right times to keep state physical or social distancing practices during a pandemic emergency

There are some types of software related to psychiatric conditions, which may be devices as defined in the FD&C Act, but FDA does not intend to impose requirements as they pose a low risk to patients. These can include

- General wellness software functions to promote, track, and/or encourage choices as part of a healthy lifestyle and may reduce the risk of certain chronic psychiatric diseases, including depression, anxiety, obsessive-compulsive disorder, autism, attention deficit hyperactive disorder
- Social function of the display, at opportune times, images or other messages for a substance abuser who wants to stop addictive behavior
- Software functions that help patients or users self-manage a disease or condition without providing treatment or treatment suggestions

- Software functions that use a checklist or a questionnaire of common signs and symptoms for a psychiatric disorder to provide a list of possible medical conditions and advise on when to consult a healthcare provider
- Software functions that guide a user to a questionnaire of signs and symptoms of a psychiatric disorder and provide a recommendation for the type of healthcare facility most appropriate to their needs.

FDA recommends that the design and development of the device software functions follow the Quality System regulation, which is discussed separately (FDA. 21 CFR 820).

Medical device data systems & medical image devices

FDA has issued targeted guidance for medical device data systems, medical image storage devices, and medical image communications devices. As per the regulation, Medical Device Data Systems (MDDS) transfer, store, convert formats and display medical device data on medical imaging data. An MDDS does not modify the data or control the functions of another connected medical device.

The MDDS can be a Device-MDDS or Non-Device MDDS. Non-device MDDS, medical image storage devices, or medical image communications devices are not devices under the FD&C Act. The software functions that are solely intended to transfer, store, convert formats, and display medical device data or medical imaging data, unless the software function is intended to interpret or analyze clinical laboratory test or other device data, results, and findings, are not devices and are not subject to FDA laws and regulations applicable to devices. This type of software function is called Non-Device-MDDS. However, the hardware products solely intended to transfer, store, convert formats, and display medical device data and results are medical devices under section 201(h) of the FD&C Act. Such hardware functions are Device-MDDS.

A Medical Image Storage Device (MISD) is a device that provides electronic storage and retrieval function for medical images. A Medical Communications Device (MCD) is a device that provides electronic transfer of medical image data between medical devices.

Software functions that generate alarms or alerts or prioritize patient-related information on multi-patient displays are considered device software functions. The characteristics of software device functions used for active patient monitoring are that the clinical context and the clinical condition require a timely response. Such devices could be displayed on the hospital wards, which display information from the bedside monitors, or devices that display information or alarms from home monitoring devices for clinical action by the caregivers. Examples of Non-device MDDS that transfer, store, convert formats, and display medical device data include apps that transmit the temperature of the child at school to parents or remote display of information from a blood glucose monitor with no intention of immediate clinical action, which is not considered active patient monitoring.

Software functions that analyze or interpret medical device data in addition to transferring, storing, converting formats, or displaying clinical laboratory test or other device data and results are subject to FDA oversight unless specifically exempt. If the hardware function of a device MDDS is limited to assisting the software functions, including electronic transfer, storage, conversion of formats, or distilled medical device data, then it is exempt from requirements under the FD&C act. The regulatory controls include registration and listing, premarket review, post-market reporting, and quality system regulation for manufacturers (FDA. 2018b).

Device software functions

As described by the FDA in the FD&C Act, the definition of the device is important to evaluate if a software app will be considered a medical device. Device means an instrument, apparatus, implement, machine, contrivance, implant, in vitro reagent, or other similar related article, including any component, part, or accessory, which is (Source: 21CFR9(II) Title 321(h)):

- Recognized in the official National Formulary, or the United States Pharmacopeia,
- Intended for use in the diagnosis of disease or other conditions, or in the cure, mitigation, treatment, or prevention of disease, in man or other animals, or
- Intended to affect the structure or any function of the body of man or other animals, and which does not achieve its primary intended purposes through chemical action within or on the body of man or other animals and which is not dependent upon being metabolized for the achievement of its primary intended purposes.
- Is determined by FDA that a software function would be reasonably likely to have serious adverse health consequences by assessing
    - the likelihood and severity of patient harm if the software function were to not perform as intended;
    - the extent to which the software function is intended to support the clinical judgment of a health care professional;
    - whether there is a reasonable opportunity for a health care professional to review the basis of the information or treatment recommendation provided by the software function; and
    - the intended user and user environment, such as whether a health care professional will use a software function

The device software functions have the potential to cause harm to the health of the public if they do not function as intended. Similarly, if the software function is intended to analyze or interpret medical data for notification for clinical intervention, perform a medical device function, including diagnosis of disease, cure, mitigation, treatment, or prevention, it is a medical device. If a mobile app interprets EKG reforms to detect heart rhythm irregularities, it will be regulated like an EKG machine.

The definition of device does not include a software function that is intended

- for administrative support of a health care facility, including the processing and maintenance of financial records, claims or billing information, appointment schedules, business analytics, information about patient populations, admissions, practice and inventory management, analysis of historical claims data to predict future utilization or cost-effectiveness, determination of health benefit eligibility, population health management, and laboratory workflow management or laboratory information systems;
- for maintaining or encouraging a healthy lifestyle and is unrelated to the diagnosis, cure, mitigation, prevention, or treatment of a disease or condition;
- to serve as electronic patient records, including patient-provided information, to the extent that such records are intended to transfer, store, convert formats, or display the equivalent of

a paper medical chart, so long as

- such records were created, stored, transferred, or reviewed by health care professionals, or by individuals working under supervision of such professionals;
- such records are part of health information technology that is certified
- such function is not intended to interpret or analyze patient records, including medical image data, for the purpose of the diagnosis, cure, mitigation, prevention, or treatment of a disease or condition;

- for transferring, storing, converting formats, or displaying clinical laboratory test or other device data and results, findings by a health care professional with respect to such data and results, general information about such findings, and general background information about such laboratory test or other device, unless such function is intended to interpret or analyze clinical laboratory test or other device data, results, and findings; or

However, the software provider is a device if the function is intended to acquire, process, or analyze a medical image or a signal from an in vitro diagnostic device or a pattern or signal from a signal acquisition system, for the purpose of-

- displaying, analyzing, or printing medical information about a patient or other medical information (such as peer-reviewed clinical studies and clinical practice guidelines);
- supporting or providing recommendations to a health care professional about prevention, diagnosis, or treatment of a disease or condition; and
- enabling such health care professional to independently review the basis for such recommendations that such software presents so that it is not the intent that such health care professional rely primarily on any of such recommendations to make a clinical diagnosis or treatment decision regarding an individual patient.

Software functions, including mobile apps that do not match the definition of the device, are not device software functions of mobile medical apps. Some examples of such software functions are:

- that provide access to medical textbooks in an e-book format
- that are used by healthcare providers as educational tools for medical training or to reinforce previous training
- those used for providing health education to patients, matching patients with appropriate research studies, or providing information about patient specific medical resources
- those used for automating medical office or healthcare back office operations
- that are general purpose products not intended for use in the diagnosis of disease, or in the cure, mitigation, treatment, or prevention of disease including mobile platform for recording audio, messaging, providing directions to medical resources
- which allow individuals to log, record, track, evaluate, or make decisions on behavioral suggestions related to developing or maintaining general wellness, health and wellness
- that provide individuals with access to health record systems allowing them the ability to view, transfer, or download the EHR data
- which allow patients to organize and track their health information
- that provide easy access to information take to a patient's health condition or treatments
- that help patients document, show, or communicate with providers regarding potential medical conditions including videoconferencing portals, web-based personal health records, immunization trackers, web based asthma records, records of blood glucose, blood pressure, heart rate, weight, or others data

- that display images from the Picture Archiving and Communication System (PACS) there may come in here and her server
- that meet the definition of non-device MDDS
- those used for transferring, storing, and converting formats for displaying clinical laboratory test or other device data without intending to interpret or analyze this data, results, and findings
- those that maintain or encourage a general state of health or a health activity
- those that reduce the risk or impact of chronic disease or conditions

Some software functions are considered devices but are subject to enforcement discretion. These meet the regulatory definition of a device but are low risk to patients and consumers. In these cases, manufacturers are not expected to submit premarket review applications or register and list their software with FDA. Generally, software functions that help patients or users self-manage their disease or condition without providing specific treatment suggestions or those that automate simple tasks for healthcare providers are included. Any low-risk software generating alerts without requiring clinical action or clinical notification are outside the purview of FDA. Specific examples could be software (FDA. 2019c):

- that help patients with diagnosed psychiatric conditions (e.g., post-traumatic stress disorder (PTSD), depression, anxiety, obsessive compulsive disorder)
- that provide periodic educational information, reminders, or motivational guidance to smokers trying to quit, patients recovering from addiction, or pregnant women
- that use GPS location information to alert asthmatics of environmental conditions that may cause asthma symptoms or alert an addiction patient (substance abusers) when near a pre-identified, high-risk location
- that use video and video games to motivate patients to do their physical therapy exercises at home
- that prompt a user to enter which herb and drug they would like to take concurrently and provide information about whether interactions have been seen in the literature and a summary of what type of interaction was reported
- that use patient characteristics such as age, sex, and behavioral risk factors to provide patient-specific screening, counseling and preventive recommendations from well-known and established authorities
- that use a checklist of common signs and symptoms to provide a list of possible medical conditions and advice on when to consult a health care provider
- that guide a user through a questionnaire of signs and symptoms to provide a recommendation for the type of health care facility most appropriate to their needs
- that are intended to allow a user to initiate a pre-specified nurse call or emergency call using broadband or cellular phone technology
- that enable a patient or caregiver to create and send an alert or general emergency notification to first responders
- that keep track of medications and provide user-configured reminders for improved medication adherence
- that provide patients a portal into their own health information, such as access to information captured during a previous clinical visit or historical trending and comparison of vital signs
- that aggregate and display trends in personal health incidents
- that allow a user to collect blood pressure data and share this data through e-mail, track and trend it, or upload it to a personal or electronic health record

- that provide oral health reminders or tracking tools for users with gum disease
- that provide prediabetes patients with guidance or tools to help them develop better eating habits or increase physical activity
- that display, at opportune times, images or other messages for a substance abuser who wants to stop addictive behavior
- that provide drug-drug interactions and relevant safety information as a report based on demographic data, clinical information, and current medications
- that provide the surgeon with a list of recommended intraocular lens powers and recommended axis of implantation based on information inputted by the surgeon

For software application regulation, in general, the lowest risk category includes the devices that inform the clinical management for nonserious conditions; the next risk level includes devices driving or informing clinical management for serious conditions and treating or diagnosing nonserious conditions. The third level is all the devices driving informing clinical management of clinical conditions or treating or diagnosing serious conditions.

Mobile medical apps

A 'mobile platform' is defined as a commercial off-the-shelf computing platform, with or without wireless connectivity, which is handheld. This includes smartphones and tablets. A 'mobile application' or 'mobile app' is a software application that can be executed on a mobile platform or a web-based software application that is tailored to a mobile platform but is executed on the server. The term 'software functions' includes mobile applications (apps). A 'mobile medical app' is a software function that meets the definition of a "device" and is deployed on a mobile platform. Software functions need to meet the definition of a device under section 201(h) of the FD&C Act for the FDA to regulate them. FDA can exercise enforcement discretion over devices that meet the definition of a medical device but are of low risk.

Mobile medical apps include only those mobile apps that made the definition of a device and either are intended to be used as an accessory to a regulated medical device or to transform a mobile platform into a regulated medical device. A 'regulated medical device' is a product that meets the definition of the device for the FD&C act that has been cleared or approved by the FDA review of premarket submission or otherwise classified by the FDA.

A 'mobile medical app manufacturer' is any person or entity that manufactures mobile medical apps in accordance with the definitions of the manufacturer as defined by the FDA, including those which create specifications, designs, labels, or create a software system or application for a regulated medical device. It also includes entities that develop specifications or requirements, procure product development, or manufacture from other third-party entities for subsequent commercial distribution unless the third-party entity has responsibilities for manufacturing and distribution.

If a software developer who provides engineering, design, and development services is contracted by the author, who either was the creator of the original idea, or initiated and developed specifications for the mobile medical app, then the author will be considered a manufacturer. Manufacturers will also include any person or entity offering cloud-based software as a service to provide users access to medical device functions and offering a combination of mobile medical labs and hardware attachments intended to be used as medical devices. The distributors of mobile medical apps, providers of tools, services, or infrastructure used in the development, distribution, or use of a mobile app are not considered manufacturers.

Licensed medical practitioners, including physicians, and dentists, who manufacture mobile medical apps or change mobile medical apps solely for professional practice and do not label or promote their mobile medical apps for general use by other licensed practitioners or other individuals are not considered manufacturers. The exemption also applies to persons who manufacture mobile medical apps solely for use in research, teaching, or analysis and who do not launch such mobile medical apps or commercial distribution (FDA. 21 CFR 807.65(d)).

As discussed earlier, a mobile app is considered a device if the intended use is for the diagnosis of disease, cure, mitigation, treatment, prevention, or of disease or is intended to affect the structure or any function of the human body. FDA's oversight is based on the functionality of the software function. It is not determined by the platform like a smartphone or desktop computer. Whether or not a mobile app meets the definition of a device depends on its intended use, shown in labeling claims, advertising materials, or oral or written statements by manufacturers.

Types of medical devices and their regulation

FDA assigns medical devices into three regulatory classes based on the level of control necessary to assure the safety and effectiveness of the device. The device's classification is based on the intended use and indications for the use of the device. Class I devices have the lowest risk, and Class III devices pose the most significant risk. All the classes are subject to General Controls, which are the baseline requirements of the Food, Drug, and Cosmetic (FD&C) Act (FDA. 2020b). The classification is based on the amount of control required to provide 'reasonable assurance of its safety and effectiveness.'

The Class I devices have minimum regulatory control. In contrast, the Class III devices have the most regulatory control. Most digital health companies under the medical device classification will go with Class I or Class II classification. Class II is generally covered by insurance as a reimbursable medical product. For example, electrocardiograph software (ECG app) which includes the Apple Watch App and iPhone App components by Apple, is a Class II medical device (FDA. CDRH. 2018a). Similarly, their photoplethysmography analysis software for notification of irregular rhythm is also Class II. Both underwent 510(k) submission (FDA. CDRH. 2018b). Class III devices include implantable devices. FDA approval has specific terminology for each Class type – Class I devices are 'cleared,' Class II devices are 'granted,' and Class III devices are 'approved.' Class I and Class II devices can get 'exemption from review' or 'enforcement discretion.' All categories of devices may be entered into the FDA Pre-Cert program, 510(k), de novo, or PMA pathways, where FDA reviews the product in detail.

Class I devices

These devices are expected to adhere to General Controls. Almost all Class I devices are exempted from Premarket Notification Requirements. These devices do not require a Premarket notification application and FDA clearance before marketing. For non-exempt Class I devices, 510k is required for marketing. This category requires a predicate with substantial equivalence.

Class II devices

These devices are expected to adhere to General Controls and Special Controls. Premarket notification (510k) is also required for non-exempt Class II devices for marketing.

Class III devices

These devices must adhere to General controls and Premarket Approval (PMA) application. The regulatory agencies may require independent evaluation of effectiveness and safety data.

General controls

The General controls include establishment registration, quality system regulation, labeling requirements, medical device reporting, premarket notification, reporting corrections and removals, and Investigational Device Exemptions (IDE) requirements. General controls for regulatory requirements apply to all medical devices unless exempted by the regulations.

FDA requires manufacturers of medical devices to adhere to specific requirements to be able to market the products. Further details can be obtained from the FDA website (FDA, 2019b). Medical app developers or medical device manufacturers creating novel technologies should engage with FDA early to get guidance about testing and development, including clinical studies. They should identify appropriate regulatory pathways like premarket submission or Investigational Device Exemption (IDE), which allows any investigational device to be used in a clinical study in order to collect safety and effectiveness data to support a Premarket Approval (PMA) application or Premarket Notification 510(k) submission (FDA, 2019f). FDA and IRB should approve these clinical studies if the device poses a significant risk and only IRB if the device poses a non-significant risk. The manufacturers should comply with the labeling requirements for medical devices.

The Quality System regulations provide a framework to ensure that the products meet the relevant requirements and specifications. The device software functions should be verified and validated to ensure safe and effective operation (FDA, 2022). The FDA intends to ensure that the medical device software meets the applicable requirements and specifications, risk management strategies, good design practices, and adequate verification and validation. These are based on industry-accepted good software development practices. FDA has stressed the importance of risk assessment and management and good design practices in software development. The manufacturers are expected to have procedures to identify, analyze, correct, and prevent software-related causes of patient or user harm. FDA has developed guidelines for the design of clinical studies to support premarket submission (FDA, 1997).

Special controls

Special controls are regulatory requirements for class II devices, including performance standards, post-market surveillance, patient registries, special labeling requirements, premarket data requirements, and guidelines.

Premarket Approval (PMA)

A premarket approval is one of the most strict requirements of the FDA to evaluate the safety and effectiveness of class III devices which are "intended to be used in supporting or sustaining human life or preventing impairment of human health, or that may present a potential unreasonable risk of illness or injury for which general controls and special controls are insufficient to provide reasonable assurance of the safety and effectiveness of a device, or for which there is insufficient information to make such a determination" (FDA, 2019h).

The documentation required for premarket submission is based on the 'level of concern' which refers to the "estimate of the severity of injury that a device could permit or inflict, either directly or indirectly, on a patient or operator as a result of device failures, design flaws, or simply by employing the device for its intended use" (FDA. 2005). The level of concern is divided into Major, Moderate, and Minor.

The level of concern is Major if "a failure or latent flaw could directly result in death or serious injury to the patient or operator." It is Moderate if "a failure or latent design flaw could directly result in minor injury to the patient or operator.". Furthermore, it is Minor "if failures or latent design flaws are unlikely to cause any injury to the patient or operator."

Generally, the medical devices that go through PMA are novel, with no equivalent Class I, II, or III. The request for Premarket Approval can be submitted by an individual, partnership, corporation, association, scientific or academic establishment, government agency or organizational unit, or other legal entity per FDA. The application needs to have a review of scientific and clinical data with detailed analysis. The technical section of the PMA includes

- Non-clinical laboratory studies section, which includes microbiology, toxicology, immunology, biocompatibility, stress, wear, shelf life, and other laboratory or animal tests.
- Clinical investigations section, which includes study protocols, safety and effectiveness data, adverse reactions and complications, device failures and replacements, patient information, patient complaints, tabulations of data from subjects, and statistical analyses.

A PMA is similar to the New Drug Application for drugs as both are necessary before the device or the drug is marketed. Examples of digital health products approved through PMA include (FDA, 2022c):

- Device management software for insertable cardiac monitors or implantable cardioverter defibrillator
- Ocular refractive surgery planning software
- Software used for individualized fit of cochlear implants.

Premarket notification 510(k)

Every Class I, II, and III device marketed for human use must submit a 510(k) application to the FDA. It requires a Premarket Approval (PMA) application or is otherwise exempt from requirements. 510(k) is a premarket submission made to the FDA to demonstrate that the device to be marketed is as safe and effective, substantially equivalent to a legally marketed device not subject to premarket approval (FDA, 2020c). The device must be compared to one or more already marketed devices (predicate devices) and demonstrate substantial equivalence. Per FDA, substantial equivalence with predicate is established if all the following criteria are satisfied:

- Same intended use
- Same technological characteristics
- Same intended use
- Different technological characteristics without raising different questions of safety and effectiveness
- Device has demonstrated same level of safety and effectiveness as the predicate device.

Some types of Class I and Class II devices are exempt from premarket notification (510(k)) requirements and Quality System Regulation (Medical Device Good Manufacturing Practices (GMPs). These devices need to comply with regulatory controls unless specifically exempt. The exempted device list can be found on Medical Device Exemptions 510(k) and the GMP Requirements website (FDA, 2022). Digital health companies are encouraged to consult FDA's website or a regulatory consultant for more details.

37 SOFTWARE AS A MEDICAL DEVICE

Digital health technologies include mobile health, health information technology, wearable devices, telehealth and telemedicine, and personalized medicine. The digital health technologies help the consumers make better-informed decisions about their own health and help in prevention, early diagnosis of life-threatening diseases, and management of chronic conditions outside of traditional care settings (FDA. 2020a).

Medical software regulation

FDA oversees software including mobile apps used to treat, diagnose, mitigate, or prevent or other conditions as medical devices under the federal Food, drug and cosmetic act (FD&A). The software used for these purposes is called 'Software as a Medical Device' (SaMD). FDA distinguishes Software as a Medical Device (SaMD) and Software in a Medical Device (SiMD) (FDA. 2018a).

FDA has created a Digital Health program that created policies and practices to support innovation in digital health. FDA's oversight is focused on mobile apps that presented higher risk to patients and doe not focus oversight on products that only promoted general wellness or technologies that receive, transmit, store or display data from medical device. 'Software as a Medical Device (SaMD)' is defined by the International Medical Device Regulators Forum as software intended to be used for one or more medical purposes that perform these purposes without being part of a hardware medical device (International Medical Device Regulators Forum. 2013) The medical purpose as defined by FDA as those purposes that are intended to treat, diagnose, cure, mitigate, or prevent disease or other conditions. The SaMD has the following components (FDA. 2019f):

- **Data sources**: Laboratory, medical devices, medical imaging devices, physiological monitors, patient reported outcomes, medical sensors, IVD devices, computer peripherals and other sensors, personal records, patient records, etc.
- **Data types**: Lab results, medical images, symptoms, genomic data, environmental signals, pictures, activity data, phenotype data, patient demographic information, progress notes, vital signs, medications, diagnoses, immunization dates, allergies, etc.
- **SaMD Algorithms**: Algorithm, inference engine, migrations, analysis engine, model-based logic, machine learning, rules on a knowledge base etc.

- **SaMD output**: Inform, Drive, Diagnose, Treat

The traditional approach used by FDA for regulation of hardware-based medical devices is not well suited to the software where developers can modify their products in response to real-world performance and incorporate user feedback to update the product in weeks or months.

Software Pre-Certification Program

The software precertification program is planned to be a voluntary pathway to assess the safety and effectiveness of software without impeding the innovation. FDA has implemented Pre-Cert Pilot program under the de novo pathway. The developer submits all applicable requirements to FDA for excellence appraisal, review determination, and streamlined review.

Software precertification pilot program is a mechanism to provide regulatory oversight of software-based medical devices. In this approach FDA evaluates the digital health technology developer first to ensure that they are able to respond to any future issues. FDA is employing a total product lifecycle approach for the software precertification program. This includes demonstration of a culture of quality and organizational excellence, continued safety, effectiveness, and performance. FDA conducts both organizational level analysis of the product level analysis to determine reasonable assurance of safety and effectiveness (FDA. 2019g). The components of Pre-Cert program are Excellence Appraisal, Review Determination, Post-Market Real-World Performance Analytics.

Excellence appraisal

The objective of Excellence Appraisal and Precertification component of the pilot program is to develop and refine the process of precertification, identify elements required for Excellence Appraisal process, and explore best practices for ongoing monitoring. Any organization that intends to develop and market software that meets the definition device as per the FD&C will be considered for Software Pre-Cert program. FDA has identified domains and elements which lead to safer and effective SaMD.

- **Leadership and Organizational Support**: This has 3 elements: 1) Providing clear accountability and responsibility to address product issues, user issues, constraints, and conflicting priorities throughout the product lifecycle, 2) Empowering staff to act regarding the decisions or issues impacting users, products, or patient safety and 3) Providing the resources and focus to assure important infrastructure and processes to assure patient safety are sustained and improved.
- **Transparency**: The 5 elements of transparency are: 1) Developing and maintaining systems or dashboards where all levels of the organization can rapidly see and understand how they are performing among metrics relevant to the organization, 2) Making defects, deviations, safety issues transparent to internal and external stakeholders, as appropriate, 3) Security and quality issues are communicated with internal and external stakeholders sufficiently to catalyze corrective and preventive action, 4) Buyers and users understand design assumptions about expected operational conditions/environment to use devices safely, securely, and effectively, and 5) Buyers and users (patients/physicians) understand expected or minimum support lifetimes and levels
- **People**: The 4 elements of people domain are 1) Developing and maintaining access to highly skilled employees with relevant/applicable clinical knowledge, 2) Involving appropriate cross

functional subject matter expertise including, engineering, clinical expertise, and user advocates, with frequent engagement and communication in product decisions and potential safety events, 3) Continuous development of employees through robust knowledge management, employee development options, coaching, training, and succession planning. This includes keeping updated with the latest clinical developments and patient safety priorities and 4) Developing and maintaining clear and objective employee performance metrics, rewards, and recognition aligning behaviors to the business goals, values, and rapidly responding to patient safety issues.

- **Infrastructure and Work Environment**: The 5 elements of infrastructure and work environment are 1) Customer engagement and providing multiple avenues for outreach, feedback, and learning, 2) Implementing the tools, automation, and test environments in development that establish a centralized and visible process, 3) Develop and maintain a robust notification and communication framework, 4) Communicate and preserve the relevant results of the activities, processes and expectations related to the SaMD lifecycle processes, and 5) Developing and maintaining processes and mechanisms for rapid learning from successes, failures, and near-misses.
- **Risk Management**: Risk management domains create patient safety focused processes and includes 1) Regularly questioning how software works by understanding, identifying, and proactively anticipating potential issues and factors that can influence what can go wrong with the software, 2) Favor rigorously tested software components (i.e. well-vetted cryptographic libraries vs roll your own) or identify risks and mitigations, 3) Identifying, receiving, and handling vulnerability reports from third parties directly (coordinated vulnerability disclosure) or from public sources, such as vulnerability databases, and 4) Accounting for support lifecycles of hardware and software components and dependencies. (i.e. If the SaMD is expected to be used longer than the operating system is supported, how will you continue to address things like security vulnerabilities?).
- **Configuration Management and Change Control**: The 3 elements in this domain are 1) Source control by establishing mechanisms for initiating, evaluating and controlling changes to software during all lifecycle processes and after deployment, 2) Good release management with a secure update process, and 3) The ability to rollback software in the event of an emergency.
- **Measurement, Analysis, and Improvement of Processes and Products**: The 5 elements in continuous improvement domain are 1) Responsive issue escalation & resolution, 2) Actively monitoring, analyzing, rapidly addressing, and implementing resulting process improvements from user feedback and product issues including safety, cyber or data issues, 3) Analyzing and providing the learning collected from real world data back to development teams throughout all lifecycle processes, 4) Developing and maintaining process performance metrics that are clear, simple, and actionable across all staff and organizational levels with integrated improvement activities, and 5) Supporting rigorous interrogation into sources of failure, error, and tampering, including tamper resistant, forensically sound evidence capture and publicly known mechanisms to perform or trigger investigations.
- **Managing Outsourced Processes, Activities, and Products**: The outsourcing related elements are 1) Comprehensive risk management of third-party and open source software throughout all lifecycle process and activities, 2) Avoid third-party software components with known vulnerabilities when less vulnerable alternatives are available, 3) Maintain and provide traceability and assurance of third-party and open source software throughout the effective lifetime of the software.
- **Requirements Management**: This section includes 3 elements 1) Understanding the clinical association between the SaMD output and a clinical condition (i.e., clinical performance) and

understanding and updating the priorities, concerns, and value to intended user based on user feedback throughout all lifecycle phases, 2) Buyers and operators understand the impact of operational isolation (e.g. which features are fully available in standalone/no network mode), and 3) Carefully manage and gate remote access to all device components and dependencies. (e.g. Avoid hardcoded default credentials within the device and enforce secure identity and access management for any provider-operated components like software update distribution servers.)

- **Design and Development**: The design and development elements are comprehensive and contain good software good product development practices including 1) Secure software development lifecycle, including adversarial resilience analysis and testing, reducing elective attack surface & complexity, and minimizing elective exposure throughout the software lifecycle, 2) Designing software based on good quality clinical evidence from research and can reference published, peer-reviewed studies that show claimed results, 3) Incorporating resilience, containment, and isolation into the design solution so that product fails safely and visibly, continue to perform as intended when there are failures in the operating environment, and assures the integrity of data input and storage, 4) Incorporating anticipated safety risks and mitigations throughout all lifecycle phases and actions taken to prevent recurrence of any unanticipated hazards, 5) Reliably identifying and removing code errors at source, 6) Integrating user experience/Human Factors and Good Clinical Practices Human Subject Protection into development in partnership with patients and caregivers, 7) Secure, prompt, and agile update mechanism and process, with high rates of prompt update adoption and clear notification and communication to stakeholders, and 8) Leadership/peer/expert review throughout lifecycle phases and at key milestones.
- **Verification and Validation**: Elements in this domain are 1) Staged release with active user testing, 2) Demonstrating software works for intended use / indications for use, and 3) Measuring quality of the output of the software on the clinical target (intended use, indication of use).
- **Deployment and Maintenance**: 1) Proactive patient and clinical outreach and education including limitations of software and FAQs addressing potential patient safety questions developed as part of release, 2) Active control mechanisms to force/push patient safety and security updates, and 3) Support dependency updates, such as routine operating system upgrades.

At the time of this writing, FDA has proposed two levels of precertification.

- Level 1 Pre-Certification will allow organizations to develop and market lower risk software without review. The organization needs to demonstrate excellence in product development in all five excellent principles and have a track record in developing, delivering and maintaining products.
- Level 2 Pre-Certification will allow developers to develop and market certain lower and moderate software without review. This level of certification will be awarded to a nomination that has a proven track record in developing, delivering, and maintaining products.

Review determination

FDA has created guidelines for determination of SaMD's which may require FDA review. The risk-based framework for developers to assess the premarket review pathway for their products is evolving at the agency. To determine the SaMD risk, the pre-certified organizations provide FDA the following information about the SaMD: 1) device description, 2) SaMD performance, 3) core functionality, 4) state of healthcare situation or condition targeted by the SaMD, and 5) significance of information provided by SaMD. Based on these, the devices are divided into category of risks. FDA is using IMDRF N12 framework to assess the significance of the information. The IMDRF risk categorization framework considers two factors: 1) The significance of information provided by the software as medical device to the healthcare decision. e.g. diagnosis, clinical management, and 2) state of healthcare situation or condition for example critical, serious, or non-serious (IMDRF. 2014).

Significance of information

Significance of information provided by SaMD means that the information obtained from the SaMD will be used for clinical actions with different levels of significance. There are three categories based on significance of information provided by SaMD to healthcare decision (IMDRF. 2014):

- **To treat or diagnose**: Treating or diagnosing means that information provided by the SaMD will be used to take an immediate or near-term action. This could include interventions to treat, prevent or mitigate by connecting to a medical devices, medical products, general-purpose actuators or other means of providing therapy to human body and to diagnose/screen/detect a disease or condition using sensors, data, or other information from other hardware or software devices
- **To drive clinical management**: The information provided by the SaMD is used to guide next diagnostics or treatment interventions, or to identify early signs of disease or condition which will be used to guide diagnostics or treatment interventions. These are used to aid in treatment by providing enhanced support to safe and effective use of medicinal products or a medical device, to aid in making a definitive diagnosis and to triage or identify early signs of a disease or conditions.
- **To inform clinical management**: The information provided will not trigger an immediate or near-term action it is not necessary to decision-making to deliver patient care. The goal for this criteria is to inform of options for treating, diagnosing, preventing, or mitigating a disease or condition and to provide clinical information by aggregating relevant information including disease, condition, medical devices, drugs etc.

State of healthcare situation

The state of the healthcare situation or condition refers to how important is the healthcare condition targeted by the SaMD. There are 3 categories for the state of healthcare situation:

- **Critical**: Critical situations or conditions of those where accurate and/or timely diagnosis or treatment action is vital to avoid death, long-term disability or other serious deterioration of health of an individual patient or to mitigate impacts to the public health.
    - Types of disease or condition: Life-threatening state of health, including incurable states; requires major therapeutic interventions; and sometimes time critical, depending on the progression of the disease or condition that could affect the user's ability to reflect on the output information.
    - Intended target population: Fragile with respect to the disease or condition
    - Intended to be used by: Specialized trained users
- **Serious**: Serious situations or conditions are those where accurate diagnosis or treatment is a vital importance to avoid unnecessary interventions, to mitigate long-term irreversible

consequences.

  - Types of disease or condition: Moderate in progression and often curable, those which do not require major therapeutic interventions and those in which intervention is normally not expected to be time critical in order to avoid death, long-term disability or other serious deterioration of health.
  - Intended target population: Not fragile with respect to the disease or condition
  - Intended to be used by: Either specialized trained users or lay users.
- **Non-Serious**: The non-serious situations or conditions are those where accurate diagnosis and treatment is important but not critical or interventions to mitigate long-term irreversible consequences on an individual patient's health condition or public health. They include conditions with an accurate and timely diagnosis, or timely treatment interventions important but not critical to prevent or mitigate long-term irreversible consequences.
  - Types of disease or condition: Slow with predictable progression of disease state which may not be curable but can be managed effectively, those requiring only minor therapeutic interventions and those interventions which are normally non-invasive in nature, providing the user the ability to detect erroneous recommendations.
  - Intended target population: Individuals who may not always be patients
  - Intended to be used by: Either specialized trained users or lay users

Streamlined premarket review

FDA considers SaMD for streamlined review if the organization has gone through Excellence Appraisal and successfully demonstrated excellence in developing, testing, maintaining, and improving software products. The objective of establishing streamlined premarket review is to identify the elements necessary for a premarket review and development premarket review process ensuring safety and effectiveness of the software is a medical device. During this stage, FDA will contract with the applicant and understand the details of the software. FDA will review software's analytical performance, clinical performance, and appropriate safety measures. After this process is complete, FDA makes a premarket decision for marketing authorization. The elements of streamlined review are (FDA. 2019g)

Administrative elements

- Cover letter
- Financial Certification and Disclosure Form
- Truthful and Accuracy Statement

Product-Specific elements

- Clinical algorithm: Information about clinical algorithms including mechanism of action
- Clinical Data Analysis and Interpretation
- Cybersecurity: Ability of a company to assess security, manage updates, perform post-market security assessments, update SaMD during the Excellence Appraisal and from Real-World Performance data
- Declaration of Conformity and Summary Reports for Vertical Standards
- Hazard Analysis: Product specific risks, hazards and subsequent mitigations.
- Instructions for use
- Labeling review
- Regulatory Pathway Specific Items (e.g., 510(k) substantial equivalence comparison)

- Requirements: Product-specific including user interface, user stories and workflow.
- Revision history
- SaMD product demo
- Software architecture: Detailed depiction of functional units and software modules and may include state diagrams as well as flow charts.
- Validation: Validation of clinical performance claims and device performance

Miscellaneous elements

- Excellence Appraisal Assessment
- Review Determination information (Indications for Use, Device Description, etc.)
- Real-world Performance Plan

FDA has also created five principles of excellence for regulating Software as a Medical Device (SaMD):

- **Patient Safety**: Demonstration of a commitment to providing a safe patient experience, and to emphasizing patient safety as a critical factor in all decision-making processes.
- **Product Quality**: Demonstration of a commitment to the development, testing, and maintenance necessary to deliver SaMD products at the highest level of quality.
- **Clinical Responsibility**: Demonstration of a commitment to responsibly conduct clinical evaluation and to ensure that patient-centric issues including labeling and human factors are appropriately addressed.
- **Cybersecurity Responsibility**: Demonstration of a commitment to protect cybersecurity, and to proactively address cybersecurity issues through active engagement with stakeholders and peers.
- **Proactive Cultures**: Demonstration of a commitment to a proactive approach to surveillance, assessment of user needs, and continuous learning.

Post-Market Real-World Performance Analytics (RWPA)

Post-Market Real-World Performance Analytics (RWPA) is used for verification of continued safety, effectiveness, performance and an organization's commitment to culture of quality. FDA is looking for evidence that organizations will demonstrate excellence for continuous improvement through proactive monitoring of real-world performance data including safety, effectiveness, and performance of the SaMD. FDA will collect the RWPA plan from the developers prior to the market launch. FDA is creating a mechanism for ongoing RWPA monitoring.

RWPA framework is a systematic computational analysis of data targeted at safety, effectiveness, and performance of a SaMD product. There are three types of analyses under RWPA – Real World Health Analytics, User Experience Analytics, and Product Performance Analytics.

Real World Health Analytics (RWHA)

Real World Health Analytics (RWHA) is the analysis of real-world clinical outputs and outcomes related to the intended use of SaMD. The advantage of RWHA is that it can help to identify additional functions of a SaMD, identify any changes required to the existing use of a SaMD, and provide early signal for any safety issues in post-market use. RWHA can be obtained from user complaints, search analytics, user errors or from medical device manufacturer submissions. RWHA can help with the following three components:

- **Human Factors and Usability Engineering**: Organizations can understand users' ability to understand and navigate the user interface and drive continuous improvement in usability engineering.
- **Clinical Safety**: The medical device manufacturer can detect early safety signals and thereby provide assurance to customers and regulators that safety risks are managed and mitigated in a timely way
- **Health Benefits**: Organizations can have positive impact on health outcomes by understanding clinical benefits which can inform product modifications.

User Experience Analytics (UXA)

User Experience Analytics (UXA) is the analysis of user experience outputs related to the real-world use of SaMD. UXA can be collected from use patterns, download rates, user feedbacks, social media platforms, search analytics. Organizations can make timely identification and correction of user issues resulting in improvements to the utilization and effectiveness of their software product. UXA helps with the following components:

- **User Satisfaction**: User satisfaction can provide indirect evidence of brand reputation and product performance
- **Issue resolution**: Faster issue resolution builds consumer confidence in the organization and their SaMD
- **User feedback channels**: by deploying multiple user feedback channels, organizations can identify and resolve user issues early and timely.
- **User engagement**: UXA helps to optimize user experience and meet business targets for user engagement

Product Performance Analytics (PPA)

Product Performance Analytics (PPA) is the analysis of outputs and outcomes demonstrating real-world accuracy, reliability, and security of SaMD. Using PPA, organizations can identify and resolve software bugs and security vulnerabilities. The connected devices have additional expectations around cybersecurity risk management. The PPA components are

- **Cybersecurity**: Organizations are expected to protect user privacy, ensure product integrity, and maintain system availability and build consumer confidence in organization and SaMD product.
- **Product Performance**: The organization is expected to continuously improve product quality.

Global digital health regulation

The EU Medical Device Regulation (MDR) provides the CE Mark to the medical devices and regulates the production and distribution of medical devices in Europe. MDR identifies four players in the medical device ecosystem – manufacturers, authorized representative, importers and distributors. The current version of the regulation (MDR 2017/745) was updated from Medical Devices Directive (MDD). As per MDR, a medical device is "any instrument, apparatus, appliance, software, implant, reagent, material or other article intended by the manufacturer to be used, alone or in combination, for human beings for one or more of the following specific medical purposes:

- diagnosis, prevention, monitoring, prediction, prognosis, treatment or alleviation of disease,
- diagnosis, monitoring, treatment, alleviation of, or compensation for, an injury or disability,
- investigation, replacement or modification of the anatomy or of a physiological or pathological process or state,
- providing information by means of in vitro examination of specimens derived from the human body, including organ, blood and tissue donations, and which does not achieve its principal intended action by pharmacological, immunological or metabolic means, in or on the human body, but which may be assisted in its function by such means."

Software has been determined to be an 'active device' per the regulation. An 'active device' is "any device, the operation of which depends on a source of energy other than that generated by the human body for that purpose, or by gravity, and which acts by changing the density of or converting that energy. Devices intended to transmit energy, substances or other elements between an active device and the patient, without any significant change, shall not be deemed to be active devices."

As per the EU regulation, "software in its own right, when specifically intended by the manufacturer to be used for one or more of the medical purposes set out in the definition of a medical device, qualifies as a medical device, while software for general purposes, even when used in a healthcare setting, or software intended for life-style and well-being purposes is not a medical device. The qualification of software, either as a device or an accessory, is independent of the software's location or the type of interconnection between the software and a device" (European Parliament. MDR 2017/745). This regulation, which came into effect in May 2021, the software applications which qualify as a medical device will have to provide clinical evaluation report including clinical data for safety, effectiveness, and performance data.

United Kingdom's National Health Service (NHS) has introduced Digital Technology Assessment Criteria (DTAS) for evaluation of digital health technologies covering clinical safety, data protection, technical security, interoperability, usability and accessibility (NHS. 2021). The National Institute for Health and Care Excellence has also developed evidence standards framework for digital health technologies (NICE. 2018). The standards cover evidence for effectiveness and economic impact.

NHS also developed Improving Access to Psychological Therapies (IAPT) assessment criteria for digitally enabled therapies. Digital enabled therapies are those applications which are designed to treat depression, generalized anxiety disorder, social anxiety disorder, panic disorder, agoraphobia, post-traumatic stress disorder, health anxiety (hypochondriasis), specific phobia, obsessive-compulsive disorder, body dysmorphic disorder, irritable bowel syndrome, chronic fatigue syndrome, or medically unexplained symptoms not otherwise specified. These applications must satisfy the DTAC for Health and social care, assessment for clinical content, and assessment for effectiveness (NHSx. 2021).

38 CLINICAL DECISION SUPPORT REGULATION

Introduction

Clinical decision support (CDS) software provides decision support to clinicians for medical diagnosis, treatment, or prevention of diseases. This may include computerized alert systems and reminders for healthcare professionals and patients. For healthcare providers, it could include clinical guidelines, order sets targeted at specific conditions, targeted and relevant patient data reports, templates for creating documentation in the electronic medical record system, encouragement and support for making diagnoses, support to clinicians for the diagnosis, treatment, cure, or mitigation (FDA. 2014).

Clinical decision support can tremendously benefit clinicians by providing them with intelligently curated, personalized, patient-specific information that can be point-of-care (FDA. 2019a). As per the Five Rights model, clinical decision support implementation can be successful in the clinical setting if it communicates the following (Sirajuddin AM et al., 2009):

- **Right information:** CDS systems should provide evidence-based appropriate information which informs the correct action relevant to the circumstance. If the provider feels that the information provided by the CDS system is irrelevant, they will dismiss the alert. The information should be relevant to the clinician and the patient. It should be very specific in addressing the action that needs to be taken. The provider should trust the information. This can be reinforced by providing citations to the sources. It is also important to make the alert clear and concise and include the right detail.
- **Right person:** CDS intervention should be available to the correct member of the care team, including providers, patients, caretakers, and other stakeholders. The alert that is relevant for a physician may not be relevant for a nurse or pharmacist. Every care team member is different, even if they respond to the same data point.
- **Right format:** CDS intervention can be an alert, filtered options in an order set, text-based reference information pertinent to the context in which it is made available. In order to do so, the set may need reference information from published literature. It is important to avoid overuse or inappropriate use of alerts which can lead to alert fatigue.
- **Right channel:** The channel could be an electronic medical record system, a personal health record, a mobile app, or a text message. The most common channel is the computerized

physician order entry system which is used to place orders by a physician.

- **Right time:** The CDS intervention needs to occur during decision-making. The clinical decision support systems must understand the clinical workflows well to identify the appropriate time to trigger the intervention. A helpful exercise is to observe the clinicians and create a process map of their actions and mental decision-making.

Success factors

The chances of successful implementation of clinical decision support can be improved by keeping the following into consideration:

- Creating governance structures and operating mechanisms.
- Creating a goal for improvement and identifying metrics to evaluate and collect baseline performance data and comparing pre and post-implementation change. The metrics that can be tracked include structural measures, process measures, and outcome measures.
- Engaging all relevant stakeholders, including physicians, nurses, administrators, clinical Informaticists, pharmacists, and other supporting departments, including quality and patient safety.
- Involving end-users of CDS interventions early in the development and deployment process as well as getting their buy-in at every step of the process.

CDS has been shown to improve the practice of clinical medicine. However, the implementation must consider the behavioral and logistical nuances to achieve this. As per research (Kawamoto K et al., 2005), the features which were associated with improved clinical outcomes included:

- Automatically providing decision support during clinician workflow
- Providing decision support at the time and location of decision-making
- Providing a recommendation rather than just an assessment
- Using a computer system to generate decision support

Device vs Non-Device CDS

Clinical decision support (CDS) can be Device CDS or Non-Device CDS. The Cures Act amended the FD&C Act to exclude certain software functions from the definition of device which meet all the following four criteria:

- CDS is not intended to acquire, process, or analyze a medical image of a signal from an in vitro diagnostic device or a pattern or signal from a signal acquisition system. Physiological signals include signals which require an in-vitro diagnostic device with software that uses electrochemical or photometric response generated by an assay or instrument or a signal acquisition system using software and including the use of electronic sensors or radiological imaging systems and biological samples such as tissue, blood, or other fluids. Examples of such systems include medical devices and software to detect abnormal heart rhythms on ECG devices, identify abnormal images, interpret genomic data, and monitor gate physiological activities.

- CDS intended for displaying, analyzing, or printing medical information about a patient or other medical information, which may include peer-reviewed clinical studies and clinical practice guidelines. General medical information could include peer-reviewed clinical studies, clinical practice guidelines, textbooks, drug or device labels, and medical society recommendations. Medical information related to patients includes demographic information, symptoms, test results, hospital documentation, and reading for medical devices such as heart rate, blood pressure, and temperature.
- CDS is intended to support or provide recommendations to a healthcare professional about preventing, diagnosing, or treating a disease or condition. Functions could include assisting healthcare professionals with treatment options for diagnostic tests targeted at specific patients. These tools are not used to treat a patient, determine a patient's treatment, or provide a definitive diagnosis of a patient's disease or condition. The software could make recommendations about possible treatment plans for diagnostic tests and help inform the healthcare professionals' decisions regarding the prevention, diagnosis, or treatment of a patient's condition. If these recommendations are for patients or caregivers, they will be considered devices.
- CDS is intended to enable healthcare professionals to independently review the basis for such recommendations that such software presents so that it is not the intent that such healthcare professionals rely primarily on any of such recommendations to make a clinical diagnosis or treatment decision regarding an individual patient. The idea is that healthcare professionals do not rely primarily on such recommendations but draw on their judgment to make clinical decisions. Per FDA, the non-device CDS software functions should have clear documentation, including the purpose or intended use of the software function, intended user, inputs used to generate the recommendations, and basis for rendering recommendations. It is important to know that the FDA expects the software developer to describe the underlying data used to develop the algorithm and the logic used by the algorithm to render recommendations. The source to develop the algorithm should be identified and available to the users.

A software function is considered CDS if it is not intended to acquire, process, or analyze; intended for displaying, analyzing, or printing medical information; and intended for supporting or providing recommendations. These exclusions do not apply if the software meets the definition of a device under FD&C Act or if the software is used in the manufacture and transfusion of blood and blood components to assist in the prevention of disease in humans, or if the software function is reasonably likely to have serious adverse health consequences. It is a Non-Device CDS if it is intended to enable the HCP to independently review the basis for such recommendations that the software makes available. However, the intent is not that the HCP will rely primarily on the recommendations to make clinical diagnoses or treatment decisions. Otherwise, it is a device CDS.

FDA uses a risk-based policy and is an approach to regulate the device's CDS functions. FDA uses IMDRF risk categorizations. The goal of the FDA is to provide regulatory oversight of high-risk device CDS software functions. These include those that intended use it is patient or caregiver except where risk categorization is informed for nonserious situations where FDA has enforcement discretion. FDA will provide oversight focus for all risk categories where the intended user is a healthcare professional, and they cannot independently review the basis of recommendations.

Examples of Non-Device CDS functions are:

- Software to provide recommendations to healthcare professionals by matching patients' signs, symptoms, and diagnoses with current treatment guidelines
- Software that identifies drug-drug interactions and drug-allergy contraindications
- Software that provides recommendations to healthcare professionals on the appropriate use of prescription drugs, o laboratory tests, medical devices
- Software that makes therapy suggestions to healthcare professionals based on patient history, test results, or patient characteristics.
- Software that provides tools, calculators, guidelines, and protocols for nutritional recommendations
- Software that provides alternatives to the healthcare professionals' orders, drugs, or therapies using practice guidelines and recommendations

Unregulated CDS

CDS is exempted from FDA oversight if the CDS is for health care providers and is used to inform clinical management of non-serious conditions or if the CDS is for patient/caregiver and is used to inform clinical management of non-serious conditions if it allowed the patients/caregivers to be able to review the basis for CDS recommendations. Examples of Device CDS for which FDA does not currently intend to enforce compliance with applicable device requirements are:

Device CDS intended for Health Care Professionals

- Software that provides recommendations about allergens and common cold symptoms based on location-specific electronic health records, environmental conditions, and patient-reported outcomes to provide healthcare professionals with different diagnoses for consideration. This is a device CDS because healthcare professionals cannot evaluate the basis of software recommendation; however, because it is intended to provide clinical information for nonserious situational conditions, FDA does not intend to enforce compliance with applicable requirements of the FD&C Act.
- Software that uses machine learning to create alerts targeted at healthcare professionals for patient-specific cholesterol management challenges. In this condition, the logic and algorithm inputs are not explained. However, FDA does not intend to enforce compliance with the applicable requirements of the FD&C act because the aggregation of data is providing clinical information for nonserious situations.
- Software that analyzes patient information to decide the most effective over-the-counter allergy drug. The software is a device CDS function because the healthcare provider is not intended to be able to evaluate the basis for the recommendation independently. However, FDA does not intend to enforce compliance with the FD&C act because the treatment options provided are for nonserious situational conditions.

Device CDS intended for patients

Examples of software which is treated as a device CDS but intended to be used by patients directly:

- Software that provides instructions to the patient about how or when to take a prescription drug based on FDA labeling without recommending any changes in those for drug discontinuation. FDA does not intend to enforce compliance with applicable requirements of the FD&C act because it aggregates data that provides clinical information for nonserious situations or conditions, and the basis for recommendation is explained to the user. The software is considered a device CDS because it is intended for patients.

- Software that helps the patient to purchase an OTC cold or allergy medication based on symptoms and past medical history. The regulation is the same as the previous example.
- Software that provides general information like general pre-and post-surgical care preparation and instructions to patients or non-healthcare professional caregivers.
- Software that recommends choosing an over-the-counter sunscreen and general information about preventing sunburn. Like the examples above, if you do not intend to enforce compliance with applicable requirements of the FD&C act because it is an aggregation of data intended to provide clinical information for nonserious situations, it enables patients to independently evaluate the basis for recommendations.

Regulated CDS

Examples of Device CDS for which FDA intends to focus its regulatory oversight are:

Device CDS intended for Health Care Professionals

- Software based on machine learning algorithms assists health providers in differentiating between common flu symptoms and other illnesses like the common cold based on electronic health record data, symptoms, and epidemiology of seasonal flu. Suppose the logic and inputs for the software are not explained in the software. In that case, it is a device CDS function because the healthcare provider cannot independently evaluate the basis for software recommendations. For FDA, the focus is regulatory oversight of the software due to its function of informing clinical management of serious situations or conditions. However, if the manufacturer had explained the logic, inputs, and basis of the predictions algorithm so that the healthcare providers could evaluate the recommendations, then this software would be considered non-device CDS.
- Software that identifies patients exhibiting opiate addiction based on patient-specific data, family history, electronic health records, prescription patterns, and referral data. If the input logic is not explained, the FDA will focus its regulatory oversight on the software because of its intention to inform clinical management of critical situations or conditions.
- Software that uses machine learning algorithms that identify hospitalized, diabetic patients with a higher risk of postoperative complications. If the logic and inputs are not explained, then the software is a device CDS function eligible for FDA oversight.

Device CDS intended for patients

- Software that data from devices like activity trackers, continuous glucose monitors, and food logs to help diabetic patients on insulin get alerts for potential hypoglycemic events and get recommendations for treatment options. FDA will focus its regulatory oversight on the software because it informs clinical management for serious condition. The software is a device CDS 's function because it is intended for patients and inform clinical management.
- Software intended for patients which is a questionnaire to evaluate patient stress and anxiety and recommends treatment options based on output of the assessment. The regulatory

approach is similar to the previous example because the patient is not expected to be able to independently evaluate the basis for software recommendation. It is a device CDS function because it is intended for patients and informs clinical management.

- Software that is targeted towards caregivers of cystic fibrosis patients in the pediatric age group to alert them when they should bring the children to the emergency room. It's the target population displays are fragile with respect to the disease or condition in the software forms clinical management for is considered a device CDS function under the purview of FDA oversight.

Device software functions that are not CDS on which FDA intends to focus its regulatory oversight are

- Software that uses CT or MRI images of patients undergoing radiation therapy treatment to create individualized treatment plans for the healthcare professionals. The software is considered device function because it analyzes a medical image and generates the treatment plan.
- Software which create 3D models of anatomical regions from radiology images for use in planning orthopedic or dental surgical interventions.
- Software that monitors physiological signals like heart rate, breathing patterns, oxygen saturation obtained from FDA regulated devices to diagnose medical events like cardiac arrests, seizures.
- Software that performs image analysis to differentiate between ischemic and hemorrhagic stroke. The software agents in the diagnosis of her disease or condition.
- Software that analyzes cerebrospinal fluid spectroscopy to diagnose different types of meningitis. The software analyzes medical signal and diagnosis of disease.
- Software that detects abnormalities and evaluates disease severity
- Software that analyzes data pathology slides to perform cell counts and review morphology of the cells. The software is considered device function because it intends to analyze a medical image
- Software that calculates the dose of insulin based on carbohydrate intake, premium blood glucose, anticipated physical activity.
- Bioinformatics software that makes patient specific recommendations after analyzing patient genomic data against reference databases. The health professional is not expected to be able to independently evaluate the basis for the software product's recommendations so that considered device functions.
- Software which provides diagnostic and treatment guidance based on genomics, proteomics, and metabolomics data.

39 MOBILE MEDICAL APP REGULATION

Introduction

Traditionally, FDA's focus has been to regulate drugs and medical devices. With the increasing use of mobile phones for healthcare applications, FDA has developed guidance documents to help inform software developers about FDA's regulatory scope targeting these applications. FDA has become involved in regulations of mobile medical applications because of the potential health risks of software functions that are device functions.

FDA considers any product a device to be regulated by the FDA based on the intended use and an indication of use. As discussed earlier, as per the Section 201(h) of the Food, Drug, and Cosmetic Act, the product is a device if it is "An instrument, apparatus, implement, machine, contrivance, implant, in vitro reagent, or other similar or related article, including a component part, or accessory which is:

- recognized in the official National Formulary, or the United States Pharmacopoeia, or any supplement to them,
- intended for use in the diagnosis of disease or other conditions, or in the cure, mitigation, treatment, or prevention of disease, in man or other animals, or
- intended to affect the structure or any function of the body of man or other animals, and which does not achieve its primary intended purposes through chemical action within or on the body of man or other animals and
- which does not achieve its primary intended purposes through chemical action within or on the body of man or other animals and which is not dependent upon being metabolized for the achievement of its primary intended purposes."

The software functions excluded from the definition of "device" are discussed elsewhere in the text. Products intended for only general wellness and which are low-risk are not actively regulated by the FDA.

Mobile medical applications

FDA differentiates between "Mobile Medical Applications" and "Software as a Medical Device."

The device software functions can be "Software as a Medical Device (SaMD)" or "Software in a Medical Device (SiMD)." The software intended for one or more medical purposes without being part of a hardware medical device is considered Software as a Medical Device. This is covered under the Software as a Medical Device chapter. (FDA. 2019b)

FDA defines a 'mobile platform' as a commercial off-the-shelf handheld computing platform, with or without wireless connectivity. The 'mobile app' is defined as the software application that either runs on the mobile platform or runs on a cloud server but is tailored to a mobile platform. 'Mobile medical apps' are software functions that meet the definition of a device and are deployed on a mobile platform to be used as an accessory to a regulated medical device or transform a mobile platform into a regulated medical device.

It is important to note that a mobile app's 'intended use' determines if that meets the definition of 'device.' The intent can be communicated to labeling claims, advertising, or statements issued by the manufacturers or their representatives.

Mobile medical apps include those mobile apps that meet the definition of a device and are either used as an accessory to a regulated medical device or to transform a mobile platform into a regulated medical device. A mobile app used in performing a medical device function, including diagnosis, mitigation, treatment, or disease prevention, is considered a medical device. If the FDA reviews the medical app and approves it, it is considered a 'regulated medical device.' A software developer or company that develops mobile medical apps is considered a 'manufacturer.' The mobile medical app manufacturer is "anyone who initiates specifications, designs, labels, or creates a software system or application for a regulated medical device in whole or from multiple software components." Similarly, persons or entities creating hardware attachments for mobile platforms and the mobile medical labs intended to be used as a medical device will be considered manufacturers. Any web-based software application designed for access on a mobile platform will fall under this definition (FDA. 2019b).

The entities which are not considered mobile medical app manufacturers include:

- Manufacturers or distributors of mobile platforms without the intention of using them as medical device functions.
- Mobile medical app stores or other app distribution channels.
- Providers of tools, services, or infrastructure used in the development, distribution, and use of the medical app.
- Physicians, dentists, and optometrists who manufacture mobile medical apps or alter mobile medical apps only for use in their professional practice with no intention of labeling or promoting the mobile medical app to be generally used by other licensed practitioners or other individuals.
- Researchers who manufacture mobile medical apps solely for use in research, teaching, or without commercially distributing them.

FDA strongly recommends that manufacturers of software and mobile apps follow the quality system regulation in the design and development of the device software functions. These govern the methods used in, and the facilities and controls used for, the design, manufacture, packaging, labeling, storage, installation, and servicing of all devices intended for human use. It has specified that each manufacturer set up and maintain a quality system appropriate for the medical device.

The manufacturer should develop a quality policy & resources and establish quality audits to ensure compliance with the quality system requirements. The manufacturer should also set up design, document, purchasing, production, and process controls. The procedures to identify and trace a product during the production lifecycle should be implemented. Further details can be obtained from 21 CFR Part 820 (FDA. 21 CFR 820).

FDA regulated mobile apps

Here are some examples of device software functions or mobile apps subject to the FDA's regulatory oversight.

- Software functions that connect to a medical device for controlling the device or analyzing the data on the medical device. Since the software device functions extend the intended use and functionality of the connected medical device, these are subject to FDA's regulatory oversight. Examples include mobile apps controlling the delivery of insulin-on-insulin pumps.
- Mobile apps which transform the regular mobile platform into a regulated medical device through attachments, display screens, or sensors. Examples include the attachment of the blood glucose strip reader to a mobile device which functions as a glucose reader, attaching ECG electrodes to a mobile device to measure, store or display ECG signals, and mobile apps that monitor the heart rate variability from a signal produced by a blood pressure monitor.
- Mobile apps which perform patient-specific data analysis and provide diagnosis or treatment recommendations. Examples include software that creates the radiation therapy dosing plan or radiology image processing software.
- Software functions using the sensors or electrodes attached to the mobile platform like accelerometer, microphone, and speaker. Examples include apps to amplify the sounds of internal organs, apps that monitor the effectiveness of CPR, apps used for diagnosing hearing disorders, measuring EKG or EEG, and apps using images of skin lesions to assess the risk of the lesion.
- Software functions that connect to an existing device to control its operation, function, or energy source. Examples include caps in which multiple functional settings of an infusion pump, apps that control gene settings, often implantable neuromuscular stimulators, and caps that are used to calibrate hearing aids and assess characteristics of sound that are produced.
- Software functions used in active patient monitoring to analyze patient-specific medical device data. Examples include software functions that process physiological signals that connect to cardiac monitors for active patient monitoring and software that remotely processes data from fetal heart rate monitors.

Non-FDA regulated medical apps

Mobile Apps may not be regulated by FDA because either they fall under FDA's enforcement discretion or because they are not considered medical devices.

Software under FDA enforcement discretion

FDA does not intend to enforce regulatory requirements (exercise enforcement discretion) as listed under the FD&C Act on software functions that help patients self-manage a disease or condition without providing specific treatment or treatment suggestions or software functions that automate simple tasks for healthcare providers. These may meet the definition of medical devices but are considered low-risk device software functions. Examples of such software functions include:

- Software functions that coach or help patients manage their health by facilitating behavioral change are educating patients about a specific disease and providing recommendations. Examples include mobile apps for patients with hypertension, diabetes, and obesity and provide recommendations about maintaining a healthy weight, managing calories, and prompt medication adherence. These apps are not intended to replace the healthcare provider and can be used by a patient needing oversight by a medical national.
- Software functions that provide contextually relevant information to users engaged in patient care. Examples include software functions that provide clinicians with treatment guidelines based on patient diagnosis and software functions that provide a drug–drug interactions drug – allergy information via an app.
- Software functions that help patients communicate with their medical providers the data or information to images, recorded audio, and video. Examples include apps that use the mobile device's camera for documenting or transmitting photos of a patient's skin lesions to augment the verbal description.
- Software functions that perform simple medical calculations used in clinical practice. Examples include medical calculators for body mass index, the NIH stroke scale, etc.
- Mobile apps which provide behavioral techniques to improve the behavior coping skills of patients with psychiatric conditions.
- Software functions that provide educational information, reminders, or motivational guidance to patients with addiction and smokers trying to quit.
- Mobile apps which alert patients with chronic disease exacerbated by environmental agents. For example, asthmatics or folks with pollen allergies when the environmental conditions become unfavorable.
- Mobile apps which use a checklist of common signs and symptoms to provide a list of medical conditions and advice about consulting a health care provider or facility.
- Software functions that allow the users to make calls or send messages to nurses and first responders.
- Patient portals, which can be used by patients to access their health information.
- Video games which motivate patients to engage in physical or mental activity.
- Mobile apps which provide information about drugs and herbs, including interactions, contraindications, adverse effects, etc.
- Mobile apps which provide information about guidelines for screening, counseling, and preventive activities.
- Mobile apps which enable patients to collect vital data information including blood pressure, heart rate, etc., and share it with the providers.
- Software functions that provide patients with chronic disease tips and reminders about managing their conditions, including physical activity, eating habits, etc.
- Software functions that provide customized messages at the right time to patients with addictive conditions to help reduce their addictions.

Software not considered a medical device

FDA does not regulate medical devices that are not considered medical devices. These are the devices that are "not intended for use in the diagnosis of disease or other conditions, or in the cure, mitigation, treatment, or prevention of disease by facilitating a health professional's assessment of the specific patient, replacing the judgment of clinical personnel, or performing any clinical assessment." Examples of these types of software applications include:

- Medical apps, which are electronic versions of medical books. These could include medical dictionaries, medical textbooks, and encyclopedias of medical specialties.
- Medical apps which are used to train and educate medical professionals. These could include surgical training videos, coaching material for medical examinations, interactive simulations for training in procedures, quizzes or flashcards using images, pictures, graphs, case studies with videos, pictures, or text.
- Medical apps for patient education, including those which are customized for patients or generic applications to improve patient awareness and education. Portals used by healthcare providers to educate patients about their disease, treatment plan, or upcoming procedures, apps that provide information about specific food products contraindicated for patients with certain foods allergies, software functions that match patients with appropriate clinical research studies, medical apps which are directories of a specific type of medical practitioners, advice lines, hotlines.
- Medical apps and software functions which help with healthcare operations. Examples of such applications can include software functions that help to identify the ICD-10 billing codes or are used for insurance claim processing; caps that analyze insurance fraud apps used for creating appointments and reminders; apps that are used for medical billing, coding, collections, payment processing.
- Enable individuals to capture and track health information and get tailored suggestions for improving fitness and wellness. Such apps include those encouraging and leaking weight loss, sleeping; apps that provide calorie counters and meeting planners; apps that provide motivational tips; apps that provide mental games or testing for cognition.
- Software functions that provide access to electronic health records, including viewing, transferring, and downloading the EHR information.
- Software functions that are used to communicate with providers regarding medical conditions, including videoconferencing portals, secured chat apps.
- Software functions that patients use to log where medication usage, exacerbation of disease conditions, measurements like diet, emotional states, exercise, heart rate, weight.
- Software functions that are non-Device-MDDS. Software functions solely intended to transfer, store, convert formats, and display medical device data or results without controlling or altering the functions are parameters of many connected medical devices. Examples of such devices include those which act as a secondary display to a medical device and medical device data on the provider's mobile platform for review.

Wellness apps

General wellness products are defined by FDA's Center for Devices and Radiological Health (CDRH) as products that are intended only for general wellness use and which present a low risk to the safety of users or other persons. The general wellness product is one which "has an intended use that relates to maintaining or encouraging a general state of health or a health activity or the role of a healthy lifestyle with helping to reduce the risk of the impact of certain chronic diseases or conditions and where it is well understood and accepted that healthy lifestyle choices may play an important role in health outcomes for the disease or condition." A low-risk device includes "instrument, apparatus, implement, machine, contrivance, implant, in vitro reagent, or other similar or related article, including any component, part, or accessory, which is ...intended for use in the diagnosis of disease or other conditions, or in the cure, mitigation, treatment, or prevention of disease, in man ... or intended to affect the structure or any function of the body of man..." (FDA. 2019d).

The software functions of low-risk devices generally target areas like weight management through healthy eating or physical activity, relaxation or stress management, sleep improvement, and improving cognitive functions like concentration, multitasking, decision-making, hand-eye coordination, learning capacity, etc. These do not make any reference to any specific disease or medical condition. So, software functions that claim diagnosis or treatment of obesity, treatment of anxiety disorders, and improvement of ambulation in amputees using prosthetics are not considered general wellness claims.

The claim that helps lifestyle choices play a role in a certain disease or condition should be substantiated by peer-reviewed studies in professional journals or statements from professional organizations. Software functions that reference specific diseases or conditions help improve functions associated with the general state of health. For example, they may have an intended use to "promote, track, and/or encourage choices which are part of a healthy lifestyle to help reduce the risk of certain chronic diseases or conditions or, in those individuals who already have certain chronic disease or conditions, improvement in quality of life or reduction in physical limitations due to these chronic diseases or conditions." Such examples could be software functions that coach about healthy sleeping habits and healthy eating practices to reduce the risk of type II diabetes and promote physical activity, which may reduce high blood pressure.

Specific examples of general wellness products which do not fall under the FDA's regulatory oversight can include software apps that play music to reduce stress, software function which records energy expenditure to improve cardiovascular health, and software functions that send reminders to users to avoid the sun when the UV index is higher than normal.

40 NATIONAL EVALUATION SYSTEM FOR HEALTH TECHNOLOGIES

Introduction

In 2016, FDA set up a national evaluation system for health technology (NEST) to generate better evidence for medical device evaluation and regulatory decision-making. Using real-world evidence in applying advanced analytics to data, NEST generates evidence across the total product life cycle of medical devices. The NEST coordinating center (NESTcc) provides governance for the NEST ecosystem, oversees infrastructure building, promotes standards, and monitors progress. It also monitors medical devices using real-world data (RWD), ensuring the quality of the source data and appropriateness of analysis methods (Krucoff MW et al., 2015).

NEST projects

FDA's Center for Devices and radiological health (CDRH) is responsible for the safety and effectiveness of medical devices in the United States. NEST has established partnerships with health providers, health fairs, and professional registries that collect, curate, and analyze RWD from electronic health records, claims, pharmacies, and other sources, including registries. NEST is funding several test cases on multiple topics, including mechanical heart valves, catheter ablation devices, lumbar interbody spinal systems, and microwave ablation devices, and will get technologies. They include technologies, including lower-risk devices designated to the 510 (K) pathway and high-risk devices, which typically require premarket approval (Fleurence RL et al., 2019).

Real-world Evidence Generation

Real-world data is generated at the point-of-care during healthcare related activities. This data includes electronic health records, claims data, billing data, pharmacy data, variables, and data from mobile devices. The real-world data has the potential to generate robust real-world evidence (RWE). FDA defines RWD as "data related to patient health status and/or the delivery of healthcare routinely collected from electronic health records, claims and billing data, data from product and disease registries, patient-generated data including home–use settings, and data gathered from other sources that can inform on health status, such as mobile devices." The applications of real-world evidence include:

- **Label expansion**: Investigate indications for use to support regulatory, coverage, and clinical decisions.
- **Post-market safety**: Determine more accurate device performance, survivorship, and outcomes.
- **Historical control group**: Provide a standard-of-care control group alongside a single-arm trial of a new device.
- **Objective performance criteria**: Scientifically develop OPC for use in pre-market and label change decisions.
- **Academic research**: Obtain quality of care information for device selection and procedural outcomes.
- **Measures creation and validation**: Develop scientifically sound measures to promote quality device assessment.
- **Safety assessments**: Evaluate suspected adverse events and investigate causation.
- **Digital health studies**: Assess the impact of digital tools on patient-reported outcomes and clinical utilization.
- **Patient diversification**: Characterize device safety and effectiveness across a broader demographic population.
- **Patient outcomes**: Characterize device performance regarding outcomes of interest for patients.
- **Device comparison**: Analyze safety and effectiveness across devices on the market.

Demonstration projects

NESTcc has conducted some demonstration projects as proof of concept for evidence generation. Some of the projects include:

- Randomized Controlled Trial Examining Real-World Effectiveness of a Prescription Digital Therapeutic for the Treatment of Insomnia and Depression
- Lung-RADS Assist: Artificial Intelligence Model Verification, Reporting, and Monitoring
- Feasibility Study to Evaluate the use of mHealth as Data Source in Post-Market Surveillance
- Electrophysiology Predictable and Sustainable Implementation of National Registries
- Developing and Implementing Sustainable Real-World Evidence (RWE) Infrastructure for In Vitro Diagnostics (IVDs) Through Systemic Harmonization and Interoperability for Enhancement of Laboratory Data (SHIELD)
- Vascular Implant Surveillance and Interventional Outcomes Network (VISION)
- Use of Linked Implantable Device/Medicare Data to Assess Association Between Device Diagnostics and Patient Outcomes
- Use of EHR-Based Data Network to Support Evidence Generation Across the Total Product Life Cycle (TPLC)
- Use of Real-World Evidence to Characterize Patients with Uncontrolled Hypertension
- Testing the Use of Real-World Data from Three Unique Sources to Expand Indications
- Testing the Feasibility of Registry and Claims Data Linkages
- Effect of Wearable Devices on Patient-Reported Outcomes and Clinical Utilization: A Randomized, Controlled Trial
- Developing Capacity to Conduct Proactive Post Marketing Safety Surveillance of Craniomaxillofacial Distractors Using Electronic Health Record Data

- Creation of a Patient-facing Mobile App for an SUI Surgery Registry
- Assessment of the Value of Electronic Health Records Data for Identifying Implantable Cardiac Lead Failures

NEST is continuing to add to its portfolio of projects. The most recent list is available on its website.

Data Quality Framework (DQF)

The data quality subcommittee of NEST has created a data quality framework for capturing and using data for post-market evaluation of medical devices. The source of data is electronic health records (NESTcc. 2020). The framework has five sections which serve as the guiding principles:

- **Governance**: Governance has been established to limit bias, unethical behavior, and undue influence by stakeholders. Stakeholders include patients, clinicians, researchers, purchasers, payers, industry, hospitals and health systems, policymakers, and training institutions. These principles to allow for reliable conversion of real-world data to generate world evidence include:

    - **Organizational transparency and integrity**: NEST provides guidelines for leadership, data stewardship, patient-centeredness, stakeholder engagement, transparency, and oversight.
    - **Data access, management, linkage and aggregation, and use**: NEST provides guidelines for data quality assurance, data storage, data permission, and data linkage.
    - **Submission, management, review, and acceptance of RWD/RWE requests**: The guidelines are for clear criteria, transparent submission and review process, commitment to possible analysis, efficiency, data use agreement, and commitment to results reporting.

- **Characteristics of data**: The limitation of PHR data is that it is retrospective observational data compared to data acquired through randomized clinical trials. NEST framework provides a structure for designing prospective clinical trials using existing real-world data sources. High-quality data is required to generate actionable insights and regulate resubmission. The accessible data must be high quality, relevant to purpose and context, convertible to evidence, and interpretable (AHRQ. 2014). High-quality data is reliable, complete, accurate, and timely. It helps to define:
    - Study population
    - Specific data elements to check medical device utilization
    - Elements to assess performance and outcomes
    - Sources of data acquisition including identification of potential bias and confounding
    - Development of standardized data sets
    - Experimental methods

- **Data Capture and Transformation**: Ideally, high-quality data should be collected at the point of entry. In reality, most information in an electronic health record is in the form of free text rather than structured data. This presents challenges to data relevance and reliability. The secondary data obtained from EHRs needs to be processed and transformed into common data models to improve reliability. There is a possibility to extract data of interest from unstructured text using natural language processing. Extraction, transformation, and loading are used prior to standardized analysis tools for creating discrete elements, semantic interoperability, and application of clinical data management specifications. RWD to RWE conversion requires robust data streams and quality control.

- **Data Curation**: The data is organized, assessed, and prepared for analysis through an iterative process. The initial step is converting the raw data to "research-ready" data. The next step is to transform the data to the specific study and make it "study ready." A series of data quality checks are performed, including the identification of missing values and outliers and the creation of frequency distributions. Finally, it is checked for conformance, completeness, and plausibility (Kahn MG. 2016).

NESTcc Data Quality Maturity Model (DQMM)

Maturity models organize the capabilities of an organization in a specific domain into a framework by considering culture, process, and/or technology with a goal of continuous improvement (Mettler. 2011). The NESTcc Data Quality Maturity Model (DQMM) targets healthcare organizations' governance, processes, and technologies. The model'smodel's scope is real-world data capture and management and has five stages of maturity (NESTcc. 2020). It has five stages:

Stage 1: **Conceptual**: "Clinical processes capture information primarily in verbose, unstructured documents, not as discrete data; lack of organizational awareness of data utility, no effort to systematically manage health care data; lack of consistent or centralized governance, policies, and/or resources; data not organized centrally; data not available for organizational use and analysis; individual data units are project-oriented or focused on immediate profits."

Stage 2: Reactive: "Able to react to requests for analysis and respond to research requests – but mostly accomplished by manual chart review and abstraction; data management inefficient and expensive, with only sporadic recognition of data utility beyond immediate use; tacit support from leadership regarding need for centralized data governance and management, but only limited allocation of resources; data not available for organizational use and analysis beyond individual requests; individual data units are project-oriented or focused on immediate profits."

Stage 3: Structured: "Clinical systems manage transactional data types (e.g., orders, transactions, laboratory results, medication prescriptions) as discrete data; clinical information (i.e., clinical documentation) largely analog text requiring abstraction into data for clinically focused analytics such as quality, performance measurements, or outcomes assessment. Support from leadership (with resources provided) for centralized data governance and management of transactional data types and limited clinical data types at the enterprise level (e.g., support for ETL among internal systems); commitment to centralized enterprise data governance, management, and curation via managed processes, people, and technologies (e.g., enterprise data warehouse [EDW]); non-administrative queries (clinical questions, research) conducted mostly as one-offs via individual queries, still a moderate-to-high cost to extract data for analysis; able to support a CDM but not done routinely and automatically; data transmission to registries still largely accomplished by manual chart review and abstraction."

Stage 4: Complete: "Granular clinical data based on standardized, semantically interoperable clinical CDEs captured in the processes of care, integrated into those care processes; less than one-quarter of clinical data submitted to registries requires chart abstraction or mañual processing;

UDI captured in the processes of care and available in the supply chain, clinical documentation, EHR, and EDW systems; EDW routinely and systematically represents data externally via various CDMs, including efficient queries, support for a large number of research projects; leadership provides centralized data governance, management, and curation at the enterprise level, ensuring performance and data quality of local units and achieving financial sustainability."

Stage 5: Advanced: "Data linkage and aggregation across systems enabled and open to external queries; semantic interoperability of the vast majority of clinical data accomplished; multiple sources of sustainable funding support for research; engagement of regulatory and industry enterprises with enterprise data; leadership responsible for centralized data governance, management, and curation at the enterprise level; business benefit well understood, with financial sustainability and recognition and participation in initiatives external to the organization."

41 HEALTHCARE AI REGULATION

Artificial intelligence and machine learning can be used for earlier disease detection, faster diagnosis, understanding human physiology, and developing personalized diagnostics and therapeutics. Software based on artificial intelligence and machine learning can improve itself by incorporating real-world feedback and, over time, improve performance by adapting to new information. FDA considers this especially valuable for medical devices. Based on the risk of software as medical advice FDA may assign it to either 510 (k) notification pathway, de novo pathway, or premarket approval application process.

Challenges of regulating AI

Any software modifications that require premarket submission include changes that either introduce any risk or modify an existing risk with the potential to cause major harm, introduce any change to risk controls to prevent significant harm or make any change that significantly affects clinical functionality or performance specifications of the device. This is challenging in artificial intelligence and machine learning-based approaches because continuous learning may modify the software medical device algorithm. In the past, FDA required that the algorithms be locked before marketing, and any algorithm changes required FDA premarket review. A "locked" algorithm is defined as one which produces the same result every time the same input is applied to it, and the result does not change over time with use. However, FDA recognized that some algorithms can adapt over time. The locked algorithms can apply a fixed function to a set of input variables using a lookup table, decision tree methodology, or a complex classifier.

On the other hand, an adaptive algorithm may have different outputs for the same set of inputs over time. The clinical situations could be optimizing performance based on the local patient population, physician preference, and understanding of the disease process. The traditional FDA approach cannot work in these situations. So, FDA has introduced a total product lifecycle (TPLC) regulatory approach to law continual improvement of algorithms. The primary objective is to evolve the regulations with innovation while ensuring patient safety.

Total Product Life Cycle (TPLC) approach

FDA's TPLC approach is a modification to AI/ML Software as a Medical Device (SaMD) approach (FDA. 2019i). FDA is developing Good Machine Learning Practices modeled on Good Clinical Practice and Good Manufacturing Practice. This is based on 4 principles:

- Culture of quality and organizational excellence
- Premarket assurance and safety and effectiveness
- Review of SaMD Pre-Specifications and Algorithm change protocol
- Real-world performance monitoring

These apply to both continuously adaptive algorithms as well as locked algorithms with discrete updates. For models which are already in production, as new data becomes available and is introduced into the deployed model, it will continuously undergo model validation and monitoring through performance evaluation and clinical evaluation. The goals for an AI/ML framework are to allow for frequent iterations, ensure that performance improves over time, and advance the standard of care.

The TPLC approach is a way to assure safety and effectiveness throughout the lifecycle of the AI/ML software product. This proposed approach will only apply to artificial intelligence or machine learning-based software medical devices that require premarket submission and will not apply to those exempt from premarket review. FDA has defined Good Machine Learning Practices (GMLP), which include data management, feature extraction, training, and evaluation, similar to good software engineering practices. These include consistent, clinically relevant, and generalizable data acquisition; separation between training, tuning, and testing data sets; and transparency of the output and the algorithm.

The developers can submit a plan for anticipated modifications to the performance of AI/ML-based SaMD when the premarket review application is submitted. An algorithm change protocol and step-by-step listing of data and procedures to be followed are created so that the modification achieves its goals and the ongoing safety and effectiveness of the device after the modification. A new premarket application is required if the modification is beyond the intended use for which the software medical device was initially authorized. The developers are expected to collect and monitor real-world data and the performance of the device and respond to safety or usability concerns. The developers are expected to provide periodic reporting to FDA through transparent means.

FDA approved AI algorithms

Every year, increasing number of AI algorithms are getting approved. So far, most of these have been in radiology, followed by cardiology. Here is a summary of major and interesting algorithms that have been approved at the time of this writing. Additional details about the algorithms can be obtained from FDA's website (FDA. 2021m):

- Algorithms that help women to track fertility during the month.
- Algorithms that can interpret recorded sounds for diagnosis of heart murmurs.
- Algorithms that can identify, optimize, measure, or flag areas of concern on images obtained through X-Ray, echocardiogram, endoscopy, ultrasound, CT scan, or MRI for stroke, coronary artery disease, retinopathy, mammograms, pulmonary nodules, fractures, ejection fraction, metastases, anatomy reconstruction, gastrointestinal lesions, pneumothorax, COPD, pneumonia, radiation treatment planning.

- Algorithms that aid in the acquisition or optimization of diagnostic signals or images.
- Algorithms that predict decompensation in patients with chronic diseases like respiratory disease.
- Algorithm for evaluation of physiological data to sleep disorders, EKG interpretation, EEG analysis, arrhythmia detection.

Regulation of healthcare AI is rapidly evolving as our understanding of potential and risks gets better. Introduction of transformers and large language models like ChatGPT has catalyzed the AI regulatory landscape including ethical considerations in regulations. A significant amount of development is expected in this domain over the next few years.

42 HITECH ACT AND HEALTH IT CERTIFICATION

Hitech Act of 2009

Health Information Technology for Economic and Clinical Health (HITECH) Act of the American Recovery and Reinvestment Act (ARRA) was a major legislation passed in 2009, which drove the adoption of Electronic Medical Records in the United States. It provided incentives of up to $27 billion for the adoption of Electronic Health Records by physicians and hospitals. Eligible Physicians (EPs) were eligible to receive $44-63k, and Eligible Hospitals (EHs) $2-9M. This spurred EHR adoption, increased revenues of EHR vendors, and spurred startup creation. The providers were required to have EMRs that were certified, and the certification was based on criteria developed by the ONC. This ensured that the adopted EHRs had certain minimum functionality. The products can be certified on each of the ONC certification criteria.

2015 certification edition is the most recent amendment of the Act, and close to 600 products have been certified in this edition. In health tech, regulatory changes are great opportunities to unlock innovation and provide opportunities for startups to develop new products and services. The incentives offered through this legislation were distributed through the provision of "Meaningful Use" of EHR based on certain requirements and criteria. Centers for Medicare & Medicaid Services and the Office of the National Coordinator for Health IT (ONC) oversee the provisions. Five policy priorities that drove the meaningful concept were:

- Improving quality, safety, efficiency, and reducing health disparities
- Engage patients and families in their health
- Improve care coordination
- Improve population and public health
- Ensure adequate privacy and security protection for personal health information

Meaningful use was implemented through three stages:

- Stage 1 created requirements for the electronic capture of clinical data by healthcare providers and the ability to provide patients with electronic patient health records. It focused on standardized formats for healthcare data to track clinical conditions, which can be communicated with other providers, patients, or family members to coordinate clinical care.
- Stage 2 expanded the Stage 1 criteria by incorporating priorities of the National Quality

Strategy. It encouraged using Certified Electronic Health Record Technology (CEHRT) and Health Information Exchange. It focused on the electronic transmission of prescriptions, lab results, and patient care summaries.

- Stage 3 was established from 2017 onwards to improve quality, safety, and efficiency to improve health outcomes. CMS added the requirement of using CEHRT to improve healthcare quality and structure health data exchange. For the reporting period beginning in 2019, the healthcare providers were required to use the 2015 edition of CEHRT. This edition focused on improving interoperability among different health systems. Some of the provisions of this stage included decision support for high-priority conditions, providing patients access to their health data, improving population health, and connecting with Health Information Exchanges.

In April 2018, CMS renamed EHR incentive programs as Promoting Interoperability Program. It introduced Quality Payment Program for Eligible healthcare professionals (EPs) or Eligible Hospitals (EHs) participating in Medical Promoting Interoperability Program. Medicare Access & Chip Re Authorization Program (MACRA) transitioned Meaningful Use into one of the four components of the new Merit-Based Incentive Payment System (MIPS).

Health IT Certification Program

The Health IT Certification Program was launched in 2010 by the Office of the National Coordinator for Health Information Technology to evaluate the health IT products which met the necessary standards, security measures, and implementation specifications under the requirements of the EHR incentive programs. The certification program is based on the International Standards Organization (ISO) principles and the International Electrotechnical Commission (IEC) framework. ONC collaborates with other designated organizations called ONC Authorized Testing Laboratories (ONC—ATLs) and ONC Authorized Certification Bodies (ONC-ACBs) to test and certify health IT systems. ONC develops test methods and approves test tools used to evaluate health IT systems, certifying them as conforming to the certification criteria (e-CFR. 45 CFR § 170.315).

The 2015 edition was created to improve interoperability and enable health information exchange through enhanced certification criteria, standards, and implementation specifications. 2015 edition has 58 certification criteria organized into eight categories (ONC. 2015). Once the health IT product has been tested by an ONC Authorized Testing Laboratory and certified by ONC Authorized Certification Body, these products are listed on the certified health IT product list. Overall, the goal of the 2015 edition is to enable patients to access and send their health information electronically to empower clinicians and hospitals to have tools for clinical processes, care coordination, and quality improvement. The developers assure their customers that the product meets standards. The final rule is available in Title 45 CFR 170.

The health IT vendors must meet the 2015 Edition Base EHR definition and the certification criteria to meet the 2015 Edition Certified EHR Technology status. The certification criteria categories are clinical processes, care coordination, clinical quality measurement, privacy and security, patient engagement, public health, health IT design performance, and electronic exchange.

Clinical processes

The category of clinical processes is related to order entry decision support, safety alerts, and management of clinical data in the EMRs. The sub-categories include:

- **Computerized provider order entry—medications**: Enable a user to record, change, and access medication orders.
- **Computerized provider order entry—laboratory**: Enable a user to record, change, and access laboratory orders.
- **Computerized provider order entry—diagnostic imaging**: Enable a user to record, change, and access diagnostic imaging orders.
- **Drug-drug, drug-allergy interaction checks for CPOE**: During CPOE, provide clinical decision support by indicating drug-disease interactions, drug–allergy interactions, Drug – frequency ranges, drug–dosage ranges, drug-drug interactions, drug–renal function adjustment, drug–laboratory monitoring requirements, and drug – nasal sales adjustments
- **Demographics**: Enable a user to record, change, and access patient demographic data, including race, ethnicity, preferred language, sex, sexual orientation, gender identity, and date of birth. In the inpatient setting, enable a user to record, change, and access the preliminary cause and date of death in the event of mortality.
- **Clinical decision support (CDS)**: CDS provides appropriate knowledge and patient-specific information at the right time to improve care quality and health outcomes. The CDS tools include relevant reference information, clinical guidelines, condition-specific order sets, patient data reports, documentation templates, and alerts. The interventions provided to a user must occur when interacting with technology. CDS must enable user roles, enable interventions, including those based on problem lists, medication lists, allergies and intolerance, laboratory tests, and vital signs. The CDS must be able to identify user diagnostic or therapeutic reference information. For evidence-based decision support, the user must be able to reference relevant clinical guidelines, translation of the clinical guidelines, funding source of the intervention development, and technical implementation and revision dates.
- **Drug formulary and preferred drug list checks**: The provision of automated drug – formulary and preferred drug list allows the clinicians to identify medications approved for prescriptions based on hospital policy as well as patient's health insurance information, thereby reducing unanticipated delays at the time of picking up the prescription as well as reducing prescription costs for the patient. This functionality is achieved through drug formulary checks and preferred drug list checks.
- **Family health history**: Enable a user to record, change, and access a patient's family health history. Capturing the family health history electronically helps in clinical decision support for screening high-risk conditions and allowing for preventive interventions. This information can also be subsequently reused once captured accurately.
- **Patient-specific education resources**: Patient-specific education resources help patients to understand their disease condition and make better decisions about their healthcare. These educational resources could be articles, videos, and images. The patient-specific education resources can be based on data included in the patient's problem list and medication list.
- **Implantable device list**: Integration of Unique Device Identifiers (UDI) in certified health IT products can help track the patients in product recall cases and allows clinicians and researchers to study outcomes associated with a particular device. To achieve this, the product must record Unique Device Identifiers associated with a patient's Implantable Devices. Information captured from UDIs include the lot or batch within which a device was

manufactured, the serial number of a specific device, the expiration date of a specific device, the date a specific device was manufactured, and for an HCT/P regulated as a device, the distinct identification code. UDI helps to describe implantable devices, including GMDN PT Name and associated SNOMED CT® description. The other attributes available are "Brand Name," "Version or Model," "Company Name," "What MRI safety information does the labeling contain?" and "Device required to be labeled as containing natural rubber latex or dry natural rubber (21 CFR 801.437)."

- **Social, psychological, and behavioral data**: The social determinants of health help the clinician to make decisions more appropriate for every patient's unique situation. Per the requirement, the software must enable a user to record, change, and access the following patient social, psychological, and behavioral data: financial resource strain, education, stress, depression, physical activity, alcohol use, social connection and isolation, and exposure to intimate partner violence.

Care Coordination

The Care Coordination category is concerned with care management and care coordination processes and data exchange.

- **Transitions of care**: The transitions of care summary and after summary provide essential information to the receiving care team and ensure healthcare continuity when patients are transferred between different clinical groups. The certification criteria assess a product's ability to create, receive, and with interoperable documents using common content and transport standard that includes necessary health data. The product must send and receive via edge protocol care/referrals summaries, receive and make available the contents of an XDM package, and demonstrate the ability to detect the valid and invalid transition of care/referrals summaries for Continuity of Care Document, Referral Note, and Discharge Summary templates. This includes the ability to parse each document type and detect errors in templates, including invalid vocabulary standards and codes. The system must allow users to be notified of the errors. The system must display the data in a human-readable format. The system must enable the user to create a transition of care/referral summary using Continue of Care Document, Referral Note, and Discharge Summary document templates with relevant data sections, including assessment and plan of treatment, goals of care, health concerns, encounter diagnosis, cognitive status, discharge instructions, patient demographics and other data classes listed in United States Core Data for Interoperability as well as content exchange standards and implementation specifications for exchanging electronic health information of 45 CFR.
- **Clinical information reconciliation and incorporation (CIRI)**: Clinical information reconciliation and incorporation help reduce errors by accurately reconciling and incorporating patient health information sent from external sources. The Consolidated Clinical Document Architecture document is one of the many methods to accomplish this goal. The transition of care/summary document is formatted based on the standards and matched with the correct patient. Reconciliation allows the user to reconcile patients' active medication list, medication allergy list, and problem list.
- **Electronic prescribing**: Electronic prescribing is a fast and efficient method to transmit prescriptions to the pharmacy. Electronic prescribing allows clinicians to send and receive prescription-related messages with the pharmacy, including prescription cancel requests as well as prescription history. The system can automatically store all the prescriptions in the patient's record, preset fields can automatically be populated, and prescriptions can be

transmitted to the patient's pharmacy of preference, which can be updated at every encounter. The system must enable a user to perform all of the following prescription-related electronic transactions: Create new prescriptions (NEWRX), Change prescriptions (RXCHG, CHGRES), Cancel prescriptions (CANRX, CANRES), Refill prescriptions (REFREQ, REFRES), Receive fill status notifications (RXFILL), and Request and receive medication history information (RXHREQ, RXHRES). It must be able to receive and transmit the reason for the prescription using the diagnosis elements in DRU Segment. It must also limit a user's ability to prescribe all oral liquid medications in only metric standard units of mL, and it must always insert leading zeroes before the decimal point for amounts less than one. It must not allow trailing zeroes after a decimal point when a user prescribes medications.

- **Common Clinical Data Set summary record—create and receive**: The system must enable a user to create and receive a transition of care/referral summary formatted in accordance with the standard.
- **Data export**: Data export allows access and ability to export patient data for use in a different health IT system, thereby facilitating the exchange of clinical data and ensuring patient data is included when creating and exporting patient health information. The system must enable a user to set the configuration options when creating the export summary and a set of export summaries for patients whose information is stored in the technology. A user must be able to execute these capabilities at any time the user chooses and without subsequent developer assistance to operate. It must have a mechanism to limit the ability of users who can create export summaries. It must enable a user to create export summaries formatted in accordance with the standard using the CCD template that includes, at a minimum: (A) The Common Clinical Data Set, Encounter diagnoses, (C) Cognitive status, (D) Functional status, (E) The reason for referral; and referring or transitioning provider's name and office contact information, and if relevant, (F) Discharge instructions.
- **Data segmentation for privacy – send and receive**: This criterion confirms that the health IT product is capable of sending and receiving a transition of care summary document with privacy metadata in the document, section, and data element that expresses the data classification and possible re-disclosure restrictions based on the data mapping of the law. Any exchange of sensitive health data via fax or paper-based methods may lead to lower quality of care as well as redundant, unnecessary, or harmful care.
- **Care plan**: A care plan provides a structured format for documenting patient information such as goals, health concerns, health status evaluations, and interventions. It helps to improve coordination of care and incorporates the patient's perspective creating a longitudinal, dynamic, shared care plan. The system must enable a user to record, change, access, create, and receive care plan information per the care plan document template, including the Health Status Evaluations and Outcomes Section and Interventions Section per the defined standard.
- **Electronic Health Information (EHI) export**: EHI export is the ability to export the EHI when requested by the patient or when migrating a patient record to another health system. The system must enable a user to timely create an export file(s) with all of a single patient's electronic health information or all the stored electronic health information that can be stored at the time of certification by the product. The export file(s) created must be electronic and in a computable format. The publicly accessible hyperlink of the export's format must be included with the exported file(s). The documentation of the export format(s) used to support paragraphs must be kept up-to-date.

Clinical Quality Measures (CQM)

The Clinical Quality Measures are "measures of processes, experiences and/or outcomes of patient care, observations or treatment that relate to one or more quality aims for health care such as effective, safe, efficient, patient-centered, equitable, and timely care" (CMS. eHR Incentive Program). The requirements related to CQMs were:

- **Clinical Quality Measures—record and export**: CQMs help improve healthcare quality and are used in quality improvement projects, public reporting, and pay-for-reporting programs. This criterion ensures that the health IT systems can record and export CQM data electronically. The data file must record all the data necessary to calculate each CQM and be formatted in accordance with the standard.
- **Clinical quality measures—import and calculate**: This criterion helps streamline clinician processes by importing CQM data in a standardized format, reducing the need for manual patient data entry. The system must enable a user to import a data file in accordance with the standard for one or multiple patients. A user must be able to execute this capability at any time the user chooses and without subsequent developer assistance to operate. The system must allow the calculation of every clinical quality measure for which it is presented for certification.
- **Clinical quality measures—report**: This criterion supports eCQM reporting using the CMS Quality Reporting Document Architecture (QRDA) Implementation Guides. The system must enable a user to electronically create a data file for transmission of clinical quality measurement data in accordance with the applicable implementation specifications specified by the CMS implementation guides for QRDA., category I, for inpatient measures, and CMS implementation guide for QRDA, category III for ambulatory measures.
- **Clinical quality measures—filter**: The filter functionality supports the ability to query eCQM results using one or a combination of data captured by the certified health IT for quality improvement and quality reporting purposes. It can also help identify health disparities, improve care quality, and support clinicians in delivering more effective care. The system must record the data per the identified standards, where specified. The data includes Taxpayer Identification Number, National Provider Identifier, Provider type, Practice site address, Patient insurance, Patient age, Patient sex, and Patient race and Ethnicity. The system must filter CQM results at the patient and aggregate levels by each one and any combination of the above data and be able to create a data file of the filtered data and display the filtered data results in a human-readable format.

Privacy and security

The requirements related to privacy and security are industry best practices for software systems around authentication, authorization, encryption, and audit controls.

- **Authentication, access control, and authorization**: This certification criterion helps protect patient information, maintain confidentiality and control access to authorized or credentialed users. The system must verify against a unique identifier(s) (e.g., username or number) that a user seeking access to electronic health information is the one claimed, that the user is permitted the type of access to EHI based on this unique identifier(s) and the actions the user is permitted to perform with the technology.
- **Auditable events and tamper-resistance**: This certification criterion requires that the actions related to health information are recorded, including who accessed a patient's information and when, where, and how that access occurred. The health IT system must be

capable of preventing audit logs from being changed, overwritten, or deleted. The technology must be able to record actions related to EHI, record the audit log status, and record the encryption status (enabled or disabled) of EHI locally stored on end-user devices by technology in accordance with the standards unless the technology prevents EHI from being locally stored on end-user devices.

- **Audit report(s)**: The system must enable a user to create an audit report for a specific time and to sort entries in the audit log.
- **Amendments**: The system must enable a user to select the record affected by a patient's request for amendment. For an accepted amendment, it must append the amendment to the affected record or include a link that indicates the amendment's location, and for a denied amendment, at a minimum, append the request and denial of the request.
- **Automatic access time-out**: The provision of automatic access time-out prevents unauthorized users from accessing electronic health information from unattended system devices after a predetermined period of inactivity and requires users to re-enter their credentials to resume or regain access.
- **Emergency access**: The system should be able to permit an identified set of users to access electronic health information during an emergency.
- **End-user device encryption**: This criterion focuses on encryption and the condition of electronic devices if the information continues to be stored on the device and is no longer connected to certified health IT. This protects patient health information if unencrypted annual devices are lost or stolen. The requirements specified in one of the following must be met to satisfy this certification criterion (i) Technology designed to store electronic health information on end-user devices locally must encrypt the electronic health information stored on such devices after use of the technology on those devices stops. Electronic health information that is stored must be encrypted, or (ii) Technology is designed to prevent electronic health information from being locally stored on end-user devices after the use of the technology on those devices stops.
- **Integrity**: Integrating ensures a patient's health record is secured, protected, and contains accurate data. This certification criterion ensures that data is not compromised during electronic exchange by creating a message digest by verifying that the information has not been altered.
- **Trusted connection**: The system can establish a trusted connection by encryption at the message or transport level.
- **Auditing actions on health information**: This certification criterion supports recording auditable events for creating audit logs that help a practice monitor access to patient health information and detect unauthorized access. Actions recorded related to electronic health information must not be capable of being changed, overwritten, or deleted by the technology. Technology must be able to detect whether the audit log has been altered.
- **Accounting of disclosures**: This certification criterion ensures health IT can record disclosures made for treatment, payment, and health care operations. This includes recording data such as the date, time, patient identification, user identification, and a description of disclosures as defined in the Health Insurance Portability and Accountability Act. The system must record disclosures made for treatment, payment, and healthcare operations in accordance with the standard.
- **Encrypt authentication credentials**: This certification criterion requires developers to attest to whether the Health IT encrypts authentication credentials.
- **Multi-factor authentication**: This certification criterion requires developers to attest to whether the Health IT supports multi-factor authentication (MFA). MFA requires users to

authenticate using multiple means to confirm their identity.

Patient engagement

The patient engagement category relates to the role of patients in accessing and sharing their health information.

- **View, download, and transmit to 3rd parties**: This requirement is to enable patients to share their health information with third parties easily. They must be able to view the data classes expressed in the standards in United States Core Data for Interoperability, the Common Clinical Data Set, and the following data classes - assessment and plan of treatment, goals, health concerns, unique device identifiers for a patient's implantable devices, provider's name and office contact information, admission and discharge dates and locations; discharge instructions; and reasons for hospitalization, laboratory test reports, diagnostic image reports. The ambulatory summary, inpatient summary, or inpatient transition of care/referral summary should be downloadable and transmissible in human-readable and CCD formats. Further, the activity history log must be recorded and accessible to the patient.
- **Secure messaging**: The system must allow any user to exchange messages with a patient in a secure manner.
- **Patient health information capture**: The system must identify, record, and access information directly when shared by a patient and link it to that patient's existing health information.

Public health

Public Health use cases including surveillance, registries, and reporting are covered under this category.

- **Transmission to immunization registries**: The system must be able to create immunization information for exchange with other systems according to applicable standards and specifications. Immunization Registries act as standardized and consolidated sources of immunization information for individuals. The system must be able to process patients' requests to access and transmit immunization history and forecast.
- **Transmission to public health agencies—syndromic surveillance**: Syndromic Surveillance Systems are set up to collect data from hospital emergency departments, urgent care clinics, and other clinicians. The system must be able to transmit data to appropriate syndromic public health surveillance infrastructure.
- **Transmission to public health agencies—reportable laboratory tests and values/results**: The system must support electronic reporting of reportable laboratory test results. Laboratories must report any test results they process on "Reportable Diseases" for public health disease surveillance.
- **Transmission to cancer registries**: The system must be able to create information in a standardized format about cancer cases for transmission. Hospital cancer registries report up to cancer registries that may be at the county or state level. The reports are sent to national-level agencies like the Centers for Disease Control and Prevention (CDC), where de-identified data is collected and analyzed.
- **Transmission to public health agencies—electronic case reporting**: The system must be able to match patient visits or encounters to trigger codes that determine which encounters are reportable to public health agencies based on predefined criteria. The transmission of specified data fields is done in the form of a case report.

- **Transmission to public health agencies—antimicrobial use and resistance reporting**: Create antimicrobial use and resistance reporting information for electronic transmission in accordance with the standard.
- **Transmission to public health agencies—health care surveys**: Create health care survey information for electronic transmission in accordance with the standard.

Health IT design and performance

This category contains general requirements related to improving the usability, administration, performance, and integration of the applications.

- **Automated numerator recording**: Clinicians participating in certain Centers for Medicare and Medicaid (CMS) payment programs, such as the Promoting Interoperability Programs and Quality Payment Program, must submit certain percentage-based measures to CMS in compliance with the program's reporting requirements. Automated numerator recording allows the creation of a report or file for easier review of the numerator in the measure and to ensure that the denominator is accurately matched to the constraints defined in the measure.
- **Automated measure calculation**: The system supports recording the numerator, denominator, and percentage of each Promoting Interoperability Program's percentage-based measure.
- **Safety-enhanced design**: This certification criterion requires compliance with specified user-center design requirements, which improve patient safety and prevent errors. The certification criterion states that user-centered design processes must be applied to each capability technology, including:
  - Number of test participants. A minimum of 10 test participants must be used for the testing of each capability;
  - One of the following must be submitted on the user-centered design process used: (A) Name, description, and citation for an industry or federal government standard and (B) Name the processes, provide an outline of the processes, a short description of the processes, and an explanation of the reasons why the use of any of the existing user-centered design standards was impractical;
  - The following information/sections from NISTIR 7742 must be submitted for each capability to which user-centered design processes were applied: (A) Name and product version; date and location of the test; test environment; description of the intended users; and total number of participants; (B) Description of participants, including: sex; age; education; occupation/role; professional experience; computer experience; and product experience; (C) Description of the user tasks that were tested and association of each task to corresponding certification criteria; (D) The specific metrics captured during the testing of each user task performed which must include: Task success (%); task failures (%); task standard deviations (%); task performance time; and user satisfaction rating or an alternative acceptable user satisfaction measure; (E) Test results for each task using the metrics identified above; and (F) Results and data analysis narrative, including: Major test finding; effectiveness; efficiency; satisfaction; and areas for improvement;
  - Submit test scenarios used in summative usability testing.
- **Quality management system**: The developers are required to identify the quality management system used in the development, testing, implementation, and maintenance of certified capabilities of the system. This QMS system is required to be consistent with QMS standards endorsed by the federal government or developed by standards-developing organizations.

- **Accessibility-centered design**: Health IT developers are encouraged to identify the accessibility standards and laws complied with during the development, testing, implementation, and maintenance of certified health IT products.
- **Consolidated CDA creation performance**: The interoperability of transition of care and referral summaries is facilitated by this certification criterion. When organizations exchange transition of care and referral summaries, the data should be accurate and complete. The data file should match the C-CDA standards and conform to the document template and vocabulary requirements.
- **Application access—patient selection**: The "application access" certification criteria are split into three separate certification criteria: A) Patient Selection, B) Data Category Request, and C) All Data Request. The "application access" certification criteria require health IT to demonstrate that it can provide application access to a common set of patient clinical data via an application programming interface (API). The technology must be able to receive a request with sufficient information to uniquely identify a patient and return an ID or other token that can be used by an application to execute requests for that patient's data subsequently. The API must include accompanying documentation that contains, at a minimum: (1) API syntax, function names, required and optional parameters and their data types, return variables and their types/structures, exceptions and exception handling methods and their returns; (2) The software components and configurations that would be necessary for an application to implement in order to be able to successfully interact with the API and process its response(s). The documentation must be available via a publicly accessible hyperlink.
- **Application access—data category or all data request**: The following technical outcome and conditions must be met through the demonstration of an application programming interface:
  - Respond to requests for patient data for each of the individual data categories or all of the data classes specified in the Common Clinical Data Set and return the complete set of data for that data category in a computable format; and
  - Respond to requests for patient data associated with a specific date and requests for patient data within a specified date range.
- **Standardized API for patient and population services**: This certification criterion requires standardized application programming interface (API) access for single patient and population services and is limited to API-enabled "read" services using the HL7® FHIR® standard. The FHIR standard and a set of adopted implementation specifications provide known and consistent technical requirements for software developers. For example, certified health IT must be able to respond to patient data requests and searches, and register, securely connect with, and authenticate an application. The API should respond to requests or search requests for patients' data according to the standard and implementation specification, including the mandatory capabilities described in the "US Core Server Capability Statement." All data elements indicated as "mandatory" and "must support" by the standards and implementation specifications must be supported. It must enable an application to register with the Health IT module's "authorization server" to establish a secure and trusted connection with an application that requests data for system, patient, and user scopes in accordance with the implementation specifications. Authentication and authorization must occur while granting access to patient data in accordance with the implementation specification and the "SMART Backend Services: Authorization Guide" section of the implementation specification. An application storing a client secret must be issued a refresh token valid for three months. Access must be granted to patient data in subsequent connections in accordance with the implementation specification without requiring re-authorization and re-authentication when the application supplies a valid refresh token. An application capable of storing a client secret

must be issued a new refresh token valid for a new period of no less than three months. The Health IT module's authorization server must be able to revoke an authorized application's access at a patient's direction. A Health IT Module's authorization server must be able to receive and validate the tokens it has issued. APIs must include complete accompanying documentation via a publicly accessible hyperlink without any preconditions or additional steps.

Electronic exchange with transport methods and other protocols

The Direct Project is a low-cost, practical, and secure mechanism for exchanging health information electronically instead of relying on archaic, slow, inconvenient, and expensive methods of exchange such as paper and faxes, providing a path to more advanced interoperability. Direct makes it possible for providers to securely email information to other trusted providers or parties, such as specialists, pharmacies, and laboratories. The system sends and receives health information in accordance with the standard, which includes ability to send and receive health information including direct messages as well as delivery notification in accordance with the ONC Applicability Statement for Secure Health Transport, ONC XDR and XDM for direct messaging, including support for both limited and full XDS metadata profiles; and ONC standards for edge protocol methods.

Common clinical data set

The common clinical data set elements are:

- Patient name
- Sex
- Date of birth
- Race
- Ethnicity
- Preferred language
- Smoking status
- Problems
- Medications
- Medication Allergies
- Laboratory tests
- Laboratory value(s)/results(s)
- Vital signs
- Procedures
- Care team member(s)
- Immunizations
- Unique device identifiers
- Assessment and plan of treatment
- Goals
- Health concerns

43 CURES ACT

Introduction

Health Information Technology for Economic and Clinical Health (HITECH) Act, part of the American Recovery and Reinvestment Act of 2009, was enacted on February 17, 2009. HITECH Act amended the Public Health Service Act (PHSA) to improve healthcare quality, safety, and efficiency through health IT and electronic health information (EHI) exchange. The 21st Century Cures Act was signed into law on December 13, 2016, and introduced changes to Public Health Service Act related to Health IT. It has provisions with the aim of providing patients and their healthcare providers secure access to health information by developing standardized application programming interfaces so patients can access their structured and unstructured health information at no cost. It established Health Information Technology Advisory Committee to advise and recommend all health IT matters to the National Coordinator.

On May 1, 2020, the Office of the National Coordinator for Health Information Technology (ONC). Department of Health and Human Services (HHS) released the Final Rule for 21st Century Cures Act: Interoperability, Information Blocking, and the ONC Health IT Certification Program (ONC. 21st Century Cures Act. 2020). In Title IV of the Cures Act, provisions to advance interoperability, support access, exchange, and use of electronic health information, and address occurrences of information blocking are under ONC's purview. It also incorporated Executive Order 13813 by the President to increase market competition, lower barriers to entry and, prevent abuses of market power, improve access and quality of information available to the patients. The rule went into effect on June 30, 2020. The ultimate goals of this regulation were:

- Promote health care cost and outcome transparency
- Enable competition in medical care
- Provide healthcare data access to smartphone apps
- Foster innovation
- Prohibit blocking of sharing of patient data
- Improve patient safety while protecting IP of health IT companies.

Updates to 2015 Edition Certification criteria

ONC also updated the 2015 Edition Certification criteria. Some of the changes were:

- "Common Clinical Data Set" definition was replaced with United State Core Data Interoperability (USCDI) standard.
- Standards Version Advancement Process (SVAP) was proposed, which allows software developers to certify their products to newer versions of USCDI.
- HL7 Quality Reporting Document Architecture was replaced with CMS QRDA Implementation Guide.
- Capability to export entire Electronic Health Information stored in a certified health IT system.
- Standardized API for patient and population service supports services for single patient as well as multiple patients using Fast Healthcare Interoperability Resource (FHIR) standard Release 4.
- Requirement of transparency attestations from developers of certified health IT were incorporated to ensure support of encrypting authentication credentials and/or multi-factor authentication (MFA).
- Records retention included the "life of particular edition" and three years after the retirement of an edition.
- Prohibition of health IT developer, as a Condition and Maintenance of Certification requirement under the Program, from any activity that is Information Blocking defined by section 3022(a) of the PHSA, any activity that may inhibit appropriate exchange access and use of EHI, restriction of communications about the performance of developers' business practices. Taking screenshots and videos could be limited.
- Exceptions to the information blocking requirements.
- Civil and Monetary Penalties.
- Requirement for Health IT developers to publish APIs that allow "Health Information from such technology to be accessed, exchanged, and used without special effort through the use of APIs or successor technology or standards as provided for under applicable law." Conditions of Certification requirements in section 4002 of the Cures Act require developers must, through API, "provide access to all data elements of a patient's electronic health record to the extent permissible under applicable privacy laws."
- Real-World Testing: "Health IT developers must successfully test the real world use of health IT for interoperability in the type(s) of setting(s) in which such technology will be marketed."
  - Other changes to the 2015 Edition included adding electronic health information export provisions, encryption of authentication credentials, multi-factor authentication, standardized API for patient and population services, and United States Core Data for Interoperability.

Definitions

Some salient definitions from the Cures Act are shared below (ONC. 21st Century Cures Act. 2020):

- **Information blocking**: A practice likely to interfere with access, exchange, or use of electronic health information identified by USCDI till May 2, 2022, and which is likely to interfere with or prevent or materially discourage access, exchange, or use of electronic health information. CMS added exceptions to the information blocking clause in its May 1, 2020 update. These exceptions are around 1) preventing patient harm, 2) protecting patient privacy, protecting the security of Electronic Health Information, 3) events that are out of control due to environmental, technical, or financial reasons, 4) temporary disruptions due to planned or unplanned maintenance activities, security related interventions, performance enhancements or preventing harm to the patient, 5) allowed criteria for charging fees for providing access, exchange or use of electronic health information, 6) permitted licensing, royalty and non-disclosure requirements.

- **API Information Source**: API Information Source organization deploys the certified API technology. Usually this includes providers and hospitals
- **API User**: A person or entity that creates or uses software applications that interact with the "certified API Developer" and deployed by an "API Information source"
- **Certified API developer**: Certified API developer creates certified API technology which is certified to provide application access through APIs for patient and population data
- **Designated record set**: Destinated record set means a group of records maintained by or for a covered entity that is (i) The medical records and billing records about individuals maintained by or for a covered health care provider; (ii) The enrollment, payment, claims adjudication, and case or medical management record systems maintained by or for a health plan; or (iii) Used, in whole or in part, by or for the covered entity to make decisions about individuals. The term record means any item, collection, or grouping of information that includes protected health information and is maintained, collected, used, or disseminated by or for a covered entity.
- **Electronic Health Information (EHI)**: Electronically protected health information which is individually identifiable health information, including genetic information that is created or received by a health care provider, health plan, public health authority, employer, life insurer, school or university, or health care clearinghouse; and relates to past, present, or future physical or mental health or condition of an individual; the provision of health care to an individual; or the past, present, or future payment for the provision of health care to an individual, that is transmitted by electronic media, maintained in electronic media or transmitted or maintained in any other form or medium.
- **Health IT Developer of certified health IT**: Individual or an entity, other than a health care provider that self-develops health IT for its own use, that develops or offers health information technology and which has one or more Health IT Modules certified under a program for the voluntary certification of health information technology that is kept or recognized by the National Coordinator pursuant to ONC Health IT Certification Program.

Conditions of Certification

Cures Act established Conditions of Certification requirements for the ONC Health IT Certification Program. These conditions apply to developer practices associated with certified API technology. Certified API technology must support the United States Core Data for Interoperability standard (USCDI). The provision of API was one of the focus areas of the Cures Act. The API conditions of certification requirements were:

- **Transparency Conditions**: Certified API developers should provide public access to the business and technical documentation necessary to interact with their certified API technology.
- **Fees Conditions:** Health IT developers that create certified API technology can charge fees to healthcare organizations that deploy certified API technology for development,

deployment, upgrade, usage, value-added services related to certified API technology.

- **Openness and Pro-Competitive Conditions**: Certified API developers must grant healthcare organizations (API Information sources) ability to permit persons and entities that create or use software applications that interact with "certified API technology" without discrimination and ensure open and competitive environment.

Information Blocking

ONC has taken a strong stance against information blocking and has modified the conditions of certification requirement and required the following from Health IT vendors:

- **Assurances**: Provide assurances on and after November 2, 2020, that Health IT vendors will not engage in information blocking conform to certification criteria, restrict access to the certified capabilities, and allow health information export
- **Communication**: Health IT developers cannot prohibit or restrict any communication regarding the usability, interoperability, security, data exchange capability, and usage of the technology. The rule allows some communications to be restricted by the developer. These include internal communications of employees or contractors, developers' IP, non-user-facing tech, screenshots and video, and premarket testing information.
- **API**: Developers must provide public APIs and allow EHI to be accessed, exchanged, and used without special effort through APIs. The business and technical documentation should be publicly made available, including terms and conditions (fees, restrictions, limitations, obligations), which are required to develop, distribute, and deploy software to interact with API to access, exchange, and use certified API technology and authenticate users. Certified API developers cannot impose fees except to cover reasonable costs for the development, deployment, upgrade, usage, and maintenance of API tech or value-added services. Developers cannot discriminate against direct or indirect competitors by charging higher fees, limiting access, or providing different terms or services, creating disruptions. Further, API developers cannot be contingent on providing access to API on license fees, royalty, revenue sharing, non-compete clause, IP ownership, require reciprocity, special certification, and testing requirements.
- **Real-world testing**: Health IT developer must successfully test the real-world use of the Health IT modules for interoperability.
- **Attestations**: The health IT developer must attest to compliance with the Conditions and Maintenance of Certification requirements relevant to their product modules.

ONC also updated the maintenance of certification requirement with expectations that the health IT developers provide the following:

- **Assurances**: Retain all records necessary to demonstrate compliance with certification program for 10 years.
- **Communication**: Provide annual notice to all customers about any provisions of certification requirement that it is not able to fulfil. Further, the health IT developer should not sign new contracts or enforce any contracts that do not satisfy condition of certification requirement.
- **API**: Certified IT developers are allowed to verify authenticity of API users in a way which is objective and standard and once verified, allow access within 5 business days. They must also publicly publish URLs where customers, API users or patients can access their eHI at no

charge.

- **Real world testing**:
  - o Plan submission: Health IT developer must annually submit a real world testing plan covering each of the certified health IT modules. ONC-ACB will publicly make this plan available by December 15th of every year. The plan should address real world testing conducted in the calendar year following the plan submission. The plan should cover the testing method to demonstrate real world interoperability and conformance to certification criterion requirements, incorporate scenario based and use-case focused testing, care settings that will be tested and the rationale, milestones, expected outcomes, metrics, justification of the approach.
  - o Results reporting: For any resting conducted in the previous year, submit results report by March 15 of the calendar year. Any non-conformity to the plan must be reported in 30 days.
  - o Updates: Health IT developer must update their certified Health IT to be compliant with criteria in 2015 edition by May 2, 2022 including USCDI, electronic prescribing, security tags, ASTM.
  - o Standards Version Advancement Process: Regulations provide recommendations to developers about voluntarily getting certified on the newer versions of standards and implementation specifications and requirements about providing updates to affected customers about the changes.
  - **Attestations**: The Health IT developer must provide ongoing attestations semiannually for all the Health IT modules that are certified under Conditions and Maintenance of requirements.

44 MACRA & MIPS

Introduction

Medicare Access and CHIP Re-authorization Act of 2015 changed how Medicare reimbursed providers, increased funding, and extended the Children's Health Insurance Program (CHIP). It also provided incentives for using health information technology by physicians and other providers (Congress.gov. 2015). MACRA replaced the Sustainable Growth Rate formula with Quality Payment Program (QPP) to reward clinicians for providing higher-value care. It provided two tracks that the providers could choose (CMS Quality Payment Program. APMs Overview).

Merit Based Incentive Program for eligible physicians (MIPS)

MACRA introduced a Merit-Based Incentive Program (MIPS) for eligible physicians (CMS. MACRA). Providers can participate in MIPS either as an individual or as a group. With MIPS, providers can earn performance-based payment adjustments for services provided to Medicare patients. Providers are eligible for MIPS if they are eligible clinicians and have a sufficient volume of services and charges. MIPS consolidated multiple quality programs into one program. These programs were

- Value Based Payment Modifier (VBM)
- Physician Quality Reporting Program (PQRS)
- Medicare EHR Incentive Program (also known as Meaningful Use)

MIPS eligible clinicians

MIPS eligible clinicians bill for Medicare Part B or Critical Access Hospital (CAH) Method II payments assigned to the CAH and meet the low volume threshold (LVT). The eligible providers include:

- Physicians (MD/DO, DDS, DDM, DPM, Optometrists, and Chiropractors)
- Physician assistants
- Nurse practitioners

- Clinical nurse specialists
- Certified registered nurse anesthetists
- Physical or occupational therapists
- Speech-language pathologists
- Audiologists
- Nurse midwives
- Clinical psychologists
- Dieticians/nutritional professionals

MIPS exempted providers

- Newly enrolled in Medicare
- Clinicians meeting a low-volume threshold ($90,000 or less in billed Medicare Part B allowed charges AND provide care for 200 or fewer Medicare Part-B enrolled patients in one year)
- Clinicians significantly participating in alternative payment models

MIPS reporting areas

MIPS has four reporting areas, each having a different number of points. The score is determined by assessing a MIPS-eligible clinician's applicable measures and activities for each performance category. The MIPS-eligible clinician's final score determines their payment adjustment. CMS applies adjustments to Medicare reimbursements for certain services based on participation and performance in MIPS. The payment is calculated based on each MIPS-eligible clinician's final score and sent to the practice that the clinician is a part of.

- **Quality:** There are six measures of performance replacing PQRS. MIPS recommended using Certified EHR Technology to capture clinical data, calculate clinical quality measures and submit quality measure reports electronically. This helps to get electronic reporting bonuses and improve reimbursements (CMS. Quality Payment Program. Quality Performance Category: Traditional MIPS Requirements). In 2020, this contributed to 45% of the final score. The six collection types for quality measures are:
    - Electronic Clinical Quality Measures (eCQMs)
    - MIPS Clinical Quality Measures (CQMs)
    - Qualified Clinical Data Registry (QCDR) Measures
    - Medicare Part B claims measures
    - CMS Web Interface measures
    - Consumer Assessment of Healthcare Providers and Systems (CAHPS) for MIPS survey

- **Promoting Interoperability (PI):** This category promotes patient engagement and electronic exchange of information using CEHRT to report ACI measures (with some exceptions). In 2020, PI contributed 25% to the final score (with some exceptions). Providers must submit data for each of the following categories:
    - Protect Patient Health Information via Security Risk Analysis
    - Electronic prescribing including use of Prescription Drug Monitoring Program
    - Health Information Exchange supporting electronic referral loops by receiving and incorporating health information
    - Provide Patient Electronic Access to their Health Information

- Public Health and Clinical Data Exchange: Send a Summary of Care for electronically submitting clinical cases, and reporting to immunization registry, clinical data registry, public health registry, and syndromic surveillance.

- **Improvement Activities (IA):** Providers can choose the type of activities to improve the clinical practice. These activities are submitted by attestation on the CMS Quality Payment Program website, a qualified clinical data registry, a qualified registry, or from the CEHRT. The IA measures are weighted at 15% of the final score and require upto 4 improvement activities to be performed out of the following categories:
  - Achieving Health Equity
  - Behavioral and Mental Health
  - Beneficiary Engagement
  - Care Coordination
  - Emergency Preparedness and Response
  - Expanded Practice Access
  - Patient Safety and Practice Assessment
  - Population Management

- **Cost:** This category can count for 15% of the final score for 2020. This allocation can change depending on the case volumes in cost measures. If the case volumes are insufficient, the 15% allocated to this category is added to the Quality category. CMS automatically calculates cost measure performance from submitted Medicare Part A and B claims, so no separate data is submitted for Cost. Cost measures include
  - Total per capita cost
  - Medicare spending per beneficiary clinician
  - Episode based measures

Advanced Alternative Payment Models (APMs)

CMS provides added incentive payments for APMs related to a specific clinical condition, care episode, or population. These apply to providers who are either Medical Homes or have arrangements where they bear significant financial risk. Providers must use CEHRT and receive payments for covered professional services based on quality measures. APM could be an Accountable Care Organization (HealthIT.gov. Advanced Alternative Payment Model). Eligible clinicians and groups which select advanced APMs do not need to participate in MIPS. The broad categories of APMs are:

- Care Coordination
- Quality Measurement
- Improving Patient/Clinician Relationships

Advanced APM track offers a 5% incentive for achieving threshold levels of payments or patients. Those providers meeting these thresholds are excluded from the MIPS reporting requirements and payment adjustment. Qualifying APM participant or entity represents one or more providers with individual NPIs under a single TIN which receives at least 50% of Medicare Part B payments or sees at least 35% of Medicare patients through an Advanced APM entity during a 12-month duration in a 2-year eligibility assessment period. 75% of practices within the Advanced APM entity need to use CEHRT. There are other categories of providers besides physicians, including PT, OT, SLP, or Audiologists in certain conditions.

The Advanced APM models include:

- Bundled Payments for Care Improvement
- Comprehensive ESRD Care
- Comprehensive Primary Care Plus
- Medicare Accountable Care Organization Model
- Medical Shared Savings Program
- Next Generation ACO Model
- Oncology Care Model
- Comprehensive Care for Joint Replacement Payment Model
- Vermont Medicare ACO Initiative
- Comprehensive ESRD Care Model
- Maryland All-Payer Model
- Maryland Total Cost of Care Model

45 TRUSTED EXCHANGE FRAMEWORK AND COMMON AGREEMENT

The US Department of Health and Human Services has developed the Trusted Exchange Framework and Common Agreement TM (TEFCATM) to address one of the 21st Century Cures Act requirements. The goal of TEFCA is to "establish a universal policy and technical floor for nationwide interoperability, simplify connectivity for organizations to securely exchange information to improve patient care, enhance the welfare of populations, generate health care value; and enable individuals to gather their health care information" (Tripathi M et al. 2022). TEFCA is based on the "network-of-networks" concept and allows individuals and organizations to securely connect with an electronic health information exchange for treatment, payment, health care operations, public health, and government benefits.

TEFCA enables the seamless exchange of health information among individuals, providers, payers, health information exchanges, pharmacies, laboratories, technology companies, and government agencies, including public health departments, to improve clinical treatment and continuity of care, case management, care coordination, adverse event monitoring, health care operations and payments, population health, epidemiological surveillance, and tracking infectious diseases. Individuals and organizations can exchange health information by connecting to the network through Qualified Health Information Networks (QHINTM). TEFCA supports HL7 FHIR-based data exchange for patient discovery, authentication, authorization, information query, and clinical data exchange.

TEFCA Organizations

Recognized Coordinating Entity (RCE)

RCE has been created to develop, update, complement, and maintain the Common Agreement and administer and monitor the Qualified Health Information Network. Sequoia Project is a Recognized Coordinating Entity (RCE) authorized by the Office of the National Coordinator for Health Information Technology to work with Qualified Health Information Networks (QHIN) to support TEFCA.

Qualified Health Information Networks (QHIN)

TEFCA is based on centralized information networks, which serve as connection points called Qualified Health Information Networks (QHINs). QHINs are Health Information Networks (HINs) that have signed the Common Agreement with the RCE and agree to a common set of principles, terms, and conditions called the Common Agreement. QHINs also adhere to functional and technical requirements as specified in the QHIN Technical Framework (QTF) to enable nationwide exchange of electronic health information (EHI). The QHIN plays a role in patient identity resolution using a centralized master patient indexing service and enables efficient QHIN-to-QHIN data exchange by keeping location records, directories, errors, and performance metrics.

QHINs can select appropriate standards and approaches based on their requirements. QHIN participants may be required to adhere to some of the principles of the Common Agreement. The QHIN participant or sub-participants can play one of the following roles:

- Query Source
- Initiating Gateway
- Initiating QHIN Directory
- Responding QHIN Directory
- Responding Gateway
- Responding Source(s)

Participants

Participants are entities that connect to a QHIN for data exchange by signing a participant-QHIN agreement. QHINs can connect with other QHINs on behalf of the participant to exchange information or messages. A participant could include a Health Information Network, a health system or a hospital, a health IT developer, a payer, or a federal agency.

Subparticipants

Subparticipants are entities that use the services of Participants to exchange information by entering into a Participant-Subparticipant agreement or a Downstream Subparticipant Agreement. A Subparticipant could be a health system, a health IT developer, a payer, or a federal agency.

Individuals

Individuals are users who could be patients, health plan members, or patient representatives and are generally the subject of EHI. Individuals can access their records from any internet-connected device through web interfaces or mobile applications that connect them with a Participant or a Subparticipant.

TEFCA Components

TEFCA is made of three main components

Common Agreement

The Common Agreement for Nationwide Health Information Interoperability is the agreement between any entity interested in being a Qualified Health Information Network and Sequoia Project. (ONC. Common Agreement for Nationwide Health Information Interoperability. 2022). The Common Agreement creates the governance and infrastructure for the sharing of information. It includes change management, confidentiality, accountability, privacy, security, data exchange, and contract administration clauses.

QHIN Technical Framework (QTF)

QHIN Technical Framework (QTF) provides the technical and functional requirements for QHIN interoperability. At a high level, it enables two features – a) query and b) message delivery. The technical framework for QHIN implementation is available on the Sequoia Project website (https://rce.sequoiaproject.org/). It uses many existing standards discussed in the chapter on Health Information Exchange. For example, the standards for query and message delivery are (ONC. QTF, 2022):

- Secure Channel: IETF TLS 1.2 w/ BCP-195 or IETF TLS 1.3 w/BCP-195
- Mutual Authentication: IETF TLS 1.2 w/ BCP-195 or IETF TLS 1.3 w/BCP-195, OAuth 2.0
- User Authentication, Authorization & Exchange Purpose: IHE XUA
- Authorization & Exchange Purpose: IHE XUA
- Query for Patients: IHE XCPD
- Document Query and Retrieve: IHE XCA
- Auditing: IHE ATNA
- Message Delivery: IHE XCDR

Trusted Exchange Framework (TEF)

Trust Exchange Framework (TEF) is a set of "non-binding, foundational principles for trust policies and practices that can help facilitate exchange among health information networks (HINs) (ONC. The Trusted Exchange Framework. 2022). TEF standardizes the connectivity services to support QHIN query and message delivery. The seven principles are reproduced from the source:

- **Standardization**: HINs should prioritize federally recognized and industry-recognized technical standards, policies, best practices, and procedures.
- **Openness and Transparency**: HINs should conduct activities openly and transparently, wherever possible.
- **Cooperation and Non-Discrimination**: HINs should collaborate with stakeholders across the continuum of care to electronically exchange digital health information, even when a stakeholder may be a business competitor.
- **Privacy, Security, and Safety**: HINs should exchange digital health information in a manner that supports privacy; ensures data confidentiality, integrity, and availability; and promotes patient safety.
- **Access**: HINs should ensure that Individuals and their authorized caregivers have easy access

to their digital health information and understand how it has been used or disclosed.

- **Equity**: HINs should consider the impacts of interoperability on different populations throughout the activity.
- **Public Health**: HINs should support public health authorities and population-level use cases to enable the development of a learning health system that improves the health of the population and lowers the cost of care.

TEF uses IHE IT1 technical framework profiles (IHE. 2020). Briefly, the following requirements are defined:

- Connectivity and remediation: Requirements for QHINs to connect with other QHINs and Participants
- Certificates policy: Requirements for using digital certificates for authentication, encryption, and signing
- Secure channel: Requirements for providing Transport Level Security (TLS) for all transactions
- Mutual authentication: Requirements for authentication of QHIN-to-QHIN and QHIN-to-Participant communication
- User authentication: Requirements for establishing authentication workflow through the multilayer hierarchy involving QHINs and Subparticipants
- Authorization & exchange purpose: Requirements for verifying network access eligibility of entities using SAML
- Patient discovery query: Requirements for searching patients from QHIN-to-QHIN by matching patient identifiers.
- Document query and retrieve: Requirements for querying, locating, and retrieving patient records and documents
- Message delivery: Requirements to enable users to send patient data and route messages using push capabilities
- Patient identity resolution: Requirements for matching patients across multiple providers using the master patient index
- Record location: Requirements to reliably record patient records across networks
- Directory services: Requirements to maintain and manage provider directories
- Auditing: Requirements to maintain records of activities and transactions supported by connectivity services
- Error handling: Requirements to generate, send, translate, receive, and respond to errors
- Constraints for query or message source(s) and responding source(s): Requirements for correct validation of the query or message service or responding source
- Testing procedure supporting requirements: Requirements for testing on an ongoing basis
- Performance measures: Requirements for data submission to RCE for monitoring of QHIN performance

Current Status

As of 2024, the designated QHINs included eHealth Exchange, Epic Nexus, Health Gorilla, Konza National Network, MedAllies, Kno2, Commonwell Health Alliance, and Surescripts. TEFCA is supporting the following applications

- Government benefits determination
- Healthcare operations
- Individual access service
- Healthcare payments
- Public health
- Treatment

Individual Access Service providers either have their own direct-to-consumer applications or they work with other consumer application creators. A typical application of this scenario is when an individual needs to get her records from a provider (Sequoia Project. TEFCA User's Guide. 2023). The individual signs up with a consumer app which is a Participant connected to a QHIN and can verify the individual's identity. The individual then uses a consumer app to make an Individual Access Services Request via a QHIN which then sends a QHIN Query to QHINs. The QHINs query their Participants and Sub-Participants. For example, a Participant could be a hospital, and Sub-Participant could be a hospital-affiliated medical practice. If a medical record is found, they are returned to the requesting QHIN, which shares them with the consumer app. The consumer apps must provide security and privacy protections applicable under HIPAA regulation. They need to obtain consent from individuals about how their information will be accessed, used, exchanged, or disclosed.

46 HEALTH INSURANCE PORTABILITY AND ACCOUNTABILITY ACT

Health Insurance Portability and Accountability Act of 1996 (HIPAA) provided provisions to the U.S. Department of Health & Human Services (HHS) to adopt national standards for electronic healthcare transactions and code sets, unique health identifiers, and security. The subsequent rules published by HHS were Privacy, Security, Enforcement, and Omnibus rules. HIPAA Administrative Simplification Rules administered and enforced by the Centers for Medicare & Medicaid Services include Transactions and Code Sets Standards, Employer Identifier Standard, and National Provider Identifier Standard.

The regulation has General, Administrative, Organization, Security, and Privacy requirements.

General Requirements

HIPAA is applicable to covered entities, including health plans and health care providers which transmits any health information in electronic form, healthcare clearinghouses (e.g., billing and medical claim services, repricing company, health information management system, community health information systems, and value-added networks which process health information), and business associates.

Business Associate

The concept of 'Business Associate' is important under HIPAA. A Business Associate is a person, corporation, professional association, or other entity representing the covered entity or any organized healthcare arrangement requiring disclosure of protected health information, who a) creates, receives, maintains, or transmits protected health information for a function or activity covered under HIPAA including claims processing or administration, data analysis, utilization review, quality assurance, patient safety activities, billing, benefit management, practice management, repricing; b) provides legal, actuarial, accounting, consulting, data aggregation, management, administrative, accreditation, or financial services. Covered entities and business associates must a) Ensure confidentiality, integrity, and availability of all electronic PHI that they create, receive, maintain, or transmit; b) Protect against any reasonably anticipated threats, hazards to the security or integrity of such information, misuse or disclosures that are not permitted; c) Compliance by the workforce with the provisions of the HIPAA regulation; and d) Compliance with all applicable security standards.

Business associate includes health information organization, e-prescribing gateway, or other person that provides data transmission services with respect to protected health information to a covered entity, a person that offers personal health record to one or more individuals on behalf of a covered entity, a subcontractor that creates, receives, maintains, or transmits protected health information on behalf of a business associate.

Types of Health Information under HIPAA

- 'Health information' means any information that relates to the past, present, or future physical or mental health or condition of an individual; the provision of healthcare to an individual; or the past, present, or future payment for the provision of healthcare to an individual that is created or received by a healthcare provider, health plan, public health authority, employer, life insurer, school or university, or a healthcare clearing house.
- 'Protected health information' is any individually identifiable information transmitted or maintained electronically or through any other medium except for some education and employment records.
- 'Individually identifiable health information' is the subset of health information collected from an individual that is created or received by a healthcare provider, health plan, employer, or healthcare clearinghouse and relates to the past, present, or future physical or mental health or condition of an individual; the provision of healthcare to an individual; or the past, present, or future payment for the provision of healthcare to an individual and that identifies the individual or can be used to identify the individual.

Administrative Requirements

Healthcare providers must identify themselves using National Provider Identifier on all standard transactions that it conducts, either directly or through business associates, where their healthcare provider identifier is required. A covered entity must use a Health Plan Identifier (HPID) to identify a health plan or a business associate conducting standard transactions on a health plan's behalf in a transaction applicable under HIPAA. Entities not eligible to obtain NPI or HPID can obtain an Other Entity Identifier (OEID) from Enumeration System to identify themselves on all covered transactions they need to be identified. If a covered entity uses a business associate to conduct a transaction covered by HIPAA on behalf of the covered entity, the business associate and its agents and subcontractors must comply with these regulations' requirements. If covered entities or health plans conduct a transaction with each other, they must ensure that the transactions comply with the applicable standard and associated operating rules adopted in the HIPAA regulation. Exemptions can be sought under specific circumstances from HHS. There are some other important concepts related to covered entities:

- **Personnel designation**: A covered entity must designate a privacy official responsible for the development and implementation of the policies and procedures of the entity and a contact person or office responsible for receiving complaints and providing further information.
- **Training**: A covered entity must provide training to each member of the covered entity's workforce and, after that, to each new member of the workforce within a reasonable period after the person joins the covered entity's workforce and to each member of the covered entity's workforce whose functions are affected by a material change in the policies or

procedures required by HIPAA Privacy subpart within a reasonable time after the material change becomes effective. The covered entity must document that the training has been provided.

- **Safeguards**: A covered entity must reasonably safeguard protected health information from any intentional or unintentional use or disclosure that violates the standards, implementation specifications, or other requirements of the HIPAA Privacy subpart. A covered entity must reasonably safeguard protected health information to limit incidental uses or disclosures made according to an otherwise permitted or required use or disclosure.
- **Complaints to the covered entity**: A covered entity must provide a process for individuals to make complaints concerning the covered entity's policies and procedures, compliance with such policies and procedures, or the HIPAA Privacy subpart requirements. A covered entity must document all complaints received, and their disposition, if any.
- **Sanctions**: A covered entity must have and apply appropriate sanctions against members of its workforce who fail to comply with the privacy policies and procedures of the covered entity or the requirements of this subpart or subpart D of this part. This standard does not apply to a member of the covered entity's workforce for actions covered by, and that meet the conditions of disclosures by whistleblowers and workforce member crime victims. A covered entity must document the sanctions that are applied, if any.
- **Mitigation**: A covered entity must mitigate any harmful effect known to the covered entity of the use or disclosure of protected health information in violation of its policies and procedures or the requirements of this subpart by the covered entity or its business associate.
- **Refraining from intimidating or retaliatory acts**: A covered entity may not intimidate, threaten, coerce, discriminate against, or take other retaliatory action against any individual for the exercise by the individual of any right established, or for participation in any process provided for, by this subpart or subpart D of this part, including the filing of a complaint under this section; and must refrain from intimidation and retaliation.
- **Waiver of rights**: A covered entity may not require individuals to waive their rights as a condition of the provision of treatment, payment, enrollment in a health plan, or eligibility for benefits.
- **Policies and procedures**: A covered entity must implement policies and procedures concerning protected health information designed to comply with the standards, implementation specifications, or other requirements of HIPAA Privacy and Subpart D (notification of breach). The policies and procedures must be reasonably designed, considering the size and the type of activities related to protected health information undertaken by a covered entity to ensure such compliance. Appropriate procedures must be followed in case of changes in law, changes to policies and procedures, or changes to privacy practices.
- **Group health plans**: A group health plan is not subject to the Administrative requirements as outlined above if the group health plan provides health benefits solely through an insurance contract with a health insurance issuer or an HMO; and the group health plan does not create or receive protected health information, except for summary health information, information on whether the individual is participating in the group health plan, or is enrolled in or has disenrolled from a health insurance issuer or HMO offered by the plan.

Healthcare transactions

Covered entities must use medical and non-medical data code sets in the transactions between healthcare systems. These include:

- International Classification of Diseases, 10th Revision, Clinical Modification (ICD-10-CM) to represent Diseases, Injuries, Impairments, Other health problems and their manifestations, causes of injury, disease, impairment, or other health problems, procedures or actions taken for prevention, diagnosis, treatment, and management
- National Drug Codes (NDC) for Drugs and Biologics
- Code on Dental Procedures and Nomenclature
- Health Care Financing Administration Common Procedure Coding System (HCPCS) and Current Procedural Terminology (CPT) for physician services, physical and occupational therapy services, radiologic procedures, clinical laboratory tests, other medical diagnostic procedures, hearing and vision services, transportation services including ambulance
- Health Care Financing Administration Common Procedure Coding System for medical supplies, orthotic and prosthetic devices, durable medical equipment

Healthcare claim encounter information transaction

'Healthcare claims or equivalent encounter information transaction' is the transmission of encounter information or a request to obtain payment and the necessary accompanying information from a healthcare provider to a health plan. The standards used to transmit this information are:

- **Retail pharmacy drugs claims**: National Council for Prescription Drug Programs (NCPDP) Telecommunication Standards Implementation Guide
- **Dental health care claims**: ASC X12 Standards for Electronic Data Interchange Technical Report Type 3 - Health Care Claim: Dental (837)
- **Professional health care claims**: ASC X12 Standards for Electronic Data Interchange - Health Care Claim: Professional (837)
- **Institutional health care claims**: ACS X12N 837 - Health Care Claim: Institutional

Referral certification and authorization transaction

'Referral certification and authorization transaction' is a request from a health care provider to a health plan to obtain authorization for health care or for referring an individual to another health care provider or a response from the health plan to the health care provider. The standards used are:

- **Retail pharmacy drugs**: NCPDP Telecommunication Standard Implementation Guide and equivalent Batch Standard Implementation Guide
- **Dental, professional, and institutional requests**: ASC X12 Standards for Electronic Data Interchange - Health Care Services Review - Request for Review and Response (278), ASC X12 Standards for Electronic Data Interchange Technical Report

Health plan transaction

'Health Plan transaction' is an inquiry or response from a health care provider to a health plan, or from one health plan to another, for information about an enrollee's benefit plan, including eligibility, coverage, and benefits. The standards for eligibility are:

- **Retail pharmacy drugs**: The NCPDP Telecommunication Standard Implementation Guide and NCPDP Batch Standard Batch Implementation Guide supporting Telecommunications Standard Implementation Guide
- **Dental, professional, and institutional health care eligibility benefit inquiry and response**: The ASC X12N 270/271–Health Care Eligibility Benefit Inquiry and Response

Health care claim status transaction

Health care claim status transaction is the transmission of an inquiry or a response between the healthcare provider and a health plan to determine the status of a healthcare claim. The standards used are ASC X12 Standards for Electronic Data Interchange Technical Report Type 3 - Health Care Claim Status Request and Response.

The enrollment and disenrollment in a health plan transaction is the transmission of subscriber enrollment information from the sponsor of the insurance coverage, benefits, or policy, to a health plan to establish or terminate insurance coverage. The standards used are:

- **Benefit Enrollment and Maintenance**: ASC X12 Standards for Electronic Data Interchange - Benefit Enrollment and Maintenance (834)

Electronic Fund Transfer transaction

'Health care electronic funds transfers (EFT) and remittance advice transactions' is the transmission of payment, information about the transfer of funds, payment processing information from a health plan to a health care provider, and explanation of benefits and remittance advice from health plan to a health care provider. The standards adopted are:

- The National Automated Clearing House Association (NACHA) Corporate Credit or Deposit Entry with Addenda Record (CCD+) implementation specifications as contained in the 2011 NACHA Operating Rules & Guidelines
- ASC X12 Standards for Electronic Data Interchange Health Care Claim Payment/Advice (835)

Health plan premium payment transaction

Health plan premium payment transaction is the transmission of payment, information about the transfer of funds, detailed remittance information about individuals for whom premiums are being paid, payment processing information like payroll deductions, group premium payments, and associated group premium payment information from an entity arranging for the provision of health care or is providing health care coverage payments for an individual to a health plan. The standards are:

- ASC X12N 820 - Payroll Deducted and Other Group Premium Payment for Insurance Products
- ASC X12 Standards for Electronic Data Interchange Technical Report - Payroll Deducted and Other Group Premium Payment for Insurance Products (820)

Coordination of benefits transaction

'Coordination of benefits transaction' is the transmission from any entity to a health plan to determine the relative payment responsibilities of the health plan or claims or payment information:

- **Retail pharmacy drug claims:** Telecommunication Standard Implementation Guide, and equivalent Batch Standard Implementation Guide; ASC X12 Standards for Electronic Data Interchange Technical Report - Health Care Claim: Dental (837); ASC X12 Standards for Electronic Data Interchange Technical Report - Health Care Claim: Professional; ASC X12 Standards for Electronic Data Interchange Technical Report - Health Care Claim: Institutional; ASC X12 Standards for Electronic Data Interchange Technical Report
- **Dental health care claims:** ASC X12N 837 - Health Care Claim: Dental
- **Professional health care claims:** ASC X12N 837 - Health Care Claim: Professional
- **Institutional health care claims:** The ASC X12N 837 - Health Care Claim: Institutional
- Quantity Prescribed (460-ET) field, as outlined in the Telecommunication Standard Implementation Guide and equivalent Batch Standard Implementation Guide, National Council for Prescription Drug Programs

Medicaid pharmacy subrogation transaction

Medicaid pharmacy subrogation transaction is the transmission of a claim from a Medicaid agency to a payer to seek reimbursement from the responsible health plan for a pharmacy claim the State has paid on behalf of the recipient. The standard is Batch Standard Medicaid Subrogation Implementation Guide, NCPDP for all covered entities.

Security Requirements

Security standards can be divided into Required (R) or Addressable (A). Required standards require compliance under all conditions, while Addressable standards allow covered entities or business associates to evaluate reasonableness or appropriateness in their specific case.

Administrative safeguards

- **Business Associate contracts and other arrangements**: A covered entity may permit a business associate to create, receive, maintain, or transmit electronic protected health information on the covered entity's behalf only if the covered entity obtains satisfactory assurances that the business associate will appropriately safeguard the information. This also applies to a business associate subcontracting to a business associate. A covered entity is not required to obtain such satisfactory assurances from a business associate that is a subcontractor.
    - **Written contract or other arrangement (R)**: Document the satisfactory assurances required as above through a written contract or other arrangement with the business associate that meets the applicable requirements listed under the Organizational Requirements section.
- **Security Management Process**: Policies and procedures to prevent, detect, contain, and correct security violations

- **Risk analysis (R)**: Conduct an accurate and thorough assessment of the potential risks and vulnerabilities to the confidentiality, integrity, and availability of electronic protected health information held by the covered entity or business associate.
- **Risk management (R)**: Implement security measures sufficient to reduce risks and vulnerabilities to a reasonable and appropriate level.
- **Sanction policy (R)**: Apply appropriate sanctions against workforce members who fail to comply with the security policies and procedures of the covered entity or business associate.
- **Information system activity (R)**: Implement procedures to regularly review records of information system activity, such as audit logs, access reports, and security incident tracking reports.

- **Assigned Security Responsibility (R)**: Identify the security official responsible for developing and implementing the policies and procedures required by this subpart for the covered entity or business associate.
- **Workforce Security**: Implement policies and procedures to ensure that all members of its workforce have appropriate access to electronic protected health information
    - **Authorization and/or Supervision (A)**: Implement procedures for the authorization and/or supervision of workforce members who work with electronic protected health information or in locations where it might be accessed.
    - **Workforce Clearance Procedure (A)**: Implement procedures to determine that the access of a workforce member to electronic protected health information is appropriate.
    - **Termination Procedures (A)**: Implement procedures for terminating access to electronic protected health information when the employment of, or other arrangement with, a workforce member ends.
- **Information Access Management**: Implement policies and procedures for authorizing access to electronic protected health information that are consistent with the applicable requirements of Privacy of individually identifiable health information
    - **Isolating Health Care Clearinghouse Function (R)**: If a health care clearinghouse is part of a larger organization, the clearinghouse must implement policies and procedures that protect the electronic protected health information from unauthorized access by the larger organization.
    - **Access Authorization (A)**: Implement policies and procedures for granting access to electronic protected health information, for example, through access to a workstation, transaction, program, process, or other mechanism.
    - **Access Establishment and Modification (A)**: Implement policies and procedures that, based upon the covered entity's or the business associate's access authorization policies, establish, document, review, and modify a user's right of access to a workstation, transaction, program, or process.
- **Security Awareness and Training**: Implement a security awareness and training program for all members of its workforce (including management).
    - **Security Reminders (A)**: Periodic security updates.
    - **Protection from Malicious Software (A)**: Procedures for guarding against, detecting, and reporting malicious software.
    - **Log-in Monitoring (A)**: Procedures for monitoring log-in attempts and reporting discrepancies.
    - **Password Management (A)**: Procedures for creating, changing, and safeguarding passwords.
- **Security Incident Procedures (R)**: Implement policies and procedures to address security incidents.

- o **Response and Reporting**: Identify and respond to suspected or known security incidents; mitigate, to the extent practicable, harmful effects of security incidents known to the covered entity or business associate; and document security incidents and their outcomes.

- **Contingency Plan**: Establish (and implement as needed) policies and procedures for responding to an emergency or other occurrence (for example, fire, vandalism, system failure, and natural disaster) that damages systems that contain electronic protected health information.
  - o **Data backup plan (R)**: Establish and implement procedures to create and maintain retrievable exact copies of electronic protected health information.
  - o **Disaster Recovery Plan (R)**: Establish (and implement as needed) procedures to restore data loss.
  - o **Emergency Mode Operation Plan (R)**: Establish (and implement as needed) procedures to enable the continuation of critical business processes to protect the security of electronic protected health information while operating in emergency mode.
  - o **Testing and Revision Procedure (A)**: Implement procedures for periodic testing and revision of contingency plans.
  - o **Application and Data Criticality Analysis (A)**: Assess the relative criticality of specific applications and data supporting other contingency plan components.
- **Evaluation (R)**: Perform a periodic technical and nontechnical evaluation, based initially upon the standards implemented under this rule and, subsequently, in response to environmental or operational changes affecting the security of electronic protected health information, that establishes the extent to which a covered entity's or business associate's security policies and procedures meet the requirements of this subpart.

Physical safeguards

- **Facility access controls**: Implement policies and procedures to limit physical access to its electronic information systems and the facility or facilities in which they are housed while ensuring that properly authorized access is allowed.
  - o **Contingency operations (A)**: Establish (and implement as needed) procedures that allow facility access in support of restoration of lost data under the disaster recovery plan and emergency mode operations plan in the event of an emergency.
  - o **Facility security plan (A)**: Implement policies and procedures to safeguard the facility and the equipment from unauthorized physical access, tampering, and theft.
  - o **Access control and validation procedures (A)**: Implement procedures to control and validate a person's access to facilities based on their role or function, including control of visitors and access to software programs for testing and revision.
  - o **Maintenance records (A)**: Implement policies and procedures to document repairs and modifications to the physical components of a facility that are related to security (for example, hardware, walls, doors, and locks).
- **Workstation use (R)**: Implement policies and procedures that specify the proper functions to be performed, how those functions are to be performed, and the physical attributes of the surroundings of a specific workstation or class of workstation that can access electronic protected health information.
- **Workstation security (R)**: Implement physical safeguards for all workstations that access electronic protected health information to restrict access to authorized users.
- **Device and media controls**: Implement policies and procedures that govern the receipt and

removal of hardware and electronic media that contain electronic protected health information into and out of a facility and the movement of these items within the facility.

  - **Disposal (R)**: Implement policies and procedures to address the final disposition of electronic protected health information and/or the hardware or electronic media on which it is stored.
  - **Media re-use (R)**. Implement procedures for removal of electronic protected health information from electronic media before the media are made available for re-use.
  - **Accountability (A)**. Maintain a record of the movements of hardware and electronic media and any person responsible therefore.
  - **Data backup and storage (A)**. When needed, create a retrievable, exact copy of electronic protected health information before moving equipment.

Technical safeguards

- **Access control**: Implement technical policies and procedures for electronic information systems that maintain electronic protected health information to allow access only to those persons or software programs that have been granted access rights
  - **Unique user identification (R)**: Assign a unique name and/or number for identifying and tracking user identity.
  - **Emergency access procedure (R)**: Establish (and implement as needed) procedures for obtaining necessary electronic protected health information during an emergency.
  - **Automatic logoff (A)**: Implement electronic procedures that terminate an electronic session after a predetermined time of inactivity.
  - **Encryption and decryption (A)**: Implement a mechanism to encrypt and decrypt electronic protected health information.
- **Audit controls (R)**: Implement hardware, software, and/or procedural mechanisms that record and examine activity in information systems that contain or use electronic protected health information.
- **Integrity**: Implement policies and procedures to protect electronic protected health information from improper alteration or destruction.
  - **Mechanism to authenticate electronic protected health information (A)**: Implement electronic mechanisms to corroborate that electronic protected health information has not been altered or destroyed in an unauthorized manner.
- **Person or entity authentication (R)**: Implement procedures to verify that a person or entity seeking access to electronic protected health information is the one claimed.
- **Transmission security**: Implement technical security measures to guard against unauthorized access to electronic protected health information transmitted over an electronic communications network.
  - **Integrity controls (A)**: Implement security measures to ensure that electronically transmitted electronic protected health information is not improperly modified without detection until disposed of appropriately.
  - **Encryption (A)**: Implement a mechanism to encrypt electronic protected health information whenever appropriate.

Breach notification

After a breach of unsecured PHI, the covered entity or the business associate can demonstrate a low probability that the PHI has been compromised based on a risk assessment of the following factors.

- Nature and extent of the PHI involved, including the type of identifiers and the likelihood of re-identification
- Unauthorized person who used the PHI or to whom the disclosure was made
- Whether the PHI was acquired or viewed
- Extent to which the risk to the protected health information has been mitigated Breach excludes:
- Any unintentional acquisition, access, or use of PHI by a workforce member or person acting under the authority of a covered entity or a business associate, if such acquisition, access, or use was made in good faith and within the scope of authority and did not result in further use or disclosure in a manner not permitted under HIPAA Privacy subpart
- Any inadvertent disclosure by a person who is authorized to access PHI at a covered entity or a business associate to another person authorized to access PHI at the same covered entity or business associate and the information received as a result of such disclosure is not further use or disclosed in a manner not permitted under HIPAA Privacy subpart.
- A disclosure of PHI where a covered entity or business associate has a good faith belief that an unauthorized person to whom the disclosure was made would not have been able to retain such information

Notifications to individuals

A covered entity shall, following the discovery of a breach of unsecured PHI, notify each individual whose unsecured PHI has been or is reasonably believed by the covered entity to have been accessed, acquired, used, or disclosed as a result of such breach. The notification should be sent no later than 60 days after discovering the breach. The written notification should include, in plain language, a brief description of what happened during the breach, the date of discovery, a description of the type of PHI that was involved, any steps required by individuals to protect themselves from potential harm due to the breach, brief description of the investigation, mitigation, and prevention of further breaches and best way to contact for additional information.

Notification to the media

For a breach of unsecured PHI involving more than 500 residents of a state or jurisdiction, a covered entity shall notify prominent media outlets serving the State or jurisdiction within 60 days of discovering the breach.

Notification to the Secretary

Notify Secretary for breaches of 500 or more individuals per HHS guidelines. For less than 500 individuals, a covered entity shall maintain a log or other documentation of such breaches and, not later than 60 days after the end of each calendar year, provide the notification for breaches discovered during the preceding calendar year.

Notification by a business associate

Following the discovery of a breach of unprotected PHI, a business associate shall notify the covered entity within 60 days. A business associate shall be deemed to know about a breach if the breach is known to any person who is an employee, officer, or other agent of the business associate. The notification should include the identification of each individual whose unsecured PHI has been accessed, acquired, used, or disclosed during the breach. The notification should include, to the extent possible, the identification of each individual whose unsecured protected health information is believed to be accessed, acquired, used, or disclosed during the breach.

Organizational Requirements

- **Business associate contracts**: The contract must provide that the business associate will a) Comply with the applicable requirements of this subpart; b) Ensure that any subcontractors that create, receive, maintain, or transmit electronic protected health information on behalf of the business associate agree to comply with the applicable requirements of this subpart by entering into a contract or other arrangement that complies with this section; c) Report to the covered entity any security incident of which it becomes aware, including breaches of unsecured protected health information.
- **Other arrangements**: The covered entity complies with the above if it has another arrangement in place that meets the following requirements:
  - If a covered entity and its business associate are both governmental entities, the covered entity may comply with requirements by entering into a memorandum of understanding with the business associate that contains terms that accomplish the objectives listed under the business associate contract section of uses and disclosures: Organizational Requirements of the Privacy Subpart as applicable. If applicable, the covered entity may comply if another law (including regulations adopted by the covered entity or its business associate) contains requirements applicable to the business associate that accomplish the objectives.
  - If a business associate is required by law to perform a function or activity on behalf of a covered entity or to provide a service to a covered entity, such covered entity may disclose protected health information to the business associate to the extent necessary to comply with the legal mandate without meeting the requirements, if applicable, provided that the covered entity attempts in good faith to obtain satisfactory assurances, if applicable, and, if such attempt fails, documents the attempt and the reasons that such assurances cannot be obtained.
  - The covered entity may omit from its other arrangements the termination authorization if such authorization is inconsistent with the statutory obligations of the covered entity or its business associate.
  - A covered entity may comply if the covered entity discloses only a limited data set to a business associate for the business associate to carry out a health care operations function and the covered entity has a data use agreement with the business associate that complies with requirements of business associate contracts and data use agreement, if applicable.
  - Business associate contracts with subcontractors: The organizational requirements apply to contracts with subcontracts in the same manner as they apply to contracts between covered entities and business associates.
- **Requirements for group health plans (R)**: A group health plan must ensure that its plan documents provide that the plan sponsor will reasonably an appropriately safeguard ePHI created, received, maintained, or transmitted to or by the plan sponsor on behalf of the group health plan, except as allowed under the provisions of Privacy subpart. The plan documents of the group health plan must be amended to incorporate provisions to require the plan sponsor to
  - Implement administrative, physical, and technical safeguards that reasonably and

appropriately protect the confidentiality, integrity, and availability of the ePHI that it creates, receives, maintains, or transmits on behalf of the group health plan.

- o Ensure that adequate separation required by Privacy subpart requirements for group health plans is supported by reasonable and appropriate security measures.
- o Ensure that any agent to whom it provides this information agrees to implement reasonable and appropriate security measures to protect the information.
- o Report any security incident to the group health plan that it becomes aware.

Policies and procedures and documentation requirements

- **Policies and procedures**: A covered entity or business associate must implement reasonable and appropriate policies and procedures to comply with the standards, implementation specifications, or other requirements of this subpart, taking into account the size, complexity, technical & infrastructure capabilities of a covered entity or business associate as well as the costs of security measures and probability and critically of potential risks to ePHI.
- **Documentation**: A covered entity or business associate must maintain the policies and procedures implemented to comply with these requirements and any required action, activity, or assessment in written or electronic form.
  - o **Time limit (R)**: Retain the documents for 6 years from the date of their creation or date when it was last in effect, whichever is later
  - o **Availability (R)**: Make documentation available to those responsible for implementing the procedures to which the documentation pertains.
  - o **Updates (R)**: Review documentation periodically and update as needed in response to environmental or operational changes affecting the security of the ePHI.

Privacy Requirements

Privacy of Individually Identifiable Health Information

Uses and disclosures: General rules and standards

- **Covered entities - Permitted uses and disclosures***:* The covered entity is permitted to use or disclose PHI to the individual with the PHI; for treatment, payment, or health care operations, in compliance with the uses and disclosures section in the Privacy Rule and incident to a use or disclosure otherwise permitted or required under the Privacy Rule.
- **Covered entities - Required uses and disclosures***:* A covered entity is required to disclose PHI to an individual when requested or required by the provisions of the Privacy rule and when required by the Secretary to investigate or determine the covered entity's compliance.
- **Business associates - Permitted uses and disclosures***:* A business associate may use or disclose PHI only as permitted or required by its business associate contract or other arrangement permitted under Privacy rule or as required by law.
- **Business associates - Required uses and disclosures***:* A business associate is required to disclose PHI when required by the Secretary to investigate or determine the business associate's compliance with the Privacy rules or to the covered entity, individual to satisfy a covered entity's obligations.
- **Prohibited uses and disclosures***:* Use and disclosures of genetic information for underwriting purposes and sale of protected health information except under specific

scenarios.

- **Minimum necessary***:* When using or disclosing protected health information or requesting PHI from another covered entity or business associate, reasonable efforts must be made to limit PHI to the minimum necessary to accomplish the intended purpose of the use, disclosure, or request. Minimum necessary does not apply to disclosures to or requests by a health care provider for treatment, uses, or disclosures to individuals, Secretary, or law enforcement as permitted under the privacy rule.
- **Uses and disclosures of PHI subject to an agreed-upon restriction***:* A covered entity that has agreed to a restriction due to a request by an individual may not use or disclose PHI covered by the restriction providing exceptions allowed under the Privacy rule.
- **Uses and disclosures to de-identified PHI***:* A covered entity may use PHI to create information that is not individually identifiable health information or disclose PHI only to a business associate for such purpose, whether or not de-identified information is to be used by the covered entity. Health information that meets the standard and implementation specifications for de-identification is considered not to be individually identifiable health information. Disclosure of a code or other means of record identification designed to enable coded or otherwise de-identified information to be re-identified constitutes disclosure of PHI.
- **Disclosures to business associates or subcontractors**: A covered entity may disclose protected health information to a business associate or business associate to a subcontractor and may allow to create, receive, maintain, or transmit protected health information on its behalf if the covered entity or business associate obtains satisfactory assurance that the business associate or subcontractor will appropriately safeguard the information. The assurance must be documented through a written contract or agreement on arrangement with the business associate.
- **Deceased individuals***:* The covered entity must comply with the requirements of the privacy subpart for the protected health information received individual for 50 years following the text of the individual.
- **Personal representative***:* The covered entity must create a personal representative as the individual for purposes of this subchapter.
- **Confidential communications***:* The covered healthcare providers or health plans must comply with the applicable requirements as listed under the confidential communication requirements standard.

Uses and disclosures: Organizational requirements

Business Associate Contracts

A covered entity would not be in compliance if the covered entity was aware of a pattern of activity or practice of the business associate that constituted a material breach or violation of the business associate's obligation under the contract with the provisions of the law, unless the covered entity took reasonable steps to cure the breach or end the violation, and, if such steps were unsuccessful, terminated the contract arrangement. The same standard applies between business associates and subcontractors.

The contract between the covered entity in a business associate must establish permitted and required uses and disclosures of protected health information by the business associate. The contract may permit the business associate to use and disclose protected health information for the management and administration of the business associate to provide services relating to the healthcare operations of the covered entity. The contract should provide that the business associate will not use or further disclose information other than as permitted by the contract or as required by the law, use appropriate safeguards, comply with the disclosure requirements, and report any breaches of unsecured protected information.

If the contract between a covered entity and business associate is terminated, it is required to return or destroy all protected health information received from or created or received by the business associate. Business associate cannot retain copies of protected health information or, if such return or destruction is not feasible, extend the protections of the contract to the information and limit further uses and disclosure.

If a covered entity and its business associate are both governmental entities, the covered entity may enter into a memorandum of understanding with the business associate. The provisions of the Privacy subpart apply to contracts and other arrangements between a business associate and a business associate that is a subcontractor.

Requirements for group health plans

A group health plan, or a health insurance issuer or HMO must ensure that the plan documents restrict uses and disclosures of PHI information by the plan sponsor. The group health plan may disclose summary health information to the plan sponsor for a) Obtaining premium bids from health plans for providing health insurance coverage under the group health plan; b) Modifying, amending, or terminating the group health plan; c) Whether the individual is participating in the health plan, or is enrolled in or has dis-enrolled from a health insurance issuer or HMO offered by the plan.

Uses and disclosures for treatment, payment, or health care operations

A covered entity may use or disclose protected health information for treatment, payment, or health care operations provided that such use or disclosure is consistent with other applicable requirements. This does not apply to uses or disclosures that require authorization or are prohibited. A covered entity may obtain consent from the individual to use or disclose PHI to carry out treatment, payment, or health care operations if no authorization or condition is required for such a disclosure. It can also disclose PHI to another covered entity or health care provider for treatment, payment, or operations activities.

Uses and disclosures requiring authorization

- **Psychotherapy notes**: The exception is the use of notes for treatment, payment, health care operations, training programs, and defense in legal action brought by an individual.
- **Marketing exception**: The exception is the communication is face-to-face made by the covered entity to an individual, a promotion gift of nominal value provided by the covered entity, and detail of remuneration to the covered entity from the third party.
- **Sale of PHI**: Authorization must state that the disclosure will result in remuneration to the covered entity.

Requirements of authorization

The specific requirements for authorization include:

- Valid authorizations satisfy the requirements of disclosures requiring authorizations. They have expiration dates, are filled out completely, have not been revoked, satisfy the requirements of compound authorizations, and are not a condition for treatment, payment, enrollment in a health plan, or eligibility for benefits. The exception can be made for research-related treatment, authorization sought for health plan's eligibility or enrollment determination relating to the individual or for its underwriting or risk rating determinations or for the provision of health care that is solely to create PHI for disclosure to a third party
- Compound authorizations combined with another document are not permitted except for research studies.
- An individual may revoke an authorization at any time, provided the revocation is in writing.
- A covered entity must document and retain any signed authorization. A copy should be provided to the individual. A valid authorization must contain
  - Description of the information to be used or disclosed that identifies the information in a specific and meaningful fashion
  - Name or other specific identification of the person(s), or class of persons, authorized to make the requested use or disclosure
  - Name or other specific identification of the person(s), or class of persons, to whom the covered entity may make the requested use or disclosure
  - Description of each purpose of the requested use or disclosure.
  - An expiration date or an expiration event related to the individual or the purpose of the use or disclosure.
  - Signature of the individual and date
  - Required statements in plain language: a) The individual's right to revoke the authorization in writing and any related exceptions; b) Statements describing the ability or inability to condition treatment, payment, enrollment, or eligibility for benefits on the authorization.

Uses and disclosures requiring the individual to agree or object

A covered entity may use or disclose protected health information, provided that the individual is informed, in writing or orally, in advance of the use or disclosure and has the opportunity to agree to or prohibit or restrict the use or disclosure.

Use and disclosure for facility directories

A covered healthcare provider may use the following information about the individual to maintain a directory of individuals in its facility. Individuals must be informed what information is available in the directory and to whom it will be disclosed and provide an option to restrict some or all of the following information: a) Name; b) Location in the provider's facility; c) General condition; d) Religious affiliation.

Use and disclosure for involvement in the individual's care and notification purposes

A covered entity may disclose PHI for the provision of an individual's health care and notify the parties designated by the individual. These include:

- A covered entity may disclose to a family member, other relative, or a close personal friend of the individual, or any other person identified by the individual, the PHI directly relevant to such person's involvement with the individual's health care or payment related to the individual's health care.

- A covered entity may use or disclose PHI to notify or assist in the notification of (including identifying or locating) a family member, a personal representative of the individual, or another person responsible for the care of the individual of the individual's location, general condition, or death.
- If the individual is present for, or otherwise available prior to, use or disclosure and can make health care decisions, the covered entity may use or disclose the PHI if it obtains the individual's agreement or allows the individual to object to the disclosure.
- If the individual is not present, or the opportunity to agree or object to the use or disclosure cannot practicably be provided because of the individual's incapacity or an emergency circumstance, the covered entity may, determine whether the disclosure is in the best interests of the individual and, if so, disclose only the protected health information that is directly relevant to the person's involvement with the individual's care or payment related to the individual's health care or needed for notification purposes.
- A covered entity may use or disclose protected health information to a public or private entity authorized by law or by its charter to assist in disaster relief efforts
- If the individual is deceased, a covered entity may disclose to a family member, or other persons who were involved in the individual's care or payment for health care prior to the individual's death, protected health information of the individual that is relevant to such person's involvement, unless doing so is inconsistent with any prior expressed preference of the individual that is known to the covered entity.

Uses and disclosures for which authorization is not required

A covered entity may use or disclose protected health information without authorization if disclosure is required by law or, in case of research studies. The covered entity obtains documentation that IRB or a privacy board has approved waiver of requirement of individual authorization.

- A covered entity may use or disclose PHI to a public health authority that is authorized by law to collect or receive such information to prevent or control disease, injury, or disability, including, the reporting of disease, injury, vital events such as birth or death, and the conduct of public health surveillance, public health investigations, and public health interventions; receive reports of child abuse or neglect;
- A covered entity may use or disclose PHI to a person subject to the jurisdiction of the Food and Drug Administration (FDA) with respect to an FDA-regulated product or activity for which that person has the responsibility to collect or report adverse events, product defects or problems, or biological product deviations; to track FDA-regulated products, to enable product recalls repairs, or replacements, to conduct post-marketing surveillance
- A person who may have been exposed to a communicable disease or may otherwise be at risk of contracting or spreading a disease or condition, if the covered entity or public health authority is authorized by law to notify such person as necessary in the conduct of a public health intervention or investigation
- A covered entity may use or disclose PHI to an employer by providing written notice to the individual that PHI is disclosed to the individual under the following scenarios:
    - About an individual who is a member of the employer's workforce, if the covered entity products health care to the individual at the request of the employer to conduct an evaluation relating to medical surveillance of the workplace and to evaluate whether the

individual has a work-related illness or injury.
  - PHI consists of findings concerning work-related illness or injury or a workplace-related medical surveillance
  - Employer needs findings to comply with legal obligations
  - A proof of immunization for current or prospective students for the school

Uses and disclosures for health oversight activities

A covered entity may disclose protected health information to a health oversight agency for oversight activities authorized by law, including audits; civil, administrative, or criminal investigations; inspections; licensure or disciplinary actions; civil, administrative, or criminal proceedings or actions; or other activities necessary for appropriate oversight of a health care system, government benefit programs, entities subject to government regulatory programs for which health information is necessary for determining compliance with program standards, or entities subject to civil rights laws for which health information is necessary for determining compliance.

A health oversight activity does not include an investigation or other activity in which the individual is the subject of the investigation or activity, and such investigation or other activity is not directly related to the receipt of health care, a claim for public benefits related to health or qualification for public benefits or services when a patient's health is integral to the claim for public benefits or services.

Uses and disclosures for research purposes

A covered entity may use or disclose protected health information for research provided that the covered entity obtains:

- Documentation that IRB or a privacy board has approved an alteration to or waiver of the individual authorization required to use or disclose PHI.
- From researcher representations that use or disclosure is sought solely to review PHI as necessary to prepare a research protocol or for similar purposes preparatory to research, and no PHI will be removed from the covered entity by the researcher during the review. Appropriate documentation must be maintained as outlined under the requirements.

Other disclosures

- Disclosures about victims of abuse, neglect or domestic violence
- Disclosures for judicial or administrative proceedings
- Disclosures for law enforcement purposes
- Uses and disclosures about decedents
- Uses and disclosures for cadaveric organ, eye or tissue donation purposes
- Uses and disclosures to avert a serious threat to health or safety
- Uses and disclosures for specialized government functions
- Disclosures for workers' compensation

Other requirements relating to the uses and disclosures of PHI

De-identification of PHI

A covered entity may determine that health information is not individually identifiable health information if

- A person with appropriate knowledge of and experience with generally accepted statistical and scientific principles and methods for rendering information not individually identifiable
- The following identifiers of the individual or of relatives, employers, or household members of the individual, are removed
  - Names
  - Geographic subdivisions smaller than state or 3-digit zip codes if it has greater than 20,000 people
  - All elements of date related to an individual except year indicating date of birth, admission, discharge, death. Individuals over the age 89 should be aggregated into a single category
  - Telephone and fax numbers
  - Email addresses
  - Social security numbers
  - Medical record numbers
  - Health plan beneficiary numbers
  - Account numbers
  - Certificate / license numbers
  - Vehicle identifiers and serial numbers, including license plate numbers;
  - Device identifiers and serial numbers;
  - Web Universal Resource Locators (URLs)
  - Internet Protocol (IP) address numbers
  - Biometric identifiers, including finger and voice prints
  - Full face photographic images and any comparable images
  - Any other unique identifying number, characteristic, or code

Re-identification

A covered entity may assign a code or other means of record identification to allow information de-identified under this section to be re-identified by the covered entity, provided that:

- **Derivation**: The code or other means of record identification is not derived from or related to information about the individual and is not otherwise capable of being translated to identify the individual
- **Security**: The covered entity does not use or disclose the code or other means of record identification for any other purpose and does not disclose the mechanism for re-identification

Minimum necessary requirements

A covered entity must identify anyone in its workforce who need access to protected health information to carry out their duties, and the category of protected health information to which access is needed and any conditions appropriate to such access. For any disclosure that it makes on a routine and recurring basis, a covered entity must implement policies and procedures that limit the protected health information disclosed to the amount reasonably necessary to achieve the purpose of the disclosure. For all other disclosures, a covered entity must develop criteria designed to limit the protected health information disclosed to the information reasonably necessary to accomplish the purpose for which disclosure is sought and review requests for disclosure on an individual basis per such criteria.

A covered entity may rely on a requested disclosure as the minimum necessary for the stated purpose when a) making disclosures to public officials, b) when another covered entity requests the information, c) when the information is requested by a professional who is a member of its workforce or is a business associate of the covered entity to provide professional services to the covered entity, and d) when documentation or representation is presented that complies with the applicable requirements of uses and disclosures for research purposes. A covered entity may not use, disclose or request an entire medical record except when the entire medical record is justified explicitly as the amount reasonably necessary to accomplish the purpose of the use, disclosure, or request.

Limited data set

A covered entity may use or disclose limited data if it enters into a data use agreement with the limited data set recipient and for research, public health, or health care operations. A covered entity may use or disclose a limited data set only it obtains satisfactory assurance in the form of a data use agreement that meets the requirement that the data use recipient will use or disclose the PHI for limited purposes. This data use agreement must establish the permitted uses and disclosures of information, establish who is permitted to use or receive the limited data set, ensure that the limited data set recipient will not sure or further disclose the information other than as permitted by the data use agreement or as otherwise required by the law, use appropriate safeguards to prevent use or disclosure of the information other than as provided for by the data use agreement, and report any unauthorized disclosures. A limited data set is protected health information that excludes the following direct identifiers of the individual or relatives, employers, or household members of the individual:

- Names
- Postal address information, other than town or city, state, zip code
- Telephone and fax numbers
- Email addresses
- Social security numbers
- Medical record numbers
- Health plan beneficiary numbers
- Account numbers
- Certificate/license numbers
- Vehicle identifiers and serial numbers, including license plate numbers
- Device identifiers and serial numbers
- Web Universal Resource Locators (URLs)
- Internet Protocol (IP) address numbers
- Biometric identifiers, including finger and voice prints
- Full face photographic images and any comparable images

Uses and disclosures for fundraising

Under specific scenarios, a covered entity may use or disclose to a business associate or an institutionally related foundation-specific PHI to raise funds for its benefit without authorization.

Uses and disclosures for underwriting and related purposes

If a health plan receives protected health information for underwriting, premium rating, or other activities relating to the creation, renewal, or replacement of a contract of health insurance or health benefits, and if such health insurance or health benefits are not placed with the health plan, such health plan may only use or disclose such protected health information for such purpose or as may be required by law, subject to the prohibition with respect to genetic information included in the protected health information.

Verification

Before any disclosure, a covered entity must verify the identity of a person requesting PHI and the authority of any such person to access PHI and obtain any documentation, statements, or representations, whether oral or written, from the person requesting the protected health information.

Notice of privacy practices for PHI

An individual has a right to notice of the uses and disclosures of protected health information that may be made by the covered entity and of the individual's rights and the covered entity's legal duties with respect to protected health information. There are exceptions for group health plans and inmates. The covered entity must provide a plain written notice containing the following elements:

- The notice must contain the following statement as a header or prominently displayed: "This notice describes how medical information about you may be used and disclosed and how you can get access to this information. Please review it carefully."
- A description, including at least one example of the types of uses and disclosures that this subpart permits the covered entity to make for each of the following purposes: treatment, payment, and health care operations.
- A description of the other purposes for which the covered entity is permitted or required by this subpart to use or disclose protected health information without the individual's written authorization.
- The description must include sufficient detail to notify the individual of the uses and disclosures permitted or required by this subpart and other applicable laws.
- If a use or disclosure for any purpose is prohibited or materially limited by other applicable law, the description must reflect the more stringent law defined in this subchapter.
- A description of the types of uses and disclosures that require authorization, a statement that other uses and disclosures not described in the notice will be made only with the individual's written authorization, and a statement that the individual may revoke an authorization.
- Include a separate statement informing the individual of the following activities, as applicable:
    - The covered entity may contact the individual to raise funds for the covered entity, and the individual has a right to opt out of receiving such communications.
    - The group health plan, or a health insurance issuer or HMO with respect to a group health plan, may disclose protected health information to the sponsor of the plan.
    - If a covered entity that is a health plan intends to use or disclose protected health information for underwriting purposes, a statement that the covered entity is prohibited from using or disclosing protected health information that is genetic information of an

individual for such purposes.

The notice must contain a statement of the individual's rights with respect to protected health information and a brief description of how the individual may exercise these rights, as follows:

- The right to request restrictions on certain uses and disclosures of protected health information, including a statement that the covered entity is not required to agree to a requested restriction, except in case of specific restricted disclosures
- The right to receive confidential communications of protected health information
- The right to inspect and copy protected health information
- The right to amend protected health information
- The right to receive an accounting of disclosures of protected health information
- The right of an individual, including an individual who has agreed to receive the notice electronically, to obtain a paper copy of the notice from the covered entity upon request.

The notice must contain a statement that a) the covered entity is required by law to maintain the privacy of protected health information, to abide by the terms of the notice currently in effect, to provide individuals with notice of its legal duties and privacy practices with respect to protected health information, and to notify affected individuals following a breach of unsecured protected health information; b) it reserves the right to change the terms of its notice and to make the new notice provisions effective for all protected health information that it maintains. The statement must also describe how it will provide individuals with a revised notice; c) individuals may complain to the covered entity and the Secretary if they believe their privacy rights have been violated; a brief description of how the individual may file a complaint with the covered entity, and a statement that the individual will not be retaliated against for filing a complaint.

The content of the notice are a) the name, title, and telephone number of a person or office to contact for further information; b) the date on which the notice is first in effect, which may not be earlier than the date on which the notice is printed or otherwise published.

A covered entity must make the notice required by this section available on request to any person and individuals. The covered entity must promptly revise and distribute its notice whenever there is a material change to the uses or disclosures, the individual's rights, the covered entity's legal duties, or other privacy practices stated in the notice. Except when required by law, a material change to any term of the notice may not be implemented prior to the effective date of the notice in which such material change is reflected.

Rights to request privacy protection for PHI

A covered entity must permit an individual to request that the covered entity restrict the uses or disclosures of protected health information about the individual to carry out treatment, payment, or health care operations. A covered entity that agrees to a restriction may not use or disclose protected health information in violation of such restriction, except that if the individual who requested the restriction needs emergency treatment and the restricted PHI is needed to provide the emergency treatment, the covered entity may use the restricted protected health information, or may disclose such information to a health care provider, to provide such treatment to the individual. If restricted protected health information is disclosed to a health care provider for emergency treatment, the covered entity must request that such health care provider not further use or disclose the information.

A covered entity must agree to the request of an individual to restrict disclosure of protected health information about the individual to a health plan if the disclosure is to carry out payment or health care operations and is not otherwise required by law, the protected health information pertains solely to a health care item or service for which the individual has paid the covered entity in full. A covered entity may terminate a restriction if the individual agrees to or requests the termination in writing or orally agrees to the termination, the oral agreement is documented, or the covered entity informs the individual that it is terminating its agreement to a restriction. A covered entity must document such a restriction. A covered health care provider or a health plan must permit individuals to request and accommodate reasonable requests to receive communications of protected health information from the covered health care provider by alternative means or at alternative locations.

Access of individuals to PHI

Right of access: Every individual can inspect and obtain a copy of PHI in a designated record set for as long as the PHI is maintained in the designated record set. There are exceptions, including for Psychotherapy notes and requests for legal purposes.

Unreviewable grounds for denial: A covered entity may deny an individual access without providing the individual an opportunity for review under the exceptions criteria, under specific circumstances to inmates, under specific research scenarios, under clauses of the Privacy Act, and to protect the source of the information if obtained from someone other than the healthcare provider.

Reviewable grounds for denial: A covered entity may deny an individual access, provided that the individual is given a right to have such denials reviewed if the access requested is likely to endanger the life or physical safety of the individual or another person. The individual has the right to have the denial reviewed by a licensed health care professional designated by the covered entity to act as a reviewing official and who did not participate in the original decision to deny. The covered entity must permit an individual to request access to inspect or obtain a copy of the PHI that is maintained in a designated record set. The covered entity may require individuals to request access in writing, provided that it informs individuals of such a requirement. If the covered entity provides an individual with access, it must provide PHI in designated record sets.

The covered entity may provide the individual with a summary of the PHI requested instead of providing access to the PHI or may explain the protected health information to which access has been provided if the individual agrees in advance to such a summary or explanation, and the individual agrees in advance to the fees imposed, if any, by the covered entity for such summary or explanation. The covered entity may impose a reasonable, cost-based fee. A covered entity must document and retain the documentation indicating the designated record sets that are subject to access by individuals; and the titles of the persons or offices responsible for receiving and processing requests for access by individuals.

Accounting of disclosure of PHI

An individual has a right to receive an accounting of disclosures of protected health information made by a covered entity in the six years prior to the date on which the accounting is requested, except for disclosures that are:

- To carry out treatment, payment, and health care operations
- To individuals of protected health information about them
- Incident to a use or disclosure otherwise permitted or required by this subpart,
- Pursuant to an authorization
- For the facility's directory or to persons involved in the individual's care or other notification purposes
- For national security or intelligence purposes
- To correctional institutions or law enforcement officials
- As part of a limited data set
- That occurred prior to the compliance date for the covered entity.

An individual may request an accounting of disclosures for a period of time less than six years from the date of the request. The covered entity must provide the first accounting to an individual in any 12-month period without charge. The covered entity may impose a reasonable, cost-based fee for each subsequent request for an accounting by the same individual within the 12-month period. The accounting must include disclosures of protected health information that occurred during the six years The accounting must include for each disclosure - the date of the disclosure, the name of the entity or person who received the protected health information and, if known, the address of such entity or person, a brief description of the protected health information disclosed, and a brief statement of the purpose of the disclosure that reasonably informs the individual of the basis for the disclosure or, instead of such statement, a copy of a written request for disclosure.

Security and Privacy Concepts

- **Access** means the ability or the means necessary to read, write, modify, or communicate data/information or otherwise use any system resource.
- **Administrative safeguards** are administrative actions, policies, and procedures to manage the selection, development, implementation, and maintenance of security measures to protect electronic protected health information and to manage the conduct of the covered entity's or business associate's workforce in relation to the protection of that information.
- **Authentication** means the corroboration that a person is the one claimed.
- **Breach** is the acquisition, access, use, or disclosure of PHI in a manner not permitted under the HIPAA Privacy subpart, compromising the security or privacy of the protected health information.
- **Common control** exists if an entity has the power, directly or indirectly, significantly to influence or direct the actions or policies of another entity
- **Common ownership** exists if an entity or entities possess an ownership or equity interest of 5 percent or more in another entity.
- **Confidentiality** means the property that data or information is not made available or disclosed to unauthorized persons or processes.
- **Covered function** means those functions of a covered entity, the performance of which makes the entity a health plan, health care provider, or health care clearing house.
- **Data aggregation** means combining PHI received by business associates from two different covered entities for data analysis related to the health care operations of the respective covered entities.

- **Designated record set** means a group of items, collection, or grouping of information that includes PHI and is maintained, collected, used, or disseminated by or for a covered entity. They include medical and billing records or enrollment, payment, claims, adjudication, and case or medical management records.
- **Direct treatment relationship** means a treatment relationship between an individual and a health care provider where the provider delivers health care services, products, and diagnostic reports to the individual.
- **Health care component** means a component or combination of components of a hybrid entity designated by the hybrid entity. The covered entity is responsible for designating the components that are part of one or more health care components of the covered entity and documenting the designation provided that, if the covered entity designates one or more health care components, it must include any component that would meet the definition of a covered entity or a business associate if it were a separate legal entity.
- **Health care operations** include the following activities related to covered functions
    - Conducting quality assessment and improvement activities, including outcomes evaluation and development of clinical guidelines, patient safety activities, population-based activities relating to improving health or reducing health care costs, protocol development, case management and care coordination, contacting health care providers, and patients with information about treatment alternatives, and related functions that do not include treatment.
    - Reviewing the competence or qualifications of health care professionals, evaluating practitioner and provider performance, health plan performance, conducting training programs in which students, trainees, or practitioners in areas of health care learn under supervision to practice or improve their skills as health care providers, training of non-health care professionals, accreditation, certification, licensing, or credentialing activities.
    - Underwriting, enrollment, premium rating, and other activities related to the creation, renewal, or replacement of a contract of health insurance or health benefits, and ceding, securing, or placing a contract for reinsurance of risk relating to claims for health care (including stop-loss insurance).
    - Conducting or arranging for medical review, legal services, and auditing functions, including fraud and abuse detection and compliance programs.
    - Business planning and development, such as conducting cost management and planning-related analyses related to managing and operating the entity, including formulary development and administration, development or improvement of methods of payment or coverage policies.
    - Business management and general administrative activities of the entity, including:
    - Implementation and compliance with HIPAA provisions
    - Customer service to policyholders, plan sponsors, or customers provided that PHI is not disclosed
    - Resolution of internal grievances
    - Due diligence activities related to mergers and acquisitions
    - Creation of de-identified health information or a limited data set and fundraising for the benefit of the covered entity
- **Hybrid entity** means a single legal covered entity whose business activities include both covered and non-covered functions and that designates health care components.
- **Information system** means an interconnected set of information resources under the same direct management control that shares common functionality. A system normally includes hardware, software, information, data, applications, communications, and people.
- **Integrity** means the property that data or information have not been altered or destroyed in

an unauthorized manner.

- **Marketing** means to make a communication about a product or service that encourages recipients of the communication to purchase or use the product or service. It does not include communication
  - Made to provide refill reminders or other communication about drugs that are currently being prescribed to an individual only if the direct or indirect payment (received from a third party whose product or service is being described by the covered entity) in exchange for making the communication is reasonably related to the covered entity's cost of making the communication.
  - For treatment of an individual by a health care provider, including case management or care coordination for the individuals, or to direct or recommend alternative treatments, therapies, health care providers, or settings of care to the individual
  - To describe a health-related product or service (or payment for such product or service) that is provided by, or included in a plan of benefits of, the covered entity making the communication, including communication about services, benefits, and options offered under the health plan
  - For case management or care coordination, contacting individuals with treatment alternatives and related functions to the extent these activities do not fall within the definition of treatment
- **Payment** means activities undertaken by a health plan to obtain premiums, provide reimbursement, determine or fulfill its responsibility for coverage and provision of benefits under the health plan, or by a health care provider to obtain reimbursement for the provision of health care. These activities include
  - Determinations of eligibility or coverage (including coordination of benefits or the determination of cost-sharing amounts) and adjudication or subrogation of health claims
  - Risk adjusting amounts due based on enrollee health status and demographics
  - Billing, claims management, collection activities, obtaining payment under a contract for reinsurance (including stop-loss insurance and excess of loss insurance), and related health care data processing
  - Review of health care services for medical necessity, coverage under a health plan, appropriateness of care, or justification of charges
  - Utilization review activities, including precertification and preauthorization of services, concurrent and retrospective review of services
  - Disclosure to consumer reporting agencies of any protected health information relating to the collection of premiums or reimbursement, including name, address, date of birth, social security number, payment history, account number, and details of health care provider and/or health plan
- **Physical safeguards** are physical measures, policies, and procedures to protect a covered entity's or business associate's electronic information systems and related buildings and equipment from natural and environmental hazards and unauthorized intrusion.
- **Plan administration functions** means administration functions performed by the plan sponsor of a group health plan on behalf of the group health plan and excludes functions performed by the plan sponsor in connection with any other benefit or benefit plan of the plan sponsor.
- **Psychotherapy notes** means notes recorded by a health care provider who is a mental health professional documenting or analyzing the contents of conversation during a private counseling session or group, joint, or family counseling session and that are separated from the rest of the individual's medical record.
- **Security or Security measures** encompass all of the administrative, physical, and technical

safeguards in an information system.

- **Security incident** means the attempted or successful unauthorized access, use, disclosure, modification, or destruction of information or interference with system operations in an information system.
- **Summary health information** means individually identifiable health information that summarizes the claims history, claims expenses, or type of claims experienced by individuals and from which health information identifiers have been removed and geographic information has been aggregated to the level of a five-digit ZIP Code.
- **Technical safeguards** are the technology and the policy and procedures for its use that protect electronic protected health information and control access to it.
- **User** means a person or entity with authorized access.

APPENDIX

CAREERS IN DIGITAL HEALTH

Career opportunities in digital health exploded after the passage of the HITECH Act. Before that, careers in digital health were limited to either joining the clinical informatics department of hospitals, a handful of large electronic medical record companies, or a few large software integration and implementation firms. However, aspiring digital health professionals now have a wide variety of options.

There is no one way to enter the digital health industry. A professional can enter the industry from a technical background, including software engineering, data analytics, system administration, or from the healthcare side, including clinical practice, nursing, healthcare quality, research, etc., or laterally from business roles like product management, sales, and marketing in non-digital health companies.

Students and professionals interested in developing technical expertise related to software development can avail of multiple options, including degree programs, online certifications, bootcamps, etc. There are tremendous resources available to guide students in developing coding proficiency. The technical courses cover the basics of programming and target full-stack web development, data analytics, computer fundamentals, specific coding languages, etc. There is also a growing movement of no-code tools which allow the development of production-ready applications within a short timeframe and wait for a relatively flat learning curve.

Someone with no background in healthcare who is interested in learning more about opportunities in healthcare for digital health applications can use books like this one to enhance their knowledge about healthcare-specific issues. Many universities have also launched online and in-person certificate and degree programs in health informatics and healthcare data analytics.

Digital health career opportunities

Digital health roles can be broadly divided into roles at healthcare organizations and at technology companies serving healthcare organizations, providers, or patients. In most cases, health systems are customers of digital health products and services, so the roles are primarily around using digital health technologies. However, many hospitals may also develop new software products blurring the line between the activities of software development companies and these organizations.

Physicians

In a healthcare delivery environment, physicians can assume the roles of physician informaticists, physician champions, medical directors of informatics, or Chief Medical Informatics Officers. Traditionally, the only qualification to get into these roles was personal interest; however, as these roles have become more specialized, physicians are expected to complete graduate or doctorate-level coursework, complete a fellowship, or have a board certification in clinical informatics. Physicians can also get into hospital informatics by gaining experience working as EHR super users, participating in quality projects using health care data, conduct clinical informatics research with a team of informatics professionals, data scientists, and biostatisticians to gain knowledge and experience.

Physicians can also target clinical informatics roles at digital health companies providing clinical input to developing software for health applications. Physicians are increasingly recruited in digital health roles in pharmaceutical and biotech industries, digital health consulting firms, digital marketing agencies, and health insurance companies. Physicians can work in digital health roles full-time or part-time.

Nurses

Nurses with bedside experience can enter health informatics through routes similar to physicians. There are more informatics positions for nurses in healthcare organizations than for individuals from other backgrounds. All the roles discussed above are available to nurses. The nurses can enter informatics roles directly or after formal degree or certification programs. In some roles, clinical professionals may help to translate the clinical guidelines into a structured, logical representation, which can be converted into clinical decision support tools. They can work closely with software developers to develop applications or codify workflows in the clinical software.

Data scientists and analysts

Health data scientists and analysts can have bachelor's or graduate degrees in Computer Science, Data Analytics, Statistics, Engineering, Health Information Management, Healthcare Administration, or a related analytics field. There are many self-taught data analysts, though a graduate degree or significant experience in analytics is required for data scientist roles. The roles are expected to be proficient in working with visualization and front-end tools, programming languages like R or Python, statistical packages like SPSS, SAS, and Matlab, or database query languages like SQL. The data analysts clean, transform, and ingest clinical/healthcare data and create reports or predictive analytics models. The data scientists are expected to generate insights and test hypotheses using statistical techniques and machine learning models.

It is helpful to have experience with cloud computing platforms. They work on data modeling, terminology normalization, metadata management, data curation, design, development, and deployment of machine learning applications. Advanced projects may require experience with deep learning frameworks like Pytorch or Tensorflow. Healthcare organizations with large databases may require experience with data governance, enterprise-scale data warehousing, data architecture, or data engineering.

Roles requiring interpretation of healthcare data will require knowledge of healthcare terminology and ontologies (ICD10, SNOMED, LOINC, RxNorm, CPT, NDC), data exchange standards (HL7/FHIR, CCDA, and others).

Researchers

The research projects are increasing in clinical informatics and digital health teams at academic medical centers, research institutions, pharmaceutical companies, consulting firms, and software and analytics companies. These roles generally require a doctorate. The researchers can come from a data science background or clinical background with requirements as noted above.

Software engineers

Individuals who have previously worked in technology companies as programmers can apply for similar roles in digital health companies. They may need to develop an understanding of healthcare data or workflows. The section about roles at software companies lists the type of positions available at digital companies developing software. They also have positions in healthcare systems, health insurance companies, and pharmaceutical and biotech firms. The requirements for this role include proficiency in one or more programming languages like C++, Python, Java, and Javascript, as well as software interface protocols, application testing, etc.

Information Systems professionals

Information Systems (IS) professionals maintain the information technology infrastructure of digital health organizations, including hospitals, pharmaceutical companies, and digital health startups. The background of professionals in the IS or IT department is diverse. Generally, it includes previous experience as system administrators, engineers, help desk support professionals, security analysts, software application analysts, and IT project managers. Organizations are also creating DevOps positions that work closely with software development, quality assurance, infrastructure, operations, and functional and operational departments to define, develop and deploy solutions for software delivery. The network management professionals are responsible for developing and maintaining the data network within the organization. The network management team may be a part of the infrastructure and cloud services responsible for managing desktops, servers, cloud-based IaaS, PaaS, and SaaS services.

Management professionals

There is an increasing demand for professionals with management experience in digital health. Generally, prior experience in a healthcare setting or technology company is required. In software companies, they can target roles like product managers overseeing the development of digital health tools, or they can assume managerial positions in specific functions like marketing, operations, regulatory affairs, and human resources and make their way up to the executive suite. In health systems, they can take on roles ranging from Director of IT to Chief Information Officer.

Medical students

Medical students who intend to work in informatics are digital health after graduation instead of pursuing residency can explore graduate degree programs or consulting firms. Students with a technical background or college-level software development or data analytics coursework can directly apply for positions in health systems, digital health companies, or informatics research.

Nursing students

Students currently in nursing school who intend to go into informatics can traverse any of the multiple paths to getting positions in digital health. They can start working as a nurse but either volunteer or find a part-time position in the informatics team as 'elbow support' or 'super-user.' After gaining some experience, they can eventually move into full-time informatics roles. These positions can lead to positions in digital health companies or consulting firms. They can also enhance their skills by completing specialized informatics, data analytics, or software development coursework.

College students

College students have little experience with the healthcare industry or operations, so the easiest way to get into digital health is through business or technical roles. Digital health companies need marketing, customer service, human resources, sales, clinical research, and operations teams. They also have traditional software development roles, including software engineering, quality assurance, user interface, user design, etc. Health systems have teams for data analytics and quality, IT support or help desk, and information services. Many college students target consulting firms focusing on healthcare technology strategy and implementation or generic strategy consulting firms. After gaining experience, they can move into the digital health industry.

Roles at health care organizations

Healthcare delivery organizations with digital health roles include hospitals, ambulatory surgery centers, and physician offices. Conventionally, the roles are divided between clinical informatics and IT departments. The IT department is responsible for creating and managing the physical IT infrastructure in the hospital, including PCs, networks, printers, etc. The clinical informatics department handles the deployment and maintenance of software systems. They are also responsible for training the clinical staff on using the software systems. Hospitals also have biomedical engineering departments which keep the medical equipment like ventilators, endoscopes, EKG machines, etc. Some of the typical roles at healthcare organizations are discussed below:

CMIO / CNIO

Chief Medical Information Officer (CMIO) is the leader of the clinical informatics team. Some organizations also have a Chief Nursing Information Officer (CNIO) who works with CMIO in the clinical informatics leadership dyad. CMIOs oversee all the clinical software in the healthcare organization. The role of the CMIO is to develop the clinical informatics strategy in association with the Chief Medical Officer (CMO) and Chief Information Officer (CIO), oversee the implementation and optimization of clinical information systems, interface with clinical and administrative leaders, serve on strategy, operational, technology, and analytics committees. CMIOs usually have previous experience as medical directors of informatics or physician champions in the informatics teams. Some roles require board certification in clinical informatics.

CIO

The Chief Information Officer is the leader of Information Services at a healthcare organization. A CIO may report to CEO, COO, or CMO. The CIO develops the technology strategy of the organization and approves all technology-related purchases by the organization. The clinical informatics department may report to the CIO.

Physician informaticist

Physician informaticists play a critical role in a health system and acts as a bridge between the chief medical information officer or the informatics team and the physicians on staff. Physician informaticists may or may not have formal training in informatics. The responsibilities of physician informaticists could vary significantly across organizations. Their responsibilities could include supporting the technical team in developing and configuring electronic medical record interfaces and order sets and providing inputs to developing clinical decision support, including algorithms for triggering alerts. The top priority for physician informaticists is building relationships with clinicians. Physician informaticists also serve on hospital-wide committees, including quality improvement, population health, and data analytics. They also worked closely with nurse informaticists to develop strategies to improve caregivers' adoption of electronic medical records. Physician informaticists may also maintain clinical practice to a varying degree.

Some organizations have medical directors of informatics who oversee informatics teams. They support provider training, informatics workflow optimization, developing relationships, and communicating with clinical specialties.

Nurse informaticists

Nurse informaticists work alongside physician informaticists and are usually bedside nurses who move into an Informaticist position full-time or part-time. They act as an interface between the nurses and the chief nurse informatics officer or informatics team. The nursing staff's documentation burden has dramatically increased over the last 10 years as EMRs have become widely deployed. Nurse Informaticists work closely with the informatics team to ensure that the informatics workflows are aligned with nursing workflows, the documentation requirements are manageable, and nurses are on appropriate and efficient use of software applications, including EMR, analytics dashboards, and patient monitoring equipment.

Physician champion

A physician champion is a physician with medical staff privileges at the hospital who is responsible for educating and guiding providers around technology issues. This is generally a part-time or temporary role. The physician champion provides elbow support during EHR go-live and subsequently provides training and consults with super users who could be nurses or other physicians. Physician champions also engage with clinical and administrative leaders to inform them about the clinical informatics projects and gather feedback.

Nurse champion

Nurse champion participates in designing, building, and testing informatics products nurses use. The role of the nurse champion is to represent the nurses on the clinical informatics and hospital technology committees. The champions also develop, review and present the training curriculum to the nursing staff. The nursing champions are the primary source of communication between the clinical informatics leadership and the front-line nursing staff.

Super user

Super users are physicians, nurses, or other clinical providers who support users of software products in a healthcare setting. They interface with clinical informaticists, end users, department leadership, and the helpdesk. They are responsible for increasing the adoption of technologies in healthcare delivery organizations. They also provide ongoing training to the staff.

Clinical informaticist

The Clinical informaticist roles can be with the clinical informatics department or with pharmacy informatics, laboratory informatics, radiology informatics, etc. Clinical informaticists play a key role in healthcare organizations and help to deploy, optimize, and maintain electronic medical record systems and other clinical applications. They are responsible for troubleshooting any issues with the clinical systems. They are the first to respond if any provider has difficulty operating the software applications inside the hospital. Clinical informaticists are also responsible for training the clinical and administrative staff on clinical applications.

Healthcare data analyst

Data analyst positions are critical roles in healthcare organizations. The data analysts can work within a dedicated analytics department or be part of an operational team of the hospital, like strategy, finance, pharmacy, quality, nursing, surgery, etc. The analyst's role varies depending on the project's needs or the department. However, generally, they work on clinical, administrative, and financial data to develop reports, dashboards, or data-driven insights to address specific business questions. Data analysts can also work on advanced predictive analytics using machine learning techniques in some roles.

Informatics researcher

The researcher positions are primarily in universities, research institutions, and academic medical centers. These positions may not require a doctorate but generally require clinical informatics and data analytics proficiency. Generally, research projects are funded by grants from government or private funding agencies, but health systems and digital health companies are increasingly funding informatics research.

Information Technology (IT) professionals

The information technology department is one of the most critical departments in healthcare. IT professionals work 24x7 to ensure that the technology powering the healthcare system does not have downtime and that all troubleshooting requests are addressed as soon as possible. Most IT roles require experience working with enterprise IT departments. Generally, a bachelor's degree is required. However, relevant experience can trump professional education credentials.

Roles at digital health companies

The roles of software companies developing digital health products and services are similar to non-healthcare software companies. They include software engineers, product managers, marketers, sales professionals, customer service representatives, operational executives, legal experts, HR professionals, etc. There is abundant literature about the roles at a typical software company, job requirements, and job descriptions. Roles requiring some healthcare domain knowledge are discussed here. For example, many companies hire clinical informaticians or healthcare data analysts to work on clinical data.

Broadly, digital health companies can be classified into enterprise-focused and consumer-focused. The customers of enterprise companies could be hospitals or healthcare systems, employers, medical device manufacturers, or pharmaceutical companies. The companies themselves could be large, mature organizations, or they could be startups. Joining either of those has its pros and cons. This book's website shows examples of specific companies in each category.

- **Administrative automation and supply chain**: Products and services to automate administrative workflows, clinical and revenue cycle workflows in hospitals or health insurance companies.
- **Analytics products and services**: These companies provide tools and services to healthcare providers, payors, or other supporting organizations for quality improvement, clinical and administrative decision support, and predictive analytics in clinical and administrative workflows.
- **Clinical research management**: Tools and services to improve patient recruitment, clinical trial data analysis, creating digital twins for control arms, and clinical trial operations management. Real World Evidence to support clinical research with clinical, genetic, molecular databases, and analytics tools.
- **Consumer health and wellness apps**: Apps that track sleep, exercise, meditation, and menstrual cycles.
- **Database and providers**: These companies provide hosted or on-premise deployment of data warehouses, data lakes, cloud storage, business continuity, and disaster recovery products and services.
- **Clinical service line information and scheduling systems**: These are information systems developed to focus on the specialized needs of different clinical service lines and departments. They include electronic medical records, scheduling, and workflow management systems. These are targeted towards Radiology, Dietary, Emergency Department, Gastroenterology/Endoscopy, Critical care, Laboratory, Pathology, Labor & Delivery, Long term care, Operating Room, Ophthalmology, Pharmacy, Rehabilitation, Respiratory care, Physical Therapy, Cardiology, and Oncology.
- **Disease management and therapeutics**: Technology-enabled platforms providing a combination of automation and human intervention for health monitoring and improvement targeting medical conditions including insomnia, obesity, diabetes, chronic pain, etc.
- **Electronic Health Records**: EHRs capture and display data captured in the hospitals. They are agnostic to the clinical area where they are used. These include acute care and ambulatory systems and home health EHRs. Some companies provide add-ons to these EHRs, like Clinical Physician Order Entry systems, electronic Prescription systems, etc.
- **Health Information Exchange systems**: Health Information Exchange platforms and

system integration solutions include interface engines and APIs to connect apps with the health systems.

- **Health Information Management systems**: They support the workflows and processes of the Health Information Management department, including patient registration and scheduling systems, Dictation, and speech recognition systems, document management systems, revenue cycle management systems, including medical billing and coding, and claims processing.
- **Health plan and benefits management**: Specialized solutions targeting health plans, third-party administrators, or health benefit managers at employers. These include tools for tracking healthcare benefits for employers, insurance plans, and actuarial tools.
- **Image management systems**: Radiology department is one of the most technology-dependent healthcare departments. The images generate a large amount of data. Some solutions include image visualization, manipulation and analysis, Picture Archival and Communication Systems, and image storage and distribution systems.
- **IT consulting firms**: These firms provide a wide gamut of services: Some of the most significant areas are implementation and training of IT systems, overall technology strategy, IT project management, technology or data integration projects, and regulatory and compliance consulting.
- **Medical content providers**: These companies create physician and nursing practice references, clinical treatment guidelines and protocols, and health education and wellness information websites or apps.
- **Patient health tracking systems**: Software developed for vital signs monitoring, behavioral and lifestyle improvement apps, symptom checking and triage apps, on-demand consultations via text, voice, or video, laboratory testing, remote patient monitoring, and medication adherence.
- **Personal health record systems**: This includes apps and websites which enable patients to track their health data on the websites or mobile apps. They may have unidirectional or bidirectional flow of data.
- **Pharma and hospital supply chain management systems**: These supply chain management are customized for pharma and hospital supply chains. They specialize in tracking drugs, devices, and medical consumables.
- **Population health management systems**: These systems track population-level data and have in-built analytics to identify trends and suggest interventions. They include public health databases, registries, and tools for CMS Value-based payment initiatives.
- **Privacy & Security providers**: These include biometric identification and single sign-on providers, anti-malware and ransomware products and services.
- **Screening and diagnostics tools**: These tools use advanced technologies for image recognition and signal analysis and are used for radiology or pathology image analysis, gene analysis, biochemistry, and microbiology test analysis.
- **Software systems associated with hardware devices**: These include software provided with imaging equipment, RFID trackers, infusion pumps, barcode scanners, biometric scanners, etc.
- **Specialty care solutions**: These are digital solutions focused on managing patients with specific diagnoses like end-stage renal disease, addiction, depression, congestive heart failure, etc. They work in conjunction with a generic or specialty focused EHR system.
- **Virtual health care delivery**: These include platforms that provide products and services for telemedicine services.

Clinical informaticists

Digital health companies are recruiting clinical informaticists to help them understand and use the clinical data appropriately in the applications. The clinical informaticists work closely with the software engineers and the product managers to help develop the product or service. Besides clinical informatics professionals, individuals with healthcare delivery experience, like MDs, RNs, NPs, or PAs, can also apply for these positions if they have experience with healthcare technology. It is helpful to have a fellowship, master's, or Ph.D. in informatics or related fields, and in some cases, experience with clinical quality measures like HEDIS, PQA, etc. may be required. It is helpful to have experience working with healthcare systems such as EHRs, Health Information Exchanges (HIEs), clinical data interface engines, or other clinical systems, including laboratory information systems (LIS), clinical decision support systems (CDSS), radiology information systems (RIS), picture archiving and communication systems (PACS), or admission, discharge & transfer (ADT) systems. It is also essential to understand healthcare terminologies like ICD-10, SNOMED, LOINC, UMLS, etc. Some organizations may require board certification in clinical informatics for physicians, ANCC Nursing Informatics Board Certification for nurses, or CPHIMS / CAHIMS certifications.

Clinical informaticists working on clinical decision support tools may be expected to know about clinical rules and rule templates, health information models, guideline representation tools like GLIF, healthcare data exchange standards like HL7 v2, FHIR, semantic definitions and relationships, terminology value sets, order set authoring tools, knowledge graphs, Web Ontology Language (OWL), Labeled Property Graphs, Business Rules Management Systems (BRMS) or decision management tools like Decision Model and Notation (DMN), Clinical Quality Language (CQL), observational data standards like Observational Medical Outcomes Partnership (OMOP), storage standards like Open EHR, clinical research standards like Clinical Data Interchange Standards Consortium (CDISC).

Health data scientists

The role of data scientists is rapidly expanding in healthcare companies. Data scientists and analysts can work at companies primarily providing data analytics products or services or join other digital health companies that embed analytics into their core products. The analysts are generally expected to understand the healthcare workflows and standards, software programming, and core data analytics skills. Some experience extracting, curating, and integrating data from multiple clinical data sources such as electronic medical record systems, disease registries, and claims databases may be required.

Clinical professionals

Clinical professionals may work in companies' business development, R&D, and product development. They may include MD, NP, PA, RN, Physical Therapist, Occupational Therapist, Dietitian, Clinical Social Worker, Respiratory Therapist, etc. Experience with either outpatient or inpatient clinical settings is helpful.

These professionals analyze, design, validate, and test workflows of provider interaction with digital health products. They may contribute to developing clinical content or algorithms based on clinical content. They may also train healthcare professionals to use digital health products.

Product managers

Product managers identify customer needs, define specifications, and ensure timely product development and ongoing iteration based on customer feedback. They may also be responsible for developing customer relationships regarding enterprise products. Product managers may have a business degree, but generally, they get promoted from technical roles. Most product managers in the digital health industry move from companies that are not in healthcare.

Roles in research and academia

Clinical informatics is a significant area of academic research in healthcare. The research programs could range from applying technology to healthcare delivery to research on clinical apps. The researchers can work on data sets from electronic medical record systems, picture archives and communication systems, administrative data, or other large healthcare data repositories, including social determinants of health data, census data, and claims data. This work requires experience and knowledge of medical vocabularies, common data models, and EHR interoperability platforms. The clinical informatics research programs at academic medical centers also work closely with the administrative and operational teams from the healthcare delivery system, supporting areas like healthcare quality, healthcare analytics, and health services research. Depending on their qualifications, individuals can join as a researcher or as operational or technical support to the research group. In many cases, the researchers in research-oriented programs are expected to obtain external funding to support the research efforts.

The clinical informatics teaching programs recruit faculty members with prior experience in applied or research domains of clinical informatics. Clinical informatics faculty are also employed in medical schools, nursing schools, and schools of allied health professions like healthcare administration, public health, etc.

These roles require MD, Ph.D., and RN with experience in informatics research. Senior research roles may require significant work experience in biomedical or health informatics with graduate degrees in computer science, computer engineering, biomedical informatics, applied mathematics, biostatistics, medicine, nursing, health services research, clinical epidemiology, public health, etc.

Roles at consulting firms

Digital health consulting firms provide a broad spectrum of services. Please refer to the chapter about digital health products and services for more details about these firms' services. Broadly, these include services to hospitals around EMR deployment or application integration, among many others, services to digital health product companies around regulatory needs or specialized domain expertise, and services to pharmaceutical, medical device, or pharmacy companies around the development and deployment of digital health products and services.

Consulting firms can provide individuals with broad exposure to digital health, especially at an early stage of the career. There are opportunities within the digital health teams at generic or digital health-only consulting firms. Interested individuals can target even further specialized consulting firms working on medical informatics, digital health apps, or enterprise applications.

Alternatively, they can work with consulting firms with most clients in healthcare delivery, health insurance, or digital health companies.

The consulting firms hire professionals from all backgrounds ranging from fresh graduates to experienced clinicians with decades of clinical experience. Any background discussed earlier can be recruited at a digital health consulting firm. Besides providing a decent learning experience, exposure to a diverse set of industry problems and opportunities to solve them, and training on technology, consulting firms may also help obtain vendor certifications which can help in career growth.

Roles in pharma and medical device companies

The digital health roles in pharmaceutical companies are quite diverse. These could be with the medical affairs, digital innovation, data science, health economics and outcomes research, biostatistics, and Health IT departments. In medical device companies, there could be roles with the core product development team if digital health technology is the core product or a significant component of the core product. Pharmaceutical and medical device companies are using healthcare data in the research and development of their product or services. Some examples include companion apps with continuous glucose monitors and apps to monitor adverse events for patients on immunotherapy agents.

Roles with pharmaceutical drug development may need to work with clinical and/or biomedical data and perform various activities, including clinical data extraction, data analysis and management, data modeling, and predictive modeling. The bioinformatics roles may be separate from the clinical informatics or in the same department.

There is also a need for information technology professionals and system administrators who manage the vast technology infrastructure powering the pharma and medical device companies. These roles are not unique to this industry; however, the size of databases may require specialist expertise in handling large-scale pharma data. The experience and qualification requirements are similar to the other roles that have been discussed previously.

Roles in health insurance

Health insurance companies are increasingly employing professionals with digital health skills as they move into offering value-based contracts, disease management, digital well-being tools, and care coordination programs. Data analysts play a key role in health insurance operations due to the large volume and management of data. The analysts are expected to have an understanding of the healthcare claims data, clinical data standards, quality, and utilization management metrics, database management including extract, transform, and loading processes, data manipulation, visualization tools, and scripting with SQL or statistical tools like SAS, SPSS, or R. The analysts also work on analytics and reporting to improve quality measures. The other common technology roles in health insurance companies include software engineering, networking engineering, database management, infrastructure services, systems analysis, application development, application maintenance and support, support, quality assurance, UI/UX designers, enterprise architects, and IT project managers.

Telemedicine and remote patient monitoring

The roles at telehealth and remote patient monitoring organizations could broadly be in three categories: clinical, administration, and technology. Clinical professionals provide clinical services to the clients. The clinical staff is responsible for establishing and maintaining policies and procedures for the medical practice affiliated with the telemedicine organization. They work with the legal team to ensure the organization complies with regulatory requirements.

The administration professionals are responsible for managing day to day operations of the organization and could include executives, department managers, and support staff. They are responsible for hiring, credentialing, and driving engagement of the staff as well as routing organizational activities like financial management, budgeting, marketing, sales, etc.

The role of technology professionals could vary depending on whether the organization is developing telemedicine technology or providing telemedicine services. In the former, the roles will be similar to any digital health software company; in the latter case, they will be similar to a healthcare delivery organization.

REFERENCES

- AAPC. CPT Codes Lookup. https://www.aapc.com/codes/cpt-codes-range. Accessed May 12, 2021
- AAPC. CPT® 0105U, Under Proprietary Laboratory Analyses. https://www.aapc.com/codes/cpt-codes/0105U. Accessed December 21, 2021
- Aapro M, Bossi P, Dasari A, Fallowfield L, Gascón P, Geller M, Jordan K, Kim J, Martin K, Porzig S. Digital health for optimal supportive care in oncology: benefits, limits, and future perspectives. Support Care Cancer. 2020 Oct;28(10):4589-4612
- Abdel-Massih RC, Mellors JW. Telemedicine and Infectious Diseases Practice: A Leap Forward or a Step Back?. Open Forum Infect Dis. 2019;6(5):ofz196
- Abdolahi A, Bull MT, Darwin KC, Venkataraman V, Grana M, Dorsey ER, Biglan KM. A feasibility study of conducting the Montreal Cognitive Assessment remotely in individuals with movement disorders. Health Informatics Journal 2016, Vol. 22(2) 304–311
- Abdolahi A, Scoglio N, Killoran A, Dorsey ER, Biglan KM. Potential reliability and validity of a modified version of the Unified Parkinson's Disease Rating Scale that could be administered remotely. Parkinsonism Relat Disord 2013;19:218-221
- Abe Y, Sato S, Kato K, Hyakumachi T, Yanagibashi Y, Ito M, et al. A novel 3D guidance system using augmented reality for percutaneous vertebroplasty: technical note. J Neurosurg Spine. 2013;19:492–501.
- Abhishek Makkar, R Michael Siatkowski, Edgardo Szyld, Abhrajit Ganguly, Kris Sekar. Scope of telemedicine in neonatology. Chin J Contemp Pediatr, 2020, 22(5): 396-408
- Abraham WT, Compton S, Haas G, Foreman B, Canby RC, Fishel R, et al. Intrathoracic impedance vs daily weight monitoring for predicting worsening heart failure events: results of the Fluid Accumulation Status Trial (FAST) Congest Heart Fail. 2011;17(2):51–5
- Abrashkin KA, Washko J, Zhang J, Poku A, Kim H, Smith KL. Providing Acute Care at Home: Community Paramedics Enhance an Advanced Illness Management Program-Preliminary Data. J Am Geriatr Soc. 2016 Dec;64(12):2572-2576
- Accenture. Artificial Intelligence: Healthcare's New Nervous System. https://www.accenture.com/us-en/insight-artificial-intelligence-healthcare Accessed September 12, 2021
- ACP. COVID-19 State and Private Payer Policies. 2/26/2021. https://www.acponline.org/practice-resources/covid-19-practice-management-resources/covid-19-state-and-private-payer-policies. Accessed January 25, 2022
- Aczon, M. et al. Dynamic mortality risk predictions in pediatric critical care using recurrent neural networks. arXiv [stat.ML] (2017)
- ADA Guide to Understanding and Documenting Teledentistry Events. Chicago, Illinois: American Dental Association, 2017
- Adam Yala, Constance Lehman, Tal Schuster, Tally Portnoi, and Regina Barzilay. A Deep Learning Mammography-based Model for Improved Breast Cancer Risk Prediction. Radiology 2019 292:1, 60-66
- Adcock AK, Kosiorek H, Parich P, et al. Reliability of robotic telemedicine for assessing critically ill patients with the Full Outline of UnResponsiveness score and Glasgow Coma Scale. Telemed. e-Health 23(7):555-560, 2017
- Adler AJ, Martin N, Mariani J, Tajer CD, Owolabi OO, Free C, Serrano NC, Casas JP, Perel P. Mobile phone text messaging to improve medication adherence in secondary prevention of cardiovascular disease. Cochrane Database Syst Rev. 2017 Apr 29;4(4):CD011851
- Agency for Healthcare Research and Quality (AHRQ). Registries for Evaluating Patient Outcomes: A User's Guide: 3rd Edition. Research Report. April 30, 2014. https://effectivehealthcare.ahrq.gov/topics/registries-guide-3rd-edition/research. Accessed October 12, 2022
- Ahmed, F. Z., Taylor, J. K., Green, C., Moore, L., Goode, A., Black, P., Howard, L., Fullwood, C., Zaidi, A., Seed, A., Cunnington, C., and Motwani, M. (2020) Triage-HF Plus: a novel device-based remote monitoring pathway to identify worsening heart failure. ESC Heart Failure, 7: 108– 117
- Ahn DT. The COVID-19 Pandemic: A "Tech"-tonic Shift Toward Virtual Diabetes Care. J Diabetes Sci Technol. 2020 Jul;14(4):708-709
- AHRQ. AHRQ Quality indicators. 2021. https://qualityindicators.ahrq.gov. Accessed August 16, 2021
- Aitken M, Gauntlett C. Patient Apps for Improved Healthcare: from Novelty to Mainstream. Parsippany, NJ: IMS Institute for Healthcare Informatics, 2013
- Aitken, M., Clancy, B. & Nass, D. The Growing Value of Digital Health: Evidence and Impact on Human Health and the Healthcare System (IQVIA Institute for Human Data Science, 2017)
- Ajami S, Arzani-Birgani A. Fast resuscitation and care of the burn patients by telemedicine: A review. J. Res. Med. Sci. 19(6):562-566, 2014 [a]
- Ajami S, Lamoochi P. Use of telemedicine in disaster and remote places. J. Educ. Health Promot. 3:26, 2014) [b]
- Ajibade A, Younas H, Pullan M, Harky A. Telemedicine in cardiovascular surgery during COVID-19 pandemic: A systematic review and our experience. J Card Surg. 2020;35(10):2773-2784
- Akazawa M, Hashimoto K. Prediction of preterm birth using artificial intelligence: a systematic review. J Obstet Gynaecol. 2022 Aug;42(6):1662-1668
- Akbari M, Lankarani KB, Naghibzadeh-Tahami A, Tabrizi R, Honarvar B, Kolahdooz F, Borhaninejad V, Asemi Z. The effects of mobile health interventions on lipid profiles among patients with metabolic syndrome and related disorders: A systematic review and meta-analysis of randomized controlled trials. Diabetes Metab Syndr. 2019 May-Jun;13(3):1949-1955
- Akhtar M, Van Heukelom PG, Ahmed A, et al. Telemedicine physical examination utilizing a consumer device demonstrates poor concordance with in-person physical examination in emergency department patients with sore throat: a prospective blinded study. Telemed. eHealth 24(10):790-796, 2018

- Akl A, Snoek J, Mihailidis A. Unobtrusive Detection of Mild Cognitive Impairment in Older Adults Through Home Monitoring. IEEE J Biomed Health Inform. 2017 Mar;21(2):339-348
- Alachram H, Chereda H, Beißbarth T, Wingender E, Stegmaier P. Text mining-based word representations for biomedical data analysis and protein-protein interaction networks in machine learning tasks. PLoS One. 2021 Oct 15;16(10):e0258623.
- Alagappan M, Brown JRG, Mori Y, Berzin TM. Artificial intelligence in gastrointestinal endoscopy: The future is almost here. World J Gastrointest Endosc. 2018;10(10):239-249
- Alammar, J (2018). The Illustrated Transformer [Blog post]. Retrieved from https://jalammar.github.io/illustrated-transformer/
- Alan F. Westin, Computers, Health Records, and Citizen Rights, National Bureau of Standards Monograph 157, p. 6 (U.S. Government Printing Office, Washington, DC, 1976)
- Alan F. Westin, Privacy and Freedom, p. 7 (Atheneum, New York, 1967)
- Al-Arkee S, Mason J, Lane DA, et al. Mobile Apps to Improve Medication Adherence in Cardiovascular Disease: Systematic Review and Meta-analysis. J Med Internet Res. 2021;23(5):e24190
- AlAzab R, Khader Y. Telenephrology application in rural and remote areas of Jordan: benefits and impact on quality of life. Rural Remote Health. 2016 Jan-Mar;16(1):3646
- Albergotti. R. "The secret history of Elon Musk, Sam Altman, and OpenAI | Semafor". Semafor.com. March 24, 2023. Retrieved April 28, 2023. https://www.semafor.com/article/03/24/2023/the-secret-history-of-elon-musk-sam-altman-and-openai
- Albert L, Capel I, García-Sáez G, Martín-Redondo P, Hernando ME, Rigla M. Managing gestational diabetes mellitus using a smartphone application with artificial intelligence (SineDie) during the COVID-19 pandemic: Much more than just telemedicine. Diabetes Res Clin Pract. 2020;169:108396
- Alessandrini EA, Alpern ER, Chamberlain JM, Shea JA, Gorelick MH. A new diagnosis grouping system for child emergency department visits. Acad Emerg Med. 2010;17(2):204–213
- Alfano G, Fontana F, Ferrari A, et al. Peritoneal dialysis in the time of coronavirus disease 2019. Clin Kidney J. 2020;13(3):265-268
- Al-Kadi A, Dyer D, Ball CG, et al. User's perceptions of remote trauma telesonography. J. Telemed. Telecare. 15(5):251-254, 2009
- Almathami HKY, Win KT, Vlahu-Gjorgievska E. Barriers and Facilitators That Influence Telemedicine-Based, Real-Time, Online Consultation at Patients' Homes: Systematic Literature Review. J Med Internet Res. 2020 Feb 20;22(2):e16407
- Alpaydin E. Introduction to Machine Learning. MIT Press, 2014.
- Alpert A., Morgani KG, Margolis G.S., Wasserman J., and Kellerman A.L. Giving EMS Flexibility in Transporting Low-Acuity Patients Could Generate Substantial Medicare Savings. Health Aff (Milwood)2013; 32(12): 2142-2148
- Alsentzer, E., Murphy, J. R., Boag, W., Weng, W. H., Jin, D., Naumann, T., & McDermott, M. (2019). Publicly available clinical BERT embeddings. arXiv preprint arXiv:1904.03323. Available at https://github.com/EmilyAlsentzer/clinicalBERT
- Alshabanat A, Otterstatter MC, Sin DD, Road J, Rempel C, Burns J, van Eeden SF, FitzGerald JM. Impact of a COPD comprehensive case management program on hospital length of stay and readmission rates. Int J Chron Obstruct Pulmon Dis. 2017; 12():961-971
- Alshabani K, Attaway AA, Smith MJ, Majumdar U, Rice R, Han X, Wang X, Hatipoğlu U. Electronic inhaler monitoring and healthcare utilization in chronic obstructive pulmonary disease. J Telemed Telecare. 2020 Aug-Sep;26(7-8):495-503
- Altamura D, Avramidis M, Menzies SW. Assessment of the optimal interval for and sensitivity of short-term sequential digital dermoscopy monitoring for the diagnosis of melanoma. Arch Dermatol. 2008;144(4):502-506
- Alvarez-Jimenez, M, Rice, S, D'Alfonso, S, et al. A Novel multimodal digital service (moderated online social therapy+) for help-seeking young people experiencing mental ill-health: pilot evaluation within a national youth e-mental health service. J Med Int Res. 2020;22(8):e17155
- Alverson DC, Edison K, Flournoy L, Korte B, Magruder C, Miller C. Telehealth tools for public health, emergency, or disaster preparedness and response: a summary report. Telemed. eHealth16(1):112-114, 2010
- AMA. CARES Act: AMA COVID-19 pandemic telehealth factsheet. April 27, 2020. https://www.ama-assn.org/delivering-care/public-health/cares-act-ama-covid-19-pandemic-telehealth-fact-sheet. Accessed Jun 20, 2021
- AMA. CPT Editorial Summary of Panel Actions. September-October 2021. https://www.ama-assn.org/system/files/september-october-2021-summary-of-panel-actions.pdf. Accessed December 28, 2021
- Amatriain, X. (2023, February 17). Transformer models: an introduction and catalog. arXiv:2302.07730 [cs.CL]
- Ambrosino N, Vitacca M, Dreher M, et al. Tele-monitoring of ventilator-dependent patients: a European Respiratory Society Statement. Eur. Respir. J. 48(3):648-663, 2016
- America's Health Insurance Plans (AHIP). Telehealth: Connecting Consumers to Care Everywhere. https://www.ahip.org/wp-content/uploads/IB_Telehealth-031219.pdf. Published 2019. Accessed February 15, 2020
- American College of Rheumatology (ACR). Medical Malpractice Coverage for Telehealth Services. March 27, 2020. https://www.rheumatology.org/Portals/0/Files/Medical-Malpractice-Insurance-Telehealth-Coverage.pdf
- American Dental Hygienists Association (ADHA). 2016. Dental Hygienists Restorative Duties - State Chart. Available at: https://www.adha.org/resources-docs/7516_Restorative_Duties_by_State.pdf. Accessed 12 February 2021
- American Medical Association. Medicare Physician Payment Schedule. 2020. https://www.ama-assn.org/practice-management/medicare-medicaid/medicare-physician-payment-schedule
- American Psychiatric Association. DSM-5 Tabe of Contents. 2013. https://www.psychiatry.org/File%20Library/Psychiatrists/Practice/DSM/APA_DSM-5-Contents.pdf. Accessed June 15, 2021
- Ames HM, Glenton C, Lewin S, Tamrat T, Akama E, Leon N. Clients' perceptions and experiences of targeted digital communication accessible via mobile devices for reproductive, maternal, newborn, child, and adolescent health: a qualitative

evidence synthesis. Cochrane Database Syst Rev. 2019 Oct 14;10(10):CD013447

- Amir Bar, Lior Wolf, Orna Bergman Amitai, Eyal Toledano, and Eldad Elnekave "Compression fractures detection on CT", Proc. SPIE 10134, Medical Imaging 2017: Computer-Aided Diagnosis, 1013440 (3 March 2017)
- Amwell. From Virtual Care to Hybrid Care: COVID-19 and the Future of Telehealth. Insights from the 2020 Amwell Physician and Consumer Survey. https://static.americanwell.com/app/uploads/2020/09/Amwell-2020-Physician-and-Consumer-Survey.pdf. Accessed November 21, 2021
- Anderson KE, Byrne CE, Crosby RD, Le Grange D. Utilizing Telehealth to deliver family-based treatment for adolescent anorexia nervosa. Int J Eat Disord. 2017 Oct;50(10):1235-1238
- Angelucci A, Aliverti A. Telemonitoring systems for respiratory patients: technological aspects. Pulmonology. 2020 Jul-Aug;26(4):221-232
- Angus DC, Kelley MA, Schmitz RJ, White A, Popovich J Jr; Committee on Manpower for Pulmonary and Critical Care Societies (COMPACCS). Caring for the critically ill patient. Current and projected workforce requirements for care of the critically ill and patients with pulmonary disease: can we meet the requirements of an aging population? JAMA. 2000 Dec 6;284(21):2762-70
- Anicas M. An introduction to OAuth 2. July 21, 2014. https://www.digitalocean.com/community/tutorials/an-introduction-to-oauth-2
- Anne L. Peters and Satish K. Garg. The Silver Lining to COVID-19: Avoiding Diabetic Ketoacidosis Admissions with Telehealth. Diabetes Technology & Therapeutics 2020 22:6, 449-453
- Anooj PK. Clinical decision support system: risk level prediction of heart disease using decision tree fuzzy rules. Int J Res Rev Comput Sci. 2012;3(3):1659–1667
- ANSI (2010). "Introduction". Implementation Guide for CDA R2 HITSP C32, C83, and C80 Summary Documents. Model-Driven Health Tools (MDHT) for CDA
- Antonio Villegas, Josep Vilalta. HL7 Reference Information Model. Rim Explorer. VICO. http://vico.org/HL7_RIM/index.html. Accessed November 21, 2021
- Anvari M, McKinley C, Stein H. Establishment of the world's first telerobotic remote surgical service: for provision of advanced laparoscopic surgery in a rural community. Ann Surg. 2005 Mar;241(3):460-4
- Arbeille P, Fornage B, Boucher A, et al. Telesonography: virtual 3D image processing of remotely acquired abdominal, vascular, and fetal sonograms. J. Clin. Ultrasound 42(2):67-73, 2014
- Arevian AC, Jeffrey J, Young AS, Ong MK. Opportunities for flexible, on-demand care delivery through telemedicine. Psychiatr Serv. 69(1):5-8, 2018
- Armstrong KA, Coyte PC, Brown M, Beber B, Semple JL. Effect of Home Monitoring via Mobile App on the Number of In-Person Visits Following Ambulatory Surgery: A Randomized Clinical Trial. JAMA Surg. 2017 Jul 1;152(7):622-627
- Arnerić SP, Cedarbaum JM, Khozin S, Papapetropoulos S, Hill DL, Ropacki M, et al. Biometric monitoring devices for assessing end points in clinical trials: developing an ecosystem. Nat Rev Drug Discov. 2017;16(10):736
- Arnold CW, El-Saden SM, Bui AAT, Taira R. Clinical Case-based Retrieval Using Latent Topic Analysis. AMIA Annual Symposium Proceedings. 2010;2010:26–30
- Arnold S, Esernio-Jenssen D. Telemedicine: reducing trauma in evaluating abuse. Chapt. 6 in: R. Madhavan, S. Khalid (eds.), Telemedicine. InTech, 2013
- ASQ (American Society for Quality). https://asq.org/. Accessed July 26, 2021
- Athanasiadis T, Beule A, Embate J. et al. Standardized video-endoscopy and surgical field grading scale for endoscopic sinus surgery: a multi-centre study. Laryngoscope 2008; 118: 314-319
- Augestad KM, Sneve AM, Lindsetmo RO. Telemedicine in postoperative follow-up of STOMa PAtients: a randomized clinical trial (the STOMPA trial). Br J Surg. 2020 Apr;107(5):509-518
- Augusterfer EF: Clinically informed telemental health in post disaster areas. In Myers K, Turvey CL (eds.): Telemental Health, Elsevier, pp. 347-366, 2013
- Avati A, Jung K, Harman S, Downing L, Ng A, Shah NH. Improving palliative care with deep learning. BMC Med Inform Decis Mak. 2018 Dec 12;18(Suppl 4):122
- Avati, A., Jung, K., Harman, S. et al. Improving palliative care with deep learning. BMC Med Inform Decis Mak 18 (Suppl 4), 122 (2018).
- Avram R, Olgin JE, Kuhar P, Hughes JW, Marcus GM, Pletcher MJ, Aschbacher K, Tison GH. A digital biomarker of diabetes from smartphone-based vascular signals. Nat Med. 2020 Oct;26(10):1576-1582
- Azuma R. A survey of augmented reality. Presence Teleoperators Virtual Environ. 1997 Aug;6(4):355–85
- Babrak LM, Menetski J, Rebhan M, Nisato G, Zinggeler M, Brasier N, Baerenfaller K, Brenzikofer T, Baltzer L, Vogler C, Gschwind L, Schneider C, Streiff F, Groenen PM, Miho E. Traditional and digital biomarkers: two worlds apart? Digit Biomark. 2019 Aug 16;3(2):92–102
- Baeßler B, Mannil M, Maintz D, Alkadhi H, Manka R. Texture analysis and machine learning of non-contrast T1-weighted MR images in patients with hypertrophic cardiomyopathy-Preliminary results. Eur J Radiol. 2018 May;102:61-67
- Bahdanau, D., Cho, K., & Bengio, Y. (2014). Neural machine translation by jointly learning to align and translate. arXiv preprint arXiv:1409.0473
- Baker, N., & Jacobs, K. (2013). Tele-ergonomics. In S. Kumar & E. Cohn (Eds.), Telerehabilitation (pp.163–174). London: Springer
- Bakker JP, Goldsack JC, Clarke M, Coravos A, Geoghegan C, Godfrey A, et al. A systematic review of feasibility studies promoting the use of mobile technologies in clinical research. NPJ Digit Med. 2019;2(1):47
- Banda JM, Halpern Y, Sontag D, Shah NH. Electronic phenotyping with APHRODITE and the Observational Health Sciences and Informatics (OHDSI) data network. AMIA Jt Summits Transl Sci Proc. 2017 Jul 26;2017:48-57

- Bar Y, Diamant I, Wolf L, Lieberman S, Konen E, Greenspan H. Chest pathology detection using deep learning with non-medical training. In: 2015 IEEE 12th International Symposium on Biomedical Imaging (ISBI). 2015. p. 294–7
- Barakat N, Bradley AP, Barakat MNH. Intelligible support vector machines for diagnosis of diabetes mellitus. IEEE Trans Inf Technol Biomed, 14 (2010), pp. 1114-1120
- Barbash IJ. Connecting the docs: telemedicine support during in-hospital cardiac arrest resuscitation. Ann. Amer. Thorac. Soc. 17(3):278-279, 2020
- Barnett JE. Key issues in telepsychology and the integration of technology into practice. APA Amplifier Magazine, November 14, 2013. https://div46amplifier.com/2013/11/14/key-issues-in-telepsychology-and-the-integration-of-technology-into-practice. Accessed January 21, 2021
- Barry DK. Representational State Transfer (REST). Service Architecture. Barry & Associates Inc. https://www.service-architecture.com/articles/web-services/representational-state-transfer-rest.html. Accessed June 24, 2021
- Barteit S, Lanfermann L, Bärnighausen T, Neuhann F, Beiersmann C. Augmented, Mixed, and Virtual Reality-Based Head-Mounted Devices for Medical Education: Systematic Review. JMIR Serious Games. 2021 Jul 8;9(3):e29080.
- Basch E, Deal AM, Dueck AC, Scher HI, Kris MG, Hudis C, Schrag D. Overall Survival Results of a Trial Assessing Patient-Reported Outcomes for Symptom Monitoring During Routine Cancer Treatment. JAMA. 2017 Jul 11; 318(2): 197–198
- Basch E, Reeve BB, Mitchell SA, et al: Development of the National Cancer Institute's patient-reported outcomes version of the Common Terminology Criteria for Adverse Events (PRO-CTCAE). J Natl Cancer Inst 106:dju244-dju244, 2014
- Bashshur RL, Shannon GW, Smith BR, Alverson DC, Antoniotti N, Barsan WG, Bashshur N, Brown EM, Coye MJ, Doarn CR, Ferguson S, Grigsby J, Krupinski EA, Kvedar JC, Linkous J, Merrell RC, Nesbitt T, Poropatich R, Rheuban KS, Sanders JH, Watson AR, Weinstein RS, Yellowlees P. The empirical foundations of telemedicine interventions for chronic disease management. Telemed J E Health. 2014 Sep;20(9):769-800
- Batastini AB, King CM, Morgan RD, McDaniel B. Telepsychological services with criminal justice and substance abuse clients: a systematic review and meta-analysis. Psychol. Serv. 13(1):20-30, 2016
- Battelino T, Danne T, Bergenstal RM, et al.: Clinical targets for continuous glucose monitoring data interpretation: recommendations from the International Consensus on Time in Range. Diabetes Care 2019;42:1593–1603
- Bayati B, Ayatollahi H. Comprehensive Review of Factors Influencing the Use of Telepractice in Stuttering Treatment. Healthc Inform Res. 2021;27(1):57-66
- Bayati B, Ayatollahi H. Speech therapists' perspectives about using tele-speech therapy: a qualitative study. Disabil Rehabil Assist Technol. 2021 Mar 16:1-6
- Beck JA, Jensen JA, Putzier RF, Stubert LA, Stuart KD, Mohammed H, Kreofsky BL, Boles KW, Colby CE, Fang JL. Developing a Newborn Resuscitation Telemedicine Program: A Comparison of Two Technologies. Telemed J E Health. 2018 Jul;24(7):481-488
- Becker CD, Dandy K, Gaujean M, Fusaro M, Scurlock C. Legal Perspectives on Telemedicine Part 2: Telemedicine in the Intensive Care Unit and Medicolegal Risk. Perm J. 2019;23:18-294
- Becker's Health IT. Health IT spending last year prioritized EMRs. January 29, 2018. https://www.beckershospitalreview.com/healthcare-information-technology/health-it-spending-last-year-prioritized-emrs.html. Accessed January 21, 2021
- Becker's Hospital Review. Telehealth to grow nearly 65% in 2020, report finds. May 19, 2020 (https://www.beckershospitalreview.com/telehealth/telehealth-to-grow-nearly-65-in-2020-report-finds.html Accessed February 10, 2021
- Bednarski BK, Nickerson TP, You YN, Messick CA, Speer B, Gottumukkala V, Manandhar M, Weldon M, Dean EM, Qiao W, Wang X, Chang GJ. Randomized clinical trial of accelerated enhanced recovery after minimally invasive colorectal cancer surgery (RecoverMI trial). Br J Surg. 2019 Sep;106(10):1311-1318
- Beeler GW. Introduction to: HL7 Reference Information Model (RIM) ANSI/HL7 RIM R3-2010 and ISO 21731. Health Level Seven International. https://www.hl7.org/documentcenter/public/calendarofevents/himss/2011/HL7 Reference Information Model.pdf. Accessed November 18, 2021
- Bell RC, Yager PH, Clark ME, et al. Telemedicine versus face-to-face evaluations by respiratory therapists of mechanically ventilated neonates and children: a pilot study. Respir. Care 61(2):149-154, 2016
- Ben Abacha A, Agichtein E, Pinter Y, Demner-Fushman D. Overview of the Medical QA Task @ TREC 2017 LiveQA Track. TREC, Gaithersburg, MD, 2017. https://lhncbc.nlm.nih.gov/LHC-publications/PDF/pub9773.pdf
- Ben Abacha A, Yim W-w, Adams G, Snider N, Yetisgen M. 2023. In Proceedings of the 5th Clinical Natural Language Processing Workshop, pages 503–513, Toronto, Canada. Association for Computational Linguistics. https://aclanthology.org/2023.clinicalnlp-1.52
- Ben Abacha A., Mrabet Y, Sharp M, Goodwin T, Shooshan SE, Demner-Fushman D. Bridging the Gap between Consumers' Medication Questions and Trusted Answers. Asma Ben Abacha, Yassine Mrabet, Mark Sharp, Travis Goodwin, Sonya E. Shooshan and Dina Demner-Fushman. MEDINFO 2019. https://github.com/abachaa/Medication_QA_MedInfo2019
- Ben-Arye E, Gressel O, Ben-Arye E, Samuels N. Feasibility of an Online Integrative Oncology Treatment Program During COVID-19. J Pain Symptom Manage. 2021 Feb;61(2):e1-e3.
- Bendixen, R., Levy, C., Olive, E., Kobb, R., & Mann, W. (2009). Cost-effectiveness of a telerehabilitation program to support chronically ill and disable elders in their homes. Telemedicine and e-Health, 15, 31–38
- Benson G.A., Sidebottom A., Hayes J. Impact of ENHANCED (diEtitiaNs Helping pAtieNts CarE for Diabetes) telemedicine randomized controlled trial on diabetes optimal care outcomes in patients with type 2 diabetes. J Acad Nutr Diet. 2019;119(4):585–598
- Ben-Zeev D, Wang R, Abdullah S, Brian R, Scherer EA, Mistler LA. Mobile behavioral sensing for outpatients and inpatients

with schizophrenia. Psychiatr Serv. (2016) 67:558–61

- Ben-Zeev, D., Scherer, E. A., Wang, R., Xie, H., & Campbell, A. T. (2015). Next-generation psychiatric assessment: Using smartphone sensors to monitor behavior and mental health. Psychiatric Rehabilitation Journal, 38, 218–226
- Benziger CP, Huffman MD, Sweis RN, Stone NJ. The Telehealth Ten: A Guide for a Patient-Assisted Virtual Physical Examination. Am J Med. 2021;134(1):48-51
- Berg EA, Picoraro JA, Miller SD, et al. COVID-19-A Guide to Rapid Implementation of Telehealth Services: A Playbook for the Pediatric Gastroenterologist. J Pediatr Gastroenterol Nutr. 2020;70(6):734-740
- Berg WT, Goldstein M, Melnick AP, Rosenwaks Z. Clinical implications of telemedicine for providers and patients. Fertil Steril. 2020;114(6):1129-1134
- Bergenstal, R. M., Johnson, M., Passi, R., Bhargava, A., Young, N., Kruger, D. F., Bashan, E., Bisgaier, S. G., Isaman, D. J. M., & Hodish, I. (2019) Automated insulin dosing guidance to optimise insulin management in patients with type 2 diabetes: a multicentre, randomised controlled trial. The Lancet, 393(10176), 1138–1148
- Bergström AL, Hanson E. An integrative review of information and communication technology based support interventions for carers of home dwelling older people. Technol Disabil. 2018;29(1-2):1-14
- Berlin A, Lovas M, Truong T, et al. Implementation and Outcomes of Virtual Care Across a Tertiary Cancer Center During COVID-19 [published online ahead of print, 2021 Jan 7]. JAMA Oncol. 2021;e206982
- Berman SJ, Wada C, Minatodani D, Halliday T, Miyamoto R, Lindo J, Jordan PJ. Home-based preventative care in high-risk dialysis patients: a pilot study. Telemed J E Health. 2011 May;17(4):283-7
- Bertini A, Salas R, Chabert S, Sobrevia L, Pardo F. Using Machine Learning to Predict Complications in Pregnancy: A Systematic Review. Front Bioeng Biotechnol. 2022 Jan 19;9:780389
- Beule AG. Telemedical Methods in Otorhinolaryngology. Laryngorhinootologie. 2019 Mar;98(S 01):S129-S172
- Bhopal RS, Parkin DW, Gillie RF, Han KH. Pattern of ophthalmological accidents and emergencies presenting to hospitals. J Epidemiol Community Health. 1993 Oct;47(5):382-7
- Billiard A, Rohmer V, Roques MA, et al.: Telematic transmission of computerized blood glucose profiles for IDDM patients. Diabetes Care 1991;14:130–134
- Binder, M. et al. Epiluminescence microscopy-based classification of pigmented skin lesions using computerized image analysis and an artificial neural network. Melanoma Res. 8, 261–266 (1998)
- Black, P. , Okun, V. and Guttman, B. (2021). Guidelines on Minimum Standards for Developer Verification of Software. NIST Interagency/Internal Report (NISTIR), National Institute of Standards and Technology, Gaithersburg, MD, [online]. https://tsapps.nist.gov/publication/get_pdf.cfm?pub_id=933350. Accessed May 15, 2022
- Blank E, Lappan C, Belmont PJ Jr, Machen MS, Ficke J, Pope R, Owens BD. Early analysis of the United States Army's telemedicine orthopaedic consultation program. J Surg Orthop Adv. 2011 Spring;20(1):50-5
- Bloomfield RA Jr, Polo-Wood F, Mandel JC, Mandl KD. Opening the Duke electronic health record to apps: Implementing SMART on FHIR. Int J Med Inform. 2017 Mar;99:1-10
- Bodenreider O. The Unified Medical Language System (UMLS): integrating biomedical terminology. Nucleic Acids Res. 2004 Jan 1;32(Database issue):D267-70
- Boesch M, Rassouli F, Baty F, Schwärzler A, Widmer S, Tinschert P, Shih I, Cleres D, Barata F, Fleisch E, Brutsche MH. Smartphone-based cough monitoring as a near real-time digital pneumonia biomarker. ERJ Open Res. 2023 May 2;9(3):00518-2022
- Boissin C, Blom L, Wallis L, Laflamme L. Image-based teleconsultation using smartphones or tablets: qualitative assessment of medical experts. Emerg. Med. J. 34(2):95-99, 2017
- Bommasani, R., Hudson, D. A., Adeli, E., Altman, R., Arora, S., von Arx, S., Bernstein, M. S., Bohg, J., Bosselut, A., Brunskill, E., et al. On the opportunities and risks of foundation models. arXiv preprint arXiv:2108.07258 [cs.LG] (2021).
- Bonavita S, Tedeschi G, Atreja A, Lavorgna L. Digital triage for people with multiple sclerosis in the age of COVID-19 pandemic. Neurol Sci. 2020;41(5):1007-1009
- Bonoto, B. C. et al. Efficacy of mobile apps to support the care of patients with diabetes mellitus: a systematic review and meta-analysis of randomized controlled trials. JMIR Mhealth Uhealth 5, e4 (2017)
- Bordes, A., Chopra, S. & Weston, J. Question answering with subgraph embeddings. In Proc. Empirical Methods in Natural Language Processing http://arxiv.org.ucsf.idm.oclc.org/abs/1406.3676v3 (2014)
- Borghese N, Mainetti R, Pirovano M, Lanzi PL. An intelligent game engine for the at-home rehabilitation of stroke patients. Proceedings of the IEEE 2nd International Conference on Serious Games and Applications for Health (SeGAH); IEEE 2nd International Conference on Serious Games and Applications for Health (SeGAH); May 2-3, 2013; Vilamoura, Portugal. 2013.
- Botella C., Banos R., Guerrero B., Juan M., Alcañiz M. Mixing realities? An augmented reality system for the treatment of cockroach phobia. CyberPsychology & Behavior. 2005;8:305–306.
- Bouchard S, Allard M, Robillard G, et al. Videoconferencing Psychotherapy for Panic Disorder and Agoraphobia: Outcome and Treatment Processes From a Non-randomized Non-inferiority Trial. Front Psychol. 2020;11:2164
- Bowe T, Hunter DG, Mantagos IS, Kazlas M, Jastrzembski BG, Gaier ED, Massey G, Franz K, Schumann C, Brown C, Meyers H, Shah AS. Virtual Visits in Ophthalmology: Timely Advice for Implementation During the COVID-19 Public Health Crisis. Telemed J E Health. 2020 Sep;26(9):1113-1117
- Bowry R, Parker S, Rajan SS, et al. Benefits of stroke treatment using a mobile stroke unit compared with standard management: the BEST-MSU study run-in phase. Stroke 2015;46:3370–4
- Bradley EH, Yuan CT. Quality of care in low-and middle-income settings: what next? International Journal for Quality in Health Care. 2012;24(6):547–9
- Brock KE, Snaman JM, Kaye EC, Bower KA, Weaver MS, Baker JN, Wolfe J, Ullrich C. Models of Pediatric Palliative Oncology

Outpatient Care-Benefits, Challenges, and Opportunities. J Oncol Pract. 2019 Sep;15(9):476-487

- Brokmann JC, Conrad C, Rossaint R, et al. Treatment of acute coronary syndrome by telemedically supported paramedics compared with physician-based treatment: a prospective, interventional, multicenter trial. J. Med.Internet Res. 18(12):e314, 2016
- Brooke LeVasseur. "How telehealth and econsults are reducing patient wait times," Patient Safety & Quality Healthcare. January 8, 2020. https://www.aristamd.com/blog/reducing-patient-wait-times-telehealth-econsults. Accessed February 21, 2021
- Brookstone A. The Impact of Inadequate Training on Use of EHRs. AmericanEHR. May 22, 2012. http://www.americanehr.com/blog/2012/05/the-impact-of-inadequate-training-on-use-of-ehrs. Accessed July 21, 2021
- Brouillette, R. M., Foil, H., Fontenot, S., Correro, A., Allen, R., Martin, C. K., et al (2013). Feasibility, reliability, and validity of a smartphone based application for the assessment of cognitive function in the elderly. PLoS ONE, 8, e65925
- Brown AM, Ardila-Gatas J, Yuan V, Devas N, Docimo S, Spaniolas K, Pryor AD. The Impact of Telemedicine Adoption on a Multidisciplinary Bariatric Surgery Practice During the COVID-19 Pandemic. Ann Surg. 2020 Dec;272(6):e306-e310
- Brown JD, Hales S, Evans TE, Turner T, Sword DO, O'Neil PM, Ballentine S, Lovelace O, DuBose-Morris RA. Description, utilisation and results from a telehealth primary care weight management intervention for adults with obesity in South Carolina. J Telemed Telecare. 2020 Jan-Feb;26(1-2):28-35
- Brown SA, Patel S, Rayan D, et al. A virtual-hybrid approach to launching a cardio-oncology clinic during a pandemic. Cardiooncology 7(1):2, 2021
- Brown TB, Mann B, Ryder N, Subbiah M et al. 2020. Language Models are Few-Shot Learners. arXiv preprint arXiv:2005.14165 (2020).
- Brunette MF, Rotondi AJ, Ben-Zeev D, et al. Coordinated technology-delivered treatment to prevent rehospitalization in schizophrenia: a novel model of care. Psychiatric Serv. 67(4):444-447, 2016
- Brunetti ND, Tarantino N, Dellegrottaglie G, et al. Impact of telemedicine support by remote pre-hospital electrocardiogram on emergency medical service management of subjects with suspected acute cardiovascular disease. Int. J. Cardiol. 199:215-220, 2015
- Bryant MS, Fedson SE, Sharafkhaneh A. Using telehealth cardiopulmonary rehabilitation during the COVID-19 pandemic. J. Med. Syst. 44(7):125, 2020
- Bsoul M, Minn H, Tamil L. Apnea MedAssist: real-time sleep apnea monitor using single-lead ECG. IEEE Trans Inf Technol Biomed. 2011 May;15(3):416-27
- Bull MT, Darwin K, Venkataraman V, Wagner J, Beck CA, Dorsey ER, Biglan KM. A pilot study of virtual visits in Huntington disease. J Huntintons Dis. 2014;3(2):189-95
- Burgess, C., Miller, C.J., Franz, A., Abel, E.A., Gyulai, L., Osser, D., Smith, E.G., Connolly, S.L., Krawczyk, L., Bauer, M. and Godleski, L. (2020), Practical lessons learned for assessing and treating bipolar disorder via telehealth modalities during the COVID-19 pandemic. Bipolar Disord., 22: 556-557
- Burke LE, Ma J, Azar KM, Bennett GG, Peterson ED, Zheng Y, Riley W, Stephens J, Shah SH, Suffoletto B, Turan TN, Spring B, Steinberger J, Quinn CC; American Heart Association Publications Committee of the Council on Epidemiology and Prevention, Behavior Change Committee of the Council on Cardiometabolic Health, Council on Cardiovascular and Stroke Nursing, Council on Functional Genomics and Translational Biology, Council on Quality of Care and Outcomes Research, and Stroke Council. Current Science on Consumer Use of Mobile Health for Cardiovascular Disease Prevention: A Scientific Statement From the American Heart Association. Circulation. 2015 Sep 22;132(12):1157-213
- Burroni, M. et al. Melanoma computer-aided diagnosis: reliability and feasibility study. Clin. Cancer Res. 10, 1881–1886 (2004)
- Büscher R, Torok M, Terhorst Y, Sander L. Internet-based cognitive behavioral therapy to reduce suicidal ideation: a systematic review and meta-analysis. JAMA Netw. Open 3(4):e203933, 2020
- Bush NE, Armstrong CM, Hoyt TV. Smartphone apps for psychological health: A brief state of the science review. Psychol Serv. 2019 May;16(2):188-195
- Business Wire. Patients prefer physicians who offer telemedicine during COVID-19 and beyond, says new everyday health and Klick health research.. https://www.businesswire.com/news/home/20200806005248/en/Patients-Prefer-Physicians-Offer-Telemedicine-COVID-19-New. August 6, 2020. Accessed January 28, 2021
- Buvik A, Bergmo TS, Bugge E, Smaabrekke A, Wilsgaard T, Olsen JA. Cost-Effectiveness of Telemedicine in Remote Orthopedic Consultations: Randomized Controlled Trial. J Med Internet Res. 2019 Feb 19;21(2):e11330 [b]
- Buvik A, Bugge E, Knutsen G, Småbrekke A, Wilsgaard T. Patient reported outcomes with remote orthopaedic consultations by telemedicine: A randomised controlled trial. J Telemed Telecare. 2019 Sep;25(8):451-459 [a]
- Buvik A, Bugge E, Knutsen G, Småbrekke A, Wilsgaard T. Quality of care for remote orthopaedic consultations using telemedicine: a randomised controlled trial. BMC Health Serv Res. 2016 Sep 8;16(1):483
- Buxbaum JL, Eloubeidi MA, Lane CJ, Varadarajulu S, Linder A, Crowe AE, Jhala D, Jhala NC, Crowe DR, Eltoum IA. Dynamic telecytology compares favorably to rapid onsite evaluation of endoscopic ultrasound fine needle aspirates. Dig Dis Sci. 2012 Dec; 57(12):3092-7
- Cabana, F, Boissy, P, Tousignant, M, Moffet, H, Corriveau, H, Dumais, R. Interrater agreement between telerehabilitation and face-to-face clinical outcome measurements for total knee arthroplasty. Telemed J E Health. 2010;16:293–298
- Cadili L, DeGirolamo K, McKevitt E, et al. COVID-19 and breast cancer at a regional breast centre: our flexible approach during the pandemic. Breast Cancer Res. Treat. 4:1–7, 2020
- Cafazzo JA. A digital-first model of diabetes care. Diabetes Technol Ther 2019 Jun;21(S2):S252-S258
- Califf RM. Biomarker definitions and their applications. Exp Biol Med (Maywood). 2018 Feb;243(3):213-221
- California Constitution. Cal. Bus. & Prof. Code §§ 22575-22579. https://leginfo.legislature.ca.gov/faces/codes_displaySection.xhtml?lawCode=BPC&sectionNum=22575. Accessed 11 January 2021
- Camden C, Silva M. Pediatric Teleheath: Opportunities Created by the COVID-19 and Suggestions to Sustain Its Use to Support

Families of Children with Disabilities. Phys Occup Ther Pediatr. 2021;41(1):1-17

- Camden, C., Pratte, G., Fallon, F., Couture, M., Berbari, J., & Tousignant, M. (2019). Diversity of practices in telerehabilitation for children with disabilities and effective intervention characteristics: Results from a systematic review. Disability and Rehabilitation, 1–13
- Cameron JR, Ahmed S, Curry P, Forrest G, Sanders R. Impact of direct electronic optometric referral with ocular imaging to a hospital eye service. Eye (Lond). 2009 May;23(5):1134-40
- Campbell AN, Nunes EV, Matthews AG, Stitzer M, Miele GM, Polsky D, Turrigiano E, Walters S, McClure EA, Kyle TL, Wahle A, Van Veldhuisen P, Goldman B, Babcock D, Stabile PQ, Winhusen T, Ghitza UE. Internet-delivered treatment for substance abuse: a multisite randomized controlled trial. Am J Psychiatry. 2014 Jun;171(6):683-90. Erratum in: Am J Psychiatry. 2014 Dec 1;171(12):1338
- Canadian Agency for Drugs and Technologies in Health (Ottawa ON). Telemedicine Consultations for Patients in Long-Term Care: Clinical Effectiveness, Cost-Effectiveness, and Guidelines. CADTH Rapid Response Report, Oct. 2015. https://www.ncbi.nlm.nih.gov/books/NBK326842/ Accessed April 12, 2021 [b]
- Canadian Agency for Drugs and Technologies in Health (Ottawa ON). Telemedicine for the treatment of urgent conditions: a review of clinical effectiveness, cost-effectiveness, and guidelines. CADTH Rapid Response Report, Oct. 2015. https://www.ncbi.nlm.nih.gov/books/NBK326842/ Accessed April 12, 2021 [a]
- Canadian Institute for Health Information (CIHI). Indicator Library. Ottawa, ON: CIHI; Accessed July 12, 2021
- Canadian Institute for Health Information (CIHI). National health expenditure trends, 2022 - Snapshot. https://www.cihi.ca/en/national-health-expenditure-trends-2022-snapshot. Accessed July 30, 2023
- Canadian Institute for Health Information, CIHI's Information Quality Framework, 2017, https://www.cihi.ca/sites/default/files/document/iqf-summary-july-26-2017-en-web_0.pdf. Accessed August 12, 2021
- Cantlupe J. BI tapping real-world data for Pradaxa. Dive Brief. BioPharmaDive. Oct 24, 2016. https://www.biopharmadive.com/news/bi-tapping-real-world-data-for-pradaxa/428880. Accessed July 28. 2021
- Caplan GA, Sulaiman NS, Mangin DA, Aimonino Ricauda N, Wilson AD, Barclay L. A meta-analysis of "hospital in the home". Med J Aust. 2012 Nov 5;197(9):512-9
- Carey B, O'Brian S, Lowe R, Onslow M. Webcam delivery of the Camperdown Program for adolescents who stutter: a phase II trial. Lang Speech Hear Serv Sch. 2014;45:314–24
- Carey B, O'Brian S, Onslow M, Block S, Jones M, Packman A. Randomized controlled non-inferiority trial of a telehealth treatment for chronic stuttering: the Camperdown Program. Int J Lang Commun Disord. 2010;45:108–20.
- Carl, J. R., Miller, C. B., Henry, A. L., Davis, M. L., Stott, R., Smits, J. A., ... & Espie, C. A. (2020). Efficacy of digital cognitive behavioral therapy for moderate-to-severe symptoms of generalized anxiety disorder: A randomized controlled trial. Depression and Anxiety, 37(12), 1168-1178
- Carlew AR, Fatima H, Livingstone JR, et al. Cognitive Assessment via Telephone: A Scoping Review of Instruments. Arch Clin Neuropsychol. 2020;35(8):1215-1233
- Carolynn Levy. Y Combinator. Safe Financing Documents. September 2018 (updated March 2021). https://www.ycombinator.com/documents/https://www.ycombinator.com/documents/ Accessed March 21, 2021
- Carter CW, Herrero CP, Bloom DA, Karamitopoulos M, Castañeda PG. Early Experience with Virtual Pediatric Orthopedics in New York CityPearls for Incorporating Telemedicine into Your Practice. Bull Hosp Jt Dis (2013). 2020 Dec;78(4):236-242
- Case T, Morrison C, Vuylsteke A. The clinical application of mobile technology to disaster medicine. Prehosp. Disaster Med. 27(5):473-480, 2012
- Casey Stewart Keck and Charles R. Doarn. Telehealth Technology Applications in Speech-Language Pathology. Telemedicine and e-Health 2014 20:7, 653-659
- Cason J, Brannon JA. Telehealth regulatory and legal considerations: frequently asked questions. Int J Telerehabil. 2011 Dec 20;3(2):15-8
- Castaneda P., Ellimoottil C. Current use of telehealth in urology: a review. World J Urol. 2020;38:2377–2384
- Castellano NN, Gazquez JA, García Salvador RM, et al. Design of a real-time emergency telemedicine system for remote medical diagnosis. Biosys. Eng. 138: 23-32, 2015
- Castro HK, Cross RK, Finkelstein J. Using a Home Automated Telemanagement (HAT) system: experiences and perceptions of patients with inflammatory bowel disease. AMIA Annu Symp Proc. 2006;2006:872
- Cavero-Redondo I, Martinez-Vizcaino V, Fernandez-Rodriguez R, Saz-Lara A, Pascual-Morena C, Álvarez-Bueno C. Effect of Behavioral Weight Management Interventions Using Lifestyle mHealth Self-Monitoring on Weight Loss: A Systematic Review and Meta-Analysis. Nutrients. 2020;12(7):1977. Published 2020 Jul 3
- Caze Ii T, Knell GP, Abt J, Burkhart SO. Management and Treatment of Concussions via Tele-Concussion in a Pediatric Setting: Methodological Approach and Descriptive Analysis. JMIR Pediatr Parent. 2020 Aug 13;3(2):e19924
- CCCPC (Central Committee of the Communist Party of China, State Council). Opinions on deepening health system reform [Chinese]. Zhongfa No 6, 2009
- CCHP (Center for Connected Health Policy). Current State Laws & Reimbursement Policies. Center for Connected Health Policy. https://www.cchpca.org/telehealth-policy/current-state-laws-and-reimbursement-policies . Accessed July 22, 2021
- CCHP (Center for Connected Health Policy). Professional Requirements. Cross-State Licensing. https://www.cchpca.org/topic/cross-state-licensing-professional-requirements. Accessed July 26, 2021
- CCHP Center for Connected Health Policy. An analysis of private payer telehealth coverage during the Covid-19 pandemic. https://www.cchpca.org/sites/default/files/2021-01/Private Payer Telehealth Coverage Reportfinal.pdf. Accessed February 15, 2021
- Celio MA, Mastroleo NR, DiGuiseppi G, et al. Using video conferencing to deliver a brief motivational intervention for alcohol

and sex risk to emergency department patients: a proof-of-concept pilot study. Addict. Res. Theory 25(4):318-325, 2017

- Ceney A, Tolond S, Glowinski A, Marks B, Swift S, Palser T. Accuracy of online symptom checkers and the potential impact on service utilisation. PLoS One. 2021 Jul 15;16(7):e0254088
- Centers for Disease Control and Prevention (CDC). Underlying Cause of Death, 1999–2018. CDC WONDER Online Database. Atlanta, GA: Centers for Disease Control and Prevention; 2018
- Centers for Medicare & Medicaid Services. Connected Care Toolkit. Chronic Care Management Resources for Health Care Professionals and Communities. Available at https://www.cms.gov/About-CMS/Agency-Information/OMH/Downloads/connected-hcptoolkit.pdf. Accessed March 21, 2021
- Centers for Medicare & Medicaid Services. List of Telehealth Services. List of Medicare Telehealth services for PHE for the COVID-19 pandemic effective March 1 2020-updated December 14 2020. . https://www.cms.gov/Medicare/Medicare-General-Information/Telehealth/Telehealth-Codes. Accessed March 15, 2021) [b]
- Centers for Medicare & Medicaid Services. US Department of Health and Human Services. Centers for Medicare & Medicaid Services. General Provider Telehealth and Telemedicine Toolkit. https://asprtracie.hhs.gov/technical-resources/resource/8526/general-provider-telehealth-and-telemedicine-toolkit. Accessed March 18, 2021 [a]
- Chai PR, Wu RY, Ranney ML, Porter PS, Babu KM, Boyer EW. The virtual toxicology service: wearable headmounted devices for medical toxicology. J. Med. Toxicol. 10(4):382-387, 2014
- Chalmers E, Hill D, Zhao V, Lou E. Prescriptive analytics applied to brace treatment for AIS: a pilot demonstration. Scoliosis. 2015 Feb 11;10(Suppl 2):S13
- Champagne-Langabeer T, Langabeer JR, Roberts KE, et al. Telehealth impact on primary care related ambulance transports. Prehosp. Emerg. Care 23:712–717, 2019
- Chan AH, Harrison J, Black PN, Mitchell EA, Foster JM. Using electronic monitoring devices to measure inhaler adherence: a practical guide for clinicians. J Allergy Clin Immunol Pract. 2015 May-Jun;3(3):335-49.e1-5
- Chang PJ, Jay GM, Kalpakjian C, Andrews C, Smith S. Patient and Provider-Reported Satisfaction of Cancer Rehabilitation Telemedicine Visits During the COVID-19 Pandemic. PM R. 2021 Jan 17:10.1002/pmrj.12552
- Chang, J.-H., Diop, M., Burgos, Y.L., Blackstock, D.M., Fernandez, H.E., Morris, H.K., Dube, G.K., Crew, R.J., Mohan, S., Husain, S.A., Cohen, D.J. and Tsapepas, D.S. (2020), Telehealth in outpatient management of kidney transplant recipients during COVID-19 pandemic in New York. Clin Transplant, 34: e14097
- Channa R, Zafar SN, Canner JK, Haring RS, Schneider EB, Friedman DS. Epidemiology of Eye-Related Emergency Department Visits. JAMA Ophthalmol. 2016;134(3):312–319
- Chapman WW, Nadkarni PM, Hirschman L, D'Avolio LW, Savova GK, et al. (2011) Overcoming barriers to NLP for clinical text: the role of shared tasks and the need for additional creative solutions. J Am Med Inform Assoc 18: 540–543
- Che, Z., Purushotham, S., Cho, K., Sontag, D. & Liu, Y. Recurrent neural networks for multivariate time series with missing values. arXiv [cs.LG] (2016)
- Chen J, Sun D, Yang W, Liu M, Zhang S, Peng J, Ren C. Clinical and Economic Outcomes of Telemedicine Programs in the Intensive Care Unit: A Systematic Review and Meta-Analysis. J Intensive Care Med. 2018 Jul;33(7):383-393
- Chen R, Stewart WF, Sun J, Ng K, Yan X. Recurrent Neural Networks for Early Detection of Heart Failure From Longitudinal Electronic Health Record Data: Implications for Temporal Modeling With Respect to Time Before Diagnosis, Data Density, Data Quantity, and Data Type. Circ Cardiovasc Qual Outcomes. 2019;12(10):e005114
- Chen X., Siebourg-Polster J., Wolf D., Czech C., Bonati U., Fischer D., Khwaja O., Strahm M. Feasibility of using Microsoft Kinect to assess upper limb movement in type III spinal muscular atrophy patients. PLoS ONE. 2017;12:e0170472.
- Chen Y, Wang C, Shang H, Yang K, Susan Norris S. Clinical practice guidelines in China. BMJ 2018;360: j5158
- Chen YH, Hung CS, Huang CC, et al. Atrial fibrillation screening in nonmetropolitan areas using a telehealth surveillance system with an embedded cloud-computing algorithm: prospective pilot study. JMIR MHealth UHealth 5(9):e135, 2017
- Chen, Z., Cano, A.H., Romanou, A., Bonnet, A., Matoba, K., Salvi, F., Pagliardini, M., Fan, S., Köpf, A., Mohtashami, A. and Sallinen, A., 2023. Meditron-70b: Scaling medical pretraining for large language models. arXiv preprint arXiv:2311.16079.
- Chen, Z., Cano, A.H., Romanou, A., Bonnet, A., Matoba, K., Salvi, F., Pagliardini, M., Fan, S., Köpf, A., Mohtashami, A. and Sallinen, A., 2023. Meditron-70b: Scaling medical pretraining for large language models. arXiv preprint arXiv:2311.16079.
- Cheng J, Novati G, Pan J, Bycroft C, Žemgulytė A, Applebaum T, Pritzel A, Wong LH, Zielinski M, Sargeant T, Schneider RG, Senior AW, Jumper J, Hassabis D, Kohli P, Avsec Ž. Accurate proteome-wide missense variant effect prediction with AlphaMissense. Science. 2023 Sep 22;381(6664):eadg7492.
- Chicchi Giglioli IA, Pallavicini F, Pedroli E, Serino S, Riva G. Augmented Reality: A Brand New Challenge for the Assessment and Treatment of Psychological Disorders. Comput Math Methods Med. 2015;2015:862942
- Chiu CC, Tripathi A, Chou K, Co C, Jaitly N, Jaunzeikare D, Kannan A, Nguyen P, Sak H, Sankar A, Tansuwan J. Speech recognition for medical conversations. arXiv preprint arXiv:1711.07274. 2017 Nov 20.
- Choi, E., Bahadori, M. T., Schuetz, A., Stewart, W. F. & Sun, J. Doctor AI: predicting clinical events via recurrent neural networks. In Proceedings of the 1st Machine Learning for Healthcare Conference, vol 56 (eds F. Doshi-Velez, J. Fackler, D. Kale and B. Wallace, J. Wiens) 301–318 (PMLR, Los Angeles, CA, 2016)
- Chong E, Yan A, Wang S. Research on the comprehensive ranking method of hospital competitiveness. Article in Chinese. Chinese Journal of Medical Management Sciences 2016;6(3):45-50
- Chopra, V. & McMahon, L. F. Jr. Redesigning hospital alarms for patient safety: alarmed and potentially dangerous. JAMA 311, 1199–1200 (2014)
- Chow CK, Redfern J, Hillis GS, Thakkar J, Santo K, Hackett ML, Jan S, Graves N, de Keizer L, Barry T, Bompoint S, Stepien S, Whittaker R, Rodgers A, Thiagalingam A. Effect of Lifestyle-Focused Text Messaging on Risk Factor Modification in Patients With Coronary Heart Disease: A Randomized Clinical Trial. JAMA. 2015 Sep 22-29;314(12):1255-63

- Chowdhury, D., Hope, K.D., Arthur, L.C. et al. Telehealth for Pediatric Cardiology Practitioners in the Time of COVID-19. Pediatr Cardiol 41, 1081–1091 (2020)
- Christiano P et al. (2017, Jun 12). Deep reinforcement learning from human preferences. arXiv:1706.03741v4
- Christo El Morr and Hossam Ali-Hassan, Analytics in Healthcare: A Practical Introduction, Springer, 2019
- Christodoulou MA, Kontogeorgou C. Collision avoidance in commercial aircraft Free Flight via neural networks and non-linear programming. Int J Neural Syst. 2008 Oct;18(5):371-87
- Churpek MM, Yuen TC, Park SY, Meltzer DO, Hall JB, Edelson DP. Derivation of a cardiac arrest prediction model using ward vital signs*. Crit Care Med. 2012 Jul;40(7):2102-8
- Cicero M, Bilbily A, Colak E, Dowdell T, Gray B, Perampaladas K, et al. Training and Validating a Deep Convolutional Neural Network for Computer-Aided Detection and Classification of Abnormalities on Frontal Chest Radiographs. Invest Radiol. 2017; 52(5):281–7
- Cimadamore A, Cheng L, Scarpelli M, Lopez-Beltran A, Montironi R. Digital diagnostics and artificial intelligence in prostate cancer treatment in 5 years from now. Transl Androl Urol. 2021 Mar;10(3):1499-1505
- Citardi MJ, Agbetoba A, Bigcas JL, Luong A. Augmented reality for endoscopic sinus surgery with surgical navigation: a cadaver study. Int Forum Allergy Rhinol. 2016 May;6(5):523-8
- Cleeland CS, Wang XS, Shi Q, Mendoza TR, Wright SL, Berry MD, Malveaux D, Shah PK, Gning I, Hofstetter WL, Putnam JB Jr, Vaporciyan AA. Automated symptom alerts reduce postoperative symptom severity after cancer surgery: a randomized controlled clinical trial. J Clin Oncol. 2011 Mar 10;29(8):994-1000
- CMS Quality Payment Program. APMs Overview. https://qpp.cms.gov/apms/overview. Accessed November 26, 2021
- CMS. (2023, April 3). Overview of the Medicare Physician Fee Schedule. https://www.cms.gov/medicare/physician-fee-schedule/search/overview
- CMS. 85 FR 84472. December 28, 2020. https://www.federalregister.gov/documents/2020/12/28/2020-26815/medicare-program-cy-2021-payment-policies-under-the-physician-fee-schedule-and-other-changes-to-part. Accessed July 4, 2021
- CMS. 85 FR 84543. December 28, 2020. https://www.federalregister.gov/d/2020-26815. Accessed July 5, 2021
- CMS. Acute Hospital Care at Home Program. Approved List of Hospitals as of 4/5/2021. Available at www.cms.gov/files/document/covid-acute-hospital-care-home-program-approved-list-hospitals.pdf. Accessed July 22, 2021
- CMS. Additional Background:Sweeping Regulatory Changes to Help U.S. Healthcare System Address COVID-19 Patient Surge. March 30, 2020. Available at https://www.cms.gov/newsroom/fact-sheets/additional-backgroundsweeping-regulatory-changes-help-us-healthcare-system-address-covid-19-patient. Accessed on July 12, 2021
- CMS. CMS Announces Comprehensive Strategy to Enhance Hospital Capacity Amid COVID-19 Surge. Nov 25, 2020. Available at https://www.cms.gov/newsroom/press-releases/cms-announces-comprehensive-strategy-enhance-hospital-capacity-amid-covid-19-surge. Accessed July 22, 2021
- CMS. eHR Incentive Program. A Quick Guide to the Clinical Quality Measures. https://www.cms.gov/regulations-and-guidance/legislation/ehrincentiveprograms/downloads/guidetocqms_remediated_2011.pdf
- CMS. Health Care Claim or Equivalent Encounter Information. May 26, 2022. https://www.cms.gov/Regulations-and-Guidance/Administrative-Simplification/Transactions/HealthCareClaimorEquivalentEncounterInformation. Accessed July 5, 2022
- CMS. Health Care Claims Status. May 12, 2022. https://www.cms.gov/Regulations-and-Guidance/Administrative-Simplification/Transactions/HealthCareClaimsStatus. Accessed July 5, 2022
- CMS. Health Care Payment and Remittance Advice and Electronic Funds Transfer. June 16, 2022. https://www.cms.gov/Regulations-and-Guidance/Administrative-Simplification/Transactions/HealthCarePaymentandRemittanceAdviceandElectronicFundsTransfer. Accessed July 5, 2022
- CMS. Health Plan Eligibility Benefit Inquiry and Response. 05/11/2022. https://www.cms.gov/Regulations-and-Guidance/Administrative-Simplification/Transactions/HealthPlanEligibilityBenefitInquiryandResponse. Accessed July 5, 2022
- CMS. Health Plan Enrollment and Disenrollment. May 11, 2022. https://www.cms.gov/Regulations-and-Guidance/Administrative-Simplification/Transactions/HealthPlanEnrollmentandDisenrollment. Accessed July 5, 2022
- CMS. ICD-10-CM/PCS MS-DRG v37.0 Definitions Manual. https://www.cms.gov/icd10m/version37-fullcode-cms/fullcode_cms/P0001.html. Accessed July 12, 2022
- CMS. MACRA. What is MACRA? April 1, 2022. https://www.cms.gov/Medicare/Quality-Initiatives-Patient-Assessment-Instruments/Value-Based-Programs/MACRA-MIPS-and-APMs/MACRA-MIPS-and-APMs.html. May 22, 2022
- CMS. Part C and D Performance Data. September 8, 2021. https://www.cms.gov/Medicare/Prescription-Drug-Coverage/PrescriptionDrugCovGenIn/PerformanceData. Accessed October 15, 2021
- CMS. Quality Measures. April 14, 2022. https://www.cms.gov/Medicare/Quality-Initiatives-Patient-Assessment-Instruments/QualityMeasures. Accessed June 26, 2022
- CMS. Quality Payment Program. Quality Performance Category: Traditional MIPS Requirements. August 30, 2022. https://qpp.cms.gov/mips/quality-measures. Accessed September 11, 2022
- CMS. Referral Certification and Authorization. June 7, 2022. https://www.cms.gov/Regulations-and-Guidance/Administrative-Simplification/Transactions/ReferralCertificationandAuthorization. Accessed July 5, 2022
- Codella, N. et al. In Machine Learning in Medical Imaging (eds Zhou, L., Wang, L., Wang, Q. & Shi, Y.) 118–126 (Springer, 2015)
- Cohen MA, Powell AM, Coleman JS, Keller JM, Livingston A, Anderson JR. Special ambulatory gynecologic considerations in the era of coronavirus disease 2019 (COVID-19) and implications for future practice. Am J Obstet Gynecol. 2020 Sep;223(3):372-378
- Colford JM Jr, Corelli RL, Ganz JW, Guglielmo BJ, Jacobs RA. Home antibiotic therapy for streptococcal endocarditis: a call for

a controlled trial. Am J Med. 1993 Jan;94(1):111-2

- Collins TA, Robertson MP, Sicoutris CP, et al. Telemedicine coverage for post-operative ICU patients. J.Telemed. Telecare 23(2):360-364, 2017
- Collobert, R., et al. Natural language processing (almost) from scratch. J. Mach. Learn. Res. 12, 2493–2537 (2011)
- Congress.gov. H.R.2 - Medicare Access and CHIP Reauthorization Act of 2015. April 16, 2015. https://www.congress.gov/bill/114th-congress/house-bill/2. Accessed: October 19, 2021
- Conners GP, Kressly SJ, Perrin JM, Richerson JE, Sankrithi UM; Committee on practice and ambulatory medicine; Committee on pediatric emergency medicine; Section on Telehealth care; Section on Emergency Medicine; Subcommittee on Urgent Care; Taskforce on pediatric Practice change. Nonemergency Acute Care: When It's Not the Medical Home. Pediatrics. 2017 May;139(5):e20170629
- Connor, M.J., Winkler, M. and Miah, S. (2020), COVID-19 pandemic – is virtual urology clinic the answer to keeping the cancer pathway moving?. BJU Int, 125: E3-E4
- Constantinescu EC, Nicolau C, Săftoiu A. Recent developments in tele-ultrasonography. Curr. Health Sci. J. 44(2):101-106, 2018
- Consumer Federation of California. California Online Privacy Protection Act. July 29, 2015. https://consumercal.org/about-cfc/cfc-education-foundation/california-online-privacy-protection-act-caloppa-3. Accessed April 21, 2021
- Conti E, Chericoni N, Costanzo V, et al. Moving Toward Telehealth Surveillance Services for Toddlers at Risk for Autism During the COVID-19 Pandemic. Front Psychiatry. 2020;11:565999
- Continuity of Care Record: The Concept Paper of the CCR (Report). American Society for Testing and Materials. 2013.
- Coravos A, Khozin S, Mandl KD. Developing and adopting safe and effective digital biomarkers to improve patient outcomes. NPJ Digit Med. 2019;2(1):14
- Corea F, Ciotti S, Cometa A, De Carlo C, Martini G, Baratta S, Zampolini M. Telemedicine during the Coronavirus Disease (COVID-19) Pandemic: A Multiple Sclerosis (MS) Outpatients Service Perspective. Neurology International. 2021; 13(1):25-31
- Correia, F.D., Nogueira, A., Magalhães, I. et al. Home-based Rehabilitation With A Novel Digital Biofeedback System versus Conventional In-person Rehabilitation after Total Knee Replacement: a feasibility study. Sci Rep 8, 11299 (2018)
- Corry M, Neenan K, Brabyn S, Sheaf G, Smith V. Telephone interventions, delivered by healthcare professionals, for providing education and psychosocial support for informal caregivers of adults with diagnosed illnesses. Cochrane Database Syst Rev. 2019 May 14;5(5):CD012533
- Costa RTD, Carvalho MR, Ribeiro P, Nardi AE. Virtual reality exposure therapy for fear of driving: analysis of clinical characteristics, physiological response, and sense of presence. Braz J Psychiatry. 2018 Feb 15;40(2):192-199
- Cottrell E, George A, Coulson C, Chambers R. Telescopic otology referrals: Evaluation of feasibility and acceptability. Laryngoscope Investig Otolaryngol. 2020;5(2):221-227
- Cox CE, Wysham NG, Walton B, et al. Development and usability testing of a Web-based decision aid for families of patients receiving prolonged mechanical ventilation. Annals Intens. Care 5:6, 2015
- Crawford I, McBeth PB, Mitchelson M, Ferguson J, Tiruta C, Kirkpatrick AW. How to set up a low cost teleultrasound capable videoconferencing system with wide applicability. Crit. Ultrasound J. 4(1):13, 2012
- Creditor MC. Hazards of hospitalization of the elderly. Ann Intern Med. 1993;118:219–23
- Cremades M, Ferret G, Parés D, Navinés J, Espin F, Pardo F, Caballero A, Viciano M, Julian JF. Telemedicine to follow patients in a general surgery department. A randomized controlled trial. Am J Surg. 2020 Jun;219(6):882-887
- Cross RK, Arora M, Finkelstein J. Acceptance of telemanagement is high in patients with inflammatory bowel disease. J Clin Gastroenterol. 2006 Mar;40(3):200-8
- Cross RK, Cheevers N, Rustgi A, Langenberg P, Finkelstein J. Randomized, controlled trial of home telemanagement in patients with ulcerative colitis (UC HAT). Inflamm Bowel Dis. 2012 Jun;18(6):1018-25
- Cruz J, Brooks D, Marques A. Home telemonitoring effectiveness in COPD: a systematic review. Int J Clin Pract. 2014 Mar; 68(3):369-78
- Cui H, Wang C, Maan H, Pang K, Luo F, Duan N, Wang B. scGPT: toward building a foundation model for single-cell multi-omics using generative AI. Nat Methods. 2024 Feb 26.
- da Mata, K.R.U., Costa, R.C.M., Carbone, É.d.S.M. et al. Telehealth in the rehabilitation of female pelvic floor dysfunction: a systematic literature review. Int Urogynecol J 32, 249–259 (2021)
- Daggubati LC, Eichberg DG, Ivan ME, et al. Telemedicine for Outpatient Neurosurgical Oncology Care: Lessons Learned for the Future During the COVID-19 Pandemic. World Neurosurg. 2020;139:e859-e863
- Daggubati LC, Eichberg DG, Ivan ME, et al. Telemedicine for Outpatient Neurosurgical Oncology Care: Lessons Learned for the Future During the COVID-19 Pandemic. World Neurosurg. 2020;139:e859-e863
- Dahiya, A. V., McDonnell, C., DeLucia, E., & Scarpa, A. (2020). A systematic review of remote telehealth assessments for early signs of autism spectrum disorder: Video and mobile applications. Practice Innovations, 5(2), 150–164.
- Dai T, Qian Q, Xin-Ying AN. Research on the Sci-tech Influence Evaluation Index System for hospitals in China. Article in Chinese. Journal of Medical Informatics. 2016;37(3):2–7
- D'Amore, John D.; Sittig, Dean F.; Wright, Adam; Iyengar, M. Sriram; Ness, Roberta B. (2011). "The Promise of the CCD: Challenges and Opportunity for Quality Improvement and Population Health". AMIA Annual Symposium Proceedings. 2011: 285–294
- D'Antoni F, Russo F, Ambrosio L, Vollero L, Vadalà G, Merone M, Papalia R, Denaro V. Artificial Intelligence and Computer Vision in Low Back Pain: A Systematic Review. Int J Environ Res Public Health. 2021 Oct 17;18(20):10909.
- Darcy A, Beaudette A, Chiauzzi E, Daniels J, Goodwin K, Mariano TY, Wicks P, Robinson A. Anatomy of a Woebot® (WB001): agent guided CBT for women with postpartum depression. Expert Rev Med Devices. 2022 Apr;19(4):287-301

- Das, Resul & Turkoglu, Ibrahim & Sengur, Abdulkadir. (2009). Effective diagnosis of heart disease through neural networks ensembles. Expert Syst. Appl.. 36. 7675-7680. 10.1016/j.eswa.2008.09.013.
- Data Mining Group. PMML 4.4.1 – General Structure. http://dmg.org/pmml/v4-4-1/GeneralStructure.html. Accessed October 27, 2021
- Datta N, Derenne J, Sanders M, Lock JD. Telehealth transition in a comprehensive care unit for eating disorders: Challenges and long-term benefits. Int J Eat Disord. 2020 Nov;53(11):1774-1779.
- Davis MC, Can DD, Pindrik J, Rocque BG, Johnston JM. Virtual Interactive Presence in Global Surgical Education: International Collaboration Through Augmented Reality. World Neurosurg. 2016 Feb;86:103-11.
- Dawson D, McCulloch K. Managing fatigue: it's about sleep. Sleep Med. Rev. 2005;9:365–380
- Day S, Shah V, Kaganoff S, Powelson S, Mathews S. Assessing the Clinical Robustness of Digital Health Startups: Cross-sectional Observational Analysis. J Med Internet Res 2022;24(6):e37677
- de Bruin EJ, Bögels SM, Oort FJ, Meijer AM. Improvements of adolescent psychopathology after insomnia treatment: results from a randomized controlled trial over 1 year. J Child Psychol Psychiatry. 2018 May;59(5):509-522.
- de Mooij MJM, Hodny RL, O'Neil DA, Gardner MR, Beaver M, Brown AT, Barry BA, Ross LM, Jasik AJ, Nesbitt KM, Sobolewski SM, Skinner SM, Chaudhry R, Brost BC, Gostout BS, Harms RW. OB Nest: Reimagining Low-Risk Prenatal Care. Mayo Clin Proc. 2018 Apr;93(4):458-466.
- De Santi L., Lanzafame P., Spano' B., D'Aleo G., Bramanti A., Bramanti P., Marino S. Pursuit ocular movements in multiple sclerosis: A video-based eye-tracking study. Neurol. Sci. 2010;32:67–71.
- DEA. Information on Telemedicine. Substance Abuse and Mental Health Services Administration. 2020. https://www.samhsa.gov/sites/default/files/programs_campaigns/medication_assisted/dea-information-telemedicine.pdf. Accessed March 18, 2021
- Deloitte. Deloitte Insights. Technology, Media, and Telecommunications Predictions 2021. Accessed March 28, 2021
- Deloitte. How digital health apps are empowering patients. Oct 19, 2021. https://www2.deloitte.com/us/en/blog/health-care-blog/2021/how-digital-health-apps-are-empowering-patients.html
- Demiris G, Parker Oliver D, Wittenberg-Lyles E, Washington K, Doorenbos A, Rue T, Berry D. A noninferiority trial of a problem-solving intervention for hospice caregivers: in person versus videophone. J Palliat Med. 2012 Jun; 15(6):653-60
- Department of Health & Human Services (DHS). Assistant Secretary for Planning and Evaluation. "Medicare beneficiary use of telehealht visits: Early data from the start of COVID-19 pandemic, February 28, 2021.)
- Department of Health Research. Health Technology Assessment in India. Welcome to the Health Technology Assessment in India. https://htain.dhr.gov.in/. Accessed August 20, 2023
- Department of Veterans Affairs. Office of Public and Intergovernmental Affairs, "VA Video Connect visits increase 1000% during COVID-19 pandemic,". June 12, 2020.
- Devlin J, Chang M-W, Lee K, Toutanova K. 2019. BERT: Pre-training of Deep Bidirectional Transformers for Language Understanding. In Association for Computational Linguistics (ACL). 4171–4186. Accessed at https://aclanthology.org/N19-1423.
- Dharmar M, Kuppermann N, Romano PS, et al. Telemedicine consultations and medication errors in rural emergency departments. Pediatrics 132(6):1090-1097, 2013
- Dharmarajan, H, Anderson, JL, Kim, S, et al. Transition to a virtual multidisciplinary tumor board during the COVID-19 pandemic: University of Pittsburgh experience. Head & Neck. 2020; 42: 1310– 1316
- Dhombres F, Bonnard J, Bailly K, Maurice P, Papageorghiou AT, Jouannic JM. Contributions of Artificial Intelligence Reported in Obstetrics and Gynecology Journals: Systematic Review. J Med Internet Res. 2022 Apr 20;24(4):e35465.
- Digital Diagnostics for Africa Network. The potential of digital molecular diagnostics for infectious diseases in sub-Saharan Africa. PLOS Digit Health. 2022 Jun 30;1(6):e0000064)
- Dijkstra HP, Ergen E, Holtzhausen L, et al. Remote assessment in sport and exercise medicine (SEM): a narrative review and teleSEM solutions for and beyond the COVID-19 pandemic. British Journal of Sports Medicine 2020;54:1162-1167
- Dille MF, McMillan GP, Helt WJ. et al. A Store-and-Forward Tele-Audiology Solution to Promote Efficient Screenings for Ototoxicity during Cisplatin Cancer Treatment. J Am Acad Audiol 2015; 26: 750-760
- Dillenseger A, Weidemann ML, Trentzsch K, Inojosa H, Haase R, Schriefer D, Voigt I, Scholz M, Akgün K, Ziemssen T. Digital Biomarkers in Multiple Sclerosis. Brain Sci. 2021 Nov 16;11(11):1519.
- Dillon, A., Kelly, M., Robertson, I. H., & Robertson, D. A. (2016). Smartphone applications utilizing biofeedback can aid stress reduction. Frontiers in Psychology, 7, 832
- Ding H, Fatehi F, Maiorana A, Bashi N, Hu W, Edwards I. Digital health for COPD care: the current state of play. J Thorac Dis. 2019;11(Suppl 17):S2210-S2220.
- Ding J., Li A., Hu Z., Wang L. (2017) Accurate Pulmonary Nodule Detection in Computed Tomography Images Using Deep Convolutional Neural Networks. In: Descoteaux M., Maier-Hein L., Franz A., Jannin P., Collins D., Duchesne S. (eds) Medical Image Computing and Computer Assisted Intervention – MICCAI 2017. MICCAI 2017. Lecture Notes in Computer Science, vol 10435. Springer, Cham
- Ding Z, Lee TL, Chan AS. Digital Cognitive Biomarker for Mild Cognitive Impairments and Dementia: A Systematic Review. J Clin Med. 2022 Jul 19;11(14):4191.
- Dinuzzi VP, Palomba G, Minischetti M, et al. Telemedicine in patients with an ostomy during the COVID-19 pandemic: a retrospective observational study. Wound Manag. Prev. 67(1):12-17, 2021
- DMG. Run your analytic anywhere. https://dmg.org/pfa. Accessed October 12, 2022
- Dobry A, Begaj T, Mengistu K, Sinha S, Droms R, Dunlap R, Wu D, Adhami K, Stavert R. Implementation and Impact of a Store-and-Forward Teledermatology Platform in an Urban Academic Safety-Net Health Care System. Telemed J E Health. 2021

M eCQI Resource Center. Digital Quality Measures. https://ecqi.healthit.gov/dqm. Nov 16, 2022. Accessed 12/18/2022ar;27(3):308-315

- Dodge HH, Zhu J, Mattek NC, Austin D, Kornfeld J, Kaye JA. Use of high-frequency in-home monitoring data may reduce sample sizes needed in clinical trials. PLoS ONE. 2015;10(9):e0138095.
- Domingues, A. (2015). Smartphone based monitoring system for long-term sleep assessment. Methods in Molecular Biology, 1256, 391–403
- Dong S, Millar R, Shi C, Dong M, Xiao Y, Shen J, Li G. Rating Hospital Performance in China: Review of Publicly Available Measures and Development of a Ranking System. J Med Internet Res. 2021 Jun 17;23(6):e17095
- Dossett EC, Benitez C, Garcia N. Perinatal mental health in community psychiatry: a reproductive psychiatry eConsult pilot project. Psychiatr. Serv. 70(11):1075-1076, 2019
- Drerup B, Espenschied J, Wiedemer J, Hamilton L. Reduced No-Show Rates and Sustained Patient Satisfaction of Telehealth During the COVID-19 Pandemic. Telemed J E Health. 2021 Dec;27(12):1409-1415.
- Drew, B. J. et al. Insights into the problem of alarm fatigue with physiologic monitor devices: a comprehensive observational study of consecutive intensive care unit patients. PLoS ONE 9, e110274 (2014)
- Driessen J, Bonhomme A, Chang W, et al. Nursing Home Provider Perceptions of Telemedicine for Reducing Potentially Avoidable Hospitalizations. J Am Med Dir Assoc. 2016;17(6):519-524
- Du L, Becher SI. Genetic and Genomic Consultation: Are We Ready for Direct-to-Consumer Telegenetics? Front Genet. 2018 Dec 3;9:550
- Dunn BE, Choi H, Recla DL, Kerr SE, Wagenman BL. Robotic surgical telepathology between the Iron Mountain and Milwaukee. Department of Veterans Affairs Medical Centers: a 12-year experience. Hum Pathol. 2009 Aug; 40(8):1092-9
- Dzmitry Bahdanau, Kyunghyun Cho, and Yoshua Bengio. Neural machine translation by jointly learning to align and translate. CoRR, abs/1409.0473, 2014
- Eberly LA, Khatana SAM, Nathan AS, Snider C, Julien HM, Deleener ME, Adusumalli S. Telemedicine Outpatient Cardiovascular Care During the COVID-19 Pandemic: Bridging or Opening the Digital Divide? Circulation. 2020 Aug 4;142(5):510-512.)
- eCQI Resource Center. Digital Quality Measures. https://ecqi.healthit.gov/dqm. Nov 16, 2022. Accessed 12/18/2022
- Edgar S, Swyka T, Fulk G, Sazonov ES. Wearable shoe-based device for rehabilitation of stroke patients. Annu Int Conf IEEE Eng Med Biol Soc. 2010;2010:3772-5
- Edirippulige S, Armfield NR, Greenup P, Bryett A. Telehealth coordinators in hospital based telehealth services: Who are they and what do they do? J. Telemed. Telecare 22(8):447-452, 2016
- Ehlers L, Müskens WM, Jensen LG, Kjølby M, Andersen G. National use of thrombolysis with alteplase for acute ischaemic stroke via telemedicine in Denmark: a model of budgetary impact and cost effectiveness. CNS Drugs. 2008;22(1):73-81
- Ehteshami Bejnordi B, Veta M, Johannes van Diest P, et al. Diagnostic Assessment of Deep Learning Algorithms for Detection of Lymph Node Metastases in Women With Breast Cancer. JAMA. 2017;318(22):2199-2210. doi:10.1001/jama.2017.14585
- Eichberg DG, Basil GW, Di L, Shah AH, Luther EM, Lu VM, Perez-Dickens M, Komotar RJ, Levi AD, Ivan ME. Telemedicine in Neurosurgery: Lessons Learned from a Systematic Review of the Literature for the COVID-19 Era and Beyond. Neurosurgery. 2020 Dec 15;88(1):E1-E12
- Eijlers R, Dierckx B, Staals LM, et al. Virtual reality exposure before elective day care surgery to reduce anxiety and pain in children: a randomised controlled trial. Eur J Anaesthesiol. 2019;36(10):728–737.
- Electronic Code of Federal Regulations (e-CFR.). Title 45. Section 170.315. 2015 Edition health IT certification criteria. https://gov.ecfr.io/cgi-bin/text-idx?SID=5d798b6bb5ef6c5ce8ee39f45366f05e&mc=true&node=se45.2.170_1315&rgn=div8. Accessed October 12, 2021
- Elena Gkrouzman, Dee Dee Wu, Hannah Jethwa, Sonya Abraham. Telemedicine in Rheumatology at the Advent of the COVID-19 Pandemic. HSS J. 2020 Nov; 16(Suppl 1): 108–111
- Elkaryoni A, Badarin FA, Khan MS, Ellakany K, Potturi N, Poonia J, et al. Implantable cardioverter-defibrillators and survival in advanced heart failure patients with continuous-flow left ventricular assist devices: a systematic review and meta-analysis. Europace 2019 Sep 01;21(9):1353-1359
- Elliott T, Shih J, Dinakar C, Portnoy J, Fineman S. American College of Allergy, Asthma & Immunology Position Paper on the Use of Telemedicine for Allergists. Ann Allergy Asthma Immunol. 2017 Dec;119(6):512-517
- Ellis DG, Mayrose J, Phelan M. Consultation times in emergency telemedicine using realtime videoconferencing. J.Telemed. Telecare 12(6):303-305, 2006
- Ellison, L.M., Nguyen, M., Fabrizio, M.D., Soh, A., Permpongkosol, S., Kavoussi, L.R. Postoperative robotic telerounding: a multicenter randomized assessment of patient outcomes and satisfaction. Arch Surg. 2007; 142: 1177
- El-Rifai O, Garaix T, Augusto V, Xie X. A stochastic optimization model for shift scheduling in emergency departments. Health Care Manag Sci. 2015 Sep;18(3):289-302
- Elson EC, Oermann C, Duehlmeyer S, Bledsoe S. Use of telemedicine to provide clinical pharmacy services during the SARS-CoV-2 pandemic. Am J Health Syst Pharm. 2020 Jun 23;77(13):1005-1006.
- Emerick T, Alter B, Jarquin S, et al. Telemedicine for chronic pain in the COVID-19 era and beyond. Pain Med. 21(9):1743-1748, 2020
- Emerick T, Alter B, Jarquin S, et al. Telemedicine for chronic pain in the COVID-19 era and beyond. Pain Med. 21(9):1743-1748, 2020
- Emezue C. Digital or digitally delivered responses to domestic and intimate partner violence during COVID-19. JMIR Public Health Surveill. 6(3):e19831, 2020
- Erica F Weiss, Rubina Malik, Teresa Santos, Mirnova Ceide, Jason Cohen, Joe Verghese, and Jessica L Zwerling. Telehealth for

the cognitively impaired older adult and their caregivers: lessons from a coordinated approach. Neurodegenerative Disease Management 2021 11:1, 83-89

- Escobar GJ, Gardner MN, Greene JD, Draper D, Kipnis P. Risk-adjusting Hospital Mortality Using a Comprehensive Electronic Record in an Integrated Health Care Delivery System. Med Care. 2013 May; 51(5):446-53
- Escobar GJ, LaGuardia JC, Turk BJ, Ragins A, Kipnis P, Draper D. Early detection of impending physiologic deterioration among patients who are not in intensive care: Development of predictive models using data from an automated electronic medical record. J Hosp Med. 2012 May-Jun; 7(5):388-95
- Escobar GJ, Turk BJ, Ragins A, et al. Piloting electronic medical record-based early detection of inpatient deterioration in community hospitals. J Hosp Med. 2016;11 Suppl 1(Suppl 1):S18-S24
- Eslami, S., de Melo, G. & Meinel, C. Does clip benefit visual question answering in the medical domain as much as it does in the general domain? arXiv preprint arXiv:2112.13906 (2021).
- Espie, C. A., Kyle, S. D., Williams, C., Ong, J. C., Douglas, N. J., Hames, P., & Brown, J. S. (2012). A randomized, placebo-controlled trial of online cognitive behavioral therapy for chronic insomnia disorder delivered via an automated media-rich web application. Sleep, 35(6), 769-781
- Estai M, Bunt S, Kanagasingam Y, Kruger E, Tennant M. Diagnostic accuracy of teledentistry in the detection of dental caries: a systematic review. J Evid Based Dent Pract. 2016 Sep;16(3):161-172
- Esteva A, Kuprel B, Novoa RA, Ko J, Swetter SM, Blau HM, Thrun S. Dermatologist-level classification of skin cancer with deep neural networks. Nature. 2017 Feb 2;542(7639):115-118. doi: 10.1038/nature21056. Epub 2017 Jan 25. Erratum in: Nature. 2017 Jun 28;546(7660):686
- EU General Data Protection Regulation (GDPR): Regulation (EU) 2016/679 of the European Parliament and of the Council of 27 April 2016 on the protection of natural persons with regard to the processing of personal data and on the free movement of such data, and repealing Directive 95/46/EC (General Data Protection Regulation), OJ 2016 L 119/1. https://eur-lex.europa.eu/legal-content/EN/TXT/HTML/?uri=CELEX:32016R0679&from=EN#d1e1489-1-1. Accessed July 12, 2021
- European Commission. Internal Market, Industry, Entrepreneurship and SMEs. European Standards. https://single-market-economy.ec.europa.eu/single-market/european-standards_en. Accessed January 7, 2023
- European Parliament. Regulation (EU) 2017/745 of the European Parliament and of the Council. 5 April 2017. https://eur-lex.europa.eu/legal-content/EN/TXT/?uri=CELEX:02017R0745-20200424. Accessed September 14, 2021
- Everitt BS, Landau S, Leese M, Stahl D. Cluster analysis. 5th ed. Chichester: Wiley; 2011; p. 321–30
- Everitt HA, Landau S, O'Reilly G, Sibelli A, Hughes S, Windgassen S, Holland R, Little P, McCrone P, Bishop F, Goldsmith K, Coleman N, Logan R, Chalder T, Moss-Morris R; ACTIB trial group. Assessing telephone-delivered cognitive-behavioural therapy (CBT) and web-delivered CBT versus treatment as usual in irritable bowel syndrome (ACTIB): a multicentre randomised trial. Gut. 2019 Sep;68(9):1613-1623
- Exarchos KP, Exarchos TP, Bourantas CV, Papafaklis MI, Naka KK, Michalis LK, Parodi O, Fotiadis DI. Prediction of coronary atherosclerosis progression using dynamic Bayesian networks. Annu Int Conf IEEE Eng Med Biol Soc. 2013;2013:3889-92
- Fahl J. Data Analytics: A Practical Guide to Data Analytics for Business, Beginner to Expert. CreateSpace Independent Publishing Platform, 2017
- Farabet, C., Couprie, C., Najman, L. & LeCun, Y. Learning hierarchical features for scene labeling. IEEE Trans. Pattern Anal. Mach. Intell. 35, 1915–1929 (2013)
- Farmer B, Stoerger L, Vyavahare M, Sharma R. A novel use of telemedicine during a hospital mass casualty drill. J. Telemed. Telecare 31:1357633X19893879, 2019
- Farrington R. August 4 2021. HCPCS Code for Billing Artificial Intelligence is Announced. https://info.hapusa.com/blog-0/hcpcs-code-for-billing-artificial-intelligence-is-announced#_edn1
- FDA. "Software as a Medical Device (SaMD). December 4, 2018. https://www.fda.gov/medical-devices/digital-health/software-medical-device-samd. Accessed May 12, 2021. [a]
- FDA. 21 CFR 807.65(d). https://www.accessdata.fda.gov/scripts/cdrh/cfdocs/cfcfr/CFRSearch.cfm?CFRPart=807. Accessed October 12, 2021
- FDA. 21 CFR 820. https://www.accessdata.fda.gov/scripts/cdrh/cfdocs/cfcfr/CFRSearch.cfm?CFRPart=820&showFR=1 Accessed September 12, 2021
- FDA. Artificial Intelligence and Machine Learning (AI/ML)-Enabled Medical Devices. September 22, 2021. https://www.fda.gov/medical-devices/software-medical-device-samd/artificial-intelligence-and-machine-learning-aiml-enabled-medical-devices. Accessed December 2, 2021 [m]
- FDA. CDRH. De Novo Classification Request for ECG App. 2018. https://www.accessdata.fda.gov/cdrh_docs/reviews/DEN180044.pdf [a]
- FDA. CDRH. De Novo Classification Request for Irregular Rhythm Notification Feature. 2018. https://www.accessdata.fda.gov/cdrh_docs/reviews/DEN180042.pdf [b]
- FDA. Classify your Medical Device. FDA. February 7, 2020. https://www.fda.gov/medical-devices/overview-device-regulation/classify-your-medical-device. Accessed 15 February 2021 [b]
- FDA. Clinical Decision Support Software. Draft Guidance for Industry and Food and Drug Administration Staff. September 27, 2019. https://www.fda.gov/media/109618/download. Accessed October 14, 2021 [a]
- FDA. Design Control Guidance For Medical Device Manufacturers. Guidance for Industry. FDA. March 1997. https://www.fda.gov/regulatory-information/search-fda-guidance-documents/design-control-guidance-medical-device-manufacturers. Accessed November 28, 2021
- FDA. Developing a Software Precertification Program: A Working Model v1.0. January 2019.

https://www.fda.gov/media/119722/download. Accessed July 12, 2021 [g]

- FDA. Examples of Software Functions for Which the FDA Will Exercise Enforcement Discretion. September 26, 2019. https://www.fda.gov/medical-devices/device-software-functions-including-mobile-medical-applications/examples-software-functions-which-fda-will-exercise-enforcement-discretion. Accessed October 22, 2021 [c]
- FDA. FDA Facts: Biomarkers and Surrogate Endpoints. 12/21/2017. https://www.fda.gov/about-fda/innovation-fda/fda-facts-biomarkers-and-surrogate-endpoints. Accessed January 21, 2023 [i]
- FDA. FDA Launches the Digital Health Center of Excellence. September 22, 2020. https://content.govdelivery.com/accounts/USFDA/bulletins/2a20211. Accessed October 12, 2021 [a]
- FDA. FDASIA Health IT Report. April 2014. https://www.fda.gov/about-fda/cdrh-reports/fdasia-health-it-report. Accessed October 22, 2021
- FDA. General Wellness: Policy for Low Risk Devices Guidance for Industry and Food and Drug Administration Staff. FDA. September 2019. https://www.fda.gov/regulatory-information/search-fda-guidance-documents/general-wellness-policy-low-risk-devices. Accessed February 12, 2022 [d]
- FDA. Guidance for the Content of Premarket Submissions for Software Contained in Medical Devices Guidance for Industry and FDA Staff. May 2005. Accessed July 28, 2021
- FDA. Investigational Device Exemption (IDE). December 12, 2019. https://www.fda.gov/medical-devices/how-study-and-market-your-device/investigational-device-exemption-ide. Accessed 23 March 2021 [f]
- FDA. Medical Device Exemptions 510(k) and GMP Requirements. September 26, 2022. https://www.accessdata.fda.gov/scripts/cdrh/cfdocs/cfpcd/315.cfm. Accessed September 29, 2022 [a]
- FDA. MedWatch: The FDA Safety Information and Adverse Event Reporting Program. https://www.fda.gov/safety/medwatch-fda-safety-information-and-adverse-event-reporting-program. Accessed October 28, 2021
- FDA. Policy for Device Software Functions and Mobile Medical Applications. Guidance for Industry and Food and Drug Administration Staff. September 27, 2019. https://www.fda.gov/regulatory-information/search-fda-guidance-documents/policy-device-software-functions-and-mobile-medical-applications. Accessed December 12, 2021 [b]
- FDA. Premarket Approval (PMA). May 16, 2019. https://www.fda.gov/medical-devices/premarket-submissions-selecting-and-preparing-correct-submission/premarket-approval-pma Accessed December 16, 2021 [h]
- FDA. Premarket Approval. September 26, 2022. https://www.accessdata.fda.gov/scripts/cdrh/cfdocs/cfPMA/pma.cfm. Accessed October 1, 2022 [c]
- FDA. Premarket Notification 510(k). March 13, 2020. https://www.fda.gov/medical-devices/premarket-submissions-selecting-and-preparing-correct-submission/premarket-notification-510k. Accessed 21 February 2021 [c]
- FDA. Proposed Regulatory Framework for Modifications to Artificial Intelligence/Machine Learning (AI/ML)-Based Software as a Medical Device (SaMD) - Discussion Paper and Request For Feedback. April 2, 2019. https://www.fda.gov/files/medical%20devices/published/US-FDA-Artificial-Intelligence-and-Machine-Learning-Discussion-Paper.pdf. Accessed December 18, 2020 [i]
- FDA. Quality System Regulations/ Medical Device Good Manufacturing Practices. February 23, 2022. https://www.fda.gov/medical-devices/postmarket-requirements-devices/quality-system-qs-regulationmedical-device-good-manufacturing-practices. Accessed July 14, 2022 [b]
- FDA. Regulatory controls. March 27, 2018. https://www.fda.gov/medical-devices/overview-device-regulation/regulatory-controls. Accessed September 12, 2021 [b]
- FDA. UDI Basics. August 17, 2022. https://www.fda.gov/medical-devices/unique-device-identification-system-udi-system/udi-basics. Accessed June 5, 2023 [c]
- FDA. Use of Real-World Evidence to Support Regulatory Decision-Making for Medical Devices: Guidance for Industry and Food and Drug Administration Staff. August 31, 2017. https://www.fda.gov/downloads/medicaldevices/deviceregulationandguidance/guidancedocuments/ucm513027.pdf. Accessed October 12, 2021)
- FDA-NIH Biomarker Working Group. BEST (Biomarkers, EndpointS, and other Tools) Resource [Internet]. Silver Spring (MD): Food and Drug Administration (US); 2016-. Co-published by National Institutes of Health (US), Bethesda (MD)
- Federal Trade Commission. Privacy Online: A Report to Congress. June 1998. https://www.ftc.gov/sites/default/files/documents/reports/privacy-online-report-congress/priv-23a.pdf. Accessed May 14, 2021
- Fernández C, Ruiz V, Couñago F. COVID-19 and information and communication technology in radiation oncology: A new paradigm. World J Clin Oncol. 2020;11(12):968-975.
- Ferranti, Jeffrey M.; Musser, R. Clayton; Kawamoto, Kensaku; Hammond, W. Ed (May–June 2006). "The Clinical Document Architecture and the Continuity of Care Record: A Critical Analysis". Journal of the American Medical Informatics Association. 13 (3): 245–252
- Ferraz Dos Santos L, Borges RF, de Azambuja DA. Telehealth and Breastfeeding: An Integrative Review. Telemed J E Health. 2020 Jul;26(7):837-846.
- Ferrua M, Mathivon D, Duflot-Boukobza A, Abbas M, Charles C, Barrais A, Legendre J, Mendes C, Pons M, Merad M, Minvielle E, Mir O, Scotté F. Nurse navigators' telemonitoring for cancer patients with COVID-19: a French case study. Support Care Cancer. 2021 Jan 18:1–8.
- Field MJ, Grigsby J. Telemedicine and remote patient monitoring. JAMA. 2002 Jul 24-31;288(4):423-5
- Fielding RT. REST APIs must be hypertext driven. Untangled. Octomber 20, 2008. https://roy.gbiv.com/untangled/2008/rest-apis-must-be-hypertext-driven. Accessed July 12, 2021

- Finkelstein J, Khare R, Vora D. Home automated telemanagement (HAT) system to facilitate self care of patients with chronic diseases. J Syst Cybernet Inform. 2003;1:1–5.
- Finkelstein J, Lapshin O, Castro H, Cha E, Provance PG. Home-based physical telerehabilitation in patients with multiple sclerosis: a pilot study. Journal of Rehabilitation Research and Development 2008;45(9):1361-73
- Firth, J. et al. Can smartphone mental health interventions reduce symptoms of anxiety? A meta-analysis of randomized controlled trials. J. Affect. Disord. 218, 15–22 (2017)
- Fix OK, Serper M. Telemedicine and Telehepatology During the COVID-19 Pandemic. Clin Liver Dis (Hoboken). 2020 May 21;15(5):187-190
- Fleurence RL, Shuren J. Advances in the Use of Real-World Evidence for Medical Devices: An Update From the National Evaluation System for Health Technology. Clin Pharmacol Ther. 2019;106(1):30-33
- Flodgren G, Rachas A, Farmer AJ, Inzitari M, Shepperd S. Interactive telemedicine: effects on professional practice and health care outcomes. Cochrane Database Syst Rev. 2015 Sep 7;2015(9):CD002098
- Flores Mateo G, Granado-Font E, Ferré-Grau C, Montaña-Carreras X. Mobile Phone Apps to Promote Weight Loss and Increase Physical Activity: A Systematic Review and Meta-Analysis. J Med Internet Res. 2015 Nov 10;17(11):e253
- Foley & Lardner. 50-State Survey of telehealth commercial insurance laws. February 2021
- Food and Drug Administration (FDA). Digital Health Technologies for Remote Data Acquisition in Clinical Investigations. Guidance of Industry, Investigators, and Other Stakeholders. Draft Guidance. December 2021. https://www.fda.gov/media/155022/download. Accessed January 7, 2023 [k]
- Fortuna K, Naslund J, LaCroix J, Bianco C, Brooks J, Zisman-Ilani Y, Muralidharan A, Deegan P. Digital Peer Support Mental Health Interventions for People With a Lived Experience of a Serious Mental Illness: Systematic Review. JMIR Ment Health 2020;7(4):e16460.)
- Fotouhi J, Alexander CP, Unberath M, Taylor G, Lee SC, Fuerst B, et al. Plan in 2-D, execute in 3-D: an augmented reality solution for cup placement in total hip arthroplasty. J Med Imaging (Bellingham) 2018;5:021205
- Francioli P, Etienne J, Hoigné R, Thys JP, Gerber A. Treatment of streptococcal endocarditis with a single daily dose of ceftriaxone sodium for 4 weeks. Efficacy and outpatient treatment feasibility. JAMA. 1992 Jan 8;267(2):264-7
- Franco I, Perni S, Wiley S, Drapek L. Equity in radiation oncology post- COVID: bridging the telemedicine gap. Int. J. Radiat. Oncol. Biol. Phys. 108(2):479-482, 2020
- Frank Desiere aet al. Digital Diagnostics and Mobile Health in Laboratory Medicine: An International Federation of Clinical Chemistry and Laboratory Medicine Survey on Current Practice and Future Perspectives, The Journal of Applied Laboratory Medicine, Volume 6, Issue 4, July 2021, Pages 969–979
- Fredrich T. Learn REST: RESTful Tutorial. https://www.restapitutorial.com. Accessed October 12, 2021
- Freeman B, Mayne S, Localio AR, et al. Using video from mobile phones to improve pediatric phone triage in an underserved population. Telemed.e-Health 23(2):130-136, 2017
- Freeman WD, Barrett KM, Vatz KA, Demaerschalk BM. Future neurohospitalist: teleneurohospitalist. Neurohospitalist.2(4):132-143, 2012
- Frick KD, Burton LC, Clark R, Mader SI, Naughton WB, Burl JB, Greenough WB, Steinwachs DM, Leff B. Substitutive Hospital at Home for older persons: effects on costs. Am J Manag Care. 2009 Jan;15(1):49-56
- Frick KD, et al. Substitutive Hospital at Home for older persons: effects on costs. Am J Manag Care. 2009;15(1):49–56
- Fryer, K., Delgado, A., Foti, T. et al. Implementation of Obstetric Telehealth During COVID-19 and Beyond. Matern Child Health J 24, 1104–1110 (2020)
- FSMB (Federation of State Medical Boards). U.S. States and Territories Modifying Requirements for Telehealth in Response to COVID-19. February 19, 2021. https://www.fsmb.org/siteassets/advocacy/pdf/states-waiving-licensure-requirements-for-telehealth-in-response-to-covid-19.pdf. Accessed February 2021
- FSMB. Telemedicine Policies - Board by Board Overview. June 2021 https://www.fsmb.org/siteassets/advocacy/key-issues/telemedicine_policies_by_state.pdf. Accessed June 30, 2021
- Fulford D, Tuot DS, Mangurian C. Electronic psychiatric consultation in primary care in the Safety Net. Psychiatr. Serv. 67(10):1160-1161, 2016
- Fusaro VA, Daniels J, Duda M, DeLuca TF, D'Angelo O, Tamburello J, Maniscalco J, Wall DP. The potential of accelerating early detection of autism through content analysis of YouTube videos. PLoS One. 2014 Apr 16;9(4):e93533.
- Futoma J, Morris J, Lucas J. A comparison of models for predicting early hospital readmissions. J Biomed Inform. 2015;56:229-238
- G. Abbadessa, F. Brigo, M. Clerico, S. De Mercanti, F. Trojsi, G. Tedeschi, S. Bonavita, and L. Lavorgna, "Digital therapeutics in neurology," J. Neurol., vol. 269, no. 3, pp. 1209–1224, May 2022
- G. K. Alexander, S. B. Canclini, J. Fripp, and W. Fripp, "Waterborne Disease Case Investigation: Public Health Nursing Simulation," (in eng), J Nurs Educ, vol. 56, no. 1, pp. 39–42, Jan 1, 2017
- G. H. Simmons, J. M. Christenson, J. G. Kereiakes, and G. K. Bahr, "A non-linear programming method for optimizing parallel-hole collimator design," (in eng), Phys Med Biol, vol. 20, no. 3, pp. 771–88, Sep 1975
- Gagnon MP, Desmartis M, Labrecque M, Car J, Pagliari C, Pluye P, Frémont P, Gagnon J, Tremblay N, Légaré F. Systematic review of factors influencing the adoption of information and communication technologies by healthcare professionals. J Med Syst. 2012 Feb; 36(1):241-77
- Gale J, Lambert D. Exploring the business case for children's telebehavioral health. Technical Assistance Network for Children's Behavioral Health, The Institute for Innovation & Implementation, March 2015. https://www.scribd.com/document/288520754/Exploring-the-Business-Case-for-Children-s-Telebehavioral-Health. Accessed March 28, 2021

- Galiero R, Pafundi PC, Nevola R, et al. The Importance of Telemedicine during COVID-19 Pandemic: A Focus on Diabetic Retinopathy. J Diabetes Res. 2020;2020:9036847
- Gallagher, T. E. (2004). Augmentation of special-needs services and information to students and teachers "ASSIST"—A telehealth innovation providing school-based medical interventions. Hawaii Medical Journal, 63, 300–309
- Gallar P, Vigil A, Rodriguez I, et al. . Two-year experience with telemedicine in the follow-up of patients in home peritoneal Dialysis. J Telemed Telecare 2007;13:288–92
- Galloway CD, Valys AV, Petterson FL, et al. Non-invasive detection of hyperkalemia with a smartphone electrocardiogram and artificial intelligence. J Am Coll Cardiol 2018;71:Suppl:A272-A272.
- Gan A, Cohen A, Tan L. Augmented reality-assisted percutaneous dilatational tracheostomy in critically Ill patients with chronic respiratory disease. J Intensive Care Med. 2019;34(2):153–155.
- Gao X, Yan X, Gao P, Gao X, Zhang S. Automatic detection of epileptic seizure based on approximate entropy, recurrence quantification analysis and convolutional neural networks. Artif Intell Med. 2020 Jan;102:101711.
- Garcia-Gancedo L, Kelly ML, Lavrov A, Parr J, Hart R, Marsden R, Turner MR, Talbot K, Chiwera T, Shaw CE, Al-Chalabi A. Objectively Monitoring Amyotrophic Lateral Sclerosis Patient Symptoms During Clinical Trials With Sensors: Observational Study. JMIR Mhealth Uhealth. 2019 Dec 20;7(12):e13433
- Gareth James, Daniela Witten, Trevor Hastie, Robert Tibshirani. An Introduction to Statistical Learning : with Applications in R. New York :Springer, 2013
- Garibaldi, M., Siciliano, G. & Antonini, G. Telemedicine for neuromuscular disorders during the COVID-19 outbreak. J Neurol 268, 1–4 (2021)
- Gaßner H, Jensen D, Marxreiter F, Kletsch A, Bohlen S, Schubert R, Muratori LM, Eskofier B, Klucken J, Winkler J, Reilmann R, Kohl Z. Gait variability as digital biomarker of disease severity in Huntington's disease. J Neurol. 2020 Jun;267(6):1594-1601.
- Gattu R, Teshome G, Lichenstein R. Telemedicine applications for the pediatric emergency medicine: a review of the current literature. Pediatr. Emerg. Care 32(2):123-130, 2016
- Genc Y, Riedel S, Souvannavong F, Akinlar C, Navab N (2002) Marker-less tracking for AR: A learning-based approach. IEEE Xplore. International symposium on mixed and augmented reality, 2002. ISMAR 2002. Proceedings.
- Ghai S. Teledentistry during COVID-19 pandemic. Diabetes Metab Syndr. 2020;14(5):933-935
- Ghandeharioun A, Fedor S, Sangermano L, Ionescu D, Alpert J, Dale C, Sontag D, Picard R. Objective assessment of depressive symptoms with machine learning and wearable sensors data. 2017. 325-332. 10.1109/ACII.2017.8273620.
- Ghassemi M, Naumann T, Doshi-Velez F, Brimmer N, Joshi R, Rumshisky A, et al. Unfolding Physiological State: Mortality Modelling in Intensive Care Units. KDD : proceedings / International Conference on Knowledge Discovery & Data Mining International Conference on Knowledge Discovery & Data Mining. 2014;2014:75–84
- Ghaznavi F, Evans A, Madabhushi A, Feldman M. Digital imaging in pathology: whole-slide imaging and beyond. Annu Rev Pathol. 2013 Jan 24; 8():331-59
- Gibby JT, Swenson SA, Cvetko S, Rao R, Javan R. Head-mounted display augmented reality to guide pedicle screw placement utilizing computed tomography. Int J Comput Assist Radiol Surg. 2019 Mar;14(3):525-535.
- Gidora H, Borycki EM, Kushniruk AW. Effects of telenursing triage and advice on healthcare costs and resource use. Stud. Health Technol. Inform. 257:133-139, 2019
- Gilbert G, Fernandes LA, Sawant A. Digital is shaping US health insurance – winners are moving fast. McKinsey & Company. January 8, 2019. https://www.mckinsey.com/industries/healthcare-systems-and-services/our-insights/digital-is-reshaping-us-health-insurance-winners-are-moving-fast. Accessed April 15, 2021
- Gilbert S, Mehl A, Baluch A, Cawley C, Challiner J, Fraser H, Millen E, Montazeri M, Multmeier J, Pick F, Richter C, Türk E, Upadhyay S, Virani V, Vona N, Wicks P, Novorol C. How accurate are digital symptom assessment apps for suggesting conditions and urgency advice? A clinical vignettes comparison to GPs. BMJ Open. 2020 Dec 16;10(12):e040269.
- Giudice A, Barone S, Muraca D, Averta F, Diodati F, Antonelli A, Fortunato L. Can Teledentistry Improve the Monitoring of Patients during the Covid-19 Dissemination? A Descriptive Pilot Study. International Journal of Environmental Research and Public Health. 2020; 17(10):3399
- Gkikopoulos N, Wenger M, Distler O, Becker M. Self-monitoring of the resting heart rate using a fitness tracker smartwatch application leads to an early diagnosis of large vessel vasculitis. BMJ Case Rep. 2022 Feb 28;15(2):e245021.
- Glas HH, Kraeima J, van Ooijen PMA, Spijkervet FKL, Yu L, Witjes MJH. Augmented Reality Visualization for Image-Guided Surgery: A Validation Study Using a Three-Dimensional Printed Phantom. J Oral Maxillofac Surg. 2021 Sep;79(9):1943.e1-1943.e10.
- Glass JE, McKay JR, Gustafson DH, Kornfield R, Rathouz PJ, McTavish FM, Atwood AK, Isham A, Quanbeck A, Shah D. Treatment seeking as a mechanism of change in a randomized controlled trial of a mobile health intervention to support recovery from alcohol use disorders. J Subst Abuse Treat. 2017 Jun;77:57-66
- Globenewswire. (November 04, 2021). Eyenuk Applauds CMS CY 2022 Medicare Physician Fee Schedule Final Rule to Establish National Price for Autonomous AI Technology [Press release]. Retrieved from https://www.globenewswire.com/news-release/2021/11/04/2328172/0/en/Eyenuk-Applauds-CMS-CY-2022-Medicare-Physician-Fee-Schedule-Final-Rule-to-Establish-National-Price-for-Autonomous-AI-Technology.html
- Gloria A. Bachmann. Applause for telemedicine as an optimal platform for specific menopausal health-care visits beyond COVID-19 .Case Rep Womens Health. 2020 Jul; 27: e00241
- Glorot, X., Bordes, A. & Bengio. Y. Deep sparse rectifier neural networks. In Proc. 14th International Conference on Artificial Intelligence and Statistics 315–323 (2011)
- GMDN. What is GMDN? https://www.gmdnagency.org/Services/GMDN
- Go BC, Brewster R, Patel R, Rajasekaran K. Using Telemedicine and Infographics for Physician-Guided Home Drain Removal.

OTO Open. 2020;4(2):2473974X20933566
- Goedeke J, Ertl A, Zöller D, Rohleder S, Muensterer OJ. Telemedicine for pediatric surgical outpatient follow-up: A prospective, randomized single-center trial. J Pediatr Surg. 2019 Jan;54(1):200-207
- Goldsack JC, Coravos A, Bakker JP, Bent B, Dowling AV, Fitzer-Attas C, Godfrey A, Godino JG, Gujar N, Izmailova E, Manta C, Peterson B, Vandendriessche B, Wood WA, Wang KW, Dunn J. Verification, analytical validation, and clinical validation (V3): the foundation of determining fit-for-purpose for Biometric Monitoring Technologies (BioMeTs). NPJ Digit Med. 2020 Apr 14;3:55
- Goldstein, B. A., Navar, A. M., Pencina, M. J. & Ioannidis, J. P. A. Opportunities and challenges in developing risk prediction models with electronic health records data: a systematic review. J. Am. Med. Inform. Assoc. 24, 198–208 (2017)
- Gómez-de-Regil L, Avila-Nava A, Gutierrez-Solis AL, Lugo R. Mobile apps for the management of comorbid overweight/obesity and depression/anxiety: a systematic review. J. Healthc. Eng. 2020:9317179, 2020
- Gómez-Martino JR, Suárez MA, Gallego SD, González PM, Covarsí AR, Castellano IC, Novillo RS, Deira JL, Marigliano NC, Giménez JJ. Telemedicina aplicada a la nefrología. Otra forma de consulta [Telemedicine applied to Nephrology. Another form of consultation]. Nefrologia. 2008;28(4):407-12
- González-Pérez R, Sánchez-Machín I, Poza-Guedes P, Matheu V, Álava-Cruz C, Mederos Luís E. Pertinence of Telehealth in a Rush Conversion to Virtual Allergy Practice During the COVID-19 Outbreak. J Investig Allergol Clin Immunol. 2021 Feb 17;31(1):78-80.
- Goran SF. A new view: tele-intensive care unit competencies. Crit. Care Nurse 31(5):17-29, 2011
- Gorin, SNS, Jimbo, M, Heizelman, R, Harmes, KM, Harper, DM. The future of cancer screening after COVID-19 may be at home. Cancer. 2021: 127: 498- 503
- Gorini A., Griez E., Petrova A., Riva G. Assessment of the emotional responses produced by exposure to real food, virtual food and photographs of food in patients affected by eating disorders. Annals of General Psychiatry. 2010;9, article 30
- Gorini A., Riva G. The potential of Virtual Reality as anxiety management tool: a randomized controlled study in a sample of patients affected by generalized anxiety disorder. Trials. 2008;9, article 25
- Gorman MJ. Telemedicine programs in ICUs are proven to drive hospitals' clinical, financial, and operational success. Chest 143(4):1184, 2013
- Gosselt IK, Nijboer TCW, Van Es MA. An overview of screening instruments for cognition and behavior in patients with ALS: selecting the appropriate tool for clinical practice. Amyotroph Lateral Scler Frontotemporal Degener. 2020 Aug;21(5-6):324-336.
- Gottlieb D, Mandel J. FHIR bulk data API – Extending FHIR to population level datasets. Smart on FHIR. September 2021. https://bit.ly/fhir-bulk-api. Accessed November 16, 2021)
- Gough F, Budhrani S, Cohn E, et al. ATA practice guidelines for live, on demand primary and urgent care. Telemed. eHealth 21(3):233-241, 2015
- Gould CE, Hantke NC. Promoting technology and virtual visits to improve older adult mental health in the face of COVID-19. Amer. J. Geriatr. Psychiatry 28(8):889-890, 2020)
- Gozalo PL, Teno JM, Spence C. Hospice Visit Patterns in the Last Seven Days of Life and the Service Intensity Add-On Payment. J Palliat Med. 2017 Dec; 20(12):1378-1384
- Grabowski DC, O'Malley AJ. Use of telemedicine can reduce hospitalizations of nursing home residents and generate savings for medicare. Health Aff (Millwood). 2014 Feb; 33(2):244-50
- Gradman AH, Vekeman F, Eldar-Lissai A, Trahey A, Ong SH, Duh MS. Is addition of vasodilators to loop diuretics of value in the care of hospitalized acute heart failure patients? Real-world evidence from a retrospective analysis of a large United States hospital database. J Card Fail 2014; 20: 853-63.
- Graham E Quinn; e-ROP Cooperative Group. Telemedicine approaches to evaluating acute-phase retinopathy of prematurity: study design[J]. Ophthalmic Epidemiol, 2014, 21(4): 256-267
- Graham Grieve. HL7 needs a fresh look because V3 has failed. Healthcare Interoperability by Graham Grieve. Health Intersections. August 15, 2011. http://www.healthintersections.com.au/?p=476. Accessed March 22, 2021
- Gray JE, Safran C, Davis RB, et al. Baby CareLink: using the internet and telemedicine to improve care for high-risk infants. Pediatrics 106(6):1318-1324, 2000
- Gray MJ, Hassija CM, Jaconis M, et al. Provision of evidence-based therapies to rural survivors of domestic violence and sexual assault via telehealth: treatment outcomes and clinical training benefits. Training Educ.Prof. Psych. 9(3): 235–241, 2015
- Green BN, Pence TV, Kwan L, Rokicki-Parashar J. Rapid Deployment of Chiropractic Telehealth at 2 Worksite Health Centers in Response to the COVID-19 Pandemic: Observations from the Field. J Manipulative Physiol Ther. 2020;43(5):404.e1-404.e10.
- Greenwood DA, Gee PM, Fatkin KJ, Peeples M. A Systematic Review of Reviews Evaluating Technology-Enabled Diabetes Self-Management Education and Support. J Diabetes Sci Technol. 2017 Sep;11(5):1015-1027
- Grenda TR, Whang S, Evans NR. Transitioning a Surgery Practice to Telehealth During COVID-19. 3rd Ann Surg. 2020 Aug; 272(2):e168-e169
- Grimes, C.L., Balk, E.M., Crisp, C.C. et al. A guide for urogynecologic patient care utilizing telemedicine during the COVID-19 pandemic: review of existing evidence. Int Urogynecol J 31, 1063–1089 (2020).
- Grinfeld J, Nangalia J, Baxter EJ, et al. Classification and personalized prognosis in myeloproliferative neoplasms. N Engl J Med 2018;379:1416-1430
- Gujjar KR, Sharma R, Jongh AD. Virtual Reality Exposure Therapy for Treatment of Dental Phobia. Dent Update. 2017 May;44(5):423-4, 427-8, 431-2, 435
- Gulshan V, Peng L, Coram M, et al. Development and validation of a deep learning algorithm for detection of diabetic retinopathy in retinal fundus photographs JAMA, 316 (2016), pp. 2402-2410
- Gustafson DH Sr, Landucci G, McTavish F, Kornfield R, Johnson RA, Mares ML, Westergaard RP, Quanbeck A, Alagoz E, Pe-

Romashko K, Thomas C, Shah D. The effect of bundling medication-assisted treatment for opioid addiction with mHealth: study protocol for a randomized clinical trial. Trials. 2016 Dec 12; 17(1):592

- Guthrie NL, Carpenter J, Edwards KL, Appelbaum KJ, Dey S, Eisenberg DM, et al. Emergence of digital biomarkers to predict and modify treatment efficacy: machine learning study. BMJ Open 2019 Jul 23;9(7):e030710
- Guttentag S. The State of Telehealth, According to Healthcare Providers and Patients. GoodRx. November 15, 2021. https://www.goodrx.com/healthcare-access/telehealth/state-of-telehealth-survey-2021. Accessed Dec 27, 2021
- H.R.34 - 21st Century Cures Act. Sec. 3060. Clarifying Medical Software Regulation. https://www.congress.gov/114/bills/hr34/BILLS-114hr34enr.xml#toc-H73E766CC72AC4EB8AAF36670EB540164. Accessed December 10, 2021)
- Ha H-G, Hong J. Augmented reality in medicine. Hanyang Med Rev 2016; 36(4): 242.
- Habak S, Bennett J, Davies A, Davies M, Christensen H, Boydell KM. Edge of the Present: A Virtual Reality Tool to Cultivate Future Thinking, Positive Mood and Wellbeing. Int J Environ Res Public Health. 2020 Dec 28;18(1):140.
- Habibi M, Weber L, Neves M, Wiegandt DL, Leser U. Deep learning with word embeddings improves biomedical named entity recognition. Bioinformatics. 2017 Jul 15;33(14):i37-i48.
- Hachesu PR, Ahmadi M, Alizadeh S, Sadoughi F. Use of data mining techniques to determine and predict length of stay of cardiac patients. Healthc Inform Res. 2013;19(2):121-129
- Haggerty JL, Reid RJ, Freeman GK, Starfield BH, Adair CE, McKendry R. Continuity of care: a multidisciplinary review. BMJ. 2003 Nov 22; 327(7425):1219-21
- Haisley KR, Straw OJ, Müller DT, et al. Feasibility of implementing a virtual reality program as an adjuvant tool for peri-operative pain control; results of a randomized controlled trial in minimally invasive foregut surgery. Complement Ther Med. 2020;49:102356.
- Hall, N., Boisvert, M., & Steele, R. (2013). Telepractice in the screening, assessment and treatment of individuals with aphasia: A systematic review. International Journal of Telerehabilitation, 5(1), 27–38.
- Halpern Y, Choi Y, Horng S, Sontag D. Using Anchors to Estimate Clinical State without Labeled Data. AMIA Annu Symp Proc. 2014;2014:606-615. Published 2014 Nov 14.
- Halpren-Ruder D, Chang AM, Hollander JE, Shah A. Quality Assurance in Telehealth: Adherence to Evidence-Based Indicators. Telemed J E Health. 2019 Jul;25(7):599-603
- Han, T., Adams, L. C., Papaioannou, J. M., Grundmann, P., Oberhauser, T., Löser, A., ... & Bressem, K. K. (2023). MedAlpaca--an open-source collection of medical conversational AI models and training data. arXiv preprint arXiv:2304.08247.
- Haque A, Guo M, Alahi A, et al. Towards vision-based smart hospitals: a system for tracking and monitoring hand hygiene compliance. Proc Mach Learn Res 2017; 68: 75-87
- Hardt D. Internet Engineering Task Force. RFC 6749. The OAuth 2.0 Authorization Framework. October 2012. https://tools.ietf.org/html/rfc6749. Accessed June 22, 2021
- Harris M, Johnson S, Mackin S, Saitz R, Walley AY, Taylor JL. Low Barrier Tele-Buprenorphine in the Time of COVID-19: A Case Report. J Addict Med. 2020;14(4):e136-e138.
- Hartl D, de Luca V, Kostikova A, Laramie J, Kennedy S, Ferrero E, Siegel R, Fink M, Ahmed S, Millholland J, Schuhmacher A, Hinder M, Piali L, Roth A. Translational precision medicine: an industry perspective. J Transl Med. 2021 Jun 5;19(1):245.
- Hayden EM, Khatri A, Kelly HR, Yager PH, Salazar GM. Mannequin-based telesimulation: increasing access to simulation-based education. Acad. Emerg. Med. 25(2):144-147, 2018
- HCPCS Codes Lookup. Codify by AAPC. https://www.aapc.com/codes/hcpcs-codes-range. Accessed November 10, 2021
- He D, Mathews SC, Kalloo AN, Hutfless S. Mining high-dimensional administrative claims data to predict early hospital readmissions. J Am Med Inform Assoc. 2014 Mar-Apr;21(2):272-9
- He, X., Zhang, Y., Mou, L., Xing, E. and Xie, P., 2020. Pathvqa: 30000+ questions for medical visual question answering. arXiv preprint arXiv:2003.10286.
- Health Level 7. Introducing HL7 FHIR. August 19, 2018. http://hl7.org/fhir/2018Sep/summary.html. (Accessed June 2020)
- Healthcare Common Procedure Coding System (HCPCS) Level II Coding Procedures. CMS pdf https://www.cms.gov/Medicare/Coding/MedHCPCSGenInfo/Downloads/2018-11-30-HCPCS-Level2-Coding-Procedure.pdf
- HealthIT.gov. Advanced Alternative Payment Model. October 22, 2019. https://www.healthit.gov/topic/meaningful-use-and-macra/advanced-alternative-payment-model. Accessed November 21, 2021
- HealthIT.gov. Office of the National Coordinator for Health Information Technology (ONC). September 2020. Available at: https://www.healthit.gov/topic/health-it-health-care-settings/telemedicine-and-telehealth. Accessed April 14, 2021
- Hedges L. EMR Pricing Explained: Your Guide to Upfront, Recurring & Hidden Costs. Software advice. February 21, 2021. https://www.softwareadvice.com/resources/emr-pricing-explained/ Accessed October 25, 2021
- Heida A, Dijkstra A, Muller Kobold A, Rossen JW, Kindermann A, Kokke F, de Meij T, Norbruis O, Weersma RK, Wessels M, Hummel T, Escher J, van Wering H, Hendriks D, Mearin L, Groen H, Verkade HJ, van Rheenen PF. Efficacy of Home Telemonitoring versus Conventional Follow-up: A Randomized Controlled Trial among Teenagers with Inflammatory Bowel Disease. J Crohns Colitis. 2018 Mar 28;12(4):432-441.
- Heidenheim PA, Muirhead N, Moist L, Lindsay RM. Patient quality of life on quotidian hemodialysis. Am J Kidney Dis. 2003;42(S1)(S1):S36-S41
- Helsel, B.C., Williams, J.E., Lawson, K. et al. Telemedicine and Mobile Health Technology Are Effective in the Management of Digestive Diseases: A Systematic Review. Dig Dis Sci 63, 1392–1408 (2018)
- Heo S, Park JH. Effects of Virtual Reality-Based Graded Exposure Therapy on PTSD Symptoms: A Systematic Review and Meta-Analysis. Int J Environ Res Public Health. 2022 Nov 29;19(23):15911.
- Hernando D., Roca S., Sancho J., Alesanco Á., Bailón R. Validation of the Apple Watch for Heart Rate Variability Measurements

during Relax and Mental Stress in Healthy Subjects. Sensors. 2018;18:2619.

- Hickey BA, Chalmers T, Newton P, Lin CT, Sibbritt D, McLachlan CS, Clifton-Bligh R, Morley J, Lal S. Smart Devices and Wearable Technologies to Detect and Monitor Mental Health Conditions and Stress: A Systematic Review. Sensors (Basel). 2021 May 16;21(10):3461.
- Hijazi HH, Harvey HL, Alyahya MS, Alshraideh HA, Al Abdi RM, Parahoo SK. The Impact of Applying Quality Management Practices on Patient Centeredness in Jordanian Public Hospitals: Results of Predictive Modeling. Inquiry. 2018 Jan-Dec;55:46958018754739
- Hillock M. Treating COPD in rural communities with telehealth. Health Recovery Solutions, Inc., 2020. https://www.healthrecoverysolutions.com/blog/treating-copd-in-rural-communities-with-telehealth. Accessed April 15, 2021.
- Hilty D. Evidence base in telepsychiatry. 2020. https://www.psychiatry.org/psychiatrists/practice/telepsychiatry/toolkit/evidence-base. American Psychiatric Association site. Accessed February 1, 2021
- HIMSS Dictionary of Health Information and Technology Terms, Acronyms and Organizations, which is sourced from Healthcare Information and Management Systems Society (HIMSS). www.himss .org. Last accessed April 2016., www.amia.org/applications-informatics/clinical-informatics. Last accessed April 2016. En.wikipedia.org. 2021. [online] Available at: <https://en.wikipedia.org/wiki/Digital_health> [Accessed 16 September 2021].
- Hinton, G. et al. Deep neural networks for acoustic modeling in speech recognition. IEEE Signal Processing Magazine 29, 82–97 (2012).
- HL7 International. SMART App Launch 2.0.0. HL7 FHIR. November 26, 2021. http://hl7.org/fhir/smart-app-launch/ Accessed: December 16, 2021)
- HL7. About HL7. https://www.hl7.org/about/index.cfm Accessed October 11, 2021
- HL7. C-CDA (HL7 CDA® R2 Implementation Guide: Consolidated CDA Templates for Clinical Notes – US Realm). http://www.hl7.org/implement/standards/product_brief.cfm?product_id=492. Accessed October 25, 2021
- HL7. CDA® Release 2 Product Brief. http://www.hl7.org/implement/standards/product_brief.cfm?product_id=7. February 27, 2015. Accessed January 15, 2022.
- HL7. Conformance. FHIR. 4.1.0. https://build.fhir.org/conformance-rules.html. Accessed: February 16, 2022)
- HL7. Extensibility. FHIR Version 4.1.0. https://build.fhir.org/extensibility.html. Accessed June 12, 2022
- HL7. Getting started with FHIR. November 1, 2019. https://www.hl7.org/fhir/modules.html. Accessed April 26, 2021
- HL7. Guide To Resources. https://www.hl7.org/fhir/resourceguide.html. Accessed November 15, 2021
- HL7. HL7 Reference Information Model. http://www.hl7.org/implement/standards/rim.cfm. Accessed September 16, 2021
- HL7. HL7 Standards – Section 1h: Cross-paradigm/Domain Analysis Models. http://www.hl7.org/implement/standards/product_section.cfm?section=17. Accessed October 21, 2021
- HL7. HL7 Version 2 Product Suite. https://www.hl7.org/implement/standards/product_brief.cfm?product_id=185. Accessed October 21, 2021
- HL7. Introduction to HL7 Standards. http://www.hl7.org/implement/standards/index.cfm?ref=nav. Accessed October 21, 2021
- HL7. Resource Patient – Content. November 1, 2019. https://www.hl7.org/fhir/patient.html. Accessed September 22, 2021
- HL7. RESTful API. March 26, 2023. https://www.hl7.org/fhir/http.html. Accessed May 1, 2023
- Ho C, Argáez C. Telehealth-Delivered Opioid Agonist Therapy for the Treatment of Adults with Opioid Use Disorder: Review of Clinical Effectiveness, Cost-Effectiveness, and Guidelines. Ottawa (ON): Canadian Agency for Drugs and Technologies in Health. 2018 Oct 5. Available from: https://www.ncbi.nlm.nih.gov/books/NBK537877. Accessed March 1, 2021
- Ho JC, Ghosh J, Steinhubl SR, Stewart WF, Denny JC, Malin BA, et al. Limestone: High-throughput candidate phenotype generation via tensor factorization. Journal of Biomedical Informatics. 2014;52:199–211
- Holland AE, Malaguti C, Hoffman M, Lahham A, Burge AT, Dowman L, May AK, Bondarenko J, Graco M, Tikellis G, Lee JY, Cox NS. Home-based or remote exercise testing in chronic respiratory disease, during the COVID-19 pandemic and beyond: A rapid review. Chron Respir Dis. 2020 Jan-Dec;17:1479973120952418.
- Hoppe IC, Lee Y, Granick MS, Scott SS. Digital store and forward imaging as a quality assessment tool for emergency plastic surgery consultations. Eplasty 14: e1, 2014
- Horng S, Sontag DA, Halpern Y, Jernite Y, Shapiro NI, et al. (2017). Creating an automated trigger for sepsis clinical decision support at emergency department triage using machine learning. Creating an automated trigger for sepsis clinical decision support at emergency department triage using machine learning. PLOS ONE 12(4): e0174708.
- Hou, Z., Niu, Y., Du, Z., Zhang, X., Liu, X., Zeng, A., Zheng, Q., Huang, M., Wang, H., Tang, J. and Dong, Y., 2024. ChatGLM-RLHF: Practices of Aligning Large Language Models with Human Feedback. arXiv preprint arXiv:2404.00934.
- Houlihan CA, Balas EA, Lobach DF. Improving clinical practice using clinical decision support systems: a systematic review of trials to identify features critical to success. BMJ. 2005;330(7494):765
- Hripcsak G., Writing Arden Syntax Medical Logic Modules, Comput Biol Med. 1994 Sep;24(5):331-63
- Hsieh JC, Hsu MW. A cloud computing based 12-lead ECG telemedicine service. BMC Med. Inform. Decis. Making 12:77, 2012
- Huang AE, Hribar MR, Goldstein IH, Henriksen B, Lin WC, Chiang MF. Clinical Documentation in Electronic Health Record Systems: Analysis of Similarity in Progress Notes from Consecutive Outpatient Ophthalmology Encounters. AMIA Annu Symp Proc. 2018 Dec 5;2018:1310-1318.
- Huang Y, McCullagh P, Black N, Harper R. Feature selection and classification model construction on type 2 diabetic patients' data. Artif Intell Med, 41 (2007), pp. 251-262
- Huang Z, Tao H, Meng Q, Jing L. Management of endocrine disease. Effects of telecare intervention on glycemic control in type 2 diabetes: a systematic review and meta-analysis of randomized controlled trials. Eur J Endocrinol. 2015 Mar;172(3):R93-101

- Humphries SM, Yagihashi K, Huckleberry J, Rho BH, Schroeder JD, Strand M, Schwarz MI, Flaherty KR, Kazerooni EA, van Beek EJR, Lynch DA. Idiopathic Pulmonary Fibrosis: Data-driven Textural Analysis of Extent of Fibrosis at Baseline and 15-Month Follow-up. Radiology. 2017 Oct;285(1):270-278
- IBM. Watson Health. 100 Top Hospitals, 2021; 28th edition. April 27, 2021. https://www.ibm.com/downloads/cas/REAWOAOD. Accessed April 21, 2022
- ICH. Introductory Guide MedDRA Version 23.0. March 2022. https://admin.meddra.org/sites/default/files/guidance/file/intguide_%2025_0_English_0.pdf. Accessed April 12, 2022
- IHE Wiki. IHE. May 4, 2022. https://wiki.ihe.net/index.php/Main_Page. Accessed June 12, 2022
- IHE. IT Infrastructure (ITI) Technical Framework Volume 2. 2022. https://profiles.ihe.net/ITI/TF/Volume2/index.html#3 Accessed March 12, 2022.
- IHE. IT Infrastructure Technical Framework Revision 17.0 – Final Text. July 20, 2020. https://www.ihe.net/resources/technical_frameworks/technical_framework_archives/#IT
- IHI (Institute for Healthcare Improvement). http://www.ihi.org/Pages/default.aspx. Accessed July 12, 2021
- IMDRF. "Software as a Medical Device": Possible framework for risk categorization and corresponding considerations. September 18, 2014. http://www.imdrf.org/docs/imdrf/final/technical/imdrf-tech-140918-samd-framework-risk-categorization-141013.pdf Accessed July 26, 2021
- IMS Institute for Healthcare Informatics. Patient Apps for Improved Healthcare: From Novelty to Mainstream. IMS. October 2013.
- Indini, A, Cattaneo, M, Ghidini, M, Rijavec, E, Bareggi, C, Galassi, B, Gambini, D, Ceriani, R, Ceriotti, F, Berti, E, Grossi, F. Triage process for the assessment of coronavirus disease 2019-positive patients with cancer: The ONCOVID prospective study. Cancer. 2020
- Information Infrastructure Task Force, Privacy Working Group, Privacy and the National Information Infrastructure: Principles for Providing and Using Personal Information, Commentary 2, (June 1995)
- Inglis SC. Clark RA. McAlister FA, et al. Structured telephone support or telemonitoring programmes for patients with chronic heart failure. Cochrane Database Syst Rev. 2009;(1):1
- Inman KJ, Dymock K, Fysh N, Robbins B, Rutledge FS, Sibbald WJ. Pressure ulcer prevention: a randomized controlled trial of 2 risk-directed strategies for patient surface assignment. Adv Wound Care. 1999 Mar;12(2):72-80.
- Institute for Healthcare Improvement. Going Lean in Health Care. IHI Innovation Series white paper. Cambridge, MA: 2005. https://www.ihi.org/resources/Pages/IHIWhitePapers/GoingLeaninHealthCare.aspx. Accessed August 12, 2021
- International Medical Device Regulators Forum (IMDRF). Final document, "Software as a Medical Device (SaMD): Key Definitions". http://www.imdrf.org/docs/imdrf/final/technical/imdrf-tech-131209-samd-key-definitions-140901.pdf. Accessed July 24, 2021)
- International Medical Device Regulators Forum. Software as a Medical Device (SaMD): Key Definitions. December 9, 2013. http://www.imdrf.org/docs/imdrf/final/technical/imdrf-tech-131209-samd-key-definitions-140901.pdf. Accessed December 14, 2021)
- International Working Group on the Diabetic Foot. COVID-19 and diabetic foot disease. https://iwgdfguidelines.org/covid-19/#1586230034438-eafd453e-4cef. Accessed March 14, 2021
- Ionescu B, Müller H, Drăgulinescu A-M, Yim W-w, Ben Abacha A, et al. 2023. Overview of the ImageCLEF 2023: Multimedia Retrieval in Medical, Social Media and Internet Applications. In Experimental IR Meets Multilinguality, Multimodality, and Interaction: 14th International Conference of the CLEF Association, CLEF 2023, Thessaloniki, Greece, September 18–21, 2023, Proceedings. Springer-Verlag, Berlin, Heidelberg, 370–396. Details available at https://www.imageclef.org/2023/medical/mediqa
- Ionescu, Bogdan & Müller, Henning & Dragulinescu, Ana & Yim, Wen-Wai & Ben Abacha, Asma & Snider, Neal & Adams, Griffin & Yetisgen, Meliha & Rückert, Johannes & Herrera, Alba & Friedrich, Christoph & Bloch, Louise & Brüngel, Raphael & Idrissi-Yaghir, Ahmad & Schäfer, Henning & Hicks, Steven & Riegler, Michael & Thambawita, Vajira & Storås, Andrea & Popescu, Adrian. (2023). Overview of the ImageCLEF 2023: Multimedia Retrieval in Medical, Social Media and Internet Applications. 10.1007/978-3-031-42448-9_25.
- Isaia G, Astengo, M. A., Tibaldi, V., Zanocchi, M., Bardelli, B., Obialero, R., Tizzani, A., Bo, M., Moiraghi, C., Molaschi, M., & Ricauda, N. A. (2009). Delirium in elderly home-treated patients: a prospective study with 6-month follow-up. Age (Dordrecht, Netherlands), 31(2), 109–117)
- Ishani A, Christopher J, Palmer D, Otterness S, Clothier B, Nugent S, Nelson D, Rosenberg ME; Center for Innovative Kidney Care. Telehealth by an Interprofessional Team in Patients With CKD: A Randomized Controlled Trial. Am J Kidney Dis. 2016 Jul;68(1):41-9
- Islam MM, Poly TN, Walther BA, Jack Li YC. Use of Mobile Phone App Interventions to Promote Weight Loss: Meta-Analysis. JMIR Mhealth Uhealth. 2020 Jul 22;8(7):e17039.
- ISO. ISO 15225:2010 Medical devices - Quality management - Medical device nomenclature data structure. 2010-05. https://www.iso.org/standard/50728.html
- ITI Technical Committee. Enabling Document Sharing Health Information Exchange Using IHE Profiles. IHE IT Infrastructure White Paper. Integrating the Healthcare Enterprise. Integrating the Healthcare Enterprise. March 19, 2021. https://profiles.ihe.net/ITI/HIE-Whitepaper/index.html Accessed: November 15, 2021.)
- Ito K, Ahadieh S, Corrigan B, French J, Fullerton T, Tensfeldt T; Alzheimer's Disease Working Group. Disease progression meta-analysis model in Alzheimer's disease. Alzheimers Dement. 2010 Jan;6(1):39-53
- Iyer S, Shafi K, Lovecchio F, Turner R, Albert TJ, Kim HJ, Press J, Katsuura Y; Sandhu H, Schwab F, Qureshi S. The Spine Physical Examination Using Telemedicine: Strategies and Best Practices. Global Spine J. 2020 Aug 5:2192568220944129

- Iyer SV, LePendu P, Harpaz R, Bauer-Mehren A, Shah NH (2013) Learning Signals of Adverse Drug-Drug Interactions from the Unstructured Text of Electronic Health Records. AMIA Summits Transl Sci Proc 2013
- J. Difede et al., "Enhancing exposure therapy for posttraumatic stress disorder (PTSD): A randomized clinical trial of virtual reality and imaginal exposure with a cognitive enhancer," Transl. Psychiatry, vol. 12, no. 1, pp. 1–9, Jul. 2022
- Jacob J, Bartholmai BJ, Rajagopalan S, Kokosi M, Nair A, Karwoski R, Walsh SL, Wells AU, Hansell DM. Mortality prediction in idiopathic pulmonary fibrosis: evaluation of computer-based CT analysis with conventional severity measures. Eur Respir J. 2017 Jan 25;49(1):1601011
- Jagannatha A, Chen J, Yu H. Mining and ranking biomedical synonym candidates from Wikipedia. In: Proceedings of the sixth international workshop on health text mining and information analysis. 2015. p. 142–51.
- Jahmunah V, Lih Oh S, Rajinikanth V, Ciaccio EJ, Hao Cheong K, Arunkumar N, Acharya UR. Automated detection of schizophrenia using nonlinear signal processing methods. Artif Intell Med. 2019 Sep;100:101698.
- Jaimon T Kelly, Dianne P Reidlinger, Tammy C Hoffmann, Katrina L Campbell, Telehealth methods to deliver dietary interventions in adults with chronic disease: a systematic review and meta-analysis, The American Journal of Clinical Nutrition, Volume 104, Issue 6, December 2016, Pages 1693–1702
- Jansen F, van Uden-Kraan CF, van Zwieten V. et al. Cancer survivors' perceived need for supportive care and their attitude towards self-management and eHealth. Support Care Cancer 2015; 23: 1679-1688
- Jason C. EHR Use Training Key to High EHR Satisfaction Across Specialists. EHR Intelligence. November 12, 2019. https://ehrintelligence.com/news/ehr-use-training-key-to-high-ehr-satisfaction-across-specialists. Accessed July 12, 2021
- Jay H. Shore, Peter Yellowlees, Robert Caudill, Barbara Johnston, Carolyn Turvey, Matthew Mishkind, Elizabeth Krupinski, Kathleen Myers, Peter Shore, Edward Kaftarian, and Donald Hilty. Best Practices in Videoconferencing-Based Telemental Health April 2018. Telemedicine and e-Health 2018 24:11, 827-832
- Jayawardena ADL, Mankarious LA, Keamy DG Jr, Cohen MS. Pediatric, Family-Centered, "At-Home" Otologic Physical Examination in the COVID-19 Era. Otolaryngol Head Neck Surg. 2020 Nov;163(5):1061-1063.
- Jean, S., Cho, K., Memisevic, R. & Bengio, Y. On using very large target vocabulary for neural machine translation. In Proc. ACL-IJCNLP http://arxiv.org.ucsf.idm.oclc.org/abs/1412.2007 (2015)
- Jensen L, Konradsen F. A review of the use of virtual reality head-mounted displays in education and training. Educ Inf Technol. 2017 Nov 25;23(4):1515–1529.
- Jensen PB, Jensen LJ, Brunak S. Mining electronic health records: towards better research applications and clinical care. Nat Rev Genet. 2012 May 2; 13(6):395-405.)
- Jeremic A, Khoshrowshahli E. Detecting breast cancer using microwave imaging and stochastic optimization. Annu Int Conf IEEE Eng Med Biol Soc. 2015;2015:89-92.
- Jessiman S. Speech and language services using telehealth technology in remote and underserviced areas. J Speech Lang Pathol Audiol 2003; 27: 45-51
- Jhaveri K, Cohen JA, Barulich M, Levin AO, Goyal N, Loveday T, Chesney MA, Shumay DM. "Soup cans, brooms, and Zoom:" Rapid conversion of a cancer survivorship program to telehealth during COVID-19. Psychooncology. 2020 Sep;29(9):1424-1426
- Jiang MYW, Upton E, Newby JM. A randomised wait-list controlled pilot trial of one-session virtual reality exposure therapy for blood-injection-injury phobias. J Affect Disord. 2020 Nov 1;276:636-645.
- Jiang Z, Jin L, Li L, Qin M, Qu C, Zheng J, et al. A CRD-WEL system for chemical-disease relations extraction. In: The fifth BioCreative challenge evaluation workshop. 2015. p. 317–26
- Jiang Z, Li L, Huang D. A general protein-protein interaction extraction architecture based on word representation and feature selection. Int J Data Min Bioinform. 2016;14(3):276–91
- Jill, J. Ashman, Pinyao Rui, and Titilayo Okeyode, "Characteristics of office-based physician visits, 2016," NCHS Data Brief No. 331, Centers of Disease Control and Prevention. January 2019. Accessed 15 January 2021
- Jin D, Pan E, Oufattole N, Weng W-H, Fang H, Szolovits P. What Disease Does This Patient Have? A Large-Scale Open Domain Question Answering Dataset from Medical Exams. Applied Sciences. 2021; 11(14):6421.
- Jin K, Khonsari S, Gallagher R, Gallagher P, Clark AM, Freedman B, Briffa T, Bauman A, Redfern J, Neubeck L. Telehealth interventions for the secondary prevention of coronary heart disease: A systematic review and meta-analysis. Eur J Cardiovasc Nurs. 2019 Apr;18(4):260-271
- Johnson AE, Pollard TJ, Shen L, Lehman LW, Feng M, Ghassemi M, Moody B, Szolovits P, Celi LA, Mark RG. MIMIC-III, a freely accessible critical care database. Sci Data. 2016 May 24;3:160035.
- Johnston DC, Mathews WD, Maus A, Gustafson DH. Using Smartphones to Improve Treatment Retention Among Impoverished Substance-Using Appalachian Women: A Naturalistic Study. Subst Abuse. 2019 Jul 8;13:1178221819861377
- Jones SM, Milroy C., Pickford MA. Telemedicine in acute plastic surgical trauma and burns. Ann. Royal Coll. Surg.Engl. 86(4): 239–242, 2004
- Jost, Beate; Ketterl, Markus; Budde, Reinhard; Leimbach, Thorsten (2014). "Graphical Programming Environments for Educational Robots: Open Roberta - Yet Another One?". 2014 IEEE International Symposium on Multimedia. pp. 381–386.
- Juan M. C., Alcañiz M., Monserrat C., Botella C., Baños R. M., Guerrero B. Using augmented reality to treat phobias. IEEE Computer Graphics and Applications. 2005;25(6):31–37.
- Jud L, Fotouhi J, Andronic O, Aichmair A, Osgood G, Navab N, Farshad M. Applicability of augmented reality in orthopedic surgery - A systematic review. BMC Musculoskelet Disord. 2020 Feb 15;21(1):103.
- Jung K, LePendu P, Chen WS, Iyer SV, Readhead B, Dudley JT, Shah NH. Automated detection of off-label drug use. PLoS One. 2014 Feb 19;9(2):e89324.
- Junyoung Chung, Çaglar Gülçehre, Kyunghyun Cho, and Yoshua Bengio. Empirical evaluation of gated recurrent neural networks on sequence modeling. arXiv:1412.3555v1, 2014

- Kahaly GJ, Bartalena L, Hegedüs L, Leenhardt L, Poppe K, Pearce SH. 2018 European Thyroid Association Guideline for the Management of Graves' Hyperthyroidism. Eur Thyroid J. 2018 Aug; 7(4):167-186
- Kahn MG, Callahan TJ, Barnard J, et al. A harmonized data quality assessment terminology and framework for the secondary use of electronic health record data. EGEMS (Wash DC). 2016;4(1):1244. https://www.ncbi.nlm.nih.gov/pmc/articles/PMC5051581. Accessed November 12, 2021)
- Kairy D, Lehoux P, Vincent C, et al. A systematic review of clinical outcomes, clinical process, healthcare utilization and costs associated with telerehabilitation. 2009. In: Database of Abstracts of Reviews of Effects (DARE): Quality-assessed Reviews [Internet]. York (UK): Centre for Reviews and Dissemination (UK); 1995-. Available from: https://www.ncbi.nlm.nih.gov/books/NBK77000/ Accessed February 2, 2021
- Kalé N, Jones N. Practical Analytics. Epistemy Press, 2015
- Kamadi V, Rao AA, Tummala S, Padmanabhuni VNR. (2014). A computational intelligence approach for a better diagnosis of diabetic patients. Computers & Electrical Engineering. 40. 1758–1765
- Kane LT, Thakar O, Jamgochian G, Lazarus MD, Abboud JA, Namdari S, Horneff JG. The role of telehealth as a platform for postoperative visits following rotator cuff repair: a prospective, randomized controlled trial. J Shoulder Elbow Surg. 2020 Apr;29(4):775-783
- Kang M, Chai K. Wearable Sensing Systems for Monitoring Mental Health. Sensors (Basel). 2022 Jan 27;22(3):994
- Kang S, Cho S, Rhee S.-j, Yu K-S. Reliable prediction of anti-diabetic drug failure using a reject option. Pattern Anal Appl, 20 (2017), pp. 883-891
- Kang S, Kang P, Ko T, Cho S, Rhee S.-j, Yu K-S. An efficient and effective ensemble of support vector machines for anti-diabetic drug failure prediction. Expert Syst Appl, 42 (2015), pp. 4265-4273)
- Kang S. Personalized prediction of drug efficacy for diabetes treatment via patient-level sequential modeling with neural networks. Artif Intell Med. 2018;85:1-6)
- Kang, S., Thomas, P.B.M., Sim, D.A. et al. Oculoplastic video-based telemedicine consultations: Covid-19 and beyond. Eye 34, 1193–1195 (2020)
- Kannan A, Chen K, Jaunzeikare D, Rajkomar A. Semi-supervised learning for information extraction from dialogue. In: Interspeech 2018. Baixas, France: International Speech Communication Association, 2018:2077-81.
- Kansagara D, Englander H, Salanitro A, Kagen D, Theobald C, Freeman M, Kripalani S. Risk prediction models for hospital readmission: a systematic review. JAMA. 2011 Oct 19;306(15):1688-98
- Kapoor S, Eldib A, Hiasat J, et al. Developing a pediatric ophthalmology telemedicine program in the COVID-19 crisis. J AAPOS. 2020;24(4):204-208.e2
- Kario, K., Harada, N. & Okura, A. The first software as medical device of evidence-based hypertension digital therapeutics for clinical practice. Hypertens Res 45, 1899–1905 (2022)
- Karisani P, Qin ZS, Agichtein E. Probabilistic and machine learning-based retrieval approaches for biomedical dataset retrieval. Database (Oxford). 2018 Jan 1;2018:bax104
- Katharina Boehm, Stefani Ziewers, Maximilian P. Brandt, Peter Sparwasser, Maximilian Haack, Franziska Willems, Anita Thomas, Robert Dotzauer, Thomas Höfner, Igor Tsaur, Axel Haferkamp, Hendrik Borgmann. Telemedicine Online Visits in Urology During the COVID-19 Pandemic—Potential, Risk Factors, and Patients' Perspective. European Urology. Volume 78, Issue 1, 2020, Pages 16-20
- Kaukonen, K.-M., Bailey, M., Pilcher, D., Cooper, D. J. & Bellomo, R. Systemic inflammatory response syndrome criteria in defining severe sepsis. N. Engl. J. Med. 372, 1629–1638 (2015)
- Kaur, H., Sohn, S., Wi, CI. et al. Automated chart review utilizing natural language processing algorithm for asthma predictive index. BMC Pulm Med 18, 34 (2018)
- Kaye R, Rosen-Zvi M, Ron R. Digitally-enabled remote care for cancer patients: here to stay. Semin. Oncol. Nurs. 19:151091, 2020
- Keefe RSE, Cañadas E, Farlow D, Etkin A. Digital Intervention for Cognitive Deficits in Major Depression: A Randomized Controlled Trial to Assess Efficacy and Safety in Adults. Am J Psychiatry. 2022 Jul;179(7):482-489
- Keely, E, Liddy, C, Afkham, A. Utilization, benefits, and impact of an e-consultation service across diverse specialties and primary care providers. Telemedicine journal and e-health : the official journal of the American Telemedicine Association 2013; 19: 733–8
- Keller JJ, Johnson JP, Latour E. Inpatient teledermatology: diagnostic and therapeutic concordance among a hospitalist, dermatologist, and teledermatologist using store-and-forward teledermatology. J Am Acad Dermatol. 2020;82(5):1262–1267
- Kerr D, Warshaw H. Clouds and Silver Linings: COVID-19 Pandemic Is an Opportune Moment to Democratize Diabetes Care Through Telehealth. J Diabetes Sci Technol. 2020 Nov;14(6):1107-1110
- Kew KM, Cates CJ. Remote versus face-to-face check-ups for asthma. Cochrane Database Syst Rev. 2016 Apr 18;4:CD011715.
- Khan F, Amatya B, Kesselring J, Galea M. Telerehabilitation for persons with multiple sclerosis. Cochrane Database Syst Rev. 2015 Apr 9;2015(4):CD010508
- Khatibi V, Montazer GA. A fuzzy-evidential hybrid inference engine for coronary heart disease risk assessment. Expert Syst Appl. 2010;37(12):8536–8542
- Kheirkhah P, Feng Q, Travis LM, Tavakoli-Tabasi S, Sharafkhaneh A. Prevalence, predictors and economic consequences of no-shows. BMC Health Serv Res. 2016 Jan 14;16:13
- Khin K, Burckhardt P, Padman R. A deep learning architecture for de-identification of patient notes: Implementation and evaluation. arXiv preprint arXiv:1810.01570. 2018 Oct 3.
- Khozin S, Coravos A. Decentralized trials in the age of real-world evidence and inclusivity in clinical investigations. Clin Pharmacol Therapeutics. 2019;106:25–27.

- Kim HG, Tashkin DP, Clements PJ, Li G, Brown MS, Elashoff R, Gjertson DW, Abtin F, Lynch DA, Strollo DC, Goldin JG. A computer-aided diagnosis system for quantitative scoring of extent of lung fibrosis in scleroderma patients. Clin Exp Rheumatol. 2010 Sep-Oct;28(5 Suppl 62):S26-35
- Kim HJ, Brown MS, Chong D, Gjertson DW, Lu P, Kim HJ, Coy H, Goldin JG. Comparison of the quantitative CT imaging biomarkers of idiopathic pulmonary fibrosis at baseline and early change with an interval of 7 months. Acad Radiol. 2015 Jan;22(1):70-80
- Kim J, Lee J, Lee Y. Data-Mining-Based Coronary Heart Disease Risk Prediction Model Using Fuzzy Logic and Decision Tree. Healthc Inform Res. 2015;21(3):167-174
- Kim YS, Baek HJ, Kim JS, Lee HB, Choi JM, Park KS. Helmet-based physiological signal monitoring system. Eur J Appl Physiol. 2009 Feb; 105(3):365-72
- Kim-Hwang, JE, Chen, AH, Bell, DS, Guzman, D, Yee, HF, Kushel, MB. Evaluating electronic referrals for specialty care at a public hospital. Journal of general internal medicine 2010; 25: 1123–8
- Kipnis P, Turk BJ, Wulf DA, LaGuardia JC, Liu V, Churpek MM, Romero-Brufau S, Escobar GJ. Development and validation of an electronic medical record-based alert score for detection of inpatient deterioration outside the ICU. J Biomed Inform. 2016 Dec;64:10-19.
- Kitsiou S, Vatani H, Paré G, Gerber BS, Buchholz SW, Kansal MM, Leigh J, Masterson Creber RM. Effectiveness of Mobile Health Technology Interventions for Patients With Heart Failure: Systematic Review and Meta-analysis. Can J Cardiol. 2021 Aug;37(8):1248-1259
- Kittler, H., Pehamberger, H., Wolff, K. & Binder, M. Diagnostic accuracy of dermoscopy. Lancet Oncol. 3, 159–165 (2002)
- Klapan I, Vranjes Z, Prgomet D. et al. Application of advanced virtual reality and 3D computer assisted technologies in tele-3D-computer assisted surgery in rhinology. Coll Antropol 2008; 32: 217-219
- Knight M. What is Data Governance?. Dataversity. October 14, 2021 https://www.dataversity.net/what-is-data-governance/ Accessed November 18, 2021
- Knox L, Dunning M, Davies CA, et al. Safety, feasibility, and effectiveness of virtual pulmonary rehabilitation in the real world. Int J Chron Obstruct Pulmon Dis. 2019;14:775-780.
- Ko MW, Busis NA. Tele-Neuro-Ophthalmology: Vision for 20/20 and Beyond. J Neuroophthalmol. 2020 Sep;40(3):378-384
- Koblauch H, Reinhardt SM, Lissau W., Jensen P. The effect of telepsychiatric modalities on reduction of readmissions in psychiatric settings: a systematic review. J. Telemed. Telecare 24(1):31-36, 2018
- Kockro RA, Killeen T, Ayyad A, et al. Aneurysm surgery with preoperative three-dimensional planning in a virtual reality environment: technique and outcome analysis. World Neurosurg. 2016;96:489–499
- Kollins SH, Childress A, Heusser AC, Lutz J. Effectiveness of a digital therapeutic as adjunct to treatment with medication in pediatric ADHD. NPJ Digit Med. 2021 Mar 26;4(1):58
- Koo BM, Vizer LM. Examining mobile technologies to support older adults with dementia through the lens of personhood and human needs: scoping review. JMIR mHealth uHealth 7(11):e15122, 2019
- Kopycka-Kedzierawski DT, Billings RJ, McConnochie KM. Dental screening of preschool children using teledentistry: a feasibility study. Pediatr Dent. 2007 May-Jun;29(3):209-13.
- Kosinski, L.R., Brill, J.V., Sørensen, M., Baum, C., Turpin, R.S., & Landsman, P.B. (2016). 824 Project Sonar: Reduction in Cost of Care in an Attributed Cohort of Patients With Crohn's Disease. Gastroenterology, 150
- Kostikis N, Hristu-Varsakelis D, Arnaoutoglou M, et al. Towards remote evaluation of movement disorders via smartphones. Conf Proc IEEE Eng Med Biol Soc, 2011 (2011), pp. 5240-5243
- Kramer F, Butler J, Shah SJ, Jung C, Nodari S, Rosenkranz S, Senni M, Bamber L, Cichos S, Dori C, Karakoyun T, Köhler GJ, Patel K, Piraino P, Viethen T, Chennuru P, Paydar A, Sims J, Clark R, van Lummel R, Müller A, Gwaltney C, Smajlovic S, Düngen HD, Dinh W. Real-Life Multimarker Monitoring in Patients with Heart Failure: Continuous Remote Monitoring of Mobility and Patient-Reported Outcomes as Digital End Points in Future Heart-Failure Trials. Digit Biomark. 2020 Jun 30;4(2):45-59
- Krishnaiah V, Narsimha G, Chandra NS. Heart disease prediction system using data mining technique by fuzzy K-NN approach. In: Satapathy SC, Govardhan A, Srujan Raju K, Mandal JK, editors. Emerging ICT for bridging the future: Proceedings of the 49th Annual Convention of the Computer Society of India (CSI) Cham, Switzerland: Springer International Publishing; 2015. pp. 371–384
- Krizhevsky, A., Sutskever, I. & Hinton, G. ImageNet classification with deep convolutional neural networks. In Proc. Advances in Neural Information Processing Systems 25 1090–1098 (2012)
- Krucoff MW et al. The Medical Device Epidemiology Network. Recommendations for a National Medical Device Evaluation System. A report from the medical device registry task force & the medical devices epidemiology network. August 20, 2015 http://mdepinet.org/wp-content/uploads/2015-08-Recommendations-for-a-National-Medical-Device-Evaluation-System.pdf. Accessed December 22, 2018
- Kruklitis RJ, Tracy JA, McCambridge MM. Clinical and financial considerations for implementing an ICU telemedicine program. Chest 145(6):1392-1396, 2014
- Krupinski E. Teleradiology: current perspectives. Reports in Medical Imaging. 2014;7:5-14
- Krupinski EA, Johnson JP, Jaw S, Graham AR, Weinstein RS. Compressing pathology whole-slide images using a human and model observer evaluation. J Pathol Inform. 2012; 3():17
- Kruse, C., Lee, K., Watson, J., Lobo, L., Stoppelmoor, A., & Oyibo, S. (2020). Measures of effectiveness, efficiency, and quality of telemedicine in the management of alcohol abuse, addiction, and rehabilitation: Systematic review. Journal of Medical Internet Research, 22(1):e13252.
- Ku PKM, Holsinger FC, Chan JYK, Yeung ZWC, Chan BYT, Tong MCF, Starmer HM. Management of dysphagia in the patient

with head and neck cancer during COVID-19 pandemic: Practical strategy. Head Neck. 2020 Jul;42(7):1491-1496.

- Kubendran S, Sivamurthy S, Schaefer GB. A novel approach in pediatric telegenetic services: geneticist, pediatrician and genetic counselor team. Genet Med. 2017;19:1260-1267
- Kuperman EF, Linson EL, Klefstad K, Perry E, Glenn K. The virtual hospitalist: a single-site implementation bringing hospitalist coverage to critical access hospitals. J. Hosp. Med. 13(11):759-763, 2018
- Kwon BC, Achenbach P, Dunne JL, Hagopian W, Lundgren M, Ng K, Veijola R, Frohnert BI, Anand V; T1DI Study Group. Modeling Disease Progression Trajectories from Longitudinal Observational Data. AMIA Annu Symp Proc. 2021 Jan 25;2020:668-676.
- Kyle Rismiller, Alexander M. Cartron & John C. L. Trinidad (2020) Inpatient teledermatology during the COVID-19 pandemic, Journal of Dermatological Treatment, 31:5, 441-443
- Labarbera JM, Ellenby MS, Bouressa P, Burrell J, Flori HR, Marcin JP. The impact of telemedicine intensivist support and a pediatric hospitalist program on a community hospital. Telemed. e-Health 19(10):760-766, 2013
- Lagu T, Pekow PS, Shieh MS, Stefan M, Pack QR, Kashef MA, Atreya AR, Valania G, Slawsky MT, Lindenauer PK. Validation and Comparison of Seven Mortality Prediction Models for Hospitalized Patients With Acute Decompensated Heart Failure. Circ Heart Fail. 2016 Aug;9(8):10.1161/CIRCHEARTFAILURE.115.002912 e002912.
- Lakhani P, Sundaram B. Deep Learning at Chest Radiography: Automated Classification of Pulmonary Tuberculosis by Using Convolutional Neural Networks. Radiology. 2017 Apr 24; 284(2):574–82
- Lanata Valenza G, Nardelli M, Gentili C, Scilingo EP. Complexity index from a personalized wearable monitoring system for assessing remission in mental health. IEEE J Biomed Health Inform. (2015) 19:132–9.
- Lanssens D, Vandenberk T, Thijs IM, Grieten L, Gyselaers W. Effectiveness of Telemonitoring in Obstetrics: Scoping Review. J Med Internet Res. 2017 Sep 27;19(9):e327
- Lapointe L, Lavallee-Bourget MH, Pichard-Jolicoeur A, Turgeon-Pelchat C, Fleet R. Impact of telemedicine on diagnosis, clinical management and outcomes in rural trauma patients: A rapid review. Can. J. Rural Med. 25(1):31-40, 2020
- Laranjo L, Ding D, Heleno B, Kocaballi B, Quiroz JC, Tong HL, Chahwan B, Neves AL, Gabarron E, Dao KP, Rodrigues D, Neves GC, Antunes ML, Coiera E, Bates DW. Do smartphone applications and activity trackers increase physical activity in adults? Systematic review, meta-analysis and metaregression. Br J Sports Med. 2021 Apr;55(8):422-432.
- Lars Grieten and others, 'Smart' solutions for paroxysmal atrial fibrillation?, EP Europace, Volume 19, Issue 7, July 2017, Page 1108
- Laskowski ER, Johnson SE, Shelerud RA, et al. The Telemedicine Musculoskeletal Examination [published correction appears in Mayo Clin Proc. 2020 Oct;95(10):2299]. Mayo Clin Proc. 2020;95(8):1715-1731.
- Lau N, O'Daffer A, Colt S, Yi-Frazier JP, Palermo TM, McCauley E, Rosenberg AR. Android and iPhone Mobile Apps for Psychosocial Wellness and Stress Management: Systematic Search in App Stores and Literature Review. JMIR Mhealth Uhealth. 2020 May 22;8(5):e17798.
- Laureanti R., Bilucaglia M., Zito M., Circi R., Fici A., Rivetti F., Valesi R., Oldrini C., Mainardi L.T., Russo V. Emotion assessment using Machine Learning and low-cost wearable devices; Proceedings of the 2020 42nd Annual International Conference of the IEEE Engineering in Medicine & Biology Society (EMBC); Montreal, QC, Canada. 20–24 July 2020; pp. 576–579.
- Lavender T, Richens Y, Milan SJ, Smyth RM, Dowswell T. Telephone support for women during pregnancy and the first six weeks postpartum. Cochrane Database Syst Rev. 2013 Jul 18;2013(7):CD009338
- Laver KE, Lange B, George S, Deutsch JE, Saposnik G, Crotty M. Virtual reality for stroke rehabilitation. Cochrane Database Syst Rev. 2017 Nov 20;11(11):CD008349.
- Laver KE, Schoene D, Crotty M, George S, Lannin NA, Sherrington C. Telerehabilitation services for stroke. Cochrane Database Syst Rev. 2013;2013(12):CD010255
- Law RK, Sheikh S, Bronstein A, Thomas R, Spiller HA, Schier JG. Incidents of potential public health significance identified using national surveillance of US poison center data (2008-2012). Clin Toxicol (Phila). 2014;52(9):958-963
- Lawrence O. Gostin, p. 454 of "Health information privacy," Cornell Law Review 80, 451–528 (1995).
- Le Goff-Pronost M, Mourgeon B, Blanchère J-P, Teot L, Benateau H, Dompmartin A. Real-world clinical evaluation and costs of telemedicine for chronic wound management. Int J Technol Assess Health Care. 2018;34(6):567-565
- Le Moing A.-G., Seferian A.M., Moraux A., Annoussamy M., Dorveaux E., Gasnier E., Hogrel J.-Y., Voit T., Vissiere D., Servais L. A movement monitor based on magneto-inertial sensors for non-ambulant patients with Duchenne muscular dystrophy: A pilot study in controlled environment. PLoS ONE. 2016;11:e0156696.
- LeCun, Y., Bengio, Y. & Hinton, G. Deep learning. Nature 521, 436–444 (2015)
- Lee C. Rogers, Lawrence A. Lavery, Warren S. Joseph, David G. Armstrong; All Feet On Deck—The Role of Podiatry During the COVID-19 Pandemic: Preventing hospitalizations in an overburdened healthcare system, reducing amputation and death in people with diabetes. J Am Podiatr Med Assoc 2020
- Lee H, Chang W, Lee J, Hwang J. Therapeutic potential of the home-based exercise program with the augmented reality system on balance in stroke patients: a preliminary report. Annals Physical Rehab Med. 2018 Jul;61(Supplement):e36.
- Lee J, Yoon W, Kim S, Kim D, Kim S, So CH, Kang J. BioBERT: a pre-trained biomedical language representation model for biomedical text mining. Bioinformatics. 2020 Feb 15;36(4):1234-40.
- Lee J.-H., Lee K.-H., Kim H.-J., Youk H., Lee H.-Y., Lee J.-H., Lee K.-H., Kim H.-J., Youk H., Lee H.-Y. Effective Prevention and Management Tools for Metabolic Syndrome Based on Digital Health-Based Lifestyle Interventions Using Healthcare Devices. Diagnostics. 2022;12:1730
- Lee M, Chun Y, Griffith DA. Error propagation in spatial modeling of public health data: a simulation approach using pediatric blood lead level data for Syracuse, New York. Environ Geochem Health. 2018 Apr;40(2):667-681

- Lee P., Stewart D., Calugar-Pop C. Technology, Media & Telecommunications Predictions: 2014. Deloitte, New York, NY2014. https://www2.deloitte.com/content/dam/Deloitte/global/Documents/Technology-Media-Telecommunications/dttl_TMT_Predictions-2014-lc2.pdf. Accessed: February 12, 2021
- Lee SK, Kang BY, Kim HG, Son YJ. Predictors of medication adherence in elderly patients with chronic diseases using support vector machine models. Healthc Inform Res. 2013;19(1):33-41
- Lee TC, Kaiser TE, Alloway R, Woodle ES, Edwards MJ, Shah SA. Telemedicine Based Remote Home Monitoring After Liver Transplantation: Results of a Randomized Prospective Trial. Ann Surg. 2019 Sep;270(3):564-572s
- Lefèvre T, Rondet C, Parizot I, Chauvin P. Applying multivariate clustering techniques to health data: the 4 types of healthcare utilization in the Paris metropolitan area. PLoS One. 2014 Dec 15;9(12):e115064
- Leff B et al. Satisfaction with hospital at home care. J Am Geriatr Soc. 2006;54(9):1355–63
- Leff B, Burton L, Guido S, Greenough WB, Steinwachs D, Burton JR. Home hospital program: a pilot study. J Am Geriatr Soc. 1999 Jun;47(6):697-702
- Leff B, Burton L, Mader S, Naughton B, Burl J, Clark R, Greenough WB 3rd, Guido S, Steinwachs D, Burton JR. Satisfaction with hospital at home care. J Am Geriatr Soc. 2006 Sep;54(9):1355-63
- Leff B, Burton L, Mader SL, Naughton B, Burl J, Greenough WB 3rd, Guido S, Steinwachs D. Comparison of functional outcomes associated with hospital at home care and traditional acute hospital care. J Am Geriatr Soc. 2009 Feb;57(2):273-8
- Leff B, Burton L, Mader SL, Naughton B, Burl J, Inouye SK, Greenough WB 3rd, Guido S, Langston C, Frick KD, Steinwachs D, Burton JR. Hospital at home: feasibility and outcomes of a program to provide hospital-level care at home for acutely ill older patients. Ann Intern Med. 2005 Dec 6;143(11):798-808
- Leff B, Burton L, Mader SL, Naughton B, Burl J, Koehn D, Clark R, Greenough WB 3rd, Guido S, Steinwachs D, Burton JR. Comparison of stress experienced by family members of patients treated in hospital at home with that of those receiving traditional acute hospital care. J Am Geriatr Soc. 2008 Jan;56(1):117-23
- Leff B. Acute? care at home. The health and cost effects of substituting home care for inpatient acute care: a review of the evidence. J Am Geriatr Soc. 2001 Aug;49(8):1123-5
- Leff J, Williams G, Huckvale M, Arbuthnot M, Leff AP. Avatar therapy for persecutory auditory hallucinations: what is it and how does it work? Psychosis 2014;6(2):166-76
- Leggett P, Graham L, Steele K, Gilliland A, Stevenson M, O'Reilly D, Wootton R, Taggart A. Telerheumatology--diagnostic accuracy and acceptability to patient, specialist, and general practitioner. Br J Gen Pract. 2001 Sep; 51(470):746-8.)
- Legrain A, Fortin MA, Lahrichi N, Rousseau LM. Online stochastic optimization of radiotherapy patient scheduling. Health Care Manag Sci. 2015 Jun;18(2):110-23.
- Lequertier V, Wang T, Fondrevelle J, Augusto V, Duclos A. Hospital Length of Stay Prediction Methods: A Systematic Review. Med Care. 2021 Oct 1;59(10):929-938.
- Leung, M. K., Xiong, H. Y., Lee, L. J. & Frey, B. J. Deep learning of the tissue-regulated splicing code. Bioinformatics 30, i121–i129 (2014)
- Levin YS, Warshaw EM. Teledermatology: A review of reliability and accuracy of diagnosis and management. Dermatol Clin, 27 (2) (2009), pp. 163-176
- Levine DM, Ouchi K, Blanchfield B, Saenz A, Burke K, Paz M, Diamond K, Pu CT, Schnipper JL. Hospital-Level Care at Home for Acutely Ill Adults: A Randomized Controlled Trial. Ann Intern Med. 2020 Jan 21;172(2):77-85
- Lew SQ, Wallace EL, Srivatana V, et al. Telehealth for Home Dialysis in COVID-19 and Beyond: A Perspective From the American Society of Nephrology COVID-19 Home Dialysis Subcommittee. Am J Kidney Dis. 2021;77(1):142-148
- Lewis ER, Thomas CA, Wilson ML, Mbarika VWA. Telemedicine in acute-phase injury management: a review of practice and advancements. Telemed. eHealth 18(6): 434–445, 2012
- Li SX, Thompson KD, Peterson T, Huneven S, Carmichael J, Glazer FJ, Darling K, Siegel CA. Delivering High Value Inflammatory Bowel Disease Care Through Telemedicine Visits. Inflamm Bowel Dis. 2017 Oct;23(10):1678-1681.
- Li Yunxiang, Li Zihan, Zhang Kai, Dan Ruilong, and Zhang You. Chatdoctor: A medical chat model fine-tuned on llama
- Li, C., Wong, C., Zhang, S., Usuyama, N., Liu, H., Yang, J., Naumann, T., Poon, H. & Gao, J. LLaVA-Med: Training a Large Language-and-Vision Assistant for Biomedicine in One Day. arXiv preprint arXiv:2306.00890 (2023).)
- Li, J., Cheng, X., Zhao, W. X., Nie, J. Y., & Wen, J. R. (2023). Helma: A large-scale hallucination evaluation benchmark for large language models. arXiv preprint arXiv:2305.11747.
- Liao M, Li Y, Kianifard F, Obi E, Arcona S. Cluster analysis and its application to healthcare claims data: a study of end-stage renal disease patients who initiated hemodialysis. BMC Nephrol. 2016 Mar 2;17:25
- Liao YY, Tseng HY, Lin YJ, Wang CJ, Hsu WC. Using virtual reality-based training to improve cognitive function, instrumental activities of daily living and neural efficiency in older adults with mild cognitive impairment. Eur J Phys Rehabil Med. 2020 Feb;56(1):47-57.
- Lih OS, Jahmunah V, San TR, Ciaccio EJ, Yamakawa T, Tanabe M, Kobayashi M, Faust O, Acharya UR. Comprehensive electrocardiographic diagnosis based on deep learning. Artif Intell Med. 2020 Mar;103:101789.
- Lilly CM, Cucchi E, Marshall N, Katz A. Battling Intensivist Burnout: A Role for Workload Management. Chest. 2019 Nov;156(5):1001-1007.
- Lilly CM, Mullen M. Critical care surge management: a role for ICU telemedicine and emergency department collaboration. Crit. Care Med. 47(9):1271-1273, 2019.
- Lin J, Paganini S, Sander L, Lüking M, Ebert DD, Buhrman M, Andersson G, Baumeister H. An Internet-Based Intervention for Chronic Pain. Dtsch Arztebl Int. 2017 Oct 13;114(41):681-688
- Lindvall C, Lilley EJ, Zupanc SN, et al. Natural Language Processing to Assess End-of-Life Quality Indicators in Cancer Patients Receiving Palliative Surgery. J Palliat Med. 2019;22(2):183-187

- Lins S, Hayder-Beichel D, Rücker G, Motschall E, Antes G, Meyer G, Langer G. Efficacy and experiences of telephone counselling for informal carers of people with dementia. Cochrane Database Syst Rev. 2014 Sep 1;2014(9):CD009126
- Lipton, Z. C., Kale, D. C., Elkan, C. & Wetzel, R. Learning to diagnose with LSTM recurrent neural networks. arXiv [cs.LG] (2015)
- Lisanne S. Pauw, Disa A. Sauter, Gerben A. van Kleef, Gale M. Lucas, Jonathan Gratch, and Agneta H. Fischer. 2022. The avatar will see you now: Support from a virtual human provides socio-emotional benefits. Comput. Hum. Behav. 136, C (Nov 2022).
- Litjens G, Kooi T, Bejnordi BE, et al. A survey on deep learning in medical image analysis. Med Image Anal. 2017;42:60-88
- Liu N. Market Analysis Report on Potential Resources for Knowledge-Based Systems. U.S. Army Institute of Surgical Research. 30 October 2018. https://apps.dtic.mil/sti/pdfs/AD1064950.pdf. Accessed January 15, 2022
- Liu S, Tang B, Chen Q, Wang X. Drug-drug interaction extraction via convolutional neural networks. Comput Math Methods Med. 2016;2016
- Liu Y, Kohlberger T, Norouzi M, et al. Artificial Intelligence-Based Breast Cancer Nodal Metastasis Detection: Insights Into the Black Box for Pathologists. Arch Pathol Lab Med. 2019;143(7):859-868
- Liu, X., Yu, H., Zhang, H., Xu, Y., Lei, X., Lai, H., ... & Tang, J. (2023). Agentbench: Evaluating llms as agents. arXiv preprint arXiv:2308.03688.
- Liu, Z., Wang, P., Li, Y., Holmes, J., Shu, P., Zhang, L., Liu, C., Liu, N., Zhu, D., Li, X. and Li, Q., 2023. Radonc-gpt: A large language model for radiation oncology. arXiv preprint arXiv:2309.10160.
- Logie K, Welsh L, Ranganathan SC. Telehealth spirometry for children with cystic fibrosis Archives of Disease in Childhood 2020;105:1203-1205.
- Logishetty K, Gofton WT, Rudran B, Beaulé PE, Cobb JP. Fully Immersive Virtual Reality for Total Hip Arthroplasty: Objective Measurement of Skills and Transfer of Visuospatial Performance After a Competency-Based Simulation Curriculum. J Bone Joint Surg Am. 2020 Mar 18;102(6):e27.
- LOINC. About LOINC. https://loinc.org/about/. Accessed March 16, 2021
- LOINC. Leukocytes [#/volume] in Cerebral spinal fluid by Manual count. https://loinc.org/806-0
- LOINC. Users' Guide. June 10, 2020. https://loinc.org/kb/users-guide. Accessed March 18, 2021
- Long N, Lei Y, Peng L, Xu P, Mao P. A scoping review on monitoring mental health using smart wearable devices. Math Biosci Eng. 2022 May 27;19(8):7899-7919
- Lopez AM. Telemedicine, telehealth, and e-health technologies in cancer prevention. In Alberts D, Hess LM (eds). Fundamentals of Cancer Prevention. Berlin: Springer, 2014;259-277.
- Lopez CD, Boddapati V, Lombardi JM, Lee NJ, Mathew J, Danford NC, Iyer RR, Dyrszka MD, Sardar ZM, Lenke LG, Lehman RA. Artificial Learning and Machine Learning Applications in Spine Surgery: A Systematic Review. Global Spine J. 2022 Sep;12(7):1561-1572.
- Low LL, Lee KH, Hock Ong ME, et al. Predicting 30-Day Readmissions: Performance of the LACE Index Compared with a Regression Model among General Medicine Patients in Singapore. Biomed Res Int. 2015;2015:169870
- Lozada KN, Morton K, Stepan K. et al. The clinical impact of bedside fiberoptic laryngoscopic recording on a tertiary consult service. Laryngoscope 2018; 128: 818-822
- Lu Y, Fu X, Chen F, Wong KKL. Prediction of fetal weight at varying gestational age in the absence of ultrasound examination using ensemble learning. Artif Intell Med. 2020;102:101748.
- Lumley HA, Flynn D, Shaw L, et al. A scoping review of pre-hospital technology to assist ambulance personnel with patient diagnosis or stratification during the emergency assessment of suspected stroke. BMC Emerg Med. 20(1):30, 2020
- Luo H, Lee PA, Clay I, Jaggi M, De Luca V. Assessment of Fatigue Using Wearable Sensors: A Pilot Study. Digit Biomark. 2020 Nov 26;4(Suppl 1):59-72.
- Luxton DD, O'Brien K, Pruitt LD, Johnson K, Kramer G. Suicide risk management during clinical telepractice. Int. J.Psychiat. Med. 48(1): 19-31,.2014
- Ma L, Zhao Z, Zhang B, Jiang W, Fu L, Zhang X, et al. Three-dimensional augmented reality surgical navigation with hybrid optical and electromagnetic tracking for distal intramedullary nail interlocking. Int J Med Robot. 2018;14:e1909
- Ma, J., Sheridan, R. P., Liaw, A., Dahl, G. E. & Svetnik, V. Deep neural nets as a method for quantitative structure-activity relationships. J. Chem. Inf. Model. 55, 263–274 (2015)
- MacIntyre CR, Ruth D, Ansari Z. Hospital in the home is cost saving for appropriately selected patients: a comparison with in-hospital care. Int J Qual Health Care. 2002 Aug;14(4):285-93
- MacKinney AC, Ward MM., Ullrich F, Ayyagari P, Bell AL, Mueller KJ. The business case for tele-emergency. Telemed. eHealth 21(12): 1005-1011, 2015
- Maduskar P, Muyoyeta M, Ayles H, Hogeweg L, Peters-BaxL, van Ginneken B. Detection of tuberculosis using digital chest radiography: automated reading vs. interpretation by clinical officers. Int J Tuberc Lung Dis Off J Int Union Tuberc Lung Dis. 2013 Dec; 17(12):1613–20)
- Mahon SM. Telegenetics: remote counseling during the COVID-19 pandemic. Clin. J. Oncol. Nurs. 24(3):244-248, 2020
- Malandraki GA, McCullough G, He X. et al. Teledynamic evaluation of oropharyngeal swallowing. J Speech Lang Hear Res 2011; 54: 1497-1505
- Malbos E, Mestre DR, Note ID, Gellato C. Virtual reality and claustrophobia: multiple components therapy involving game editor virtual environments exposure. Cyberpsychol Behav. 2008 Dec;11(6):695-7.
- Maldonado F, Moua T, Rajagopalan S, Karwoski RA, Raghunath S, Decker PA, Hartman TE, Bartholmai BJ, Robb RA, Ryu JH. Automated quantification of radiological patterns predicts survival in idiopathic pulmonary fibrosis. Eur Respir J. 2014 Jan;43(1):204-12

- Mandall NA, O'Brien KD, Brady J, Worthington HV, Harvey L. Teledentistry for screening new patient orthodontic referrals. Part 1: A randomised controlled trial. Br Dent J. 2005;199(10):659-662
- Mandel JC, Kreda DA, Mandl KD, Kohane IS, Ramoni RB. SMART on FHIR: a standards-based, interoperable apps platform for electronic health records. J Am Med Inform Assoc. 2016 Sep;23(5):899-908.
- Manenti R, Gobbi E, Baglio F, Macis A, Ferrari C, Pagnoni I, Rossetto F, Di Tella S, Alemanno F, Cimino V, Binetti G, Iannaccone S, Bramanti P, Cappa SF, Cotelli M. Effectiveness of an Innovative Cognitive Treatment and Telerehabilitation on Subjects With Mild Cognitive Impairment: A Multicenter, Randomized, Active-Controlled Study. Front Aging Neurosci. 2020 Nov 16;12:585988.
- Mann, W. C., & Milton, B. R. (2005). Home automation and SMART homes to support independence. In W.C. Mann (Ed.), Smart technology for aging, disability, and independence (pp. 33–66). Hoboken, NJ: Wiley
- Mantovani E, Zucchella C, Bottiroli S, et al. Telemedicine and virtual reality for cognitive rehabilitation: a roadmap for the COVID-19 pandemic. Frontiers Neurol. 11:926, 2020
- Maragatham G, Devi S. LSTM Model for Prediction of Heart Failure in Big Data. J Med Syst. 2019;43(5):111. Published 2019 Mar 19
- Marcin, J., Shaikh, U. & Steinhorn, R. Addressing health disparities in rural communities using telehealth. Pediatr Res 79, 169–176 (2016)
- Marcucci, BreAnne. (2018). Use of Telehealth to Increase Breastfeeding Exclusivity and Duration. Clinical Lactation. 9. 66-71.
- Maroongroge S, Smith B, Bloom ES, et al. Telemedicine for radiation oncology in a post-COVID world. Int. J.Radiat. Oncol. Biol. Phys. 108(2):407-410, 2020
- Marquard B, Haas E, Dolin G, Grieve G, Bashyam N. US Core Implementation Guide. 4.0.0 – STU4 Release. HL7 FHIR. HL7 International. June 28, 2021. http://www.hl7.org/fhir/us/core/. Accessed November 24, 2021.
- Marra DE, Hoelzle JB, Davis JJ, Schwartz ES. Initial changes in neuropsychologists clinical practice during the COVID-19 pandemic: a survey study. Clin. Neuropsychol. 29:1-16, 2020
- Marsch LA, Borodovsky JT. Technology-based Interventions for Preventing and Treating Substance Use Among Youth. Child Adolesc Psychiatr Clin N Am. 2016 Oct; 25(4):755-68.),
- Martinez-Martin N, Kreitmair K. Ethical issues for direct-to-consumer digital psychotherapy apps: addressing accountability, data protection, and consent. JMIR Ment. Health 5(2):e32, 2018
- Marttos A, Kelly E, Graygo J, et al. Usability of telepresence in a level 1 trauma center. Telemed. eHealth 19(4):248-251, 2013)
- Mary Helmer-Smith, Celeste Fung, Amir Afkham, Lois Crowe, Mohamed Gazarin, Erin Keely, Isabella Moroz, Clare Liddy. The Feasibility of Using Electronic Consultation in Long-Term Care Homes. Journal of the American Medical Directors Association. Volume 21, Issue 8, 2020, 1166-1170.e2
- Mason M, Ola B, Zaharakis N, Zhang J. Text messaging interventions for adolescent and young adult substance use: a meta-analysis. Prev Sci. 2015 Feb; 16(2):181-8.
- Masood, A. & Al-Jumaily, A. A. Computer aided diagnostic support system for skin cancer: a review of techniques and algorithms. Int. J. Biomed. Imaging 2013, 323268 (2013)
- MassHealth Pharmacy Program. The Prescriber e-letter. December 2021 Volume 11, Issue 4. https://www.mass.gov/doc/issue-4-december-2021-0/download#:~:text=reSET%20and%20reSET%2DO%20are,and%20opioid%20use%20disorder%2C%20respectively. Accessed February 21, 2022
- Mathis Friesdorf, Ulrike Deetjen, Ajit Sawant, Greg Gilbert, Florian Niedermann. Digital health ecosystems: A payer perspective. McKinsey & Company. July 2019. Available at https://healthcare.mckinsey.com/digital-health-ecosystems-payer-perspective. Accessed April 12, 2021
- McCambridge J, Witton J, Elbourne DR. Systematic review of the Hawthorne effect: new concepts are needed to study research participation effects. J Clin Epidemiol. 2014 Mar;67(3):267-77.
- McCarthy M, Munoz K, White KR. Teleintervention for infants and young children who are deaf or hard-of-hearing. Pediatrics 2010; 126 (Suppl. 01) S52-S58
- McCarthy, J. (2007). What Is Artificial Intelligence? Stanford University, Stanford, CA. Retrieved from http://jmc.stanford.edu/articles/whatisai/whatisai.pdf Accessed September 12, 2021
- McCool RR, Davies L. Where Does Telemedicine Fit into Otolaryngology? An Assessment of Telemedicine Eligibility among Otolaryngology Diagnoses. Otolaryngol Head Neck Surg 2018; 158: 641-644
- McDermott K, Elixhauser A, Sun R. Trends in hospital inpatient stays in the United Sates, 2005-2014. HCUP. 2017; Agency for Healthcare Research and Quality, Rockville, MD. www.hcup-us.ahrq.gov/reports/statbriefs/sb225-Inpatient-US-Stays-Trends.pdf
- McDougall JA, Ferucci ED, Glover J, Fraenkel L. Telerheumatology: A Systematic Review. Arthritis Care Res (Hoboken). 2017 Oct; 69(10):1546-1557
- McDuff, D., Schaekermann, M., Tu, T., Palepu, A., Wang, A., Garrison, J., ... & Natarajan, V. (2023). Towards accurate differential diagnosis with large language models. arXiv preprint arXiv:2312.00164.
- McGillicuddy JW, Gregoski MJ, Weiland AK, Rock RA, Brunner-Jackson BM, Patel SK, Thomas BS, Taber DJ, Chavin KD, Baliga PK, Treiber FA. Mobile Health Medication Adherence and Blood Pressure Control in Renal Transplant Recipients: A Proof-of-Concept Randomized Controlled Trial. JMIR Res Protoc. 2013 Sep 4;2(2):e32
- McGinn MM, Roussev MS, Shearer EM, et al. Recommendations for using clinical video telehealth with patients at high risk for suicide. Psychiatr. Clin. North Amer. 42(4):587-595, 2019
- McKay JR, Lynch KG, Shepard DS, Pettinati HM. The effectiveness of telephone-based continuing care for alcohol and cocaine dependence: 24-month outcomes. Arch Gen Psychiatry. 2005 Feb; 62(2):199-207.

- McLaughlin WJ, Schifman RB, Ryan KJ, Manriquez GM, Bhattacharyya AK, Dunn BE, Weinstein RS. Telemicrobiology: feasibility study. Telemed J. 1998 Spring;4(1):11-7
- McLean S, Nurmatov U, Liu JL, Pagliari C, Car J, Sheikh A. Telehealthcare for chronic obstructive pulmonary disease: Cochrane Review and meta-analysis. Br J Gen Pract. 2012 Nov;62(604):e739-49
- McManus DD, Chong JW, Soni A, Saczynski JS, Esa N, Napolitano C, Darling CE, Boyer E, Rosen RK, Floyd KC, Chon KH. PULSE-SMART: Pulse-Based Arrhythmia Discrimination Using a Novel Smartphone Application. J Cardiovasc Electrophysiol. 2016 Jan;27(1):51-7
- MDN web docs. An overview of HTTP. Mozilla. December 4, 2021. https://developer.mozilla.org/en-US/docs/Web/HTTP/Overview. Accessed December 28, 2021
- MedDRA. ICH. MedDRA Hierarchy. https://www.meddra.org/how-to-use/basics/hierarchy. Accessed April 12, 2022
- Medeiros NB, Fogliatto FS, Rocha MK, Tortorella GL. Forecasting the length-of-stay of pediatric patients in hospitals: a scoping review. BMC Health Serv Res. 2021 Sep 8;21(1):938. doi: 10.1186/s12913-021-06912-4.
- Medicaid.gov. State Overviews. https://www.medicaid.gov/state-overviews/state-profiles/index.html. Accessed July 24, 2021
- Menon PR, Stapleton RD, McVeigh U, Rabinowitz T. Telemedicine as a tool to provide family conferences and palliative care consultations in critically ill patients at rural health care institutions: a pilot study. Amer. J. Hosp. Palliat. Care 32(4):448-453, 2015
- Merchant R, Szefler SJ, Bender BG, Tuffli M, Barrett MA, Gondalia R, Kaye L, Van Sickle D, Stempel DA. Impact of a digital health intervention on asthma resource utilization. World Allergy Organ J. 2018 Dec 3;11(1):28.
- Merrell RC, Cone SW, Rafiq A. Telemedicine in extreme conditions: disasters, war, remote sites. Stud. Health Technol. Inform.131:99-116, 2008
- Merritt Hawkins. Survey: Physician Practice Patterns Changing As A Result Of COVID-19. https://www.merritthawkins.com/news-and-insights/media-room/press/-Physician-Practice-Patterns-Changing-as-a-Result-of-COVID-19/ April 22, 2020. Accessed January 23, 2021
- Mettler T. Maturity assessment models: a design science research approach. Int J Soc Syst Sci. 2011;3(1/2):213–222. https://www.alexandria.unisg.ch/214426/1/IJSSS0301-0205%2520METTLER.pdf Accessed October 12, 2022
- Metzinger TK. Why Is Virtual Reality Interesting for Philosophers? Front Robot AI. 2018 Sep 13;5:101
- Meuret AE, Wilhelm FH, Ritz T, Roth WT. Feedback of end-tidal pCO2 as a therapeutic approach for panic disorder. J Psychiatr Res. 2008 Jun;42(7):560-8.
- Meyer BC, Raman R, Chacon MR, Jensen M, Werner JD. Reliability of site-independent telemedicine when assessed by telemedicine-naive stroke practitioners. J Stroke Cerebrovasc Dis. 2008 Jul-Aug;17(4):181-6
- Meyers DJ, Ozonoff A, Baruwal A, Pande S, Harsha A, Sharma R, Schwarz D, Schwarz RK, Bista D, Halliday S, Maru DS. Combining Healthcare-Based and Participatory Approaches to Surveillance: Trends in Diarrheal and Respiratory Conditions Collected by a Mobile Phone System by Community Health Workers in Rural Nepal. PLoS One. 2016 Apr 25;11(4):e0152738
- Mhajna M, Schwartz N, Levit-Rosen L, Warsof S, Lipschuetz M, Jakobs M, Rychik J, Sohn C, Yagel S. Wireless, remote solution for home fetal and maternal heart rate monitoring. Am J Obstet Gynecol MFM. 2020 May;2(2):100101
- Miao F, Wen B, Hu Z, Fortino G, Wang XP, Liu ZD, Tang M, Li Y. Continuous blood pressure measurement from one-channel electrocardiogram signal using deep-learning techniques. Artif Intell Med. 2020 Aug;108:101919.
- Michelle Finneran Dennedy, Jonathan Fox, and Thomas Finneran. 2014. The Privacy Engineers Manifesto: Getting from Policy to Code to QA to Value (1st. ed.). Apress, USA.
- Migoya-Borja M, Delgado-Gómez D, Carmona-Camacho R, Porras-Segovia A, López-Moriñigo JD, Sánchez-Alonso M, Albarracín García L, Guerra N, Barrigón ML, Alegría M, Baca-García E. Feasibility of a Virtual Reality-Based Psychoeducational Tool (VRight) for Depressive Patients. Cyberpsychol Behav Soc Netw. 2020 Apr;23(4):246-252.
- Mikolov, T., Deoras, A., Povey, D., Burget, L. & Cernocky, J. Strategies for training large scale neural network language models. In Proc. Automatic Speech Recognition and Understanding 196–201 (2011).
- Milgram P, Kishino F (1994) A Taxonomy of Mixed Reality Visual-Displays. Ieice T Inf Syst E77d:1321–1329
- Miller JB, Barr WB. The Technology Crisis in Neuropsychology. Arch Clin Neuropsychol. 2017 Aug 1;32(5):541-554.
- Miller JC, Skoll D, Saxon LA. Home monitoring of cardiac devices in the era of COVID-19. Curr. Cardiol. Rep.23(1):1, 2020
- Miller LE, Buzi A, Williams A, Rogers RS, Ortiz AG, Jones-Ho KO, Elden LM. Reliability and Accuracy of Remote Fiberoptic Nasopharyngolaryngoscopy in the Pediatric Population. Ear Nose Throat J. 2020 Apr 13:145561320919109
- Miotto, R., Li, L., Kidd, B. A. & Dudley, J. T. Deep patient: an unsupervised representation to predict the future of patients from the electronic health records. Sci. Rep. 6, 26094 (2016)
- model using medical domain knowledge. arXiv preprint arXiv:2303.14070, 2023.
- Moessner M, Bauer S. Maximizing the public health impact of eating disorder services: A simulation study. Int J Eat Disord. 2017 Dec;50(12):1378-1384
- Mohammad Naseem, Saman Naseem, 'International', (2022), pp.1-268 in Herman Nys (ed.), IEL Medical Law, (Kluwer Law International BV, Netherlands), https://kluwerlawonline.com/EncyclopediaChapter/IEL+Medical+Law/MEDI20190002
- Mohammadpour RA, Abedi SM, Bagheri S, Ghaemian A. Fuzzy Rule-Based Classification System for Assessing Coronary Artery Disease. Comput Math Methods Med. 2015;2015:564867
- Mohebali D, Kittleson MM. Remote monitoring in heart failure: current and emerging technologies in the context of the pandemic. Heart 2021;107:366-372
- Mohr NM, Young T, Harland KK, Skow B, Wittrock A, Bell A, Ward MM. Emergency Department Telemedicine Shortens Rural Time-To-Provider and Emergency Department Transfer Times. Telemed J E Health. 2018 Aug;24(8):582-593
- Molfenter T, Boyle M, Holloway D, Zwick J. Trends in telemedicine use in addiction treatment. Addict Sci Clin Pract. 2015 May 28; 10():14.

- Molfenter T, Brown R, O'Neill A, Kopetsky E, Toy A. Use of Telemedicine in Addiction Treatment: Current Practices and Organizational Implementation Characteristics. Int J Telemed Appl. 2018;2018:3932643.
- Molini-Avejonas DR, Rondon-Melo S, Amato CA, Samelli AG. A systematic review of the use of telehealth in speech, language and hearing sciences. J Telemed Telecare. 2015 Oct;21(7):367-76
- Montalto M. How safe is hospital-in-the-home care? Med J Aust. 1998 Mar 16;168(6):277-80
- Moon SJ, Hwang J, Hill HS, Kervin R, Birtwell KB, Torous J, McDougle CJ, Kim JW. Mobile device applications and treatment of autism spectrum disorder: a systematic review and meta-analysis of effectiveness. Arch Dis Child. 2020 May;105(5):458-462
- Moore K. CMS: Patients can self-report vitals for Medicare AWV telehealth visits. Family Practice Medicine, May 28, 2020. https://www.aafp.org/journals/fpm/blogs/gettingpaid/entry/medicare_awv_vitals.html. Accessed February 12, 2021
- Moore SL, Portz JD, Santodomingo M, Elsbernd K, McHale M, Massone J. Using Telehealth for Hospice Reauthorization Visits: Results of a Quality Improvement Analysis. J Pain Symptom Manage. 2020;60(3):e22-e27
- Morano B., Jimenez-Mejia J., Sanon M., Morano C., DeCherrie L.V. (2020) Acute Care in the Home Setting: Hospital at Home. In: Chun A. (eds) Geriatric Practice. Springer, Cham.
- Moreno L, Peck JL. Nurse Practitioner-Led Telehealth to Improve Outpatient Pediatric Tracheostomy Management in South Texas. J Pediatr Health Care. 2020 May-Jun;34(3):246-255
- Mori Y, Kudo SE, Berzin TM, Misawa M, Takeda K. Computer-aided diagnosis for colonoscopy. Endoscopy. 2017;49(8):813-819
- Mori Y, Kudo SE, Misawa M, et al. Real-time use of artificial intelligence in identification of diminutive polyps during colonoscopy: a prospective study. Ann Intern Med 2018;169:357-366
- Moring JC, Dondanville KA, Fina BA, Hassija C, Chard K, Monson C, LoSavio ST, Wells SY, Morland LA, Kaysen D, Galovski TE, Resick PA. Cognitive Processing Therapy for Posttraumatic Stress Disorder via Telehealth: Practical Considerations During the COVID-19 Pandemic. J Trauma Stress. 2020 Aug;33(4):371-379.
- Morland LA, Greene CJ, Rosen CS, Foy D, Reilly P, Shore J, He Q, Frueh BC. Telemedicine for anger management therapy in a rural population of combat veterans with posttraumatic stress disorder: a randomized noninferiority trial. J Clin Psychiatry. 2010 Jul; 71(7):855-63
- Moro C, Birt J, Stromberga Z, Phelps C, Clark J, Glasziou P, Scott A. Virtual and augmented reality enhancements to medical and science student physiology and anatomy test performance: a systematic review and meta-analysis. Anat Sci Educ. 2021 May;14(3):368–376
- Morrison D, Wyke S, Agur K, Cameron EJ, Docking RI, Mackenzie AM, McConnachie A, Raghuvir V, Thomson NC, Mair FS. Digital asthma self-management interventions: a systematic review. J Med Internet Res. 2014 Feb 18;16(2):e51
- Morrison KS, Paterson C, Toohey K. The Feasibility of Exercise Interventions Delivered via Telehealth for People Affected by Cancer: A Rapid Review of the Literature. Semin Oncol Nurs. 2020 Dec;36(6):151092
- Mortara A, Vaira L, Palmieri V, et al. Would You Prescribe Mobile Health Apps for Heart Failure Self-care? An Integrated Review of Commercially Available Mobile Technology for Heart Failure Patients. Card Fail Rev. 2020;6:e13.
- Motahari-Nezhad H, Al-Abdulkarim H, Fgaier M, Abid MM, Péntek M, Gulácsi L, Zrubka Z. Digital Biomarker-Based Interventions: Systematic Review of Systematic Reviews. J Med Internet Res. 2022 Dec 21;24(12):e41042
- Mousa AY, Broce M, Monnett S, Davis E, McKee B, Lucas BD. Results of Telehealth Electronic Monitoring for Post Discharge Complications and Surgical Site Infections following Arterial Revascularization with Groin Incision. Ann Vasc Surg. 2019 May;57:160-169.
- Mozgai, S., Rizzo, A. & Hartholt, A. Persuasive Technology for Suicide Prevention: A Virtual Human mHealth Application. In Proceedings of the 18th International Conference on Persuasive Technologies, 2023.
- Mueller KJ, Potter AJ, MacKinney AC, Ward MM. Lessons from tele-emergency: improving care quality and health outcomes by expanding support for rural care systems. Health Aff (Millwood). 2014 Feb;33(2):228-34
- Muraco L. Improved medical photography: key tips for creating images of lasting value. JAMA Dermatol. 2020;156(2):121
- Murphy AC, Meehan G, Koshy AN, Kunniardy P, Farouque O, Yudi MB. Efficacy of Smartphone-Based Secondary Preventive Strategies in Coronary Artery Disease. Clin Med Insights Cardiol. 2020 Jun 5;14:1179546820927402.
- Murray MA, Penza KS, Myers JF, Furst JW, Pecina JL. Comparison of eVisit Management of Urinary Symptoms and Urinary Tract Infections with Standard Care. Telemed J E Health. 2020 May;26(5):639-644
- Myers K, Nelson EL, Hilty D, Rabinowitz T. Practice guidelines for telemental health with children and adolescents. American Telemedicine Association, March 2017
- Nabutovsky I, Ashri S, Nachshon A, Tesler R, Shapiro Y, Wright E, Vadasz B, Offer A, Grosman-Rimon L, Klempfner R. Feasibility, Safety, and Effectiveness of a Mobile Application in Cardiac Rehabilitation. Isr Med Assoc J. 2020 Jun;22(6):357-363.
- Nagayo Y, Saito T, Oyama H. A Novel Suture Training System for Open Surgery Replicating Procedures Performed by Experts Using Augmented Reality. J Med Syst. 2021 Apr 7;45(5):60.
- Nagpal K, Foote D, Tan F, et al. Development and Validation of a Deep Learning Algorithm for Gleason Grading of Prostate Cancer From Biopsy Specimens. JAMA Oncol. Published online July 23, 2020
- Nahm WJ, Gwillim EC, Badiavas EV, Nichols AJ, Kirsner RS, Boggeln LH, Shen JT. Treating Melanoma in Situ During a Pandemic with Telemedicine and a Combination of Imiquimod, 5-Fluorouracil, and Tretinoin. Dermatol Ther (Heidelb). 2021 Feb;11(1):307-314
- Najafi B. Post the Pandemic: How will COVID-19 Transform Diabetic Foot Disease Management? J Diabetes Sci Technol. 2020 Jul;14(4):764-766
- Nakamura N, Koga T, Iseki H. A meta-analysis of remote patient monitoring for chronic heart failure patients. J Telemed Telecare. 2014 Jan;20(1):11-7
- Nakamura Y, Ghaibeh AA, Setoguchi Y, et al. On-admission pressure ulcer prediction using the nursing needs score. JMIR Med

Inform. 2015;3(1):e8. Published 2015 Feb 11

- National Center for Health Statistics. 2020 Mar 11. Nursing Home Care URL: https://www.cdc.gov/nchs/fastats/nursing-home-care.htm. Accessed January 18, 2021
- National Coverage Determination (NCD) for Intensive Behavioral therapy for Obesity. CMS. https://www.cms.gov/medicare-coverage-database/details/ncd-details.aspx?NCDId=353 Accessed March 12, 2021)
- National Drug Codes List. NDC 50580-496-98 Tylenol Regular Strength Acetaminophen Tablet Oral. https://ndclist.com/ndc/50580-496/package/50580-496-98
- National Evaluation System for health Technology Coordinating Center (NESTcc). Data Quality Framework. February 2020. A Report of the Data Quality Subcommittee of the NEST Coordinating Center – An initiative of MDIC. Accessed November 12, 2022
- National Health Systems Resource Center (NHSRC). Quality Assurance Scores & Key Performance Indicators. http://qi.nhsrcindia.org/quality-assurance-scores-and-key-performance-indicators. Accessed March 23, 2021
- National Health Systems Resource Center (NHSRC). About NHSRC. https://nhsrcindia.org/sites/default/files/NHSRC.pdf. Accessed August 20, 2023
- National Institute of Standards and Technology (NIST). Security Requirements for Cryptographic Modules. May 25, 2001. https://csrc.nist.gov/publications/detail/fips/140/2/final
- National Institutes of Health. U.S. National Library of Medicine. RxNorm Overview. January 3, 2022. https://www.nlm.nih.gov/research/umls/rxnorm/overview.html. Accessed 22 March 2022.
- National Library of Medicine. SNOMED-CT. https://www.nlm.nih.gov/healthit/snomedct/index.html . Accessed March 15, 2021
- National Library of Medicine. Unified Medical Language System (UMLS). https://www.nlm.nih.gov/research/umls/index.html. Accessed March 20, 2022
- National Research Council, Committee on Maintaining Privacy and Security in Health Care Applications of the National Information Infrastructure, Computer Science and Telecommunications Board, For the Record: Protecting Electronic Health Information, p. 1-1 (National Academy Press, Washington, DC, March 1997)
- NCQA. HEDIS and Performance Measurement. 2021. Available at https://www.ncqa.org/hedis. Accessed August 15, 2021
- Negrini S, Donzelli S, Negrini A, Negrini A, Romano M, Zaina F. Feasibility and Acceptability of Telemedicine to Substitute Outpatient Rehabilitation Services in the COVID-19 Emergency in Italy: An Observational Everyday Clinical-Life Study. Arch Phys Med Rehabil. 2020;101(11):2027-2032.
- Nelson BP, Melnick ER, Li J. Portable ultrasound for remote environments, Part I: Feasibility of field deployment. J. Emerg. Med. 40(2):190-197, 2011
- NEST. Real-World Evidence Generation. https://nestcc.org/real-world-evidence. Accessed October 12, 2022
- Newton, K. M. et al. Validation of electronic medical record-based phenotyping algorithms: results and lessons learned from the eMERGE network. J. Am. Med. Inform. Assoc. 20, e147–e154 (2013)
- NHPCO. Facts and figures: hospice care in America. Alexandria, VA: National Hospice and Palliative Care Organization; 2016
- NHS Digital. Quality and Outcomes Framework. September 30, 2021. Available at https://digital.nhs.uk/data-and-information/publications/statistical/quality-and-outcomes-framework-achievement-prevalence-and-exceptions-data. Accessed October 30, 2021
- NHS. Digital Technology Assessment Criteria for Health and Social Care (DTAC) - Version 1.0. 22 February 2021. https://transform.england.nhs.uk/key-tools-and-info/digital-technology-assessment-criteria-dtac. Accessed Sept 15, 2021.)
- NHSx. Draft IAPT assessment criteria for digitally enabled therapies. August 2021. https://www.nhsx.nhs.uk/key-tools-and-info/digital-technology-assessment-criteria-dtac/draft-iapt-assessment-criteria-for-digitally-enabled-therapies. Accessed October 15, 2021
- NICE. Evidence standards framework for digital health technologies. December 10, 2018. https://www.nice.org.uk/corporate/ecd7. Accessed October 15, 2021
- NICE. Quality Standards. https://www.nice.org.uk/standards-and-indicators/quality-standards. Accessed November 15, 2021
- Nichols KR. Teledentistry overview: United States of America. J Int Soc Telemed eHealth 2019;7:e9
- Nicol G, Wang R, Graham S, Dodd S, Garbutt J. Chatbot-Delivered Cognitive Behavioral Therapy in Adolescents With Depression and Anxiety During the COVID-19 Pandemic: Feasibility and Acceptability Study. JMIR Form Res. 2022 Nov 22;6(11):e40242
- NIH Health Care Systems Research Collaboratory (HCSRC). Informed consent. In Rethinking Clinical Trials: A Living Textbook of Pragmatic Clinical Trials. [Septmeber 5th, 2016]. Available from: http://sites.duke.edu/rethinkingclinicaltrials/informed-consent-in-pragmatic-clinical-trials/
- Nixon, J., & McGough, A. (2001). Principles of patient assessment: Screening for pressure ulcers and potential risk In Morison M. (Ed.), The prevention and treatment of pressure ulcers (pp. 17–36). Edinburgh: Mosby.
- Noffs G., Boonstra F.M.C., Perera T., Kolbe S.C., Stankovich J., Butzkueven H., Evans A., Vogel A., Van Der Walt A. Acoustic Speech Analytics Are Predictive of Cerebellar Dysfunction in Multiple Sclerosis. Cerebellum. 2020;19:691–700.
- Norris RM. Fatality outside hospital from acute coronary events in three British health districts, 1994–1995. BMJ 1998;316:1065.
- Novara G, Checcucci E, Crestani A, et al. Telehealth in Urology: A Systematic Review of the Literature. How Much Can Telemedicine Be Useful During and After the COVID-19 Pandemic?. Eur Urol. 2020;78(6):786-811.
- Nygaard G.O., Benavent S.A.D.R., Harbo H.F., Laeng B., Sowa P., Damangir S., Nilsen K.B., Etholm L., Tønnesen S., Kerty E., et al. Eye and hand motor interactions with the Symbol Digit Modalities Test in early multiple sclerosis. Mult. Scler. Relat. Disord. 2015;4:585–589.
- O'Connor M. CMS renews payment coverage for Viz.ai's stroke CT platform. HealthImaging. August 4, 2021.

https://www.healthimaging.com/topics/medical-imaging/computed-tomography/vizai-stroke-ct-payment-cms

- Office of National Coordinator for Health Information Technology (ONC). United States Core Data for Interoperability (USCDI). Version 1. February 2020. https://www.healthit.gov/isa/united-states-core-data-interoperability-uscdi. Accessed May 20, 2021
- Office of the National Coordinator for Health Information Technology (ONC). 2015 Edition Health Information Technology (Health IT) Certification Criteria, 2015 Edition Base Electronic Health Record (EHR) Definition, and ONC Health IT Certification Program Modifications. October 16, 2015. https://www.healthit.gov/topic/certification-ehrs/2015-edition. Accessed November 25, 2021
- Office of the National Coordinator for Health Information Technology (ONC). 21st Century Cures Act: Interoperability, Information Blocking, and the ONC Health IT Certification Program. May 1, 2020. https://www.federalregister.gov/documents/2020/05/01/2020-07419/21st-century-cures-act-interoperability-information-blocking-and-the-onc-health-it-certification. Accessed November 15, 2021.
- Office of the National Coordinator for Health Information Technology (ONC). Department of Health and Human Services. January 2022. The Trusted Exchange Framework (TEF): Principles for Trusted Exchange). https://www.healthit.gov/sites/default/files/page/2022-01/Trusted_Exchange_Framework_0122.pdf
- Office of the National Coordinator for Health Information Technology (ONC). January 2022. Common Agreement for Nationwide Health Information Interoperability. Version 1. https://www.healthit.gov/sites/default/files/page/2022-01/Common_Agreement_for_Nationwide_Health_Information_Interoperability_Version_1.pdf
- Office of the National Coordinator for Health Information Technology (ONC). Strategic Health IT Advanced Research Projects (SHARP). 2013. http://www.healthit.gov/policy-researchers-implementers/strategic-health-it-advanced-research-projects-sharp. Accessed June 2020
- O'Hara VM, Johnston SV, Browne NT. The paediatric weight management office visit via telemedicine: pre- to post-COVID-19 pandemic. Pediatr Obes. 2020;15(8):e12694
- Okamoto T, Onda S, Yanaga K, et al. Clinical application of navigation surgery using augmented reality in the abdominal field. Surg Today 2015; 45(4): 397–406.
- Oliveira JAQ, Wolff IS, Ribeiro LD, Silva MVRS, Silva LTD, Marcolino MS. Teledermatology: current perspectives. Smart Homecare Technology and TeleHealth. 2017;4:61-73
- ONC TEFCA Recognized Coordinating Entity. Trusted Exchange Framework and Common Agreement. Qualified Health Information Network (QHIN) Technical Framework (QTF). Version 1.0. January 2022. https://rce.sequoiaproject.org/wp-content/uploads/2022/01/QTF_0122.pdf. Accessed November 27, 2022
- Oregon State Government. Statement of Work (SOW) Writing Guide. DAS Procurement Services, Version 2. 2018-04-02. https://www.oregon.gov/das/Procurement/Guiddoc/SOWWritingGuide.pdf. Retrieved 2021-02-10.
- Orlando JI, Prokofyeva E, Del Fresno M, Blaschko MB. An ensemble deep learning based approach for red lesion detection in fundus images. Comput Methods Programs Biomed. 2018;153:115-127
- Ostacher MJ, Fischer E, Bowen ER, Lyu J, Robbins DJ, Suppes T. Investigation of a Capnometry Guided Respiratory Intervention in the Treatment of Posttraumatic Stress Disorder. Appl Psychophysiol Biofeedback. 2021 Dec;46(4):367-376.
- Oswald D, Sherratt F, Smith S. Handling the Hawthorne effect: The challenges surrounding a participant observer. Review of Social Studies. 2014 Nov;1(1):53-73.
- Ouslander JG, Bonner A, Herndon L, Shutes J. The Interventions to Reduce Acute Care Transfers (INTERACT) quality improvement program: an overview for medical directors and primary care clinicians in long term care. J Am Med Dir Assoc. 2014 Mar;15(3):162-170.
- Overbeek DL, Hogikyan EM, Davis M, McGillicuddy DC. A unique case of bradycardia recognized by wearable technology as first presentation of complete heart block. Am J Emerg Med. 2019 Oct;37(10):1989.e5-1989.e7.
- Ozaslan B., Patek S.D., Breton M.D. Impact of Daily Physical Activity as Measured by Commonly Available Wearables on Mealtime Glucose Control in Type 1 Diabetes. Diabetes Technol. Ther. 2020;22:742–748.
- Padley RH, Di Pace B. Touch-ups, Rejuvenation, Re-dos and Revisions: Remote Communication and Cosmetic Surgery on the Rise. Aesthetic Plast Surg. 2021 Apr 2:1–3. doi: 10.1007/s00266-021-02235-1. Epub ahead of print.
- Palacín-Marín, F, Esteban-Moreno, B, Olea, N, Herrera-Viedma, E, Arroyo-Morales, M. Agreement between telerehabilitation and face-to-face clinical outcome assessments for low back pain in primary care. Spine (Phila Pa 1976). 2013;38:947–952
- Palaniappan S, Awang R. Intelligent heart disease prediction system using data mining techniques; Proceedings of IEEE/ACS International Conference on Computer Systems and Applications (AICCSA2008); 2008 Mar 31-Apr 4; Doha, Qatar. pp. 108–115
- Paleri V, Hardman J, Tikka T, Bradley P, Pracy P, Kerawala C. Rapid implementation of an evidence-based remote triaging system for assessment of suspected referrals and patients with head and neck cancer on follow-up after treatment during the COVID-19 pandemic: Model for international collaboration. Head Neck. 2020 Jul;42(7):1674-1680
- Palmer MJ, Henschke N, Bergman H, Villanueva G, Maayan N, Tamrat T, Mehl GL, Glenton C, Lewin S, Fønhus MS, Free C. Targeted client communication via mobile devices for improving maternal, neonatal, and child health. Cochrane Database Syst Rev. 2020 Jul 14;8:CD013679
- Panda N, Solsky I, Huang EJ, et al. Using smartphones to capture novel recovery metrics after cancer surgery. JAMA Surg, 155 (2) (2019), pp. 123-129
- Pantanowitz L, Dickinson K, Evans AJ, et al. American Telemedicine Association clinical guidelines for telepathology. J Pathol Inform. 2014;5(1):39
- Parecki A. OAuth 2.0. https://oauth.net/2/. Accessed July 2, 2021)
- Park J, Edington DW. A sequential neural network model for diabetes prediction. Artif Intell Med. 2001 Nov;23(3):277-93
- Parker S, Prince A, Thomas L, et al. Electronic, mobile and telehealth tools for vulnerable patients with chronic disease: a

systematic review and realist synthesis. BMJ Open. 2018;8(8):e019192.

- Parsons T. D., Rizzo A. A. Affective outcomes of virtual reality exposure therapy for anxiety and specific phobias: a meta-analysis. Journal of Behavior Therapy and Experimental Psychiatry. 2008;39(3):250–261.
- Paruthi S. Telemedicine in Pediatric Sleep. Sleep Med Clin. 2020;15(3S):e1-e7
- Pastora-Bernal JM, Martín-Valero R, Barón-López FJ, Estebanez-Pérez MJ. Evidence of Benefit of Telerehabitation After Orthopedic Surgery: A Systematic Review. J Med Internet Res. 2017;19(4):e142
- Patil B, Joshi R, Toshniwal D. (2010). Hybrid prediction model for Type-2 diabetic patients. Expert Systems with Applications. 37. 8102–8108. 10.1016/j.eswa.2010.05.078.
- Paul M, Bullock K, Bailenson J. Virtual Reality Behavioral Activation for Adults With Major Depressive Disorder: Feasibility Randomized Controlled Trial. JMIR Ment Health. 2022 May 6;9(5):e35526.
- Pauly RP, Gill JS, Rose CL, Asad RA, Chery A, Pierratos A, Chan CT. Survival among nocturnal home haemodialysis patients compared to kidney transplant recipients. Nephrol Dial Transplant. 2009 Sep;24(9):2915-9
- Pawlikowska T, et al. Population based study of fatigue and psychological distress. BMJ. 1994;308:763–766
- Payne, H. E., Lister, C., West, J. H. & Bernhardt, J. M. Behavioral functionality of mobile apps in health interventions: a systematic review of the literature. JMIR Mhealth Uhealth 3, e20 (2015)
- Peahl AF, Smith RD, Moniz MH. Prenatal care redesign: creating flexible maternity care models through virtual care. Am J Obstet Gynecol. 2020;223(3):389.e1-389.e10
- Pediatric Musculoskeletal Matters International. Virtual or Video-pGALS (V-pGALS). Available at http://www.pmmonline.org/doctor/approach-to-clinical-assessment/examination/v-pgals. Accessed March 12, 2021
- Peissig PL, Santos Costa V, Caldwell MD, Rottscheit C, Berg RL, Mendonca EA, et al. Relational machine learning for electronic health record-driven phenotyping. Journal of Biomedical Informatics. 2014;52:260–70
- Penner I-K, Paul F. Fatigue as a symptom or comorbidity of neurological diseases. Nat. Rev. Neurol. 2017;13:662.
- Penteado SP, Ramos Sd E L, Battistella LR, Marone SA, Bento RF. Remote hearing aid fitting: Tele-audiology in the context of Brazilian Public Policy. Int Arch Otorhinolaryngol. 2012;16(3):371-381
- Pérez Alonso N, Pardo Rios M, Juguera Rodriguez L, Vera Catalan T, Segura Melgarejo F, Lopez Ayuso B, Martí Nez Riquelme C, Lasheras Velasco J. Randomised clinical simulation designed to evaluate the effect of telemedicine using Google Glass on cardiopulmonary resuscitation (CPR). Emerg Med J. 2017 Nov;34(11):734-738
- Persell SD, Doctor JN, Friedberg MW, Meeker D, Friesema E, Cooper A, Haryani A, Gregory DL, Fox CR, Goldstein NJ, Linder JA. Behavioral interventions to reduce inappropriate antibiotic prescribing: a randomized pilot trial. BMC Infect Dis. 2016 Aug 5;16:373. doi: 10.1186/s12879-016-1715-8. PMID: 27495917; PMCID: PMC4975897.
- Pervez MA, Silva G, Masrur S, et al. Remote supervision of IV-tPA for acute ischemic stroke by telemedicine or telephone before transfer to a regional stroke center is feasible and safe. Stroke 2010;41:e18–24
- Pesce E, Joseph Withey S, Ypsilantis PP, Bakewell R, Goh V, Montana G. Learning to detect chest radiographs containing pulmonary lesions using visual attention networks. Med Image Anal. 2019;53:26-38
- Peterson KM, Ibañez VF, Volkert VM, Zeleny JR, Engler CW, Piazza CC. Using telehealth to provide outpatient follow-up to children with avoidant/restrictive food intake disorder. J Appl Behav Anal. 2021 Jan;54(1):6-24
- Pew Research Center, "Internet/broadband fact sheet," https://www.pewresearch.org/internet/fact-sheet/internet-broadband. April 7, 2021. Accessed May 12, 2021
- Pfeifer AC, Uddin R, Schröder-Pfeifer P, Holl F, Swoboda W, Schiltenwolf M. Mobile Application-Based Interventions for Chronic Pain Patients: A Systematic Review and Meta-Analysis of Effectiveness. J Clin Med. 2020 Nov 5;9(11):3557
- Pham T., Tran T., Phung D., Venkatesh S. (2016) DeepCare: A Deep Dynamic Memory Model for Predictive Medicine. In: Bailey J., Khan L., Washio T., Dobbie G., Huang J., Wang R. (eds) Advances in Knowledge Discovery and Data Mining. PAKDD 2016. Lecture Notes in Computer Science, vol 9652. Springer, Cham. ++++ Pham T, Tran T, Phung D, Venkatesh S. Predicting healthcare trajectories from medical records: A deep learning approach. J Biomed Inform. 2017;69:218-229
- Phongtankuel V, Adelman RD, Trevino K, Abramson E, Johnson P, Oromendia C, Henderson CR Jr, Reid MC. Association Between Nursing Visits and Hospital-Related Disenrollment in the Home Hospice Population. Am J Hosp Palliat Care. 2018 Feb; 35(2):316-323
- Piao C, Terrault NA, Sarkar S. Telemedicine: An Evolving Field in Hepatology. Hepatol Commun. 2019;3(5):716-721.
- Piau A, Wild K, Mattek N, Kaye J. Current State of Digital Biomarker Technologies for Real-Life, Home-Based Monitoring of Cognitive Function for Mild Cognitive Impairment to Mild Alzheimer Disease and Implications for Clinical Care: Systematic Review. J Med Internet Res. 2019 Aug 30;21(8):e12785.
- Pivetta E, Girard E, Locascio F, Lupia E, Martin JD, Stone M. Self-Performed Lung Ultrasound for Home Monitoring of a Patient Positive for Coronavirus Disease 2019. Chest. 2020;158(3):e93-e97
- Place S, Blanch-Hartigan D, Rubin C, Gorrostieta C, Mead C, Kane J, Marx BP, Feast J, Deckersbach T, Pentland AS, Nierenberg A, Azarbayejani A. Behavioral Indicators on a Mobile Sensing Platform Predict Clinically Validated Psychiatric Symptoms of Mood and Anxiety Disorders. J Med Internet Res. 2017 Mar 16;19(3):e75.
- Polinski JM, Barker T, Gagliano N, Sussman A, Brennan TA, Shrank WH. Patients' Satisfaction with and Preference for Telehealth Visits. J Gen Intern Med. 2016 Mar;31(3):269-75
- Poncette AS, Mosch L, Spies C, Schmieding M, Schiefenhövel F, Krampe H, Balzer F. Improvements in Patient Monitoring in the Intensive Care Unit: Survey Study. J Med Internet Res. 2020 Jun 19;22(6):e19091.
- Portnoy JM, Waller M, De Lurgio S, Dinakar C. Telemedicine is as effective as in-person visits for patients with asthma. Ann Allergy Asthma Immunol. 2016 Sep;117(3):241-5
- Posadzki P, Mastellos N, Ryan R, et al. Automated telephone communication systems for preventive healthcare and management of long-term conditions. Cochrane Database Syst Rev. 2016;12(12):CD009921.

- Powell RE, Henstenburg JM, Cooper G, Hollander JE, Rising KL. Patient Perceptions of Telehealth Primary Care Video Visits. Ann Fam Med. 2017 May;15(3):225-229
- Prasad, N., Cheng, L., Chivers, C., Draugelis, M., & Engelhardt, B. (2017). A Reinforcement Learning Approach to Weaning of Mechanical Ventilation in Intensive Care Units. ArXiv, abs/1704.06300
- Press, G. Cleaning big data: most time-consuming, least enjoyable data science task, survey says. Forbes (2016). Available at: https://www.forbes.com/sites/gilpress/2016/03/23/data-preparation-most-time-consuming-least-enjoyable-data-science-task-survey-says. Accessed October 12, 2021
- Pronovost PJ, Angus DC, Dorman T, Robinson KA, Dremsizov TT, Young TL. Physician staffing patterns and clinical outcomes in critically ill patients: a systematic review. JAMA. 2002 Nov 6;288(17):2151-62
- Pronovost PJ, Thompson DA, Holzmueller CG, Dorman T, Morlock LL. The organization of intensive care unit physician services. Crit Care Med. 2007 Oct;35(10):2256-61
- Proton Technologies. Writing a GDPR-compliant privacy notice. https://gdpr.eu/privacy-notice/ Accessed April 23, 2021
- Puiatti, A., Mudda, S., Giordano, S., & Mayora, O. (2011). Smartphone centered wearable sensors network for monitoring patients with bipolar disorder. Conference Proceedings of the IEEE Engineering in Medicine and Biology Society, 2011, 3644 – 3647
- Purnell S, Zheng F. Safety of Surgical Telehealth in the Outpatient and Inpatient Setting. Surg Clin North Am. 2021 Feb;101(1):109-119
- Pyysalo, S., Ginter, F., Moen, H., Salakoski, T., & Ananiadou, S. (2013). Distributional Semantics Resources for Biomedical Text Processing. In Proceedings of LBM 2013 (pp. 39-44) https://bio.nlplab.org/pdf/pyysalo13literature.pdf
- Quinn CC, Clough SS, Minor JM, Lender D, Okafor MC, Gruber-Baldini A. WellDoc mobile diabetes management randomized controlled trial: change in clinical and behavioral outcomes and patient and physician satisfaction. Diabetes Technol Ther. 2008 Jun;10(3):160-8
- Quinn CC, Shardell MD, Terrin ML, Barr EA, Ballew SH, Gruber-Baldini AL. Cluster-randomized trial of a mobile phone personalized behavioral intervention for blood glucose control. Diabetes Care. 2011 Sep;34(9):1934-42
- Rabatin AE, Lynch ME, Severson MC, Brandenburg JE, Driscoll SW. Pediatric telerehabilitation medicine: Making your virtual visits efficient, effective and fun. J Pediatr Rehabil Med. 2020;13(3):355-370
- Rahemi H, Nguyen H, Lee H, Najafi B. Toward Smart Footwear to Track Frailty Phenotypes-Using Propulsion Performance to Determine Frailty. Sensors (Basel). 2018 Jun 1;18(6):1763
- Rahul Saxena and Anand Srinivasan, Business Analytics: A Practitioner's Guide, International Series in Operations Research & Management (New York: Springer Science+Business Media, 2013)
- Raina R, Nair N, Sharma A, Chakraborty R, Rush S; Delphi Panelists. Telemedicine for Pediatric Nephrology: Perspectives on COVID-19, Future Practices, and Work Flow Changes. Kidney Med. 2021 May-Jun;3(3):412-425.
- Rajakumar K, Weisse M, Rosas A, Gunel E, Pyles L, Neal WA, Balian A, Einzig S. Comparative study of clinical evaluation of heart murmurs by general pediatricians and pediatric cardiologists. Clin Pediatr (Phila). 1999; 38:511–518
- Rajendra Acharya U, Meiburger KM, Wei Koh JE, Vicnesh J, Ciaccio EJ, Shu Lih O, Tan SK, Aman RRAR, Molinari F, Ng KH. Automated plaque classification using computed tomography angiography and Gabor transformations. Artif Intell Med. 2019 Sep;100:101724.
- Rajkomar A, Dean J, Kohane I. Machine Learning in Medicine. N Engl J Med. 2019;380(14):1347-1358
- Rajkomar A, Oren E, Chen K, et al. Scalable and accurate deep learning for electronic health records. arXiv. January 24, 2018
- Rajkomar A, Yim JW, Grumbach K, Parekh A. Weighting Primary Care Patient Panel Size: A Novel Electronic Health Record-Derived Measure Using Machine Learning. JMIR Med Inform. 2016;4(4):e29. Published 2016 Oct 14.
- Rajpurkar P, Irvin J, Ball RL, Zhu K, Yang B, Mehta H, et al. (2018) Deep learning for chest radiograph diagnosis: A retrospective comparison of the CheXNeXt algorithm to practicing radiologists. PLoS Med 15(11): e1002686
- Ramos A, Rodriguez C, Martinez-Beneyto P, Perez D, Gault A, Falcon JC, Boyle P. Use of telemedicine in the remote programming of cochlear implants. Acta Otolaryngol. 2009 May;129(5):533-40.
- Ramsey RR, Plevinsky JM, Kollin SR, Gibler RC, Guilbert TW, Hommel KA. Systematic Review of Digital Interventions for Pediatric Asthma Management. J Allergy Clin Immunol Pract. 2020;8(4):1284-1293
- Rangel E, Martinez F. A Parkinsonian Digital Biomarker Learned as an Anomaly Deep Generative Representation. Annu Int Conf IEEE Eng Med Biol Soc. 2022 Jul;2022:4188-4191.
- Rao S.M., Leo G.J., Bernardin L., Unverzagt F. Cognitive dysfunction in multiple sclerosis: I. Frequency, patterns, and prediction. Neurology. 1991;41:685–691.
- Rasmussen MB, Frost L, Stengaard C, et al. Diagnostic performance and system delay using telemedicine for prehospital diagnosis in triaging and treatment of STEMI. Heart 100(9):711-715, 2014
- Rassouli F, Tinschert P, Barata F, Steurer-Stey C, Fleisch E, Puhan MA, Baty F, Kowatsch T, Brutsche MH. Characteristics of Asthma-related Nocturnal Cough: A Potential New Digital Biomarker. J Asthma Allergy. 2020 Dec 3;13:649-657
- Rathi S, Tsui E, Mehta N, Zahid S, Schuman JS. The Current State of Teleophthalmology in the United States. Ophthalmology. 2017 Dec;124(12):1729-1734
- Ray M, Dayan PS, Pahalyants V, Chernick LS. Mobile health technology to communicate discharge and follow-up information to adolescents from the emergency department. Pediatr. Emerg. Care 32(12):900-905, 2016
- Raymond E, Chong E, Winikoff B, Platais I, Mary M, Lotarevich T, Castillo PW, Kaneshiro B, Tschann M, Fontanilla T, Baldwin M, Schnyer A, Coplon L, Mathieu N, Bednarek P, Keady M, Priegue E. TelAbortion: evaluation of a direct to patient telemedicine abortion service in the United States. Contraception. 2019 Sep;100(3):173-177
- Raymond Liu, Tilak Sundaresan, Mary E. Reed, Julia R. Trosman, Christine B. Weldon, and Tatjana Kolevska. Telehealth in Oncology During the COVID-19 Outbreak: Bringing the House Call Back Virtually. JCO Oncology Practice 2020 16:6, 289-293

- Razak F, Shin S, Pogacar F, et al. Modelling resource requirements and physician staffing to provide virtual urgent medical care for residents of long-term care homes: a cross-sectional study. CMAJ Open. 2020;8(3):E514-E521.
- Razavian N, Sontag D. Temporal Convolutional Neural Networks for Diagnosis from Lab Tests. arXiv:1511.07938, 2015.
- Razavian, N., Marcus, J. & Sontag, D. Multi-task prediction of disease onsets from longitudinal laboratory tests. In Proceedings of the 1st Machine Learning for Healthcare Conference, (eds F. Doshi-Velez, J. Fackler, D. Kale and B. Wallace, J. Wiens) Vol. 56, pp 73–100 (PMLR, Los Angeles, CA, 2016)
- Ream E, Hughes AE, Cox A, Skarparis K, Richardson A, Pedersen VH, Wiseman T, Forbes A, Bryant A. Telephone interventions for symptom management in adults with cancer. Cochrane Database Syst Rev. 2020 Jun 2;6(6):CD007568
- Reese G. (2000). "Distributed Application Architecture". Database Programming with JDBC and Java, Second Edition. O'Reilly Media Inc. https://web.archive.org/web/20110406121920/http:/java.sun.com/developer/Books/jdbc/ch07.pdf.. Archived on 6 April 2011. Accessed September 16, 2021
- Regueiro MD, Greer JB, Binion DG, Schraut WH, Goyal A, Keljo DJ, Cross RK, Williams ED, Herfarth HH, Siegel CA, Oikonomou I, Brand MH, Hartman DJ, Tublin ME, Davis PL, Baidoo L, Szigethy E, Watson AR; IBD LIVE Physician Group. The inflammatory bowel disease live interinstitutional and interdisciplinary videoconference education (IBD LIVE) series. Inflamm Bowel Dis. 2014 Oct;20(10):1687-95
- Regulation (EU) 2016/679 of the European Parliament and of the Council of 27 April 2016. http://data.europa.eu/eli/reg/2016/679/2016-05-04 Accessed April 23, 2021)
- Reis Ben Y, Kohane Isaac S, Mandl Kenneth D. Longitudinal histories as predictors of future diagnoses of domestic abuse: modelling study BMJ 2009; 339 :b3677
- Ren M, Yi PH. Artificial intelligence in orthopedic implant model classification: a systematic review. Skeletal Radiol. 2022 Feb;51(2):407-416. doi: 10.1007/s00256-021-03884-8. Epub 2021 Aug 5. PMID: 34351457.
- Report of the Task Force on the Regulation of Telepharmacy Practice. Model rules for the Practice of Pharmacy. Available at https://nabp.pharmacy/wp-content/uploads/2017/05/2016_2017_TelepharmacyTF_Report.pdf. Accessed March 21, 2021
- Rhapsody. Understanding the Continuity of Care Record. https://rhapsody.health/resources/understanding-continuity-care-record/. vAccesed January 15, 2022
- Rhee H, Belyea MJ, Sterling M, et al: Evaluating the validity of an automated device for asthma monitoring for adolescents: Correlational design. J Med Internet Res 17:e234, 2015
- Rhoads DD, Habib-Bein NF, Hariri RS, et al. Comparison of the diagnostic utility of digital pathology systems for telemicrobiology. J Pathol Inform. 2016;7:10 [b]
- Rhoads DD, Mathison BA, Bishop HS, da Silva AJ, Pantanowitz L. Review of Telemicrobiology. Arch Pathol Lab Med. 2016;140(4):362-370 [a]
- Rhoads DD, Novak SM, Pantanowitz L. A review of the current state of digital plate reading of cultures in clinical microbiology. J Pathol Inform. 2015;6:23
- Ricauda NA, Bo M, Molaschi M, Massaia M, Salerno D, Amati D, Tibaldi V, Fabris F. Home hospitalization service for acute uncomplicated first ischemic stroke in elderly patients: a randomized trial. J Am Geriatr Soc. 2004 Feb;52(2):278-83
- Richards SH, Coast J, Gunnell DJ, Peters TJ, Pounsford J, Darlow MA. Randomised controlled trial comparing effectiveness and acceptability of an early discharge, hospital at home scheme with acute hospital care. BMJ. 1998 Jun 13;316(7147):1796-801
- Rincon TA, Manos EL, Pierce JD. Telehealth intensive care unit nurse surveillance of sepsis. Comput.Inform. Nurs. 35(9):459-464, 2017
- Riva G. Virtual reality in eating disorders and obesity: state of the art and future directions. CyberPsychology & Behavior. 2005;8:p. 351
- Rivera J, McPherson A, Hamilton J, et al. Mobile Apps for Weight Management: A Scoping Review. JMIR Mhealth Uhealth. 2016;4(3):e87
- Robert P Murphy, Karen A Dennehy, Maria M Costello, Evelyn P Murphy, Conor S Judge, Martin J O'Donnell, Michelle D Canavan, Virtual geriatric clinics and the COVID-19 catalyst: a rapid review, Age and Ageing, Volume 49, Issue 6, November 2020, Pages 907–914
- Rock Health. Q3 2021 digital health funding: To $20B and beyond! October 4, 2021. https://rockhealth.com/insights/q3-2021-digital-health-funding-to-20b-and-beyond/. Accessed January 8, 2022
- Rogante M, Grigioni M, Cordella D, Giacomozzi C. Ten years of telerehabilitation: a literature overview of technologies and clinical applications. NeuroRehabilitation 2010;27(4):287-304
- Rogers H, Madathil KC, Agnisarman S, Narasimha S, Ashok A, Nair A, Welch BM, McElligott JT. A Systematic Review of the Implementation Challenges of Telemedicine Systems in Ambulances. Telemed J E Health. 2017 Sep;23(9):707-717
- Roginiel AC, Dhruva SS, Ross JS. Evidence supporting FDA approval and CMS national coverage determinations for novel medical products, 2005 through 2016: A cross-sectional study. Medicine (Baltimore). 2018 Oct;97(40):e12715.
- Rogove HJ, McArthur D, Demaerschalk BM, Vespa P. Barriers to telemedicine: survey of current users in acute care units. Telemed J E Health. 2012 Jan-Feb; 18(1):48-53.)
- Romanov, A., & Shivade, C. (2018). Lessons from Natural Language Inference in the Clinical Domain. arXiv preprint arXiv:1808.06752. https://jgc128.github.io/mednli/ Available at https://physionet.org/content/mednli/1.0.0/ and https://github.com/jgc128/mednli_baseline
- Romare C, Skär L. Smart glasses for caring situations in complex care environments: scoping review. JMIR mHealth uHealth 8(4):e16055, 2020
- Root cause analysis [Internet] Rockville, MD: Agency for Healthcare Research and Quality Patient Safety Network AHRQ PSN; 2018. updated September 2019 Jan [Accessed February 21, 2021]. Available from: https://psnet.ahrq.gov/primers/primer/10/Root-Cause-Analysis

- Rosado, B. et al. Accuracy of computer diagnosis of melanoma: a quantitative meta-analysis. Arch. Dermatol. 139, 361–367, discussion 366 (2003)
- Rosner MH, Ronco C. Remote monitoring for the wearable artificial kidney. Contrib Nephrol. 2011;171:243-247
- Rostom K, Smith CD, Liddy C, Afkham A, Keely E. Improving Access to Rheumatologists: Use and Benefits of an Electronic Consultation Service. J Rheumatol. 2018 Jan;45(1):137-140
- Rothman SA, Laughlin JC, Seltzer J, Walia JS, Baman RI, Siouffi SY, Sangrigoli RM, Kowey PR. The diagnosis of cardiac arrhythmias: a prospective multi-center randomized study comparing mobile cardiac outpatient telemetry versus standard loop event monitoring.J Cardiovasc Electrophysiol. 2007; 18:241–247
- Rotmensch M, Halpern Y, Tlimat A, Horng S, Sontag D. Learning a Health Knowledge Graph from Electronic Medical Records. Sci Rep. 2017 Jul 20;7(1):5994.
- Ruggiero A, Megna M, Annunziata MC, et al. Teledermatology for acne during COVID-19: high patients' satisfaction in spite of the emergency. J Eur Acad Dermatol Venereol. 2020;34(11):e662-e663
- Rui X, Dong F, Ma X, Su L, Shan G, Guo Y, Long Y, Liu D, Zhou X; China-NCCQC Group. Quality metrics and outcomes among critically ill patients in China: results of the national clinical quality control indicators for critical care medicine survey 2015-2019. Chin Med J (Engl). 2022 May 5;135(9):1064-1075
- Run Yu. Successful Management of Pheochromocytoma and Thyroiditis With Fever by Telemedicine During the COVID-19 Pandemic. Endocrine Practice. Volume 26, Issue 9. 2020. Pages 1042-1043.
- Rushton S, Boggan JC, Lewinski AA, et al. Effectiveness of Remote Triage: A Systematic Review [Internet]. Washington (DC): Department of Veterans Affairs (US); 2019 Jul. Available from: https://www.ncbi.nlm.nih.gov/books/NBK553039/). Accessed March 20, 2021
- Russell TG. Physical rehabilitation using telemedicine. J Telemed Telecare. 2007;13(5):217-20
- Russell, TG, Blumke, R, Richardson, B, Truter, P. Telerehabilitation mediated physiotherapy assessment of ankle disorders. Physiother Res Int. 2010;15:167–175
- RVS Update Committee. RBRVS overview. American Medical Association. https://www.ama-assn.org/about/rvs-update-committee-ruc/rbrvs-overview. Accessed May 14, 2021
- Saba, Virginia and McCormick, Kathleen. Essentials of Nursing Informatics, 6th Edition. New York: McGraw-Hill Education, 2015. Pg 232
- Saeb, S., Zhang, M., Karr, C. J., Schueller, S. M., Corden, M. E., Kording, K. P., & Mohr, D. C. (2015). Mobile phone sensor correlates of depressive symptom severity in daily-life behavior: An exploratory study. Journal of Medical Internet Research, 17, e175.
- Safaee MM, Scheer JK, Ailon T, Smith JS, Hart RA, Burton DC, Bess S, Neuman BJ, Passias PG, Miller E, Shaffrey CI, Schwab F, Lafage V, Klineberg EO, Ames CP; International Spine Study Group. Predictive Modeling of Length of Hospital Stay Following Adult Spinal Deformity Correction: Analysis of 653 Patients with an Accuracy of 75% within 2 Days. World Neurosurg. 2018 Jul;115:e422-e427
- Saffer SI, Mize CE, Bhat UN, Szygenda SA. Use of non-linear programming and stochastic modeling in the medical evaluation of normal-abnormal liver function. IEEE Trans Biomed Eng. 1976 May;23(3):200-7
- Said M, Ngo V, Hwang J, Hom DB. Navigating telemedicine for facial trauma during the COVID-19 pandemic. Laryngoscope Investig Otolaryngol. 2020 Jul 9;5(4):649-656
- Sainath, T., Mohamed, A.-R., Kingsbury, B. & Ramabhadran, B. Deep convolutional neural networks for LVCSR. In Proc. Acoustics, Speech and Signal Processing 8614–8618 (2013)
- Sakimura N, Bradley J, Jones MB, de Medeiros B, Mortimore C. OpenID Connect Core 1.0 Incorporating Errata set 1. OpenID Foundation. 2014. http://openid.net/specs/openid-connect-core-1_0.html. Accessed March 14, 2021
- Salawu A, Green A, Crooks MG, Brixey N, Ross DH, Sivan M. A Proposal for Multidisciplinary Tele-Rehabilitation in the Assessment and Rehabilitation of COVID-19 Survivors. International Journal of Environmental Research and Public Health. 2020; 17(13):4890
- Salisbury ML, Lynch DA, van Beek EJ, Kazerooni EA, Guo J, Xia M, Murray S, Anstrom KJ, Yow E, Martinez FJ, Hoffman EA, Flaherty KR; IPFnet Investigators. Idiopathic Pulmonary Fibrosis: The Association between the Adaptive Multiple Features Method and Fibrosis Outcomes. Am J Respir Crit Care Med. 2017 Apr 1;195(7):921-929
- Salmhofer, W, Hofmann-Wellenhof, R, Gabler, G, et al. Wound teleconsultation in patients with chronic leg ulcers. Dermatology. 2005;210:211-217
- Samwald, Matthias; Fehre, Karsten; De Bruin, Jeroen; Adlassnig, Klaus-Peter (2012). "The Arden Syntax standard for clinical decision support: Experiences and directions". Journal of Biomedical Informatics. 45 (4): 711–8
- Sanchez D, Reiner JF, Sadlon R, Price OA, Long MW. Systematic Review of School Telehealth Evaluations. J Sch Nurs. 2019 Feb;35(1):61-76
- Sánchez-Peralta LF, Bote-Curiel L, Picón A, Sánchez-Margallo FM, Pagador JB. Deep learning to find colorectal polyps in colonoscopy: A systematic literature review. Artif Intell Med. 2020 Aug;108:101923.
- Saner H, Knobel SEJ, Schuetz N, Nef T. Contact-free sensor signals as a new digital biomarker for cardiovascular disease: chances and challenges. Eur Heart J Digit Health. 2020 Nov 27;1(1):30-39.
- Sarasohn-Kahn J. Making sense of sensors: how new technologies can change patient care. California Healthcare Foundation. Available at: http://www.chcf.org/publications/2013/02/making-sense-sensors. 2013. Accessed February 1, 2021
- Sayeed, R., Gottlieb, D. & Mandl, K.D. SMART Markers: collecting patient-generated health data as a standardized property of health information technology. npj Digit. Med. 3, 9 (2020)
- Schädler MR, Warzybok A, Kollmeier B. Objective Prediction of Hearing Aid Benefit Across Listener Groups Using Machine Learning: Speech Recognition Performance With Binaural Noise-Reduction Algorithms. Trends Hear. 2018 Jan-

Dec;22:2331216518768954

- Schindewolf, T. et al. Classification of melanocytic lesions with color and texture analysis using digital image processing. Anal. Quant. Cytol. Histol. 15, 1–11 (1993)
- Schmidhuber J (2015) Deep learning in neural networks: an overview. Neural Netw 61:85–117
- Schneider, J. E., Parikh, A., & Stojanovic, I. (2018). Impact of a Novel Insulin Management Service on Non-insulin Pharmaceutical Expenses. Journal of Health Economics and Outcomes Research, 6(1), 53–62.
- Schoenfeld AJ, Davies JM, Marafino BJ, et al. Variation in quality of urgent health care provided during commercial virtual visits. JAMA Intern. Med. 176(5):635-642, 2016
- Schoeppe, S. et al. Efficacy of inte rventions that use apps to improve diet, physical activity and sedentary behaviour: a systematic review. Int. J. Behav. Nutr. Phys. Act. 13, 127 (2016)
- Schoonhoven L, Grobbee DE, Donders AR, et al. Prediction of pressure ulcer development in hospitalized patients: a tool for risk assessment. Qual Saf Health Care. 2006;15(1):65-70.
- Schwamm LH, Holloway RG, Amarenco P, et al. A review of the evidence for the use of telemedicine within stroke systems of care: a scientific statement from the American Heart Association/American Stroke Association. Stroke 2009;40:2616–34
- Scuffham PA, Steed M. An economic evaluation of the Highlands and Islands teledentistry project. J Telemed Telecare. 2002;8(3):165-177
- Scurlock C, Becker C. Telemedicine for trauma and emergency: The eICU. Curr. Trauma Rep. 2(3): 132–137, 2016
- Scurlock C, D'Ambrosio C. Telemedicine in the intensive care unit: state of the art. Crit Care Clin. 2015 Apr;31(2):187-95
- SEC. Renalytix Reports Full Year Fiscal 2021 Results. https://www.sec.gov/Archives/edgar/data/1811115/000119312521303481/d164692dex991.htm. Accessed November 12, 2021
- Segal M, Rollins E, Hodges K, Roozeboom M. Medicare-Medicaid eligible beneficiaries and potentially avoidable hospitalizations. Medicare Medicaid Res Rev. 2014; 4(1)
- Sekhon H, Sekhon K, Launay C, Afililo M, Innocente N, Vahia I, Rej S, Beauchet O. Telemedicine and the rural dementia population: A systematic review. Maturitas. 2021 Jan;143:105-114.
- Seneviratne MG, Banda JM, Brooks JD, Shah NH, Hernandez-Boussard TM. Identifying Cases of Metastatic Prostate Cancer Using Machine Learning on Electronic Health Records. AMIA Annu Symp Proc. 2018;2018:1498-1504.
- Seoane F., Mohino-Herranz I., Ferreira J., Alvarez L., Buendia R., Ayllón D., Llerena C., Gil-Pita R. Wearable biomedical measurement systems for assessment of mental stress of combatants in real time. Sensors. 2014;14:7120–7141.
- Sepp Hochreiter and Jürgen Schmidhuber. Long short-term memory. Neural computation, 9(8):1735–1780, 1997
- Sequeira N, D'Souza D, Angaran P, Aves T, Dorian P. Common wearable devices demonstrate variable accuracy in measuring heart rate during supraventricular tachycardia. Heart Rhythm. 2020 May;17(5 Pt B):854-859.
- Sequoia Project. March 24, 2023. User's Guide to the Trusted Exchange Framework and Common Agreement – TEFCA. Versions 1.1. https://rce.sequoiaproject.org/wp-content/uploads/2023/03/Common-Agreement-Users-Guide-version-1.1-dated-3.22.2023.pdf. Accessed 12 April 2023.
- Serper M, Volk ML. Current and Future Applications of Telemedicine to Optimize the Delivery of Care in Chronic Liver Disease. Clin Gastroenterol Hepatol. 2018;16(2):157-161.e8.
- Setio AAA, Ciompi F, Litjens G, Gerke P, Jacobs C, Riel SJ van, et al. Pulmonary Nodule Detection in CT Images: False Positive Reduction Using Multi-View Convolutional Networks. IEEE Trans Med Imaging. 2016 May; 35(5):1160–9.
- Sezgin E, Huang Y, Ramtekkar U, Lin S. Readiness for voice assistants to support healthcare delivery during a health crisis and pandemic. NPJ Digit. Med. 3:122, 2020
- Shah MN, Gillespie SM, Wood N, et al. High-intensity telemedicine-enhanced acute care for older adults: an innovative healthcare delivery model. J. Amer. Geriatr. Soc. 61(11):2000-2007, 2013
- Shah RV, Grennan G, Zafar-Khan M, Alim F, Dey S, Ramanathan D, Mishra J. Personalized machine learning of depressed mood using wearables. Transl Psychiatry. 2021 Jun 9;11(1):338.
- Shah T, Churpek MM, Coca Perraillon M, Konetzka RT. Understanding why patients with COPD get readmitted: a large national study to delineate the Medicare population for the readmissions penalty expansion Chest. 2015 May; 147(5):1219-1226.
- Shahid SM, Anguita R, daCruz L. Telemedicine for postoperative consultations following vitrectomy for retinal detachment repair during the COVID-19 crisis: a patient satisfaction survey. Can J Ophthalmol. 2021;56(2):e46-e48
- Shamloul N, Ghias MH, Khachemoune A. The Utility of Smartphone Applications and Technology in Wound Healing. Int J Low Extrem Wounds. 2019 Sep;18(3):228-235
- Shannon RJ, Brown L, Chakravarthy D. Pressure Ulcer Prevention Program Study: a randomized, controlled prospective comparative value evaluation of 2 pressure ulcer prevention strategies in nursing and rehabilitation centers. Adv Skin Wound Care. 2012 Oct;25(10):450-64.
- Shannon, KM, Emmet, MM, Rodgers, LH, Wooters, M, Seidel, ML. Transition to telephone genetic counseling services during the COVID-19 pandemic. J Genet Couns. 2020; 00: 1– 5.
- Shao C, et al. Telemedicine Associated with Decreased No-show Visits among Surgical Specialties, Scientific Forum, American College of Surgeons Clinical Congress 2022.
- Sharda R, Delen D, Turban E, Aronson J, Liang TP. Business Intelligence and Analytics: Systems for Decision Support. 2014
- Sharma S, Parness IA, Kamenir SA, Ko H, Haddow S, Steinberg LG, Lai WW. Screening fetal echocardiography by telemedicine: efficacy and community acceptance.J Am Soc Echocardiogr. 2003; 16:202–208.
- Shaukat-Jali R., van Zalk N., Boyle D.E. Detecting Subclinical Social Anxiety Using Physiological Data from a Wrist-Worn Wearable: Small-Scale Feasibility Study. JMIR Form. Res. 2021;5:e32656.
- Shea S, Weinstock RS, Teresi JA, Palmas W, Starren J, Cimino JJ, Lai AM, Field L, Morin PC, Goland R, Izquierdo RE, Ebner S,

Silver S, Petkova E, Kong J, JP; IDEATel Consortium. A randomized trial comparing telemedicine case management with usual care in older, ethnically diverse, medically underserved patients with diabetes mellitus: 5 year results of the IDEATel study. J Am Med Inform Assoc. 2009 Jul-Aug;16(4):446-56

- Sheikh M, Qassem M, Kyriacou PA. Wearable, Environmental, and Smartphone-Based Passive Sensing for Mental Health Monitoring. Front Digit Health. 2021 Apr 7;3:662811.
- Sheng J, Manjunath S, Michael M, Gajera P, Wang E, Sendelbach D, Greilich P, Ambardekar A. Integrating handover curricula in medical school. Clin Teach. 2020 Dec;17(6):661-668
- Shenoi, S., Hayward, K., Curran, M.L. et al. Telemedicine in pediatric rheumatology: this is the time for the community to embrace a new way of clinical practice. Pediatr Rheumatol 18, 85 (2020)
- Sherman RE, Anderson SA, Dal Pan GJ, et al. Real-World Evidence - What Is It and What Can It Tell Us?. N Engl J Med. 2016;375(23):2293-2297
- Sherwood BG, Han Y, Nepple KG, Erickson BA. Evaluating the Effectiveness, Efficiency and Safety of Telemedicine for Urological Care in the Male Prisoner Population. Urol Pract. 2018;5(1):44-51.
- Shields AD, Wagner RK, Knutzen D, Deering S, Nielsen PE. Maintaining access to maternal fetal medicine care by telemedicine during a global pandemic. J Telemed Telecare. 2020 Sep 26:1357633X20957468
- Shin B, Oh J, Kim BH, Kim HE, Kim H, Kim S, Kim JJ. Effectiveness of Self-Guided Virtual Reality-Based Cognitive Behavioral Therapy for Panic Disorder: Randomized Controlled Trial. JMIR Ment Health. 2021 Nov 22;8(11):e30590.
- Shin EK, Mahajan R, Akbilgic O, et al. Sociomarkers and biomarkers: predictive modeling in identifying pediatric asthma patients at risk of hospital revisits. NPJ Digit Med 2018;1
- Shivank Garg, Noelle L. Williams, Andrew Ip, and Adam P. Dicker. Clinical Integration of Digital Solutions in Health Care: An Overview of the Current Landscape of Digital Technologies in Cancer Care. JCO Clinical Cancer Informatics 2018 :2, 1-9
- Shokri T, Lighthall JG. Telemedicine in the Era of the COVID-19 Pandemic: Implications in Facial Plastic Surgery. Facial Plast Surg Aesthet Med. 2020 May/Jun;22(3):155-156
- Shor, J., Bi, R. A., Venugopalan, S., Ibara, S., Goldenberg, R., & Rivlin, E. (2023). Clinical BERTScore: An Improved Measure of Automatic Speech Recognition Performance in Clinical Settings. arXiv preprint arXiv:2303.05737.
- Shortreed SM, Laber E, Lizotte DJ, Stroup TS, Pineau J, Murphy SA. Informing sequential clinical decision-making through reinforcement learning: an empirical study. Mach Learn. 2011;84(1-2):109-136
- Shotorbani S, Miller L, Blough DK, Gardner J. Agreement between women's and providers' assessment of hormonal contraceptive risk factors. Contraception 2006;73:501–6.
- Sibert K, Ricci MA, Caputo M, et al. The feasibility of using ultrasound and video laryngoscopy in a mobile telemedicine consult. Telemed. eHealth14(3):266-272, 2008
- Sicotte C, Lehoux P, Fortier-Blanc J. et al. Feasibility and outcome evaluation of a telemedicine application in speech-language pathology. J Telemed Telecare 2003; 9: 253-258
- Sieberts SK, Schaff J, Duda M, Pataki BÁ, Sun M, Snyder P, Daneault JF, Parisi F, Costante G, Rubin U, Banda P, Chae Y, Chaibub Neto E, Dorsey ER, Aydın Z, Chen A, Elo LL, Espino C, Glaab E, Goan E, Golabchi FN, Görmez Y, Jaakkola MK, Jonnagaddala J, Klén R, Li D, McDaniel C, Perrin D, Perumal TM, Rad NM, Rainaldi E, Sapienza S, Schwab P, Shokhirev N, Venäläinen MS, Vergara-Diaz G, Zhang Y; Parkinson's Disease Digital Biomarker Challenge Consortium; Wang Y, Guan Y, Brunner D, Bonato P, Mangravite LM, Omberg L. Crowdsourcing digital health measures to predict Parkinson's disease severity: the Parkinson's Disease Digital Biomarker DREAM Challenge. NPJ Digit Med. 2021 Mar 19;4(1):53.
- Simon LE, Shan J, Rauchwerger A, Reed S, Warton ME, Vinson DR, et al. Paramedics' perspectives on telemedicine in the ambulance: a survey study. JEMS. 2020;4(30):20
- Simpson CL, Kovarik CL. Effectively engaging geriatric patients via teledermatology. J Am Acad Dermatol. 2020 Dec;83(6):e417-e418
- Sims TW, Wilson K. Telehealth Management of Urostomy Postoperative Complications: A Case Study. J Wound Ostomy Continence Nurs. 2020;47(5):456-457.
- Singh J, Badr MS, Diebert W, Epstein L, Hwang D, Karres V, Khosla S, Mims KN, Shamim-Uzzaman A, Kirsch D, Heald JL, McCann K. American Academy of Sleep Medicine (AASM) Position Paper for the Use of Telemedicine for the Diagnosis and Treatment of Sleep Disorders. J Clin Sleep Med. 2015 Oct 15; 11(10):1187-98.
- Singhal A. 2012. Introducing the knowledge graph: things, not strings. https://blog.google/products/search/introducing-knowledge-graph-things-not/
- Singhal K, Azizi S, Tu T, Mahdavi SS, Wei J, Chung HW, Scales N, Tanwani A, Cole-Lewis H, Pfohl S, Payne P, Seneviratne M, Gamble P, Kelly C, Babiker A, Schärli N, Chowdhery A, Mansfield P, Demner-Fushman D, Agüera Y Arcas B, Webster D, Corrado GS, Matias Y, Chou K, Gottweis J, Tomasev N, Liu Y, Rajkomar A, Barral J, Semturs C, Karthikesalingam A, Natarajan V. Large language models encode clinical knowledge. Nature. 2023 Aug;620(7972):172-180.
- Siniscalchi M, Zingone F, Savarino EV, D'Odorico A, Ciacci C. COVID-19 pandemic perception in adults with celiac disease: an impulse to implement the use of telemedicine. Dig Liver Dis. 2020;52(10):1071-1075
- Siouras A, Moustakidis S, Giannakidis A, Chalatsis G, Liampas I, Vlychou M, Hantes M, Tasoulis S, Tsaopoulos D. Knee Injury Detection Using Deep Learning on MRI Studies: A Systematic Review. Diagnostics (Basel). 2022 Feb 19;12(2):537.
- Sirajuddin AM, Osheroff JA, Sittig DF, Chuo J, Velasco F, Collins DA. Implementation pearls from a new guidebook on improving medication use and outcomes with clinical decision support. Effective CDS is essential for addressing healthcare performance improvement imperatives. J Healthc Inf Manag. 2009;23(4):38-45.
- Sirintrapun SJ, Rudomina D, Mazzella A, et al. Robotic Telecytology for Remote Cytologic Evaluation without an On-site Cytotechnologist or Cytopathologist: An Active Quality Assessment and Experience of Over 400 Cases. J Pathol Inform. 2017;8:35

- Skandarajah A, Sunny SP, Gurpur P, Reber CD, D'Ambrosio MV, Raghavan N, James BL, Ramanjinappa RD, Suresh A, Kandasarma U, Birur P, Kumar VV, Galmeanu HC, Itu AM, Modiga-Arsu M, Rausch S, Sramek M, Kollegal M, Paladini G, Kuriakose M, Ladic L, Koch F, Fletcher D. Mobile microscopy as a screening tool for oral cancer in India: A pilot study. PLoS One. 2017 Nov 27;12(11):e0188440
- Skarzynski PH, Swierniak W, Pilka A. et al. A Hearing Screening Program for Children in Primary Schools in Tajikistan: A Telemedicine Model. Med Sci Monit 2016; 22: 2424-2430
- Slotwiner D, Varma N, Akar JG, Annas G, Beardsall M, Fogel RI, Galizio NO, Glotzer TV, Leahy RA, Love CJ, McLean RC, Mittal S, Morichelli L, Patton KK, Raitt MH, Ricci RP, Rickard J, Schoenfeld MH, Serwer GA, Shea J, Varosy P, Verma A, Yu CM. HRS Expert Consensus Statement on remote interrogation and monitoring for cardiovascular implantable electronic devices. Heart Rhythm. 2015 Jul;12(7):e69-100
- SMART Standards and Specifications. 2020. https://docs.smarthealthit.org. Accessed: September 26, 2021
- Smith C, Gold J, Ngo TD, Sumpter C, Free C. Mobile phone-based interventions for improving contraception use. Cochrane Database Syst Rev. 2015 Jun 26;2015(6):CD011159
- Smith CJ, Rozga A, Matthews N, Oberleitner R, Nazneen N, Abowd G. Investigating the accuracy of a novel telehealth diagnostic approach for autism spectrum disorder. Psychol Assess. 2017 Mar;29(3):245-252.
- Smith SW, Tiu J, Caspers CG, et al. Virtual Urgent Care Quality and Safety in the Time of Coronavirus. Jt Comm J Qual Patient Saf. 2021;47(2):86-98
- SNOMED. SNOMED CT Starter Guide. https://confluence.ihtsdotools.org/display/DOCSTART/7.+SNOMED+CT+Expressions. Accessed June 25, 2021
- Snoswell CL, Rahja M, Lalor AF. A Systematic Review and Meta-Analysis of Change in Health-Related Quality of Life for Interactive Telehealth Interventions for Patients With Asthma. Value Health. 2021 Feb;24(2):291-302.
- Sodhi M. Lessons from the field: How rural clinics, FQHCs can use telehealth, eConsults during the COVID-19 emergency. Medical Group Management Association News, July 2020. https://www.mgma.com/resources/quality-patient-experience/lessons-from-the-field-how-rural-clinics,-fqhcs-c. Accessed March 15, 2021
- Softpath. 2021 EHR project report. Available at https://softwarepath.com/guides/ehr-report. Accessed March 14, 2021
- Solomon SD, Chew E, Duh EJ, Sobrin L, Sun JK, VanderBeek BL, Wykoff CC, Gardner TW.Diabetic Retinopathy: A Position Statement by the American Diabetes Association. Diabetes Care. 2017 Mar; 40(3):412-418
- Somanchi, Sriram & Adhikari, Samrachana & Lin, Allen & Eneva, Elena & Ghani, Rayid. (2015). Early Prediction of Cardiac Arrest (Code Blue) using Electronic Medical Records. 2119-2126. 10.1145/2783258.2788588.
- Song, B.; Wolf, K.-H.; Gietzelt, M.; Al Scharaa, O.; Tegtbur, U.; Haux, R.; Marschollek, M. (2009). "Decision Support for Teletraining of COPD Patients". Methods of Information in Medicine. 49 (1): 96–102
- Sorknaes AD, Madsen H, Hallas J, Jest P, Hansen-Nord M. Nurse tele-consultations with discharged COPD patients reduce early readmissions--an interventional study. Clin Respir J. 2011 Jan; 5(1):26-34
- South Florida Water Management District. Statement of Work (SOW) Examples. 2007-02-28. https://www.sfwmd.gov/sites/default/files/documents/aws_examples_sows.pdf. Retrieved 2021-02-10.
- Spiegel B. 2015 American Journal of Gastroenterology Lecture: How Digital Health Will Transform Gastroenterology. Am J Gastroenterol. 2016 May;111(5):624-30
- Sposaro F, Danielson J, Tyson G. iWander: An Android application for dementia patients. Annu Int Conf IEEE Eng Med Biol Soc. 2010;2010:3875-8
- Staicu ML, Holly AM, Conn KM. et al. The Use of Telemedicine for Penicillin Allergy Skin Testing. J Allergy Clin Immunol Pract 2018
- Standard Specification for Continuity of Care Record (CCR) (Active standard). ASTM International. 2012. https://www.astm.org/Standards/E2369.htm Accessed September 18, 2021
- Steel K, Cox D, Garry H. Therapeutic videoconferencing interventions for the treatment of long-term conditions. Journal of Telemedicine and Telecare 2011;17(3):109-17
- Steinkamp JM, Goldblatt N, Borodovsky JT, et al. Technological interventions for medication adherence in adult mental health and substance use disorders: a systematic review. JMIR Ment. Health 6(3):e12493, 2019
- Stephan S, Lever N, Bernstein L, Edwards S, Pruitt D. Telemental health in schools. J. Child Adolesc Psychopharmacol. 26(3):266-272, 2016
- Stephanie Hugie Barello, "Consumer spending and U.S. employment from the 2007–2009 recession through 2022," Monthly Labor Review, U.S. Bureau of Labor Statistics, October 2014. https://www.bls.gov/opub/mlr/2014/article/consumer-spending-and-us-employment-from-the-recession-through-2022.htm. Accessed June 15, 2021
- Stifani BM, Avila K, Levi EE. Telemedicine for contraceptive counseling: An exploratory survey of US family planning providers following rapid adoption of services during the COVID-19 pandemic. Contraception. 2021 Mar;103(3):157-162
- Stockdill ML, Barnett MD, Taylor R, Dionne-Odom JN, Bakitas M. Telehealth in palliative care: communication strategies from the COVID-19 pandemic. Clin. J. Oncol. Nurs. 25(1):17-22, 2021
- Stone JM, Gibbons TE. Telemedicine in Pediatric Gastroenterology: An Overview of Utility. Telemed J E Health. 2018 Aug;24(8):577-581
- Stoyanov SR, Hides L, Kavanagh DJ, Zelenko O, Tjondronegoro D, Mani M. Mobile app rating scale: a new tool for assessing the quality of health mobile apps. JMIR Mhealth Uhealth. 2015;3(1):e27
- Strauss JA, Chao CR, Kwan ML, Ahmed SA, Schottinger JE, Quinn VP. Identifying primary and recurrent cancers using a SAS-based natural language processing algorithm. J Am Med Inform Assoc. 2013;20:349–355
- Strnad K, Shoulders BR, Smithburger PL, Kane-Gill SL. A Systematic Review of ICU and Non-ICU Clinical Pharmacy Services Using Telepharmacy. Ann Pharmacother. 2018 Dec;52(12):1250-1258

- Strome TL. Healthcare analytics for quality and performance improvement. Hoboken, NJ: Wiley, 2013
- Stucki, R. A., Urwyler, P., Rampa, L., Müri, R., Mosimann, U. P., & Nef, T. (2014). A web-based non-intrusive ambient system to measure and classify activities of daily living. Journal of Medical Internet Research, 16, e175
- Sturesson L, Groth K. Clinicians' Selection Criteria for Video Visits in Outpatient Care: Qualitative Study. J Med Internet Res 2018;20(11):e288
- Subhi, M.A., Ali, S.H., & Mohammed, M.A. (2019). Vision-Based Approaches for Automatic Food Recognition and Dietary Assessment: A Survey. IEEE Access, 7, 35370-35381
- Sumant Ugalmugle, Rupali Swain. Healthcare IT Report. August 2020. Global Market Insights
- Sun P, Zhao Y, Men J, Ma ZR, Jiang HZ, Liu CY, Feng W. Application of Virtual and Augmented Reality Technology in Hip Surgery: Systematic Review. J Med Internet Res. 2023 Mar 10;25:e37599.
- Sun, H. et al. Semantic processing of EHR data for clinical research. J. Biomed. Inform. 58, 247–259 (2015)
- Suresh, H. et al. Clinical intervention prediction and understanding using deep networks. arXiv [cs.LG] (PMLR, Los Angeles, CA, USA, 2017)
- Susan J. Daniel, Lin Wu, Sajeesh Kumar. Teledentistry: A Systematic Review of Clinical Outcomes, Utilization and Costs. American Dental Hygienists' Association Dec 2013, 87 (6) 345-352
- Sutskever, I. Vinyals, O. & Le. Q. V. Sequence to sequence learning with neural networks. In Proc. Advances in Neural Information Processing Systems 27 3104–3112 (2014)
- Sveistrup H. Motor rehabilitation using virtual reality. J Neuroeng Rehabil. 2004 Dec 10;1(1):10
- Swezey, L . 5 techniques for accurate wound measurement. Wound Source. https://www.woundsource.com/blog/5-techniques-accurate-wound-measurements. Accessed March 11, 2021
- Switzer JA, Hall C, Gross H, Waller J, Nichols FT, Wang S, Adams RJ, Hess DC. A web-based telestroke system facilitates rapid treatment of acute ischemic stroke patients in rural emergency departments. J Emerg Med. 2009 Jan;36(1):12-8
- Sylvia ML, Terhaar MF. Clinical Analytics and Data Management for the DNP, Second Edition. Springer Publishing Company, 2018
- Talal AH, Andrews P, Mcleod A, Chen Y, Sylvester C, Markatou M, Brown LS. Integrated, Co-located, Telemedicine-based Treatment Approaches for Hepatitis C Virus Management in Opioid Use Disorder Patients on Methadone. Clin Infect Dis. 2019 Jul 2;69(2):323-331.
- Tan AJ, Yamarik R, Brody AA, Chung FR, Grudzen C; EMPallA Telephonic Working Group. Development and protocol for a nurse-led telephonic palliative care program. Nurs Outlook. 2021 Jan 20:S0029-6554(20)30718-1
- Tan K, Lai NM. Telemedicine for the support of parents of high-risk newborn infants. Cochrane Database Syst. Rev. (6):CD006818, 2012
- Tanaka MJ, Oh LS, Martin SD, Berkson EM. Telemedicine in the Era of COVID-19: The Virtual Orthopaedic Examination [published correction appears in J Bone Joint Surg Am. 2020 Oct 21;102(20):e121]. J Bone Joint Surg Am. 2020;102(12):e57
- Tanenbaum LN. A Brighter Future Lies Ahead for AI Funding in Radiology. Appl Radiol. 2020;49(6):32-33. https://www.appliedradiology.com/communities/Artificial-Intelligence/a-brighter-future-lies-ahead-for-ai-funding-in-radiology
- Tang B, Cao H, Wang X, Chen Q, Xu H. Evaluating word representation features in biomedical named entity recognition tasks. Biomed Res Int. 2014;2014.
- Tang MSS, Moore K, McGavigan A, Clark RA, Ganesan AN. Effectiveness of Wearable Trackers on Physical Activity in Healthy Adults: Systematic Review and Meta-Analysis of Randomized Controlled Trials. JMIR Mhealth Uhealth. 2020 Jul 22;8(7):e15576
- Tauber J, Ayoub S, Shah P, Wu M, Tsui E, Schuman JS, Rathi S. Assessing the Demand for Teleophthalmology in Florida Emergency Departments. Telemed J E Health. 2020 Dec;26(12):1500-1506
- Tauschmann M, Allen J, Wilinska M, Thabit H, Stewart Z, Cheng P, et al. Day-and-Night Hybrid Closed-Loop Insulin Delivery in Adolescents With Type 1 Diabetes: A Free-Living, Randomized Clinical Trial. Diabetes Care 2016 Dec;39(7):1168-1174
- Tavris DR, Dey S, Albrecht-Gallauresi B, et al. Risk of local adverse events following cardiac catheterization by hemostasis device use — phase II. J Invasive Cardiol 2005; 17: 644-50
- Taylor-Gjevre R, Nair B, Bath B, Okpalauwaekwe U, Sharma M, Penz E, Trask C, Stewart SA. Addressing rural and remote access disparities for patients with inflammatory arthritis through video-conferencing and innovative inter-professional care models. Musculoskeletal Care. 2018 Mar; 16(1):90-95.
- Teh SK, Rawtaer I, Tan HP. Predictive Accuracy of Digital Biomarker Technologies for Detection of Mild Cognitive Impairment and Pre-Frailty Amongst Older Adults: A Systematic Review and Meta-Analysis. IEEE J Biomed Health Inform. 2022 Aug;26(8):3638-3648
- Telehealth in Occupational Therapy. Am J Occup Ther 2018;72(Supplement_2):7212410059
- Telehealth. Am J Occup Ther 2013;67(6_Supplement):S69–S90
- Teng G, He Y, Zhao H, Liu D, Xiao J, Ramkumar S. Design and development of human interface using electrooculogram with deep learning. Artif Intell Med. 2020 Jan;102:101765.
- The Data Governance Institute. Definitions of Data Governance. 2021 https://datagovernance.com/the-data-governance-basics/definitions-of-data-governance/. Accessed September 15, 2021
- The Joint Commission. Performance Measurement. https://www.jointcommission.org/measurement) Accessed September 12, 2021
- Theodoris CV, Xiao L, Chopra A, Chaffin MD, Al Sayed ZR, Hill MC, Mantineo H, Brydon EM, Zeng Z, Liu XS, Ellinor PT. Transfer learning enables predictions in network biology. Nature. 2023 Jun;618(7965):616-624.
- Theurer L, Bashshur R, Bernard J, et al. American Telemedicine Association guidelines for teleburn. Telemed. eHealth 23(5):365-375, 2017

- Thottakkara P, Ozrazgat-Baslanti T, Hupf BB, et al. Application of Machine Learning Techniques to High-Dimensional Clinical Data to Forecast Postoperative Complications. PLoS One. 2016;11(5):e0155705. Published 2016 May 27
- Thrall MJ, Rivera AL, Takei H, Powell SZ. Validation of a novel robotic telepathology platform for neuropathology intraoperative touch preparations. J Pathol Inform. 2014;5:21
- Timmers T, Janssen L, van der Weegen W, Das D, Marijnissen WJ, Hannink G, van der Zwaard BC, Plat A, Thomassen B, Swen JW, Kool RB, Lambers Heerspink FO. The Effect of an App for Day-to-Day Postoperative Care Education on Patients With Total Knee Replacement: Randomized Controlled Trial. JMIR Mhealth Uhealth. 2019 Oct 21;7(10):e15323
- Timmers, C., Maeghs, A., Vestjens, M., Bonnemayer, C., Hamers, H., & Blokland, A. (2014). Ambulant cognitive assessment using a smartphone. Applied Neuropsychology Adult, 21, 136–142
- Tison GH, Sanchez JM, Ballinger B, et al. Passive Detection of Atrial Fibrillation Using a Commercially Available Smartwatch. JAMA Cardiol. 2018;3(5):409–416.
- Tofighi B, Abrantes A, Stein MD. The role of technology-based interventions for substance use disorders in primary care: a review of the literature. Med. Clin. North Amer. 102(4):715-731, 2018
- Toma, A., Lawler, P.R., Ba, J., Krishnan, R.G., Rubin, B.B. and Wang, B., 2023. Clinical camel: An open-source expert-level medical language model with dialogue-based knowledge encoding. arXiv preprint arXiv:2305.12031.
- Tompson, J., Jain, A., LeCun, Y. & Bregler, C. Joint training of a convolutional network and a graphical model for human pose estimation. In Proc. Advances in Neural Information Processing Systems 27 1799–1807 (2014)
- Towey MP. Speech telepractice: installing a speech therapy upgrade for the 21st century. Int J Telerehabil. 2012;4(2):73-78.
- Triana AJ, Vyas R, Shah AS, Tiwari V. Predicting Length of Stay of Coronary Artery Bypass Grafting Patients Using Machine Learning. J Surg Res. 2021 Aug;264:68-75.
- Tripathi M, Yeager M. 3…2…1…TEFCA is Go for Launch. HealthITbuzz. January 18, 2022. https://www.healthit.gov/buzz-blog/interoperability/321tefca-is-go-for-launch. Accessed November 21, 2022
- Trondsen MV, Bolle SR, Stensland GØ, Tjora A. Video-confidence: a qualitative exploration of videoconferencing for psychiatric emergencies. BMC Health Serv. Res. 14:544, 2014
- Tsanas A, Woodward E, Ehlers A. Objective characterization of activity, sleep, and circadian rhythm patterns using a wrist-worn actigraphy sensor: insights into posttraumatic stress disorder. JMIR MHealth UHealth. (2020) 8:e14306.
- Tseng VW, Valliappan N, Ramachandran V, Choudhury T, Navalpakkam V. Digital biomarker of mental fatigue. NPJ Digit Med. 2021 Mar 11;4(1):47.
- Tu, T., Palepu, A., Schaekermann, M., Saab, K., Freyberg, J., Tanno, R., ... & Natarajan, V. (2024). Towards conversational diagnostic ai. arXiv preprint arXiv:2401.05654.
- Tu, Tao & Azizi, Shekoofeh & Driess, Danny & Schaekermann, Mike & Chang, Pi-Chuan & Carroll, Andrew & Lau, Charles & Tanno, Ryutaro & Ktena, Sofia Ira & Palepu, Anil & Mustafa, Basil & Chowdhery, Aakanksha & Liu, Yun & Kornblith, Simon & Fleet, David & Mansfield, Philip & Prakash, Sushant & Wong, Renee & Natarajan, Vivek. (2024). Towards Generalist Biomedical AI. NEJM AI. 1. 10.1056/AIoa2300138.
- Twomey C, O'Reilly G, Bültmann O, et al. Effectiveness of a tailored, integrative internet intervention (deprexis) for depression: updated meta-analysis. PLoS One. 2020;15(1):e0228100)
- Tzanetakos, George, Fred Ullrich, and Keith Mueller (2018). "Telepharmacy Rules and Statutes: A 50-State Survey," American Journal of Medical Research 5(2): 7–23
- Uberoi RS, Gupta U, Sibal A. Root Cause Analysis in Healthcare. Apollo Medicine, vol. 1, no. 1, pp. 60–63, 2004/09/01/ 2004
- UMLS. UMD (UMDNS) - Statistics. https://www.nlm.nih.gov/research/umls/sourcereleasedocs/current/UMD/stats.html
- UMLS. UMD (UMDNS) - Synopsis. https://www.nlm.nih.gov/research/umls/sourcereleasedocs/current/UMD/ index.html#:~:text=UMDNS%20is%20a%20standard%20international,of%20data%20about%20medical%20devices
- Umoren RA, Gray MM, Handley S, et al. In-Hospital Telehealth Supports Care for Neonatal Patients in Strict Isolation. Am J Perinatol. 2020;37(8):857-860.
- United States Census Bureau. 2020 Feb 13. U.S. Census Bureau Releases National Population Projections Reports on Life Expectancy and Alternative Migration Scenarios URL: https://www.census.gov/newsroom/press-releases/2020/population-projections.html. Accessed February 10, 2021)
- United States Department of Agriculture. Sample Template Statement of Work. 2006-06-30. https://www.nrcs.usda.gov/Internet/FSE_DOCUMENTS/16/stelprdb1041239.pdf. Retrieved 2021-02-10.
- University of South Florida (USF). Informed Consent for Telemedicine Consultation. SP CH6 Consent for Telemedicine Consult 3-16-2020. https://www.usf.edu/student-affairs/student-health-services/documents/consent-for-telemedicine-consultation.pdf. Accessed September 5, 2021)
- Upadhyay UD, Grossman D. Telemedicine for medication abortion. Contraception. 2019 Nov;100(5):351-353.
- Ursprung R, Gray J. Random safety auditing, root cause analysis, failure mode and effects analysis. Clin Perinatol. 2010 Mar;37(1):141-65
- US Census Bureau. Health Insurance Coverage in the United States: 2019. United States Census Bureau Web site. https://www.census.gov/library/publications/2020/demo/p60-271.html. Published 2020. Updated 2020/09/15/. Accessed July 12, 2021
- US Department of Health and Human Services. Prescribing controlled substances via telehealth. DHHS, January 28, 2021. https://telehealth.hhs.gov/providers/policy-changes-during-the-covid-19-public-health-emergency/prescribing-controlled-substances-via-telehealth/. Accessed April 15, 2021
- US Department of Justice, Drug Enforcement Administration. Diversion Control Division. United States Code (U.S.C.) Controlled Substances Act, Title 21, Section 802(54). Source: https://www.deadiversion.usdoj.gov/21cfr/21usc/802.htm Accessed February 12, 2021)

- US Department of Justice. United States Government Interagency Guidance Document. How to protect your networks from Ransomware. Available at https://www.justice.gov/criminal-ccips/file/872771/download. Accessed October 15, 2021
- Uscher-Pines L, Huskamp HA, Mehrotra A. Treating Patients With Opioid Use Disorder in Their Homes: An Emerging Treatment Model. JAMA. 2020 Jul 7;324(1):39-40
- Uscher-Pines L, Sousa J, Raja P, Mehrotra A, Barnett ML, Huskamp HA. Suddenly Becoming a "Virtual Doctor": Experiences of Psychiatrists Transitioning to Telemedicine During the COVID-19 Pandemic. Psychiatr Serv. 2020 Nov 1;71(11):1143-1150.
- Uthman OA, Nduka CU, Abba M, Enriquez R, Nordenstedt H, Nalugoda F, Kengne AP, Ekström AM. Comparison of mHealth and Face-to-Face Interventions for Smoking Cessation Among People Living With HIV: Meta-Analysis. JMIR Mhealth Uhealth. 2019 Jan 7;7(1):e203.
- Valentine AZ, Hall SS, Young E, Brown BJ, Groom MJ, Hollis C, Hall CL. Implementation of Telehealth Services to Assess, Monitor, and Treat Neurodevelopmental Disorders: Systematic Review. J Med Internet Res. 2021 Jan 20;23(1):e22619.
- Valle CG, Deal AM, Tate DF: Preventing weight gain in African American breast cancer survivors using smart scales and activity trackers: A randomized controlled pilot study. J Cancer Surviv 11:133-148, 2017
- Van Dillen C, Silvestri S, Haney M, et al. Evaluation of an off-the-shelf mobile telemedicine model in emergency department wound assessment and management. J. Telemed. Telecare19(2):84-88, 2013
- van Netten JJ, Clark D, Lazzarini PA, Janda M, Reed LF. The validity and reliability of remote diabetic foot ulcer assessment using mobile phone images. Sci Rep. 2017; 7(1):9480.
- van Veen T, Binz S, Muminovic M, et al. Potential of mobile health technology to reduce health disparities in underserved communities. West. J. Emerg. Med. 20(5):799-802, 2019.
- van Walraven C, Dhalla IA, Bell C, Etchells E, Stiell IG, Zarnke K, Austin PC, Forster AJ. Derivation and validation of an index to predict early death or unplanned readmission after discharge from hospital to the community. CMAJ. 2010 Apr 6;182(6):551-7.
- Vanisree K, Jyothi S (2011) Decision support system for congenital heart disease based on signs and symptoms using neural networks. Int J Comput Appl 19(6):6-12
- Varrell JR, Boyce G, Baker S, Robinson B, Boyce OC. Telepsychiatry for hospital systems—White Paper. In Sight Telepsychiatry, Inc, 2015
- Vasudevan, S., Saha, A., Tarver, M.E. et al. Digital biomarkers: Convergence of digital health technologies and biomarkers. npj Digit. Med. 5, 36 (2022).
- Vaswani, A., Shazeer, N., Parmar, N., Uszkoreit, J., Jones, L., Gomez, A. N., Kaiser, Ł. & Polosukhin, I. (2017). Attention is all you need. Advances in Neural Information Processing Systems (pp. 5998--6008)
- Verburg, G., Borthwick, B., Bennett, B., & Rumney, P. (2003). Online support to facilitate the reintegration of students with brain injury: Trials and errors. NeuroRehabilitation, 18, 113–123
- Verduzco-Gutierrez M, Bean AC, Tenforde AS, Tapia RN, Silver JK. How to Conduct an Outpatient Telemedicine Rehabilitation or Prehabilitation Visit. PM R. 2020 Jul;12(7):714-720
- Viers BR, Lightner DJ, Rivera ME, Tollefson MK, Boorjian SA, Karnes RJ, Thompson RH, O'Neil DA, Hamilton RL, Gardner MR, Bundrick M, Jenkins SM, Pruthi S, Frank I, Gettman MT. Efficiency, satisfaction, and costs for remote video visits following radical prostatectomy: a randomized controlled trial. Eur Urol. 2015 Oct;68(4):729-35.
- Villa L, Matz O, Olaciregui Dague K, Kluwig D, Rossaint R, Brokmann JC. The assessment of dermatological emergencies in the emergency department via telemedicine is safe: a prospective pilot study. Intern Emerg Med. 2020 Oct;15(7):1275-1279
- Vinolo Gil MJ, Gonzalez-Medina G, Lucena-Anton D, Perez-Cabezas V, Ruiz-Molinero MDC, Martín-Valero R. Augmented Reality in Physical Therapy: Systematic Review and Meta-analysis. JMIR Serious Games. 2021 Dec 15;9(4):e30985.
- Vitkovski T, Bhuiya T, Esposito M. Utility of telepathology as a consultation tool between an off-site surgical pathology suite and affiliated hospitals in the frozen section diagnosis of lung neoplasms. J Pathol Inform. 2015; 6():55
- Vreeman DJ. LOINC from Regenstrief. Introduction and Overview. December 6, 2012. https://www.ehealth.gov.hk/filemanager/content/pdf/en/LOINC_Workshop_2013/1_LOINC_Overview_Part1.pdf. Accessed April 13, 2021
- W3CWeb Accessibility Initiative. Web Content Accessibility Guidelines (WCAG) Overview. 11 December 2008. https://www.w3.org/WAI/standards-guidelines/wcag/ Accessed April 21, 2021
- Wade SL, Raj SP, Moscato EL, Narad ME. Clinician perspectives delivering telehealth interventions to children/families impacted by pediatric traumatic brain injury. Rehabil Psychol. 2019 Aug;64(3):298-306.
- Wakefield BJ, Scherubel M, Ray A, Holman JE. Nursing interventions in a telemonitoring program. Telemed J E Health. 2013;19(3):160-165
- Wall LR, Ward EC, Cartmill B. et al. Adherence to a Prophylactic Swallowing Therapy Program During (Chemo) Radiotherapy: Impact of Service-Delivery Model and Patient Factors. Dysphagia 2017; 32: 279-292
- Wallace W, Chan C, Chidambaram S, Hanna L, Iqbal FM, Acharya A, Normahani P, Ashrafian H, Markar SR, Sounderajah V, Darzi A. The diagnostic and triage accuracy of digital and online symptom checker tools: a systematic review. NPJ Digit Med. 2022 Aug 17;5(1):118.
- Waller G, Pugh M, Mulkens S, Moore E, Mountford VA, Carter J, Wicksteed A, Maharaj A, Wade TD, Wisniewski L, Farrell NR, Raykos B, Jorgensen S, Evans J, Thomas JJ, Osenk I, Paddock C, Bohrer B, Anderson K, Turner H, Hildebrandt T, Xanidis N, Smit V. Cognitive-behavioral therapy in the time of coronavirus: Clinician tips for working with eating disorders via telehealth when face-to-face meetings are not possible. Int J Eat Disord. 2020 Jul;53(7):1132-1141.
- Wallis LA, Fleming J, Hasselberg M, Laflamme L, Lundin J. A smartphone app and cloud-based consultation system for burn injury emergency care. PLoS One11(2):e0147253, 2016
- Walsh WA, Meunier-Sham J, Re C. Using telehealth for sexual assault forensic examinations: a process evaluation of a national pilot project. J. Forensic Nurs. 15(3):152-162, 2019

- Walsh, Simon L F., et al. "Deep Learning for Classifying Fibrotic Lung Disease On High-resolution Computed Tomography: a Case-cohort Study." The Lancet. Respiratory Medicine, vol. 6, no. 11, 2018, pp. 837-845
- Wang C, Goel R, Noun M, Ghanta RK, Najafi B. Wearable Sensor-Based Digital Biomarker to Estimate Chest Expansion During Sit-to-Stand Transitions-A Practical Tool to Improve Sternal Precautions in Patients Undergoing Median Sternotomy. IEEE Trans Neural Syst Rehabil Eng. 2020 Jan;28(1):165-173
- Wang C, Li L, Wang L, Ping Z, Flory MT, Wang G, Xi Y, Li W. Evaluating the risk of type 2 diabetes mellitus using artificial neural network: an effective classification approach. Diabetes Res Clin Pract. 2013 Apr;100(1):111-8.
- Wang C, Li X, Sun W, Li J, Wang Y, Bao X, et al.Weekly variation in quality of care for acute ST-segment elevation myocardial infarction by day and time of admission: a retrospective observational study. BMJ Qual Saf. 2021;30:500-8.
- Wang P, Berzin TM, Glissen Brown JR, et al. Real-time automatic detection system increases colonoscopic polyp and adenoma detection rates: a prospective randomised controlled study. Gut. 2019;68(10):1813-1819
- Wang P, Xiao X, Glissen Brown JR, Berzin TM, Tu M, Xiong F, Hu X, Liu P, Song Y, Zhang D, Yang X, Li L, He J, Yi X, Liu J, Liu X. Development and validation of a deep-learning algorithm for the detection of polyps during colonoscopy Nat Biomed Eng. 2018 Oct; 2(10):741-748
- Wang S, Lee SB, Pardue C, et al. Remote evaluation of acute ischemic stroke: reliability of National Institutes of Health Stroke Scale via telestroke. Stroke 2003;34:e188–91
- Wang TC, Tsai CL, Tang TW, Wang WL, Lee KT. The Effect of Cycling Through a Projection-Based Virtual Environment System on Generalized Anxiety Disorder. J Clin Med. 2019 Jul 4;8(7):973.
- Wang X, Sontag D, Wang F. 2014. Unsupervised learning of disease progression models. In Proceedings of the 20th ACM SIGKDD international conference on Knowledge discovery and data mining (KDD '14). Association for Computing Machinery, New York, NY, USA, 85–94
- Wang Y, Liu S, Afzal N, Rastegar-Mojarad M, Wang L, Shen F, et al. A comparison of word embeddings for the biomedical natural language processing. J Biomed Inform. 2018;87:12–20.
- Wang ZJ, Shi QL, Liu YL, Ren MJ, Zhao SY, et al. Evaluation of Chinese Clinical Practice Guidelines Published in Medical Journals in 2019: status of the Authorship and Guideline Development Group. Med J PUMCH 2021;12: 552–559
- Wang, B., Min, S., Deng, X., Shen, J., Wu, Y., Zettlemoyer, L. & Sun, H. Towards Understanding Chain-of-Thought Prompting: An Empirical Study of What Matters. arXiv:2212.10001 [cs.CL] (2022)
- Wang, H., Liu, C., Xi, N., Qiang, Z., Zhao, S., Qin, B. and Liu, T., 2023. Huatuo: Tuning llama model with chinese medical knowledge. arXiv preprint arXiv:2304.06975.
- Wang, Z., Wu, Z., Agarwal, D. & Sun, J. Medclip: Contrastive learning from unpaired medical images and text. arXiv preprint arXiv:2210.10163 (2022).
- Wantlin, K., Wu, C., Huang, S.-C., Banerjee, O., Dadabhoy, F., Mehta, V. V., Han, R. W., Cao, F., Narayan, R. R., Colak, E., et al. BenchMD: A Benchmark for Modality-Agnostic Learning on Medical Images and Sensors. arXiv preprint arXiv:2304.08486 (2023).
- Ward MM, Jaana M, Natafgi N. Systematic review of telemedicine applications in emergency rooms. Int J Med Inform. 2015 Sep;84(9):601-16
- Warner JL, Levy MA, Neuss MN, Warner JL, Levy MA, Neuss MN. ReCAP: Feasibility and Accuracy of Extracting Cancer Stage Information From Narrative Electronic Health Record Data. J Oncol Pract. 2016 Feb;12(2):157-8; e169-7.
- Watts, KA, Malone, E, Dionne-Odom, JN, et al. Can you hear me now?: Improving palliative care access through telehealth. Res Nurs Health. 2021; 44: 226– 237.
- Wechsler TF, Kümpers F, Mühlberger A. Inferiority or Even Superiority of Virtual Reality Exposure Therapy in Phobias?-A Systematic Review and Quantitative Meta-Analysis on Randomized Controlled Trials Specifically Comparing the Efficacy of Virtual Reality Exposure to Gold Standard in vivo Exposure in Agoraphobia, Specific Phobia, and Social Phobia. Front Psychol. 2019 Sep 10;10:1758.
- Wedekind L, Sainani K, Pershing S. and perceived demand for teleophthalmology in triage and consultations in California emergency departments. JAMA Ophthalmol. 134(5):537-543, 2016
- Weidner, Kristen & Lowman, Joneen. (2020). Telepractice for Adult Speech-Language Pathology Services: A Systematic Review. Perspectives of the ASHA Special Interest Groups. 5. 1-13
- Weinstein MM, Dunivan G, Guaderrama NM, Richter HE. Digital Therapeutic Device for Urinary Incontinence: A Randomized Controlled Trial. Obstet Gynecol. 2022 Apr 1;139(4):606-615
- Weinstein RS. Static image telepathology in perspective. Hum Pathol. 1996 Feb; 27(2):99-101
- Weiss P, Kizony R, Feintuch U, Katz N. Virtual reality in neurorehabilitation. In: Selzer M, Cohen L, Gage F, Clarke S, Duncan P editor(s). Textbook of Neural Repair and Rehabilitation. Cambridge University Press, 2006:182-97
- Weiyan Jian, Winnie Yip, William Hsiao et al. 2014. "A Win-Win-Win Provider Payment Policy Innovation: The Case of Yanchi County Hospital," China Health Economics 11: 8–10
- Wells SY, Morland LA, Wilhite ER, et al. Delivering prolonged exposure therapy via videoconferencing during the COVID-19 pandemic: an overview of the research and special considerations for providers. J. Trauma Stress 33(4):380-390, 2020
- Weng SF, Reps J, Kai J, Garibaldi JM, Qureshi N (2017) Can machine-learning improve cardiovascular risk prediction using routine clinical data? PLoS ONE 12(4): e0174944
- Wesendahl T. Hearing aid fitting: application of telemedicine in audiology. Int Tinnitus J. 2003;9(1):56-8.
- Whetten J, van der Goes DN, Tran H, Moffett M, Semper C, Yonas H. Cost-effectiveness of Access to Critical Cerebral Emergency Support Services (ACCESS): a neuro-emergent telemedicine consultation program. J Med Econ. 2018 Apr;21(4):398-405
- WHO Global Observatory for eHealth. (2011). mHealth: new horizons for health through mobile technologies: second global

survey on eHealth. World Health Organization. https://apps.who.int/iris/handle/10665/44607

- WHO International Programme on Chemical Safety Biomarkers in Risk Assessment: Validity and Validation. 2001. http://www.inchem.org/documents/ehc/ehc/ehc222.htm. Accessed January 14, 2023
- WHO. International Classification of Diseases 11th Revisions. https://icd.who.int/en. Accessed May 12, 2022
- Widmer RJ, Collins NM, Collins CS, West CP, Lerman LO, Lerman A. Digital health interventions for the prevention of cardiovascular disease: a systematic review and meta-analysis. Mayo Clin Proc. 2015 Apr;90(4):469-80
- Wilbright, WA, Birke, JA, Patout, CA, Varnado, M, Horswell, R. The use of telemedicine in the management of diabetes-related foot ulceration: a pilot study. Adv Skin Wound Care. 2004;17(5 pt 1):232-238
- Williams AM, Bhatti UF, Alam HB, Nikolian VC. The role of telemedicine in postoperative care. Mhealth. 2018;4:11
- Winburn AS, Brixey JJ, Langabeer J 2nd, Champagne-Langabeer T. A systematic review of prehospital telehealth utilization. J. Telemed. Telecare 24(7):473-481, 2018
- Winegard B, Miller EG, Slamon NB: Use of telehealth in pediatric palliative care. Telemed J E Health 23:938-940, 2017)
- Woehrle H, Arzt M, Graml A. et al. Effect of a patient engagement tool on positive airway pressure adherence: analysis of a German healthcare provider database. Sleep Med 2018; 41: 20-26
- World Bank Group; World Health Organization; Ministry of Finance, P.R.C.; National Health and Family Planning Commission, P.R.C.; Ministry of Human Resources and Social Security, P.R.C.. 2016. Deepening Health Reform in China: Building High-Quality and Value-Based Service Delivery. © Washington, DC: World Bank. http://hdl.handle.net/10986/24720
- World Health Organization, 1998. A health telematics policy in support of WHO's Health-For-All strategy for global health development: report of the WHO group consultation on health telematics, 11–16 December, Geneva, 1997
- Wshah S, Skalka C, Price M. Predicting Posttraumatic Stress Disorder Risk: A Machine Learning Approach. JMIR Ment Health. 2019 Jul 22;6(7):e13946
- Wu JR, Wang ML, Liu KC, Hu MH, Lee PY. Real-time advanced spinal surgery via visible patient model and augmented reality system. Comput Methods Programs Biomed. 2014 Mar;113(3):869-81.
- Wu S, Chen T, Pan Q, Wei L, Xuan Y, Li C, Wang Q, Song J. Establishment of a comprehensive evaluation system on medical quality based on cross-examination of departments within a hospital. Chin Med J (Engl) 2017 Dec 05;130(23):2872–2877
- Wu X, Oliveria SA, Yagerman S, et al. Feasibility and Efficacy of Patient-Initiated Mobile Teledermoscopy for Short-term Monitoring of Clinically Atypical Nevi. JAMA Dermatol. 2015;151(5):489–496
- Wu Y, Doi K, Metz CE, Asada N, Giger ML. Simulation studies of data classification by artificial neural networks: potential applications in medical imaging and decision making. J Digit Imaging. 1993 May;6(2):117-25
- Wu Y, Yao X, Vespasiani G, Nicolucci A, Dong Y, Kwong J, et al. Mobile app-based interventions to support diabetes self-management: a systematic review of randomized controlled trials to identify functions associated with glycemic efficacy. JMIR Mhealth Uhealth 2017 Mar 14;5(3):e35
- Wu YR, Chou TJ, Wang YJ, Tsai JS, Cheng SY, Yao CA, Peng JK, Hu WY, Chiu TY, Huang HL. Smartphone-Enabled, Telehealth-Based Family Conferences in Palliative Care During the COVID-19 Pandemic: Pilot Observational Study. JMIR Mhealth Uhealth. 2020 Oct 28;8(10):e22069
- Wu, C., Zhang, X., Zhang, Y., Wang, Y., & Xie, W. (2023). Pmc-llama: Further finetuning llama on medical papers. arXiv preprint arXiv:2304.14454.
- X12. X12 EDI examples. https://x12.org/examples. Accessed March 16, 2021
- Xiong X, Gao J, Zhang B, Lu J, Luo L. Introduction of Chinese hospital ranking method from the aspect of theoretical framework, practical choice and social effect. J Hosp Manag Health Policy. 2017 Nov 6;1:4–400
- Xiong, H. Y. et al. The human splicing code reveals new insights into the genetic determinants of disease. Science 347, 6218 (2015)
- Xu H, Long H. The Effect of Smartphone App-Based Interventions for Patients With Hypertension: Systematic Review and Meta-Analysis. JMIR Mhealth Uhealth. 2020 Oct 19;8(10):e21759
- Xu S, Perez M, Yang K, Perrenot C, Felblinger J, Hubert J. Determination of the latency effects on surgical performance and the acceptable latency levels in telesurgery using the dV-Trainer(®) simulator. Surg Endosc. 2014 Sep;28(9):2569-76
- Y. Wu, K. Doi, C. E. Metz, N. Asada, and M. L. Giger, "Simulation studies of data classification by artificial neural networks: potential applications in medical imaging and decision making," (in eng), J Digit Imaging, vol. 6, no. 2, pp. 117–25, May 1993
- Yang N, Chen YL. Survey and evaluation of clinical practice guidelines in China in 2019. Med J PUMCH 2021;12: 407–410.
- Yang YT, Weintraub E, Haffajee RL. Telemedicine's role in addressing the opioid epidemic. Mayo Clin.Proc. 93(9):1177-1180, 2018
- Yao JJ, Yao D, Givens G. A Browser-Server-Based Tele-audiology System That Supports Multiple Hearing Test Modalities. Telemed J E Health 2015; 21: 697-704
- Yap KY, Low HX, Koh KS, Un M, Shih V, Chan A. Feasibility and acceptance of a pharmacist-run tele-oncology service for chemotherapy-induced nausea and vomiting in ambulatory cancer patients. Telemed J E Health. 2013 May;19(5):387-95
- Yarnitsky D, Dodick DW, Grosberg BM, Burstein R, Ironi A, Harris D, Lin T, Silberstein SD. Remote Electrical Neuromodulation (REN) Relieves Acute Migraine: A Randomized, Double-Blind, Placebo-Controlled, Multicenter Trial. Headache. 2019;59(8): 1240-1252
- Yellowlees P, Burke MM, Marks SL, Hilty DM, Shore JH. Emergency telepsychiatry. J. Telemed Telecare 14(6):277-281, 2008
- Yellowlees P, Nakagawa K, Pakyurek M, et al. Rapid conversion of an outpatient psychiatric clinic to a 100% virtual telepsychiatry clinic in response to COVID-19. Psychiatr. Serv. 71(7):749-752, 2020
- Yellowlees P, Parish MB, Gonzalez A, et al. Asynchronous telepsychiatry: a component of stepped integrated care. J. Telemed. Telecare 24(5):1-4, 2017

- Yen H.Y., Huang W.H. The efficacy of commercial smartwatches with a blood pressure-monitoring feature: A pilot randomized controlled trial. J. Nurs. Scholarsh. 2022;54:324–331.
- Yeo CT, Ungi T, UT P, Lasso A, RC MG, Fichtinger G. The effect of augmented reality training on percutaneous needle placement in spinal facet joint injections. IEEE Trans Biomed Eng. 2011;58:2031–2037.
- Yim, J., Chopra, R., Spitz, T., Winkens, J., Obika, A., Kelly, C., Askham, H., Lukic, M., Huemer, J., Fasler, K., et al. Predicting conversion to wet age-related macular degeneration using deep learning. Nature Medicine 26, 892–899 (2020).
- Yip J, Vescan AD, Witterick IJ. et al. The personal financial burden of chronic rhinosinusitis: A Canadian perspective. Am J Rhinol Allergy 2017; 31: 216-221
- Youn BY, Ko Y, Moon S, Lee J, Ko SG, Kim JY. Digital Biomarkers for Neuromuscular Disorders: A Systematic Scoping Review. Diagnostics (Basel). 2021 Jul 15;11(7):1275.
- Young LB. Telemedicine interventions for substance-use disorder: a literature review. J Telemed Telecare. 2012 Jan; 18(1):47-53.
- Yulzari R, Bretler S, Avraham Y. et al. Mobile Technology-Based Real-Time Teleotolaryngology Care Facilitated by a Nonotolaryngologist Physician in an Adult Population. Ann Otol Rhinol Laryngol 2018; 127: 46-50
- Yunxiang, L., Zihan, L., Kai, Z., Ruilong, D., & You, Z. (2023). Chatdoctor: A medical chat model fine-tuned on llama model using medical domain knowledge. arXiv preprint arXiv:2303.14070.
- Zangbar B, Pandit V, Rhee P, et al. Smartphone surgery: how technology can transform practice. Telemed. e-Health 20(6): 590-592, 2014)
- Zarski, A.-C., Berking, M., & Ebert, D. D. (2021). Efficacy of internet-based treatment for genito-pelvic pain/penetration disorder: Results of a randomized controlled trial. Journal of Consulting and Clinical Psychology, 89(11), 909–924
- Zegarelli BM. FDA Updates Digital Health Guidances to Align with 21st Century Cures Act. Lexology. Oct 9, 2019. https://www.lexology.com/library/detail.aspx?g=d6a36196-7705-4394-bea5-b4ee62e58989 Accessed December 12, 2021
- Zeng, A., Liu, X., Du, Z., Wang, Z., Lai, H., Ding, M., Yang, Z., Xu, Y., Zheng, W., Xia, X. and Tam, W.L., 2022. Glm-130b: An open bilingual pre-trained model. arXiv preprint arXiv:2210.02414.
- Zhan, A. et al. Using smartphones and machine learning to quantify Parkinson disease severity: the mobile Parkinson disease score. JAMA Neurol. 75, 876–880 (2018).
- Zhang J, Lu V, Khanduja V. The impact of extended reality on surgery: a scoping review. Int Orthop. 2023 Mar;47(3):611-621.
- Zhang T, Kishore V, Wu F, Weinberger KQ, Artzi Y. 2019. BERTScore: Evaluating Text Generation with BERT. arXiv e-prints, arXiv:1904.09675.
- Zhang, K., Yu, J., Yan, Z., Liu, Y., Adhikarla, E., Fu, S., Chen, X., Chen, C., Zhou, Y., Li, X., et al. BiomedGPT: A Unified and Generalist Biomedical Generative Pre-trained Transformer for Vision, Language, and Multimodal Tasks. arXiv preprint arXiv:2305.17100 (2023)
- Zhang, S., Xu, Y., Usuyama, N., Xu, H., Bagga, J., Tinn, R., Preston, S., Rao, R., Wei, M., Valluri, N. and Wong, C., 2023. BiomedCLIP: a multimodal biomedical foundation model pretrained from fifteen million scientific image-text pairs. arXiv preprint arXiv:2303.00915.
- Zhang, Y., Chen, Q., Yang, Z. et al. BioWordVec, improving biomedical word embeddings with subword information and MeSH. Sci Data 6, 52 (2019). Data available at https://github.com/ncbi-nlp/BioSentVec
- Zhao Z, Poyhonen J, Chen Cai X, Sophie Woodley Hooper F, Ma Y, Hu Y, Ren H, Song W, Tsz Ho Tse Z. Augmented reality technology in image-guided therapy: State-of-the-art review. Proc Inst Mech Eng H. 2021 Dec;235(12):1386-1398.
- Zhou H, Della PR, Roberts P, Goh L, Dhaliwal SS. Utility of m all odels to predict 28-day or 30-day unplanned hospital readmissions: an updated systematic review. BMJ Open. 2016;6(6):e011060
- Zhu H, Paschalidis IC, Tahmasebi A. Clinical concept extraction with contextual word embedding. arXiv preprint arXiv:1810.10566. 2018 Oct 24.
- Zhu J, Xie Q, Zheng K. An improved early detection method of type-2 diabetes mellitus using multiple classifier system Inf Sci, 292 (2015), pp. 1-14
- Zoder-Martell KA, Markelz AM, Floress MT, Skriba HA, Sayyah LEN. Technology to facilitate telehealth in applied behavior analysis. Behav. Anal. Pract. 2020 Sep; 13(3): 596–603.
- Zoom Video Communications Inc. HIPAA Compliance Datasheet. https://zoom.us/docs/doc/Zoom-hipaa.pdf. Accessed August 21, 2021 [b]
- Zoom Video Communications Inc. System requirements for Windows, macOS, and Linux. https://support.zoom.us/hc/en-us/articles/201362023-System-requirements-for-Windows-macOS-and-Linux. Accessed April 21, 2021 [a]
- Zoom Video Communications Inc. Zoom and PIPEDA/PHIPA Compliance Guide. https://zoom.us/trust/legal-compliance#certifications. August 21, 2021. Accessed August 22, 2021 [c]
- Zork NM, Aubey J, Yates H. Conversion and optimization of telehealth in obstetric care during the COVID-19 pandemic. Semin Perinatol. 2020 Oct;44(6):151300
- Zorron Cheng Tao Pu L, Singh G, Rajadurai A, Terbah R, De Silva R, Vaughan R, Efthymiou M, Chandran S. Benefits of phone consultation for endoscopy-related clinics in the COVID-19 pandemic. J Gastroenterol Hepatol. 2021 Apr;36(4):1064-1080.
- Zubatsky M, Berg-Weger M, Morley J. Using Telehealth Groups to Combat Loneliness in Older Adults Through COVID-19. J Am Geriatr Soc. 2020 Aug;68(8):1678-1679
- Zuniga C, Grossman D, Harrell S, Blanchard K, Grindlay K. Breaking down barriers to birth control access: An assessment of online platforms prescribing birth control in the USA. J Telemed Telecare. 2020 Jul;26(6):322-331

INDEX

Printed in Great Britain
by Amazon

effca351-b667-4f4b-854d-9d5155802ec3R01